Forty Studies that Changed Criminal Justice

Forty Studies that Changed Criminal Justice

Explorations into the History of Criminal Justice Research

Amy B. Thistlethwaite

Northern Kentucky University

John D. Wooldredge

University of Cincinnati

Prentice Hall
Upper Saddle River, New Jersey
Columbus, Ohio

Library of Congress Cataloging-in-Publication Data

Thistlethwaite, Amy B.

   Forty studies that changed criminal justice : explorations into the history of criminal justice research /
Amy B. Thistlethwaite, John D. Wooldredge.—1st ed.

     p. cm.

Includes bibliographical references.

ISBN-13: 978-0-13-234975-8 (alk. paper)

ISBN-10: 0-13-234975-2 (alk. paper)

1. Criminal justice, Administration of—History.   2. Criminal justice, Administration of—Philosophy.
3. Criminology—Philosophy.   4. Police administration—Philosophy.   5. Court administration.
6. Corrections.   I. Wooldredge, John.   II. Title.

K5001.T45 2010

364.9—dc22

                             2008052089

Vice President and Executive Publisher: Vernon Anthony
Senior Acquisitions Editor: Tim Peyton
Editorial Assistant: Alicia Kelly
Media Project Manager: Karen Bretz
Director of Marketing: David Gesell
Marketing Manager: Adam Kloza
Marketing Coordinator: Alicia Dysert
Production Manager: Wanda Rockwell
Creative Director: Jayne Conte
Cover Design: Susan Behnke
Cover Illustration/Photo: Getty Images, Inc.
Full-Service Project Management/Composition: Integra Software Services, Ltd.
Printer/Binder: Command Web/Bind-Rite Graphics

Credits and acknowledgments borrowed from other sources and reproduced, with permission, in this textbook
appear on appropriate page within text.

Pearson Education Ltd., London
Pearson Education Singapore, Pte. Ltd
Pearson Education, Canada, Inc.
Pearson Education–Japan
Pearson Education Australia PTY, Limited

Pearson Education North Asia, Ltd., Hong Kong
Pearson Educación de Mexico, S.A. de C.V.
Pearson Education Malaysia, Pte. Ltd
Pearson Education Upper Saddle River,
  New Jersey

Prentice Hall
is an imprint of

www.pearsonhighered.com

10 9 8 7 6 5 4 3 2
ISBN-13: 978-0-13-234975-8
ISBN-10:   0-13-234975-2

We dedicate this book to all the pioneers
of criminal justice research whose contributions
continue to enlighten and inspire.

CONTENTS

CONTENTS

Kalven, H. Jr., and H. Zeisel (1966). *The American Jury.* Boston: Little, Brown (shortly thereafter published by University of Chicago Press).

Greenwood, P., with A. Abrahamse (1982). *Selective Incapacitation.* Santa Monica, CA: Rand Corporation.

Wilsnack, R. (1976). "Explaining Collective Violence in Prisons: Problems and Possibilities." In *Prison Violence,* edited by A. Cohen, G. Cole, and R. Bailey. Lexington, MA: Lexington Books.

Jacobs, J., and L. Kraft (1978). "Integrating the Keepers: A Comparison of Black and White Prison Guards in Illinois." *Social Problems* 25:304–18.

Unobtrusive Research

Wilson, J., and G. Kelling (1982). "Broken Windows: The Police and Neighborhood Safety." *Atlantic Monthly* March:29–38.

Milton, C., J. Halleck, J. Lardner, and G. Abrecht (1977). *Police Use of Deadly Force.* Washington, DC: Police Foundation.

Albonetti, C. (1987). "Prosecutorial Discretion: The Effects of Uncertainty." *Law and Society Review* 21:291–313.

Hagan, J. (1974). "Extra-legal Attributes and Criminal Sentencing: An Assessment of a Sociological Viewpoint." *Law and Society Review* 8:357–83.

Steffensmeier, D., J. Ulmer, and J. Kramer (1998). "The Interaction of Race, Gender, and Age in Criminal Sentencing: The Punishment Cost of Being Young, Black, and Male." *Criminology* 36:763–97.

Wilkins, L., J. Kress, D. Gottfredson, J. Calpin, and A. Gelman (1978). *Sentencing Guidelines: Structuring Judicial Discretion.* Washington, DC: National Institute of Law Enforcement and Criminal Justice, U.S. Department of Justice.

Moore, C., and T. Miethe (1986). "Regulated and Unregulated Sentencing Decisions: An Analysis of First-year Practices Under Minnesota's Felony Sentencing Guidelines." *Law and Society Review* 20:253–77.

Martinson, R. (1974). "What Works? Questions and Answers About Prison Reform." *The Public Interest* 35:22–54.

Ehrlich, I. (1975). "The Deterrent Effect of Capital Punishment: A Question of Life and Death." *American Economic Review* 65:397–417.

Zedlewski, E. (1987). *Making Confinement Decisions.* Washington, DC: National Institute of Justice.

Petersilia, J., S. Turner, J. Kahan, and J. Peterson (1985). *Granting Felons Probation: Public Risks and Alternatives.* Santa Monica, CA: Rand Corporation.

Burgess, E. (1928). "Factors Determining Success or Failure on Parole." In *The Workings of the Indeterminate-Sentence Law and the Parole System in Illinois,* edited by A. Bruce, E. Burgess, and A. Harno, 205–49. Springfield: Illinois Board of Parole.

Fuller, D., and T. Orsagh (1977). "Violence and Victimization within a State Prison System." *Criminal Justice Review* 2:35–55.

PREFACE

The idea for this book is credited to Roger Hock who authored *Forty Studies that Changed Psychology* (Prentice Hall). Hock created a book that provides students with thorough yet concise summaries of the major research studies that have shaped the field of psychology. We wanted to do the same for criminal justice. Like other social science disciplines, knowledge in criminal justice is based upon research. Introductory textbooks provide students with an excellent overview of this material; however, they fail to offer students more than a cursory synopsis of the significant empirical studies that established the foundation of our discipline. This book will provide students with a richer understanding of some of the important research published in each of the three areas of criminal justice: policing, courts, and corrections.

HISTORY OF CRIMINAL JUSTICE EDUCATION

Academic disciplines grew out of the shift in higher education from a generalist approach to a focus on more specialized knowledge. Criminal justice is a relatively new discipline (compared to other social and behavioral science disciplines such as psychology, sociology, and political science). The origins of criminal justice education can be traced back to schools of police science.[1] In 1908, Berkeley police chief August Vollmer (a pioneer of police professionalism) helped establish the Berkeley Police School to provide formal education and training to police recruits (Morn 1995). He taught courses in evidence and investigation and implemented a curriculum that was the most advanced in the country. Vollmer believed an education was the most important asset for a police officer to have. In 1916, the program was expanded to include courses in criminology that all of his officers were encouraged to take. He took his curriculum to the University of Chicago in 1929 and put into operation a similar program in police studies (Morn 1995). He returned to Berkeley one year later and continued teaching in the newly created School of Criminology. That same year, San Jose State College advertised a two-year police curriculum that was soon expanded into a four-year degree. The idea of an educated police force caught on in other states as well. In 1935, a police studies program was established at Michigan State University. In addition to courses on policing, students took classes in science and math. In the mid-1930s, Indiana University also started a four-year degree program in police science. Twenty years later, the City College of New York followed suit and police science became a recognizable field of study (Morn 1995).

Vollmer and some of his colleagues formed an organization known as the National Association of College Police Training Officials (NACPTO) in 1941 (Morris 1975). The purpose of the organization was to create a standardized curriculum with minimum standards for all policing students. This organization was renamed the Society for the

---

[1] Criminology as a discipline traces its roots back to 1893 when the University of Chicago began offering sociological courses on the study of crime. Although the terms criminology and criminal justice are sometimes used interchangeably, criminology is the study of the correlates and causes of criminal behavior while criminal justice explores the operations, functions, and practices of the criminal justice system.

Advancement of Criminology in 1946 and later became the American Society of Criminology (ASC) in 1957. A second professional organization, the Academy of Criminal Justice Sciences (ACJS), was established in 1963.

In the 1960s, many police science programs expanded their curriculums to include courses in courts and corrections. A major impetus for criminal justice education came from federal legislation that established the Omnibus Crime Control and Safe Streets Act, which included the creation of the Law Enforcement Assistance Administration (LEAA). The program designated funds to be used for tuition grants and research to explore the operation of the various agencies within criminal justice: policing, courts, and corrections. For the first time, people starting thinking about the agencies within criminal justice as constituting a single criminal justice system with the goals of controlling crime and administering justice. Criminal justice programs flourished as the demand for college-educated personnel in criminal justice increased. Unlike other social science disciplines, the role of federal funding in promulgating the growth of criminal justice was unique (Morn 1995). There were 50 criminal justice programs in 1960, but by 1970 there was over 600 and by 1978, there were 1200-degree programs in criminal justice (Crank 2003). Today, there are close to 2000 with 32 universities conferring doctoral degrees (Frost and Clear 2007). Criminal justice has become an established discipline in higher education.

CRIMINAL JUSTICE RESEARCH

Criminal justice education continues to be interdisciplinary in nature drawing from the fields of sociology, psychology, and political science. As such, the knowledge base was created and continues to grow using the same principles of scientific inquiry that became the foundation of the older disciplines. At the same time criminal justice programs were prospering, crime was becoming a serious problem in communities across the United States. The institutions responsible for crime control (police, courts, and corrections) were deemed ineffective in their efforts. There appeared to be no clear consensus on how to address the problem and policy makers voiced concern about a lack of scientific knowledge on the functioning of the criminal justice system. According to the President's Commission on Crime and Administration of Justice (1967), ". . . revolution of scientific discovery has largely bypassed the problems of crime and crime control." One year later, Congress took action and established the National Institute of Justice to support research that would fill the void in knowledge and offer ideas to improve the police, courts, and corrections. Other agencies such as the Police Foundation and the American Correctional Association were created with similar missions. Privately funded research groups (i.e., the Rand Corporation and the Vera Institute) also started to conduct criminal justice research on the operation of the criminal justice system.

Types of Research

Applying the principles of scientific inquiry to the study of criminal justice involves the same methods and techniques utilized by other social science disciplines. Science allows us to investigate, identify, and answer questions about people, groups and institutions. Science can be used to develop and test theories and can also be used to develop programs and policies to solve problems. Scientific or *empirical* research involves understanding through observation. Researchers utilize different modes of observation in their inquiries depending upon the topic studied and purpose of the study: exploration, description, explanation, or application. *Exploratory* research is typically conducted when researchers are unfamiliar with a topic or there is a lack of prior research. Exploration is sometimes needed to provide a framework for future research endeavors. A lot of research in criminal justice is *descriptive* in nature where the researcher describes some phenomenon of interest. Descriptive research can also be used as a foundation to develop a more sophisticated type of study. The third type of research is *explanatory*. Social scientists are often interested in explaining the "why" of something. For example, why are the elderly more fearful of crime than younger people despite their low rates of victimization? Finally, *applied* research involves evaluating the effectiveness or impact of a program or policy. Criminal justice research can also be categorized into qualitative or quantitative. *Qualitative* research involves detailed information about some social issue or problem to provide thorough understanding. *Quantitative* research is designed to formulate and utilize theories and hypotheses pertaining to our social world. Again, the choice is dictated by what the researcher is studying and how the information will be used.

Methods of Observation

Methods of observation include experiments, surveys, field research, and unobtrusive research. All of these have been used to study the criminal justice system. *Experiments* allow researchers to determine whether or not one variable produces change in another variable. Two important features of an experiment are treatment and control. A researcher introduces some type of treatment to a variable of interest while controlling for extraneous influences. Experiments are ideal for establishing cause and effect. *True* experiments (those meeting all of the requirements of experimental design) are rarely utilized in criminal justice research. *Quasi-experiments* (experiments lacking one or more of the essential components of a true experiment) are more common given the difficultly controlling the settings in which criminal justice research takes place. These difficulties will be addressed in each of the studies presented that utilizes an experimental design. The most common method of observation in criminal justice research is survey research. *Survey* research typically involves administering a standardized questionnaire to a sample of respondents. Respondents are selected through some type of sampling procedure based on characteristics reflective of a population. Responses are then numerically coded and analyzed using statistical techniques. Surveys are conducive for making generalizations from a selected sample to a population of interest. *Field* research is used to gain firsthand knowledge of a social phenomenon. Field research is also called *observational* or *ethnographic* research because the researcher gathers data by observing subjects in their naturally occurring environments. Observers may participate by becoming actively engaged with the subjects or have no direct interaction with the subjects. The last mode of observation, *unobtrusive* research, involves examining data that has already been collected by another researcher or institution. Criminal justice agencies collect an enormous amount of information as part of their daily operations, and researchers can learn more about how these agencies function by using this *archival* data.

Research Design

Research design is an important part of research. It is a plan for how a research study will be carried out. The steps involved in the research process are presented below:

- **Step 1 Select Topic**

  What is the research question you would like to answer? Topic must be specific and stated in such a way that concepts (variables) can be measured.

- **Step 2 Review Prior Research**

  How have others studied your topic? What did they find? How will your study improve upon prior research?

- **Step 3 Observation**

  Which mode of observation will you use to collect data on your topic: experiment, survey, field or an unobtrusive design? What type of study are you conducting and how will the research be used?

- **Step 4 Analyze Data**

  What statistical techniques will you use to make sense out of your data? Will you be describing your data or making inferences from a sample to population?

- **Step 5 Report Findings**

  What are the results of your study? How do these results fit into the existing body of knowledge on your topic?

Steps in the Research Process

Ethical Considerations

Some of the research discussed in this book has been criticized for ethical violations. Regardless of the type of research or mode of observation, researchers must follow certain ethical principles when conducting research. Every academic discipline has a standard of ethics that members are expected to adhere to. The most common ethical considerations include avoiding harm to subjects and being truthful in reporting. Research involving human subjects falls under the greatest scrutiny. Universities and other sponsoring agencies have institutional review boards that oversee these projects to make sure there is no potential for physical, psychological, or legal harm. Researchers must not deceive their subjects, and they should obtain informed consent. All promises of anonymity and confidentiality must be kept. Researchers must also be truthful in reporting how their research was conducted, and they have a responsibility to report the agency that is sponsoring their research. Results must be thoroughly and accurately reported.

Selecting the Research

Choosing 40 studies for inclusion in this book was an easy task. Thousands of studies have been published in each of the three areas of criminal justice: police, courts, and corrections. Choosing *which* 40 studies was more difficult. We believe the studies that are included in this book represent some of the most significant published research in criminal justice and provide students with examples of a variety of research designs used in criminal justice research.[2] We consider the studies significant for various reasons. First, we include several "pioneering" works. These are

---

[2] Only studies that included a thorough description of the research methodology were considered for inclusion.

studies that were the first of their kind and changed the way we think about criminal justice topics. Second, we include studies that have generated a considerable amount of other research. Third, we include studies that have had a major influence on the operation of the criminal justice system. Fourth, some of the studies are notable because of the controversy surrounding the research design and/or the findings. Most of the studies selected are considered "classics" in the field as evidenced by their inclusion in most textbooks and reading lists in criminal justice courses. Many of the studies have also been listed in various studies reporting on the frequency of the most cited research in criminal justice.[3]

Organization of the Research

The studies selected for the book will include a complete citation for where the original study can be located as well as the following information:

an introduction that includes background information to provide a context in which the study was conducted;

a thorough description of how the study was designed and carried out, including the type of research undertaken and any problems the researchers may have encountered;

a detailed summary of the results and how the authors interpreted the results;

a discussion of any follow up research, criticisms and/or ethical issues raised with the research; and

summaries of a selection of more recent studies conducted on the same topic, including references and suggestions for additional reading.

References

Crank, J. (2003). *Imagining Justice.* Cincinnati: Anderson.

Frost, N., and T. Clear (2007). "Doctoral Education in Criminology and Criminal Justice." *Journal of Criminal Justice Education* 18:35–52.

Morn, F. (1995). *Academic Politics and the History of Criminal Justice Education.* Westport, CT: Greenwood.

Morris, A. (1975). "The American Society of Criminology: A History, 1941–1974." *Criminology* 13:123–67.

President's Commission on Law Enforcement and Administration of Justice (1967). *The Challenge of Crime in a Free Society.* Washington, DC: Government Printing Office.

Reviewers

Ronald Ialouetta
Witchita State University, KS

Robert B. Jenkot
University of Alabama, AL

Christine Tartaro
Richard Stockton College, NJ

Carlos E. Posadas
New Mexico State University, NM

Debra Ross
Grand Valley State University, MI

Donald Faggiani
University of Wisconsin-Oshkosh, WI

---

[3] For example, Wright, R. and J. Miller (1998). "The Most-Cited Scholars and Works in Police Studies." *Policing: An International Journal of Police Strategies & Management* 21:240–254 and Wright, R. and J. Miller (1999). "The Most-Cited Scholars and Works in Corrections." *The Prison Journal* 79:5–22.

ACKNOWLEDGMENTS

We offer our sincere gratitude to all those from Prentice Hall who have guided and supported us throughout this endeavor: Tim Peyton, Daniel Trudden, Alicia Kelly, Jessica Sykes, and Shiji Sashi. It has been a pleasure working with all of you. Thank you for your patience and for making this experience so enjoyable for us. We would also like to thank the reviewers for providing useful and valuable feedback.

ABOUT THE AUTHORS

Amy Thistlethwaite is an associate professor in the Department of Political Science and Criminal Justice at Northern Kentucky University. She earned her Ph.D. from the University of Cincinnati in 1999. Her research interests include domestic violence, sentencing, and corrections. Her research has appeared in *Criminology, Journal of Quantitative Criminology, Crime and Delinquency* and *Public Health Reports.* She is currently working on the development of a Mental Health Court for the Northern Kentucky region.

John Wooldredge is a professor in the Division of Criminal Justice at the University of Cincinnati. He received his Ph.D. in Sociology in 1986 from the University of Illinois. His research and publications focus on institutional corrections (crowding, inmate violence, inmate adaptation), and criminal case processing (sentencing and recidivism, extra-legal disparities in case processing and outcomes). He is currently involved in research on inter-judge variability in sentencing, victim-based disparities in case processing, and official responses to prison inmate rule violations. Related work has recently appeared or is forthcoming in *Criminology, Journal of Research in Crime and Delinquency, Justice Quarterly, Crime and Delinquency,* and *Journal of Criminal Justice.*

FORTY STUDIES THAT CHANGED CRIMINAL JUSTICE

PART

I

Police

Policing in the United States evolved from English traditions and practices. In colonial America, law enforcement was the responsibility of the local community, and individual citizens assumed the role of maintaining order and keeping the peace. In 1845, the city of New York established the first police department, and the concept of an organized police force spread quickly to other major cities. The first police officers were unskilled and untrained and served at the whim of local political leaders. Officers were selected from their own communities and were expected to meet the needs of the community, particularly those of the less fortunate. The police helped the poor by working in soup kitchens and shelters (Travis and Langworthy 2007). Law enforcement took a backseat to service. Service to the poor gave way to service to the politicians by the end of the 19th century. The police became entangled in local politics, and many turned to corruption as a way to supplement their incomes.

Efforts to reform the police after the turn of the 20th century resulted in a new generation of officers. A civil service system was put into place to select more qualified recruits. Retention and promotion would be based upon job performance, not political ties. Advances in science and technology opened the door for police officers to become true crime fighters using such techniques as fingerprint analysis to identify suspects. A new breed of police administrators emerged as well. The International Association of Chiefs of Police became a forum for sharing knowledge and generating ideas and innovations in police work (Johnson 1981). By the mid-20th century, policing had become a professionalized occupation. The police were seen as highly specialized crime fighters responsible for protecting the public and keeping communities safe. An unfortunate consequence of the efforts to transform the police from political pawns to professionalized law enforcement officers, however, was that the police became isolated from their communities.

The social turmoil of the 1960s created a division between the police and the public. Large segments of the population began to express discontent with their government in the form of protests and demonstrations. The police were charged with responding to these actions. Through their efforts to keep the peace, the police were often viewed as the strong arm of the government infringing upon the rights of citizens to voice their opinions. Many people started to question the legitimacy and authority of the police. By the early 1970s, police community relations were strained. A second reform movement took place to help bridge the gap between the public and the police (Roberg et al. 2005). The poor relationships were having an impact on police work. The police could not function effectively as crime fighters without the assistance of the public. The police rely upon the public to report crime and provide information that helps identify suspects. Police departments all across the country implemented various programs to build public confidence in the police and improve police community relations. In some departments, police returned to their roots of patrolling on foot to increase face-to-face interactions with the public. In other neighborhoods, the police set up community station houses to make the police more accessible. These efforts were also designed to make people feel safe. Fear of crime was at an all time high and the strained relations between the public and the police were believed responsible. Recruitment strategies changed to attract more women and minorities into police work. Agencies wanted a more diverse police force that was representative of the communities in which they worked. While the role of the police has changed over the years, what has not is the continuous struggle to achieve a balance between protecting the public without infringing upon our individual liberties (Travis and Langworthy 2007).

Research on Policing

Until the late 1960s, police departments allocated resources and deployed the police according to customary practices and widely held assumptions about what the police do and how they should do it (Weisburd and Braga 2006). In 1968, the federal government began funding innovative police programs and research on traditional police practices. Hundreds of millions of dollars were spent examining different aspects of the criminal justice system. An enormous body of research was created that not only provided valuable insight into what works in policing, but also challenged many commonly held assumptions about police work. It was also during this time that criminal justice as an academic discipline began to flourish. The growth of Ph.D. programs and police research institutes helped contribute to this body of knowledge.

Policing today can be characterized with some of the same attributes as the 19th century police. Police agencies remain decentralized and police work is still primarily reactive in its focus. The research studies presented in this section are landmark studies in policing. The knowledge produced from this research continues to have major impacts on how the police function in our society. Policing has evolved into an empirical field of study. Modern day police administrators base their decisions on scientific evidence and police officers work in an environment that continues to encourage innovation and more proactive strategies to combat crime and make us feel safe (Sherman 1998). This section includes research on the different aspects of policing in the United States. Studies of police officer behavior, roles, and use of discretion as well as police operations are presented.

References

Johnson, D. (1981). *American Law Enforcement: A History*. St. Louis: Forum Press.

Sherman, L. (1998). "Evidence-Based Policing." *Ideas in American Policing Series*. Washington, DC: The Police Foundation.

Travis, L., and R. Langworthy (2007). *Policing in America: A Balance of Forces* (4th ed.). Upper Saddle River, NJ: Prentice Hall.

Roberg, R., K. Novak, and G. Cordner (2005). *Police and Society* (3rd ed.). Los Angeles: Roxbury.

Weisburd, D., and A. Braga (eds.) (2006). *Police Innovation: Contrasting Perspectives*. Cambridge: University Press.

Further Reading

Berg, B. (1992). *Law Enforcement: An Introduction to Police in Society*. Boston: Allyn and Bacon.

Johnson, H., and N. Wolfe (2003). *History of Criminal Justice*. Cincinnati: Anderson

Klockers, C. (1985). *The Idea of Police*. Beverly Hills, CA: Sage.

Tonry, M. and N. Morris (eds.) (1993). *Modern Policing: Crime and Justice*, Volume 15 in Crime and Justice: A Review of Research. Chicago: University of Chicago Press.

Walker, S. (1977). *A Critical History of Police Reform: The Emergence of Professionalism*. Lexington, MA: DC Health.

Walker, S. (2004). "Science and Politics in Police Research: Reflections on Their Tangled Relationship." *The Annals of the American Academy of Political and Social Science* 593:137–55.

1

Police Behavior

A substantial amount of policing research has focused on the behavior of police officers. Beginning in the 1960s, researchers started to examine the various types of police conduct (proper and improper) and decision-making. One of the earliest observations was that the attitudes and behavior of police officers were different from other citizens. Two competing perspectives have been put forth to explain these differences. According to the first perspective, individuals with particular attitudes, characteristics, and beliefs are attracted to policing as an occupation. Any observed differences between the police and general public are due to personality traits that existed *before* the individual became a police officer. Others believe that the differences are attributed to the unique characteristics of the police occupation itself. Individuals become socialized into a profession and through their work experiences develop certain characteristic attitudes and traits. The socialization process includes both formal and informal processes. The formal socialization consists of the recruitment, selection, and training of police while the informal processes include the interactions between new recruits and more experienced officers (Roberg et al. 2005). The three studies included in this section each support the socialization perspective and have considerably advanced our understanding of police behavior. In 1966, Jerome Skolnick offered insight into how the occupational environment shaped the "working personality" of police. James Q. Wilson (1968) created the first typology of police behavior by examining the different functions police perform in our society. Finally, John Van Maanen (1973) explored the early socialization of police by conducting an observational study of recruits as they enter into their profession.

POLICE PERSONALITY: ARE POLICE OFFICERS DIFFERENT FROM THE REST OF US?

Skolnick, J. (1966). *Justice Without Trial: Law Enforcement in Democratic Society.* New York: Wiley.

Background

One of the inherent conflicts within our criminal justice system is the attempt to maintain social order within the limits proscribed by law. It is within this context that the police are expected to perform their duties as law enforcement officers and peacekeepers. The burden of public safety falls primarily upon the shoulders of the police because of their responsibility to enforce the law. We authorize the police to stop and question citizens on the street and in their cars, to conduct searches of their person and property, and to take them into custody. In each of these situations, the police are infringing upon an individual's freedom and liberty. While this infringement may be permissible, the police are required to follow certain procedures designed to protect an individual's constitutional rights. This apparent contradiction was noted by Herbert Goldstein in 1977 when he wrote, "The police, by the very nature of their function, are an anomaly in a free society" (p. 1). In the early 1960s, the courts took on a more active role in examining police behavior in response to concerns that the police were overstepping their authority and abusing their power. During the *due process revolution*, the US. Supreme Court under Chief Justice Earl Warren redefined the police function in our society. The Court handed down several rulings that favored the rights of individuals over the tactics traditionally used by police to fight crime. In 1966, sociologist Jerome Skolnick published an empirical assessment of the conflict between law and order based on his observations of the daily activities police officers. The police were faced with organizational pressures to enforce the law, however there were procedural restraints that interfered with this objective. It was within this context Skolnick believed that police developed their patterns of behavior.

The Study

Data for the study were derived from Skolnick's (1966) observations of police officers employed in a medium-sized police department located in California. The department consisted of 616 police officers that served the city of Westville (a fictitious name to keep the identity of the department confidential). Westville's population was around 400,000 with a 30 percent nonwhite population. The department was well respected and maintained a good reputation in the community. Skolnick also collected data from Eastville—a comparison city (also fictitiously named) of the same size and similar demographic characteristics. There were, however, a few important differences between the police departments that were mentioned. Eastville spent more money on its police services than Westville, but Westville officers were paid higher salaries and had better benefits. Both departments had experienced decreases in the number of officers, but the decline was more dramatic in Westville. The departments differed in their organizational structure as well. Administration was much more centralized in Westville. The entire police force was contained in one building and functioned under the authority of a single police chief. In Eastville, officers were divided among five precincts, each with its own police captain.

Gaining access to the police department turned out to be an easy task. Permission was obtained from the *gatekeeper*. In *observational* or *ethnographic* research, the gatekeeper has the authority to grant access to a researcher. For this study, the gatekeeper was the Westville police chief. The chief welcomed the opportunity to participate in the study. He was proud of the department's accomplishments over the past decade. The department had previously been known as a "tainted police department," but now had a reputation of being well organized and trustworthy. The chief assigned one Lieutenant Doyle to assist with the introductions and to help familiarize Skolnick with the department. The first observations took place with the patrol division. These officers patrolled in one-officer vehicles and held one of three ranks: patrolman, sergeant, or supervising detective. Skolnick observed officers for a total of eight shifts. The observations took place mostly on the weekends and all were during the second shift (7:00 P.M. to 3:00 A.M.). The objective of the study was to gain firsthand knowledge of the police officers' perceptions, attitudes, and behaviors. Skolnick also interviewed each of the officers he rode with. Using an unstructured interview format, Skolnick questioned the officers' actions, their encounters with the public, their attitudes and perceptions about work and home life.

In addition to observing patrol officers, Skolnick also spent about a week observing officers from the traffic division and 6 weeks with the vice squad. The detectives working vice were especially accommodating. Skolnick was allowed to observe interrogations and conversations with informants. Detectives would even call him at home when an important development with a case occurred. Skolnick's role as observer turned into that of *participant-observer* on more than one occasion. As a participant-observer, Skolnick became an active participant in the daily activities of the study subjects. He accompanied officers on "raids" and was even mistaken for a detective by suspects and officers from neighboring police departments. He also provided assistance to the officers by helping them locate suspects or gain access to some private location.

Skolnick also administered a survey to the police officers working for the Westville Police Department. The questionnaire was distributed to patrol officers during their "preduty briefing." The detectives were called to a special meeting and asked to complete the question-naire. A total of 285 policemen answered the survey. Questions were asked about the officers' demographic characteristics, family background, job satisfaction, attitudes, and beliefs. Most of the responses came from officers who had been working for the department for 9 years or more. Forty-one percent of the officers had graduated from high school and 45 percent had some college training. Most of the officers were married and considered themselves to be "middle-class."

There are several *ethical considerations* that arise when a researcher becomes a partici-pant in the activities of the individuals under observation. Skolnick addressed these in his book. First, there was a concern that Skolnick's participation might somehow influence the outcome of the encounters between police and suspects. For example, the police might have responded more harshly with suspects in an attempt to impress an observer with their author-ity or the police might have been more laidback and informal. During the study period, there were times when a detective would ask Skolnick for his opinion on information received from an informant. Skolnick offered his opinions and justified doing so on the grounds that detec-tives regularly solicit advice from their partners and offering a second opinion might have been beneficial to the detective. He also signed confessions as a witness for the detectives. The suspects Skolnick encountered during the study naturally assumed him to be a detective and this assumption was never corrected. The suspects never gave their *consent* to be studied, which violates one of the *ethical principles* of research. When a researcher becomes a partici-pant-observer, one of the difficult decisions to make is how much to become involved in the activities of those being observed. Skolnick relied on his own professional and moral judgment in making that decision. According to Skolnick, he did not believe that his participation resulted in any unfair or in any different treatment of the suspects by the police.

Skolnick's role as a researcher and the purpose of the study were never kept secret from the participating officers. Skolnick was reporting on their activities, but some of the activities engaged in by police were illegal and could have had adverse consequences for the officers involved. Researchers have an obligation to make sure that their study does not inflict *harm* upon the participants. In his reporting, Skolnick protected the officers' *confidentiality* by never revealing their names (just as he kept the names of the departments confidential). Skolnick also solicited feedback from the officers before publishing his findings. For the most part, the study participants indicated that Skolnick's description and assessment of their behavior was fair and accurate.

Conclusions

Based on his observations of police officers at work (particularly their enforcement patterns) and the officers' responses to his survey, Skolnick offered a description of the "working personality" of police officers. There were certain characteristics of police work that influenced how the police did their job and could be observed in their interactions with the public. The characteristics that shaped the "working personality" included danger and authority. The police were continually aware of the potential danger in their associations with violent suspects and lawbreakers. This awareness caused the police to act in a manner that was "suspicious." The police were trained to be on the constant lookout for suspicious activity. Individuals outside of the policing occupation perceived the police as apprehensive and always on guard. These traits assisted the police in identifying probable threats of danger while on duty; however, they isolated the police from the general public. Police tended to use "perceptual shorthand" in identifying potential sources of danger. Prior experience and the socialization they received from other officers equipped them with "danger cues". Police were frequently put into situations where they had to make quick assessments of danger so they relied upon cues that were readily available, such as a citizen's demeanor, mannerisms, language, dress, and appearance. Citizens became "symbolic assailants" to the police regardless of their actual potential for violence or even past violent behavior. Interestingly enough, when questioned about the dangers of police work, most officers deemphasized their risk of being injured or killed in the line of duty, yet the police expressed a preference for dangerous assignments. One-half of the police officers surveyed indicated that their ideal job assignment within the department was that of detective.

The police are given the authority to enforce the law including laws that the public does not necessarily want enforced (i.e., speeding and public drinking). According to Skolnick, in these situations the public often refused to acknowledge the officers' authority and pressured the police to focus their attention on the dangerous threats instead. The public expected the police to enforce the laws, but challenged their authority to do so when the law was enforced against them. This only further isolated the police from the public. The police were acutely aware of the distance between them and the communities in which they worked. When asked what the most serious problem facing the police was, most officers indicated a problem with public relations (i.e., the publics' disrespect of police, mistrust, lack of cooperation and understanding). Nearly three-fourths of the police officers responded that the public ranked the status of the police as "fair" or "poor". The police feel rejected, alienated, and taken for granted from the very people they are trying to serve.

Skolnick observed a high level of solidarity among police officers. Coworkers in all occupations tend to be united by their common work experiences and problems, but for police officers this solidarity became much more intensified. Police officers spent more time engaged in social activities with other police officers. Over half of the officers' surveyed had participated in three or more police social functions during the past year. The characteristic traits of danger and authority reinforced this solidarity. The public failed to understand the daily risks of being a police officer. Only the police understood the dangers of police work. There was also an unwillingness of the public to assist the police in their law enforcement duties leaving the police to rely only upon each other for backing and support. Efforts to enforce minor law violations (i.e., traffic laws) were frequently met with resistance and resentment from the public. The police were often required to meet organizational demands of performance that tended to result in more aggressive law enforcement tactics. Skolnick used the example of departments setting quotas for traffic citations. While some police preferred to issue warnings to speeders, they were faced with pressures to conform to department standards that required them to write tickets. In addition, the police found themselves enforcing laws that they themselves had broken, for example, speeding and public intoxication. The police were aware of this hypocrisy and so were the citizens who found themselves in trouble for the same conduct. This generated a considerable amount of public criticism toward the police. As a result, police solidarity increased as the police sought out approval and acceptance from other officers. In his interviews with police officers, Skolnick discovered that most officers were conservative in their beliefs and political ideologies. He attributed this to their suspicious personalities. Police found comfort in maintaining the status quo and aligned themselves with conventional values and norms.

Skolnick examined several instances of discretionary justice during his observations. Police were charged with enforcing the law, but the police used their discretion to determine which laws were enforced and against which individuals. The organizational pressures to be efficient and productive influenced the officers' use of discretion. Officers used the threat of an arrest to gather information on other suspects, informants were rewarded with reduced or dropped charges, and suspects were often pressured into confessing to multiple crimes only to have most of them later dismissed. What mattered to the department was that the police maintained adequate clearance rates, which were determined by the number of arrests, not convictions. Skolnick also witnessed the police using their discretion in ways that had adverse effects on minorities. Most of the officers studied openly expressed their dislike of blacks although very few believed that their attitudes resulted in disparate treatment. It was noted that the negative attitudes of police officers were similar to those articulated by other whites in the community. Skolnick pointed out that the biased treatment of blacks also stemmed from factors other than race that the police use in their decision-making. For example, Skolnick observed that traffic warrant police were more likely to arrest suspects with outstanding warrants who were on welfare. The police perceived these suspects as "bad risks." A large proportion of the welfare recipients were black, resulting in harsher treatment for black suspects.

Criticisms

Skolnick provided one of the first empirical analyses of police behavior. He observed and surveyed police officers from two California police departments. One of the major limitations of this research is the *generalizability* of his findings to police working in other jurisdictions. Most of the data came from Westville, a police department described as more efficient and professional than most departments in the United States. The department also enjoyed a high amount of public trust and confidence after cleaning up a lot of the corruption that was prevalent a decade before. Skolnick spent 2 weeks collecting data from the comparison city of Eastville but because of time constraints, limited resources was not able to provide a complete case study of this department (Skolnick 1966).

Skolnick based most of his conclusions on his observations and surveys of police detectives, a group he credits with having the greatest responsibility for law enforcement. He minimized the patrol function and described patrol officers as "peace" officers. Patrol officers play an important role by maintaining order within the community. In some communities the police spend more time maintaining order than enforcing the law, therefore the work of a patrol officer is significant to understanding how the police function in our society (Bordua 1967). Skolnick's observations were made at a time when most people operated under an assumption that detectives were the ones primarily responsible for solving crimes. This assumption would be refuted several years later.

Roger Hood (1967) took issue with the *validity* of Skolnick's findings that were based upon observations of police behavior. One of the major concerns with *observational* research is that the presence of an observer influences the behavior of the study participants. Hood believed this to be true in Skolnick's study particularly when he reported witnessing only one incidence of police violence. This is a criticism of several police studies that utilize observers to collect data (Spano 2005). In addition, the findings were based upon the observations of a single observer. Having only one observer limited the number of subjects and settings selected for observation. Using multiple observers not only increases the number of observations, but it allows the researcher to determine any *observer bias* (Reiss 1971). Observer bias is the tendency of an observer to pay too much attention to expected behaviors and not enough attention to behaviors not perceived as relevant to the study.

Skolnick believed that the behavior of the police was shaped primarily by their occupational experiences. Police officers were socialized in their occupations in similar ways. The elements of "danger" and "authority" influenced the interactions between the police and the public. Organizational pressures to issue tickets and arrest influenced police decision-making. An alternative explanation for police behavior suggested that the characteristics, values, and opinions an officer brings with them to their job were better predictors of behavior. Police work attracted certain types of people whose behavior was more a product of their general personality, not any "working personality" formed on the job. A study of experienced police officers working for the Denver, Colorado Police Department found that officers were actually *less* authoritarian than a control sample of individuals outside of police work (Bayley and Mendelsohn 1969). Research by Milton Rokeach, Martin Miller, and John Snyder (1971) supported this perspective. They administered the Rokeach Value Survey to 153 white male police officers who worked for a medium-sized midwestern police department in 1968. The same survey instrument was administered to a group of citizens by the National Opinion Research Center. The researchers surveyed a random sample of Americans aged 21 and older. A total of 561 white male citizens and 93 black male citizens completed the survey that consisted of questions to assess end goals, terminal values, and instrumental values. The values held by police officers were similar to those held by the general public on several end values (i.e., family security and freedom). No significant differences were found between the police and the public on half of the terminal values (i.e., comfortable life, pleasure, self-respect) or on 6 of the 18 instrumental values (i.e., courageous, loving, polite). To determine the source of the differences between the groups, researchers matched the sample of police officers with members of the general public on such characteristics as age and education. *Matching* is a technique used when a researcher is unable to randomly assign cases to an experimental and control group. The procedure helps to control for preexisting differences between cases that may influence the results of a study. A comparison of values among the matched sample revealed that police differed from the general public on only eight values. In addition, the values held by older police officers were similar to those held by younger officers. According to Rokeach et al. (1971) these findings suggested that social backgrounds and preexisting personality traits were better predictors of police behavior than the socialization of officers on the job (Rokeach et al. 1971). Research published by Jihong Zhao, Ni He, and Nicholas Lovrich in 1998 and by Michael Caldero and Anthony Larose in 2001 supported these findings as well.

Significance and Subsequent Research

Justice Without Trial was one of the first comprehensive studies of police behavior, and its content remains relevant to our understanding of police behavior today. Skolnick's book remains the second most highly cited work in the policing literature (Wright and Miller 1998). Skolnick's description of the "working personality" provides valuable insight into the daily activities of police. Skolnick believed that the occupational elements of danger and authority influence the encounters between the police and the public. Jonathan Rubinstein (1973) provided a description of police work consistent with Skolnick. Based on his observations of the police in Philadelphia, Rubinstein reported that officers were taught to be suspicious as part of their academy training but the on-the-job socialization provided officers with the knowledge to identify potential sources of danger. Research that followed offered support for the contention that police officers developed certain personality characteristics as a result of their experiences on the street. Arthur Niederhoffer (1967) found that police officers were also *cynical.* He developed a 20-item scale to measure levels of cynicism among police and administered the instrument to over 200 New York City police officers. Results showed a *curvilinear* relationship between degree of cynicism and years of experience. Cynicism was lowest among police recruits, progressively increased for officers until about year 10, and then declined with additional years of service. Despite the decline in cynicism for officers with considerable experience, levels never decreased back to those held by recruits. William Westley (1970) identified an additional personality trait based on his observations of police officers from Gary, Indiana. Westley found that police officers were *secretive* about their daily activities primarily because of their perception that the public did not support them. Police experienced feelings of alienation and believed that the public could not be trusted.

Suspicion is an integral part of police work. Police are trained to be on the constant lookout for suspicious activity. While the public may observe this to be an unfavorable personality trait, it helps the police identify possible sources of danger. The courts have also recognized the legitimacy of police suspicion. In the landmark case of *Terry v. Ohio* (1968), the US Supreme Court upheld the stop and frisk of a suspect based on the "reasonable suspicion" of the officer. This decision was recently reaffirmed in the 1989 case of *U.S. v. Sokolow* and with the Court's decision in *U.S. v. Arvizu* (2002). In Arvizu, the Court ruled that permitting an officer to use reasonable suspicion to stop a person or vehicle ". . . allows officers to draw on their own experiences and specialized training to make inferences from and deductions about the cumulative information available" (U.S. Arvizu, 534 U.S. 266 2002).

Skolnick's concept of the "symbolic assailant" becomes particularly relevant in light of recent discussions of racial profiling by police. Skolnick believed that certain citizens became "symbolic assailants" and were perceived as dangerous to the police based on little or no information as to their actual potential for violence. According to Skolnick, "The patrolman in Westville, and probably most communities, has come to identify the black man with danger" (p. 49). Furthermore, most of the officers studied expressed negative attitudes toward the blacks in their community (Skolnick 1966). Little appears to have changed 40 years later. In a recent article, Delores Jones–Brown (2007) wrote ". . . the police are conditioned to suspect blacks, and black males in particular, of wrong-doing even in the absence of actual criminality" (p. 103). Gregory Alpert, John MacDonald, and Roger Dunham (2005) observed police officers in Savannah, Georgia in an effort to understand *how* officers form their suspicions. Over an 8-month period, observers recorded officers forming suspicions a total of 174 times. Suspicions were categorized by researchers as "behavioral" or "nonbehavioral." When the police became suspicious because of some specific action by a citizen, the suspicion was considered behavioral. Nonbehavioral was based on an ". . . individual's appearance, the time and place, and descriptive information provided to an officer" (p. 419). The results showed that police were four times more likely to form "nonbehavioral" suspicions of black suspects compared to white suspects. As part of a large-scale study of racial profiling carried out in conjunction with the Miami–Dade County Police Department, Michael Smith, Matthew Makarios, and Geoffrey Alpert (2006) examined police suspicion in the context of traffic stops. Between April and October 2001, patrol officers were required to fill out a citizen contact card for every traffic stop. Over 66,000 cards were completed that included information on reasons for the stop as well as suspects' demographic data. Researchers found police to be more suspicious of black motorists. In addition, the police were more suspicious of male drivers and drivers of older vehicles. The police were also more suspicious during nighttime hours.

Skolnick's analysis of police behavior helped generate considerable interest among scholars interested in explaining the manners and customs of police officers. Understanding the underlying influences on police behavior has significantly improved our knowledge of the police function in our society. The policing literature today contains a wealth of information identifying the various individual, situational, organizational, and neighborhood influences on behavior. This field of study has also benefited from contributions made by different academic disciplines including sociology, political science, and psychology.

References

Alpert, G., J. MacDonald, and R. Dunham (2005). "Police Suspicion and Discretionary Decision Making During Citizen Stops." *Criminology* 43:407–34.

Bayley, D., and H. Mendelsohn (1969). *Minorities and the Police.* New York: Free Press.

Bordua, D. (1967). "Justice Without Trial: Law Enforcement in Democratic Society, Book Review." *American Sociological Review* 32:492–93.

Caldero, M., and A. Larose (2001). "Value Consistency Within the Police: The Lack of a Gap." *Policing: An International Journal of Police Strategies and Management* 24:162–80.

Goldstein, H. (1977). *Policing a Free Society.* Cambridge, MA: Ballinger.

Hood, R. (1967). "Justice Without Trial: Law Enforcement in Democratic Society, Book Review." *British Journal of Sociology* 18:109–10.

Jones-Brown, D. (2007). "Forever the Symbolic Assailant: The More Things Change, The More They Remain the Same." *Criminology and Public Policy* 6:103–22.

Niederhoffer, A. (1967). *Behind the Shield.* New York: Doubleday.

Roberg, R., K. Novak, and G. Cordner. (2005). *Police and Society* (3rd ed.). Los Angeles: Roxbury.

Rokeach, M., Miller, M. and J. Snyder (1971). "The Value Gap Between Police and Policed." *Journal of Social Issues* 27:155–71.

Rubinstein, J. (1973) *City Police*. New York: Farrar, Straus, and Giroux.

Skolnick, J. (1966). *Justice Without Trial: Law Enforcement in Democratic Society*. New York: Wiley.

Smith, M., M. Makarios, and G. Alpert (2006). "Differential Suspicion and Gender Effects in the Traffic Stop Context." *Justice Quarterly* 23:271–95.

Spano, R. (2005). "Potential Sources of Observer Bias in Police Observational Data." *Social Science Research* 34:591–617.

Westley, W. (1970). *Violence and the Police*. Cambridge, MA: MIT Press.

Wright, R. and J. Miller (1998). "The Most-Cited Scholars and Works in Police Studies." *Policing: An International Journal of Police Strategies & Management* 21:240–54.

Zhao, J., N. He, and N. Lovrich (1998). "Individual Value Preferences Among American Police Officers the Rokeach Theory of Human Values Revisited." *Policing* 21:22–37.

Further Reading

Balch, R. (1972). "The Police Personality: Fact or Fiction." *The Journal of Criminal Law, Criminology, and Police Science* 63:106–19.

Brunson, R. (2007). "Police Don't Like Black People: African-American Young Men's Accumulated Police Experiences." *Criminology and Public Policy* 6:71–102.

Brunson, R. and J. Miller (2006). "Young Black Men and Urban Policing in the United States." *British Journal of Criminology* 46:613–40.

Crank, J. (1998). *Understanding Police Culture*. Cincinnati: Anderson.

Evans, B., G. Coman, and R. Stanley (1992). "The Police Personality: Type A Behavior and Trait Anxiety." *Journal of Criminal Justice* 20:429–41.

Harris, D. (2007). "The Importance of Research on Race and Policing: Making Race Salient to Individuals and Institutions Within Criminal Justice." *Criminology and Public Policy* 6:5–24.

Herbert, S. (1998). "Police Subculture Reconsidered." *Criminology* 36:343–69

Hickman, M., N. Piquero, and A. Piquero (2004). "The Validity of Niederhoffer's Cynicism Scale." *Journal of Criminal Justice* 32:1–13.

Langworthy, R. (1987). "Police Cynicism: What We Know From the Niederhoffer Scale." *Journal of Criminal Justice* 15:17–35.

Reuss-Ianni, E. (1983). *Two Cultures of Policing: Street Cop and Management Cop*. New Burnswick, NJ: Transaction.

Skolnick, J. (2007). "Racial Profiling: Then and Now." *Criminology and Public Policy* 6:65–70.

Weitzer, R. (2000). "Racialized Policing: Residents' Perceptions in Three Neighborhoods." *Law and Society Review* 34:129–56.

POLICE STYLES: WHY ARE THERE DIFFERENCES IN POLICE BEHAVIOR ACROSS COMMUNITIES?

Wilson, J. (1968). *Varieties of Police Behavior: The Management of Law and Order in Eight Communities*. Cambridge, MA: Harvard UP.

Background

The police perform a variety of functions in our society. Police organizations were established with the primary task of reducing crime and disorder. The first police agencies were more involved in maintaining order than fighting crime. This all changed in the early 1900s with the rise of police professionalism. Police became more focused in their law enforcement efforts. While the police continue to fight crime and maintain order, departments today have become much more interested in serving their neighborhoods as part of the shift toward community policing. Police officers perform each of these functions—order maintenance, law enforcement, and service on a daily basis; however, there are observable differences across departments with respect to which function is most apparent. Beginning in the 1960s, researchers became interested in exploring the different functions of police. One such researcher was a political scientist by the name of James Q. Wilson. Wilson recognized that the police performed their duties within the larger organizational context of a bureaucracy. Police agencies were organized according to a hierarchical structure with functional divisions of labor. According to Wilson (1968), the police were a prime example of the "bureaucracy problem." We are all dependent upon some system of law enforcement, and most people agree that this function should be the responsibility of the government. The police provide a variety of services in addition to law enforcement to a large segment of the population. Police agencies across the United States are organized in similar ways, but each responds to a different jurisdiction and operates within a unique political and institutional environment. Wilson believed that how the police performed their duties had obvious implications for the ability to balance the needs of law and order in society.

The Study

Wilson's objective was to provide a detailed description of how patrol officers performed their duties and to determine if there were any differences in performance from one department to another. The study was offered as an *exploratory* study because of the void in research on differences in police function. Exploratory research is appropriate when little is known about a particular topic. Wilson utilized a variety of data sources for his research including observations, interviews with police officers, and official police records. In selecting the departments for his study, he first wanted to determine if there were differences in how police departments responded to minor crimes. During the summer of 1964, he arranged to have a group of his students conduct research on police departments and local courts in 12 cities. The departments were selected as a matter of convenience in that they were located near where the students lived. *Convenience* sampling is often used during the early stages of a research project to identify potential units for study. Half of the cities were described as "working class" and the other half as "high-income" suburbs. The following year, several additional departments were selected at random for his study. *Random* samples are selected through a process that gives each unit in the population an equal chance of being selected. Random samples are more likely to be representative of the population from which the sample is selected. Wilson's research assistants visited 17 cities to collect data and interview police and court personnel. Wilson then selected eight cities for his detailed analysis. Six of the cities were located in New York: Albany, Amsterdam, Brighton, Nassau, Newburgh, and Syracuse. The other two cities were Highland Park, Illinois, and Oakland, California. The eight study sites were selected using *purposive* sampling where the researcher relies on his or her expert judgment in selecting units that are representative of some population. Wilson selected cities with different characteristics such as population size, social class, and type of city government that he believed would explain differences in the police function. Each department was visited between two and four times, with each visit lasting from 3 to 8 weeks. Five of the cities: Albany, Amsterdam, Newburgh, Oakland, and Syracuse were described as "industrial, working-class cities." Each had a median household income below the state average, and each was ethnically diverse. With the exception of Amsterdam, these cities also had a large proportion of black residents. The remaining three cities: Brighton, Highland Park, and Nassau were "well-to do suburban areas" whose residents were predominately white. Wilson categorized four of the cities as "high crime" cities: Albany, Newburgh, Oakland, and Syracuse.

Wilson focused his attention on minor crimes for three reasons. First, these were the most commonly committed offenses. Less than 10 percent of all suspects arrested were charged with an index crime. Second, these were crimes that impacted the largest number of citizens. Third, police officers exercised a considerable amount of discretion with less serious offenses. Wilson was particularly interested in the discretionary decisions of police. Unlike most bureaucracies where discretion was greatest among the top ranking officials, it was actually the patrol officer who used the most discretion in police work. In addition to enforcing the law, patrol officers were also responsible for maintaining order, keeping the peace, and preventing crime by looking out for suspicious activity. It was with the latter activities—maintaining order, peacekeeping, and crime prevention—that patrol officers used the most discretion.

Findings

Because of the *exploratory* nature of the study, Wilson did not test any specific *hypotheses*. The objective of his study was to describe in-depth the work of a patrol officer, including their use of discretion. He also wanted to identify the relevant factors that influenced differences in patrol across jurisdictions. The findings presented below were based on information obtained from a 3-year examination of eight police departments located in three states.

Police functions. Patrol officers perform three major functions in our society: law enforcement, order maintenance, and service. Law enforcement involves responding to violations of the legal code by making an arrest, thereby invoking the criminal justice process. In performing this function, the police respond to crimes reported by the public (referred to by Wilson as "citizen-invoked law enforcement") or as a result of the officer's own initiative ("police-invoked law enforcement"). Order maintenance activities consist of peacekeeping efforts. The police respond to many situations where there is no obvious violation of the law and often the officer relies on an informal response (i.e., command to go home). Wilson believed that the patrol officer's position in society was defined more by his order maintenance function than his law enforcement activities. Not only were these situations more common, but also officers had to rely on their discretion in deciding on an appropriate response. The broadest police function is the service function. Police are often called upon to perform a variety of services (i.e., assisting motorists and providing information) primarily because of their accessibility. A common assumption underlying police work was that patrol officers spent most of their time fighting crime. In the large, socially diverse cities, Wilson found that patrol officers spent *more* time engaged in order maintenance and service activities than law enforcement. An examination of dispatch records for the Syracuse Police Department revealed that 37.5 percent of calls were service related and 30.1 percent were related to order maintenance. Law enforcement accounted for only 10.3 percent of all calls. Given the varied and unpredictable nature of responding to order maintenance calls, patrol officers perceived this activity to be most dangerous (Wilson was not able to determine the number of officers killed or injured while performing this function). For example, when a patrol officer responded to a domestic disturbance, he did not know the suspect's potential for violence. The officer may have appeared to be anxious and standoffish to the suspect who then misinterpreted the officer's behavior as aggressive. Public order laws tended to be vague putting the officer in a position where he must determine first if any law was broken and second how to respond (i.e., arrest or a command to go home). In many of these situations, there was no victim or complaining party present leaving the police to rely on their judgment as to how to handle things. The presence of a victim, however, did not necessarily make things easier for the police. In many states, the police were unable to arrest someone for a misdemeanor unless the crime occurred in the presence of the officer or the victim made a sworn complaint. Wilson reviewed police reports in Oakland and discovered that in a one-month period, there were 163 batteries reported to the police. The victim knew their attacker in most of these cases; however, less than a third resulted in arrest. Victims frequently refused to press charges, but they wanted the police to take some type of action that the police were not authorized to do (i.e., throw a husband out of their home). Encounters between the police and citizens rarely ended in either party walking away satisfied. Wilson found this to be especially true in lower-class communities where crimes of violence were more frequent.

Police discretion. Wilson conceptualized four different situations that a patrol officer was called upon to use their discretion. The first situation involved *police-invoked law enforcement.* The police discovered that a crime had been committed or an innocent bystander reported it. There was typically no victim expressing a preferred response so the police relied upon departmental policies and community standards to determine what action (if any) would be taken. One example of this type of situation was traffic enforcement. In his analysis of traffic citations across all eight communities, Wilson found significant variation in the rate at which officers wrote tickets. Syracuse had a rate that was 10 times greater than Albany, despite the fact that these cities had similar characteristics. Wilson attributed the variation to differences in department policies, not community characteristics. Some of the departments had recently purchased speed radar equipment, and others had a quota system in place to measure performance. The enforcement of vice crimes such as prostitution and gambling was also influenced by departmental policies, but community standards also played a role. Vice crimes were rare occurrences in the suburbs compared to the small industrial cities. In large cities, police typically were provided more resources for enforcing vice laws.

The second situation included *citizen-invoked law enforcement.* The victim reported a crime to the police who took down a report. If the suspect was also present at the time the police responded, the officer then had to decide whether or not to arrest. Police exercised the least amount of discretion in these situations. The seriousness of the offense and the suspect's age as well as the department's policies influenced the officer's decision-making. Wilson found that departments with specialized juvenile units took these offenses more seriously than those without. Officers had time to keep track of the juveniles and had access to resources to help them deal with problem juveniles. Wilson also discovered differences in arrest rates for larceny (the most common victim-reported crime). In Oakland and Syracuse, several juveniles were arrested for larceny, while very few were in Albany and Newburgh. Albany and Newburg had no specialized juvenile patrol officers. Juvenile arrests in these two cities were primarily for serious offenses such as robbery, aggravated assault, burglary, and auto theft. Interviews with patrol officers in the suburban communities revealed that juvenile crime was taken seriously because officers had time to respond to them and the officers received input from the community.

Other situations were *police-invoked order maintenance.* Here the police just happened upon a disorderly situation. Without a victim, the police were afforded a tremendous amount of discretion in deciding how to respond. Because these situations were so varied, there was often a lack of department procedures to guide discretion. The most common type of disorderly behavior was public drunkenness. Most departments preferred officers not to arrest these suspects unless the person had no place to go and was involved in some other type of problem behavior (i.e., fighting). The typical police response was to take the person home or to the stationhouse to sober up. There were observable differences in arrest rates for public drunkenness across the eight cities. Significantly more people were arrested in the suburban communities compared to the industrial cities. Suburban communities were less tolerant of this behavior and residents were more likely to turn to the police for action.

The last situation was *citizen-invoked order maintenance.* A citizen would call the police to complain about a public or private disorder. The police still had the discretion to decide on an appropriate course of action, but their discretion was influenced by input provided by the citizen. These situations were governed less by departmental policies because there was often no legal basis for an arrest unless the citizen swore out a complaint. Wilson, however, uncovered differences in misdemeanor assault rates that he attributed to differences in departmental policies across departments. Oakland had a high assault rate compared to the other jurisdictions. Officers in Oakland were permitted to take the suspect into custody once the victim signed a complaint that the officer had in his possession. In New York, the victim had to wait until morning to sign the complaint. Newburg also had a high number of assaults. Wilson attributed this to police officers arresting suspects for third-degree battery when in fact the evidence justified a felony charge. The officers believed that suspects would receive a harsher penalty from the city court compared to the county court that maintained jurisdiction over felony offenses.

Styles of policing. Wilson identified three organizational "styles" of policing based upon how the police performed their order maintenance function. The specific "style" displayed by a department was explained by the use of discretion by its patrol force, the organization, and political culture of a community. The "watchman style" characterized departments concerned primarily with keeping the peace by controlling illegal and disruptive behavior. These departments were typically found in communities without a serious crime problem. The term "watchman" exemplified police work in the early 19th century. Officers patrolled their beats in an effort to "keep the peace" in the community. Under this model, police exercised a considerable amount of discretion in deciding between formal and informal police action. Discretion was controlled by departmental policies only to the extent that police administrators permitted the officers to ignore certain minor law violations. Offenses that were tolerated by the public tended to also be tolerated by the department and the police typically relied on an informal response. This did not mean that communities operating under a watchmen style necessarily looked the same, nor did it mean that serious laws were not enforced. Factors such as the socioeconomic structure and political system influenced community standards of public order. Albany, Amsterdam, and Newburg all displayed the watchman style of policing. A downside to this arrangement was that the police tended to use their discretion in ways that had adverse effects on certain members of the community. Wilson found that in Albany and Newburg, police were more likely to arrest blacks for disorderly conduct compared to Oakland. The political culture in the watchman cities had several things in common. Government was in the hands of local community leaders. Local politicians responded to the concerns of their constituency that were primarily working-class residents. Party ties and individual networks, as well as keeping taxes low were important considerations.

The "legalistic style" involved a strict adherence to the criminal law. The police saw themselves as crime fighters. Officers issued a large number of traffic tickets, arrested a large number of juveniles, and misdemeanor offenders. These departments placed a high premium on technical efficiency. Officers were encouraged to work harder and smarter to achieve a desired outcome. The use of discretion was minimized because the police operated under the principle that if a law had been violated they had an obligation to enforce it. Oakland,

Highland Park, and Syracuse had departments with this style. Strict enforcement of the law did not mean that the police did not respond informally to certain types of crimes. These departments all had some officers who preferred to handle minor offenses with an informal response. Wilson found that legalistic departments were usually ones with prior histories of corruption and poor public image. Adopting a legalistic style was a way for a "reform chief" to reduce negative publicity and criticism. The legalistic style could also be problematic for black residents. Wilson found that over 38 percent of all blacks in Oakland and 29 percent of blacks in Syracuse had a formal involvement with the police in 1965. This number was significantly higher than in the watchman departments. Two of the three legalistic communities (Oakland and Highland Park) were governed by highly professional city managers assisted by a mayor and an elected city council. In Syracuse, the top ranking official was the mayor.

The "service style" emphasized the delivery of police services (requests for law enforcement and order maintenance) in response to community needs. Police relied heavily on citizen input and informal action in helping communities address the problems of crime and disorder. This style was most likely to be found in middle-class homogenous communities such as the cities of Brighton and Nassau. Here, residents shared common values and definitions of disorder. Serious crime was minimal, but the police still devoted sufficient resources to their prevention. In Nassau, officers were assigned to specialized investigative units that were responsible for particular types of crime. The department implemented a public education campaign to combat drug use. One concern in a service-oriented department was that police would play favorites with the more prestigious residents. This was difficult for Wilson to examine because arrest reports did not include a suspect's income. Service departments were concerned with maintaining a positive image in the community and typically had a no-tolerance policy of favoritism. The number of black residents in these communities was small, but they expressed favorable attitudes toward the police. In the service communities, politicians were most responsive to the middle- and upper-class residents who had high expectations of their city government. Leaders were expected to sustain a thriving business community, offer an excellent school system, and work to preserve the community's positive reputation.

Drawing from his training in political science, Wilson was particularly interested in how the political culture of a community had an influence over the "style" of police work. To help substantiate this premise further, Wilson analyzed data from 188 cities across the United States. Cities were categorized according to four types of local government: professional council-manager, nonprofessional council-manager, partisan mayor-council, and non-partisan mayor-council. Next, he classified each police department according to one of his three "styles." Wilson used arrest rates for crimes that typically involved the use of discretion (i.e., larceny, simple assault, public drunkenness). Wilson speculated that the professional council-manager cities would be more likely to have legalistic police departments while the partisan mayor-council cities would be more likely to have watchman departments. The data supported both claims. For the other two cities, nonprofessional council-manager and non-partisan mayor-council, there was no relationship with style of police work.

Policy Implications

Even though Wilson's study was offered as an exploratory study of police functions, he put forth several policy recommendations based on his findings. Because patrol officers were afforded a tremendous amount of discretion, there was always the potential for abuse. Officers may exceed their authority or rely on extralegal factors in their decision-making. To reduce this probability, Wilson suggested that departments work on recruiting and selecting better police officers, particularly those with a college education. While this might have improved the decision-making abilities of officers in the long run, in the short term departments must control the use of discretion with rules and regulations. Adopting a more legalistic style would reduce the amount of discretion used by police, but would likely be met with resistance from the officers themselves. In addition to being trained in when to use discretion, officers needed guidance in *how* to use their discretion.

Criticisms

Wilson's analysis of police departments in eight US cities provided a detailed description of the differences in police function and offered possible explanations for those differences. Wilson himself acknowledged that the eight cities were not representative of all cities across the country. Cities were selected using a *non-probability* (or non-random) sampling procedure. Departments were selected according to characteristics Wilson believed would help explain the different styles of police work. Only small and medium-sized cities were included. One of the drawbacks of using a non-probability sample is that the results may not *generalize* to other units of analysis (in this case to other police departments) particularly departments in large cities. According to Patrick Murphy (1970), Wilson's study ignored two important problems faced by police departments in large urban areas: the large proportion of lower-class black residents and poor police community relations. The ability of the police to control crime was often hindered by the tense relationship between citizens and the police (Murphy 1970, Galliher 1971). What had yet to be determined at the time of Wilson's study was the impact on crime resulting from efforts to repair these relationships. Daniel Glaser (1969) also took issue with Wilson's limited number of cities. Despite Wilson's effort to expand his analysis to examine differences in political structure for 188 other cities, the cities all had similar characteristics as the original eight. This could have created a problem for Wilson's typology. According to Glaser (1969), the legalistic and watchman styles were ". . . the extremes of a single main dimension. The service style is an optimum middle range between these extremes . . ." (p. 137).

Critics also took issue with Wilson's source of data. A significant portion of his study was based upon official statistics that can present an inaccurate count of crime. Wilson utilized arrest statistics to support many of his contentions, but very few police-citizen encounters ended in arrest (Black 1969). Wilson's study also ignored an important element of the police function—the interactions between police and citizens. Limited resources prevented him from examining such encounters (Wilson 1968). If Wilson had supplemented his research with observations of police-citizen interactions, he may have been able to more accurately measure the extent to which police abused their discretion. This was something Wilson believed to be beyond the scope of social science research, despite the fact that other researchers have drawn conclusions regarding the abuse of discretion from such an approach (Black 1969). Thomas Smith (1969) also criticized Wilson for not exploring the role of *police legitimacy* in his analysis of police functions. Police legitimacy refers to the degree of public trust in the police. The extent to which citizens perceived the actions of the police as fair may be related to the "style" of policing found in a particular community.

Significance and Subsequent Research

Wilson developed a typology of four types of discretionary situations and explained differences in the way police performed their order maintenance function in terms of three styles of policing. Differences were explained from both organizational and political perspectives. Wilson's study was the first to provide a comprehensive analysis of police behavior across multiple departments. Wilson's study also offered a thorough look at the work of a patrol officer who Wilson observed to hold the greatest responsibility for enforcing the law. Patrol officers exercised a considerable amount of discretion that could be abused if departments failed to become proactive in their efforts to control it. Wilson's styles of policing have also been used to understand differences in individual police officer behavior (Coates 1972). A *legalistic abusive officer* perceived himself as a guardian of community norms and values. Officers tended to be rigid in their jobs and had no problem using coercive power. The *task-oriented officer* was more concerned with enforcing the law according to department rules and regulations, while the *community service officer* relied less on law enforcement and believed instead that the role of the police should be to help the community with their everyday problems.

Varieties of Police Behavior remains one of the most highly cited books in the police literature (ranked third behind Skolnick in terms of the number of times the work has been cited (Wright and Miller 1998). Wilson's ideas, however, have also been among the least empirically tested (Hassell et al. 2003). Ten years after Wilson published his findings, Susette Talarico and Charles Swanson (1978) conducted an empirical study to determine the extent to which departmental and individual styles of policing were related. A questionnaire was mailed to a randomly selected sample of 18 police departments across the United States. Six hundred and fifty useable surveys were returned (*response rate* of 72.2%). Respondents included uniformed patrol officers who were asked questions to assess their perceptions of what style of policing existed within their department as well as their own individual style of policing. The largest percentage of officers (43.4%) viewed their department as service oriented, followed by legalistic (32.7%) and watchman (23.9%). The study found that perceptions were consistent between patrol officers and their supervisors.

Wilson's premise that the political culture of a community influenced the style of policing adopted by the police department has also been the subject of subsequent research. Political culture was not well defined by Wilson who used a typology of local government political systems. In his 1968 study, Wilson found that professional council-manager cities were more likely to have legalistic police departments while the partisan mayor-council cities were more likely to have watchman departments. In 1978, Wilson and Barbara Boland used a similar indicator of political culture in a study of police practices across 35 large American cities and found additional support for Wilson's original measure. Cheryl Swanson (1978) examined three indicators of community political culture: the percentage of white-collar, the percentage of foreign-born or mixed parentage, and the percentage of membership in the League of Women Voters across 40 cities in the United States with populations between 300,000 and 1,000,000. She found that the third indicator (membership in the League of Women Voters) had an influence on the arrest rate for simple assault, driving while intoxicated, and disorderly conduct (Swanson 1978). More recently, Kimberly Hassell, Jihong Zhao, and Edward Maguire (2003) wanted to determine if Wilson's findings would apply to an understanding of modern police organizations. Four hundred and one police departments with at least 100 full-time officers participated in a mail survey to determine the influence of local political culture on police function. Data did not support such a relationship (Hassell et al. 2003). This suggested that police departments might not be subject to the same political pressures that existed when Wilson undertook his study.

Additional typologies of police organizations emerged after Wilson. In 1984, Doug Smith published a study using data from 21 police departments across three states. He classified police agencies according to their level of bureaucratization and professionalism. Four distinct types emerged: legalistic, service, militaristic, and fraternal. Legalistic and service departments were consistent with Wilson's description. *Legalistic* departments were high on professionalism and were highly bureaucratic. *Service* departments were highly professional with low bureaucratization. *Militaristic* departments were nonprofessional, highly bureaucratic agencies while *fraternal* departments were both nonprofessional and had low bureaucratization. He then analyzed a total of 5,688 police-citizen encounters to determine if police organization type influenced arrest probabilities even after such factors as suspect characteristics, victim preferences, presence of a police supervisor, and offense type were taken into account. These factors were found to have different influences depending on the type of police department. For example, juveniles were more likely to be arrested in legalistic departments, while suspects who acted in a manner described as "antagonistic" toward police were less likely to be arrested in legalistic departments compared to the other department types. Victim preferences were related to the arrest decision across all types of police departments. In both militaristic and legalistic police agencies, officers were more likely to arrest in the presence of their supervisors. Finally, the police were more likely to arrest suspects for violent offenses in fraternal and legalistic departments compared to service and fraternal departments.

Researchers also set out to determine whether or not Wilson's findings applied to cities with different characteristics than the eight examined in his book. Robert Langworthy offered a *replication* of Wilson's study in 1985. He analyzed data from 152 police agencies located in cities with populations over 100,000. Cities were categorized as "good" government cities (those with council-managers), "traditional" government cities (mayor-council elected on partisan tickets), and "mixed" government cities (those that hold partisan elections *or* have a mayor-council). Information used to categorize the cities was obtained from the municipal Yearbook. Arrest data for each city was acquired from the FBI. Findings from the study supported Wilson's conclusions. Arrest rates for larceny and driving while intoxicated were higher in "good" government cities, while arrests for disorderly conduct were highest in "traditional" cities. Contrary to Wilson, however, this study found there was only a general *tendency* for political culture to influence police style. In other words, departments were not "restricted" by that culture. John Crank (1990) studied police styles across departments in Illinois and found that the same factors that influenced police style in urban communities did not apply equally to rural areas. Organizational characteristics maintained a greater influence on police style in urban communities, whereas environmental factors had a greater influence in rural communities.

After examining local police departments across eight different communities, Wilson conceptualized the role of police in terms of three major functions: law enforcement, order maintenance, and service. His description of each function is as relevant to our understanding of the police function today as it was in 1968. Wilson was among the first to examine and explain the discretionary decisions of patrol officers. He believed that departments could exercise greater control over these decisions by improved recruiting and selection procedures. Hiring officers with some college would help improve police decision-making. Currently, 15 percent of all local police departments require at least a 2-year college degree (Hickman and Reaves 2003). Research has found that college-educated officers maintain higher performance standards and receive fewer citizen complaints compared to less educated officers (Roberg et al. 2005). With his focus on order maintenance, Wilson drew attention to an area of police work that had previously been ignored in the literature. Less serious offenses are by far the most numerous and impact the largest number of people. It is also with less serious offenses that police exercise most of their discretionary decisions. This does not mean that the theory is limited in scope. John Crank (1992) found that Wilson's styles also applied to more serious crimes.

References

Black, D. (1969). "Varieties of Police Behavior: The Management of Law and Order in Eight Communities" (Book Review). *Administrative Science Quarterly* 14:321–23.

Coates, R. (1972). *The Dimension of Police-Citizen Interaction: A Social Psychological Analysis.* Ph.D. Dissertation, University of Michigan.

Crank, J. (1990). "The Influence of Environmental and Organizational Factors on Police Style in Urban and Rural Environments." *Journal of Research in Crime and Delinquency* 27:166–89.

Crank, J. (1992). "Police Style and Legally Serious Crime: A Contextual Analysis of Municipal Police Departments." *Journal of Criminal Justice* 20:401–12.

Galliher, J. (1971). "Explanations of Police Behavior: A Critical Review and Analysis." *Sociological Quarterly* 12:308–18.

Glaser, D. (1969). "Varieties of Police Behavior: The Management of Law and Order in Eight Communities" (Book Review). *Social Forces* 48:136–37.

Hassell, K., J. Zhao, and E. Maguire (2003). "Structural Arrangements in Large Municipal Police Organizations: Revisiting Wilson's Theory of Local Political Culture." *Policing: An International Journal of Police Strategies and Management* 26:231–50.

Hickman, M., and B. Reaves (2003). *Local Police Departments, 2000.* Washington, DC: Bureau of Justice Statistics.

Langworthy, R. (1985). "Wilson's Theory of Police Behavior: A Replication of the Constraint Theory." *Justice Quarterly* 2:89–98.

Murphy, P. (1970). "Varieties of Police Behavior: The Management of Law and Order in Eight Communities" (Book Review). *Harvard Law Review* 83:1943-47.

Roberg, R., K. Novak, and G. Cordner (2005). *Police and Society* (3rd ed.). Los Angeles: Roxbury.

Smith, D. (1984). "The Organizational Context of Legal Control." *Criminology* 22:19–38.

Smith, T. (1969). "Varieties of Police Behavior: The Management of Law and Order in Eight Communities" (Book Review). *American Journal of Sociology* 75:160–62.

Swanson, C. (1978). "The Influence of Organization and Environment on Arrest Policies in Major U.S. Cities." *Policy Studies Journal* 7:390–98.

Talarico, S., and C. Swanson, Jr. (1978). "Styles of Policing: A Preliminary Mapping." *Policy Studies Journal* 7:398–406.

Wilson, J. (1968). *Varieties of Police Behavior: The Management of Law and Order in Eight Communities.* Cambridge, MA: Harvard UP.

Wilson, J., and B. Boland (1977–78). "The Effect of the Police on Crime." *Law and Society Review* 12:368–90.

Wright, R., and J. Miller (1998). "The Most-Cited Scholars and Works in Police Studies." *Policing: An International Journal of Police Strategies & Management* 21: 240–54.

Further Reading

Brown, M. (1981). *Working the Street: Police Discretion and the Dilemmas of Reform.* New York: Russell Sage Foundation.

Crank, J. (1994). "Watchman and Community: Myth and Institutionalization in Policing." *Law and Society Review* 28:325–52.

Crank, J., and R. Langworthy (1992). "An Institutional Perspective of Policing." *The Journal of Criminal Law and Criminology* 85:338–63.

Langworthy, R. (1986). *The Structure of Police Organizations.* Westport, CT: Praeger.

Maguire, E. (1997). "Structural Change in Large Municipal Police Organizations During the Community Policing Era." *Justice Quarterly* 14:547–76.

Pursley, R. (1976). "Community Characteristics and Policy Implementations: Some Exploratory Findings About Two Categories of Municipal Police Chiefs." *Journal of Criminal Justice* 4:291–301.

Slovak, J. (1986). *Styles of Urban Policing: Organization, Environment, and Police Styles in Selected American Cities.* New York: New York UP.

POLICE OFFICER SOCIALIZATION: WHY ARE POLICE OFFICERS DIFFERENT FROM THE REST OF US?

Van Maanen, J. (1973). "Observations on the Making of Policemen." *Human Organization* **33:407–18.**

Background

Initial studies of police behavior were based on patrol officers and detectives who had already been working in the police field. Much of this research examined the working environments that played a role in the socialization of police. Skolnick (1966) and others identified personality traits that distinguished police from individuals in other occupations. The "working personality" of police was shaped by the occupational characteristics of danger and authority. In 1973, John Van Maanen extended this research by offering a "backstage perspective." He explored the early socialization of police officers as they began their careers by observing police recruits throughout their academy training and probationary assignment to patrol. Police recruits acquired certain attitudes and behaviors characteristic of officers with years of experience. The socialization process was marked by four phases that explained the attitudes, behaviors, and values shared by many police officers.

The Study

In order to better understand the *process* of becoming a police officer, Van Maanen became a police recruit for the Union City (a fictitious name for a large urban city located in California) Police Department. Union City was not his first choice. Van Maanen had a difficult time finding a department willing to allow him access. Fourteen departments turned him down before a colleague helped him convince Union City administrators the value of his study. The Union City Police Department consisted of over 1,500 uniformed personnel. The department fit the legalistic description offered by Wilson in 1968. The applicant screening process in Union City was similar to other large departments across the country. Once an applicant successfully passed the civil service exam, background investigation, medical and psychology exam, strength and agility test, and oral interview they were hired as positions opened up. Recruits were then sent to the police academy for training. Very few recruits failed to graduate from training.

Van Maanen spent 3 months in the Union City Police Academy as a "fully participating member." He attended all classes and participated in training exercises. Van Maanen made every attempt to fit in and gain acceptance from his fellow recruits. Van Maanen deliberately aligned with the recruits. There were times when the academy staff invited him to sit at their lunch table or go out drinking after work and Van Maanen avoided these situations (Van Maanen 1988). Upon completion of the academy, Van Maanen became a "backseat observer" accompanying other recruits and their field-training officers on patrol. He observed these officers over a 4-month period (8–10 hours per day, 6 days per week). He purposely chose the shift with the most police activity (7 P.M. to 3 A.M.) and rode with officers assigned to the most active parts of the city. Van Maanen made no effort to conceal his role as a researcher. The recruits, instructors, and supervisors all knew his true identity. His objective was to develop an in depth understanding of the police from the "street level" (Van Maanen 1988). While on patrol, he dressed like the other officers and even carried several tools of the trade (i.e., flashlight and nightstick). His primary source of data for the study came from personal observations and interactions with all the various police personnel. In addition, Van Maanen had the opportunity to observe court officials, reporters, and family members of the officers. Structured interviews were also used for some study participants.

As mentioned in the earlier discussion of Skolnick's study, one of the most important decisions made in *field* research is how involved in the activities should a participant become. This decision becomes even more complicated when the activities are inappropriate, unethical, or illegal. In a book written several years after his 1973 study was published, titled *Tales From the Field: On Writing Ethnography*, Van Maanen provided examples of such activities. During his academy training, he became aware that several recruits engaged in cheating by accepting and/or providing answers on assignments. In order to gain their acceptance, Van Maanen did the same (Van Maanen 1988). In another situation, Van Maanen was observing an officer on patrol. During their shift, he accompanied the officer home and drank a few beers (while the officers were still on duty). Later that same night they received a call from dispatch requesting assistance with a car pursuit (police had attempted to pull over a suspected car thief who refused to stop). Van Maanen and the officer located the vehicle and pulled the car over. The suspect fled into some bushes. Van Maanen drew his gun on the suspect and ordered him out of the bushes. He admitted getting so caught up in the chase that he lost sight of his observer role (Van Maanen 1988). Field researchers have a name for this— it is called *going native*.

Findings

After observing police recruits during their early months on the job, Van Maanen reached several conclusions related to the socialization of an officer into the police organization. He identified four distinct stages of initiation into the department. Officers progressed through the stages as they became socialized into their new occupation.

Preentry choice. The recruits in Van Mannen's study became interested in police work for a variety of reasons. Prior studies of police recruits revealed that most were local, white males from working-class backgrounds who were attracted to police work primarily because of the job security and compensation. Van Maanen uncovered other motivations. Recruits expressed a desire to become part of an occupation that was perceived as important to society. Recruits also indicated that they were looking for an exciting career with diverse work experiences. Van Maanen speculated that this motivation was probably influenced to some extent by popular culture. A third reason was derived from the selection process itself. Recruits were made to feel special and accepted as they successfully progressed through the early screening phases (application, qualifying exam, background check etc.). The entire process (which took up to 6 months) projected a message that the department was very selective in hiring; therefore police work must be important. Potential recruits were also made to feel sought after and valued by the department. They were encouraged and supported throughout the entire application process.

Admittance: introduction. Applicants became police recruits upon their appointment to the department. Each recruit had to attend and successfully complete police academy training. This was the first real introduction into the police officer subculture. The police subculture consisted of norms and values that set the police apart from other citizens. Training academies bore a strong resemblance to the stressful environment of a military boot camp. Recruits were subjected to rigorous physical exercise, discipline, and training. Strict adherence to the rules was expected at all times. Recruits wore a uniform that distinguished them from veteran officers and enhanced their group solidarity. The curriculum was designed to teach recruits the technical aspects of law enforcement including patrol techniques, use of force, vehicle operations, first aid, self defense, criminal law, and criminal procedure. In addition to their formal training, recruits started to become familiar with the culture of the department. Veterans spent hours telling their "war stories" of the realities of police work. These shared experiences helped recruits feel as if they already belonged to the police organization and further solidified their occupational status. As their training progressed, recruits became more enmeshed into the police subculture. They learned to count on their fellow recruits for support. Van Maanen wrote,

> "The main result of such stress training is that the recruit soon learns it is his peer group rather than the 'brass' which will support him and which he, in turn must support. For example, the newcomers adopt covering tactics to shield the tardy colleague, develop cribbing techniques to pass exams, and become proficient at constructing ad hoc explanations of a fellow-recruit's mistake." (p. 411)

Change encounter. Upon completion of their academy training, recruits were assigned a Field Training Officer (FTO) who accompanied them on patrol during their probation period. This on-the-job training was where recruits learned the realities of police work for themselves. They quickly came to realize that their academy training was more of a "rite of passage" and now their FTO was going to teach them the ins and outs of police work. Recruits were further socialized into their occupation by learning appropriate standards of behavior as well as the expectations and norms of the department. Each and every decision of the recruit was scrutinized by their FTO who was evaluating not only their technical ability but also their adherence to certain subculture values such as dependability and loyalty.

Continuance: metamorphosis. The final stage for a new police officer was a period of adjustment. New officers began to recognize that police work was not as glamorous and exciting as portrayed on television. In reality, most of their time was spent engaged in routine service assignments. Despite this recognition, officers did not become unenthusiastic about their jobs. They continued to be motivated by the *potential* for something exciting to happen. Patrol work could be unpredictable and risky and this was precisely what stimulated the officers and made them feel good about themselves and their jobs. Van Maanen discovered that police officers became disillusioned with two aspects of their jobs during this stage. The first was with the police organization itself. Officers grew irritated at a bureaucracy that made it difficult to get straight answers to their questions about police policies and procedures. Officers were taught not to "make waves" and to "stay out of trouble" by becoming complacent. The second was with the general public. Through increased contacts with the public, officers started to feel alienated and disconnected from their communities (just as Skolnick had described in his earlier study). Officers became even more reliant upon each other for understanding and support.

Limitations

Van Maanen set out to conduct an empirical study of police socialization by participating as a recruit himself in a police academy training program. Upon graduating from the academy, he continued his study by observing rookie officers during their field training. *Observational* research is ideal for gaining an insider's view of naturally occurring social events. Van Maanen's observations and interactions provided valuable insight into the *process* of becoming part of the police subculture. As with all observational studies, however, the *generalizability* of Van Mannen's findings was uncertain. Van Maanen's study was carried out in a single police department. The department itself was not *randomly* selected (he contacted several before finding one that would grant him access). While collecting data on police during their field training, Van Maanen did not randomly select officers to ride along with. He deliberately chose officers who worked second shift (the most active time) and patrolled in the most active parts of the city. In addition, his findings were based upon the observations of a single observer. Having only one observer limits the number of subjects and settings selected for observation. Using multiple observers not only increases the number of observations, but it allows the researcher to determine any *observer bias* (Reiss 1971). There was also the issue that the behavior of the study subjects was altered because of the observer's presence. Van Maanen described a police subculture that was isolated from the rest of society, and yet we are to assume that the subculture members accepted the presence of an outsider.

Significance and Subsequent Research

Van Maanen described in great detail the process by which recruits became socialized into the police occupation. During their academy training, recruits took on the behaviors, values, and norms held by veteran officers and became initiated into a police subculture. Several other studies have examined the early socialization process of recruits and have produced consistent results. Richard Harris (1973) published a book that same year titled *The Police Academy: An Inside View.* Like Van Maanen, Harris became a participant observer in a police academy in order to examine the early socialization of police recruits. Gaining access also proved difficult for Harris. He contacted several police agencies before finding one willing to allow his participation, and he had harder time being accepted by his fellow recruits. Harris observed a discrepancy between the classroom instruction and the informal culture that developed at the academy. Recruits felt they were wasting their time in the classroom and the instructors reinforced this sentiment. Recruits were told that their real training began once they completed the academy and were assigned to patrol. Consistent with Van Maanen's observations, Harris described the group solidarity that emerged among recruits during their academy training. Recruits became socialized into an organization characterized by "defensiveness" and "depersonalization." According to Harris, recruits started to think of themselves as different because of the "dirty" nature of police work. These differences were reinforced by the hierarchical structure of police authority where recruits held little organizational status. The impersonal treatment of recruits at the academy and on the job explained the formal and sometimes unfriendly interactions between police and members of the public.

Researchers were not only interested in observing the process of becoming a police officer, but they also wanted to determine if the attitudes of police officers remained constant or changed throughout their careers. Van Maanen (1975) published findings from a separate study of police socialization 2 years after his original article appeared in print. This time he administered a survey to police recruits to measure their occupational attitudes. He also utilized a *longitudinal* research design to determine the attitudinal *changes* among police recruits as they progressed through the early stages of their careers. Longitudinal research is ideal for examining such patterns of change. Van Maanen surveyed 136 police recruits who were at various stages of their policing careers (ranging in experience from 0 to 30 months). Survey questions measured the recruits' motivations, organizational commitments, and need satisfaction. In addition, Van Maanen collected performance measures from each of the recruits' supervisors. Survey responses revealed declines in the motivation measures for recruits with more months on the job. The decline appeared to be the result of decreased job expectancies. Recruits with more months on the job were more likely to feel their efforts were not rewarded by their department, peers, and community and their overall motivation to work hard was lower than for new recruits who perceived their efforts were rewarded. An interesting relationship emerged between motivation and the recruits' performance measures. Officers with high job expectations received the lowest ratings by their supervisors. Organizational commitment levels also decreased over time for recruits, however, the overall commitment measure remained high compared to employees in other occupations. Performance ratings were higher for recruits with greater organizational commitments. Measures of need satisfaction remained fairly constant across careers and performance measures were higher for officers who perceived their needs satisfied. Based on these findings, Van Maanen concluded that the socialization process for police recruits occurred gradually as recruits progressed in their careers. Recruits were socialized into an occupation that stressed a "don't make waves" perspective.

Richard Bennett (1984) also conducted a longitudinal analysis of police socialization using a sample of police recruits in three medium-sized police departments located in the southeast. To explain the socialization process for recruits, he put forth a model that included three stages and recognized changes in the recruits' affiliation with various "occupational reference groups." Recruits learned about police work from a variety of sources including their friends, family, and the media as well as by other police officers. Bennett's data only partially supported his model. He found that the values held by recruits changed during their academy training in a manner consistent with those held by officers with more experience on the job. Between graduation and completion on their field training, however, values became less similar. Bennett attributed this finding to the "reality shock" that recruits faced once on the street. The influence of the recruits' reference groups also played a role in explaining the change in values.

Several studies have confirmed that a change in values takes place among recruits during their academy training. In 2003, Robert Ford offered an explanation for how these values were acquired by recruits. He examined the use of parables or "war stories" that were frequently used by academy instructors. Police academy instructors were typically veteran or retired police officers. They told stories of their past personal experiences or the experiences of their peers on the street. The content usually portrayed policing as dangerous and glamorous by focusing on ". . . the heroic, the extreme, and the cynically humorous" aspects of police work (p. 86). According to Elizabeth McNulty (1994), war stories were used to help recruits develop "commonsense knowledge" of police work. In his study, Ford asked a sample of police officers to relate any war stories they remembered from their academy training and to indicate whether or not the stories had influenced their values. He then analyzed the stories' content to determine its purpose and the underlying message conveyed to recruits (this type of study is known as a *content analysis*). Over half of the stories were used to teach police skills. Stories were also used to warn recruits of potential sources of danger, citizen complaints, and administrative difficulties. All but two officers reported that the stories influenced their values. War stories were also examined for their underlying themes. Ford found that the majority of stories conveyed messages consistent with police subculture values.

Van Maanen and Harris described the early socialization process of police in terms of the shared experiences of a group of police recruits participating in a training academy program. According to Marianne Hopper (1977), recruits were likely to have had different experiences based on their different backgrounds. Recruits were varied in their prior law enforcement experiences. The variation explained differences in the experiences of the recruits as they progressed through their training. In her study of 28 training academy recruits, Hopper described the academy training as a "rite of passage" for new police officers. Officers learned not only the necessary technical skills necessary to perform their jobs but the role conceptions as well. Recruits were in an unusual position caught between the civilian life they once occupied and the police officers already working the street. After reviewing background information for each recruit, Hopper identified four groups of recruits. The first group consisted of recruits with some prior experience working as a law enforcement officer. These recruits came to the academy with a basic understanding of police work. The second group of recruits had worked as military police officers in one of the armed services. This group also had prior knowledge of police work, but understood that there would be differences between their prior assignment and working as a civilian police officer. The third group consisted of recruits who had previously worked as "police aides." They had prior experience working in a law enforcement agency but unlike the first group had never performed any law enforcement duties. The last group consisted of novices. They came from various occupations and had no real law enforcement experience. Hopper also noted differences among recruits in their long-range perspective of police work. Many of the novices articulated an "idealistic" perspective. These recruits were drawn to police work because of the potential to help others. They also believed that their training would not change their outlook; however, this group experienced difficulty accepting some of the contradictions between their academy training and their perceptions of police work. Two of the recruits ended up resigning from the program. Other novices, along with the former police aids and former military police, displayed a "practical" perspective. These recruits indicated that they were drawn to police work because they found it appealing even though they did not know exactly what the job would entail. The ambiguous nature of police work presented a challenge for this group. Practical recruits learned to accept their responsibilities as officers while at the same time realized how little authority they would have on the street. Two of the practical officers were dropped from the course based on their performance. Former law enforcement officers expressed a "realistic" perspective. These recruits were familiar with the job expectations and showed a genuine interest in police work. The realistic officers had already dealt many of the issues facing the other two groups. The officers did, however, have trouble adjusting to their recruit status because they had already worked as law enforcement officers.

Richard Lundman (1980) extended the research on police socialization by examining the influence of changes in recruitment, selection, and training procedures that occurred in the 1970s. Federal legislation required departments to modify selection criteria. The result was an increase in the number of minority and female recruits. Many departments also began recruiting officers with at least some college education. The outcome of these changes was a more demographically diverse group of police recruits. The academy experience changed as well. The academy experience described by Van Maanen, Harris, and Hopper was altered for recruits in the late 1970s. Several academies became less militaristic and more college oriented.

While the on-the-job training process remained unchanged, departments started to carefully screen and train their FTOs. According to Lundman, these changes have produced additional styles or personalities of policing. To support this contention, Lundman cited the typology put forth by William Muir in 1977. According to Muir, police officers differed in their levels of compassion and in how comfortable they were using coercive control. Based on these differences, Muir observed four types of police officers. The *professional-style* officer was both compassionate and comfortable asserting his authority. These officers would use coercive force only when alternative methods failed. The *enforcer* was comfortable using force but displayed little compassion. *Reciprocators* were highly compassionate but not comfortable asserting their authority, particularly when it involved the use of force. Finally, the *avoiders* lacked compassion and were not comfortable asserting their authority. These officers tended to steer clear of risky situations. Forty-three percent of the officers studied by Muir were either enforcers or avoiders. These two types matched Skolnick's (1966) description of the working personality of the police (i.e., suspicious). The other two types (reciprocators and professionals) displayed very little of the traits described by Skolnick. Muir attributed the differences to changes in the police academy experience. In 1984, Charles Bahn also reported that changes in the demographic make-up of police recruits were likely to have an influence on the socialization of police.

Van Maanen's study offered further support for the contention that the observed differences between the police and the general public (identified by Skolnick) are a result of the unique occupational experiences of police. He gave a firsthand look at how recruits become socialized into the police occupation during their academy training and probationary assignment to patrol. Wilson's study helped us to understand why there are differences in police behavior across communities. The pioneering research of Skolnick, Wilson, and Van Mannen, as well as numerous qualitative and quantitative studies that followed has significantly improved our understanding of police practices and decision-making.

References

Bahn, C. (1984). "Police Socialization in the Eighties: Strains in the Forging of an Occupational Identity." *Journal of Police Science and Administration* 12:390–94.

Bennett, R. (1984). "Becoming Blue: A Longitudinal Study of Police Recruit Occupational Socialization." *Journal of Police Science and Administration* 12:47–58.

Ford, R. (2003). "Saying One Thing, Meaning Another: The Role of Parables in Police Training." *Police Quarterly* 6:84–110.

Harris, R. (1973). *The Police Academy: An Inside View.* New York: Wiley.

Hopper, M. (1977). "Becoming a Policeman: Socialization of Cadets in a Police Academy." *Urban Life* 6:149–70.

Lundman, R. (1980). *Police and Policing: An Introduction.* New York: Holt, Rinehart, and Winston.

McNulty, E. (1994). "Generating Common Sense Knowledge Among Police Officers." *Symbolic Interaction* 17:281–94.

Muir, W. (1977). *Police: Streetcorner Politicians.* Chicago: University of Chicago Press.

Reiss, A., Jr. (1971). "Systematic Observation of Natural Social Phenomena." *Sociological Methodology* 3:3–33.

Van Maanen, J. (1973). "Observations on the Making of Policemen." *Human Organization* 33:407–18.

Van Maanen, J. (1975). "Police Socialization: A Longitudinal Examination of Job Attitudes in an Urban Police Department." *Administrative Science Quarterly* 20:207–28.

Van Maanen, J. (1988). *Tales from the Field: On Writing Ethnography.* Chicago: University of Chicago Press.

Further Reading

Chappell, A. (2007). "Community Policing: Is Field Training the Missing Link?" *Policing: An International Journal of Police Strategies & Management* 3:498–517.

Lefkowitz, J. (1975). "Psychological Attributes of Policemen: A Review of Research and Opinion." *Journal of Social Issues* 31:3–26.

Manning, P. (1977). *Police Work*. Cambridge, MA: MIT Press.

Pitts, S., R. Glensor, and K. Peak (2007). "The Police Training Officer (PTO) Program: A Contemporary Approach to Postacademy Recruit Training." *The Police Chief* 74:114.

Van Maanen, J. (1978). "The Asshole." In *Policing: A View From the Streets*, edited by P. Manning and J. Van Maanen, 221–38. Santa Monica, CA: Goodyear.

Van Maanen, J. (1984). "Making Rank: Becoming an American Police Sergeant." *Urban Life* 13:155–76.

2

Police Discretion

The police are afforded a tremendous amount of discretion. We rely on the police to use their professional judgment in their encounters with criminals and with law-abiding members of the community. Every day the police are confronted with situations that require them choose between official police action and some type of informal response. Their decision-making has important implications for what happens to offenders, victims, and the community. When the police make an arrest they are making a decision to invoke the criminal justice process. The police are the "gatekeepers" of the criminal justice system. They decide which criminals are brought in and which criminals are let go. An arrest often leads to lengthy court proceedings, and conviction could mean a loss of freedom. All of this is avoided when an officer chooses an informal response such as issuing a warning or an order to leave the premises. Police officers have always used discretion in their decision-making, but the extent to which it was used, how it was used, and the consequences were largely ignored until the 1960s. It was not until the results of a landmark study of the criminal justice system were published that researchers began to address these questions. That study was the *American Bar Foundation Survey* published in 1958.

The *American Bar Foundation Survey* involved a comprehensive examination of the entire criminal justice system. The idea for the project is credited to Supreme Court Justice Robert H. Jackson, who in a speech delivered to the American Bar Association in 1953 urged the ABA to develop a research agenda to explore the operations of the police, courts, and correctional agencies (Walker 1992). One of the topics to be included in this proposal was the use of discretion by police. Jackson pointed out to his audience that there were two police goals: enforce the law *and* defend our constitutional rights (Walker 1992). When researchers began the task of analyzing the enormous amount of data collected as part of the survey, they were ". . . overwhelmed by the pervasiveness of discretionary decision-making" and the extent of ". . . lawlessness, racism, and casual unprofessional conduct" (Walker 1992). Irving Piliavin and Scott Briar published one of the first empirical studies of police discretion and its consequences in 1964. They examined police encounters with juveniles and reported on several legal and extralegal factors that influenced police decision-making.

A second major study of police discretion was published in 1984. One of the major factors that have a huge influence over a police officer's use of discretion is the seriousness of the crime. Police use less discretion with more serious crimes. Crimes that result in injury or significant damage to or loss of property typically end in an arrest. With less serious crimes, there are often extralegal factors that determine what type of police response is taken. Factors such as the demeanor of a suspect, victim preferences, and community norms all help us to understand how the police use their discretion and which encounters end in an arrest. One of the most frequent types of crime encountered by the police involves violence between intimates. In many situations, when the police respond to cases of domestic violence there is no apparent physical injury and the parties may give conflicting information as to who is at fault. These types of situations call for the police to utilize their discretion in deciding on an appropriate cause of action. In the early 1980s a research study was undertaken that dramatically altered traditional police responses to domestic violence. Lawrence Sherman and Richard Berk (1984) conducted a controlled experiment (the first of its kind) in Minneapolis to determine which police response—arrest, separation, or mediation—yielded the largest decrease in domestic violence.

POLICE OFFICERS' USE OF DISCRETION: WHAT INFLUENCES POLICE DECISION-MAKING?

Piliavin, I., and S. Briar (1964). "Police Encounters with Juveniles." *American Journal of Sociology* 70:206–14.

Background

The recognition that discretion was such an integral part of the criminal justice system and that discretion could lead to discriminatory decision-making generated interest in additional research. A few early discussions of police discretion were published and are worth noting. Joseph Goldstein published one in a 1960 issue of the *Yale Law Review*. Goldstein argued that police decisions not to invoke the law were "low visibility" decisions with little oversight from the department or community. He called for the creation of a Policy Appraisal and Review Board to develop guidelines to assist the police in their nonenforcement decisions. In 1962, Wayne LaFave published two articles for the *Wisconsin Law Review* in which he debated the issue of whether or not the police should have discretion over the arrest decision and what would be the best way to control it. Finally, Herman Goldstein added to the debate, arguing that it would be a mistake to try and eliminate discretion, but that it could be regulated by department rules and procedures (Walker 1992).

Each of the scholars mentioned above made important contributions to the study of police discretion and it would have been worthwhile to discuss any one of them at length in this book. The decision to include this next study was difficult because there have been many notable studies of police discretion. Irving Piliavin and Scott Briar were among the first to conduct an empirical study of how the police use their discretion and the consequences of their decision-making. Their article, titled "Police Encounters with Juveniles," has been cited in over 300 other published works.[1]

The Study

Piliavin and Briar (1964) conducted their study of police discretion by observing police officers working in the Juvenile Bureau of a metropolitan police department. The unnamed department served an industrial city with a population around 450,000. The department had a good reputation in the community and was known for its high standards of recruitment and training. Reports of police corruption and excessive use of force were rare in the 10 years prior to the study being completed. There were approximately 30 police officers assigned to the Juvenile Bureau. In addition to their law enforcement duties, the officers worked with other community groups on delinquency prevention activities. Assignment to the Bureau was considered to be a privileged position because it was used as consideration in promotion. Bureau officers were perceived to be among the best in the department.

Data for the study came from observations and interviews with police officers. Researchers looking at interactions between individuals and groups frequently use *observational* or *field* research. This method of data collection allows a researcher to witness the interactions as they are taking place in their natural setting, something that cannot be achieved with a survey. Furthermore, researchers could examine the interactions not resulting in any official action by the police. All 30 officers working in the Juvenile Bureau were included as study subjects. Piliavin and Briar had the opportunity to observe each of the officers during a 9-month study period, but most of their observations focused on the officers who had been working with the Bureau for at least a year. All but two of the officers were white. Observations took place on a variety of days and shifts, but more observations occurred in the evenings and on weekends, when police officers were most likely to interact with juveniles. Observations made during the first several months of the study period were used to develop procedures and a data collection instrument to record the observations. A total of 76 systematic observations were analyzed for the actual study.

Researchers rode along with the officers while they patrolled their beats and observed the interactions between officers and juveniles. The interactions occurred as a result of the following circumstances:

1. An officer came across a juvenile "wanted" by the police (i.e., there was an outstanding warrant for their arrest or they were wanted for questioning).
2. An officer encountered a juvenile who was present at the scene when the officer responded to a call for service.
3. An officer observed the juvenile engaged in illegal or suspicious activity.

In the first circumstance, police officers were directed to take the juvenile into custody. Officers exercised little, if any, discretion in these encounters. It was with the other two encounters that officers exercised their discretion in deciding what action to take. Officers could choose between five possible outcomes:

1. The officer could simply release the juvenile without any formal action.
2. The officer could question the juvenile and then file a "field interrogation report" describing the events that led up to the encounter.

---

[1] According to the Social Science Citation Index.

3. The officer could issue an "official reprimand" and then release to the juvenile to the custody of a parent or guardian.
4. The officer could issue a citation to appear in juvenile court.
5. The officer could arrest the juvenile and take them to the juvenile detention facility.

The outcomes ranged from least severe (no action) to most severe (arrest and detention). Outcomes three, four, and five were distinct from one and two in that the juvenile would have an official record.

Results

Piliavin and Briar analyzed data from 76 separate police juvenile encounters. Their findings, however, were based on 66 of the observations because 10 of the encounters involved circumstances where the police stopped a juvenile without legal cause. Piliavin and Briar systematically observed the interactions between the police and juveniles and recorded the outcome for each encounter. Their observations provided valuable insight into the discretionary decisions of police.

Seriousness of the offense has always been a factor in the police decision to invoke the criminal justice process or initiate an informal response. More serious crimes result in an arrest while officers are more likely to use their discretion with less serious offenses. Researchers, however, observed the five possible outcomes presented above for *all* types of crimes. Interviews with officers revealed that many of them were hesitant to initiate formal action regardless of the offense. Officers expressed concern over stigmatizing the juveniles with a negative label, and many were skeptical that the juveniles would be helped by the juvenile justice system. In fact, all of the officers believed that bringing the youth into the juvenile justice system could possibility make their behavior worse. The department authorized the wide latitude of discretion exercised by officers. Researchers reviewed training manuals produced by the department. Despite the fact that it was department policy to arrest all juveniles involved in felony or misdemeanor crimes, the manual listed "considerations" that justified an informal response by police. Considerations included age, attitude, and prior criminal record. Officially, the department rationalized the use of discretion on the grounds that the police were there to help the juvenile and to act in their best interest. If it was in the best interest of the juvenile to be released, then this was the action the police should take. In other words, police officers were an extension of the juvenile court that was established based on the philosophy of "parens patria." Decisions were made in the court system according to the best interests of the child. Researchers uncovered a second "unofficial" justification for affording officers discretion. Strict adherence to the "total enforcement" policy would overburden the juvenile court and correctional facilities. A high juvenile crime rate would also make the department look bad in the eyes of the community.

It was the contention of Piliavin and Briar that departmental policy required officers to use discretion in deciding on appropriate outcomes and that this created problems for the officers. Officers had to justify their decisions not only on legal grounds, but also with *extra legal* factors. Choosing the outcome of the encounter meant that the officer was no longer acting in a law enforcement capacity but in a judicial capacity. The policy was also unclear exactly *how* the officers were to use the special considerations. In other words, which outcomes were most appropriate for particular types of offenders? Piliavin and Briar observed the police arresting juveniles for minor offenses based on the officers' perception that the juveniles were serious delinquents. Others were released because the officers' believed the juveniles were not likely to commit another crime and did not deserve to be punished.

The police were making decisions based on their own perceptions and very little other information. At the time these decisions were made, the officer usually did not know if the juvenile had a prior record, came from a stable family, or performed well in school. Instead, the officers' perceptions were based on how the offenders dressed, who their friends were, age, race, and the juveniles' demeanor. Piliavin and Briar observed the police using the more severe outcomes for older, black juveniles who were affiliated with juvenile gangs, wore black jackets and dirty jeans, and were disrespectful and uncooperative with the police. The most significant extralegal factor was the juveniles' demeanor or attitude toward the police. A juvenile's demeanor was measured by observing their responses to the police officer's questions and requests, the extent to which the juvenile demonstrated respect to the police officer, and based on how the police officer perceived the juvenile. To obtain an objective assessment of demeanor, this information was turned over to a researcher not affiliated with the study. This researcher classified each of the juveniles as "cooperative" or "uncooperative." In 14 of the 16 arrests and four out of the five official reprimands, the juvenile was judged to be uncooperative with the police. All but one of the cooperative suspects was released with only a verbal reprimand. According to Piliavin and Briar, police officers believed that they were entitled to the respect of the community because they were providing an important public service.

Piliavin and Briar's observations also led them to conclude that blacks were receiving unfair treatment by the police. As previously mentioned, 10 of the encounters between the police and juveniles were without any legal basis. The officers had stopped and questioned the juveniles simply because they looked suspicious. Seven of the 10 juveniles were black. Blacks were also more likely to receive one of the more severe outcomes. This finding was attributed to police officer prejudice against minorities. Researchers interviewed 27 police officers, and 18 of them candidly expressed their disapproval of blacks. They rationalized their feelings based on their prior experience on the streets. Most of the juveniles with whom the police had encounters with were black. These juveniles fit the stereotype of what the police thought a delinquent looked like (i.e., black, dressed to look tough, and acted disrespectful to the police). Was the stereotype justified? Piliavin and Briar analyzed the delinquency rates of all juveniles processed in the Bureau in 1961 and found that 40 percent were black (in a city where blacks comprised 22.7% of the population). This overrepresentation of blacks in the juvenile justice system may have resulted from unfair police practices. Concentrating police patrol in predominately black communities and having officers target black juveniles increased the number of blacks brought into the juvenile justice system. Blacks were not committing more crimes; they were just being arrested more often than their white counterparts.

In their study of police encounters with juveniles, Piliavin and Briar discovered that police officers exercised a considerable amount of discretion in their decision-making. This was not only allowed, but also encouraged by the department. Discretionary decision-making resulted in the unfair treatment of some juveniles based on their appearance and demeanor. The police discriminated against blacks and the police felt justified in doing so because of the significant amount of delinquency committed by black juveniles. According to Piliavin and Briar, regardless of whether or not the official counts of crime supported the stereotype, the discriminatory police practice produced "self-fulfilling consequences." The more the police stopped and questioned black juveniles without cause and arrested them for minor offenses, the more resentment these juveniles displayed toward the police. The resentment expressed toward the police only reinforced their stereotype that uncooperative, disrespectful black juveniles were delinquent.

Criticisms

Piliavin and Briar offered one of the first empirical studies of police discretion by observing police encounters with the public. They based their conclusions, however, on a small sample of police observations. The 76 encounters recorded for the study were not *randomly* selected. Researchers purposely selected shifts that maximized the number of encounters and spent most of their time riding along with the more experienced officers. These limitations are fairly common with observational research. Subjects or settings tend to be selected based on accessibility as opposed to any type of random sampling procedure. These limitations—small sample size and nonrandom sample—brought the *generalizability* of findings into question. What the researchers observed in this particular city with these officers may not apply in other jurisdictions with different officers.

Observational research is highly dependent upon the observer's expertise in knowing *what* data to record as well as *how* the data are recorded. Most of the juvenile characteristics recorded by Piliavin and Briar were not subject to any interpretation. The juveniles' age and race were apparent (or the information was provided by the juvenile himself), but whether or not the juvenile was cooperative and respectful to the police could be highly subjective. Researchers did use an outside consultant to record the data on demeanor, but their interpretation of the data may have been different from another person's interpretation. One of the considerations used in categorizing juveniles as "cooperative" or "uncooperative" was the police officers' perception of the encounter. A more tolerant police officer could have perceived behavior as cooperative, while a less tolerant officer would have perceived the behavior as uncooperative. According to David Klinger (1994), one of the biggest problems with early research on demeanor and arrest was the failure to take into account any criminal conduct that occurred *during* the interaction. In the police discretion literature, demeanor has usually been conceptualized as disrespectful or uncooperative behaviors. These behaviors, however, were "legally permissible" (Klinger 1994). In other words, citizens were not (nor are they now) legally required to respect the police and citizens were not under any legal obligation to answer their questions. A suspect that threatened or assaulted a police officer during a field interrogation has committed a crime. If these criminal behaviors were being considered indicators of demeanor, then demeanor was no longer an extralegal factor. There was no mention of juveniles committing crimes during the encounters in Piliavin and Briar's research, but if this was not taken into account, the results may be misleading (Klinger 1994). However, Robert Worden and Robin Shepard (1996) found that even when criminal behavior that occurred during an encounter was considered, demeanor continued to influence the arrest decision.

In Piliavin and Briar's study, their role as observers was known to the police officers under study. The police knew exactly who they were and that their encounters with the juveniles were being examined. A potential source of bias with this type of observational research is known as the *Hawthorne effect*. When research subjects are aware that their behavior is being observed, the observation itself may influence their behavior. The Hawthorne effect was discovered in 1939 when researchers conducted an experiment testing the impact of altered work conditions on productivity. Regardless of how the researchers changed the conditions (i.e., increased or decreased the lightening or number of breaks), productivity increased. The subjects increased their productivity because they knew they were being watched, not because of the changes introduced in the work environment (Roethlisberger and Dickson 1939). The extent to which the police officers in Piliavin and Briar's study altered their behaviors because they were aware they were being observed was unknown, but the Hawthorne effect has been documented in other studies involving observations of police data (Spano 2005).

Significance and Subsequent Research

William Westley in 1953 and Howard Becker in 1963 had previously recognized the relationship between demeanor and police use of discretion. In his study of police violence, Westley (1953) found that officers felt justified in using unnecessary force against suspects who were disrespectful. In his classic work *The Outsiders*, Becker stated that an individual might acquire a deviant label not because they broke the law but because they behaved in a manner that was disrespectful toward the police. Piliavin and Briar (1964) observed the police using more severe outcomes with disrespectful and uncooperative juveniles. In their study, police officers used their discretion to take formal or informal action based upon a stereotype that included a juvenile's demeanor. They further found that black juveniles were much more likely to act disrespectful and uncooperative than white juveniles and that this helped explain the disproportionate number of black juveniles who were arrested. Richard Sykes and John Clark (1975) put forth an explanation for *why* demeanor might influence police discretion. Police citizen encounters were influenced by an "asymmetrical status norm." The police occupied a higher occupational status than most citizens because they have been charged with enforcing the law. In most instances, the police were also of a higher socioeconomic status. The police expected citizens to respect them and when they failed to show respect, the police were likely to respond with formal police action.

Several other studies of police discretion have been published since 1964 that examined other factors (in addition to demeanor) believed to influence discretion. In 1970, Donald Black and Albert Reiss, Jr., published findings from an observational study of police-juvenile encounters in Boston, Chicago, and Washington, DC. There were many different situations that brought the police in contact with an alleged juvenile offender. Most of these situations did not involve a serious crime. Black and Reiss reported that 5 percent of the encounters involved an alleged felony crime and only 15 percent ended in an arrest. Differences between blacks and whites were noted in the arrest data. Twenty-one percent of the black juveniles were arrested, while the police only arrested 8 percent of the white juveniles. Minorities committed all of the alleged felony offenses, however, differential arrest rates were found across the less serious crimes as well. Juvenile demeanor was also associated with the decision to arrest. The arrest rate for "civil" juveniles was 16 percent and 22 percent for juveniles who were hostile. They noted, however, that in their study the arrest rate was also 22 percent for "very deferential" juveniles. Black and Reiss also conducted a separate analysis excluding felony offenses and found the same result for black juveniles, but not for whites. The variation in demeanor was limited. Very few juveniles were extremely hostile or extremely civil. Most of the behaviors could be classified as *neither* civil nor hostile. This could reflect how demeanor was measured. Piliavin and Briar examined only two categories of demeanor: cooperative and uncooperative. Black and Reiss examined four: very deferential, civil, antagonistic, and not ascertained. Black and Reiss also observed that when the complaining citizen was present during the encounter, the police were more likely to arrest. This finding was consistent more for blacks than whites. The arrest rate for blacks in the presence of a citizen complainant was 21 percent and for whites only 8 percent. Not only did the presence of the complainant influence the police decision to arrest, but also the preference of the complainant was important. In their encounters with white juveniles, complainants were more likely to request an informal police action. When the juvenile was black, more complainants pushed for arrest. These findings suggested that differential arrest rates for blacks and whites had more to do with situational differences such as the presence of a complainant and the complainants' preferences than differences in demeanor or the prejudices of individual police officers.

Douglas Smith and Christy Visher published results from a large-scale study of police decision-making in 1981. Data were collected from 5,688 police-citizen encounters from 24 police departments across three states: Florida, Missouri, and New York. Seriousness of the offense was an important predictor of arrest, but extralegal factors including race, demeanor, victim preferences, and the presence of bystanders were also significant. Their data revealed that black suspects were more likely to be arrested, independently from demeanor and offense seriousness. These findings had important implications for research that examined decision-making later on in the criminal justice system (i.e., decisions to charge, set bail, offer plea deals, and sentencing). The group of people brought into the system did not necessarily reflect the true criminal population. Arrest statistics become biased when they are derived from biased arrest practices.

Recent research has also focused on improving the way demeanor is measured. Richard Lundman (1994) recently analyzed data collected as part of the Midwest City Police-Citizen Encounters Study. Demeanor was measured in terms of whether or not the suspect was "impolite" (the suspect made one or more impolite statements and no deferent statements), "deferent" (the suspect made one or more deferent statements and no impolite statements), or "mixed" (the suspect made both impolite and deferent statements). Only verbal statements were used in this classification. A fourth indicator of demeanor was included that consisted of the number of impolite statements made to the police. This fourth indicator—the number of impolite statements—was not found to be significant across several studies of police discretion, but suspects who provided mixed statements to the police or had an above average number of impolite statements were significant across studies.

These early studies of police discretion focused almost exclusively on individuals who were part of the encounters between police and citizens. Lundman (1979) wanted to expand upon this literature by exploring whether or not the organizations in which police work influenced these interactions. Lundman examined the most common type of interaction between the police and the public: traffic stops. Most police departments utilized data on traffic stops as a performance indicator of the police. In fact, many departments established quotas for their patrol officers. While departmental policy may dictate the number of traffic tickets or citations each officer is required to issue, it did not determine *which* citizens would be ticketed. In his study, Lundman randomly assigned observers to ride along with patrol officers in a large midwestern city. In this department, patrol officers were required to issue two traffic citations per shift. At the end of each month, tallies were posted in the roll call room to remind officers of their quotas. Lundman quickly discovered that many officers put off their traffic enforcement duties until the end of the month and then worked forcefully to meet their quotas. Lundman analyzed 293 traffic stops and found that during periods when the police were working aggressively to meet their quotas, blacks were issued more citations than whites as well as motorists who offered "verbal resistance."

Piliavin and Briar were among the first to conduct an empirical study that explored the influence of demeanor on police decision-making. Their systematic observations of police-juvenile encounters revealed that the police were more likely to arrest uncooperative juveniles. Over the past 45 years, numerous studies of police discretion have demonstrated the relationship between suspect demeanor and formal police action (i.e., arrest). This body of knowledge has been expanded to include other situational and organizational factors that help us better understand how police officers use their discretion. Piliavin and Briar also observed that police unfairly targeted black juveniles because they fit a stereotype held by the police that most delinquents were black. Race was also found to influence demeanor. Black suspects were more disrespectful and uncooperative with police and were also more likely to be arrested, making it difficult to determine the individual effects of each. Today, the influence of race and police discretion centers on the topic of *racial profiling*. Racial profiling involves police practices that target minorities (with traffic stops and field interrogations) based on an assumption that minorities are more involved in crime. Racial profiling made the headlines in 1985 when Florida Highway Patrol officers started using race and ethnicity as one of the criteria for stopping motorists suspected of drug trafficking. The practice was rationalized on the grounds that police made more arrests compared to random stops. Research refuted this argument. According to David Harris (1997), targeting black motorists over white motorists did not increase the number of drug arrests. Racial profiling has become a legal, political, and public relations issue. Many police departments have been ordered by courts or legislatures to collect data on traffic stops and field interrogations while other departments are voluntarily gathering information. Several research studies have uncovered disparities in police contacts (see Harris 1999 and Spitzer 1999). Blacks and Hispanics continue to be stopped and questioned by the police at rates that are disproportionate to their representation in the population. What is unclear from this research is exactly *why* minorities become targets.

References

Becker, H. (1963). *The Outsiders.* New York: Free Press.

Black, D., and A. Reiss, Jr. (1970). "Police Control of Juveniles." *American Sociological Review* 35:63–77.

Goldstein, J. (1960). "Police Discretion Not to Invoke the Criminal Process: Low-Visibility Decisions in the Administration of Justice." *Yale Law Journal* 69:543–88.

Harris, D. (1997). "'Driving While Black' and All Other Traffic Offenses: The Supreme Court and Pretextual Traffic Stops." *Journal of Criminal Law and Criminology* 87:544–82.

Harris, D. (1999). "The Stories, the Statistics, and the Law: Why 'Driving While Black' Matters." *Minnesota Law Review* 84: 265–326.

Klinger, D. (1994). "Demeanor or Crime? Why 'Hostile' Citizens are More Likely to be Arrested." *Criminology* 32:475–93.

LaFave, W. (1962). "The Police and Nonenforcement of the Law—Part I." *Wisconsin Law Review* (January) pp. 104–37.

Lundman, R. (1979). "Organizational Norms and Police Discretion: An Observational Study of Police Work with Traffic Law Violators." *Criminology* 17:159–71.

Lundman, R. (1994). "Demeanor or Crime? The Midwest City Police-Citizen Encounters Study." *Criminology* 32:631–52.

Piliavin, I., and S. Briar (1964). "Police Encounters with Juveniles." *American Journal of Sociology* 70:206–14.

Roethlisberger, F., and W. Dickson (1939). *Management and the Worker: An Account of a Research Program Conducted by the Western Electric Co. Hawthorne Works, Chicago.* Cambridge, MA: Harvard UP.

Smith, D., and C. Visher (1981). "Street-Level Justice: Situational Determinants of Police Arrest Decisions." *Social Problems* 29:167–77.

Spano, R. (2005). "Potential Sources of Observer Bias in Police Observational Data." *Social Science Research* 34:591–617.

Spitzer, E. (1999). *The New York City Police Department's 'Stop and Frisk' Practices: A Report to the People of the State of New York from the Office of the Attorney General.* Albany, NY: New York Attorney General's Office.

Sykes, R., and J. Clark (1975). "A Theory of Deference Exchange in Police-Civilian Encounters." *American Journal of Sociology* 81:584-600.

Walker, S. (1992). "Origins of the Contemporary Criminal Justice Paradigm: The American Bar

Foundation Survey, 1953-1969." *Justice Quarterly* 9:47–76.

Westley, W. (1953). "Violence and the Police." *American Journal of Sociology* 59:34–41.

Worden, R., and R. Shepard (1996). "Demeanor, Crime, and Police Behavior: A Reexamination of the Police Services Data." *Criminology* 34:83–105.

Further Reading

Bazemore, G., and S. Senjo (1997). "Police Encounters with Juveniles Revisited: An Exploratory Study of Themes and Styles in Community Policing." *Policing: An International Journal of Police Strategy and Management* 20:60–82.

Bittner, E. (1967). "The Police on Skid-Row: A Study of Peacekeeping." *American Sociological Review* 32:699–715.

Lundman, R., R. Sykes, and J. Clark (1978). "Police Control of Juveniles." *Journal of Research in Crime and Delinquency* 15:74–91.

Mastrofski, S. (2004). "Controlling Street-Level Police Discretion." *Annals of the American Academy of Political and Social Science* 593:100–18.

Maurer, M. (1993). *Young Black Men and the Criminal Justice System: A Growing National Problem.* Washington, DC: The Sentencing Project, US Government Printing Office.

Reiss, A. (1971). *The Police and the Public.* New Haven, CT: Yale UP.

Smith, D., C. Visher, and L. Davidson (1984). "Equity and Discretionary Justice: The Influence of Race on Police Arrest Decisions." *Journal of Criminal Law and Criminology* 75:234–49.

Van Maanen, J. (1978). "The Asshole." In *Policing: A View From the Street,* edited by P. Manning and J. Van Maanen, 221–38. Santa Monica, CA: Goodyear.

THE MINNEAPOLIS DOMESTIC VIOLENCE EXPERIMENT: DOES ARREST DETER CRIME?

Sherman, L., and R. Berk (1984). "The Specific Deterrent Effects of Arrest for Domestic Assault." *American Sociological Review* 49:261–72.

Background

Domestic violence is the most common form of violence encountered by the police. More woman are injured by a spouse or partner than by any other source. Despite this fact, the traditional police response was that of nonintervention. The public perceived domestic violence as a "private" matter and the police were reluctant to get involved formally by making an arrest. Police officers would utilize their discretion by either separating the parties (having the suspect leave for a "cooling-off" period) or would attempt some type of counseling to help mediate the situation. Interest in protecting the victims of domestic violence increased in the 1970s as battered women's groups and victims' rights groups organized to provide shelters and legal assistance (Pleck 1989). These same groups were also responsible for calling attention to the lack of formal police response. From 1970 to 1983, 36 states and the District of Columbia passed laws to modify official responses to domestic violence (Buzawa and Buzawa 1985). Several states passed laws permitting an officer to make a warrantless arrest *if* the officer had probable cause to believe that a protection order had been violated. Other states imposed additional responsibilities upon officers such as remaining with the victim until she was out of danger or taking the victim to a shelter.

In spite of these legislative changes, the police remained largely apathetic toward domestic violence and it was considered a low priority (Sherman et al. 1992, Zorza 1992). Most police departments had explicit nonarrest policies and officers were instructed to discourage victims from pressing charges. The most common police responses were to order the perpetrator to leave for a cooling-off period or attempt mediation. These actions often led to an escalation of violence. According to a study on spousal homicides conducted by the police foundation in 1977, 85 percent of the sample had called for police assistance at least once in the proceeding 2 years and 54 percent had called five or more times (Sherman et al. 1992). There was also an increase in litigation during the 1970s. Several lawsuits were filed against police departments for their failure to arrest when the police had probable cause that an assault had occurred. The threat of liability was enough for many police departments to implement voluntary changes in their domestic violence policies; however, most departments still did not allow their officers to make a warrantless arrest in cases where there was no apparent physical injury. In 1982, only five states *required* the police to arrest if the officer had probable cause that the assault had taken place (Zorza 1992).

The Experiment

The most significant change in police response to domestic violence can be attributed to an experiment conducted by Lawrence Sherman and Richard Berk (1984) with the assistance of the Police Foundation and the Minneapolis Police Department. Beginning in 1978, police officers in Minneapolis were allowed to arrest in cases of misdemeanor domestic violence but it was left up to the officer's discretion to arrest, separate the parties, or attempt mediation. The experiment began on March 17, 1981, and lasted until August 1, 1982. The purpose of the experiment was to determine which three police responses: arrest, separation (involving an 8 hour cooling-off period), or mediation produced the lowest recidivism rates for offenders. The study involved an *experimental* design in which the responses were randomly selected prior to each shift. Police officers were given color-coded report forms and were instructed to respond to each case of misdemeanor domestic violence according to the predetermined response. Encounters involving felony domestic assault, those involving physical injury, were excluded from the study because officers were required to arrest. The *random* selection of responses enabled the researchers to control for any preexisting differences between offenders so that the exact influence of each response could be determined. Research assistants were assigned to ride along with the officers during a sample of shifts to make sure that the officers complied with the random selection process. Participation by the officers was voluntary. During the study period, 314 cases of misdemeanor domestic violence were reported. The experiment was conducted in two of the city's precincts with the highest concentration of domestic violence to yield a large number of cases in a short period of time. Two measures of recidivism were examined: official police reports indicating whether or not a suspect was rearrested and follow-up interviews with the victims indicating any repeat occurrence. The victim interview data was collected to address one of the major problems with official measures of crime: the fact that many crimes go unreported to the police. Victims are often reluctant to report abuse for reasons that include embarrassment, fear or retaliation, economic concerns, or the perception that the police will not help. Victimization studies often reveal a higher incidence of domestic violence compared to police reports and the researchers wanted to accurately determine the extent of repeat violence.

The experiment raised a potential *ethical* concern as well. Police officers were responding to cases of domestic violence differently. The responses were predetermined which meant that the police would not be permitted to use their discretion in choosing perhaps the most appropriate response. For example, if a police office arrived on the scene with the predetermined response of counseling but felt that separation would be a better response after observing interactions between the offender and the victim, the officer was supposed to just counsel. The separation may have prevented violence in the future, whereas counseling might not. In medicine, this issue frequently arises with experimental trials to determine the effectiveness of new medications or treatment. Doctors must randomly assign patients to either the experimental group (patients who receive the treatment) or a control group (patients receiving a placebo). The ethical problem is that some patients may not receive treatment that makes them better. With the domestic violence experiment, some offenders may not have received the response that might have prevented future violence. This issue was addressed by Sherman who argued that randomly assigning suspects to one of three dispositions was appropriate because at the time there was no evidence to suggest one response was better than the other two (Sherman et al. 1992). In this case, *random assignment* was no different than the police officers' professional judgment.

Results

Both the official measures and victim interviews revealed that the arrested suspects were *less* likely to recidivate compared to offenders that were separated or counseled. It appeared as if by arresting a suspect, the arrest served as a deterrent for future violence. The results are presented in the graph below.

Based on their conclusions, the researchers made three recommendations. First, it was suggested that all states adopt policies *permitting* a police officer to make warrant-less arrests for domestic violence. Second, although the researchers cautioned against a policy of mandatory arrest, they did contend ". . . an arrest should be made unless there are good, clear reasons why an arrest would be counterproductive." (Sherman and Berk 1984, p. 270). Finally, the researchers recommended that the study be replicated in other locations across the United States.

Criticisms

Experimental research involving human subjects outside of a controlled setting is rare in criminal justice and the Minneapolis Domestic Violence Experiment remains one of the best examples of this type of research. The researchers, however, did run into a problem inherent in *field experiments:* the difficulty of ensuring *random* selection to the treatment groups. With any experiment it is important to establish *internal validity.* Internal validity means that the researcher was able to control for all *extraneous* influences. The Minneapolis police chief determined that certain encounters between the police and a domestic violence suspect should end in an arrest. For example, the police were instructed to arrest based on the preference of the victim or if the suspect physically attacked the officer, regardless of what the color-coded card indicated. There was also the possibility that some officers may have just refused to follow the cards. The discrepancy in *random assignment* could have led to certain types of suspects being arrested more often making it difficult to determine the true effect of each police response (Berk et al. 1988). Eighty-two percent of the suspects did receive the proscribed treatment. Reasons for not following the predetermined response included many of the exceptions mentioned above. In cases where the officer was assaulted or the victim requested arrest, an arrest was made (Berk et al. 1988).

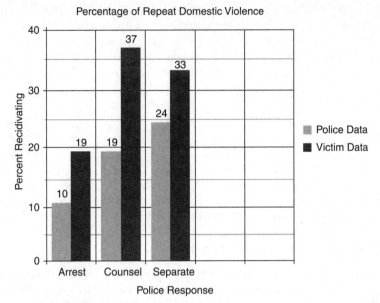

FIGURE 1.1 **Minneapolis Domestic Violence Recidivism**

Collecting the official measures of recidivism proved easy in comparison to the victim interview data. Many of the victims could not be located or refused to cooperate with researchers. Only 62 percent of the victims were interviewed, which raises the risk of *selection bias* if victim characteristics influenced who participated in the interviews and who did not. The researchers were able to examine victim characteristics and a thorough examination of the data revealed no significant differences between the victim participants and nonparticipants (Sherman and Berk 1984). Critics also took issue with the implication that just because arrest "worked" better than separating or counseling that arrest should be best response (Binder and Meeker 1988). The Minneapolis study only examined three police interventions, yet the influence on police policy was significant. Domestic violence is a social issue that many believe requires a much broader response than simply arresting the offenders.

The biggest challenge to the experiment's results came from the *replication* studies. Replication is crucial to the *generalizability* of an experiment's results. Establishing that the findings would be consistent across different police agencies in different cities is an important element of experimental research. The experiment was replicated 6 times in five different cities: Omaha, Charlotte, Milwaukee, Colorado Springs, and Miami. All of these replication studies utilized an experimental design and were close approximations (although not exact) of the original Minneapolis study. Only two of the replication cities produced findings consistent with Minneapolis. In Colorado Springs and Miami, the arrested offenders had the lowest incidence of repeat domestic violence, but data from the other three cities, Milwaukee, Omaha, and Charlotte, revealed that the arrested suspects had the *highest* occurrence of domestic violence (Sherman et al. 1992).

Explaining the inconsistent results. The relationship between arrest and recidivism for domestic violence was obviously more complex than originally thought. It was possible that the inconsistent findings were a result of treatment and/or methodological differences between studies. The arrested suspects across cities spent different amounts of time in jail following their arrest (Garner et al. 1995, Sherman et al. 1992). In some of the cities, the police (like in Minneapolis) followed color-coded cards to ensure *random assignment*, in other cities a police dispatcher or a civilian made the assignment (Sherman et al. 1992). One alternative explanation provided by the researchers was that arrest only reduced domestic violence among suspects who had something to lose if arrested—suspects with a stake in conformity. A subgroup analysis of the data from each of the cities revealed that the arrested suspects who were employed were *less* likely to commit domestic violence in the future, but the unemployed arrested suspects were *more* likely to recidivate. A similar finding was also found for suspects who were married at the time of the arrest (Pate et al. 1991). Employment and martial status appeared to have an influence over the effectiveness of an arrest. A second explanation given was to attribute the differences in findings to what actually happened to the suspects after arrest. Not all arrested suspects are prosecuted and convicted. Offenders were also subject to different forms of punishment. Some received a jail sentence, others were placed on probation, and some were required to participate in treatment. The Minneapolis Domestic Violence Experiment and the replication studies only explored differences in the outcome of arrest.

Significance and Subsequent Research

Dramatic changes in domestic violence policy occurred following the release of the experiment's results. By 1989, 84 percent of police agencies in large urban areas adopted policies favoring arrest, and 76 percent imposed a mandatory arrest policy (Sherman 1992). The 1994 Crime Bill advocated the adoption of mandatory arrest policies throughout the United States as well. The Minneapolis Domestic Violence Experiment was the first controlled experiment to examine the effectiveness of arrest. The results of the study along with the replication research helped us to appreciate the connection between research and policy making. Domestic violence was no longer perceived to be a private matter but a social issue deserving official action. Arrest remained the predominate police response in domestic violence situations, but the failure of arrest to work for all offenders has led to the investigation of other police and court practices that have been shown to be effective in reducing domestic violence.

David Ford and Mary Regoli (1993) conducted an experiment in the early 1990s to determine the effectiveness of *prosecution* on domestic violence recidivism in Indianapolis. Prosecution did not reduce the likelihood of repeat violence in general, but there was an important exception worth mentioning. Cases that were initiated by the victim and involved "severe violence" did benefit from prosecution. The study also found that most (90%) of the offenders arrested for misdemeanor domestic violence were never charged or had their charges dropped. Prosecutors dismissed cases for a variety of reasons, including insufficient or improperly obtained evidence or at the request of a victim. Dropping charges at the request of the victim was especially problematic in misdemeanor domestic violence cases because often there was no physical evidence. Prosecutors were left to make their cases on the testimony provided by the victim. Several jurisdictions operated under a "no-drop policy" with regard to prosecuting domestic violence. Regardless of whether or not the victim cooperated with prosecutors, prosecutors were encouraged to pursue charges. The implementation of these policies varied significantly across jurisdictions. Ford and Regoli's experiment compared two types of no-drop policies. With the "soft" no-drop policy, victims had input into whether or not charges could be dropped against their perpetrator, but only after the abuser had appeared before a judge. With the "hard" drop policy, victims were informed that once charges were filed, they could not be dropped at the request of the victim. The study found that allowing the victim to drop charges actually resulted in less recurrent domestic violence compared to the more strict no-drop policy.

Research has also been conducted examining the differences in whether or not domestic violence defendants were convicted, participated in some type of diversionary treatment, or received other sanctions. Ford and Regoli (1993) found no difference in the Indianapolis data between arrestees randomly assigned to pretrial diversion with counseling, probation with counseling, or a combination of fines, probation, and/or jail. Research on the effectiveness of court-mandated batterer intervention programs has produced mixed results. One study conducted by Lynette Feder and Laura Dugan (2002) involved random assignment of 404 convicted domestic violence offenders to either probation or probation with weekly counseling sessions. There were no significant differences in recidivism rates between the two groups. Research by Robert Davis et al. (2000), however, found that participants who had completed a 6-month treatment problem recidivated less compared to offenders who only completed an 8-week program or received community service.

Several jurisdictions have implemented "specialized" courts for processing domestic assault offenders and to provide greater assistance to victims. Victims today have greater access to court enforced protection orders, shelters, and other resources designed to help them separate from their abusive partners. Offenders are provided greater opportunities to participate in treatment programs. Policy makers now have access to an enormous body of research that explores the causes and correlates of domestic violence and the effectiveness of criminal justice responses to the problem. Furthermore, the Minneapolis Domestic Violence Experiment provided important insight into how police officers used their discretion and the outcome of policies designed to reduce police discretion.

References

Berk, R., G. Smyth, and L. Sherman (1988). "When Random Assignment Fails: Some Lessons from the Minneapolis Spouse Abuse Experiment." *Journal of Quantitative Criminology* 4:209–23.

Binder, A., and J. Meeker (1988). "Experiments as Reforms." *Journal of Criminal Justice* 16:347–58.

Buzawa, E., and C. Buzawa (1985). "Legislative Trends in the Criminal Justice Response to Domestic Violence." In *Crime and the Family*, edited by A. Lincoln and M. Straus, 134–47. Springfield: Charles C. Thomas.

Davis, R., B. Taylor, and C. Maxell (2000). *Does Batterer Treatment Reduce Violence? A Randomized Experiment in Brooklyn*. Washington, DC: National Institute of Justice.

Feder, L. and L. Dugan (2002). "A Test of the Efficacy of Court-Mandated Counseling for Domestic Violence Offenders: The Broward Experiment." *Justice Quarterly* 19:343–75.

Ford, D. and M. Regoli (1993). *The Indianapolis Domestic Violence Prosecution Experiment*. Washington, DC: National Institute of Justice.

Garner, J., J. Fagan, and C. Maxwell (1995). "Published Findings From the Spouse Assault Replication Program: A Critical Review." *Journal of Quantitative Criminology* 11:3–29.

Pate, A., E. Hamilton, and S. Annan (1991). *Metro-Dade Spouse Abuse Replication Project Draft Final Report*. Washington, DC: Police Foundation.

Pleck, E. (1989). "Criminal Approaches to Family Violence, 1640–1980." In *Family Violence*, vol. 11, *Crime and Justice: An Annual Review of Research*, edited by L. Ohlin and M. Tonry, 19–57. Chicago: University of Chicago.

Sherman, L., and R. Berk (1984). "The Specific Deterrent Effects of Arrest for Domestic Assault." *American Sociological Review* 49:261–72.

Sherman, L. (1992). "The Influence of Criminology on Criminal Law: Evaluating Arrests for Misdemeanor Domestic Violence." *Journal of Criminal Law and Criminology* 83:1–45.

Sherman, L., with J. Schmidt and D. Rogan (1992). *Policing Domestic Violence: Experiment and Dilemmas*. New York: Free Press.

Zorza, J. (1992). "The Criminal Law of Misdemeanor Domestic Violence, 1970–1990." *Journal of Criminal Law and Criminology* 83:240–79.

Further Reading

Berk, R., and P. Newton (1985). "Does Arrest Really Deter Wife Battery? An Effort to Replicate the Findings of the Minneapolis Spouse Abuse Experiment." *American Sociological Review* 50:253–62.

Fagan, J. (1996). *The Criminalization of Domestic Violence: Promises and Limits.* Washington, DC: National Institute of Justice.

Ferraro, K. (1989). "Policing Women Battering." *Social Problems* 36:61–73.

Garner, J. (2005). "What Does 'The Prosecution' of Domestic Violence Mean?" *Criminology and Public Policy* 4:567–73.

Hirschel, J., I. Hutchinson, and C. Dean (1992). "The Failure of Arrest to Deter Spouse Abuse." *Journal of Research in Crime and Delinquency* 29:7–33.

Maxwell, C., J. Garner, and J. Fagan (2001). *The Effects of Arrest on Intimate Partner Violence: New Evidence From the Spouse Assault Replication Program.* Washington, DC: National Institute of Justice.

McCord, J. (1992). "Deterrence of Domestic Violence: A Critical Review of the Research." *Journal of Research in Crime and Delinquency* 29:229–39.

Wooldredge, J., and A. Thistlethwaite (2005). "Court Dispositions and Rearrest for Domestic Violence Assault." *Crime and Delinquency* 51:75–102.

3

Police Operations

PATROL

Patrol is considered to be the "backbone of policing" (Wilson and McLaren 1977). When the first police officers took to the streets centuries ago, a large amount of their time was spent simply maintaining a visible presence in the community. Today, all new police officers working in a state or local police agency begin their law enforcement careers as a patrol officer, and most of a department's manpower and resources are spent engaged in patrol activities. These activities include responding to calls for service, questioning suspects, witnesses, and victims, and probing suspicious circumstances. When a crime is committed, it is most frequently the patrol officer who is the first to arrive at the scene, and nearly all arrests are at the hands of a patrol officer. For most of our law enforcement history, police agencies operated under several commonly held assumptions about the patrol function. A considerable amount of time was spent maintaining a visible police presence because police administrators believed that a visible police presence could deter crime. Potential law-breakers would think twice before committing a crime in close proximity to a police officer. The visibility of the police lets people know that there is a very good likelihood they will be caught. The presence of the police also reduces fear of crime. Having a police officer in sight or knowing one is close by makes us feel safe. If we are unfortunate enough to be victimized, we can rest assured the police are there to respond quickly. The importance of rapid response time was also a high priority among police departments. Another common assumption underlying police patrol was that it was critical for the police to respond as quickly as possible when summoned by the public. Police administrators believed that rapid response was essential in making the public feel safe and satisfied with the police. It was also thought that a fast response time improved the chances of apprehending a suspect and enhanced the deterrent value of patrol. A third assumption underlying the patrol function had to do with patrol staffing. Administrators believed that having two police officers in a vehicle was safer for the officers and enhanced the efficiency and effectiveness of patrol. Two heads are better than one, right? A fourth assumption was that removing officers from foot and placing them in cars significantly improved the patrol function. Automobile patrol was considered to be a major advancement in the delivery of police services. The police could patrol larger areas, respond faster, and deter more crime through their increased visibility. These assumptions remained unchallenged until the early 1970s when several important empirical studies were conducted on police patrol. Results from the research included in this section refuted these assumptions, which led to several important changes in the patrol function.

THE KANSAS CITY PREVENTIVE PATROL EXPERIMENT: CAN THE POLICE PREVENT CRIME AND MAKE US FEEL SAFE?

Kelling, G., T. Pate, D. Dieckman, and C. Brown (1974). *The Kansas City Preventive Patrol Experiment: A Summary Report.* Washington, DC: Police Foundation.

Background

By the early 1960s, police administrators and researchers started to question the true effectiveness of preventive patrol strategies. Crime rates were on the rise, as were police expenditures. Police departments wanted to make sure their limited resources were being utilized in the most cost-effective way possible. To address this issue, departments needed a better understanding of what patrol actually provided a community. The difficult question was, how exactly do you measure the true impact of patrol? Every single police department across the United States utilized patrol, but few were willing to alter patrol strategies in an effort to determine its effectiveness. Departments were concerned that any attempt to manipulate levels of patrol or patrol activities might lead to an increase in crime. This would violate one of the *ethical standards* of research: no *harm* to subjects. This concern would have to be addressed in the research design.

A team of researchers headed by George Kelling of the Police Foundation approached the Kansas City Police Department about conducting a study of their patrol practices (Kelling et al. 1974). Known for its innovative and progressive strategies, the Kansas City Police Department welcomed the opportunity to participate in a study that would shed light on preventive patrol strategies. In 1972, there were approximately 1,300 police officers working for the department, which served a city of around half a million people. The department was already in the process of collecting information from task forces established within each of the department's three patrol divisions. These task forces were comprised of patrol officers and supervisors who were instructed to identify problems within each division and to recommend solutions. One of the task forces actually raised the issue of whether preventive patrol was the best use of an officer's time and if it really made the community feel safe. The task force then decided it would be a worthwhile endeavor to design a research experiment that would test the true impact of preventive patrol.

The Experiment

The experiment began on July 19th, 1972, and included the participation of over 200 police officers. Kansas City was divided into 15 police beats. The 15 beats were randomly split into 3 groups of 5 beats each. In one group, preventive patrol was eliminated. The police were instructed to go into these areas *only* if they were called for assistance. In the second group, the concentration of preventive patrol was *increased* from two to three times the normal level and in the third or control group the amount of preventive patrol remained the same.

Researchers made sure that the three groups of beats were very similar to each other in terms of population demographics such as income and ethnicity, crime rates, and calls for service. This allowed the researchers to determine how changes in patrol levels influenced crime and other outcome measures. Specifically, five research questions (*hypotheses*) were tested:

1. There would be *no differences* in crime across the three levels of patrol.
2. There would be *no differences* in public perceptions of police services across the three levels of patrol.
3. There would be *differences* in public perceptions of safety across the three levels of patrol.
4. There would be *differences* in police response time and in the public's satisfaction with response time across the three levels of patrol.
5. There would be an *increase* in traffic incidents in the areas without preventive patrol.

To accurately assess the differences in patrol, several outcome measures were examined by the researchers, including official police data, victimization surveys, and surveys of citizens and area businesses. Examining different sources of crime measurement enabled researchers to address potential biases with any one particular source. For example, many assaults go unreported to the police, but victimization surveys help to better estimate this type of crime. Researchers were also interested in determining how much of a police officer's time was spent *not* responding to calls for service when they were on patrol and how the police spent their "noncommitted" time. Observers followed the officers around over a 10-week period and kept track of their activities across each of the three study areas. It was also decided that the police

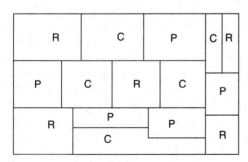

P = Proactive
C = Control
R = Reactive

FIGURE 1.2 Schematic Representation of the 15 Beat Areas

Source: Kelling, G., T. Pate, D. Dieckman, and C. Brown (1974) *The Kansas City Preventive Patrol Experiment: A Summary Report.* Washington, DC: Police Foundation.

officers participating in the experiment would be given a questionnaire to determine their attitudes and perceptions about patrol and the experiment itself.

Once the research questions were agreed upon, it was time to address the *ethical consideration* involved in this study. Researchers would be manipulating what was believed to be a vital police function in the community. In order to determine the impact of patrol, a critical component of the experiment was to eliminate this function to see what would happen. The researchers and police participants were concerned that by purposely eliminating patrol in the reactive beats, they would be responsible for an increase in crime. The researchers decided to monitor the crime data weekly, and if crime suddenly increased, they would immediately stop the experiment. Fortunately, no sudden increase in crime occurred so no *harm* resulted in the reactive communities.

As with most experiments conducted in the field, researchers ran into some problems. One month into the experiment, it was discovered that some of the experimental conditions were being compromised. In one division, there were too few patrol officers to meet the requirements of the experiment. Some officers were also not following procedures. The experiment was temporarily suspended to address these issues. More police officers were reassigned to some of the study districts and the police received additional training to make sure that the procedures were being followed. One problem unique to the reactive beats was that the police officers became bored. The researchers modified their original procedures to allow these officers more opportunities for activity when assigned to the proactive beats. The experiment started up again in October and ran uninterrupted for 12 months, ending on September 30, 1973.

Results

The sheer volume of data collected as part of the Kansas City Preventive Patrol experiment was impressive. After careful analysis of all of the different data sources, the researchers concluded that increasing or decreasing the level of patrol in an area had *no* measurable influence on crime. The results showed no change in reported crime, arrest trends, or self-reported victimization. Crime did not increase in the areas without preventive patrol and crime did not go down in the areas with increased patrol. Not only was there no change in crime, but the public's perception of crime remained unchanged as well. Fear of crime remained the same across all three areas, and neither the residents nor the business community reported any changes in behavior that corresponded with increased feelings of fear or safety. Public attitudes toward the police also remained unchanged. Finally, no differences in response time or in the number of traffic accidents were reported across the three study areas.

Data collected from the police observers revealed that only about 40 percent of a police officer's time was spent responding to calls for service. It was during the other 60 percent that officers were engaged in preventive patrol. The activities of the police during their "noncommitted" time varied little between the three areas. Police assigned to the areas without patrol did spend a little more of their time in non-police-related activities such as eating, resting, and making personal phone calls. Regarding the officers' attitudes toward patrol, 42 percent strongly agreed that patrol was the most important police function. Before the experiment began, several officers cautioned the researchers to expect an increase in crime and fear in the neighborhoods without preventive patrol. Researchers discovered that this perception was shaped by the informal socialization that new police recruits received during their first few months on the street.

Criticisms

One year after the results were made public, MIT professor, Richard Larson (1975), published an article in the *Journal of Criminal Justice* criticizing the Kansas City study. Some of the criticisms concerned a lack of adequate information provided in the study. For example, there was no mention of any changes in dispatch procedures that according to Larson would have had to change to meet the criteria of the experimental conditions. Changes in travel times and responses to calls for service were factors that could have influenced the actual amount of patrol taking place in each of the study areas. Larson also questioned whether or not the experimental design used in the study really resulted in a lack of preventive patrol in the reactive areas. The reactive beats were surrounded by either proactive beats or control beats. Residents in the reactive beats may have still witnessed preventive patrol in the areas surrounding their neighborhoods. The experiment in Kansas City was a test of the "spatial redistribution" of patrol, not a true test of whether or not reductions or increases in patrol had measurable effects. Patrol presence was scarce to begin with, so adding or taking away a few more officers went unnoticed. Despite these criticisms, Larson acknowledged the value in utilizing an experimental design to study differences in police patrol:

> ". . . the seed effect of the Kansas City Experiment may be its most important contribution. The experiment has sparked a lively debate in police circles and has prompted others to want to test their own hypotheses regarding preventive patrol in their own cities." (Larsen 1975, p. 269)

Issues were also raised regarding the use of police observers to collect data. *Observer bias* exists when the phenomenon being studied is influenced by the presence of an observer. The police officers that participated in the experiment may have altered their behavior to meet the expectations of the observers. This is a criticism of several police studies that utilize observers to collect data (Spano 2005).

Significance and Subsequent Research

The Kansas City Preventive Patrol Experiment provided the first systematic assessment of the effectiveness of routine preventive patrol. Researchers examined several *hypotheses* that were derived from common assumptions about the role of the police in our communities. Results failed to support the contention that simply increasing the number of police would reduce crime and make people feel safer in their communities. When the results were made public, many people misinterpreted the findings to imply that patrol officers were an unnecessary resource in the community. Others refused to believe the findings and some newspapers editorialized that the experiment was used to justify a reduction in police. Despite the fact that the results were not presented in the most favorable light, the findings did lead police and researchers to explore other ways to utilize department manpower and resources. Preventive patrol was part of a long-standing tradition of reactive policing in the United States. After the experimental findings were published, many departments began moving toward more proactive police strategies such as hot spot policing, police crackdowns, and directed patrols. These strategies have been shown to be effective in preventing crime and demonstrate the critical role of the police in keeping our neighborhoods safe (Weisburd and Braga 2006).

James Levine (1975) also examined the assumption that adding more police reduces crime. Levine examined the relationship between increasing the number of police officers and crime rates in 10 cities across the United States. He found no evidence that increasing the size of a city's police force had any appreciable impact on crime. Not everyone was quick to dismiss the value of added patrol. Among the skeptics of the Kansas City findings was Lawrence Sherman. Along with Patrick Gartin and Michael Buerger, Sherman (1989) researched 9-1-1 calls in the city of Minneapolis. Over a one-year period, the Minneapolis Police Department logged over 300,000 calls and the police were dispatched to approximately 115,000 places. Sixty-four percent of the calls to police were placed from only 5 percent of the city's residences. These areas were called "hot spots" of crime because these were areas where the police were spending most of their time. The high number of police visits to a relatively small number of places suggested that crime was not evenly distributed throughout a city, but rather was concentrated in certain areas called "hot spots" of criminal activity. A few years later, Lawrence Sherman and David Weisburd (1995) designed an experiment that provided a possible explanation for the findings from the Kansas City Preventive Patrol Experiment. Working with the Minneapolis Police Department, Sherman and Weisburd wanted to determine if varying levels of patrol made a difference in "hot spot" crime areas. One hundred and ten "hot spots" were randomly assigned to either the treatment areas or control areas. In the treatment areas, researchers increased the level of preventive patrol two to three times the normal level. The control areas maintained the usual level of patrol. The experiment ran for 8 months, after which researchers examined the number of crime related calls to the police. There were significantly fewer calls in the areas with increased patrol. Sherman and Weisburd (1995) attributed these findings to a deterrent effect in which the increased presence of the police prevented criminal activity. Equally significant was their finding that preventive patrol (implemented in the right areas) reduced crime. The Minneapolis Hot Spots Experiment generated an interest in additional research on "hot spots" and several government-funded research studies in cities across the United States followed. Most of the studies produced findings similar to Minneapolis leading the National Academy of Sciences to conclude: "Studies that focused police resources on crime hot spots provide the strongest collective evidence of police effectiveness that is now available" (Weisburd and Braga 2006).

During the 1980s, several police departments implemented various types of "crackdowns." A police crackdown involved short-term, intensive law enforcement efforts. These efforts could be focused in one particular area with a high crime rate or could be designed to target a specific type of crime, such as drunk driving. Police utilize the crackdown strategy as way to increase arrests during a short period of time. The logic behind a crackdown is that by increasing the certainty of arrest, potential offenders would be deterred and crime will decrease. A comprehensive study by Sherman in 1990 examined 18 case studies of different crackdown programs across the United States. The studies supported the use of crackdowns as a deterrent police strategy. Crackdowns continue to be used by police departments as an efficient use of resources and an effective strategy to reduce crime.

Recent advances in technology have also been used to aid police departments in their allocation of patrol resources. Computerized crime analysis and crime-mapping software allows the police to accurately determine where patrol should be concentrated to achieve maximum results. By 1999, 73 percent of surveyed police departments reported using some type of crime analysis and 36 percent of large police departments were using crime-mapping technology (Mamalian and LaVigne 1999). Police departments are increasingly using directed patrol as part of the "noncommitted" time of patrol officers. The Kansas City Preventive Patrol experiment also facilitated a movement within policing toward *evidence-based policing*. Police agencies now rely upon scientific research to help address issues of crime and public fear. Police agencies now have access to an expansive body of empirical studies on what works and does not work in policing. Evidence-based policing provides standards for conducting policing research and can also be used to improve training of police personnel (Sherman 1998).

References

Kelling, G., T. Pate, D. Dieckman, and C. Brown (1974). *The Kansas City Preventive Patrol Experiment: A Summary Report.* Washington, DC: Police Foundation

Larson, R. (1975). "What Happened to Patrol Operations in Kansas City? A Review of the Kansas City Preventive Patrol Experiment." *Journal of Criminal Justice* 3:267–97.

Levine, J. (1975). "Ineffectiveness of Adding Police to Prevent Crime." *Public Policy* 23:523–45.

Mamalian, C., and N. LaVigne (1999). *The Use of Computerized Crime Mapping by Law Enforcement: Survey Results.* Washington, DC: National Institute of Justice.

Sherman, L., P. Gartin, and M. Buerger (1989). "Hot Spots of Predatory Crime: Routine Activities and the Criminology of Place." *Criminology* 27:27–55.

Sherman, L., and D. Weisburd (1995). "General Deterrence Effects of Police Patrol in Crime 'Hot Spots:' A Randomized, Controlled Trial." *Justice Quarterly* 12:625–48.

Sherman, L. (1998). *Evidence-Based Policing.* Washington, DC: The Police Foundation.

Spano, R. (2005). "Potential Sources of Observer Bias in Police Observational Data." *Social Science Research* 34: 591–617.

Weisburd, D., and A. Braga (2006) "Hot Spots Policing as a Model for Police Innovation." In *Police Innovation: Contrasting Perspectives,* edited by D. Wiesburd and A. Braga, 225–44. New York: Cambridge UP.

Wilsons, O. and R. McLaren (1977). Police Administration (3rd Ed.). New York: McGraw-Hill.

Further Reading

Brown, C. (1975). "Discussion: Evaluative Research on Policing—the Kansas City Experience." *Police Chief* XLII (June):40.

Davis, E. M., and L. Knowles (1975). "A Critique of the Report: An Evaluation of the Kansas City Preventive Patrol Experiment." *Police Chief* XLII (June):22.

Farmer, D. (1984). *Crime Control: The Use and Misuse of Police Resources.* New York: Plenum.

Feinberg, S. E., L. Kinley, and A. Reiss (1976). "Redesigning the Kansas City Preventive Patrol Experiment." *Evaluation* 3:124–31.

Kelling, G. L., and T. Pate (1975) "Response to: The Davis-Knowles Critique of the Kansas City Preventive Patrol Experiment." *Police Chief* XLII (June):22.

Risman, B. (1980). "The Kansas City Preventive Patrol Experiment: A Continuing Debate." *Evaluation Review* 4:802–08.

POLICE RESPONSE TIME: HOW IMPORTANT IS IT FOR THE POLICE TO RESPOND QUICKLY WHEN WE CALL?

Pate, T., A. Ferrara, R. Bowers, and J. Lorence (1976). *Police Response Time: Its Determinants and Effects.* **Washington, DC: Police Foundation.**

Background

The importance of rapid response was conveyed in a 1973 National Commission on Productivity Report despite the fact that there was very little empirical evidence upon which to base this assumption. In fact, the Commission stated ". . . there is no definitive relationship between response time and deterrence, but professional judgment and logic do suggest that the two are related in a strong enough manner to make more rapid response important" (p. 19). Departments allocated substantial resources attempting to improve response time with the use of the 9-1-1 telephone number, computer-assisted dispatch, and beat assignment systems (Caiden 1977). The few studies of police response time that had been conducted produced mixed results. In Los Angeles and Seattle, rapid response appeared to be related to the likelihood of arrest (Pate et al. 1976). In Ottawa, Ontario, however, police response time had no impact on arrest (Pate et al. 1976). The President's Commission on Law Enforcement and the Administration of Justice was left to conclude that while rapid response time may be *correlated* with arrest, it had yet to be established as the *cause* (Isaacs 1967). Causation is more difficult to establish in social science research, but it is important if police departments intend to alter resources or change procedures in an effort to improve response time. Otherwise, changes will have no impact.

Experimental research is considered to be the best way to establish *causation*. Experiments allow the researcher to control for *extraneous* or unrelated influences that can produce a spurious (false) relationship. In the early 1970s, the opportunity to examine police response time using experimental data (although this study is not considered to be an experiment in and of itself) presented itself to a group of researchers from the Police Foundation. Tony Pate had recently finished working with George Kelling on the Kansas City Preventive Patrol Experiment. As part of that experiment, researchers collected data on police response time that was subsequently analyzed in a separate report by Tony Pate and Police Foundation staff Amy Ferrara, Robert Bowers, and Jon Lorence (1976). Their study of police response time was the first to examine not only the factors impacting police time, but the effects of improving response time as well. The results of the study provided valuable insight into the real importance of rapid response time and what can and should be done to improve it.

The Study

The data for the project was collected as part of a larger experiment on preventive patrol carried out in Kansas City, Missouri, between October 1972 and September 1973. The study was presented as an *exploratory* study because very little was known on the subject of police response time. The researchers were interested in exploring the determinants of response time and the impact on citizen satisfaction and police performance. Because the study was only exploratory, the researchers did not test any specific *hypotheses*. They did, however, offer several possible influences of police response time, including:

> type of call (i.e., burglary, robbery, or assault)
>
> the officers' activity at the time of receiving the call (whether they were engaged in preventive patrol or responding to another call for service)
>
> the elapsed time before the officer initiated a response
>
> the elapsed time waiting for an assisting officer
>
> driving speed
>
> distance to the call

To determine the impact of response time, researchers speculated that the following variables would be influenced by response time: the outcome of the response, citizen satisfaction with response time, citizen satisfaction with responding officer, and the general attitude of the citizen toward the police. Researchers also looked at citizen perceptions of safety and several demographic variables such as the citizens' race, gender, age, education, and income because many of these had been shown in prior research to be related to citizen satisfaction with police.

Four data sources were used for this project. All of data were derived from surveys that had been administered to police officers and citizens during the Kansas City Patrol Experiment. *Surveys* are ideal for *exploratory* research. Researchers can ask a wide variety of questions to find out more information on a topic. Surveys can also be used in *explanatory* research when the researcher is interested in establishing relationships between variables. Furthermore, surveys are ideal for measuring attitudes among a large group of people. The first survey was the *Response Time Survey*. Observers who accompanied patrol officers in the experimental beat areas completed the surveys. The experimental beats were divided into three areas with different amounts of police patrol (beats were randomly divided into regular, no preventive patrol, and increased patrol). Researchers also included surveys from nine beats that were not part of the experimental area. In the nonexperimental beat, the patrol officers themselves completed the surveys. The surveys were completed after all citizen-initiated calls that involved contact with a police officer. Only contacts where a police officer was the first to arrive on the scene were included. Automobile accident calls were excluded because researchers were only interested in calls having to do with some type of crime. Both the observers and the police officers were provided with survey guidelines for completing and/or administering the surveys. The survey instrument consisted of questions to assess the length of time to respond to a call, how fast the officer drove, whether or not the officer used emergency equipment (i.e., lights and sirens) in responding, and the outcome of the call (i.e., arrest). One thousand, one hundred and six questionnaires were completed (576 from the experimental area and 530 from the nonexperimental area). A follow-up questionnaire was also mailed to citizens whom the police had contacted during their response. These surveys asked questions to assess citizen satisfaction with response time and outcome. Four hundred and twenty-seven (39%) of these surveys were returned.

The second survey was known as the *Encounter Survey*. This survey was only administered in the 15 experimental beat areas. Three sets of questionnaires were constructed: one for observers, one for police officers, and one for citizens. The Encounter Survey contained the same type of questions as the first survey, however, was used to collect more detailed information regarding the type of call received by the police. A total of 299 surveys were completed. The last two surveys were administered to a sample of households located within the 15 experimental beat areas. One survey was administered in 1972 and another in 1973. Approximately 1200 households were contacted and respondents were asked when was the last time they had called the police for service during the past year. In 1972, 270 respondents indicated they had called the police and in 1973, there were 315 respondents. Only the respondents who had contacted the police were asked to complete the survey. Questions were consistent with the Response Time and Encounter Surveys.

Results

Researchers examined several variables believed to have an influence on police response time. Data from the four groups of surveys revealed which variables maintained a *significant* relationship with response time. The distance an officer traveled to respond to a call for service as well as the elapsed time between when the call was received and when the officer left to respond was correlated with response time. The average distance traveled to respond was 3.5 miles in the nonexperimental areas and 1.7 miles in the experimental areas. In most cases, very little time (less than one minute) elapsed before an officer initiated a response. The data also revealed that any delays were usually because the police was involved in another activity at the time they received the call. Prior research by Jonathan Rubinstein (1973) indicated that the police responded quicker to certain types of calls where they believed they had a good chance of apprehending a suspect or saving a life. Robbery, burglary, prowler, and ambulance calls were the ones police thought a fast response time made a difference. Data from Kansas City showed that in 88 percent of these types of calls, the police responded in less than one minute. Despite conventional logic, there was little *correlation* between driving speed and response time. Researchers attributed this to the fact that the average speed examined in the study only ranged from 20 to 35 miles per hour.

To determine the effects of response time, researchers examined whether or not response time (measured in minutes from the time a citizen called the police to the time an officer arrived) had any influence over four *dependent* variables: outcome of the response, citizen satisfaction with response time, citizen satisfaction with the responding officer, and citizen attitudes toward the police. The results for each outcome measure are summarized below.

Outcome of police response. Police departments operated for a long time under the assumption that rapid response time improved the ability of the police to solve crime. Data from all four surveys refuted this notion. Response time did not determine whether or not the police made an arrest or recovered stolen property. This was the most surprising finding from the study because it challenged one of the basic underlying principles of patrol. Researchers attributed the lack of significance to the fact that most citizens waited before calling the police. Rapid response simply did not matter in situations where citizens delayed in reporting the crime.

Citizen satisfaction with response time. Rapid response time was not only believed to be important in determining the outcome of a response, but it was also considered an important predictor of citizen satisfaction. Data from the Encounter Survey and both community surveys showed that when the police arrived sooner than expected, citizens were more satisfied with the response time. The race and age of the citizen were significant predictors of satisfaction. Older, white citizens tended to be more satisfied compared to younger, nonwhite citizens.

Citizen satisfaction with the responding officer. Not only was response time the best predictor of citizen satisfaction with police response, it was also the best predictor of how satisfied a citizen was with the responding officer. It was further revealed that citizens became dissatisfied with the police when they were not informed of the outcome (i.e., was someone arrested).

Citizen attitudes toward the police. Several variables were significant predictors of citizen attitudes toward the police in general, including response time and whether or not a citizen was satisfied with the response time and the responding police officer. Data also showed that citizens' perceptions of safety predicted their attitudes toward the police. Citizens who felt safe in their neighborhood expressed more positive attitudes toward the police.

Based on the results of the response time study, Pate et al. (1976) concluded that rapid response was not as important as police administrators thought it was. Response time was not related to an officer's ability to make an arrest or recover stolen property. The most likely explanation for this was citizen's delay in reporting the crime. While citizen satisfaction with response time was an important predictor of their overall satisfaction with police, the study revealed that the most significant factor influencing citizen satisfaction with response time was the difference between *expected* and *observed* response time. Police departments could improve satisfaction levels by simply providing the public with realistic expectations of response time. Departments that continued allocating resources in an effort to improve response time were not likely to see a return on their investment.

Limitations

The data for the police response study were collected as part of the Kansas City Preventive Patrol Experiment. Surveys were administered in 15 police beats that varied the amount of preventive patrol (the experimental areas). Surveys were also administered in an additional nine beats involving no differences in preventive patrol (non-experimental areas). Data collected for one purpose then subsequently used for another is subject to criticism. The *validity* of the findings was suspect because the data might not have measured concepts the researcher was reportedly studying. In this study, data on response times was collected to test *hypotheses* related to variations in preventive patrol. The data was then used to study factors predicting response times and the impact of response times on police outcomes and citizen satisfaction with the police. In the published findings, Pate et al. (1976) acknowledged this limitation as well as other flaws of the study. The response time survey itself was not administered to a *random* selection of respondents in the experimental beats (only the beats were randomly divided into different levels of patrol). The observers who completed the survey rode with police officers during the busiest part of the day and primarily in the most active beats. The lack of random selection raises the possibility that beat characteristics and time of day influenced the results. In the non-experimental areas, researchers selected police officers that they believed would fill out the questionnaire accurately. Officer characteristics became a potential source of bias with the results as well. Researchers also reported that the guidelines for completing the questionnaires were not always adhered to.

One of the biggest problems with mail surveys is the low *response rate*. In this study, questionnaires were mailed to each citizen who had contacted the police during the study period. Only 39 percent of the surveys were completed and returned. The low response rate could have biased the results if the respondents who completed the survey were significantly different from the respondents who did not. Researchers discovered two differences when they compared the two groups. Younger, nonwhite respondents were over represented in the group that returned the surveys. Participants of the 1972 and 1973 community surveys were *randomly* selected, however, females and nonwhites were over represented in the sample. Researchers attributed this to two possibilities: females were more likely the ones who answered the phone and a high concentration of nonwhites residing in the study areas. Another potential source of bias with the study had to do with differences in beat size and in the number of patrol officers in each beat. Beats in the non-experimental areas were larger and had fewer officers. Both of these differences could have influenced response time.

Significance and Subsequent Research

Results from the response time study challenged traditional beliefs about the allocation of patrol in our communities. Police departments operated under the assumption that rapid response was a crucial factor for the ability of an officer to solve a crime and an important predictor of citizen satisfaction. Beginning in the late 1960s, departments took advantage of technological advances such as the 9-1-1 telephone and computer dispatch systems in an effort to improve response time. The response time analysis was offered as an *exploratory* study to generate additional research on the importance of response time. Shortly after Pate et al. (1976) published the findings, William Bieck (1977) published findings from a similar, but larger study of response time in Kansas City. Beick utilized trained observers who recorded travel times while riding with police officers in beats that had high rates of robbery and assaults (two crimes where response time should improve the chances of an arrest). Researchers also collected dispatch data and interviewed victims and citizens who had requested police service. Bieck's findings were consistent with Pate et al. (1976). The likelihood of an arrest had more to do with the reporting time by citizens than police response time; however, he did find that when reporting time and response time was short, the likelihood of arrest increased in crimes with a victim or witness present at the scene.

William Spelman and Dale Brown (1984) carried out a multistate study of response time between 1979 and 1980. Data were collected from cities in California, Florida, Illinois, and New York. Over 4,000 citizens, victims and witness who were involved in over 3,300 serious crimes were interviewed for the study. The researchers drew an important distinction between "discovery crimes" and "involvement crimes." Seventy-five percent of all crimes were discovery crimes (crimes that were discovered by a victim or witness some-time after they were committed). Improving response time had no impact on the ability of police to make an arrest for these crimes. The remaining 25 percent were involvement crimes or crimes where the victim was confronted by the offender. The police had a better chance of making an arrest with these crimes, but only when there was little delay in calling the police. Police had a 35 percent chance of making an arrest when the victim called the police while the crime was being committed and an 18 percent chance if the call was made within the first minute. Their study found that even with the involvement crimes, most people delayed in reporting the crime to police and this delay reduced the likelihood that the police would make an arrest. It appeared that rapid patrol only mattered for some crimes. Richard Coupe and Laurence Blake (2005) recently published a study of police response carried out in the United Kingdom. They examined only "in progress" residential burglaries. Their research found that the police were twice as likely to catch the offender if they arrived within 4 minutes of being called than if the police arrived after 6 minutes. Response times were largely a product of patrol deployment and workloads.

In response to the research on preventive patrol and rapid response, many police departments changed the way they responded to calls for service. Thomas Repetto (1980) surveyed police departments and found that 74 percent changed their allocation of patrol resources. Many departments adopted a differential police response approach. Differential police response programs allow departments to prioritize calls and rapidly dispatch an officer only when an immediate response is needed (i.e., a crime in progress). For nonemergency calls, an officer is either dispatched at a later, more convenient time or a report is taken over the phone. Differential police response has been shown to save departments money and gives patrol officers more time to engage in community oriented policing activities (Roberg et al. 2005). The benefits for a department are not at the expense of the public. A study by Robert Worden (1993) found a high degree of citizen satisfaction with differential police response across all racial and ethnic groups.

Police departments have also started implementing nonemergency call systems to reduce the burden on the current 9-1-1 system. The 9-1-1 system was introduced in the United States in 1968 as a uniform emergency contact number to summon police, fire, and/or emergency personnel. In the 1980s, it became apparent that many people were using the 9-1-1 system for nonemergency calls to the police. Between 40 and 80 percent of 9-1-1 calls were to request nonemergency services (Mazerolle et al. 2002). In 1996, the city of Baltimore introduced a 3-1-1 nonemergency call system to alleviate the burden on the 9-1-1 system and to make it easier for police to differentiate between calls for service. An evaluation of the system by Mazerolle et al. (2002) showed that 9-1-1 calls declined after the system went into effect and police response time to 9-1-1 calls was slightly faster. The ability of a department to distinguish between emergency and nonemergency calls appears to improve the delivery of police services. Over 50 cities across the United States have implemented 3-1-1 nonemergency systems and in 1997 the Federal Communications Commission reserved 3-1-1 as a national nonemergency phone number.

References

Bieck, W. (1977). *Response Time Analysis: Synopsis, Executive Summary, Methodology and Analysis.* Kansas City, MO: Kansas City PD.

Caiden, G. (1977). *Police Revitalization.* Lexington, MA: Lexington Books.

Coupe, R., and L. Blake (2005). "The Effects of Patrol Workloads and Response Strength on Arrests at Burglary Emergencies." *Journal of Criminal Justice* 33:239–55.

Isaacs, H. (1967). "A Study of Communications, Crimes, and Arrests in a Metropolitan Police Department." In *President's Commission on Law Enforcement and Administration of Justice* pp. 88–106.

Mazerolle, L., D. Rogan, J. Fran, C. Famega, and J. Eck (2002). "Managing Citizen Calls to the Police: The Impact of Baltimore's 3-1-1 Call System. *Criminology and Public Policy* 2:97–124.

National Commission on Productivity (1973). *Opportunities for Improving Productivity in Police Services.* Washington, DC: United States Government Printing Office.

Pate, T., A. Ferrara, R. Bowers, and J. Lorence (1976). *Police Response Time: Its Determinants and Effects.* Washington, DC: Police Foundation.

Repetto, T. (1980). "Police Organization and Management." In *Progress in Policing: Essays on Change,* edited by R. Staufenberger, 65–85. Cambridge, MA: Ballinger.

Roberg, R., K. Novak, and G. Cordner (2005). *Police and Society* (3rd ed.). Los Angeles: Roxbury.

Rubinstein, J. (1973). *City Police.* New York: Farrar, Straus & Giroux.

Spelman, W., and D. Brown (1984). *Calling the Police.* Washington, DC: Police Executive Research Forum.

Worden, R. (1993). "Toward Equity and Efficiency in Law Enforcement: Differential Police Response." *American Journal of Police* 12:1–32.

Further Reading

Bayley, D. (1998). *What Works in Policing.* New York: Oxford UP.

Clawson, C., and S. Chang (1977). "The Relationship Between Response Time and Arrest Rates." *Journal of Police Science and Administration* 5:53–68.

Farmer, M. (1981). *Differential Police Patrol Strategies.* Washington, DC: Police Executive Research Forum.

Sherman, L. (1998). "Policing for Crime Prevention." In *Preventing Crime: What Works, What Doesn't and What's Promising,* edited by L. W. Sherman, D. Gottfredson, D. MacKenzie, J. Eck, P. Reuter, and S. Bushway. Washington, DC: US Department of Justice.

Sparrow, M., M. Moore, and D. Kennedy (1990). *Beyond 9-1-1: A New Era for Policing.* New York: Basic Books.

PATROL STAFFING WHICH IS BETTER: ONE- OR TWO-OFFICER PATROL UNITS?

Boydstun, J., M. Sherry, and N. Moelter (1977). *Patrol Staffing in San Diego: One- or Two-Officer Units.* Washington, DC: Police Foundation.

Background

Two-officer patrol units became standard in the United States when the automobile replaced foot patrol. Foot patrol officers walked their beats alone. Departments assigned two officers to a car for safety reasons. Officers in cars patrolled larger areas and were spending more time engaged in law enforcement activities which were perceived as more dangerous (Boydstun et al. 1977). In 1953, the Kansas City (Missouri) Police Department became the first Metropolitan police department to assign a single police officer to vehicle patrol (Brannon 1956). One-officer patrol was believed to be more efficient. With each officer having their own vehicle, officers could cover more area, respond quicker, and increase the visible presence of the police in the community. Several other departments across the country adopted one-officer patrol based on these same beliefs. Departments deciding against the change held firm to the traditional view that two-officer units were safer. Advocates of the two-officer units also argued that they were more effective in fighting crime. Two-officer units were more proactive in their investigations of suspicious activities compared to one-officer units (Boydstun et al. 1977). None of these arguments had ever been empirically tested and the debate over the use of one- versus two-officer units continued for the next 20 years.

The San Diego Police Department assigned two officers to each patrol car up until 1954. Following the example set by the Kansas City Police Department, San Diego gradually implemented a one-officer patrol system over the next few years. The civil unrest of the early 1960s caused administrators in the San Diego Police Department to rethink their position on one-officer units (Boydstun 1977). Concern over police officer safety resulted in two-officer units being assigned to patrol certain areas of the city perceived as high risk. Beginning in 1964, the department started to use a combination of one- and two-officer units. In response to the energy crises of 1974, the San Diego Police Department started working on a patrol allocation plan that would help save on fuel costs without increasing personnel costs (Boydstun 1977). The obvious solution seemed to be to revert back to an entirely two-officer patrol force. This would have considerably reduced fuel costs (assuming the number of vehicles on the street was reduced) while keeping the same number of officers on the street. Many officers and administrators perceived two-officer units to be inefficient and resisted the proposal (Boydstun 1977). The department had no empirical evidence to help guide this decision until the Police Foundation contacted them that same year. The Foundation was interested in conducting a comprehensive study on the use of one- and two-officer patrol units and wanted the study to take place in San Diego as a joint effort with the police department. The objective of the study was to determine the most effective, efficient, and safe allocation of patrol resources by comparing the use of one- and two-officer patrol units.

The planning phase of the project lasted over a year. Because this was the first major study of patrol staffing, the San Diego Police Department and the Police Foundation conducted a nationwide survey of police departments to determine their use and justification of one- and two-officer units. Surveys were mailed to 65 police departments serving populations from 36,000 to 8 million. Fifty-two surveys were returned (80% *response rate*). The information obtained from the survey was used to develop the research design for the study of patrol staffing in San Diego.

The Experiment

A team of researchers led by John Boydstun (1977) used a *quasi-experimental* research design to determine the effects of one-officer and two-officer patrol units on several patrol operations in San Diego, California. In 1977, the city had a population of approximately 697,000 residents with a police force of 1,077. Like most departments, patrol operations were divided into three, 8-hour shifts. Seventy-one percent of officer assignments were one-officer units and the remaining 29 percent two-officer units. Two-officer units were primarily used in areas designed as "high risk." The department utilized a computer-assisted dispatch system for assigning calls for service to the officers. To control for preexisting differences across patrol areas, a sample of 16 police beats with a total of 44 patrol units were selected. Beats differed according to police officer perceptions of risk. This allowed researchers to assess differences in outcome in areas the police perceived as safe compared to areas perceived as higher risk. The beats were then divided into four groups based on the existing type of patrol. The first area involved no change in officer assignment. One-officer units were assigned in previously one-officer areas (control group). In the second area, one-officer units were assigned in areas where there were previously two-officer units (experimental group). Two-officer units were assigned in areas that were previously one-officer in the third area (experimental group). The final area consisted of two-officer units in previously two-officer areas (control group). Dividing the beats into these groups allowed researchers to compare one-officer units with two-officer units across all study areas. Beats were assigned to one of the four groups according to socio-economic and demographic variables to control for population differences between areas. A total of 306 police officers patrolled the study areas.

The experiment officially began on October 26, 1975, and lasted an entire year. The start date itself was randomly determined (to control for time of year). Some of the data, however, were derived from 12, 7-day study periods selected throughout the year. Four weeks separated each study period so that researchers were able to collect data at different time periods all throughout the year. This was done out of concern that researchers would be collecting an unmanageable amount of data. Researchers used several data sources, including dispatch and departmental records, crime statistics, officer journals, and surveys. Four outcome measures were examined: patrol unit performance, patrol unit efficiency, patrol officer safety, and officer attitudes and perceptions.

Results

A substantial amount of data was collected for this experiment (despite efforts to reduce the amount of data). Findings for each of the outcome measures are summarized below.

Patrol unit performance. Data from dispatch records, officer journals, and arrest and complaint reports were used to determine the impact of one- versus two-officer units on patrol until performance. Several performance indicators were examined, including the number of calls for service, number of arrests, traffic warnings, field interrogations, open business checks, citizen contacts, and total miles patrolled. No significant differences were found between the one-officer and the two-officer patrol units, with the exception that calls for service assigned to one-officer units resulted in more arrests and formal reports and two-officer units had more traffic citations. Findings were consistent across shifts, beats, and previous patrol staffing areas.

Researchers also examined the number of citizen complaint reports filed against officers and found that two-officer units received more complaints. In a more thorough analysis, researchers separated out two-officer ambulance units from regular two-officer patrol units because of the differences in activities between the two types of units. This analysis refuted the differences in number of arrests, formal reports, traffic citations, and citizen complaints.

Patrol unit efficiency. Researchers examined dispatch and department records as well as police officer activity reports to determine if there were any differences in the use of police officer backup, response time, officer initiated activities, and cost-effectiveness between one-officer and two-officer patrol units. One-officer units requested backup more frequently than two-officer units, but only on the second shift (3 P.M. to 11 P.M.). No differences were found overall in response time; however, it was revealed that there was a delay in dispatch time for one-officer units. This finding was attributed to two-officer units receiving more high urgency calls. Two-officer units were more efficient in their responses (spending less time serving calls for assistance), and had more time (almost one hour more per shift) available for officer initiated activities. This finding suggested that two-officer units were more efficient in their response and activities, but it was important to also consider that there were no differences found for the performance indicators. To determine the patrol unit cost, researchers considered the cost of servicing calls for service and the cost of officer initiated activities. One-officer units were more cost-effective except for calls where two-officer units were recommended (40% of all calls).

Patrol officer safety. Crime, vehicle accident, and injury reports were used to assess patrol officer safety between one- and two-officer units. Two-officer units were involved in more resisting arrest confrontations and critical incidents, but were not more likely to be assaulted or injured. No differences were found in the number of vehicle accidents.

Police officer attitudes. Surveys were administered to the entire central patrol division (390 officers). As mentioned in the previous study of response time, surveys are ideal for measuring attitudes and perceptions. Researchers included both *closed-* and *open-ended* questions. A closed-ended question provides a list of items from which the responded is instructed to select. Open-ended questions leave a blank space for the respondent to write in their response. One-half of the police officers responded that unit staffing was important or very important to police work. Officers who had previously worked two-officer units were more likely to indicate that unit staffing was important. A little more than half (52.4%) of all the officers indicated a personal preference for two-officer units, while 74.6 percent of the officers who participated in the study expressed a personal preference for two-officer units. Survey results further revealed that younger officers with lower ranks more likely to prefer the two-officer units. Researchers also wanted to determine if personal preference depended upon such factors as salary implications, partner, shift and beat assignments. Fewer officers indicated a preference for two-officer units with these considerations. Questions regarding perceptions of performance advantage and unit efficiency revealed that officers only slightly favored the two-officer units. Police officers were neutral in their perceptions that two-officer units were safer, with a few exceptions. One-officer units felt stronger that two-officer units were safer as well as officers of a lower rank with more patrol experience. No significant differences were found in the questions measuring officer morale and job satisfaction between one-officer and two-officer units. Officers indicated that two-officer units were less likely to use excessive force against a suspect. Finally, researchers discovered that officers with experience working two-officer units in beats perceived as high risk expressed the strongest preference for two-officer units.

Researchers concluded that the data did not support the continued use of two-officer patrol units in San Diego. One-officer units performed just as well, and on some measures, better than two-officer units. One-officer units would also allow the department to save money. According to the study, 18 one-officer units cost less than 10 two-officer units. The only exception to this recommendation was a suggestion to continue the practice of assigning two-officers to the police ambulance units where the research showed that two-officers were needed.

Limitations

There was one major obstacle that had to be addressed by researchers in the San Diego study. A key feature of the *experimental* design is the ability of the researcher to exercise control over all of the experimental conditions. This would have required the *random assignment* of police officers to the study units to control for police officer characteristics that might be related to the outcome measures. Random assignment was not feasible because it would have disrupted existing staffing patterns and personnel policies (i.e., the department allowed officers to pick their beats based on seniority). The inability to control for officer assignment brings into question whether officer characteristics influenced the results of the study. To help address this issue, the researchers devised a hypothetical staffing assignment (which would have been used if the existing system of unit assignments had been suspended during the study period) and compared it to the actual assignments. No significant differences were found leading researchers to conclude that individual officer characteristics would not bias their results. Because of the lack of random assignment, the study was offered as a *quasi-experiment.*

Boydstun et al. measured police officers' attitudes and perceptions of both one- and two-officer units, but their research did not address the attitudes and perceptions held by police administrators who were responsible for making decisions on patrol staffing. A study by Richard Larson and Thomas Rich (1985) found that police administrators believed one-officer units were safer because officers were more alert and used better judgment in their decision-making. Another drawback to the San Diego study had to do with the data collected on officer injuries. Boydstun et al. reported only on the number of injuries, not the type or severity of the injuries (Wilson and Brewer 1992).

Significance and Subsequent Research

For several decades, the San Diego Police Department had been staffing patrol units according to traditional assumptions of the advantages and disadvantages of one- and two-officer units. Department administrators were faced with the pressure of allocating their patrol resources in the most effective and efficient manner possible, without compromising the safety of their officers. With assistance from the Police Foundation, the department participated in a study that would better inform their decision-making. The experiment involved a highly sophisticated research design that allowed researchers to control for type of area, shift differences, and former patrol staffing and assignments. Results challenged the belief that two-officer units were better and safer for the officers. The findings provided the department (as well as others around the country) the justification needed to employ one-officer units, however, this would be going against the personal preferences of many of their own police officers. Police officer unions dictated patrol staffing in some departments. Changing police practice on the basis of a single study can be problematic if the results cannot be replicated. *Replication* is important in establishing the *external validity* of experimental findings. The extent to which results from one experiment can be repeated with other experimental studies strengthens the *generalizability* of the findings. Results from replication studies of patrol staffing have produced findings consistent with the San Diego study. Edward Kaplan (1979) offered a model-based evaluation of one- versus two-officer patrol units. He used data from the San Diego study to demonstrate some of his mathematical models. Several performance measures were examined, and his results favored the use of one-officer units. One-officer units covered more area, had faster response times, and increased patrol frequency and visibility, all while reducing costs and without increasing the risk of injury.

Using data from the Kansas City Response Time study (discussed above), David Kessler (1985) replicated the San Diego study. In his analysis, he included additional *control* variables in an effort to explain one of the findings from San Diego: that response time for two one-officer cars was faster than one two-officer car. This finding could have been attributed to the type of call patrol units were dispatched to, whether or not a patrol unit was patrolling outside of their assigned beat, whether or not the officer(s) were inside of their cars when dispatched, or whether or not the patrol unit waited for a "cover" car. Even with the additional control variables, the response time for two one-officer cars was significantly faster.

The replication studies discussed so far all involved an examination of the impact of patrol staffing on police-related outcome measures. In 1982, Scott Decker and Allen Wagner wanted to expand this research by exploring the influence of patrol staffing on citizens. The data for their study were from a medium-sized city in the United States. They found that in situations where citizens filed a complaint against a police officer, more citizens were injured as a result of the police-citizen encounters compared to police officers. The chances of injury were higher when citizens encountered a two-officer unit than for a one-officer unit. Citizens were also more likely to be arrested and charged with assaulting a police officer as a result of their encounters with two-officer units. Decker and Wagner's findings were significant regardless of how dangerous the area was (measured by the violent crime rate). Patrol staffing appeared to have significant implications for citizens as well as the police. It was also suggested that two-officer units approached their encounters with citizens differently. A study of over 1,000 Australian police officers found that two-officer units were more likely to encounter citizens who failed to comply with the officers' requests/commands (Wilson and Brewer 2001).

Recent research has shown that perceptions have not changed much since results from the San Diego experiment were published. Alejandro del Carmen and Lori Guevara (2003) published a study of police officer attitudes related to one- and two-officer patrol units. Surveys were administered to 50 police officers in a North Texas police department. The officers' responses indicated that their perceptions of performance did not depend on whether they were working as part of a one- or two-officer patrol unit. Officers expressed a preference for two-officer units in certain circumstances. Officers believed that two-officer units should be used in the evening and at night as well as in communities where a significant number of residents were suspicious of the police. The perception that two-officer units were more effective was prevalent also. A majority of the officers indicated that two-officer units could observe more, respond faster to calls for service, increase police visibility, and deter more crime than one-officer units. With regard to perceptions of safety, however, most officers believed that one-officer units were just as safe as two (provided the officers were properly trained).

Today, the use of one-officer patrol dominants small- to medium-size police departments while larger departments continue to use a combination of one- and two-officer patrol units. The San Diego study of patrol staffing, along with the replication studies, provided police departments the knowledge to make more informed decisions. Police departments no longer have to allocate resources based on traditional assumptions of how to achieve the most effective, cost-efficient use of their patrol resources.

References

Boydstun, J., M. Sherry, and N. Moelter (1977). *Patrol Staffing in San Diego: One-or Two-Officer Units*. Washington, DC: Police Foundation.

Brannon, B. (1956). "A Report on One-Man Police Patrol Cars in Kansas City, Missouri." *Journal of Criminal Law, Criminology & Police Science* July–August:238–52.

Decker, S., and A. Wagner (1982). "The Impact of Patrol Staffing on Police-Citizen Injuries and Dispositions." *Journal of Criminal Justice* 10:375–82.

del Carmen, A., and L. Guevara (2003). "Police Officers on Two-Officer Units: A Study of Attitudinal Responses Towards a Patrol Experiment." *Policing: An International Journal of Police, Strategies & Management* 26:144–61.

Kaplan, E. (1979). "Evaluating the Effectiveness of One-Officer Versus Two-Officer Patrol Units." *Journal of Criminal Justice* 7:325–55.

Kessler, D. (1985). "One- or Two-Officer Cars? A Perspective From Kansas City." *Journal of Criminal Justice* 13:49-64.

Larson, R., and T. Rich (1985). *Use of Operational Models in Considering Implementation Strategies for Combined Use of Two- and One-Officer Cars*. Washington, DC: National Institute of Justice.

Wilson, C., and N. Brewer (1992). "One- and Two-Person Patrols: A Review." *Journal of Criminal Justice* 20:443–54.

Wilson, C., and N. Brewer (2001). "Working in Teams: Negative Effects on Organizational Performance in Policing." *Policing: An International Journal of Police, Strategies & Management* 24:115–27.

Further Reading

Chelst, K. (1981). "Deployment of One- vs. Two-Officer Patrol Units: A Comparison of Travel Times." *Manage Science* 27:213–230.

Elliott, J., J. O'Connor, and T. Sardino (1969). "The Detection and Interception Capability of One- and Two-Man Patrol Units." *Police* 5:24–26.

Hale, C. (2003). *Police Patrol: Operations and Management*, 3rd ed. Upper Saddle Ridge, NJ: Prentice Hall.

Larson, R. (1972). *Urban Police Patrol Analysis*. Cambridge, MA: MIT Press.

THE NEWARK FOOT PATROL EXPERIMENT: SHOULD THE POLICE PATROL IN CARS OR ON FOOT?

Police Foundation (1981). *The Newark Foot Patrol Experiment*. Washington, DC: Police Foundation.

Background

When police officers started patrolling in motorized vehicles in the 1930s, it was viewed as a major advancement in police work. The use of motorized police patrol actually dates back to the early 1900s, but the expense prohibited most departments from adopting it until automobiles could be mass-produced. The shift to motorized patrol was assumed to have several advantages over foot patrol. Police officers could patrol larger areas with faster response times. Crime and fear would decrease because of the increased visibility. The use of a car would allow the police to carry more equipment, such as first-aid kits and a wider variety of weapons. It was believed that accountability would be improved because of the increased supervision over officers. The original intent was not to completely replace foot patrol but enhance it. The police would continue the same level of face-to-face interactions with the public (Wilson 1953). The police would drive to their assigned areas, park their vehicles, and spend most of their time walking around. This all changed when the police took on a greater role fighting crime during the professional era. With the help of technology, police departments started allocating patrol resources according to sophisticated analyses of crime patterns. Dispatch practices were computerized, and soon after vehicles were equipped with computers that allowed the police to check identifications and vehicle registrations quickly (Police Foundation 1981). Suspects could also be easily transported to the station after arrest. All of these changes were seen as improvements that assisted the police in their law enforcement efforts.

By the 1960s, the police had become highly skilled professionals, but unfortunately, the police had also become isolated from the communities in which they worked. Along with the social turmoil that strained police community relations, the use of motorized patrol significantly reduced the one-on-one interactions between the police and the public. The police could be seen driving through the neighborhood, but the police officer became invisible. Despite these setbacks, most police administrators believed the benefits of motorized patrol outnumbered the shortcomings. Both the International Association of Chiefs of Police and the President's Commission on Crime Control supported the use of motorized patrol over foot patrol (Police Foundation 1981). By the 1970s, most police administrators viewed foot patrol as useless and expensive.

It was not until the result of the Kansas City Preventive Patrol Experiment (1974) were published, that administers began to question the reliance on motorized patrol to reduce crime and make people feel safe. Several departments including Baltimore, Boston, Washington, DC, and Fort Worth had already implemented a system of foot patrol as a way to improve police community relations, but there was little research on its effectiveness (particularly research utilizing an experimental design) (Police Foundation 1981). The research that had been conducted produced mixed results in terms of its effect on crime and fear of crime. The opportunity for a large-scale empirical study of the foot patrol presented itself when the Governor of the New Jersey began inquiring about whether or not a state funded initiative that included the use of foot patrol was achieving its goals.

In early 1973, New Jersey implemented *public law 1979*, known as the "Safe and Clean Neighborhood Act." The state allocated 12 million dollars (with another 12 million in matched funds from municipal governments) to the project that was considered "unique" in the United States (Police Foundation 1981). The program included resources to improve the physical appearance and stability of low-income communities *and* funds to bring back the use of foot patrol. The use of foot patrol would increase the accessibility and visibility of the police, which would make people feel safe. Twenty-eight communities took part in the program during the first year. The program provided funds to hire and outfit 775 walking police officers (Police Foundation 1981). The officers were required to wear uniforms at all times and were instructed to spend most of their time on the street. They were assigned a geographical area that could be covered within a 45 minute time period. The Department of Community Affairs provided oversight of the program to ensure that funds were being used appropriately, but there were still variations in foot patrol practices. Differences in how officers were assigned and the length of assignment were found across jurisdictions. The majority of the departments coordinated foot patrol activities with those of motor patrol (Police Foundation 1971).

The Experiment

A team of researchers from the Police Foundation was recruited in 1976 to evaluate the effectiveness of the use of foot patrol in New Jersey. Prior to conducting the *experiment,* researchers visited several of the police departments participating in the foot patrol program. Researchers interviewed police administrators and officers, examined existing data sources, and even accompanied the officers on patrol to gain firsthand knowledge of the foot patrol in practice. Task forces were then established in four cities that would become evaluation sites. The task forces determined the research design and the specific *hypotheses* that would be tested in late 1977. Data were collected from 28 cities with Newark being selected as the primary study location. Several hypotheses were examined related to crime, fear of crime, and police officer job satisfaction. The specific *hypotheses* were:

1. Citizens would report more positive attitudes toward the police in communities with foot patrol compared to communities without foot patrol.
2. Citizens in communities with foot patrol would report less fear of crime compared to communities without foot patrol.
3. Crime would be less in communities with foot patrol compared to communities without foot patrol.
4. Victimization would be less in communities with foot patrol compared to communities without foot patrol.
5. Citizens in communities with foot patrol would be more likely to report crime compared to communities without foot patrol.
6. The number of arrests would be greater in communities with foot patrol compared to communities without foot patrol.
7. Police officers would report greater job satisfaction in communities with foot patrol compared to communities without foot patrol.

Three separate research designs were used to test the above *hypotheses.*[1] The first design compared police officer attitudes for officers assigned to foot and motorized patrol. The second design was implemented in the single city of Elizabeth where the use of foot patrol already existed in parts of the city before the Safe and Clean Neighborhoods program began. Researchers wanted to compare reported crime *between* these areas and the other areas that incorporated foot patrol only *after* the Safe and Clean Neighborhoods program went into effect. Finally, the researchers conducted an experiment in the city of Newark to determine if there were any changes in reported crime, victimization, or residents' perceptions of safety after the foot patrol program went into effect. *Experimental* research designs are ideal for establishing cause and effect. In this study, researchers wanted to determine whether or not the use of foot patrol resulted in changes to the crime rate or reported fear. Eight patrol beats were selected. These beats had consistently utilized foot patrol as part of the Safe and Clean

---

[1] The Police Foundation attempted a cost-benefit analysis of foot patrol versus motor patrol for officials in New Jersey as part of their research but was unable to accurately determine the appropriate outcomes or benefits.

Before	After	
T₁	**T₂**	**CONDITION**
O	X	4 Beats which Add Foot Patrol
*R X	O	4 Beats which Drop Foot Patrol
*R X	X	4 Beats with a Steady Level of Foot Patrol

*As Campbell and Stanley (1963) represent experimental designs, the designation "R" indicates random assignment to a condition.

FIGURE 1.3   Quasi Experimental Research Design

Source: The Newark Foot Patrol Experiment. Police Foundation.

Neighborhoods program. The eight beats were divided into four groups of two beats. Beats were "matched" based on the number of residential and commercial establishments in each beat. *Matching* is an attempt to eliminate preexisting differences between groups. Within each pair, foot patrol continued in one beat but was removed from the other. Beats were randomly assigned to either the control (no foot patrol) or experimental (foot patrol) group. Like matching, *random assignment* makes it easier to infer that any observed change was the result of foot patrol and not some *extraneous* factor. Foot patrol was also initiated in four beats that had not previously used it. These four beats were selected to be similar to the other eight beats. The research design was actually a *quasi-experimental* design because it lacked all of the essential components of a true experiment. Beats were selected according to preexisting characteristics. Beats were selected that had already been using foot patrol officers while others were selected because they were not. Any findings could have been influenced by the preexisting conditions of the areas prior to the start of the study.

A considerable amount of data was collected from surveys, crime statistics, observations, and departmental data. Researchers also wanted to gain insight into the daily activities of foot patrol officers. Each of the officers was required to fill out and turn in log sheets to their supervisors. These log sheets were reviewed by researchers who wanted to determine if activities differed from officers on motorized patrol.

Some potential problems had to be addressed before the experiment began. The research team, not the police departments, assigned the police beats to the control and experimental groups to ensure objectivity. This was a significant departure from the normal departmental allocation policies. Researchers met with representatives from the participating police departments and were able to convince them of the necessity of *random assignment*. There were also concerns that residents and business owners might complain about the removal of the foot patrol officers. This occurred on more than one occasion. Public meetings were held where police administrators explained the importance of evaluating police policies. As with any *experiment,* researchers monitored conditions closely to make sure the introduced treatment (foot patrol) was being implemented properly. To help with this, foot patrol officers were assigned two-way radios and were contacted several times during a shift and asked to report their locations to the department. Each of the beats also had a call box that the officers were required to use once per hour to report to the department. Officers who failed to comply with these reporting requirements faced disciplinary action from the department. Officials from the Department of Community Affairs (the office responsible for overseeing the Safe and

Clean Neighborhoods program) also continued their "unannounced inspections" of the foot patrol posts to make sure the officers were present. Finally, a group of civilian observers were recruited to keep track of the number of people on the streets and they also reported on the presence of the officers.

To determine the influence of foot patrol on both residents' perception of crime, victimization, fear, and overall satisfaction with the police, surveys were administered to a sample of community residents within each beat. Researchers decided to use separate pretest and posttest samples to avoid the problem of *testing treatment interaction.* This occurs when responses on the posttest (administered after the treatment is introduced) are influenced by the pretest measurement. When surveying separate samples, however, researchers have to make sure both samples are comparable. In the foot patrol study, researchers analyzed both samples and found both were similar in terms of demographic characteristics such as age, race, and gender. Respondents from commercial establishments were also sampled and surveyed using the same questions as residents.

Foot patrol officers in all 28 cities participating in the Safe and Clean Neighborhoods Program were asked to complete a survey form asking about their perceptions of foot patrol to assess job satisfaction. Researchers also accessed certain performance indicators from department records, including absenteeism and the number of citations an officer received for meritorious action.

Results

The evaluation period ended in February 1979, and the final report was published 2 years later. Findings from the study are presented below.

Visibility of officers and citizen attitudes. One of the most significant findings uncovered by researchers had to do with the visibility of the foot patrol officers. Residents were aware of the officers' presence or lack of presence in their communities. Unlike motorized patrol, foot patrol was a good way to maintain or increase police visibility. Commercial respondents, however, indicated less awareness across all three groups. This was attributed to the fact that many establishments were closed during the time when the levels of foot patrol were altered. Residents in the added beats also reported more positive attitudes toward the police.

Crime, victimization, reporting, and fear. Foot patrol appeared to have no influence on reported crime or victimization. No significant differences existed between the three groups on these measures. Perceptions of crime did change. In the areas where foot patrol was added, residents indicated that the serious crimes appeared to be *less* of a problem. The opposite trend occurred with commercial respondents. In the added foot patrol areas, respondents indicated that serious crime was greater. Foot patrol appeared to have no influence on the reporting of crime across beats and official measures of crime showed no change across the three beats. Residents also reported feeling safer in the added beats and took less precautionary measures, while commercial respondents across all beats reported feeling less safe.

Patrol officer job satisfaction. In addition to determining the effectiveness of foot patrol on levels of crime and fear, researchers also wanted to find out how police officers felt about its use. Most (81%) of the officers surveyed had been assigned to foot patrol at least once in their careers. Very few (16%) volunteered for their assignment. Foot patrol assignments typically went to officers with less seniority. Seventy-six percent of the officers received no special foot patrol training. Foot patrol officers were more likely to view the public as supportive and cooperative. Foot patrol officers also indicated they felt their work was an important police function that should be expanded. Motor patrol officers perceived the work of foot patrol as easy and reported that its use should *not* be expanded. Helping the public was perceived as a more important police function for foot patrol officers than officers engaged in motor patrol activities. Overall, foot patrol officers indicated a greater level of job satisfaction compared to their motor counterparts. Performance indicators revealed that foot patrol officers had less absenteeism but fewer citations compared to officers on motor patrol. Researchers attributed the finding for citations to opportunity and departmental perceptions. Motor officers received more action calls and supervisors may have been biased against foot patrol officers.

Patrol officer activity logs. The activity logs completed by each of the foot patrol officers shed light on how these officers spent their time. Foot patrol officers reported little in terms of law enforcement. They issued few citations and rarely made an arrest. They spent most of their time interacting with citizens on the street and checking on commercial establishments.

Policy recommendations. Based on their findings, researchers made several policy recommendations. First, they suggested that departments using (or considering the use of) foot patrol maintain the same status for foot patrol officers as motor patrol. This would help with recruitment and would bolster their status in the community. Second, foot patrol officers should be allowed to respond to calls for service. This would not only increase interactions between the public and the police but might also help the police uncover valuable information needed to solve crimes. Third, specialized training programs should be developed for foot patrol officers. This training would be in addition to the regular training a patrol officer received while at the police academy. Fourth, departments needed to develop a system for collecting and using information collected by foot patrol officers. Foot patrol officers were in a position to gather information that could be used in solving crime. Fifth, foot patrol officers needed to become more involved in community activities. They should take on the role of community "consultants" helping residents with their crime and public order problems. Finally, departments should assign foot patrol officers to shifts that would bring them into contact with the most residents possible.

Criticisms

The Newark Foot Patrol Experiment was the first large-scale study of its kind to explore this police function in the United States. The study utilized three different research designs including a *quasi-experimental* design to test the effectiveness of foot patrol on several outcome measures. Researchers made a concerted effort to maintain control over all of the experimental conditions, however, as with most experiments conducted in natural settings, *extraneous* influences created problems. Researchers anticipated that members of the business community in the beats where foot patrol was removed might express concern and discontentment. Researchers and police officials tried to alleviate those concerns through public meetings, but it remained unknown whether this influenced the findings derived from commercial respondents (Police Foundation 1981). Survey responses from the commercial respondents were consistently different from the residential responses. Commercial respondents indicated they were less aware of the police presence across all study areas, not just in the areas where foot patrol was dropped. It was possible that the publicity of the experiment influenced their responses. Another problem related to the commercial respondents was that business owners had contact with the police only when the officer was on foot—regardless of whether or not the officer drove to their establishment (Police

Foundation 1981). Commercial respondents may not have been able to accurately differentiate between foot and motor patrol.

Perhaps the biggest threat to the *validity* of the findings was the layoff of police officers toward the end of the experiment. *History* is a threat caused by events or changes in the subject's environment that could influence the outcome of the study. Due to fiscal problems, the mayor of Newark announced the layoffs of 200 officers. The announcement was met with strong public opposition from police unions. Union representatives warned communities that the reduction in police would compromise safety. Researchers also speculated that police officers complained about the layoffs to business owners. It was unclear if this unanticipated event biased the public's perceptions of police services (Police Foundation 1981).

Another criticism of the Newark Foot Patrol Study was the use of reported crime as an outcome measure. Many crimes go unreported to the police, and even if a crime is reported, police departments may not accurately record the offense. Researchers also examined arrest data that are suspect because not all crimes resulted in arrest and not all arrests were legitimate. Researchers examined victimization data to help address these sources of error. The victimization data showed consistent results with the official counts of crime (no increases occurred in any of the study areas). Victimization data provides a good source of validation for official counts of crime. Data collected from the activity logs were subject to a similar problem. The accuracy of this information relied on the truthfulness of officers in reporting their activities.

Significance and Subsequent Research

Once the automobile was introduced to police work, there appeared to be no going back. Motorized vehicles had a tremendous impact on the delivery of police services, particularly the patrol function. Police could patrol larger areas in less time, carry more equipment, and transport suspects more efficiently. Foot patrol soon became viewed as outdated and peripheral to police work. The social turmoil of the 1960s sparked a renewed interest in the foot patrol as a way to improve strained police community relationships. Increasing the face-to-face interactions could help change negative attitudes and increase citizen cooperation. After the findings from the Newark experiment were published, police agencies across the United States took notice. By 2003, 59 percent of police agencies used foot patrol on a routine basis (Bureau of Justice Statistics 2007). Many communities also currently have police officers on bicycles, horses, and scooters.

One year after the Newark results were published, Robert Trojanowicz and Dennis Banas (1982) from Michigan State University published results from a 3-year evaluation of the Neighborhood Foot Patrol Program developed in Flint, Michigan. The program went into effect in 1979 as part of a 2.6 million dollar grant by the Charles Stewart Mott Foundation. Fourteen neighborhoods were selected as experimental sites for the program. Foot patrol would be established across the city with the goal of improving police community relations and to get the public involved in crime prevention efforts. Results from the study revealed consistent findings with Newark. In areas where foot patrol was implemented, residents felt safer and were more satisfied with police services. A greater number of citizens indicated that they had either seen their foot patrol officer or had contact with them. In Flint, however, a reduction in officially recorded crime also occurred in the foot patrol areas. Residents in these areas were more likely to report crime to the police. Less victimization was also reported after foot patrol was implemented.

Given the inconsistent findings between Newark and Flint with regard to crime and victimization, William Bowers and Jon Hirsch (1987) conducted an evaluation of Boston's foot patrol program. In 1983, the Boston Police Department put into operation a new patrol plan that allocated 300 police officers to foot patrol. Foot patrol became the predominate form of patrol throughout the city. No significant reduction occurred in violent or property crime after the reallocation of patrol went into effect. Their research did not examine levels of fear or citizen satisfaction with the police. Finn Esbensen (1987) conducted a study of foot patrol in a medium-sized city located in the southwest. Overall there was no reduction in crime with the exception of public order crimes (i.e., vagrancy, disorderly conduct). This study also uncovered a potential problem with the implementation of foot patrol in limited areas within a city. While disorder crimes went down in foot patrol areas, these crimes increased in surrounding areas. This is known as *crime displacement* and can be an important factor in evaluation studies of police practices. Esbensen also examined community levels of satisfaction with the police and found no improvements, however, noted that satisfaction was high to begin with. It may be that foot patrol only had a positive impact when implemented in communities where residents were discontented with the police.

Each of the studies presented in this section challenged many commonly held assumptions about the patrol function. Findings from the Kansas City Preventive Patrol Experiment, the Kansas City Response Time Study, the San Diego Patrol Staffing Experiment, and the Newark Foot Patrol Experiment, and other important empirical studies offered valuable insight into the patrol function that were used to improve the delivery of police services. This research also marked the beginning of a new era of policing where administrators no longer had to rely on best guess practices of what works in policing.

References

Bowers, W., and J. Hirsch (1987). The Impact of Foot Patrol Staffing On Crime and Disorder in Boston: An Unmet Promise." *American Journal of Police* 6:17–44.

Bureau of Justice Statistics (2007). *Census of State and Local Law Enforcement Agencies 2004*. Washington, DC: US Department of Justice.

Esbensen, F. (1987). "Foot Patrols: Of What Value?" *American Journal of Police* 6:45–65.

Police Foundation (1981). *The Newark Foot Patrol Experiment*. Washington, DC: Police Foundation.

Trojanowicz, R., and D. Banas (1982). *An Evaluation of the Neighborhood Foot Patrol Program in Flint, Michigan*. East Lansing, MI: National Neighborhood Foot Patrol Center, Michigan State University.

Wilson, O (1953). "Put the Cop Back on the Beat." *Public Management* June.

Further Reading

Esbensen, F., and C. Taylor (1984). "Foot Patrol and Crime Rates." *Southern Journal of Criminal Justice* 8:184–94.

Pate, A., A. Ferrara, and G. Kelling (1981). "Foot Patrol: A Discussion of the Issues." *The Newark Foot Patrol Experiment*. Washington, DC: Police Foundation.

Trojanowicz, R., and D. Banas (1985). *The Impact of Foot Patrol on Black and White Perceptions of Policing*. East Lansing, MI: National Neighborhood Foot Patrol Center, Michigan State University.

Trojanowicz, R., and D. Banas (1985). *Job Satisfaction: A Comparison of Foot Patrol Versus Motor Patrol Officers*. East Lansing, MI: National Neighborhood Foot Patrol Center, Michigan State University.

INVESTIGATION

Investigation is an important part of police work constituting the second largest allocation of police resources (second behind patrol). Investigators, frequently called *detectives*, help solve the crimes that have been reported to the police. The role of an investigator is varied and depends upon the unique circumstances of each crime. Investigators collect evidence to help identify and locate suspects. Once a suspect has been arrested, investigators assist prosecutors in securing convictions by compiling evidence against the suspect, locating witnesses, questioning victims, and testifying in court. The entertainment media has always glorified the image of a detective by portraying them as smart, sophisticated crime fighters who can maneuver through complex mazes of evidence to find out who committed the crime, how the crime was committed, and for what reason. The news media also presents detectives in a favorable light. When we turn on the local news or pick up the newspaper it is the face of a detective we see describing the crime or explaining how a suspect was apprehended. This image influences how the public perceives the detectives' role in our society. Individuals aspiring for a career in law enforcement typically want to be detectives (not patrol officers) because of the assumption that detectives are the ones who actually solve crimes.

The very first police officers did little in terms of criminal investigation. Until the 1920s, the police were primarily reactive in their presence in the community (Travis and Langworthy 2007). Police were charged with the mandate of maintaining a police presence to make people feel safe and secure. The police were available to respond to calls for service, provide assistance to those in need, and to arrest suspected criminals. In 1846, the Boston Police department became the first department in the United States to promote patrol officers to detectives. As part of a reform to professionalize police work in the early 1900s, police saw their role as that of a crime fighter and became more focused on enforcing the law. Selection and training standards were implemented in police departments all across the United States. The leadership structure within departments resembled a military hierarchy. The police also focused their attention on solving crimes not immediately cleared by an arrest. Advances in technology gave the police the necessary tools and techniques to collect evidence such as fingerprints and crime labs were established to assist the police in their efforts to identify suspects. Large police departments created specialized investigation divisions where detectives worked to gather information and collect evidence. The detectives were assigned cases that they worked on until they secured an arrest and conviction or until the case was dropped. Over the next 50 years, the investigation function continued to develop and expand.

THE RAND STUDY OF INVESTIGATION: DO DETECTIVES REALLY SOLVE CRIMES?

Greenwood, P., and J. Petersilia (1975). *The Criminal Investigation Process.* Santa Monica, CA: Rand.

Background

By 1970, expenditures on investigation had reached an annual cost of one billion dollars (Greenwood and Petersilia 1975). Despite this growth, research on the effectiveness of investigation was sparse. Departments were once again operating under a widely held assumption as to the utility of this police function. The initial approach taken to determine the effectiveness of the investigation function was to examine the arrest and clearance rates for a given department or jurisdiction (Greenwood and Petersilia 1975). The argument was made that an investigator or unit that made a large number of arrests or had a high clearance rate was productive. The President's Commission on Law Enforcement and the Administration of Justice sponsored one of the first studies to examine the effectiveness of investigation. The study found that only 25 percent of all crimes resulted in arrest or were cleared through other means (Silver 1968). Most of the cleared crimes were at the hands of patrol officers, but information obtained from investigators was responsible for 25 percent of the arrests made (Silver 1968). Using arrest and clearance rates was problematic given that this information did not always reflect a "solved crime." Suspects could be arrested without being charged and departments operated under different criteria for clearing crimes. In some departments, crimes were cleared by an arrest. In others, recovery of stolen property meant a cleared crime. Department policies and procedures were a major determinant of clearance rates, and there was too much variation across departments to use these rates as a measure of effectiveness (Greenwood and Petersilia 1975). Furthermore, arrest and clearance rates had more to do with the work of the patrol force and information provided by the public than the work of an investigator.

The Study

The limitations of arrest and clearance rates as indicators of effectiveness prompted researchers to consider other types of information to learn about the investigation function. In 1974, the National Institute of Law Enforcement and Criminal Justice asked the Rand Corporation (a privately funded research group) to provide assistance in gathering information on the investigation process. The purpose of the study was to collect data on what investigators do and how they do it. The 2-year study involved collecting a massive amount of information from police departments and officers all across the country. This information led to a better understanding of the function of investigation in police work, but it also refuted some widely held beliefs about the role of the investigator in solving crime.

In order to gather such a large amount of data, Rand researchers Peter Greenwood and Joan Petersilia (1975) decided to administer a *mail* survey to police departments around the United States. Surveys are used extensively in criminal justice research. Surveys are an ideal way to collect large amounts of data used to describe the characteristics and behaviors of large populations. Only large police departments with at least 150 full-time employees that served jurisdictions with over 100,000 were selected for the study. The decision to exclude smaller departments was made because in smaller departments the investigation function was usually not separate from patrol. In small police departments, the officers were more generalists. Investigators were usually patrol officers who *sometimes* performed investigator duties. In a larger department, the role of investigation was separate and more specialized (the same is true in departments today). Researchers also wanted to make sure the information collected could be *generalized* to a large number of departments around the country. Three hundred police departments were asked to participate in the study, but only 153 complied with the request. Survey questions were constructed to collect information on the following aspects of investigation:

> procedures for allocating resources and assigning cases
>
> the organizational structure of investigation
>
> the level of specialization with investigation

training and evaluation of investigators

use of technology in the investigation process

crime, clearance and arrest rates

To enhance the quality of the information collected, *on-site* interviews were conducted in several of the departments that participated in the survey. Interviews are used to gather more detailed information than can normally be obtained from a survey instrument. Interviewers not only visited these departments, they also observed and participated in the operations of the investigation units. This type of data collection is known as *field* or *observational* research. Field research is valuable for gaining an insider's perspective often missed with survey research. It is one thing to ask an investigator the question, "how much interaction do you have with the prosecuting attorneys office?" Imagine the type of information a researcher could collect by observing the interactions between the police and prosecutors. Field research permits researchers to gain firsthand knowledge of these interactions.

Several police departments supplied additional information by providing written evaluations of their investigative programs. Some of the departments also permitted access to existing data the departments were already collecting on their own. The Kansas City Missouri Police Department had maintained a Detective Case Assignment File since 1971. This information assisted researchers in identifying the activities of the detectives, how much time detectives spent engaged in these activities, and whether their efforts resulted in an arrest. Finally, researchers utilized information from the 1972 Uniform Crime Report and victimization survey data. Given the magnitude of the study (in terms of the number of police departments participating and the multiple sources of data), researchers wanted to make sure to protect the integrity of the information. An advisory board was appointed that consisted of a prosecuting attorney and currently employed and retired police investigators. The advisory board worked closely with the Rand researchers on all aspects of the project from survey design to assisting with the interpretation of the results.

Findings

Investigators were always believed to be essential in solving crime. The results from the Rand Study of Investigation questioned the validity of this belief. Data collected from police departments all across the United States revealed that investigators spent very little time engaged in activities that resulted in the arrest of a suspect and the clearance of crime. Greenwood and Petersilia reported that investigators were responsible for clearing less than 3 percent of all index crimes (reported in the Uniform Crime Report). The crimes that investigators had the most impact on were robbery, commercial burglary, and homicide. Less than half of all index crimes received significant attention by an investigator. Most of an investigator's time (40%) was spent engaged in such activities as locating and questioning victims and witnesses for crimes that would never be solved or gathering evidence and preparing cases for prosecution.

If investigators had such a limited role to play in solving most crimes, the obvious question raised was, "who was responsible for solving crime?" The data from this project revealed that information taken by the patrol officer first on the scene was the most important factor in determining whether an arrest was made. More specifically, if the patrol officer was able to obtain information that identified a suspect, chances were good the suspect would be subsequently located and arrested. For crimes in which no suspect was identified at the scene, routine police procedures became important. Recovering stolen property, having witnesses view pictures of suspects, and searching fingerprint databases were procedures responsible for solving a lot of these crimes. These routine police activities required no special training beyond what a patrol officer received. The study found that patrol officers had an important role to play in solving the crimes that had any chance of *ever* being solved.

The Rand study also revealed that police departments were actively involved in gathering evidence from crime scenes—usually too much evidence. Most departments did not have the resources to analyze all of the information collected. Another widely held assumption underlying the investigation function was that fingerprints were key pieces of evidence necessary to solve crime. Fingerprints could help identify suspects and could be used as physical evidence to secure a conviction. The ability to collect fingerprints depended primarily on how quickly a department could dispatch an officer or crime scene technician to the scene, however the study found that fingerprints were rarely the determining factor in whether or not a crime was solved. Researchers compared the processing of fingerprint evidence in four police departments that participated in the study and found that fingerprints rarely helped with the initial identification of a suspect. Departments were usually lacking in the search capabilities necessary to efficiently and effectively use the fingerprints lifted from crime scenes. Fingerprints appeared to be more useful in securing convictions than in solving the crime.

One of the advantages of collecting information from a large number of police agencies was the ability to make comparisons between departments. The researchers were able to examine data across departments to determine whether or not there were any unique departmental characteristics related to their findings. There were observed *differences* in the size, organization, training, caseload assignment, and procedures, but none of these differences had any real influence on the ability of the investigators to solve crime. The finding that investigators played only a minor role in arrest and clearance rates was consistent across all departments in each of the jurisdictions studied. Once it was revealed how much time an investigator spent engaged in activities designated as "post clearance"(after a suspect has been arrested and/or the crime was labeled as "cleared") researchers explored these activities further. Investigators spent a great deal of their time—half of their time spent on casework—involved in activities that assisted prosecutors in securing convictions. These activities consisted of collecting additional evidence against a defendant, report writing, and testifying in court. Prosecutors used this information in plea negotiations and during trials. After all, what good was an arrest that would not stand up in court? Assisting prosecutors secure their convictions was an important aspect of police work and provides a good example of the exchange relationships between police and prosecutors. Prosecutors, however, frequently blamed the police when a case did not result in a conviction. Dismissals, plea bargains, acquittals, and lenient sentences were because the police failed to gather enough evidence, the right type of evidence, or violated the suspect's constitutional rights.

To better understand the support role that investigators played in securing convictions, Rand researchers developed a checklist with the help of prosecutors and investigators that included 39 evidentiary items prosecutors would like to have to assist them in their case screening decisions. The checklist was taken to two prosecuting attorney offices in California and compared against the evidence turned over by the investigators in a series of robbery cases. In the first office, investigators in 45 percent of the cases satisfied the 39 evidentiary items; but in the second office only 26 percent of cases were satisfied. Researchers also examined the rate of dismissals and plea bargaining in each office and found that dismissals and lenient plea offers were more prevalent in the office with fewer cases meeting the checklist criteria. This information suggested that the failure of a prosecutor to obtain convictions with harsh sentences *might* have been attributed to ineffective police investigations. This finding was issued as a cautionary conclusion because prosecutors dismissed cases for other reasons that had nothing to do with the police and these factors were not examined as part of the study.

Police departments often defended the investigation function as important to police community relations. Investigators maintained contact with crime victims; therefore they provided a valuable service to the public. To assess this function, researchers observed the interactions between investigators and victims. These observations revealed that investigators *rarely* had any contact with a victim beyond the initial contact to obtain a statement. Victims were *seldom* informed of the progress of an investigation or what happened to a defendant in the court system. To explore this function further, a telephone survey was carried out on a sample of robbery and burglary victims. Questions were asked regarding a victim's preference for being informed on the progress of their case. Most of the victims surveyed indicated that they wanted to be updated on the status of their case; however, their responses also indicated that certain types of information would not be favorably perceived. When investigators contacted victims to tell them that the investigation was being suspended, their reaction was less than positive (very few victims actually pursued any type of formal complaint against the investigator).

Investigation, like patrol, was considered to be reactive police work. Investigators responded to the crimes that had already occurred. Some of the departments selected for this study had started to experiment with more proactive investigative strategies to try and improve arrest and clearance rates in their jurisdictions. Special investigation units were established to target specific types of crime such as burglary and robbery (the crimes that investigators have a better chance of solving). Instead of being assigned a specific caseload, investigators were instructed to use informants, surveillance, and other information-gathering techniques to help identify serious criminals. Arrest and clearance rates were higher for these units compared to traditional investigation activities, however, the increase was short lived. Once the targeted efforts diminished, Greenwood and Petersilia found arrest and clearance rates returned to normal.

Criticisms

One year after the Rand study on criminal investigation was published, Daryl Gates and Lyle Knowles (1976) published an article in *Police Chief* that questioned the results. Their criticisms focused on the Rand researchers' failure to include sufficient information on their analyses, inadequate data, and conclusions that were not supported by their data. For example, in their sample of police departments, Greenwood and Petersilia mailed surveys to 300 police departments, but only half responded. Gates and Knowles questioned whether the findings were truly representative of police departments across the United States. A 50 percent *response rate* was not uncommon with mail surveys, but a concern was whether departments that failed to respond differ significantly from the departments that participated. The characteristics of the departments that participated in the study may have biased the findings. *Response bias* is a common problem with survey research. The sample consisted only of large police departments in urban areas. A consequence of such is that the findings may not have applied to smaller departments in less populated jurisdictions. Selecting an appropriate sample is important to the *generalizability* of findings in survey research. Greenwood and Petersilia defended their sample on the grounds that the data were for the most part consistent across study sites. Also, the decision to sample large departments was based on the fact that investigation was not a specialized function in smaller departments. Furthermore, the findings were not disputed by senior level police officers that worked in the study departments.

Gates and Knowles also criticized the Rand report's conclusion that investigators spent most of their time (40%) on cases that would never be solved. This was misleading because investigators only spent 60 percent of their time actually investigating crimes (not 100%). This meant that investigators only spent 24 percent (40% of 60) of their time on unsolved crimes. Rand researchers also failed to consider any deterrent value associated with the investigation function.

Significance and Subsequent Research

The Rand study of investigation offered the first comprehensive examination of the investigation function of a police department. Researchers collected a substantial amount of information through their surveys, interviews, and observations. Police agencies as well as the general public assumed that detectives were assigned cases to investigate and were responsible for solving them. Information collected from over 150 police departments across the United States revealed how limited the role of an investigator really was. Patrol officers were typically the first dispatched to a crime scene and the ability of a patrol officer to identify a suspect was what usually determined if a crime would be solved. Investigators collected a lot of evidence, but it was usually more than the department could analyze and was usually not the evidence needed to identify a suspect. Investigators spent a considerable amount of time preparing cases for prosecution. Prosecutors, however, found their efforts insufficient in securing a conviction resulting in strict punishment. Based on these findings, Rand researchers offered several recommendations for how police departments might more effectively utilize their investigators and reallocate resources to improve arrest and clearance rates. Proposed reforms included creating specialized proactive investigation forces to target specific crimes, enhancing the evidence processing capabilities of departments, and requiring prosecutors assume the responsibility of post arrest investigations.

These recommendations were not presented as justifications to reducing police personnel, but rather as suggestions for how departments should use their detectives. Several departments took the suggestions and tried to implement changes to improve the investigation function. The National Institute of Justice funded projects for police departments under the Managing Criminal Investigations program. Five police departments participated in the program and were subsequently evaluated to see if the reforms were successful. The changes failed to produce an increase in arrest, clearance or conviction rates. The program was implemented on a larger scale as part of a funding initiative by the LEAA (Wycoff and Cosgrove 2001). Reforms were put into practice in 15 cities in 1980. Unfortunately, funding ran out with the termination of the LEAA, so there was no large-scale evaluation of the sites (Wycoff and Cosgrove 2001). Even though it remained unclear whether the reforms were successful, the program appeared to have influence over the investigation functions in police departments across the United States. Departments were equipped with a better understanding of the investigation function that could be monitored and evaluated.

The Rand study itself was *replicated* 9 years later. Mark Willman and John Snortum (1984) gathered data from a Los Angeles suburban police department. Their findings were consistent with the Rand study, but they also found that the work of an investigator during the interviewing and interrogation stage to be important in obtaining information that subsequently led to an arrest. For cases in which no suspect was identified at the crime scene, 37 percent resulted in an arrest after an interrogation by a detective. This finding suggested that investigators played an important role in helping to solve crimes. Several other studies of investigation emerged in the 1980s as well. John Eck (1983) analyzed burglary and robbery investigations from 26 police departments and found that investigators performed an important role in solving these types of crime even when the patrol officer was unable to ascertain the identification of a suspect. Investigators were able to uncover the identification of a suspect in 14 percent of the cases, and an arrest occurred in 8 percent.

Changes in police practices occurred following the publication of the Rand study. Patrol officers were given greater responsibility in conducting investigations when they responded to a crime scene and in many departments were permitted to conduct follow-up investigations (Eck 1983). One Iowa police department eliminated the promotion option to detective and instead rotated patrol officers into the investigation function (Roberg et al. 2005). Departments also started to better screen cases to determine early on which cases were likely to be solved and which were not. This allowed investigators to concentrate on those cases likely to result in an arrest and conviction. Investigation also became more focused with sting operations and crackdowns. These proactive strategies typically result in an increase in arrests and produce short-term reductions in crime. Other technological advances such as the automated fingerprint identification system and DNA testing currently provide investigators with important tools to assist them with their efforts to solve crime (Roberg et al. 2005).

The Rand study of investigation and subsequent research provided valuable information on this police function. Empirical research on investigation contributed to the growing body of knowledge on police functions. While the study dispelled many commonly held assumptions about the role of an investigator, the findings were used to improve police practices in departments across the country.

References

Eck, J. (1983). *Solving Crimes: The Investigation of Burglary and Robbery.* Washington, DC: Police Executive Research Forum.

Gates, D., and L. Knowles (1976). An Evaluation of the Rand Corporation's Analysis of the Criminal Investigation Process. *The Police Chief* 43:20–23; 74–77.

Greenwood, P., and J. Petersilia (1975). *The Criminal Investigation Process.* Santa Monica, CA: Rand.

Roberg, R., K. Novak, and G. Cordner (2005). *Police and Society* (3rd ed.). Los Angeles: Roxbury.

Silver, I. (1968). *The Challenge of Crime in a Free Society: A Report by the President's Commission on Law Enforcement and the Administration of Justice.* New York: Avon.

Travis, L., and R. Langworthy (2007). *Policing in America: A Balance of Forces* (4th ed.). Upper Saddle River: Prentice Hall.

Willman, M., and J. Snortum (1984). "Detective Work: The Criminal Investigation Process in a Medium-size Police Department." *Criminal Justice Review* 9:33–39.

Wycoff, M., and C. Cosgrove (2001). *Investigating in the Community Policing Context, Executive Summary.* Washington, DC: National Institute of Justice.

Further Reading

Bloch, P., and D. Weidman (1975). *Managing Criminal Investigations*. Washington, DC: U.S. Government Printing Office.

Eck, J. (1979). *Managing Case Assignments: The Burglary Investigation Decision Model Replication*. Washington, DC: Police Executive Forum.

Eck, John E. (1996). Rethinking Detective Management or, Why Investigative Reforms are Seldom Permanent or Effective. Larry T. Hoover, ed., *Quantifying Quality in Policing*. Washington, DC: Police Executive Forum.

Lyman, M. (2007). *Criminal Investigation: The Art and the Science* (5th ed.). Upper Saddle River: Prentice Hall.

Petersilia, J. (1987). *The Influence of Criminal Justice Research*. Santa Monica, CA: Rand.

Weisburd, D., and A. Braga, eds. (2006). *Police Innovation: Contrasting Perspectives*. Cambridge, UK: Cambridge UP.

4

The Police Role

Findings from the studies on patrol and investigation raised doubts about the effectiveness of several traditional police practices. This research uncovered the limitations of the police as crime fighters. The police had always been evaluated based on their ability to fight crime. Research not only challenged common police practices, but also questioned the role of the police in our society. If the police are limited in their ability to fight crime then what should the police be doing in our communities? The social turmoil of the 1960s had put a strain on police community relations that also made it difficult for the police to perform their law enforcement duties. By the late 1970s, it became apparent that the role of the police would have to change. Through their efforts to rebuild trust and form partnerships with the community, the police became more focused on crime prevention. Residents were concerned with their safety and the police were eager to respond. Police officers worked closely with neighborhood organizations and civic groups on programs to increase safety, improve the physical appearance of areas, and enhance the overall quality of life for residents. Many police departments began to embrace the idea that communities should have a voice in determining the delivery of police services. By the early 1980s, a new paradigm emerged in police work known as *community policing*. Under this approach, the community provides input on the problems that need to be addressed and they work with the police in developing strategies and programs to alleviate these problems. This requires the police to take on a broader role in the community beyond law enforcement. Issues such as fear, disorder, and physical decay may require more from the police than simply making an arrest. Two important contributions helped generate interest in community policing. The first was *problem-oriented policing* put forth by Herbert Goldstein and the second was Wilson and Kelling's *broken windows policing*.

PROBLEM-ORIENTED POLICING: CAN THE POLICE FIX THE UNDERLYING PROBLEMS RESPONSIBLE FOR CRIME?

Goldstein, H. (1979). "Improving Policing: A Problem-Oriented Approach." *Crime and Delinquency* 24:236–58.

Background

What should the role of the police be in our communities? Herbert Goldstein (1979) provided one answer when he outlined a new police strategy known as *problem-oriented policing*. Goldstein published an article in the 1979 edition of *Crime and Delinquency* titled "Improving Policing: A Problem-Oriented Approach." In the article, Goldstein discussed the "means over ends syndrome" that occurred in policing during the professional era. The emphasis in policing was on improving the organization of the police through better recruitment, training, and supervision. While these changes were necessary improvements, police administrators lost sight of the end results or the goals of police work. According to Goldstein, the police were called upon to respond to a wide variety of problems. Some of these problems were crime related, but many were not. The police were expected to maintain order in our communities and provide assistance when we asked for help. Many of the non-crime-related problems stemmed from the fact that people called the police when they did not know whom else to call. The problems faced by police officers also tended to be repetitive. Communities dealt with the same problems over and over because no one had bothered to address the reasons why the problems existed in the first place. Problem-oriented policing offered the police a method for alleviating many of the issues that plagued our communities: crime, disorder, and fear. The approach focused police attention on a problem with the goal of the police to help solve it (Goldstein recognized that not all problems could be solved, but the police could help to reduce or minimize the problem).

Problem-oriented policing involved a systematic process. One such model commonly used in problem-oriented policing is SARA, which stands for scanning, analysis, response, and assessment (Center for Problem Oriented Policing: http://www.popcenter.org). The first step, *scanning*, is to clearly identify the nature and extent of the problem. This requires soliciting input from the community to help the police understand exactly what the problem is. Once the problem is identified, the next step is to thoroughly *analyze* the problem. The police try to determine how long the problem has existed, what solutions have already been tried, what resources exist to address the problem, and any existing research on the problem. The third step is to develop and implement a *response* or solution to remedy the problem. Responses will be varied, and the police are encouraged to utilize as many resources as possible (including those outside of the criminal justice system). The last step is to conduct an evaluation or *assessment* of the solution to determine its effectiveness. Evaluations should be ongoing and measure both short- and long-term effects. Problem-oriented policing was not put forth as a "one size fits all" model. Different communities may require different responses to the same problem.

Goldstein's problem-oriented policing model developed out of his work with the American Bar Foundation and the Chicago Police Department. His model was not derived from any particular research design; however, Goldstein did conduct an empirical study of his model 2 years later. The first application of problem-oriented policing took place in Madison, Wisconsin, in 1980 where Goldstein was teaching at the University of Wisconsin Law School. He teamed up with sociologist, Charles Susmilch who had experience in *evaluation research* (research designed to measure the effectiveness of a program and policy). Together they worked with the Madison Police Department to implement a problem-oriented approach to improve police services. The project was one of several that were funded by the National Institute of Justice on problem-oriented policing. The first task was to identify a specific problem for the police to address. Goldstein and Susmilch (1982) solicited ideas from police officers whose overwhelming choice was driving under the influence of alcohol. It was decided that this would be an appropriate issue to explore because of its seriousness and the fact that it was a regularly occurring problem. The police indicated that a considerable amount of department resources were spent confronting the problem without much success. Another problem became the focus of their second project: repeat sexual offenders (for a complete description of this project see Goldstein, H., and C. Susmilch (1982) *The Repeat Sexual Offender in Madison: A Memorandum on the Problem and the Community's Response.* Madison, WI: Law School, University of Wisconsin).

Problem-Oriented Policing in Action

Goldstein and Susmilch (1982) worked very closely with the Madison Police Department on all aspects of the project that took 6 months to complete. The project involved a type of *field* research known as a *case study*. Case studies involve extensive observations of a single person or group. In this study, researchers observed how a single police agency would use problem-oriented policing. There were five objectives of the study:

1. To examine a problem as a community concern, not just as a police issue.
2. To consider the actual behavior of those responsible for the problem, not just the behavior that comes to the attention of the police.
3. To look at police responses to underlying problems, not just to crimes.
4. To separate problems into categories if different police responses are needed.
5. To improve police and community effectiveness in responding to the problem.

Consistent with the SARA model discussed above, the first step for researchers was to develop a complete understanding of the drinking driver problem in Madison. To do this, they collected data from three sources: observations, interviews, and existing data. Researchers spent many hours riding along with police officers and observing their interactions with individuals suspected of drinking and driving. The observers gathered information on the investigation and processing of these suspects through the court system. Observations were also made of the interactions between servers and patrons at local bars and restaurants. Researchers further conducted interviews with several individuals both within and outside of the criminal justice system who had contact with drinking drivers. Police officers, prosecutors, judges, defense attorneys, insurance providers, bar owners, servers, victims, and convicted drunk drivers were all interviewed. Finally, researchers gathered information from the National Highway Traffic Safety Administration, the Department of Transportation, police and court records, jail statistics, and data from the local Group Dynamics Program (a court imposed school for drinking drivers). The amount of data collected for the project was extensive and time-consuming, but it helped researchers and the police develop a more thorough understanding of the drinking driver problem.

The most serious consequence resulting from drinking and driving are car accidents resulting in serious injury or death. In their report, Goldstein and Susmilch provided a detailed analysis (step two of the SARA model) of the incidence of drinking and driving and the extent of traffic accidents and fatalities. Fifty-three percent of the total number of traffic fatalities was the result of drinking drivers from 1975 to 1980. Twenty-five percent of all vehicle accidents with serious injuries involved a drunk driver. Researchers also uncovered that most accidents involving drunk drivers occurred between the 12:00 A.M. and 3:00 A.M. and a majority of accidents took place on a weekend. The arrest data revealed that most drinking driver suspects deemed at fault in accidents were young males who lived in or near Madison. A significant number of suspects were arrested on their way home after leaving a bar or restaurant. Some consistent findings for blood alcohol content (BAC) were found as well. In fatal accidents, the BAC was .15 and above. For accidents with serious injuries the BAC for most drivers was less than .13 (in Wisconsin a BAC of .10 or higher is considered legally impaired). One of the most significant findings was that almost one-third of the impaired drivers involved in a serious injury accident had numerous prior traffic violations and license suspensions. All of this information prove useful in the development of a better police response.

Problem-oriented policing involves the police working with the community to find out the underlying causes of recurring problems. Goldstein and Susmilch extended their research beyond exploring the incidence of drinking and driving and resulting car accidents to the impact this crime had on the community. They interviewed family members of those who had been killed in drunken driving accidents and even spoke with a minister who assisted the police in notifying family members of accident victims. Researchers also had the opportunity to listen to accident survivors testify before the state legislature. Fatal car accidents leave behind grieving family and friends. Survivors may be left with limited mobility and the inability to return to work. Many survivors were left with financial burdens from the lack of income and medical expenses. Some of these individuals expressed resentment toward for the criminal justice for not doing enough to stop repeat drinking drivers and for not keeping the victims or families informed when suspects were arrested and prosecuted. One additional piece of information uncovered by researchers during the course of these interviews was the fact that individuals who had been exposed to the problem of drinking and driving altered their behavior out of fear that they might fall victim to this crime. They stayed off of the streets during certain hours and avoided areas where they knew accidents had occurred.

A thorough analysis of the drinking driver problem required researchers to take into consideration the offenders. In addition to criminal justice sanctions, many faced financial hardships from loss of work and higher insurance premiums. Regardless of the argument that offenders deserved these hardships, it was important to include them in the analysis. Problem-oriented policing is about identifying *all* of the underlying dimensions of a problem in order to implement the most appropriate solution. The final consideration taken into account for the analysis was the examination of past and current strategies used to combat the problem. The traditional response to the drinking driver problem had been to use the criminal justice system as a deterrent. Increasing the certainty of punishment with increased police patrols and harsh sentences were intended to deter the offender from committing the crime again and others who might be contemplating such a crime. In 1978, Wisconsin implemented a new law that provided drinking driver offenders the option of completing a treatment program (or the Group Dynamics program) in place of an automatic suspension and a portion of their fine. In addition, the law included what was known as an "implied consent" provision. If a police officer had probable cause that a driver had been drinking, the officer had the authority to request a breath test. If the suspect refused, he or she faced automatic suspension of their driving privileges. The new law was nationally recognized as an innovative approach to deal with the driving driver problem, however, received considerable public criticism for being soft on offenders. The law was amended in 1981 with the provision for reduced penalties removed.

In 1979, 1,203 people were arrested for operating a motor vehicle while impaired. The number of offenders grew significantly during the 1970s. The increase was attributed to the new legislation and the police becoming more proactive in stopping suspected drinking drivers. The arrest rate started to decline in 1979. Researchers discovered that there was wide variation in the use of proactive arrests among police officers. An informal department norm was also uncovered. Despite the legal limit of .10, officers were reluctant to arrest for anything below .13. The officers rationalized this practice on the grounds that there was a margin of error with the tests and that prosecutors were only *required* to charge offenders with a level of .13 or higher. Interviews with officers also revealed that a typical arrest led to one to two hours of processing time. Some officers indicated that the processing time discouraged them from arresting drinking drivers (a handful of officers actually viewed it as a way to earn overtime and get out of other duties). An enormous amount of information was collected on the processing of drinking driver suspects. The key summary points are listed below:

1. A majority of suspects spent some time in jail prior to arraignment.
2. Charging first time offenders in nonaccident cases followed a fairly routine pattern, but charging became more complex with repeat offenders and in accident cases.
3. Most suspects were convicted (usually through plea bargaining).
4. Sentencing was fairly predictive (because of legislatively determined limits).
5. Many offenders failed to comply with court-imposed sanctions (refused to pay their fine or complete treatment).
6. Jail space was typically reserved for offenders with prior convictions, those who willfully disobeyed their court orders and/or those who caused a serious injury or death.
7. License revocation was standard for repeat offenders, but offenders could apply for a restricted license if needed for employment.
8. The Group Dynamics Program was not being fully utilized.

According to Goldstein and Susmilch, an analysis of the data presented above might have left one with the impression that the solution to the problem would have been to simply arrest more suspects, put more offenders in jail and restrict more licenses. This type of thinking was consistent with the traditional "means over end" policing. Problem-oriented policing is about achieving a result—one that will have a lasting impact on reducing the number of drinking drivers and car accidents. Goldstein and Susmilch reviewed numerous studies evaluating the effectiveness of criminal justice sanctions as well as education and treatment and found no reliable evidence that any of these strategies were successful. There were limits to what the criminal justice system could accomplish because of too few police officers compared to the number of drinking drivers, the use of discretion by the police in handling drinking driver suspects, the court systems' inability to efficiently process large numbers of cases, and the limited amount of space to house offenders within the correctional system.

Goldstein and Susmilch collected a considerable amount of information to better understand the problem of drinking drivers in Madison. After a thorough examination of the data collected from *field observations, interviews,* and *existing data* they proposed five programs to help alleviate the problem. In their report to the Madison Police Department, each program was described in detail with clearly established objectives, rationales, and procedures for implementation. The five proposals are briefly described below.

Proposal one: significantly increase the number of police contacts with suspected drinking drivers. Given the variation among officers in the use of proactive police stops; the department needed to *officially* endorse the use of proactive stops. Furthermore, the department should provide officers with more options than arrest or letting the suspect go. In their analysis, Goldstein and Susmilch discovered that suspects with a BAC between .10 and .13 were frequently let go by the police. Alternatives might have included allowing a passenger in the car to drive or calling a cab to take the driver home. These nonarrest alternatives were important because they immediately removed a dangerous driver from the street and thereby protected the community. The advantage for the police would be time saved on case processing. Increasing proactive stops may also have a deterrent value. Police were encouraged to "educate" each suspect on the dangers of drinking and driving. Increased contacts would also help in the identification of repeat offenders. To help make sure the increased contacts would not infringe upon due process, researchers also provided the department with a guide of visual cues to assist officers in their determination of probable cause to justify a stop.

Proposal two: enhance police capabilities to determine whether alcohol is a cause of car accidents. Departments needed to develop guidelines and detailed procedures for investigating accidents when alcohol was believed to be a factor. Once developed, the procedures should be consistently followed in all accident cases. Departments were encouraged to work with prosecutors so that officers had a clearer understanding of the evidence used in charging decisions. Regular communication with emergency room personnel should occur so that they would be informed of the evidence required in drinking driver cases. Finally, the researchers recommended the police work on the development of proposed legislation that would *require* a BAC test on drivers involved in any vehicle accident.

Proposal three: create a program to target repeat drinking drivers. Such a program would require screening procedures for identifying the repeat offenders. Once identified, there should be some type of continuous monitoring by police. Regular communication with prosecutors should take place to ensure that the prior record of these offenders was known at all stages in the court process. Efforts to increase the speed of case processing for these offenders would also remove them from the streets before they caused a serious accident. Prosecutors were encouraged to use the habitual offender statute in charging these offenders because under the statute offenders faced an added penalty. The department was encouraged to consider using involuntary commitment proceedings for offenders with serious alcohol addictions. Police were also encouraged to work with legislators in instigating a law that would require a minimum term of probation in addition to jail time for repeat offenders. The use of probation would provide additional supervision for repeat offenders.

Proposal four: increase more control over the individuals who serve alcohol to drinking drivers. In their analysis, Goldstein and Susmilch discovered that 66 percent of drinking drivers had their last drink in a bar or restaurant. The Madison Police Department should expand the existing "bartenders' school." This would require staffing the program with a full-time officer who would conduct classes on a regular basis for bar owners and workers. The classes were informational and included lessons on the problem of drinking drivers, legal responsibilities and consequences. Police needed to identify establishments that continually served intoxicated individuals and conduct regular investigations to look for legal violations that could result in a loss of license (i.e., extending happy hours, serving to minors).

Proposal five: strengthen and expand community education programs. Goldstein and Susmilch acknowledged the limitations and failures of previous education programs designed to reduce the occurrence of drinking and driving. The goal of such programs tended to be narrowly defined so as to focus only on the behavior. The focus should be on changing community norms and attitudes about drinking while under the influence. The police department should take the lead on these efforts because they were already the agency the community turned to for help with this problem. The police, however, should not assume sole responsibility. Police needed to work to mobilize community groups and enlist their help in educating the public on the problem of drinking and driving.

The proposals set forth by Goldstein and Susmilch were based upon an extensive analysis of information collected from a variety of sources. Data were obtained from police officers, department records, citizens, and other community groups with a vested interest in the problem of drinking and driving. A draft copy of the final report was submitted to the police department and discussed at an all day meeting. Overall the feedback from officers and supervisors was positive. The report was perceived as comprehensive and accurate, however, reactions from some of the officers left researchers wondering if the drinking driver problem was as high of a priority as they were led to believe in the beginning. It became apparent that some officers were more interested in the results than others. Despite efforts to involve the department as much as possible in the project, many officers referred to the report as an "outside study." The officers with extensive prior experience working with drinking drivers were the most interested. The Madison police chief endorsed the report and articulated support for the proposals outlined by Goldstein and Susmilch, but did not want to begin implementation on any of the suggestions. Instead he appointed a task force to examine the report and make recommendations to the command staff on which proposals (if any) should be pursued.

Lessons Learned

The goal of the project was not to evaluate the effectiveness of the proposed responses to the drinking driver problem, but rather to examine the feasibility of incorporating a problem-oriented model into police work. The case study carried out by Goldstein and Susmilch explored how police departments could use problem-oriented policing to take action against one of the most commonly experienced problems faced by officers: the problem of drinking drivers. In their final report, Goldstein and Susmilch described their experiences working with the Madison Police Department and they discussed some important lessons learned from the project.

Problem-oriented policing was a change in the way police traditionally responded to crime. Instead of a reactive approach where the police responded to the same crimes over and over again, police were encouraged to think about crimes as problems with underlying causes. The police would become proactive by identifying what the underlying causes were. When researchers met with members of the Madison Police Department there was clear consensus on what problem should be addressed. Drinking and driving had been a long-standing problem for the department, and the department was having little success with their efforts. It was also an important issue for the community who expected the police to take an active stance in the fight to reduce the occurrence of drunk driving accidents. Researchers ran into some problems early on in the project. Researchers collected a massive amount of information to develop a thorough understanding of the nature and extent of drinking and driving, but discovered that some critical data did not exist or was unusable. Researchers also had a difficult time recognizing the traditional department response to the problem because individual officers had their own informal procedures for enforcement. Some of the data appeared to contradict data from other sources, but once all of the data were collected most of the discrepancies were resolved. Establishing *validity* with findings from a case study is difficult because of limited *generalizability*. The study involved a single police department. Goldstein and Susmilch presented their results to those who had contributed to the project and the results were not challenged. Although they recognized that this was not a substitute for a formal measurement of validity, they expressed confidence in their findings.

Most of the objectives Goldstein and Susmilch set out to accomplish with their study were achieved. Approaching the problem of drinking drivers as a community issue, not just a police matter, allowed researchers the ability to more fully understand the problem. Information gathering extended beyond police records and interviews with officers to health officials, bar and restaurant servers, insurance agents, prosecutors, judges, treatment providers, and even vehicle crash survivors and family members of accident victims. Efforts to focus on the actual behavior (not just the criminal behavior) of those who drink and drive gave researchers a more accurate assessment of the problem. In addition, it helped the police realize that the burden of responding to the problem was not solely on their shoulders. The police expressed a sense of relief in response to this recognition. Police departments tended to rely on official counts of crime; however, with this particular offense arrest rates grossly underestimated the true extent of drinking and driving. Most people who engaged in this behavior were never caught, yet their behavior posed a huge threat to public safety. Researchers utilized data collected by the National Highway Traffic Safety Administration to estimate the number of people who drive under the influence of alcohol. Instead of approaching the issue of drinking drivers as an incident requiring a particular police response, researchers focused on the broader problem of drunk drivers—the car accidents caused by this behavior. This allowed researchers to develop a more thorough understanding of the issue.

Once researchers began their analysis, the magnitude of the problem became apparent. Researchers became aware that there was more than one problem to be addressed. First, there was the issue of catching drunk drivers who had not yet been involved in an accident and second, the issue of accidents caused by drunk drivers. Dividing up the problem into two separate problems allowed researchers to develop specific strategies for each one. Goldstein and Susmilch had difficulty achieving their last objective: to improve police and community effectiveness in responding to the problem. Their proposals were each based upon a solid framework of data collected over a 6-month period. Careful attention was paid to make sure the proposals were feasible. Despite this, they were not able to persuade the Madison Police Department to implement their recommendations. The department was more interested in proposals that had already been implemented and evaluated somewhere else. Administrators expressed concerns over how the proposed changes would disrupt current police protocols. The department's unwillingness to experiment with new ideas demonstrated the inherent difficultly of trying to implement change within a bureaucracy. Police departments had been following established procedures and routines for decades. Anything introduced as "new" was likely to be met with skepticism.

Criticisms

Goldstein and Susmilch acknowledged that the development of a problem-oriented approach to police work in Madison involved extensive assistance from them and their research team. The ability of a police department to undertake such an approach on their own was not part of their case study, but most of the criticisms centered on this concern. The systematic procedures were often ignored by police agencies and very few were equipped to implement such an endeavor. The ability of a department to thoroughly analyze problems and develop innovative responses was limited. Police officers typically looked for expedient solutions to problems that had not been correctly identified (Clarke 1998, Scott 2000). In a recent study of problem-oriented policing practiced in San Diego, Gary Cordner and Elizabeth Biebel (2005) found that officers engaged in activities that were considered problem solving, however, they did not follow any systematic process advocated by Goldstein's theory. This was surprising given that San Diego had been engaged in problem-oriented policing for more than 15 years. In fact, all police supervisors in this department were required to complete a 16-hour training program on problem-oriented policing (Roberg et al. 2005). There was also the tendency to skip the evaluation process. According to Anthony Braga and Davis Weisburd (2006), "There is substantial evidence that, too often, the principles envisioned by Herman Goldstein are not being practiced in the field" (p. 133). Proponents of problem-oriented policing took issue with this criticism. John Eck believed that problems with implementation were not good reasons to abandon the model. In other words, "problem-solving 'light' is better than no problem solving at all" (Eck 2006, p. 128).

Goldstein advocated a shift away from traditional reactive police work to more proactive strategies. The police would become more focused in their efforts to prevent crime rather than simply respond to it. Crime prevention is an appealing concept but it can be a challenge in a democratic society (Vaughn 1992). Many proactive police tactics result in a more intrusive police presence in the community. There is also the potential for abuse when giving police officers even greater discretion in responding to community problems (Vaughn 1992). Extralegal factors might influence decisions of who is arrested and who is dealt with informally. It should be pointed out; however, that Goldstein and Susmilch recognized this potential problem when working with the Madison Police Department and took steps to minimize it.

Critics also took issue with the fact that Goldstein did not provide a clear operational definition of what problem-oriented policing was (Vaughn 1992). According to Goldstein (1979), the concept was difficult to define because it applied differently depending on the community and the specific problem. This presented a challenge for researchers interested in empirically testing the core ideas of Goldstein's model. Goldstein himself elaborated on his model in his 1990 book *Problem-Oriented Policing*. While there have been numerous case studies describing problem-oriented policing in practice, there are few empirical tests of its effectiveness as a police intervention (Cordner and Biebel 2005).

Significance and Subsequent Research

Introduced in 1979, problem-oriented policing represented a radical change in the way police function in our society. The model was proposed as a way to improve the delivery of police services by expanding the role of police officers to take on problems that continually plague our communities. Police become problem solvers by responding to the underlying causes and not just the symptoms of crime and disorder. After Goldstein's studies of problem-oriented policing in 1981, two police agencies formally introduced his model into their departments. Baltimore County had recently established its Citizen-Oriented Police Enforcement Unit (COPE) to respond to growing public fear of crime. The Unit operated without much direction and success until the chief of police brought Goldstein in to train supervisors on the use of his problem-oriented policing model. Goldstein helped the unit better understand community sources of fear and develop programs to target the sources. For example, officers discovered that among the most fearful residents were elderly people who worried about their physical safety after dark. Police helped residents organize neighborhood associations, enlisted the help of the electric and gas company to replace broken streetlights, and worked with other agencies to improve the physical appearance of the area. As a result of the police initiatives, citizens reported less fear (Cordner 1986).

One year later, problem-oriented policing was implemented on an agency wide level in Newport News, Virginia. One of the more reoccurring problems faced by this department was theft from vehicles around the shipyards. Careful analysis of the problem revealed that a few repeat offenders were responsible for many of the thefts. Efforts to target these repeat offenders resulted in a 55 percent decrease in this particular crime (Eck and Spelman 1987). By the early 1990s, several police departments around the country had implemented at least some aspect of problem-oriented policing into police work. The model has been applied to a wide variety of problems including youth violence, domestic violence, drugs, prostitution, robbery, and disorderly conduct. Evaluations of these efforts demonstrate their effectiveness (Braga and Weisburd 2006). In addition, there are other benefits that can result when departments adopt a problem-oriented approach to their police response. Goldstein and Susmilch (1982) found that officers in Madison uncovered some deficiencies in their routine procedures when analyzing the problems of drinking drivers and repeat sex offenders. The analytical process was also useful for the court and correctional officials who participated in the study.

Since Goldstein first introduced the concept in 1979, problem-oriented policing has evolved into an elaborate framework for police operations and administration. *Routine Activities Theory* has been incorporated into the model to provide a theoretical foundation for thinking about problems (Eck 2006). According to the theory, crime occurs when there is a motivated offender, a suitable target, and the absence of capable guardians (Cohen and Felson 1979). The theory became basis for the "problem-analysis triangle," which is an analytical tool used by the police in their problem solving.

Police departments today have access to a wealth of technical information in the form of manuals, research reports, problem-oriented policing agencies, and training institutes to assist them in their problem-solving endeavors. Problem-oriented policing was

FIGURE 1.4 The Problem-Analysis Triangle

Source: Office of Community Oriented Policing Services

introduced during the time when police departments were becoming more community oriented. The two concepts are sometimes mistaken for each other. Community policing involves collaboration between the police and community in efforts to respond to crime, help prevent crime, and make people feel safe. These efforts can certainly be incorporated into a problem-oriented approach, but this is not always going to be the case. With problem-oriented policing, the specific problem determines whether or not the police work with the community in its response. Problem-oriented policing is one method that can be used under a community-policing model. Community policing became the dominant reform movement of the 1990s and continues to be an integral part of police work.

References

Braga, A., and D. Weisburd (2006). "Problem-Oriented Policing: The Disconnect Between Principles and Practice." In *Police Innovation: Contrasting Perspectives*, edited by D. Weisburd and A. Braga, 133–52 Cambridge, UK: Cambridge UP.

Center for Problem Oriented Policing: http://www.popcenter.org.

Clark, R. (1998). "Defining Police Strategies: Problem Solving, Problem-Oriented Policing and Community-Oriented Policing." In *Problem-Oriented Policing: Crime-Specific Problems, Critical Issues, and Making POP Work*, edited by T. O'Connor Shelley and A. Grant 315–30 Washington, DC: Police Executive Research Forum.

Cohen, L., and Felson, M. (1979). "Social Change and Crime Rate Trends: A Routine Activity Approach." *American Sociological Review* 44:588–608.

Cordner, G., and E. Biebel (2005). "Problem-Oriented Policing in Practice." *Criminology and Public Policy* 4:155–80.

Cordner, G. (1986). "Fear of Crime and the Police: An Evaluation of a Fear-Reduction Strategy." *Journal of Police Science and Administration* 14:223–33.

Eck, J. (2006). "Science, Values, and Problem-Oriented Policing: Why Problem-Oriented Policing?" In *Police Innovation: Contrasting Perspectives*, edited by D. Weisburd and A. Braga, 117–32 Cambridge: Cambridge UP.

Eck, J., and W. Spelman (1987). *Problem-Solving: Problem-Oriented Policing in Newport News*. Washington, DC: Police Executive Research Forum.

Goldstein, H. (1979). "Improving Policing: A Problem-Oriented Approach." *Crime and Delinquency* 24:236–58.

Goldstein, H., and C. Susmilch (1982). *The Drinking-Driver in Madison: A Study of the Problem and the Community's Response*. Madison, WI: University of Wisconsin Law School.

Roberg, R., K. Novak, and G. Cordner (2005). *Police and Society* (3rd ed.). Los Angeles: Roxbury.

Scott, M. (2000). *Problem-Oriented Policing: Reflections on the First 20 Years*. Washington, DC: U.S. Department of Justice, Office of Community Oriented Policing Services.

Vaughn, M. (1992). "Problem-Oriented Policing: A Philosophy of Policing for the 21st Century." *Criminal Justice and Behavior* 19:343–54.

Further Reading

Braga, A., D. Kennedy, E. Waring, and A. Piehl (2001). "Problem-Oriented Policing, Deterrence, and Youth Violence: An Evaluation of Boston's Operation Ceasefire." *Journal of Research in Crime and Delinquency* 38:195–225.

Buerger, M. (1994). "The Problems of Problem Solving: Resistance, Interdependencies, and Conflicting Interests." *American Journal of Police* 13:1–36.

Eck, J. and W. Spellman (1987). "Who Ya Gonna Call? The Police as Problem-Busters." *Crime and Delinquency* 33:31–52.

Goldstein, H. (1990). *Problem Oriented Policing*. Philadelphia, PA: Temple UP.

Goldstein, H., and C. Susmilch (1982). *The Repeat Sexual Offender in Madison: A memorandum on the Problem and the Community's Response.* Madison, WI: Law School, University of Wisconsin.

Goldstein, H., and C. Susmilch (1982). *Experimenting with the Problem-Oriented Approach to Improve Police Service: A Report and Some Reflections on Two Case Studies.* Madison, WI: Law School, University of Wisconsin.

Office of Community Oriented Policing Services (1998). *Problem-Solving Tips: A Guide to Reducing Crime and Disorder Through Problem-Solving Partnerships.* Washington, DC: US Department of Justice, Office of Community Oriented Police Services.

Webster, B., and E. Connors (1993) "Police Methods for Identifying Community Problems." *American Journal of Police* 12:75–102.

BROKEN WINDOWS: DOES URBAN BLIGHT LEAD TO CRIME?

Wilson, J., and G. Kelling (1982). "Broken Windows: The Police and Neighborhood Safety." *Atlantic Monthly* March:29–38.

Background

James Q. Wilson is one of the leading policy analysts of our time. His 1968 book *Varieties of Police Behavior* (previously discussed) outlined the three major police functions: law enforcement, order maintenance, and service. These functions help us to understand the different "styles" or types of police we experience in our communities. George Kelling was a member of the research team from the Police Foundation that evaluated foot patrol in Newark, New Jersey. Kelling spent a considerable amount of time observing the foot patrol officers at work and gained valuable insight into the order maintenance function of the police. The finding that foot patrol had no effect on crime rates came as little surprise to researchers or police administrators. Foot patrol was perceived as more of a public relations tactic than a strategy to reduce crime. It was surprising, however, that foot patrol made residents feel safer and more satisfied with the quality of police services. How could people feel safe and content when crime did not decrease? Together, Wilson and Kelling (1982) would provide an explanation that would become one of the most widely influential (and controversial) ideas in criminal justice.

"Broken Windows" Theory

In 1982 an article appeared in the March issue of the *Atlantic Monthly* titled "Broken Windows: The Police and Neighborhood Safety." The authors, James Q. Wilson and George L. Kelling, outlined a theory to explain why some communities were more crime prone than others. Known as the "broken windows" theory, the basic premise was quite simple: neighborhood deterioration and disorder led to crime. Image an abandoned building on your street with a single broken window. If the window is not repaired, it is assumed that no one cares about the building. If no one cares, it is just a matter of time before all of the windows are broken. The physical appearance of the area surrounding the property will start to deteriorate as well. Criminals seek out these areas because they assume their crimes will go undetected–just like the broken window. Broken windows theory did not develop out of one distinct empirical study, but rather was based on the professional experiences and data collected through the prior research of its authors. The theoretical propositions of broken windows are discussed below.

Fear and crime. Criminologists have been aware that crime and fear of crime are two distinct experiences since the first victimization surveys were conducted in the 1970s. Fear of crime has little to do with the actual crime rate as evidenced by recent crime trends. When violent crime decreased in the 1990s, reported levels of fear increased. The increase in fear was believed to be a consequence of the extensive media coverage of crime. Newspapers and televised news programs bombard us everyday with stories of horrific acts of violence and vicious criminals that threaten our safety. While the threat of violence is very real in some communities, it is not the only source of fear. According to Wilson and Kelling, people also feared "disorderly" people. People who were perceived as unpredictable and unruly (i.e., panhandlers, prostitutes, drunks, drug addicts, and noisy teenagers) maintained a strong presence in some neighborhoods that made residents feel insecure and anxious—not necessarily because of something they had done, but because of what they *might* do. It was precisely this disorderly population that foot patrol officers were in a position to manage. Kelling himself observed this during his interactions with foot patrol officers in Newark (Police Foundation 1981). The officers had become acquainted with the community and knew the regular troublemakers. Officers were also attentive to community norms and tolerance levels. For example, residents put up with drunks as long as they did not lie on the front steps and kept their alcohol in paper bags. Panhandlers were tolerated, but not permitted to approach people waiting at bus stops. Foot patrol officers enforced these "rules" either formally by arresting these disorderly people, or more often informally through orders to move along or be quiet. Foot patrol officers were successful in maintaining order within the community, which in turn made people feel safe and satisfied with the police.

Disorder and crime. Wilson and Kelling further contended that at the neighborhood level, there was a relationship between disorder and crime. If an area became run down and deteriorated, crime soon followed (broken windows metaphor). Criminals viewed these areas as desirable targets because no one paid attention to them. Crimes went undetected, and therefore, unreported to the police. In support of this argument, Wilson and Kelling cited an experiment conducted by Philip Zimbardo in 1969. He placed a car with no license plate on the street with its hood raised in the Bronx and a second car in Palo Alto, California. Within 10 minutes, people started removing parts from the car in the Bronx. Once the parts were all taken, vandals started smashing the car. The car in Palo Alto remained untouched for more than a week so Zimbardo smashed it himself with a sledgehammer. Soon after, others joined in and a few hours later the car was completely destroyed. Differences in community standards helped explain why it took longer for vandals to target the car in Palo Alto. Abandoned cars were nothing new in the Bronx and vandalism a common occurrence. A deserted vehicle was less typical in Palo Alto and vandalism was rare, but it only took one person to instigate the vandalism before others joined in. It became acceptable to smash the car, because someone else had already done it and no one seemed to care.

The car experiment illustrated the importance of community norms as a source of informal social control and what could happen when that control broke down. A disorderly population coupled with the physical deterioration of a neighborhood could progressively become more dangerous if these problems were not addressed. Law abiding residents either moved or altered their behaviors out of fear and their presence soon dissipated. Criminals noticed not only the physical appearance of an area, but also the lack of law-abiding residents who were likely to call the police. Unable to defend itself, the neighborhood became susceptible to crime.

Role of the Police

The shift away from foot patrol to motor patrol corresponded with the change in police work away from order maintenance to law enforcement. The motor vehicle became a tool to assist the police in their crime fighting efforts, but it also reduced the face-to-face interactions between the police and the public. Not only did police community relations suffer as a consequence, but the ability of the police to maintain order in the community was compromised as well. Without the informal interactions, the police lost sight of what was important to residents—their perception of safety. Motor vehicle police were less accessible to residents, and it was more difficult for the motor police to keep track of disorderly people. When a person approached a foot patrol officer with a complaint the police response tended to be immediate. For example, if I complain about the noisy teenagers in front of my house, an officer is likely to send them away. If I call the police to report that my house was burglarized, it may take hours before an officer arrives and it is unlikely my property will be returned. This insight into the role of the police in our community provided an explanation for the findings of the Newark Foot Patrol Experiment. Residents felt safer and more satisfied with the police *because* the police were maintaining order. According to Wilson and Kelling this had important implications for the informal social control of the community. The presence of the police was not a substitute for informal social control, but the police reinforced community standards and norms that were the basis of that control. Wilson and Kelling wrote: "Above all, we must return to our long-abandoned view that the police ought to protect communities as well as individuals" (p. 38).

Fixing Broken Windows

In their original article, Wilson and Kelling suggested that for the police to be effective in their efforts to reduce crime, they must first address community disorder. Concentrating on disorderly populations and minor offenses could have long-term positive benefits for crime control. Fourteen years later, Kelling and Catherine Coles (1996) offered more detailed strategies in the book *Fixing Broken Windows: Restoring Order and Reducing Crime in Our Communities.* Their plan of action was more about crime prevention than crime control. If the police remained diligent in their order maintenance function, not only would minor offenses decrease, serious crime would be prevented. Criminals would be deterred from committing crimes in neighborhoods where there was a visible police presence and the police were united with law-abiding residents who demonstrated an interest in keeping the community safe. Many of the strategies had already been put into practice by Kelling when he was hired as a consultant for the New York Transit Authority. Kelling and Transit Authority Police Chief William Bratton launched a major anti-graffiti campaign to clean up the subways and they put into practice a program to target vandalism and panhandling. The goal was to restore order to the subway system. Not only was this goal accomplished, felony crime was significantly reduced.

Criticisms

The logic underlying the broken windows theory was straightforward. Physical decay and disorderly people shaped perceptions of neighborhood safety and ultimately led to crime. Wilson and Kelling identified some potential drawbacks to their theory that others have turned into criticisms. Allowing a community to determine how order is maintained may not be the same as what the law indicates. Wilson and Kelling raised the concern that community participation in the order maintenance function could turn into vigilantism. Critics took issue with the focus on disorderly people that are typically poor. Efforts to reduce the presence of the disorderly would unfairly target those individuals who were least able to defend themselves. Bernard Harcourt (2001) outlined several criticisms of the broken windows theory in his book *The Illusion of Order: The False Promise of Broken Windows Policing.* The police are afforded tremendous discretion in situations involving their order maintenance function, and a concern was that extralegal factors such as economic status or even race and ethnicity might influence police practice. Harcourt argued that many efforts designed to maintain order resulted in aggressive police practices that infringed upon the constitutional rights of citizens. Redirecting patrol tactics to order maintenance might be more harmful to police community relations. Harcourt found an increase in citizen complaints of police misconduct when the police concentrated on public order and misdemeanor crimes. His research also showed that the targets of police crackdowns on misdemeanor crimes tended to be minorities. Gary Stewart (1989) also voiced concerns that broken windows would have negative consequences for minorities. Minority groups were already overrepresented in the criminal justice system and affording the police greater authority to combat neighborhood disorder could lead to even more minorities acquiring a criminal label.

Broken windows policing has been equated with "zero tolerance policing." Zero-tolerance policing involves the police aggressively enforcing minor crimes to achieve a deterrent effect for more serious offenses. According to Kelling, this was a misrepresentation of broken windows theory. Communities might desire a zero-tolerance approach to order maintenance, but it was not the only approach that could be taken (Sousa and Kelling 2006). Under a broken windows model, residents would have a voice in deciding which minor crimes would be enforced and if the enforcement was formal or informal. Samuel Walker (1984) took issue with many of the assumptions underlying broken windows theory. He challenged the notion that returning to the watchman style of policing would be good for many communities. There were justifiable reasons why this type of policing was abandoned in the early 1900s. Corruption, inefficiency, and a lack of political legitimacy led to the reforms that Wilson and Kelling proposed we get rid of. It was questionable whether or not the police could effectively maintain order in neighborhoods where there were conflicting norms and standards of behavior. Nineteenth-century police officers were no more in tune with the needs of their communities than they are today.

Much of the criticism directed at Wilson and Kelling focused on the lack of empirical support for their key theoretical concepts. The theory developed out of their previous research on police functions (Wilson) and the allocation of foot patrol officers in the community (Kelling). The alleged causal relationship between disorder and crime remained in dispute. While Kelling and Cole (1996) offered support for the theory with evidence from the Newark Foot Patrol Experiment as well as the New York Transit Authority study, other scholars have failed to establish anything more than a *correlation* between disorder and crime. In a large-scale study of urban decay in communities in Chicago, Robert Sampson and Stephen Raudenbush (1999) failed to find support that disorder leads to crime. Neighborhoods with high crime rates tended to have significant signs of disorder (visible garbage, vandalism, abandoned cars, etc.), but disorder was not the *cause* of crime—both disorder and crime resulted from high concentrations of poverty and low levels of collective efficacy. Disorder and crime flourished in communities where there was a breakdown in informal social control. A lack of trust and cohesion among neighbors made it difficult for residents to intervene in situations that would prevent disorder and crime. Efforts to reduce disorder and crime needed to also address the lack of informal social control mechanisms within the community. Research by Yili Xu, Mora Fielder, and Karl Flaming (2005) questioned the assertion that collective efficacy was responsible for both disorder and crime. Their data from Colorado Springs revealed that neighborhood deterioration contributed to more serious types of crime regardless of collective efficacy. Establishing *causation* in social science research is a difficult but necessary task when theories such as broken windows become the basis for police practice and policy making. Programs that target only the *correlates* of crime rarely succeed. David Thacher (2004), however, asserted that the police should pursue some order maintenance functions even if more serious crimes were not prevented. Taking action against vandalism and graffiti could help improve the quality of life for neighborhood residents and might lead to increased property values.

Bratton and Kelling (2006) argued that efforts to discredit broken windows theory were politically motivated. Many of the proponents of broken windows were conservative while most of the attacks came from liberals. A lot of liberal criminologists held firm to their beliefs that poverty, disadvantage, and discrimination were the root causes of crime and the only way to combat crime was through broad social policies designed to remedy these problems. At the community level, broken windows theory provided the police with strategies and tactics that had the potential to reduce crime, but fell short of addressing larger social problems.

Significance and Subsequent Research

Wilson and Kelling's article generated considerable interest for the idea that neighborhood disorder and decay were related to crime. Much of the subsequent empirical research has focused on determining the exact causal ordering of these concepts. In 1990, Wesley Skogan tested the broken windows theory and published the results in *Disorder and Decline: Crime and the Spiral Decay in American Neighborhoods*. Skogan's (1990) study included surveys and field research from 40 neighborhoods located within six American cities (Atlanta, Chicago, Houston, Newark, Philadelphia, and San Francisco). He discovered that residents tended to agree on the sources of disorder and perceptions of safety were shaped by similar circumstances. Even in heterogeneous communities there appeared to be consensus over the definitions of disorder. Skogan found that communities described as "disorderly" lacked the essential elements of informal society control necessary to respond to crime. Neighbors were less likely to offer assistance and help supervise unattended homes. Levels of fear were also higher in disorderly communities and fear altered the behaviors of many residents. The fearful stayed inside after dark and did not like being outside alone. Residents' fear was justified. According to Skogan, disorderly neighborhoods did have more crime. Addressing the disorder or repairing the broken windows was an important step to help residents reclaim their communities.

Broken windows theory has had a major impact on policing in the United States. According to the circulation department at the *Atlantic Monthly, Broken Windows* was their most reproduced article (Sousa and Kelling 2006). Several large cities including New York, Boston, Chicago, Baltimore, Los Angeles, and San Francisco adopted aggressive police crackdowns on disorderly conduct and misdemeanor offenses. The most public display of broken windows in action took place in New York City when Rudolph Guiliani became mayor in 1994. Guiliani, along with his new police chief, William Bratton, introduced a comprehensive broken windows program in the city. Police officers were instructed to maintain a zero-tolerance policy regarding the enforcement of misdemeanor crimes. When serious crime started to decline, broken windows received the credit, and New York became a model for the rest of the country (Center on Juvenile and Criminal Justice 2002). New York City experienced a 60 percent decline in violent crime and a 50 percent reduction in property crime between 1990 and 1998. According to Kelling and Sousa (2001), broken windows policing was a factor in the decrease. Their study also found that while the number of citizen complaints increased for a short period in the mid-1990s, complaints decreased from 1995 to 1999.

Not everyone was convinced that the significant decline in crime in New York City could be attributed to police practices derived from broken windows theory. Ben Bowling (1999) analyzed murder rates in New York City and found that the rates spiked between 1990 and 1991 when crack cocaine use was at an all time high. Beginning in the 1992, the city witnessed a decrease in the crack cocaine market, and murder rates subsequently dropped. It is important to consider the fact that significant reductions in crime occurred throughout the United States during the 1990s. San Francisco's violent crime rate dropped even more than New York City *without* the police cracking down on neighborhood disorder (Center on Juvenile and Criminal Justice 2002).

Broken windows and problem-oriented policing helped the community policing movement gain momentum in the early 1980s. Police departments all across the country looked for ways to improve the public's image of the police and increase citizen cooperation and involvement in efforts to keep communities safe. Broken windows and problem-oriented policing provided such tools. Police officers today work closely with residents to learn what the sources of disorder are and how much they are willing to tolerate. Under a problem-oriented policing model, police can work with the community to address the underlying causes of crime and disorder. Both perspectives also helped to redefine the role of police in our communities. The police now assume a role in building and maintaining valuable informal social control networks that help foster a sense of safety among residents.

References

Bowling, B. (1999). "The Rise and Fall of New York Murder: Zero Tolerance or Crack's Decline?" *British Journal of Criminology* 39:531–54.

Bratton, W., and G. Kelling (2006). "There Are No Cracks in Broken Windows: Ideological Academics Are Trying to Undermine a Perfectly Good Idea." *National Review Online.* February.

Center on Juvenile and Criminal Justice (2002). *Shattering 'Broken Windows': An Analysis of San Francisco's Alternative Crime Policies.* San Francisco, CA.

Harcourt, B. (2001). *Illusion of Order: The False Promise of Broken Windows Policing.* Cambridge, MA: Harvard UP.

Kelling, G., and W. Sousa (2001). "Do Police Matter: An Analysis of the Impact of New York City's Police Reforms." *Civic Report* No. 22. New York: Manhattan Institute.

Kelling, G., and C. Coles (1996). *Fixing Broken Windows: Restoring Order and Reducing Crime in Our Communities.* New York: Free Press.

Police Foundation (1981). *The Newark Foot Patrol Experiment.* Washington, DC: Police Foundation.

Sampson, R., and S. Raudenbush (1999). "Systematic Social Observation of Public Spaces: A New Look at Disorder in Urban Neighborhoods." *American Journal of Sociology* 105:603–51.

Skogan, W. (1990). *Disorder and Decline: Crime and the Spiral Decay in American Neighborhoods.* New York: Free Press.

Sousa, W.. and G. Kelling (2006) "Of 'Broken Windows', Criminology, and Criminal Justice." In *Police Innovation: Contrasting Perspectives,* edited by A. Weisburd and A. Braga 77–97 Cambridge, UK: Cambridge UP.

Stewart, G. (1998). "Black Codes and Broken Windows: The Legacy of Racial Hegemony in Anti-Gang Civil Injunctions." *Yale Law Journal* 107:2249–79.

Walker, S. (1984). "Broken Windows' and Fractured History: The Use and Misuse of History in Recent Patrol Analysis." *Justice Quarterly* 1:57–90.

Wilson, J., and G. Kelling (1982). "Broken Windows: The Police and Neighborhood Safety." *Atlantic Monthly* March:29–38.

Xu, Y., M. Fiedler, and K. Flaming (2005). "Discovering the Impact of Community Policing: The Broken Windows Thesis, Collective Efficacy, and Citizens' Judgment." *Journal of Research in Crime and Delinquency* 42:147–86.

Thacher, D. (2004). "Order Maintenance Reconsidered: Moving Beyond Strong Causal Reasoning." *Journal of Criminal Law and Criminology* 94:101–33.

Further Reading

Cordner, G. (1986). "Fear of Crime and the Police: An Evaluation of a Fear Reduction Strategy." *Journal of Police Science and Administration* 14:223–33.

Harcourt, B. (1998). "Reflecting on the Subject: A Critique of the Social Influence Conception of Deterrence, the Broken Windows Theory, and Order Maintenance Policing New York Style." *Michigan Law Review* 97:291–389.

Herbert, S. (2001). "Policing the Contemporary City: Fixing Broken Windows or Shoring Up Neo-Liberalism?" *Theoretical Criminology* 5:445–66.

Kelling, G. (1999). *Broken Windows and Police Discretion*. Research Report. Washington, DC: National Institute of Justice.

Taylor, R. (2001). *Breaking Away From Broken Windows*. Boulder, CO: Westview.

Weisburd, D. and J. Eck (2004). "What Can Police Do To Reduce Crime, Disorder, and Fear?" Annals *of the American Academy of Political and Social Science* 593:42–65.

5

Police Use of Deadly Force

Police officers are authorized by law to use deadly force against the public. The FBI defines deadly force as "the intentional use of a firearm or other instrument resulting in a high probability of death" (Lathrop 2000). The use of deadly force by police is a rare occurrence but can have serious implications for the officer, department, and community. All police decisions to use force against a citizen are subject to review and can result in disciplinary action against the officer. Departments can be held liable if a police officer fails to follow legal and departmental rules governing the use of force. Police community relations often suffer as a consequence of the police using force against a member of the community. Police shootings were blamed for many of the urban riots that took place during the 1960s and 1970s. According to data from the National Center for Health Statistics, there were 4,649 civilians killed by police between 1960 and 1974 (Milton et al. 1977). Up until the 1970s, research on police deadly force was scarce. The FBI kept data on the number of citizens killed by police but the information was not included in the Uniform Crime Report and was not publicized. Very little was known about the extent of deadly force, factors that influenced its use, and its consequences for officers and the community. The few studies that did exist were usually limited to a single city and were either conducted by the police department or from an outside organization without the cooperation of the department (Milton et al. 1977).

DEADLY FORCE: WHAT EXPLAINS THE VARIATION IN POLICE SHOOTINGS ACROSS DEPARTMENTS?

Milton, C., J. Halleck, J. Lardner, and G. Abrecht (1977). *Police Use of Deadly Force.* Washington, DC: Police Foundation.

Background

Significant differences in the use of deadly force were found across cities in the United States, yet there was little interest in trying to explain these differences. Laws governing police use of deadly force differed from state to state and across departments within the same state. Gerald Robin (1963) published one of the first empirical studies of police use of deadly force in 1963. Robin analyzed police killings in Philadelphia from 1950 to 1960. During that time, there were 32 instances of police use of deadly force. All but two were deemed "justifiable." Robin found that victims were disproportionately young and black. A majority of the victims were suspected of committing a Part I offense at the time they were shot and three-fourths had prior contacts with police. Robin then examined police homicides across other large cities and found considerable variation in the number of citizens killed by police. In Boston, the rate of justifiable homicides was 1.4 per 10,000 officers, while in Akron, Ohio, the rate was 63 per 10,000 officers. The findings from Robin's study drew little attention from police administrators or scholars (Fyfe 1988). It was not until 1967 when the President's Commission on Law Enforcement and the Administration of Justice report was released that interest in the subject increased. The report expressed concerns over the fact that officers were using deadly force without administrative guidance (Fyfe 1988). One consistent trend that had emerged from previous research was the wide variation across states and departments in the number of instances police used deadly force. In the mid-1970s, the Police Foundation undertook a comprehensive study to explore the differences across jurisdictions and departments in the use of deadly force by police.

The Study

Catherine Milton, Jeanne Halleck, James Lardner, and Gary Abrecht (1977), researchers from the Police Foundation, wanted to fill the void in the literature by conducting a *multi-jurisdictional* study that would help explain the differences across cities in the number of police shootings. This information could then be used to assist in the development of policies and procedures for reducing the number of police shootings. In preparation of the study, researchers reviewed prior studies of deadly force and interviewed police administrators in several cities. An advisory board was assembled that consisted of university professors and police administrators. The Board would assist with setting the research agenda and the research design. The first task was to select the police departments that would participate in the study. Researchers contacted 45 departments across the country and interviewed various administrators and supervisors to determine which agencies kept detailed records of their officers' shootings and would be willing to supply this information. Departments were also asked questions about their deadly force policies, procedures, and training. The goal was to select departments from different regions with dissimilarities in their crime rates and in their use of deadly force. Researchers were also interested in cities with different deadly force policies and particularly those that had recently changed their policies. Listed below are the seven departments selected for the study. The number of police shootings during the 2-year (1973–1974) study period is included as well as the department characteristics that appealed to researchers.

Birmingham, Alabama (41 shootings). The department operated without a written deadly force policy. Officers were guided by Alabama case law that involved a 50-year-old court decision authorizing police to use deadly force in apprehending an escaping worker of an illegal whisky still. This was the smallest city examined with a population around 300,000.

Detroit, Michigan (179 shootings). This was the largest city selected with a population of approximately 1.4 million. The city had a high occurrence of gun-related crime and police shootings. Under a new mayor, the department had recently eliminated a program that involved the use of plainclothes and decoy officers.

Indianapolis, Indiana (36 shootings). This department seemed to operate under a less restrictive deadly force policy. The police chief had recently created a deadly force review board.

Kansas City, Missouri (26 shootings). The department had just put into place a new deadly force policy, giving researchers the opportunity to examine its effectiveness.

Oakland, California (17 shootings). The city had a high crime rate and was known for racial tension, yet had a small number of police shootings. The department had in place a conflict management program.

Portland, Oregon (9 shootings). State law restricted police officers in their use of deadly force, and the department had a low rate of shootings.

Washington, DC (70 shootings). The department had adopted a strict firearms policy and was one of the first to establish a review board, however, had experienced a high rate of shootings in the preceding few years. Each of these departments agreed to fully cooperate with researchers.

The data for the study came from police department records, interviews, and observations over a 2-year period beginning in 1973. Administrators granted access to files, answered questions and allowed researchers to observe their officers at work. Researchers only examined police shootings that resulted in the death or injury of a civilian.

Findings

The goal of the Police Foundation was to conduct a *descriptive* study of police use of deadly force because of the limited amount of research on the topic. Using *archival data* from seven police departments across the United States, researchers provided an analysis of the variation in police shootings across departments giving special attention to differences in departmental policies and procedures. One of the major advantages of research using existing data that was collected for some other purpose is *nonreactive measurement.* Researchers do not have to be concerned that their observations might influence study participants. During the study period, there were 378 police shootings. Researchers gathered information on 320 incidents. Detroit had such a large number of shootings that researchers only gathered data during an 18-month period instead of 2 years. Most of the police shootings were nonfatal (79%). According to data collected by the National Center for Health Statistics, in 1973 there were 376 civilians killed by police officers in the United States (Milton et al. 1977). Fourteen percent of those occurred in the study cities. The combined population of these cities represented *only* 1.9 percent of the total population.

Victim characteristics. Demographic information was available for most of the shooting victims. A majority was male (only six victims were identified as female) and more than one-third were between the ages of 19 and 24. The youngest victim was 14 and the oldest 73. A disproportionate number of victims were black (79%), however, this percent was consistent with black arrest rates. The demographic findings were consistent with prior studies of police deadly force. Over half of the suspects were also armed (57%). All but 10 of the victims were involved in a criminal offense or were acting suspicious when the shooting occurred. Almost one-third involved police responding to some type of disturbance call (i.e., domestic disturbance or assaults). One of the victims was attempting suicide when shot by the police. Four of the victims were bystanders and five were other police officers. The data did not permit a clear determination of whether the victims were "confronting" the officer(s), "resisting," or "fleeing."

Officer characteristics. This information was more difficult to obtain. Demographic information on the officers involved in the shootings was not readily available from all departments. Researchers were able to access information on the officers' status at the time of the shootings. In 17 percent of the shootings, the officer was off-duty, while 21 percent involved plainclothes officers. Researchers speculated that these officers were not easily identified and were more likely to become involved in situations where a crime was in progress. The officers did not initiate most of the off-duty shootings. They came upon a crime scene and stopped to help. Ninety-two percent of these shootings were considered justified and resulted in no disciplinary action taken against the officer (this percent excluded the city of Detroit because no data on officer disposition was available).

City characteristics. Overall, the cities with a larger population had more shootings than smaller populations, but according to researches, population size alone could not explain the difference in rates, because cities of the same size had significantly different numbers of shootings. Size of the police force within a city was not related to the number of shootings. Fluctuations in crime rates also failed to correspond with changes in the use of deadly force, although the researchers noted the difficulty establishing trends over a limited (2-year) time period.

Departmental regulations. At the time of the study, many police departments had implemented (or were in the process of implementing) policies and procedures that restricted the use of deadly force (some even beyond what the law specified). One reason why some departments avoided the more restrictive policies was the threat of civil liability. If a court found that an officer acted outside of the policy the department could be held liable. The more narrow the policy, the easier it was to establish the officer was at fault. The regulations in place within each of the seven study departments varied significantly. Furthermore, most departments lacked a single comprehensive policy on the use of force. Instead, policies and procedures were spread across multiple documents that lacked organization. Birmingham had no formal policy beyond the 1915 court decision and police officers in Indianapolis operated only under state law. In Oakland, department regulations prohibited police from shooting at burglars and auto thieves, but the rule did not mention any other non-violent felons. Every department authorized the use of deadly force in self-defense situations or in defense of third parties, but there were language differences. For example, in Oakland, officers could only use deadly force "when all other available means have failed" and in Detroit, there had to be a threat of "serious bodily harm or death." Each department permitted officers to shoot fleeing felons but differed with regard to which felons could be shot. All of the departments had more restrictive policies in place for juvenile suspects. It appeared from the data that this particular policy had achieved its desired effect. After the Kansas City Police Department implemented their regulation, the number of juveniles shot by police significantly decreased. None of the departments required officers to first fire a warning shot. In fact, all of the departments prohibited it based on the risk of harm to innocent bystanders. Two departments—Indianapolis and Washington, DC—actually required officers to carry their firearms when off-duty. In Detroit and Indianapolis, the officers were allowed to carry a second gun.

Departmental reviews. All decisions to use deadly force were subject to review, but the nature and extent of the reviews differed across departments. Every department required its officers to immediately report a shooting or firearm discharge. In some departments the report was made to dispatch while in others the watch commander. Departments also differed in how police shootings were investigated. Some departments used a chain of command system where a preliminary investigation was made by a supervisor who submitted a report that was reviewed by everyone up through the administrative hierarchy. Other departments allowed the internal affairs unit to conduct the investigation or convened an investigative committee to review the shootings. Beginning in 1970, a handful of departments established police firearms review boards. The concept quickly took off. Composition of these boards varied by department but they usually consisted of police administrators, investigators, patrol officers, and members of the community. Detroit, Oakland, Washington, DC, Portland, and Indianapolis all had review boards in place at the time of the study. When the use of deadly force was found to be "unjustified," the most common sanction received by an officer was a verbal or written reprimand. Seldom were officers suspended or ordered to surrender their days off. It was even more unusual for an officer to be criminally prosecuted.

Recommendations. The variation in police use of deadly force and the limited number of departments studied, prevented researchers from drawing any definitive conclusions that would have explained the differences in use. The researchers did, however, suggest several factors that were worth pursuing in subsequent research. State statutes, department policies, training, and review procedures *appeared* to be related to differences in rates across cities. Based on their findings, researchers made several recommendations for departments interested in reducing the number of police shootings and considering changes to their deadly force regulations. Policies that were clearly written and provided specific guidelines for when officers were authorized to shoot were preferable to vague policies that required the officers to make too many assessments of the situation before deciding if deadly force was appropriate. Researchers advocated policies that limited the use of deadly force by police to the following two situations:

> "To defend himself or herself, or another person, from what the officer reasonably perceives as an immediate threat of death or serious injury, when there is no apparent alternative." (Milton et al. p. 131) **and** "To apprehend an armed and dangerous subject, when alternative means of apprehension would involve a substantial risk of death or serious injury, and when the safety of innocent bystanders will not be additionally jeopardized by the officer's actions." (Milton et al. p. 131)

Researchers recommended against any policy that required officers to make distinctions based on the seriousness of the crime committed or a suspect's age. Not all felony suspects posed a threat to an officer's safety, and age became relevant only if it was related to the suspect's *ability* to inflict harm upon the officer. Other recommendations included prohibiting officers from firing upon moving vehicles (shots were rarely accurate and posed a risk to innocent bystanders) and firing warning shots (because of the risk to other officers and innocent bystanders). Officers should also be restricted in their ability to "draw and display" a firearm. Given the significant percentage of shootings by off-duty police officers, departments should implement guidelines specifying the circumstances in which off-duty officers were permitted to involve themselves in a situation (i.e., only in serious crimes).

It was important for departments to include representatives from all ranks in the discussion of changes. Rules that further restrict the ability to use deadly force were likely to be perceived as a threat to the officers' safety. Involving as many officers as possible in the discussions could help alleviate these concerns. All regulations, rules, and procedures needed to be compiled into a single policy document that was periodically reviewed and revised as needed. In addition to the recommendations for policy changes, researchers also suggested ways to increase officer compliance to the regulations. Improved training, increased accountability, and meaningful review procedures would help ensure that officers followed the rules.

Limitations

The Police Foundation report was the first large-scale study of police use of deadly force. Researchers analyzed data from seven police departments across the United States in an effort to provide information on the character and extent of police shootings. Special attention was given to departmental policies and review procedures. The data for the study came primarily from police department records. Research using available data is often cost-effective and less time-consuming than collecting original data, and the data can be ideal for examining changes in a phenomenon under study (in this case researchers wanted to examine changes in deadly force policies). A major disadvantage, however, to using existing data is that the data may be insufficient to achieve the research objectives. The findings from the Police Foundation study of deadly force were derived from data supplied by police departments that were not *randomly* selected. Departments were chosen based on their availability of data and willingness to cooperate with researchers (*convenience* sampling). In addition, the seven study departments were selected to be representative of a variety of departments of different sizes from different geographical areas (*purposive* sampling). The extent that findings would *generalize* to other departments was questionable. Because of the limited availability of information on police officer characteristics, researchers were unable to determine how much of the differences across departments were due to the individual characteristics of police officers. Furthermore, the data did not allow researchers to determine the context in which deadly force was used (i.e., were victims fleeing or resisting an arrest).

Another problem identified with the Police Foundation study had to do with the fact that that police departments provided the data. Data on the number of police shootings was considered suspect when obtained from department records, particularly when the data were used to make comparisons across departments. Many small police departments did not keep accurate records of their police shootings, and departments differed in how they defined and classified police shootings (Sherman and Langworthy 1979). In the Police Foundation study, researchers only examined police shootings that resulted in a civilian death or injury. They did not examine the number of discharges where no civilian was shot. According to William Waegel (1984) prior research on police use of deadly force should have included discharges in their analyses because the circumstances that led up to a discharge incident may have been the same as for police shootings.

Significance and Subsequent Research

In addition to providing a detailed description of the use of deadly force across departments in multiple cities, researchers from the Police Foundation also set forth a research agenda to guide future inquires. High priority was given to establishing uniform data collection procedures for keeping track of all police shootings. Minnesota had already implemented a mandatory reporting system for all police agencies within the state (Sherman and Langworthy 1979). Research on police shootings needed to also include data on harmless discharges (situations where the police fired their weapon but hit no target), characteristics of officers involved in shootings, and information on the shooting incidents (locations, time of day, precipitating factors, etc.). Researchers also suggested that future inquiries should consider the role of opportunity on police shootings. Did more police-citizen contacts increase the number of police shootings? Finally, *longitudinal* research to determine the impact of legislative and department changes in policies as well as more multijurisdictional studies were needed. Police administrators and scholars took note of the recommendations. Numerous studies of police deadly force followed that addressed these issues.

The only two community characteristics examined by Police Foundation researchers were community size and crime rate, and neither factor was related to the number of police shootings. Other studies have produced *correlation*s between community characteristics and the number of police shootings. Richard Kania and Wade Mackey (1977) examined all police shootings that resulted in death in the United States from 1961 to 1970 and found that levels of public violence and homicide produced the strongest relationships. Communities with greater amounts of violence were more likely to experience a greater number of police shootings. Several other studies have produced the same relationship (Fyfe 1980a, Alpert, 1989, Jacobs and O'Brien 1998). Kenneth Matulia (1985) examined police shootings across 57 large cities in the United States and also found that a cities' robbery rate and number of police officers murdered were related to the number of police shootings.

In their study, researchers form the Police Foundation discovered that a significant number of police shootings were at the hands of off-duty police officers. Officers were encouraged and sometimes required to arm themselves at all times. This practice was based on an assumption that a police officer was *always* a police officer. Arming the police off-duty would keep them safe and possibly deter potential criminals. James Fyfe (1980b) examined this practice among New York police officers who were required to carry guns at all times. Three-fourths of the 681 shootings by off-duty officers were justified (i.e., defense of self or others), but 12.6 percent were accidental. Four out of every 10 shootings resulted in disciplinary action or criminal prosecution. It may not be in the best interests of a department to mandate their officers carry guns at all times. Milton et al. (1977) also uncovered in their research that a disproportionate number of victims were black. Several other studies reported similar findings in cities across the United States (Meyer 1980, Fyfe 1988, Blumberg 1981, Geller and Karales 1981, and Binder, Scharf, and Galvin 1982). Explanations for the disparity are divided. Some scholars attributed the differences to the higher number of contacts minorities had with police. Others believed that officers were more likely to shoot black suspects than white suspects. Research has shown a decline in the racial disparity as a result of more restrictive deadly force policies (Sparger and Giacopassi 1992). In his research Fyfe (1981) also discovered that in New York City, black police officers were twice as likely as white officers to use deadly force. The difference, however, was attributed to the environment in which black officers worked (areas with a high amount of violence) and to differences in rank and assignment. Age and experience was not related to the use of deadly force.

According to the Police Foundation report, much of the variation in police use of deadly force was attributed to departmental policies and state statutes. In 1979, Fyfe published a study that evaluated the impact of changes in deadly force policies within the New York City Police Department. Fyfe, a former lieutenant with the department, had just completed his doctorate in criminal justice. In 1972, the department had implemented a new regulation that restricted the use of deadly force beyond the state statute. The regulation stipulated that officers must rely on a minimum amount of force necessary to achieve a desired result. Officers were prohibited from firing warning shots, firing upon moving vehicles (unless occupants were firing at the officers), and discharging their weapon in such a manner that would endanger the lives of innocent bystanders. The regulation also created a Firearms Discharge Review Board to "investigate and adjudicate all officer firearms discharges" (p. 311). Fyfe analyzed over 3,800 firearm discharge reports between 1971 and 1975 and found a significant reduction in the occurrence of police shootings after the new regulation was implemented. Most noteworthy was the reduction in instances where police shot "fleeing felons." The analysis also showed officer compliance with the regulation evidenced by the decrease in warning shots fired. The importance of departmental policies in controlling police use of deadly force has been well documented in the literature (Meyer 1980 and Scharf and Binder 1983).

The Police Foundation study focused attention on the wide variation of deadly force laws across states. Differences were especially pronounced in the rules for apprehending "fleeing felons." Some states allowed officers to shoot at *any* fleeing felon, while others limited the use of deadly force to violent or armed fleeing felons. Waegel (1984) examined police shootings in Philadelphia for the period 1970–1978. Pennsylvania adopted a more restrictive statute governing police use of deadly force in 1973. Police officers were no longer permitted to shoot unarmed, fleeing felons. Waegel determined that the statutory change had little impact on police use of deadly force. Twenty percent of the shootings that occurred in the 5 years after the law went into effect violated the statute. In 1980, a new deadly force policy was implemented within the Philadelphia Police Department. Unlike the statute, the departmental policy achieved its goal of reducing the number of police shootings (White 2001). In 1985, the US Supreme Court intervened with its decision in the case of *Tennessee v. Garner*. The Court declared the use of deadly force to apprehend an unarmed, nonviolent felon a violation of the Fourth Amendment. Police shot Garner, an unarmed 15-year-old boy, after he had committed a residential burglary. The impact of the Court's decision was significant. The number of police homicides dropped 16 percent across the country (Tennenbaum 1994).

Police scholars and administrators have learned a great deal about the use of deadly force by police since the Police Foundation published their findings in 1977. Results from several empirical studies have helped fill the knowledge gaps outlined by Milton and her colleagues. Furthermore, subsequent research moved beyond *describing* the variation in police shootings to *explaining* the differences. This information has led to more restrictive policies, improved police training, and a greater availability of alternative nonlethal weapons that have significantly reduced the number of police shootings. The 1994 Crime Control Act required the Attorney General to compile information on police shootings making police agencies today more accountable for their decisions to use deadly force.

References

Alpert, G. (1989). "Police Use of Deadly Force: The Miami Experience." In *Critical Issues in Policing*, edited by R. Dunham and G. Alpert. Prospect Heights, IL: Waveland Press.

Binder, A., P. Scharf, and R. Galvin (1982). *Use of Deadly Force By Police Officers: Final Report*. Washington, DC: National Institute of Justice.

Blumberg, M. (1981). "Race and Police Shootings: An Analysis of Two Cities." In *Contemporary Issues in Law Enforcement*, edited by J. Fyfe, 152–66 New York: Sage.

Fyfe, J. (1979). "Administrative Interventions on Police Shooting Discretion: An Empirical Examination." *Journal of Criminal Justice* 7:309–23.

Fyfe, J. (1980a). "Geographic Correlates of Police Shooting." *Journal of Research in Crime and Delinquency* 17:101–113.

Fyfe, J. (1980b). "Always Prepared: Police Off-Duty Guns." *Annals of the American Academy of Political and Social Science* 452:72–81.

Fyfe, J. (1988). "Police Use of Deadly Force: Research and Reform." *Justice Quarterly* 5:165–205.

Geller, W., and K. Karales (1981). *Split-Second Decisions: Shootings of and by Chicago Police*. Chicago: Chicago Law Enforcement Study Group.

Jacobs, D., and R. O'Brien (1998). "The Determinants of Deadly Force: A Structural Analysis of Police Violence." *American Journal of Sociology* 103:837–62.

Kania, R., and W. Mackey (1977). "Police Violence as a Function of Community Characteristics." *Criminology* 15:27–48.

Matulia, K. (1985). *A Balance of Forces: Model Deadly Force Policies and Procedure* (2nd ed.). Gaithersburg, MD: International Association of Chiefs of Police.

Meyer, M. (1980). "Police Shootings at Minorities: The Case of Los Angeles." *Annals of the American Academy of Political and Social Science* 452:98–110.

Milton, C., J. Halleck, J. Lardner, and G. Abrecht (1977). *Police Use of Deadly Force*. Washington, DC: Police Foundation.

Robin, G. (1963). "Justifiable Homicide by Police Officers." *Journal of Criminal Law, Criminology, and Police Science* 54:225–31.

Scharf, P., and A. Binder (1983). *The Badge and the Bullet*. New York: Praeger.

Sherman, L., and R. Langworthy (1979). "Measuring Homicide by Police Officers." *Journal of Criminal Law and Criminology* 70:546–60.

Sparger, J. and D. Giacopassi (1992). "Memphis Revisited: A Reexamination of Police Shootings After the Garner Decision." *Justice Quarterly* 9:211–25.

Tennenbaum, A. (1994). "The Influence of the Garner decision on Police Use of Deadly Force." *Journal of Criminal Law and Criminology* 85:241–60.

Waegel, W. (1984). "The Use of Lethal Force by Police: The Effect of Statutory Change." *Crime and Delinquency* 30:121–40.

White, M. (2001). "Controlling Police Decisions to Use Deadly Force: Reexamining the Importance of Administrative Policy." *Crime and Delinquency* 47:131–51.

Further Reading

Bayley, D., and J. Garofalo (1989). "The Management of Violence by Police Patrol Officers." *Criminology* 27:1–25.

Binder, A., and P. Scharf (1980). "The Violent Police-Citizen Encounter." *Annals of the American Academy of Political and Social Science* 452:111–21.

Geller, W. (1983). "Deadly Force: What We Know." In *Thinking About Police*, edited by C. Klockers, 313–31. New York: McGraw Hill.

MacDonald, J., R. Kaminski, G. Alpert, A. Tennenbaum (2001). "The Temporal Relationship Between Police Killings of Civilians and Criminal Homicide: A Refined Version of the Danger-Perception Theory." *Crime and Delinquency* 47:155–72.

Reiss, A. (1980). "Controlling Police Use of Deadly Force." *Annals of the American Academy of Political and Social Science* 452:122–34.

White, M. (2002). "Identifying Situational Predictors of Police Shootings Using Multivariate Analysis." *Policing: An International Journal of Police Strategies and Management* 25:726–51.

6

Female Police Officers

Policing has traditionally been a male-dominated profession. Women were originally restricted from working as police officers. Women began working as matrons in local jails as early as 1845. The Chicago Police Department was hiring females by the late 1800s; however, they were the widows of police officers who had been killed in the line of duty. The department had no formal provision for paying death benefits so this was a way to compensate them. In 1905, the Portland (Oregon) Police Department was the first department to employ a female officer (Walker 1977). Lola Baldwin was hired more as a social worker than police officer. She was given the responsibility of protecting the city's young women. Alice Stebbin Wells was the first female to actually be called a *policewoman*. She was hired by the Los Angeles Police Department in 1910. Like Baldwin, she occupied a social worker role helping young women in trouble and working with delinquency prevention programs (Walker 1977). Wells became an advocate for women interested in police work, and by 1916 women were employed in 16 departments across the country. She founded and became the first president of the International Association of Policewomen in 1915 (Schulz 1993). The number of female police officers significantly increased in the 1950s, and by 1967 there were almost 1,800 female officers. As impressive as this number may seem, women made up less than 2 percent of the police workforce (Melchionne 1967). Women continued to occupy social work positions aimed at addressing stereotypical female offenses (i.e., prostitution and shoplifting). Women were also hired to fill clerical and dispatch positions. Women were excluded from patrol work because they were perceived as weak and unable to handle the demands and stress of law enforcement. Minimum height and weight requirements significantly reduced the pool of eligible female recruits. In 1968, the Indianapolis Police Department became the first department to assign females to patrol. Up until 1972, departments utilized different selection criteria for females. Amendments to the 1964 Civil Rights Act (passed in 1972) created real opportunities for women in policing. By law, police agencies could not discriminate against women in their recruiting, hiring, and job assignments. Many more women went to work as police officers and women started performing the same tasks as their male counterparts.

FEMALE POLICE OFFICERS: DO FEMALE OFFICERS PERFORM AS WELL AS MALE OFFICERS?

Bloch, P., and D. Anderson (1974). *Policewomen on Patrol.* Washington, DC: Police Foundation.

Background

As women began establishing themselves as police officers, some police administrators remained skeptical of their performance. Should women perform the same duties as men? Would women perform their duties as well as men? Would hiring a large number of women police officers change the nature of police work? These were all questions that had no answers. The first effort to address those questions came from a comprehensive study of women in police work conducted by the Police Foundation and the Urban Institute in the early 1970s. In collaboration with the Metropolitan Police of the District of Columbia, Peter Bloch and Deborah Anderson (1974) carried out an *experiment* to compare the job performance of male and female police officers. Results from the study were published in 1974 under the title "Policewomen on Patrol: Final Report."[1]

The Metropolitan Police Department in Washington, DC, was well known for its progressive policies regarding female officers. Beginning in 1969, the department under the direction of Chief Jerry Wilson, advocated expanding the role of women in policing. He allowed women to work as investigators and assigned them to the technical squad. In 1972, Wilson hired a large number of female police officers and assigned them to patrol. It was a significant move that went against national trends of only allowing a few women to work as patrol officers. It also presented a unique opportunity for researchers to assess the female officers' job performance.

The Experiment

The Washington, DC, Metropolitan Police Department hired 86 women between 1971 and 1973 (referred to in the study as "new women"). No special recruitment strategies were used to attract the female applicants (the starting salary of $8500 to $10,000 appeared to be motivation enough). Another 25 women hired between 1969 and 1971 ("reassigned women") also participated in the study. Each of them had undergone a "retraining" period to prepare them for reassignment to patrol. Each of the new female officers was "matched" to a male officer who had graduated from the same police academy training class. *Matching* is frequently used in experimental research when the researcher is not able to *randomly* select study participants. Matching can help control for prior differences between groups (i.e., age, experience). The

---

[1] A preliminary report was published one year earlier.

police department served a total of seven districts within Washington, DC. Each district consisted of two platoons with three sections each. Each section was broken into five squads with about 10 to 12 officers for each squad. The "new women" officers were assigned to two districts: one and seven. These districts would be the "experimental districts" where the women comprised more than 10 percent of the personnel. Each of the women was "matched" to a male officer ("comparison men") from districts five and six ("comparison districts"). The females could not be matched to officers within their own district because the women made up a significant proportion of the patrol force within these districts. Districts five and six were selected because they were the most similar to districts one and seven in terms of crime rate and demographic characteristics. No females were assigned to the comparison districts. This allowed researchers to examine the performance of new male police officers assigned to what had always been all male districts. Because the prior job assignments of the reassigned women were different from the male officers, they could not be matched.

Researchers ran into a few problems during the initial stage of the experiment. Some of the male officers were reporting to dispatch that they were patrolling alone even though they had been assigned a female partner. Several women who were required to wear skirts complained about the cold weather and were reassigned to station house duties. To address these problems, Chief Wilson set forth guidelines that prohibited any special treatment for the women. Women would receive the same type of assignments (i.e., foot patrol, two officer units) and the same number of assignments. For the most part, officers complied with the guidelines for the rest of the study period.

Researchers collected an impressive amount of data from department records, surveys, and observations over a 2-year period. Data were used to answer three important research questions:

1. Could women perform patrol work as well as men?
2. Were there any benefits or drawbacks to hiring women as patrol officers?
3. What was the impact of hiring a large number of women on police functioning?

The police department provided personnel information for each of the study participants. Researchers had access to performance reviews, civil service scores, as well as selection, interview and training data. Included in each file was demographic information and prior criminal history (if applicable).

Six different *surveys* were developed for this study. Chief Wilson himself administered the first survey. A questionnaire was mailed to each of the districts with female officers. Supervisors were asked to report assignment information: patrol, investigation, or station duty. Supervisors were also asked to rate each of the officers on a variety of performance indicators. Surveys were completed for 71 new women officers and 54 comparison men (for a 91% *response rate*). The second survey was a service survey. Researches contacted 131 people who had been in contact with the officers during the study period. A combination of telephone and face-to-face interviews were used to assess general attitudes about female police offices and how these groups rated the officers' performance. A general community survey was also administered to 129 residents to measure citizen attitudes about policewomen. A *random* sample of respondents was selected by a computer-generated random telephone number system. The advantage of using a computer to select the phone numbers as opposed to the phone book was the inclusion of unlisted numbers. The fifth survey was administered directly to those who supervised study participants. Eighty-four sergeants, captains, and lieutenants completed an *anonymous* questionnaire to determine their attitudes and opinions about working with women. The supervisors were also asked to rate each of the officers (both male and female) participating in the study. Study participants (new women, comparison men, and other male patrol officers) were asked to complete a similar survey to assess their attitudes and opinions as well.

Researchers paid observers to accompany both the male and female police officers on their shifts. *Observational* data is often used to enhance survey data because researchers can collect data on interactions as they are occurring. Two groups of observers were recruited: civilian and police. Police observers were selected from officers not participating as subjects in the study. Each had at least one-year experience. Observers received detailed instructions, a set of uniform procedures for collecting data, and attended training meetings prior to the start of the project. Using a structured data collection form, the observers recorded demographic information on each officer and then completed a separate form for each observed incident or encounter. Observers recorded the actions and conversations of both officers and citizens. This provided another measure of officer performance and citizen attitudes. Observers recorded information from 191 shifts from late June through September 1, 1973. They observed shifts with single female officers and single male officers, shifts with male-female teams, and shifts with both two male and two female teams. This allowed researchers to examine a variety of work assignments. To guarantee enough incidents would be recorded observers only accompanied officers from the evening shifts.

Results

At the end of 1972, Chief Wilson issued a public statement acknowledging the success of the experiment. He stated that in the future men and women would be hired from the same civil service list and in an effort to recruit more female applicants, lowered the minimum height requirement from 5'7" to 5'0". The guidelines issued earlier in the experiment to ensure equal treatment were no longer being enforced meaning that supervisors were free to assign officers as they felt appropriate. This resulted in some observed differences in assignment beginning mid-1973. Only 45 of the new women continued as patrol officers compared to 71 percent of the comparison men. Thirty-one percent of the females had been assigned to "inside" details such as clerical, juvenile division, or public relations. Only 12 percent of the men were assigned to these duties. The survey administered by Chief Wilson uncovered some differences in assignment that occurred *during* the study period as well. Men were once again less likely to be assigned to station duties and were more likely assigned to one-officer patrol cars. Women were more likely assigned to one-officer foot patrol. Researchers were not able to determine if the differences were because females requested these assignments or supervisors felt them more appropriate for women. By October 1973, there were 228 (5% of the police force) women working for the Metropolitan Police Department in Washington, DC. Sixty-one percent of these women were assigned to patrol.

To answer the research questions put forth above, researchers analyzed a large quantity of data from department records, surveys, and observations. Results from the experiment are presented below.

Job performance. There were few differences in the overall job performance or work-load between male and female police officers. The new women responded to slightly fewer incidents than the comparison men. Observations revealed that women had 4.40 incidents per hour while the men responded to 5.28. This difference was attributed to the comparison men initiating more traffic stops. Women, however, responded to more dispatch incidents than men, which took longer than traffic stops. This could also have explained the differences in patrol activity. No differences were found in the amount of time it took to respond to each incident. Few differences were reported in the type of calls for service with the exception that new women responded to more disorderly or drunk persons calls. There were no differences between new women and comparison men in terms of the emotional states of the citizens involved in the encounters or in the occurrence of threatening behavior. In other words, police officer gender had no influence on the behavior of the citizens. Police officer gender was also not related to the officers' ability to respond to a threatening citizen. No differences in the officers' attitudes toward citizens were found either.

The most commonly used measures of job performance in police work are the number of arrests and the number of traffic citations by a single officer. These two items were readily available to researchers and could easily be quantified. A review of the Chief's survey data found that comparison men made more felony and misdemeanor arrests and issued more traffic citations than the new women. Researchers attributed the difference to the more varied work assignments of women. Female officers were engaged in more nonpatrol activities that reduced their opportunity to arrest and ticket suspects. Researchers also noted that 20 percent of the female officers made as many, if not more, arrests as the male officers. While the number of arrests and citations provided an assessment of how productive an officer was, the numbers by themselves revealed nothing about whether or not the arrests and tickets were valid. To address this issue, researchers assessed the *quality* of the arrests by examining data from the prosecutor's management information system for all serious offenses. While cases brought in by new women were more likely to be dismissed immediately, comparison men had more charges dropped later in the process. There were no differences in conviction rates.

A review of personnel records found no difference in the departmental ratings for new women and comparison men. Departmental reviews took place one year after an officer's appointment and included such assessment items as attitude and behavior, learning ability, technical knowledge and abilities, willingness to accept responsibility and communication skills. The chief's survey included questions to assess patrol ability only. A few of the items produced differences that favored the male officers. Males performed better on the following items: protecting a partner from violence, responding to a public fight, or responding to a disorderly male citizen. Supervisors were also administered an *anonymous* survey to assess patrol performance for each of the new officers. Male officers once again received slightly higher ratings than the females, but the 1973 data found no differences in general competence, ability to respond to violence, or take care of injured and distressed people.

Contrary to many stereotypes about women in the workforce, female officers did not take sick leave more often, were not injured on the job more frequently, and were just as skillful in their driving ability (although it did take the women longer to pass their driving test). Comparison men were more likely to have been involved in "serious unbecoming conduct" (i.e., giving false statements to a police official or being arrested for disorderly conduct while off-duty) and mild misconduct (i.e., sleeping during a police academy class or not completing an assignment). New women were more likely to have been cited for being late to work. There were no differences in the resignation rate for men and women. Observers reported very few differences in the reactions of citizens toward the male and female officers. Survey data also showed a high level of citizen satisfaction with both the males and females. Sixty-three percent of the people who had contact with a female officer reported that she was "very good" or "good" and 33 percent reported "average." These figures were comparable to the male officers.

Several citizens reported that their experience with the female officer had improved their general attitudes toward women.

Community and officer attitudes. In addition to comparing job performance between male and female police officers, researchers also assessed community and police officer attitudes toward women assigned to patrol. Results from the community survey (administered one year after the new women were assigned to patrol) showed a considerable amount of acceptance toward females in their new role. Ninety percent of the citizens surveyed indicated that they had seen a female officer in person and most citizens indicated that women should be afforded the opportunity for police work. Citizens were somewhat skeptical about the ability of a female police officer to respond to a violent situation, but felt that a male and female patrol team would be effective in responding to male-female disputes. The police officer surveys revealed some interesting differences. Supervisors, patrolmen, and patrol women all indicated that males were better at responding to a disorderly male, but women were better at questioning rape victims. Supervisors and male patrol officers believed men were better at handling armed robbery victims, responding to noisy teenagers and drunks, and reacting to armed suspects. The female patrol officers did not share their opinions. They reported no differences. Patrolmen indicated that they would be better at responding to family disputes, disorderly females, and traffic accidents as well as gathering information from a crime scene (even though the females reported more cooperation from citizens). Female officers and supervisors agreed there was no difference. Females indicated they were better report writers, but the males and supervisors did not agree.

When the first patrol survey was administered in 1972, researchers discovered a problem with *reliability.* The order of the questions appeared to have an influence on the responses. To correct this problem of *response bias* with the 1973 survey, researchers administered two questionnaires with the same questions only in a different order. Researchers found that both males and supervisors expressed a preference for working with other male officers. Even the females indicated a slight preference for male partners. Fifty-five percent of the officers felt that it was "a good idea to have women as a regular part of the patrol force." Supervisors and male and female patrol officers were also asked about the desirable personality traits of a police officer. All three groups felt it was important for officers to be "calm and cool in tough situations," followed by "thinks and acts decisively," and "observant." The supervisors and males reported that it was important for officers to be "emotionally stable" and "intelligent" while the females felt that it was important for officers to be "understanding." Females reported that their supervisors were more critical of their performance and that they received lower performance ratings than their male counterparts. The males believed the females received higher ratings. Researchers also assessed whether or not these attitudes changed from 1972 to 1973. Over time, the supervisors reported fewer differences in their perceptions that males could perform better than women. Very little change occurred in the attitudes of the patrol officers.

Based on their findings, researchers concluded that in terms of job performance, women performed equally well as men and should be hired on the same basis. According to the report, ". . . sex is not a bona fide occupational qualification for doing police patrol work" (Bloch and Anderson 1974, p. 3). Researchers also noted several advantages to hiring women police officers, including a larger pool of applicants, police officers that were more representative of the communities in which they served, and fewer cases of misconduct that could tarnish the public's image of the police. Aside from these advantages, assigning females to patrol brought departments into compliance with civil rights legislation. Would a significant number of policewomen change the nature of police work? Researchers believed it would. Departments with female officers may be less aggressive than all male departments. Researchers believed females to be less aggressive and less tolerant of aggression.

Criticisms

The Police Foundation study of women on patrol provided answers to questions about the ability of women to perform the same duties as male patrol officers. The hiring of a large number of female officers and assigning them to patrol gave researchers a unique opportunity to conduct an *experiment* to determine if there were any observable differences in performance. The new women were all assigned to one of two police districts and then *matched* with a male police officer from a different district. The matched male officers had graduated from the same training academy at the same time as the females so they were equal in training and rank. In this study, matching was used to eliminate the influence of preexisting differences on the outcome measure. As useful as matching is, it is not a replacement for *random assignment*—a key component of experimental research. The fact that the females had to be matched to males outside of their district raised the possibility that differences in the districts biased the findings. Researchers did make an effort to select districts that resembled the female districts but the conditions were not identical. Despite efforts to make sure that males and females were treated the same throughout the duration of the experiment; females were more likely to be assigned station duties and "other patrol" responsibilities that reduced their opportunity to make arrests and issue tickets. Males did outperform females in the study on these measures, but the results may be biased because of the unequal duty assignments.

One of the inherent difficulties with any experiment carried out in a natural environment is the ability to control for all *extraneous* influences. In their report, researchers described some difficulties with the police observations. The intent was to observe each new woman and each comparison man at least once during the study period. This did not happen because procedures for assigning observers were not strictly followed. Supervisors took it upon themselves to make the assignments based on their own judgment. For example, the department had a prior rule prohibiting female civilians from riding alone with a male officer (the department was concerned about sexual harassment allegations). The rule had been suspended for the experiment, however; only male observers were assigned to the male one-officer units and to the male-female officer units.

When multiple observers are used to record information, researchers should always test for *intercoder reliability*. Intercoder reliability is used to determine the similarity of results recorded by different observers. If males and females differed in their recorded observations, the findings may be misleading. Researchers performed a *reliability check* by comparing the data colleted by male and female observers and found no apparent differences in their ratings of male and female officers, but there were differences in their reported activities. Female observers reported more total incidents per hour than the male observers. Researchers also discovered that females were being deliberately assigned particular shifts in order to accommodate the observer.

One of the biggest challenges with survey research is obtaining an adequate *response rate*. Response rates usually vary according to the type of survey administered. Face-to-face interviews typically have higher response rates than telephone and mail surveys. Response rates were an issue with the survey administered to police supervisors. In 1972, the response rate was fairly high (79%), however, in 1973 the rate dropped to 52 percent. A larger percentage of surveys were administered in 1973, but it appeared that officials were less willing to complete and return the surveys in 1973 (despite the fact that it was an anonymous survey). Response rates become an issue when the characteristics of those who complete the survey differ significantly from those who do not. In this study, supervisors from the experimental districts were less likely to respond than those from the comparison districts. A different set of problems emerged from the Chief's Survey. Ninety-one percent of the surveys were returned, but seven were duplicates. Officers who had been reassigned to another district during the study period were evaluated twice. This was only a problem for the female officers. Researchers decided to use the instrument with the greatest number of evaluation days for their analysis. Researchers also found out that several patrol officers had completed a portion of the survey themselves at the request of their supervisors. An attempt was made to return the surveys with strict instructions that they were to be completed by a supervisor, but this was unsuccessful. Researchers tried to identify the problematic surveys so that they could be excluded from the analysis. The suspected self-ratings were higher than the ratings by supervisors and males rated themselves higher than the females who had completed their own ratings.

Merry Morash and Jack Greene (1986) criticized the research design used in the Police Foundation study (along with other studies evaluating the performance of policewomen). Many of items used to measure performance were indicators derived from male stereotypes that were not necessarily job related (i.e., willingness to use force and physical effort). In addition, performance indicators did not reflect the wide range of police activities. Women were being evaluated based on their ability to respond to crime, however, police officers spend a considerable amount of time in service and order maintenance functions.

Significance and Subsequent Research

The Police Foundation study of women on patrol was the first comprehensive study comparing male and female patrol officers. Utilizing an *experimental* design, researches were able to compare job performance and attitudes for male and female officers. As more females entered into the policing occupation, additional research followed. Lawrence Sherman published a similar study of female patrol officers one year after the Police Foundation study. Sherman (1975) evaluated the performance of 16 women who had just been assigned to the patrol division in the St. Louis County Police Department. The females were "matched" to a group of 16 men who were part of the same academy training class. Data from field observations, interviews, surveys and department records produced findings consistent with Bloch and Anderson (1974). Policewomen performed their duties as well as the policemen. According to Sherman, females tended to display a different style of policing compared to men. Women were less aggressive and made fewer arrests and traffic stops. Citizen satisfaction surveys revealed that women tended to be more receptive to citizen needs. The National Institute of Justice funded a comparison study of male and female patrol offices in New York City. Forty-one female patrol officers were "matched" with 41 male officers. Data from over 3600 hours of observations found very few differences in performance. Both males and females used similar techniques to assert control (Sichel et al. 1978). There were no significant differences in the likelihood of using force and displaying a weapon between the males and females. Consistent with Sherman's findings, female officers made fewer arrests and were found to be more deferential in their interactions with citizens. Performance indicators revealed that women officers took more sick time, but this was attributed to a problem with officer morale within the department (Sichel et al. 1978).

While research has shown women to be equal to men in their ability to perform as patrol officers, attitudes have been slow to change. In 1976, Joann McGeorge and Jerome Wolfe published results from their study of police officer attitudes toward policewomen. Only a small percentage of male officers (18.1%) "strongly agreed" or "agreed" with the statement "Women make as good police officers as men," compared to almost 63 percent of the female officers. They also found that almost half of the female officers were "undecided" when asked if their coworkers respected and admired them. Differences in attitudes have also been found with surveys of undergraduate criminal justice college students. Christina Johns (1979) found that males believed females should be given limited police responsibilities; however, should be subject to the same selection requirements as men. Kathryn Golden (1982) examined the attitudes of 134 male criminal justice majors and also found that males continued to express doubt about the ability of a female to adequately perform many police duties. Ten years later, a study by Thomas Austin and Donald Hummer (1994) revealed that not much had changed. Surveys of students enrolled in criminal justice courses found that almost half continued to express negative attitudes about female police officers.

The negative attitudes expressed by male police officers were also reflected in their behavior. Policewomen were frequently subjected to hostile work environments created by their male coworkers. In her book *Breaking and Entering: Policewomen on Patrol,* Susan Martin (1980) reported that many female officers avoided interactions with their male counterparts because of the sexual jokes and harassment. Robin Haarr (1997) interviewed female officers employed by a Midwest police department and found that women were "marginalized" in the department. Male officers held negative attitudes about the females' ability to perform their duties, and many women were teased with sexual jokes, pornography, unwanted sexual advances, and sexual harassment. These negative workplace conditions were frequently a source of anxiety for female officers who typically reported greater stress than male officers. Ni He, Jihong Zhao, and Carol Archbold (2002) examined sources of stress among male and female police officers in Baltimore and found that women police officers exhibited more stress symptoms than male officers. Workplace problems continue to be a significant predictor of female police officer stress (Morash et al. 2006).

When the Police Foundation conducted its experiment beginning in 1972, women comprised only 2 percent of the uniformed police force in the United States. By 1978 the percentage increased to 4.2 percent and by 1986, 8.8 percent. Susan Martin conducted a follow-up study for the Police Foundation in 1987 that was published in 1990. The goal of the follow-up study was to assess the progress and changes that had occurred for women in policing since the original study. A mail survey was sent to all state and local police agencies in cities with a population over 50,000. In addition, case studies were completed for five major police department within cities with a population over 100,000: Birmingham, Chicago, Detroit, Phoenix, and Washington, DC. Martin (1990) found that the implementation of the 1972 Equal Employment Opportunity Act occurred gradually during the 1970s. One contributing factor was the large number of civil cases filed against police agencies for sex discrimination. By the end of the 1970s, most police agencies had abandoned the minimum height and weight selection requirements. Many departments had in place affirmative action plans. Despite the increases in the number of women police officers across the country, women still occupied a small percentage of the police labor force. This was especially true for supervisory ranks where women only made up 3 percent of these positions. According to Martin, there did not appear to any widespread discrimination in hiring practices for female applicants. Women officers did, however, have higher turnover rates compared to men. Possible reasons included unrealistic job expectations and rotating shifts. Performance evaluations were comparable for men and women, despite the fact that women tend to be evaluated differently. Females were still less likely to be assigned to patrol and utilized more sick leave than their male counterparts.

According to the National Center for Women and Policing, in 2001 women made up less than 13 percent of all sworn law enforcement personnel in the United States (among agencies with 100 or more officers). This represented a four-percentage point increase since 1990. Among smaller departments, females comprised approximately 8 percent of all sworn law enforcement personnel. While some progress had been made since 1990 in the percentage of females occupying supervisory positions, over half of all large police agencies had no women in their top command positions. Many departments that want to increase their female police force find recruitment difficult. Police work continues to be viewed as masculine and physically strenuous despite the fact that in the current era of community policing, communication and problem solving are the desired traits of a police officer. Several studies have shown that females are effective communicators, and many segments of the community have expressed a preference for female police officers (Sulton and Townsey 1981). Numerous studies have also shown women to be less aggressive and less inclined to use force against the public (Grennan 1987, Brandl et al. 2001 and Bazley et al. 2007). Research continues to document the valuable contribution made by female police officers. Departments that are active in the recruitment and retention of female police officers benefit not only themselves but also the overall communities in which they serve.

References

Austin, T., and D. Hummer (1994). "Has a Decade Made a Difference? Attitudes of Male Criminal Justice Majors Towards Female Police Officers." *Journal of Criminal Justice Education* 5:229–39.

Bazley, T., K. Lersch, T. Mieczkowski (2007). "Officer Force Versus Suspect Resistance: A Gendered Analysis of Patrol Officers in an Urban Police Department." *Journal of Criminal Justice* 35:183–92.

Bloch, P., and D. Anderson (1974). *Policewomen on Patrol.* Washington, DC: Police Foundation.

Brandl, S., M. Stroshine, and J. Frank (2001). "Who Are The Complaint-Prone Officers? An Examination of the Relationship Between Police Officers' Attributes, Arrest Activity, Assignment, and Citizens' Complaints About Excessive Force." *Journal of Criminal Justice* 29:521–29.

Golden, K. (1981-1982). "Women as Patrol Officers: A Study of Attitudes." *Police Studies: International Review of Police Development* 4:29–33.

Grennan, S. (1987). "Findings on the Role of Officer Gender in Violent Encounters with Citizens." *Journal of Police Science and Administration* 15:78–85.

Haarr, R. (1997). "Patterns of Interaction in a Police Patrol Bureau: Race and Gender Barriers to Integration." *Justice Quarterly* 14:53–85.

He Ni, J. Zhao, C. Archbold (2002). "Gender and Police Stress: The Convergent and Divergent Impact of Work Environment, Work-Family Conflict, and Stress Coping Mechanisms of Female and Male Police Officers." *Policing: An International Journal of Police Strategies and Management* 25:687–708.

Johns, C. (1979). "The Trouble with Women in Policing: Attitudes Aren't Changing." *Criminal Justice Review* 4:33–40.

Martin, S. (1980). *Breaking and Entering: Policewomen on Patrol.* Berkeley: University of California Press.

Martin, S. (1990). *On the Move: The Status of Women in Policing.* Washington, DC: Police Foundation.

McGeorge, J., and J. Wolfe (1976). "A Comparison of Attitudes Between Men and Women Police Officers: A Preliminary Analysis." *Criminal Justice Review* 1:21–33.

Melchionne, T. (1967). "Curent Status and Problems of Women Police." *Journal of Criminal Law, Criminology and Police Science* 58:257–60.

Morash, M., and J. Greene (1986). "Evaluating Women on Patrol: A Critique of Contemporary Wisdom." *Evaluation Review* 10:231–55.

Morash, M., D. Kwak, and R. Haarr (2006) "Gender Differences in the Predictors of Police Stress." *Policing: an International Journal of Police Strategies and Management* 29:541–63.

National Center for Women and Policing (2002). *Equality Denied: The Status of Women in Policing 2001.* Arlington, VA.

Schulz, D. (1993). "From Policewoman to Police Officer: An Unfinished Revolution." *Police Studies: International Review of Police Development* 16:90–98.

Sherman, L. (1975). "Evaluation of Policewomen on Patrol in a Suburban Police Department." *Journal of Police Science and Administration* 3:434–38.

Sichel, J., L. Friedman, J. Quint, and M. Smith (1978). *Women on Patrol—A Pilot Study of Police Performance in New York City.* New York: Vera Institute of Justice.

Sulton, C., and R. Townsey (1981). *A Progress Report on Women in Policing.* Washington, DC: Police Foundation.

Walker, S. (1977). *A Critical History of Police Reform.* Lexington, MA: Lexington Books.

Further Reading

Hoffman, P., and E. Hickey (2005). "Use of Force by Female Police Officers." *Journal of Criminal Justice* 33:145–51.

Horne, P. (1980). *Women in Law Enforcement* (2nd ed.). Springfield, IL: Charles C. Thomas.

Martin, S. (1994). "Outsider Within the Station House: The Impact of Race and Gender on Black Women Police." *Social Problems* 41:383–400.

Milton, C. (1972). *Women in Policing.* Washington, DC: Police Foundation.

Morash, M., and R. Haarr (1995). "Gender, Workplace Problems and Stress in Policing." *Justice Quarterly* 12:113–40.

Raganella, A., and M. White (2004). "Race, Gender and Motivation for Becoming a Police Officer: Implications for Building a Representative Police Department." *Journal of Criminal Justice* 32:501–13

A n emphasis on decentralized government in the United States is reflected in the country's organization of trial courts. It is a trifurcated system based on the separate jurisdictions of federal, state, and local governments. There are 94 federal trial courts which follow United States federal district boundaries, over 3,000 state trial courts of general jurisdiction that typically operate at the county level, and several thousand municipal courts with limited jurisdiction at the city level. These courts of original jurisdiction deal with both criminal and civil actions and are distinguished from appellate (appeals) courts where persons convicted by the courts of original jurisdiction can challenge their conviction or their sanctions. At the local government level, the trial court of general jurisdiction serves as the appeals court for municipal cases. Separate courts for juveniles also exist and operate primarily through the general jurisdiction trial courts, although in some jurisdictions they operate as stand-alone courts or within municipal family courts. Family courts and drug courts, in addition to other "specialized" courts, also exist in many areas at the municipal level.

Despite the complexity of court organization and the seemingly eclectic body of research that mirrors that complexity, court research in the field of criminal justice has focused heavily on *criminal* case processing in courts of *original jurisdiction* at the *state* and *federal* levels, and even most of those studies examined "county" courts (the trial courts of general jurisdiction, also referred to as circuit courts, common pleas courts, or superior courts). Although courts are synonymous with judges (i.e., judicial decisions are "court" decisions), here we also include prosecutors and defense attorneys as "court actors" because many studies have focused on their roles in criminal case processing and case outcomes. The courts of original jurisdiction constitute the intermediate stage between the apprehension and punishment of a criminal offender and are responsible for determining the guilt or innocence of those individuals. It is during this stage that (a) prosecutors determine what criminal charges (if any) to file against arrested suspects based on the evidence, (b) decisions are made regarding what must be done with a formally charged defendant prior to trial (i.e., bail and pre-trial detention), (c) formal charges may actually be dropped based on the weakness of evidence and/or the unwillingness of victims and witnesses to cooperate with prosecutors, (d) discussions and negotiations take place between prosecutors and defense attorneys in the hope that both sides will come to a mutual agreement on the convicted charges and/or sentence to be served by the defendant, and (e) trials are held when such negotiations do not occur or are not successfully resolved. At the trial stage, where proportionately very few cases are heard, the evidence of the prosecution and the defense is presented to and reviewed by a jury and/or a judge and a decision regarding innocence or guilt is determined. Sentencing often follows in a separate appearance, usually by a judge but sometimes by a jury (with judicial oversight).

Research on Courts

The field of criminal justice has devoted much less attention to the study of criminal courts per se relative to the study of police and corrections. The relevance of courts may seem obvious today but was originally limited to studies of criminal law and its impact on policing and corrections. The concepts of "justice" and "due process" appear to be the primary foci of court research today. The evolution of these concepts has implications for both policing, in terms of how the police treat criminal suspects, and corrections, in terms of the punishments administered to convicted criminals and their (in)consistencies with other legal philosophies. Since most of the attention paid to criminal courts has dealt either directly or indirectly with the concept of "justice," this might explain why court research is most often associated with legal scholars and political scientists. Nonetheless, the barriers to achieving "justice" (or the equitable treatment of offenders based on guiding punishment philosophies) are a primary interest of scholars who recognize the impact of the courts on both effective policing and the successful management of criminal offenders.

Early on, primarily law professors and political scientists conducted empirical research on courts. This research area continues to be a major interest of both legal scholars and political scientists although it has become much more interdisciplinary since the 1970s. Generally speaking, legal scholars and political scientists have focused primarily on court organization and the dynamics of criminal case processing. The interests of sociologists and economists, on the other hand, tend to focus more on criminal case outcomes and the factors that help to shape those outcomes. Psychologists and social psychologists have also studied issues related to *both* process and outcome, but with a more narrow focus on jury deliberations and decision-making as well as a focus on the psychological aspects of a criminal defense (e.g., guilty by reason of insanity). Broadly speaking, therefore, this area of research can be divided into studies of court cultures and processes versus case outcomes. The casual reader could easily confuse the two, although there are important differences between them in terms of applicable theories and dominant research methodologies. Also contributing to the confusion is a growing research interest in the effects of sentencing policy (e.g., sentencing guidelines) on process *and* outcome, as well as continued interest in the role of plea bargaining and how it is affected by differences in court cultures and, in turn, how it affects case outcomes.

Part II is organized into five sections reflecting these various topics of court research, including pre-conviction dispositions (bail and pre-trial release, numbers and types of charges, full prosecution versus dropped charges, etc.), the guilty plea process (convictions via plea bargains), jury trials (convictions by juries), sentencing (equities and inequities in case outcomes), and structuring sentencing decisions (to reduce inequities in case outcomes). The first three sections fall primarily into our broader categorization of research on court organization and case processing, whereas the last two sections reflect the broader category of case outcomes. This particular organization of research topics is not meant to trivialize a vast body of research that reflects the complexity of court organization described above. This complexity has generated a seemingly eclectic body of research encompassing topics related to all levels and types of courts, the different actors involved in case processing and sentencing (defense attorneys, prosecutors, judges, and juries), the different stages of case processing (indictment versus full prosecution versus the guilty plea process versus bench and jury trials), the impact of courts on corrections, and the effects of policies and policy change on legal decision-making. However, much of this research can either be categorized into one of our five groupings, is purely *descriptive* without contributing to theory development, or can be classified as *evaluation* studies of the impact of courts on corrections. The categories we identified as well as the studies included under each are of both policy and theoretical relevance and are distinct from corrections research.

Further Reading

Holten, N., and L. Lamar (1991). *The Criminal Courts: Structures, Personnel, and Processes.* New York: McGraw-Hill.

Zimring, F., and R. Frase (1980). *The Criminal Justice System: Materials on the Administration and Reform of the Criminal Law.* Boston: Little, Brown.

1

Preconviction Dispositions

"**P**opular" attention paid to the court system by the media and the general public has focused primarily on problems and issues related to the trial process and sentencing. The stages of case processing prior to trial and conviction have largely been ignored; a likely consequence of their more hidden nature as well as the general public's preoccupation with just deserts and whether criminal offenders receive their appropriate punishments. The decisions made in the early stages of processing, however, are very important for shaping what actually happens to defendants (i.e., whether or not they are convicted and actually receive those "appropriate" punishments). Specifically, these decisions include whether to release an arrested suspect prior to trial and, if so, under what conditions, whether to formally charge a defendant with a crime, the seriousness of the charge(s) to file against a defendant, and whether to fully prosecute (or to *not* subsequently drop the criminal charges once they have been filed). Pretrial release decisions have implications for a defendant's ability to prepare an adequate defense and, in turn, for his or her odds of being convicted, and charging decisions ultimately reflect the most serious offense that a defendant *could* be punished for. Aside from the implications of what happens during these early stages for decisions that the general public actually cares about, the hidden nature of these decisions can lead to corruption in the decision-making process because there are no formal checks on those dispositions. As a result, pre-conviction dispositions can ultimately lead to case outcomes that are either too harsh or too lenient relative to the crimes involved, possibly reflecting violations of defendants' due process rights.

PRETRIAL RELEASE

After apprehension by the police, the preliminary hearing is the first step in the court process for an arrested suspect. At this hearing, a magistrate or judge informs the defendant of the arrested charges, decides whether to dismiss those charges, and (in cases that are not dismissed) determines the conditions for *pretrial release*. This process involves determination of whether a suspect is eligible for release prior to trial and, if so, under what conditions. The vast majority of suspects are either *released on their own recognizance* (*ROR*) or they obtain release by posting a financial *bond* to the court (which is a portion of the total *bail* amount imposed by a magistrate or judge).

ROR means that suspects are released with only having to promise to return to court for trial, although some of these suspects might be supervised by probation officers to ensure their appearance. ROR is an advantage to persons of lower socioeconomic status (SES) who cannot afford bond yet are "good risks" for release. By contrast, bail is designed for suspects who might be inclined to not show up for trial. Failure to do so would then entail forfeiture of the total dollar amount of bail to the court, either by the defendant (when eventually found) or by the third party who put up the initial bond. Bail amounts are usually determined at preliminary hearings in lower courts although certain types of more serious (felony) offenses require that a superior court judge determine bail. There is no constitutional right to bail in the United States and some suspects are denied bail and the opportunity for release altogether due to their extremely high flight risk and/or their potential dangerousness to the community.

BARRIERS TO PRETRIAL RELEASE: ARE SUSPECTS PUNISHED BEFORE GUILT IS DETERMINED?

Foote, C. (1954). "Compelling Appearance in Court: Administration of Bail in Philadelphia." *University of Pennsylvania Law Review* **102:1031–79.**

Background

Permitting suspects to be released prior to trial stems from the due process concern that suspects should not be punished (by serving time in jail) before they have been found guilty in court. This process also helps defendants to work freely with attorneys in preparing their defense while freeing up limited jail space for convicted criminals. Pre-trial release enables defendants to continue working at their jobs and to support their families, which also reduces tax burdens by reducing a suspect's reliance on pubic assistance for both family support and legal fees. Aside from these seemingly benevolent intentions, however, the bail system exists to increase the odds that suspects show up to their trials. Failure to appear at trial means that a suspect must forego the entire bail amount whereas the posted bond is given back to the defendant who shows up to trial. Suspects deemed eligible for bail are supposedly protected from having to pay "excessive bail" via a constitutional provision implied by the Eighth Amendment to the US Constitution, which states that "excessive bail shall not be required." This provision is intended to prohibit the practice of setting very high bail amounts in order to prevent defendants from being released. Such a practice is analogous to denying bail altogether even though the suspect is deemed eligible for release.

Legal controversies have emerged over the system of pre-trial release because it reflects a basic conflict between our interests in due process (protecting the rights of the defendant) versus crime control (protecting the community). Moreover, the way the system operates in practice is far from ideal. For example, despite the protection against excessive bail, most suspects cannot afford to post their own bond and must seek assistance through a *surety company* or a *bail bondsman*. This and other aspects of the system introduce many opportunities for abusing the rights of defendants while also ignoring the interests of the community. As early as the 1930s, the US federal government recognized the moral problem posed by housing criminal defendants in jail even though they have not yet been found guilty in a court of law. Such detainment constitutes punishment even though some detainees subsequently may be found innocent, meaning that they suffered needlessly. In its review of the US bail system, the Wickersham Commission (1931) concluded that research on bail is needed in order to see what can be done to ensure that bail decisions are fair and more "individualized," taking into account the "history, character, standing, personality and record of the accused" (p. 12).

The Study

Caleb Foote's (1954) *descriptive* investigation into bail practices in Philadelphia constituted the first empirical study of the topic and led to a series of more rigorous studies, subsequent debates, and policy changes related to both state and federal pretrial release practices. Regarding the determination of a defendant's eligibility for bail and the amount of bail, Foote underscored the importance of being able to balance the need to ensure the suspect's appearance at trial with the desire to avoid needless punishment given that the defendant is presumed innocent until the conclusion of his or her trial. Foote's study was designed to examine how this balance was struck in noncapital cases in Philadelphia courts (both state and federal) during 1951. He identified the methods of determining bail, the proportion of defendants detained prior to trial, differences in the case dispositions and sentences of defendants who made bail versus those who did not, and the effectiveness of various forms of pre-trial release for ensuring appearance at trial. Foote's *quantitative* analyses involved some very basic descriptions of court data, and his *qualitative* analysis focused on interviews with magistrates, attorneys, and defendants, in addition to his observations of bail settings across various Philadelphia police precincts.

Findings

Foote initially observed two major problems with bail practices in Philadelphia. First, the percentage of defendants who did not make bail rose consistently as bail amounts increased. Whereas only 15 percent of defendants did not obtain release when bail was set at or below $500, as much as 68 percent of defendants were detained when bail amounts exceeded $1,000. For defendants charged with state crimes, 73 percent overall obtained pretrial release versus only 53 percent overall in the federal court. Most of us would take this observation for granted, but it underscores how counterintuitive the process is to making sure that bail is not excessive *to the individual*. That is, any specific bail amount might not appear excessive relative to the crime committed, but it might be excessive to the defendant if s/he does not have the means to raise the money. Since criminal defendants are drawn disproportionately from the underclass, many of these defendants cannot make bail even when the amounts appear reasonable. The second problem initially observed by Foote dealt with the sometimes lengthy delays between arrest and pre-trial release across the Philadelphia precincts. He argued that bail should be determined very soon after arrest and that the defendant should have had immediate access to the means of posting bond (i.e., access to non-corrupt bail bondsmen and more efficient methods to post bond).

The methods used by magistrates for determining bail primarily involved consideration of the offense, although in some cases the defendant's history of bail jumping and whether the current charge involved being a fugitive from justice were also examined. Consideration of offense severity was consistent with the idea that bail amounts should increase in more serious cases because the defendant was more likely to flee the jurisdiction and needed a greater incentive to show up at trial. Such an approach, however, ignored the individualization of the decision based on particular facts and circumstances surrounding both the offense and the suspect. The range of bail also appeared somewhat arbitrary to Foote, who noted that it was unclear how these amounts per offense were determined. Despite higher bail amounts for more serious offenses, virtually all bail jumping in Philadelphia was for minor offenses. Foote observed that any effort to "individualize bail determination must be plagued by the treacherous *uncertainty* inherent in predicting future human behavior" (p. 1035, emphasis added). This observation foreshadowed the theoretical perspectives of Celesta Albonetti (1987) and Darrell Steffensmeier et al. (1998), who focused heavily on the idea that court actors were constantly seeking clues to inform them of a defendant's risk of future criminality even if such clues fell outside the information that was allowed to be considered in the decision-making process. Despite the absence of individualization in bail decisions, Foote also found that pre-trial detainees rarely challenged their detention since defendants who could not afford bail also could not afford an appeal.

Bail was determined by one of two methods for suspects arrested on state charges in Philadelphia. For the vast majority of these defendants, bail was set by a magistrate at preliminary hearings that took place each morning in lower (police) courts across the city. For particular types of more serious offenses, bail was set by a superior court judge. (United States Commissioners determined bail in federal cases.) Only 15 percent of defendants processed through the lower courts were represented by legal counsel. The options available to a magistrate at the preliminary hearing included dismissing the case, setting bail, or (for particular types of serious cases) holding the defendant without bail until a superior court judge could determine the amount. Foote noted the difficulty in determining what standards magistrates applied when determining bail since the process occurred very quickly and seemed to be driven primarily by court culture and "custom." There were indications, however, that magistrates often introduced personal objectives into their decisions, such as making sure that a defendant could not make bail in order to keep him in jail for the purpose of protecting the public or even for punishment. Foote provided quotes from magistrates who admitted during the proceedings that certain defendants should be punished for their actions or that examples needed to be made of these suspects. A clever bail-setting practice to this end was to charge an amount for each offense instead of charging one amount for all offenses combined, thus inflating the bail amount. Foote also observed that magistrates set high bail in order to punish defendants who they knew would not be convicted based on the evidence and/or the crimes committed. Based on these observations, it was not surprising to Foote that different magistrates assigned different bail amounts to similarly situated defendants. These amounts varied by as much as 40 percent across magistrates (more commonly by 20%). Bail amounts were actually lower than recommended in nearly 40 percent of the cases, yet were higher than recommended in nearly 20 percent. Bail amounts were determined primarily by the offenses charged in both state and federal courts. What remained unclear to Foote was why this was the case, if bail jumping was more likely to occur in *less* serious cases.

Foote also examined the speed of implementing bail because the need to avoid unnecessary punishment requires that bail be determined swiftly (in order to reduce time spent in jail). Time to bail is affected by the amount of time between arrest and the preliminary hearing, and by the amount of time until a circuit court judge can set bail in cases where the magistrate cannot. The time that typically elapsed between arrest and the preliminary hearing was not long in Philadelphia since these hearings took place each morning in lower courts around the city. On the other hand, it took an average of five days for bail to be set when a circuit court judge was involved. Also, when magistrates told these individuals at the preliminary hearing that their cases were "without bail for court," many defendants assumed this meant that they were ineligible for bail and did not understand that they could apply for bail at a second hearing in the superior court.

The role of bail bondsmen in the process was also a concern to Foote. The defendants often obtained the necessary bail money from a bail bondsman by providing 10 percent of the total amount. The bondsman was then responsible for ensuring that the defendant appeared at trial or else he would forego the entire bail amount to the court. This process was subject to abuse, however, because some bondsmen worked in collusion with attorneys where they recommended particular attorneys to their clients, and then those attorneys split their fees with the bondsmen as payment for the recommendations. This raised a question about the quality of legal representation by such attorneys. Foote also noted that the deterrent effect of bail might become weaker when the defendant uses a bondsman as opposed to his own money or that of family members or friends.

Another problem with pre-trial detention was that it might interfere with a defendant's ability to assist in the preparation of his or her defense. Yet, in "serious" cases where a poor defense had the greatest possible consequences for a defendant, 75 percent of those defendants stayed in jail until trial. Foote conducted an analysis of case outcomes for 1,000 defendants detained prior to trial and found that 47 percent were convicted and imprisoned, 32 percent were convicted but not imprisoned, and roughly 20 percent were not convicted. This last figure was important because it reflected defendants who were deemed legally innocent, yet were punished by serving jail time prior to trial. Pretrial detainees served an average of 33 days in jail between preliminary hearing and trial. Defendants who made bail fared much better by comparison, based on an examination of 946 cases, with 48 percent not convicted (versus 20% of detainees), and 22 percent convicted and sent to prison (versus 47% of detainees). Foote observed that the difference in imprisonment rates for convicted defendants might lie in detainees losing their jobs prior to trial, thus providing less incentive for judges to administer probation so that offenders are able to keep their jobs.

Foote also observed problems with the treatment of arrested suspects prior to their preliminary hearings, such as suspects complaining about not being permitted to make a phone call. (He noted that this was probably more likely among minorities and "poorly dressed" suspects.) Some suspects also were not allowed to write letters, were limited in the number they could write, or were not granted access to writing materials. Such delays in communications with family and attorneys necessarily interfered with a suspect's ability to obtain pre-trial release, thus prolonging unnecessary punishment. Some of the conditions of confinement were also poor, including bug-infested cells, confinement in crowded facilities where suspects shared a cell with another person even though cells were designed for single occupancy, the absence of mattresses, and inmates having to buy their own food.

Problems also existed in the determination of "true" bail jumpers versus those who did not appear at trial based on advice from their legal counsel. An initial failure to appear at trial led to the surety being allowed five days to produce the defendant or else forfeit the entire bail amount.

Some attorneys abused this process and encouraged defendants to not show up for their court date in order to delay trials and/or to reschedule trials with different (perhaps more lenient) judges. Foote noted that assigning the same judge to the retrial would eliminate the second incentive for delay. Actual bail forfeitures were rare in *serious* cases, even though initial failures to appear were relatively common. Considering all types of cases, forfeitures were least common when bail was put up by private sources (13% forfeitures), whereas bail amounts paid by bondsmen and surety companies were much more likely to be forfeited (by roughly 30% for each type). Although private bail coincided with higher appearance rates, it was the *least* likely to be collected for defendants who became fugitives. This was ironic given that it was the threat of bail forfeiture that should have provided the deterrent for bail jumping, which was why some jurisdictions made efforts to improve collection rates during the 1940s. Foote introduced the idea that such efforts would not necessarily increase the odds of trial appearances.

Foote speculated about why private bail was so much more effective for increasing the rate of trial appearances. First, the defendant who puts up a private bond might believe that failure to appear would result in efforts by the court to collect bail from relatives or friends (i.e., individuals the defendant cares about). On the other hand, defendants typically did not maintain close ties to bondsmen. Second, relatives and friends who were willing to put up bond for defendants might better understand the defendants' risk for flight and were more likely to put up bond for "better risks." Finally, relatives and friends had more frequent contact with defendants and were better able to supervise their actions whereas it was too costly for bondsmen to police their clients. On the other hand, improving collection rates for bail jumpers who used bondsmen would provide the bondsmen with greater incentives to find their fugitive clients, but these incentives were lacking in Philadelphia due to low collection rates. Foote argued that there was an incentive for the court to increase collection rates from bondsmen because they often had access to resources for more effectively tracking down defendants compared to defendants' families and friends (through the bondsmen's various ties to both police and persons involved in organized crime). Rather than imposing financial sanctions for bail jumping, the jurisdiction simply imposed harsher sentences for the original crimes when defendants were found guilty. After Foote's study, most jurisdictions as well as the federal system implemented laws against bail jumping where defendants are now charged with "escape" and face separate punishments.

Foote's analysis exposed several weaknesses of the bail system at both state and federal levels. In particular, the absence of "individualized" bail decisions was most troubling to Foote because he believed that the ability to guarantee appearance at trial relied on the court's consideration of a number of different and unique factors that more adequately reflected a defendant's risk of flight. He also inferred from his analyses and observations that tying risk of flight to bail amounts did not seem to improve appearance rates, and that other methods might be more useful to this end. The bail system in Philadelphia during the early 1950s was fraught with abuses based on how it actually operated, and it was not set up to prevent "excessive" bail. Foote's specific recommendations for improving the system included:

1. Making nonappearance a criminal offense (providing a potentially more effective deterrent than bail itself).
2. Improving the bail process at the preliminary hearing and increasing the proportions of defendants eligible for release without bond (ROR).
3. Lowering going-rate bail amounts for some offenses.
4. Enabling pretrial detainees to communicate more regularly and effectively with outsiders.

This last recommendation would entail regular use of telephones, permission to meet with visitors as they choose, and being supplied with writing materials and postage for a "reasonable number of letters per week." The first recommendation was Foote's response to the inherent bias of the bail system against persons of lower SES. He believed that trial appearances could be guaranteed by nonfinancial means. Related to this, Foote believed that bail should not be used at all for minor cases. Technically, he argued, bail is "excessive" if a defendant cannot afford it, no matter how small the amount.

Limitations

Foote conducted a pioneering study of bail practices that impacted how academics thought about the topic, their subsequent research, and various bail reform efforts. Considering the time period (early 1950s), the study was also unique in its application of both *qualitative* and *quantitative* analyses to a political process. There are three important caveats to these observations, however, related to the type of quantitative analysis employed by Foote, his focus on a single jurisdiction, and his theoretical assumptions.

Foote's quantitative analysis involved examination of *zero-order relationships*, or relationships between variables that did not *control for* (hold constant) other factors that might affect both of the variables involved. The practice of controlling for such *extraneous* effects on the variables of interest can generate misleading relationships between variables. For example, Foote's description of what happened to defendants who are held in jail prior to trial versus those who obtained release indicated that pretrial detainees faced much higher odds of being convicted and of being sentenced to incarceration. His observations raised very important concerns over the potentially damaging effects of pretrial detention on the quality of defense preparations and the images of detained defendants as more "dangerous" offenders in the eyes of judges and jurors. It is possible, however, that Foote overlooked other factors that were related to both the odds of a defendant not making bail and the odds of being convicted and sent to prison. Although he argued that most bail decisions "appeared" to be made based on the seriousness of the offense, it is possible that magistrates were in fact individualizing their decisions based on other factors. Suspects deemed to be more dangerous would be forced to put up higher bond amounts, thus decreasing their odds of release, yet more dangerous offenders are more likely to be guilty of the offense(s) charged. Certain types of crimes are also, by their nature, more likely to have better evidence, which would also reduce doubt about guilt while raising bail amounts. Possession of large quantities of drugs, motor vehicle theft, and certain violent crimes involving multiple victims are examples of crimes with readily available evidence. Failure to control for these and other factors related to both pre-trial detention and case outcomes could generate the appearance of a significant relationship between detention and sentence severity, but this could be a *spurious relationship* if it would otherwise not exist when these other factors are controlled. A more rigorous analysis, for example, might involve a comparison of pretrial detainees versus suspects who obtained release in cases involving the same types of crimes, thereby holding constant the type of crime committed (such as comparing suspects arrested for motor vehicle theft only, drug possession only, etc).

Another drawback to Foote's study involved his focus on a single jurisdiction. Failure to include just one more jurisdiction prevented him from evaluating how similar or unique Philadelphia might have been relative to other jurisdictions. Sampling experts have underscored the much larger contribution to knowledge that can result from simply increasing the number of study sites from one to two (Kish 1965, Sudman 1976). The practice of examining at least two sites (preferably three or more) helps to prevent researchers from making *generalizations* based only on a single site that might not be representative of others. A researcher who selects one study site might do so because s/he is intrigued by the behaviors of individuals within that site, yet it is those interesting behaviors and processes that might make the site an exception to the rule. This practice is not unique in criminal justice research, and is evident in many of the studies described in this book, but it increases the odds of becoming too preoccupied with research findings that are interesting yet atypical. The work of James Eisenstein and Herbert Jacob (1977) demonstrated the importance of being able to compare court practices across multiple jurisdictions due to differences in politics and court cultures that ultimately affected how cases were processed and how defendants were treated.

A less obvious (and possibly less important) criticism of Foote's study focused on the assumption of deterrence that underlies both a system of bail and Foote's observations on the use of non-financial methods for ensuring a defendant's appearance at trial. The idea of deterrence is grounded in a belief that human beings calculate their actions and tend to make choices that will produce the greatest pleasure or "gain." The logic of using bail as a deterrent to "flight" is that defendants have much to gain by not showing up to trial and escaping justice, so the threat of having to forfeit potentially large sums of money should compel them to show up to trial. This logic might be flawed because it rests on faulty premises such as (a) all persons engage in these types of calculations in order to maximize their gains, (b) these individuals also ascribe equal importance to the threat of monetary loss, and (c) bail amounts determined by magistrates actually reflect what is intrinsically valuable to defendants. Foote recognized some of these flaws in logic, which, in part, led him to favor nonfinancial solutions to improving the odds of trial appearances. The fundamental problem with this approach, however, is the assumption that a defendant's interest in appearing at trial can somehow be tied to other factors that reflect a deterrent, or calculated effect on his or her behavior. For example, Foote recommended, "making non-appearance a criminal offense" (which it is today in all US jurisdictions). If intended as a deterrent to flight, however, it has not succeeded because the rate of non-appearances has not declined over the years. Such an intention also implies that a defendant is concerned about being charged with one more offense in addition to a possible laundry list of charges. In reality, the concept of deterrence originated among philosophers who imposed their own foresight on others, yet the nature of criminality may involve an absence of foresight and an inability to forego short-term gratification for long-term gains (Gottfredson and Hirschi 1990).

Significance and Subsequent Research

Foote was the first scholar to examine discrepancies in case outcomes between pre-trial detainees and suspects released prior to trial, and this was perhaps the most important contribution of his work. Arthur Beeley was actually the first scholar to study the bail system, focusing on Chicago in 1927. Although he did not examine these types of discrepancies in case outcomes, there were many similarities between the two studies in both the methods employed, the problems identified with bail, and the authors' recommendations (such as a greater use of summons instead of arrests, and the need to individualize bail decisions). Beeley's study had very little impact on bail practices, however, but he influenced subsequent researchers including Foote. In contrast to Beeley, Foote's analysis received much more attention and had a much greater impact on the field, possibly due to his analysis and observations regarding differences in the treatment of pretrial detainees versus released suspects, and perhaps due to the timing of his research when criticisms of the bail system were much more widespread among both scholars and practitioners.

Foote's study ultimately raised the question of whether a system of bail can ever be constitutional, especially since it so clearly violates the assumption of equal protection of due process when applied to indigent defendants. Foote's observations from this as well as from his subsequent research with graduate students up through the mid-1960s (Foote 1965) contributed greatly to a national pretrial release reform movement that emerged in the 1960s (Thomas 1976, Walker 1993). Despite the criticism above regarding his analysis of *zero-order relationships*, many scholars who subsequently conducted more rigorous analyses came to similar conclusions regarding the ideas that pre-trial detainees were more likely than released defendants to plead guilty, to be convicted at trial, and to be sent to prison upon conviction (Ares et al. 1963, Clarke and Henry 1997, Goldkamp 1979, Gottfredson and Gottfredson 1988, Wald 1964).

Regarding specific changes to pretrial release policies, some of Foote's influence could be seen in the Bail Reform Act of 1966. The reform stipulated that even in capital cases, and even for defendants who had been convicted and are awaiting sentencing in such cases, defendants had the right to be released unless a judge determines that no conditions of release could possibly ensure their appearance at trial. Also, defendants in non-capital cases had the (on-going) right to pre-trial release under ROR or bail, with the added stipulation that judges *could not* deny release based on considerations of their dangerousness to the community (except for convicted defendants who were awaiting sentencing). This last aspect of the Reform Act was challenged in the District of Columbia after many violent offenders committed crimes while out on bail. In several cases these offenders were re-arrested and bailed out again, only to commit more crimes. This subsequently led to the District of Columbia Court Reform and Criminal Procedure Act of 1970, which allowed judges to consider a defendant's threat to the community in noncapital cases. The Bail Reform Act of 1966 eventually was replaced altogether in 1984 with a new law that incorporated the same type of revision implemented in the District of Columbia in 1970 (United States Code, Title 18, Sections 3141–3150). An important difference was that judges could only consider dangerousness to the community for certain types of defendants including those accused of committing violent crimes, any crime with possible life imprisonment or execution, and very serious drug crimes with sentences greater than 10 years. Judges could also consider dangerousness for defendants with histories of habitual offending, who were very likely to flee the jurisdiction upon release, who engaged in the obstruction of justice, and who engaged in witness intimidation. All other defendants were eligible for bail. Although bail laws currently differ to some extent across states, defendants charged with non-capital crimes are generally deemed eligible for bail.

As will be discussed later, there has been a heavy emphasis in court research on whether sentencing decisions are influenced by the extralegal characteristics of defendants such as their race and sex. Several scholars have criticized the research focus on sentencing as being "narrow" because sentencing constitutes only one stage of case processing, and biases against defendants can emerge at earlier decision points which are subjected to even less scrutiny than sentencing decisions (e.g., Albonetti 1987, Hagan 1972, LaFree 1985, Petersilia 1983, Spohn et al. 1987, Zatz 1985). Foote's work had a significant impact on this perspective and underscored the importance of examining earlier stages of case processing which affect larger numbers of defendants relative to just those who are convicted. Moreover, Foote's observations regarding biases against socially and economically disadvantaged suspects, such as his observation regarding higher bail amounts for African-Americans and "poorly dressed" suspects, set the stage for subsequent debates on racial disparities in the treatment of defendants. Other studies of racial disparities in pre-trial release have produced conflicting results, however. Some scholars found that release decisions were not related to a defendant's race once the seriousness of the offense and a defendant's criminal history were controlled (Albonetti et al. 1989, Frazier et al. 1980, Holmes et al. 1987, 1996, Nagel 1983, Stryker et al. 1983). On the other hand, several scholars found a connection between race and release even when controlling for legal factors (Ayres and Waldfogel 1994, Chiricos and Bales 1991, Demuth 2003, Demuth and Steffensmeier 2004, Katz and Spohn 1995, LaFree 1985, Patterson and Lynch 1991). Of course, differences in the jurisdictions examined across these studies might have contributed to some of the different findings (Peterson and Hagan 1984), which further underscores the "limitation" noted earlier regarding the importance of examining and comparing multiple jurisdictions in a single study.

References

Albonetti, C. (1987). "Prosecutorial Discretion: The Effects of Uncertainty." *Law and Society Review* 21:291–313.

Albonetti, C. (1989). "Bail and Judicial Discretion in the District of Columbia." *Sociology and Social Research* 74:40–47.

Ares, C., A. Rankin, and H. Sturz (1963). "The Manhattan Bail Project: An Interim Report on the Use of Pre-trial Parole." *New York University Law Review* 38:67–95.

Ayres, I., and J. Waldfogel (1994). "A Market Test for Race Discrimination in Bail Setting." *Stanford Law Review* 46:987–1047.

Chiricos, T., and William Bales (1991) "Unemployment and Punishment: An Empirical Assessment." *Criminology* 29:701–24.

Clarke, J., and D. Henry (1997). "Pretrial Release Decision." *Judicature* 81:76–81.

Demuth, S. (2003). "Racial and Ethnic Differences in Pretrial Release Decisions and Outcomes: A Comparison of Hispanic, Black, and White Felony Arrestees." *Criminology* 41:873–907.

Demuth, S., and D. Steffensmeier (2004). "The Impact of Gender and Race/Ethnicity in the Pretrial Release Process." *Social Problems* 51:222–42.

Eisenstein, J., and H. Jacob (1977). *Felony Justice: An Organizational Analysis of Criminal Courts.* Boston: Little, Brown.

Foote, Caleb (1954). "Compelling Appearance in Court: Administration of Bail in Philadelphia." *University of Pennsylvania Law Review* 102:1031–79.

Foote, C. (1965). "The Coming Constitutional Crisis in Bail." *University of Pennsylvania Law Review* 113:959–69.

Frazier, C., W. Bock, and J. Henretta (1980). "Pretrial Release and Bail Decisions: The Effects of Legal Community and Personal Variables." *Criminology* 18:162–81.

Goldkamp, J. (1979). *Two Classes of Accused.* Cambridge, MA: Ballinger.

Gottfredson, M., and D. Gottfredson (1988). *Decisionmaking in Criminal Justice: Towards the Rational Exercise of Discretion.* New York: Plenum.

Gottfredson, M., and T. Hirschi (1990). *A General Theory of Crime.* Stanford, CA: Stanford UP.

Holmes, M., H. Daudistel, and R. Farrell (1987) "Determinants of Charge Reductions and Final Dispositions in Cases of Burglary and Robbery." *Journal of Research in Crime and Delinquency* 24:233–54.

Holmes, M., H. Hosch, H. Daudistel, D. Perez, and J. Graves (1996). "Ethnicity, Legal Resources, and Felony Dispositions in Two Southwestern Jurisdictions." *Justice Quarterly* 13:11–30.

Katz, C., and C. Spohn (1995). "The Effect of Race and Gender on Bail Outcomes: Test of an Interactive Model." *American Journal of Criminal Justice* 19:161–84.

Kish, L. (1965). *Survey Sampling.* New York: Wiley.

LaFree, G. (1985). "Official Reactions to Hispanic Defendants in the Southwest." *Journal of Research in Crime and Delinquency* 22:213–37.

Nagel, I. (1983). "The Legal/Extra-legal Controversy: Judicial Decisions in Pretrial Release." *Law and Society Review* 17:481–515.

Patterson, M. and E. Lynch (1991). "Bias in Formalized Bail Procedures." In *Race and Criminal Justice,* edited by M. Lynch and E. Patterson. New York: Harrow and Heston.

Peterson, R., and J. Hagan (1984). "Changing Conceptions of Race: Towards an Account of Anomalous Findings of Sentencing Research." *American Sociological Review* 49:56–70.

Steffensmeier, D., J. Ulmer, and J. Kramer (1998). "The Interaction of Race, Gender, and Age in Criminal Sentencing: The Punishment Cost of

Being Young, Black, and Male." *Criminology* 36:763–97.

Stryker, R., I. Nagel, and J. Hagan (1983). "Methodological Issues in Court Research: Pretrial Release Decisions for Federal Defendants." *Sociological Methods and Research* 11:469–500.

Sudman, S. (1976). *Applied Sampling.* New York: Academic Press.

Thomas, W. (1976). *Bail Reform In America.* Los Angeles: University of California Press.

Wald, P. (1964). "Pre-trial Detention and Ultimate Freedom: A Statistical Study." *New York University Law Review* 39:631–55.

Walker, S. (1993). *Taming the System: The Control of Discretion in Criminal Justice 1950-1990.* New York: Oxford UP.

Wickersham Commission (1931). *Report on Lawlessness in Law Enforcement.* Washington DC: National Commission on Law Observance and Enforcement.

Further Reading

Cohen, T., and B. Reaves. (2007). *Pretrial Release of Felony Defendants in State Courts.* Washington, DC: Bureau of Justice Statistics Special Report.

Thomas, W. Jr. (1977). *Bail Reform in America.* Berkley, CA: University of California Press.

Wheeler, C., and G. Wheeler (1981). "Two Faces of Bail Reform: An Analysis of the Impact of Pretrial Status on Disposition, Pretrial Flight and Crime in Houston." *Policy Studies Review* 1:168–82.

DECISIONS TO PROSECUTE

Prosecuting attorneys are considered to be the most powerful figures in our court system because of their discretion over charging decisions. Prosecutors exercise a considerable amount of discretion in deciding which suspects are charged and the nature of those charges. For the most part, the decisions made by prosecutors are hidden from public scrutiny. Underlying a *deterministic approach* to understanding prosecutorial decision-making is the assumption that a particular phenomenon or process (such as a prosecutor's decision to formally charge an arrested suspect) can be predicted by other pieces of information (seriousness of the offense, the suspect's prior record, the quality of evidence both for and against the suspect, etc.). Also implied is that what is being predicted (the outcome or *dependent* variable) is caused by these other factors (the *independent* variables). The prosecutor's decision to move forward with charges, therefore, is not a decision entirely driven by free will, but instead is constrained or shaped in part by factors external to the prosecutor. Prosecutors' decisions will change, therefore, based on differences in these other factors. For example, a prosecutor may file charges against one suspect because the police were able to gather physical evidence during the arrest, yet may decide to not file charges against another suspect because there was no physical evidence gathered.

A critical assumption underlying a deterministic model of prosecutorial decisions is that the same factors influence the decisions of different prosecutors. This assumption implies that there exists an objective reality, or a world that different people perceive in similar fashion. Related to this assumption is that such a reality can be studied objectively. (The perspective that individual and social processes can be studied dispassionately or *scientifically* is referred to as *positivism*.) Not all scholars share this perspective because they believe that particular phenomena are incapable of being objectified (or measured empirically). Court scholars such as Albert Alschuler (1975) and David Sudnow (1965) might maintain this view because their focus on *interrelationships* between court actors would be difficult to measure, and different researchers attempting to observe these relationships might derive very different interpretations of their substance and relevance. This is the ethnographer's primary criticism of *quantitative* research because it requires the ability to measure theoretical concepts that are often highly abstract, and so researchers may settle for observable proxies for the concepts of interest. These proxies may not capture the full essence of the original idea, as when sentencing researchers use different measures of a defendant's criminal history to reflect how judges might perceive their "risk" for future offending. Different measures, however, may reflect different levels of risk, such as a history of serving prison time as opposed to a history of misdemeanor arrests.

Prior to the mid-1980s, studies of differences in the severity of criminal case outcomes based on the extralegal characteristics of defendants focused primarily on the sentencing stage, with a major emphasis on the race of defendants, and were grounded in traditional "conflict" perspectives. By the 1980s, however, there were several drawbacks to continuing related research in the same fashion. First, focusing only on the sentencing stage ignores all prior decisions in case processing that ultimately shapes the demographic composition of the pool of convicted defendants. Second, a conflict perspective focuses primarily on an individual's "class status" for shaping his or her treatment by the criminal justice system, yet by the 1980s it was questionable whether a person's race could still be considered a class-based characteristic in many areas of the United States. Finally, even the traditional conflict perspective itself was drawing more criticism for its outdated emphasis on Marxian views of western culture.

Conflict theory has not disappeared entirely from court research and, in fact, currently plays an important role in a somewhat revised version (as will be described in a subsequent section). Some of the original concepts, however, are questionable in terms of their applicability to an understanding of decision-making in criminal courts today. The conflict paradigm stems from Karl Marx and Friedrich Engels' perspective that crime in western cultures was to some extent a symptom of a decline in social solidarity. They attributed the decline in solidarity to the economics of capitalism that generated a division of labor reflecting the unjust exploitation of one social class by another. Generally speaking, therefore, conflict theories focus on the struggles between groups in society in terms of economic power differentials. The three key propositions of this perspective include recognition that (1) conflict of interests between different groups will be increased by inequality in the distribution of scarce resources (food, clothing, shelter, etc.), (2) those receiving less of the needed resources would eventually become aware of the inequitable exchange and begin to question the arrangement, and (3) these groups would then be more likely to organize and to bring conflict out in the open, after which there would be violence leading to the redistribution of the scarce resources so that they can be shared by everyone. This broader perspective has been applied to an understanding of both crime and the treatment of criminal defendants by the criminal justice system. Conflict theorists see "crime" as a social construction of reality whereby members of the wealthy class are able to translate their interests into laws, which, in turn, are more likely to be violated by members of the underclass because they do not necessarily share the same interests. For example, crimes against pan handling and trespassing are necessarily counter to the interests of poor and homeless persons. As a result, members of the underclass are disproportionately over-represented in the criminal justice system. Part of this overrepresentation might also be due to the differential treatment of suspects who are economically disadvantaged relative to those who are not. Police might be more likely to arrest such persons, prosecutors more likely to charge, juries more likely to convict, and judges more likely to send to prison. The apprehension and removal of these people from society serves to remove their "threat" to the interests of the upper class.

PROSECUTORS' USE OF DISCRETION IN DECISION-MAKING: DO PROSECUTORS CONSIDER EXTRALEGAL FACTORS IN THEIR DECISIONS?

Albonetti, C. (1987). "Prosecutorial Discretion: The Effects of Uncertainty." *Law and Society Review* 21:291–313.

Background

The appeal of the conflict perspective has grown weaker since the 1960s for several reasons. First, since the 1960s and the civil rights movement, it is questionable whether the prevailing definition of morality reflects *only* the interests of the powerful. Second, desegregation in many parts of the country has contributed to substantial gains in the economic status of many African Americans, thus weakening the link between a person's race and his or her economic status. Third, the traditional conflict perspective may be a better explanation of misdemeanor crimes and the treatment of misdemeanants relative to felony crimes and the treatment of felons. Felony crimes reflect more serious harms that are innately more offensive to human beings (i.e., the *mala in se* crimes described in introductory criminal justice textbooks). These types of crimes (murder, sex offenses, other violence, stolen property) are the offenses that all citizens agree should be outlawed. In other words, western societies operate on the basis of broad social consensus when it comes to outlawing the most serious offenses, which, by definition, also demand the most serious punishments. These criticisms imply that attorney' decisions may be driven not so much by potential biases toward the underclass due to competition for scarce resources, but rather by other factors that may actually involve legally relevant criteria. In the 1980s, Celesta Albonetti offered a refreshing alternative to this body of research because she emphasized two important ideas. First, the prosecutors are perhaps the most powerful court actors due to the virtual absence of any supervision over their decisions to file charges against arrested suspects, making them more important than judges for shaping court caseloads. Second, explanations of discretionary decision-making in the courts do not have to rely solely on sociological explanations grounded in either a conflict perspective or symbolic interactionism. Perhaps it is not the characteristics of defendants that shape case outcomes, but rather differences in legal factors surrounding their cases. After all, related research consistently demonstrates that legal factors are far superior to extra-legal factors when predicting the severity of case outcomes (Ulmer 1997).

The Study

Albonetti (1987) examined prosecutors' decisions to file formal charges against arrested suspects. Prosecutors faced much less scrutiny than judges in their decision-making, and the initial filing of formal charges was an "invisible" decision. As such, this decision was subject to abuse. Albonetti developed and tested a theory of prosecutorial discretion that would shed light on this first stage of court processing. She observed that prosecutors in the United States were somewhat unique from those in other countries because they were "free of accountability" (p. 292) when determining (a) whether to file charges, (b) the severity of filed charges, and (c) whether to subsequently drop some or all charges against defendants. Albonetti was not the first scholar to examine prosecutorial discretion, although there were only about 15 related studies by that time with less than half providing *quantitative* analyses and only two involving relatively large samples. This body of research suggested that, much like sentencing severity, the decision to charge was shaped most heavily by legal factors such as evidence, offense seriousness, and criminal history (Blumberg 1967, Eisenstein and Jacob 1977, Mather 1979, Miller 1969, Neubauer 1974, Swigert and Farrell 1977).

Albonetti adopted an organizational perspective to explain prosecutorial decision-making, arguing that a "fully rational" decision could only be made when all relevant information was available to the decision-maker. This situation did not exist in practice, particularly in the criminal justice system, and so rationality was "bounded" to some extent in that there was a level of uncertainty to these decisions (March and Simon 1958, p. 169). Decision-makers attempted to reduce uncertainty and compensate for the absence of all necessary information by basing their decisions on past decisions in similar circumstances/cases, and settling "for satisfactory rather than optimal solutions" (Albonetti 1987, p. 294). Albonetti applied two additional ideas, borrowed from James Thompson (1967), in order to complete her theory of prosecutorial decision-making. First, the filing of charges did not guarantee conviction because the prosecutor could not control the actions of all parties involved. That is, s/he could not perfectly predict the actions of the defendant and other court actors (defense attorney, judge, and/or jurors). The prosecutor's "beliefs about cause and effect relations" (p. 294) would therefore influence the decision to file charges. Second, the prosecutor's "preferences regarding possible outcomes" (p. 294) also played a role in that prosecutors would assess their chances of success in obtaining a conviction and would *not* file charges based on particular "cues" associated with non-convictions (such as offenses involving less harm, weaker evidence, and defendants with whom jurors are more likely to sympathize). Integrating these ideas, Albonetti theorized that prosecutors sought to remove uncertainty in their decisions by focusing on information that had corresponded with the odds of conviction in the past. Their use of discretion in this decision actually permitted them to gain control over uncertainty by allowing them to consider factors that they believed were relevant for improving the prediction of case outcomes (convictions versus acquittals).

Albonetti examined over 6,000 felony cases processed during 1974 in the Superior Court of the District of Columbia. She focused on prosecutors who were responsible for determining whether charges would be filed against arrested suspects (including those arrested by police as well as by warrants). Several measures were developed in order to facilitate her examination of the "uncertainty" thesis. Perhaps the most important of these involved three "evidence" measures, which had never been examined previously. She *hypothesized* that the presence of "exculpatory evidence" (the first evidence measure) would coincide with lower odds of prosecution because such evidence raised doubts about whether a crime actually occurred, thus increasing uncertainty in the outcome. By contrast, the existence of "corroborative evidence" (the second evidence measure) should *reduce* uncertainty by removing ambiguity regarding whether a crime actually occurred, thereby increasing the odds of prosecution. The presence of "physical evidence" (the third measure) should be the most salient of the three, especially at trial (although Albonetti noted that between 80 and 90% of these cases were disposed by defendants pleading guilty to the original or reduced charges).

Noting the importance of witnesses to the prosecution, Albonetti also examined whether more witnesses increased the odds of prosecution. Having to rely on one witness, especially when the witness was the victim, increased the uncertainty of conviction at trial. Multiple witnesses were desirable to compensate for the possibility that any single witness might not come across as credible to a judge or jurors. She also *hypothesized* that the relationship between the defendant and victim would be relevant in that there was greater uncertainty when the two persons knew each other because the victim was less likely to follow through as a cooperative witness for the prosecution (especially when the victim and the defendant were intimates). Crimes involving strangers, by contrast, were perceived as less likely to have been fabricated by the victim, thus reducing uncertainty that a crime actually occurred. Also related to this theme, prosecutors might be more likely to pursue charges when the victim was an organization as opposed to an individual because the former was more likely to cooperate with prosecutors since they were not (personally) tied to the defendant. In other words, organizations were more reliable and reduced the uncertainty of conviction.

Uncertainty about the odds of conviction might also be reduced for a defendant who was arrested at the scene of the crime, which helped to establish the person's link to the event, as well as for a defendant who had a prior record of felony convictions, assuming that such a history would be seen as increasing the likelihood of their involvement in yet another criminal offense. If violent crimes were perceived as more threatening to others, prosecutors might also be more zealous in their pursuit of prosecution when the crimes involved personal harm as opposed to property crimes and victimless crimes. Finally, uncertainty was greater for prosecutors when faced with victims who provoked their assailants because such cases automatically generated doubts about the defendant's culpability.

Findings

Albonetti's analysis produced evidence favoring all but one of her predictions described above. The exceptional finding was that the odds of prosecution were *lowered* by 65 percent when the defendant was arrested at the scene of the crime, which contradicted her hypothesis that arrests made by police would coincide with *higher* odds of prosecution. Albonetti speculated that the contrary finding could have resulted if prosecutors had greater doubts about whether warrantless arrests would stand up in court, especially if they resulted from "hasty police decisions" (p. 309). With arrest warrants, on the other hand, the prosecutor had greater control over the investigation and the collection of evidence leading up to the actual arrest.

Not only did Albonetti find empirical support for most of the effects of interest, some of those effects were quite strong. Specifically, the existence of exculpatory evidence reduced the odds of prosecution by 34 percent, whereas corroborative evidence increased those odds by 15 percent. Physical evidence was also a significant predictor of prosecution, although the odds of prosecution in such cases were higher by only 4 percent relative to other cases (which represents a fairly modest impact). Perhaps the most dramatic effect involved the number of witnesses, where the odds of prosecution for cases with no witness or only one witness were 64 percent lower than the odds for cases with two or more witnesses. Regarding victim characteristics, prosecution odds for cases involving strangers were 18 percent higher relative to non-stranger cases. Defendants who were provoked by victims had considerably lower odds of prosecution (by 59%), and cases involving organizations as victims had higher odds by 9 percent.

Albonetti interpreted these findings as support for her contention that prosecutors were concerned with reducing uncertainty in their decisions regarding whether to prosecute arrested suspects. The more general finding that prosecutors weighed various aspects of a case differently implies that each aspect may be assessed by prosecutors relative to its perceived impact on the odds of conviction at trial, suggesting the use of discretionary decision-making designed to reduce uncertainty in case outcomes.

Limitations

Specific criticisms of Albonetti's study have not appeared in print although it is subject to the more general criticism of *quantitative* analyses of decision-making in the courts and the questionable utility of deterministic models. Court researchers who have adopted the *ethnographic* approach to understanding the dynamics of case processing have argued that case studies are essential for placing quantitative findings in their proper perspective (see Ulmer 1997). Otherwise, researchers run the risk of giving greater meaning to particular findings that may only reflect *correlations* as opposed to *causal* relationships. A correlation between two factors merely reflects that the two factors are related to each other, and not that one factor necessarily causes the other (recall our discussion of possible *spurious relationships* in Foote's study of bail practices in Philadelphia). Without observing the courts under study, a researcher might infer causal relationships that do not really exist. For example, Albonetti gave ex-post facto meaning to her counterintuitive finding that suspects who were arrested at the scene of the crimes were *less* likely to be prosecuted compared to warranted arrests. Her interpretation implied that prosecutors consciously considered whether an arrest was made with or without a warrant, but this empirical relationship might have resulted from another process altogether. For example, there may be particular types of crimes where police are more likely to make an arrest on the spot, such as in cases of men threatening physical harm to women. These types of cases more often involve spouses or intimates, and so prosecutors might have considered the higher odds of victims subsequently dropping charges against their assailants in such cases. Similarly, any incident involving a victim where both the suspect and the victim are present when the police arrive might be more likely to result in an on-the-scene arrest at the victim's request. As tempers cool, however, victims may reconsider their interest in filing formal charges. Thus, failure to actually interview prosecutors in order to verify the causal nature of the empirical relationships leaves open the question of causality.

Somewhat related to the above is the common tendency in these types of studies to infer prosecutorial motives based on analyses of imperfect measures. All empiricists do this to some extent, but some tend to be bolder than others in ascribing greater meaning to statistical findings. There are both conceptual and mathematical reasons why theories can never be "proven" in the social sciences, and this is a good example of one conceptual reason. Albonetti's "uncertainty avoidance" theory is an explanation of prosecutorial decision-making and motivation. Rigorous tests of such a theory requires more direct measures of prosecutors' *intentions*, perhaps with self-report data from prosecutors, in order to avoid *inferences* of intentions based on the evidence measures examined by Albonetti. In other words, much of her discussion regarding "support" for the uncertainty avoidance perspective involved inferences made from the significant empirical relationships to the mind-sets of prosecutors. Whether prosecutors were consciously driven by the goal of reducing uncertainty was never established, and many of the significant relationships found by Albonetti had alternate interpretations. For example, Albonetti interpreted the findings for exculpatory evidence as suggesting that prosecutors were less likely to charge suspects in cases with such evidence because the odds of winning a guilty verdict at trial were weaker. This interpretation implied that the motivation of these prosecutors was to always formally charge defendants, regardless of their own assessments of a suspect's actual guilt. Exculpatory evidence would raise doubts in the minds of jurors regarding whether the suspect actually committed the crime, but would not such evidence also raise doubts in the prosecutor's mind regarding a suspect's guilt? Albonetti's theory assumes that prosecutors' motivations were geared only toward obtaining convictions rather than pursuing the truth of a case. While this might be true once charges were filed, there is a real possibility that prosecutors failed to prosecute because it was the "right" thing to do. Again, such inferences to uncertainty avoidance might have been stronger if backed up with some *ethnography* of the court under study.

Significance and Subsequent Research

Albonetti's findings, particularly the strength of some of the relationships she examined, demonstrated the utility of conducting *quantitative* analyses of decision points prior to sentencing, thereby defusing potential criticisms of her deterministic approach. More broadly, her work underscored the relevance of examining stages of case processing prior to sentencing due to the less visible nature of those decisions (see also LaFree 1985, Petersilia 1983, Spohn et al. 1987, Zatz 1985). Focusing only on sentencing as a measure of how severely a criminal defendant is treated by the courts ignores the treatment of all other defendants who do not reach the sentencing stage. Although the treatment of non-convicted defendants is clearly less severe relative to those who are convicted, each stage of case processing still imposes a form of punishment on the defendant by forcing him or her to endure some manner of inconvenience (Feeley 1979). Dispositions that "push" a defendant further into the system, such as filing formal charges and full prosecution, might be considered less favorable for defendants compared to the respective alternatives of not filing charges and subsequently dropping formal charges. Albonetti established that empirical analyses of prosecutorial decision-making might add considerably to our understanding of how discretionary decision-making affects defendants *throughout* the system of case processing.

Albonetti's study had a significant impact on subsequent quantitative research on case processing in general, and on disparities in case processing based on the race and ethnicity of defendants in particular, including her own work on the guilty plea process. For example, in a study of the guilty plea process in Norfolk, Virginia, Albonetti (1990) found significant race differences in the odds of pleading guilty. Specifically, the effects on pleading guilty of being single, being represented by court-appointed counsel, using a weapon, having a prior felony record, and having fewer charges differed between African American and white defendants. Guilty pleas were less common among African Americans with more prior felony convictions; yet prior record was *not* a predictor of guilty pleas for whites. Also, African Americans with more charges were *more* likely to plead guilty, whereas whites with more charges were *less* likely to do so. Albonetti speculated that African Americans with more priors might have been less willing to plead guilty because they did not trust the process and feared harsh sentences. In contrast, attorneys might have "encouraged" guilty pleas for African Americans with more *charges* if prosecutors saw them as dangerous and wanted to secure their convictions through plea bargains.

In related studies conducted by other scholars, Malcolm Holmes, Howard Daudistel, and Ronald Farrell (1987) found that African Americans in Delaware County, Pennsylvania, were *more* likely than whites to obtain charge reductions in plea agreements, perhaps due to the initial overcharging of African Americans. By contrast, these authors found no differences in charge reductions between Anglos and Latinos in Pima County, Arizona. Terance Miethe and Charles Moore (1986), however, found that African Americans charged with more serious offenses were less likely than whites to receive negotiated sentences in Minnesota courts. In a study of bail decisions, Gary LaFree (1985) found that Latinos received more favorable pretrial release decisions than whites in Tucson, Arizona, but less favorable decisions in El Paso County, Texas (perhaps due to differences in language barriers between the two jurisdictions which, in turn, might have interfered with a Latino defendant's ability to comprehend the proceedings). As a final example, Cassia Spohn, John Gruhl, and Susan Welch (1987) found no significant ethnic differences in likelihoods of subsequently dropped charges in Los Angeles, but they did find that Latino males had their charges *rejected* by the prosecutor less often than Anglo males (perhaps because charge rejections were subjected to less scrutiny by the court compared to subsequently dropped charges).

Albonetti eventually extended her theoretical framework of "uncertainty avoidance" to an understanding of judicial discretion and possible disparities in sentencing based on the race of defendants (Albonetti 1991). Just as prosecutors seek to reduce uncertainty in the key decisions upon which they are evaluated, such as whether to formally charge a suspect, judges also seek to reduce uncertainty in the decisions that matter most in the public's eyes, such as whether a sentence is appropriate for protecting the community. Similar to prosecutors who rely on particular case characteristics in order to improve prediction of their success if they should pursue formal charges against a defendant, thus reducing uncertainty in their decision to prosecute, judges also rely on particular "cues" which might suggest whether a defendant should be incarcerated in order to protect the community. An important distinction between these court actors, however, is that prosecutors might rely solely on legal factors in their decisions based on their unique goal of enhancing their own credibility to others *within* the system, yet judges might introduce their own biases and stereotypes regarding "dangerous" offenders based on their distinct goal of enhancing their credibility in the eyes of the public. Racial bias in treatment, therefore, might be more likely to emerge at the sentencing stage due to judges' considerations of a defendant's race as an indicator of risk. This particular application of uncertainty avoidance incorporates an element of conflict theory, but in a more subtle and realistic manner. That is, racial disparities in sentencing might not be a consequence of *overt* bias due to conscious efforts by judges to reduce competition for scarce economic resources, but instead might result from subconscious biases rooted in societal stereotypes of criminal offenders. Under pressure to dispose of cases efficiently, and lacking perfect knowledge of offenders' amenability to rehabilitation or likelihood of recidivism, sentencing judges instinctively default to criminal stereotypes in assessing threat, and young, African American males could be more readily regarded as falling into a high-risk category. Similarly, *unemployed* (and young) minorities could face higher odds of incarceration and longer sentences if their lack of gainful employment combined with minority status flags them as "social dynamite" (Spitzer 1975), or individuals whose social "failure" makes them potentially unstable in the eyes of sentencing judges (Steffensmeier et al. 1998). The implication of this argument is that it is not African Americans *in general* who are biased against, but particular subgroups of African Americans who possess other characteristics that, in conjunction with race, constitute these criminal offender stereotypes that are reinforced by the media and others with less tolerance for ambiguity. The argument subsequently became a focus of most research on sentencing disparities.

Earlier we mentioned that court studies can be divided into two broad camps reflecting a more qualitative focus on court organization and the dynamics of criminal case processing versus a more *quantitative* focus on criminal case outcomes and the factors that affect those outcomes. Albonetti's work might be considered a merging of these two areas, where she used quantitative methods to examine factors that affect case processing decisions prior to sentencing in order to better understand how attorneys exercise their discretion. Her focus on decision points prior to sentencing taps into the dynamics of case processing because such decisions are more discretionary than sentencing, yet they ultimately culminate to shape the pool of convicted defendants eligible to be sentenced.

Albonetti's efforts to model prosecutorial discretion were very useful and well received. As a result, she has contributed greatly to this body of research and to scholarly interest in quantitative research on decision points prior to sentencing (ranging from prosecutors' decisions to initially file formal charges against arrested suspects to the magnitude of charge reductions between indictment and conviction). Her work has also been more realistically framed relative to the works of other sociologists, who often ground their research in a conflict perspective, thus offering a more credible perspective to policy makers. This might have helped to offset her willingness to subject such topics to quantitative analysis, at least in the eyes of some court scholars who have not placed much faith in a deterministic approach to studying case processing.

References

Albonetti, C. (1987). "Prosecutorial Discretion: The Effects of Uncertainty." *Law and Society Review* 21:291–313.

Albonetti, C. (1990). "Race and the Probability of Pleading Guilty." *Journal of Quantitative Criminology* 6:315–34.

Albonetti, C. (1991). "An Integration of Theories to Explain Judicial Discretion." *Social Problems* 38:247–66.

Alschuler, A. (1975). "The Defense Attorney's Role in Plea Bargaining." *Yale Law Journal* 84:1179–1314.

Blumberg, A. (1967). "The Practice of Law as a Confidence Game: Organizational Cooptation of a Profession." *Law and Society Review* 1:15–39.

Eisenstein, J., and H. Jacob (1977). *Felony Justice: An Organizational Analysis of Criminal Courts.* Boston: Little, Brown.

Feeley, M. (1979). *The Process is the Punishment.* New York: Russell Sage.

Holmes, M., H. Daudistel, and R. Farrell (1987). "Determinants of Charge Reductions and Final Dispositions in Cases of Burglary and Robbery." *Journal of Research in Crime and Delinquency* 24:233–54.

LaFree, G. (1985). "Official Reactions to Hispanic Defendants in the Southwest." *Journal of Research in Crime and Delinquency* 22:213–37.

Mather, L. (1979). *Plea Bargaining or Trial?* Lexington, MA: Lexington Books.

March, J., and H. Simon (1958). *Organizations.* New York: Wiley.

Miethe, T., and C. Moore (1986). "Racial Differences in Criminal Processing: The Consequences of Model Selection on Conclusions About Differential Treatment." *Sociological Quarterly* 27:217–37.

Miller, F. (1969). *Prosecution: The Decision to Charge a Suspect with a Crime.* Boston: Little, Brown.

Neubauer, D. (1974). "After the Arrest: The Charging Decision in Prairie City." *Law and Society Review* 8:495–517.

Petersilia, J. (1983). *Racial Disparities in the Criminal Justice System.* Santa Monica, CA: Rand.

Spitzer, S. (1975). "Toward a Marxian Theory of Deviance." *Social Problems* 22: 638–51.

Spohn, C., J. Gruhl, and S. Welch (1987). "The Impact of the Ethnicity and Gender of Defendants on the Decision to Reject or Dismiss Felony Charges." *Criminology* 25:175–91.

Steffensmeier, D., J. Ulmer, and J. Kramer (1998). "The Interaction of Race, Gender, and Age in Criminal Sentencing: The Punishment Cost of Being Young, Black, and Male." *Criminology* 36:763–97.

Sudnow, D. (1965). "Normal Crimes: Sociological Features of the Penal Code in a Public Defender Office." *Social Problems* 12:255–76.

Swigert, V., and R. Farrell (1977). "Normal Homicides and the Law." *American Sociological Review* 42:16–32.

Thompson, J. (1967). *Organizations in Action.* New York: McGraw Hill.

Ulmer, J. (1997). *Social Worlds of Sentencing: Court Communities under Sentencing Guidelines.* Albany: SUNY Press.

Zatz, M. (1985). "Pleas, Priors, and Prison: Racial/ Ethnic Differences in Sentencing." *Social Science Research* 14:169–93.

Further Reading

Joseph, R. (1975). "Review Ability of Prosecutorial Discretion: Failure to Prosecute." *Columbia Law Review* 75:130–61.

LaFave, W. (1970). "The Prosecutor's Discretion in the United States." *American Journal of Comparative Law* 18:532–48.

2

The Guilty Plea Process

The vast majority of convicted defendants choose to plead guilty as opposed to exercising their constitutional right to trial and challenging the state's accusations in front of a judge and a jury. Although not formally documented in any publication, we have seen anywhere from 95 to 99 percent of all felony case convictions consist of guilty pleas in various jurisdictions across the United States. This fact tends to fly in the face of the public's image that trials are the dominant mode of criminal case disposal (although trials can take up an enormous amount of time and resources even when they constitute fewer than 5% of all convictions). Such a scenario necessarily begs the question of *why* most defendants are willing to simply plead guilty rather than fight the charges against them. The answers to this question, in a nutshell, are that most defendants are in fact guilty and can engage in the process of *plea bargaining* in order to obtain less severe sentences relative to what they would otherwise get if they were convicted at trial. Plea bargaining involves negotiations between the defense and the prosecution that ultimately lead to an agreement, subject to judicial approval, whereby a defendant agrees to plead guilty in exchange for a reduced charge and/or sentence. *Charge bargaining* involves reducing the severity of the formal charges filed by the prosecutor, which necessarily results in a reduced sentence. *Sentence bargaining* focuses solely on reducing the sentence that corresponds with the original charges (which is not feasible in states with mandatory sentencing guidelines). It must also be recognized that a fair number of defendants simply plead guilty to the original charges at their arraignment. Even in those cases, however, their sentences are more likely to be reduced as a "reward" for not wasting the court's time and resources. Given that most convictions are obtained via guilty pleas rather than trials, both scholars and practitioners have raised general concerns regarding whether the guilty plea process is counterintuitive to due process and just deserts, and more specific concerns about how the process might be coercive to defendants and ultimately lead to the conviction of innocent persons. Some of the most interesting *ethnographic* research on courts has focused on these issues, providing us with detailed perspectives on the subject offered by defense attorneys, prosecutors, and, most importantly, by defendants.

"GOING RATE" SENTENCES FOR DEFENDANTS WHO PLEAD GUILTY: HOW DO ATTORNEYS USE THE PENAL CODE IN CASE PROCESSING?

Sudnow, D. (1965). "Normal Crimes: Sociological Features of the Penal Code in a Public Defender Office." *Social Problems* 12:255–76.

Background

Arrested suspects who cannot afford to hire a private defense lawyer must be allowed access to legal representation. This may involve the appointment by the court of a private attorney who receives compensation for their work in the form of court fees, or it may involve representation by a salaried attorney from a Public Defenders Office. Although found in only one-third of all counties in the United States, public defenders represent over two-thirds of all indigent defendants because these offices are found in most metropolitan counties. As a consequence, public defenders are overworked and underpaid. Whereas private attorneys, especially those working in large law firms, are typically of higher socioeconomic status (SES) and are drawn from more prestigious law schools, public defenders (and other pro bono attorneys) are more likely to come from lower status law schools and may not possess the skills of more savvy trial attorneys. This situation has generated concern that indigent clients are unable to take full advantage of their constitutional rights if public defenders are more concerned with moving their caseloads as opposed to providing their clients with the best possible legal defense. Scholars have paid considerable attention to this issue, especially with regard to the guilty plea process and how attorneys may use plea bargaining to avoid time-consuming trials. This situation ultimately shapes case outcomes, creating a situation where a defendant's SES becomes linked to their odds of being convicted and the severity of their sentences. The very notion that case outcomes are tied to non-legal factors such as a defendant's economic status and possibly his race or ethnicity, in areas where minorities are disproportionately overrepresented in the poverty class, is contradictory to the notion of "blind justice" and equal due process for all persons accused of committing crimes.

Concerns about the equitable application of due process rights emerged almost as soon as these rights appeared, but the attention of academics toward this issue escalated during the 1960s and 1970s. Perhaps this comes as no surprise, since the 1960s marked the heyday of political liberalism, greater public awareness of human inequalities and the oppression of minorities and women (made possible by the civil rights movement, the women's movement for equal rights with men, and skepticism regarding United States involvement in Vietnam), and attention by a more liberal Supreme Court toward the physical and psychological abuses endured by prison inmates. Academic interest in the treatment of criminal defendants seemed to grow most noticeably among sociologists, perhaps because political scientists and legal scholars were following these issues already, but the interest of sociologists brought unique perspectives to the topic. The three major paradigms of sociology, namely symbolic interactionism, conflict theory, and structural functionalism, were all brought to bear on the topic. Due to the more liberal era, however, these discussions were grounded primarily in the conflict and symbolic interactionist perspectives. In particular, the idea that poor defendants are often stereotyped and "labeled" by government officials in order to fit with their preconceived notions of life among the underclass led to some of the more interesting explanations for why inequities exist in the court system. The inherent problem with such perspectives, however, is the inability to empirically assess their validity. David Sudnow offered one of the first and more compelling *ethnographic* studies of the topic which subsequently led to academic interest in court cultures, the dynamics of case processing, and the disparate treatment of criminal defendants based on their class status.

The Study

In order to provide a more empirical approach to evaluating the relevance of symbolic interactionism for an understanding of how the penal code is perceived and used in the administration of justice, Sudnow (1965) carried out an *ethnographic* study of attorneys working in a Public Defenders Office in an urban California jurisdiction. Ethnography involves the *qualitative* study of social groups or (sub)cultures by which researchers compile detailed descriptions of processes and outcomes related to the topics of interest. Sudnow observed and recorded the interactions between public defenders and their clients, interactions between public defenders and prosecutors, and court proceedings for both trials and guilty plea submissions. These observations took place in both the Public Defenders Office and in courtrooms, encompassing the types of cases dealt with by public defenders, the perceptions of attorneys toward the defendants involved in those cases, perceptions of attorneys toward their jobs, working relationships between public defenders and prosecutors, and how all of these factors ultimately affected case processing. He synthesized this information to generate a symbolic interactionist perspective of case processing. Critical to the success of this endeavor was Sudnow's objectivity in making and recording his observations. Without a dispassionate orientation, a researcher runs the risk of adopting a subject's perspective and definition of his or her social world. This, in turn, can bias how these observations are recorded and subsequently interpreted. While the possibility of subjective interpretation is a common criticism of ethnographic research, Sudnow's *third-party observational* approach is superior to interviews in this regard because he did not actually participate in any of the recorded dialogues.

Sudnow's work preceded all of the more frequently cited *ethnographic* studies of case processing and the use of discretion by court actors, yet Sudnow contributed to the ideas of many of those researchers by capturing several themes that ultimately became important for academic discussions of court actors' perceptions of offenders, how those perceptions are formed, their impact on court dispositions (particularly plea bargaining) which potentially feed extra-legal disparities in case outcomes, the use and abuse of discretion in case processing, and what this all meant for the potential successes and failures of legal reforms designed to create more formal rationality in legal decision-making. His work offered valuable insights into a topic that remains hotly debated today, namely the role of a defendant's personal attributes in case processing and outcome. Although a symbolic interactionist ("labeling") perspective was most often used to predict greater *dis*advantages to more socially and economically disadvantaged defendants, Sudnow's work suggested that how attorneys stereotype offenders might actually generate more lenient treatment of particular groups of "disadvantaged" defendants who engaged in particular types of large-volume crimes.

Findings

Sudnow set out to specifically understand how the penal code was applied by public defenders on a routine basis, the role of plea bargaining in this process, the quality of representation offered to the accused and the uniformity of representation across defendants, and the processes involved in preparing a defense. He began with a very simple integration of two basic ideas, the fact that most cases were disposed of *without* formal trials and the limitations of the penal code (using the common scenario of "necessary included lesser offenses" and how vague the penal code was regarding their interpretation), in order to underscore the discretionary nature of case processing which could generate more or less favorable outcomes for defendants. It was in their interpretations of the penal code that public defenders acted on their stereotypes of both particular types of offenses and offenders in order to guide their decisions regarding plea agreements. As Sudnow observed, many times defendants plead guilty to offenses that would not even be formally considered as "lesser included offenses" in the penal code (such as reducing "burglary" to "petty theft," even though the former refers to removing money or property from a physical structure, whereas the latter refers to theft of money or property from a person). The processes guiding these types of agreements, therefore, fell outside legitimate interpretations of the penal code and may have reflected instead other commonly shared values of attorneys stemming from their unique "cultural" goals, such as the need to persuade offenders to plead guilty in order to move caseloads and avoid time-consuming trials. If not driven by formal (legal) rationality, however, these practices must be legitimized in other ways by attorneys. Sudnow further described how attorneys came to rationalize the dramatic reductions in charges that took place in the guilty plea process. His focus centered on how these attorneys derived and acted on stereotyped perceptions of offenders involved in large-volume crimes, which was an essential ingredient to efficient case processing when attorneys had neither the time nor resources to carefully scrutinize the particular characteristics and circumstances surrounding every offense. For example, the "typical" burglar was often apprehended for petty theft, thereby justifying the reduced charge as long as other cues were present and consistent with their stereotypes of the "typical" burglary. These characteristics or cues tapped the methods of the crime as well as attributes of offenders, victims, and places or areas where the crimes occurred. Yet, when asked to describe these offenders, attorneys referred more generically to the stereotypical offense types as opposed to the attributes of offenders.

Particular types of plea agreements therefore became commonplace, with very little "negotiation" actually taking place. Sudnow labeled these types of large-volume cases "normal" crimes, which shared several common attributes. First and foremost, these cases reflected commonly committed crimes (e.g., burglary, narcotics offenses, petty theft, and drunkenness). Second, consistent with police encounters, these cases must be common in the courtroom. Third, the offenses must occur in "typical locales," or areas characterized by high rates of the offenses (particular neighborhoods, parks, bars, etc.). The ecological distribution of these crimes was also commonly linked to socioeconomic variables when described by attorneys. Fourth, the offenders themselves also shared some common criminal and social attributes, the latter also tied to socioeconomic variables. Sudnow also offered an important qualification to these criteria, noting that what was "typical" versus "atypical" could vary from one jurisdiction to the next. Nonetheless, these aspects of normal crimes helped public defenders to make sense of their caseloads and became part of the unique culture of the Public Defenders Office. Sudnow described how new attorneys were socialized in this regard in terms of how to recognize these characteristics and what the expectations were regarding the going-rate plea agreements.

Sudnow's description also focused heavily on the interactions between public defenders and prosecutors from the District Attorney's Office who also shared these stereotypes and expectations. These common definitions resulted in what he called "unstated recipes for reducing original charges to lesser offenses" (p. 262), and were the mainstay of efficient case processing. Such unstated agreements were an advantage to both sides, as prosecutors gained convictions while defense attorneys gained substantial charge reductions that (most often) kept their clients out of jail or prison. Sudnow was quick to point out that both sides were concerned with avoiding injustices, such as offenders not receiving their due punishment (prosecution) versus offenders facing significantly reduced punishments relative to those associated with the original offenses (defense). Related to the latter, it was the goal of achieving a significant reduction that accounted for the legal discrepancies between the original and convicted charges (i.e., discrepancies that were not evident in a strict interpretation of the penal code).

Despite the heavy focus on guilty plea "agreements" and what charge reductions were appropriate for which cases, Sudnow observed that public defenders did not communicate much with their clients. After the initial contact and interview, most interactions occurred in court. (On the rare occasions when public defenders had to prepare for trial, those preparations were minimal and occurred within an hour before the trial began.) A public defender's perceptions of a defendant, therefore, was formulated quickly based on the first interview. Sudnow underscored that public defenders conducted these interviews under the assumption that their client was guilty, even though a confession was never sought. Rather, attorneys sought "reasonableness" in the hopes of getting their client to agree to a guilty plea. The issue of "guilt" only came up when a defendant proclaimed his innocence.

During the interview, much was determined by the defendant's appearance that may or may not have been consistent with the aspects of "normal" crimes described above. The defendant's responses to questions about the circumstances of the offense also helped establish whether the offense fell into this group. By allowing the defendant to fill in any gaps to the attorney's story, the attorney could assess how different this particular defendant was relative to others brought in under the same charges. Once the public defender established the case as routine, the typical plea bargain was described to the defendant, often with an added "threat" of what might happen if the defendant took a chance at trial (conviction and sentencing on the original charge, a jury would not be as sympathetic, etc.). This process operated under the assumption that a defendant was typical, and it was only the information provided to the public defender by the district attorney that might flag a defendant as atypical. These "clues" were provided in the prosecutor's description of the original complaint, usually suggesting that the going-rate plea agreement would be too lenient in a particular case. Charge reductions may still have occurred, but generally the lesser charges were dropped while the most serious charge remained.

Based on the willingness of prosecutors to reduce charges, most of a public defender's trial caseload included defendants who refused to bargain (the so-called stubborn defendants). Public defenders did not enter a courtroom with the idea that they were actually going to win, but were concerned instead with following legal procedures and of avoiding a determination that they had behaved in a negligent fashion. "Stubborn" defendants stood in contrast to the much smaller proportion of defendants who went to trial because the crimes they committed were atypical or the way in which a crime was committed was atypical. Homicides, gang rapes, drug rings, and other more sensational crimes did not receive the label of "normal" crimes and, therefore, attorneys were less apt to follow the typical interview process described above. These were also cases that received a lot of media and public attention that could generate pressures to go to trial. These types of "atypical" cases were uncomfortable to attorneys because they must compete in the courtroom, yet for most of their cases they maintained cooperative working relationships. For this reason, so as not to sour working relationships, both the PD's office and the DA's office reserved particular (more "seasoned") attorneys for trials.

Sudnow concluded his article by noting that how attorneys actually perceived and used the penal code could be quite different than the substance of that code, and that an understanding of those perceptions and processes were critical for an empirical understanding of criminal case processing. Formal categories of crime, as stated in penal codes, were merely "shorthand reference terms" for what they actually reflected in the eyes of attorneys. As such, the relevance of a symbolic interactionist perspective was underscored without being formally stated by Sudnow. The social world of the public defender was driven by stereotypes of both "typical" crimes and "typical" offenders which, in conjunction with their somewhat "assembly line" view of case processing, helped attorneys to make sense of their world in order to expedite the movement of their caseloads through the system.

Limitations

Although Sudnow's work implied that many lower SES offenders actually received greater leniency in sentencing due to the reduced charges offered by attorneys who saw those cases as stereotypical of large-volume crimes, such observations stood in rather stark contrast to many academics' assumptions that lower SES defendants received *harsher* sentences in the courts. Ironically, while Sudnow adopted a symbolic interactionist perspective in his work, others have also used the same perspective to explain *more* severe outcomes for defendants with lower SES. This seeming contradiction is a result of a difference in the focus of research, however, where Sudnow applied the perspective to an understanding of court culture and plea bargaining practices while others have applied the perspective to an understanding of sentencing. Regarding the latter focus, the labeling perspective is often used to explain how judges may consider defendants' personal attributes when assessing risk for subsequent offending with limited available information (Albonetti 1991, 1997, Hawkins 1981, Steffensmeier et al. 1998). Defendants who fit judges' stereotypes of higher risk offenders may be sentenced more severely, such as individuals with characteristics reflecting greater social and economic disadvantage (Nobiling et al. 1998, Spohn and Holleran 2000, Steffensmeier et al. 1998). Darnell Hawkins (1981) referred to this type of decision-making as "perceptual shorthand," and Albonetti (1991) described how judges might consider extralegal attributes in order to reduce uncertainty in their decisions. Darrell Steffensmeier, Jeffery Ulmer, and John Kramer (1998) have also discussed these considerations in the context of "focal concerns" and how judges weighed the impact of their decisions for crime control. However, these perspectives seem to downplay the fact that the vast majority of cases are disposed with guilty pleas, and attorneys play a key role in the guilty plea process (as demonstrated by Sudnow). Judges must ultimately approve the charge reductions accompanying guilty pleas, but the fact that attorneys derive those bargains means that they have a powerful influence on the sentences ultimately distributed in court. In short, judicial perceptions of defendants may matter less than attorneys' perceptions.

Sudnow's use of *ethnography* and *qualitative* data also contrast with the trends in *quantitative* research, which followed soon after his work was published in 1965 and that contributed to the research focus on sentencing. Yet, ethnography remains a more powerful tool for understanding court cultures and may generate very different findings from quantitative research focusing solely on the sentencing stage. Whereas ethnography involves compiling detailed verbal accounts of various phenomena of interest, quantitative research involves gathering information and attaching numerical values to each piece. Variables are generated from these numerical data and then analyzed with statistics in order to make sense of the information for subsequent interpretation. In contrast to qualitative information, statistical information is a more general summary of the information gathered by a researcher. Whereas a researcher remains "open" to new information throughout a qualitative study, the types of information gathered from a quantitative study are determined before data collection begins. This is one reason why quantitative research is used primarily for *theory/hypothesis* testing, because such research involves collecting information that has already been described in a specifically worded hypothesis derived from a testable theory.

Sudnow's *ethnographic* approach is more compatible with *exploratory* research intended to generate an explanation for some unknown phenomenon, to provide new observations never previously described by others, and/or to understand how more general processes operate in unique environments (such as case processing in a public defender's office). It is for these reasons that related studies of case processing were often conducted in this fashion. Critical to the success of any ethnographic study, however, is a researcher's objectivity toward their subjects. The risk of becoming subjective during the course of study can be very high, and one method of reducing the risk is by relying on *third-party observations* rather than on interviews between the researcher and his subjects. Interviews permit subjects to try and convince the interviewer that their actions (e.g., how attorneys treat defendants) are logical in their social world and, if they are persuasive, might hinder a researcher's ability to convey an interpretation of process that is different (more objective) than the interpretation provided by their subjects. Interviews aside, such bias can easily emerge during the course of criminal justice research because many academics in the discipline are ex-practitioners, ideologues, or even ex-offenders with strong opinions regarding the topics they study.

Significance and Subsequent Research

Like Sudnow's study, research on court cultures and processes are most often ethnographic in their design and focus on the dynamics of case processing within particular sociopolitical contexts, especially regarding plea negotiations in large-volume cases (such as Sudnow's study of plea agreements in a California urban jurisdiction) (e.g., Alschuler 1983, Casper 1972, Eisenstein and Jacob 1977, Eisenstein et al. 1988, Fleming et al. 1992, Heumann 1978, Nardulli et al. 1988, Ulmer 1997). Ethnographic studies have focused less on actual sentences and more on the processes leading to them such as plea bargaining. Nevertheless, this approach has generated observations with clear implications for understanding extralegal disparities in case outcomes. However, predictions based on those arguments are not necessarily consistent with the common perspective described above that economically disadvantaged defendants actually receive harsher treatment by courts.

Studies of court cultures which followed Sudnow's also focused heavily on several of his themes, including the more "common" characteristics of criminal defendants, how court actors might have perceived those characteristics, and the more "typical" ecological contexts in which large-volume crimes occurred. These ethnographic accounts also described organizational and political influences on how attorneys and judges ("courtroom workgroups") processed large-volume cases within particular jurisdictions (e.g., Eisenstein and Jacob 1977, Nardulli et al. 1988). These cases must be moved quickly through the courts to moderate caseloads, and attorneys in some jurisdictions informally established "going rates" (Eisenstein and Jacob 1977) to accompany guilty pleas (see also Flemming et al. 1992, Emerson 1983, Nardulli et al. 1988, Ulmer 1997). These involved charge and or sentence recommendations that were often less severe than those formally recommended by law. Defendants may therefore plead guilty rather than take their chances at trial, saving the state both time and money. Very little negotiation actually takes place in these circumstances, which also saves valuable time, because the charges and sentences accompanying guilty pleas are most often understood (referred to by Nardulli et al. 1988, as "consensus mode" guilty pleas). Note how closely these ideas coincide with Sudnow's observations.

Some scholars have also pursued more heavily the idea that "atypical" defendants, or those who do not fit Sudnow's concept of "normal crime," might be treated more severely by the courts. As described by Farrell and Holmes (1991), when faced with atypical defendants, such as individuals of higher SES, attorneys may spend more time evaluating culpability, future risk, and appropriate outcomes because such evaluations are not readily dictated by any preconceptions. This opens the possibility that atypical defendants could experience outcomes that differ significantly from informal going rates, but whether these outcomes are more or less severe depends on the argument. Case outcomes for atypical defendants could be more severe if judges maintain higher expectations of these individuals and are less likely to tolerate excuses for their behaviors (Peterson and Hagan 1984, Weisburd et al. 1991, Wheeler et al. 1982), or if atypical defendants are more likely to risk trials and face sentences that approximate those recommended by law (relative to going rates that accompany guilty pleas) (Eisenstein and Jacob 1977, Emerson 1983, Nardulli et al. 1988, Ulmer 1997). Atypical defendants could also experience more severe outcomes if refusal to negotiate leads to criminal investigations uncovering more evidence of culpability, providing the state with greater leverage in subsequent negotiations. Reluctance to initially accept a plea could also lead to harsher treatment even if these defendants subsequently plead guilty. Eisenstein and Jacob (1977) found that, in Chicago, prosecutors offered less attractive plea bargains as trial dates approached. By contrast, criminal investigations involving atypical defendants could lead to *less* severe outcomes if details about a defendant's background are revealed that either reinforce preconceptions that the offense might have been an aberration in the life of an otherwise law-abiding citizen, or if uncovered details raise questions about guilt (Farrell and Swigert 1978). Extrapolations of arguments found in this literature therefore leave open the possibility that relationships between extralegal characteristics of defendants and case outcomes may operate to the advantage or disadvantage of higher status defendants. This stands in contrast to extant *quantitative* studies most often grounded in theories leading to the prediction of harsher treatment for persons with lower status.

Also similar to Sudnow's work, discussions of large-volume crimes offered by Eisenstein and Jacob (1977), Roy Flemming et al. (1992) and Peter Nardulli et al. (1988) included mention of more typical ecological contexts in which these crimes occurred, such as poor or poverty-stricken neighborhoods, further demonstrating the relevance of considering neighborhood characteristics as "defendant related factors" (Ulmer 1997).

Scholars adopting a quantitative approach have argued that court actors' stereotypes of defendants are fed by class status indicators, such as a defendant's race and economic status. Sudnow's (1965) observation that "ecological patterns (of normal crime) are seen as related to socioeconomic variables and these in turn to typical modes of criminal and noncriminal activities" (p. 261) further underscored the idea that such class-based stereotypes included the social and economic attributes of the neighborhoods in which these crimes occurred. However, in contrast to arguments most often found in the quantitative studies, arguments derived from the literature on court communities left open the possibility that defendants from lower SES neighborhoods could be treated more leniently (as implied by Sudnow).

As noted previously, the second research focus on empirical links between extralegal characteristics of defendants and case outcomes are more often quantitative in design. Scholars of this approach directly examine extralegal disparities expected under particular theories, but do not directly examine the underlying social and political processes of interest to scholars like Sudnow. Nonetheless, a focus on disparate treatment based on extralegal characteristics is consistent with arguments of how case processing practices vary by the sociopolitical context in which court actors operate (Eisenstein and Jacob 1977, Eisenstein et al. 1988, Fleming et al. 1992, Nardulli et al. 1988, Ulmer 1997). Moreover, several sentencing scholars have also underscored the importance of examining decision points prior to sentencing because of the less visible nature of those decisions (for example, Albonetti 1990, Spohn et al. 1987, Zatz 1985). This is consistent with Sudnow's appreciation for the role of plea bargaining in case outcomes.

References

Albonetti, C. (1990). "Race and the Probability of Pleading Guilty." *Journal of Quantitative Criminology* 6:315–34.

Alschuler, A. (1983). "Implementing the Criminal Defendant's Right to Trial: Alternatives to the Plea Bargaining System." *University of Chicago Law Review* 50:931–1050.

Casper, J. (1972). *Criminal Courts: The Defendant's Perspective.* Washington, DC: National Institute of Law Enforcement and Criminal Justice.

Eisenstein, J., and H. Jacob (1977). *Felony Justice: An Organizational Analysis of Criminal Courts.* Boston: Little, Brown.

Eisenstein, J., R. Flemming, and P. Nardulli (1988). *The Contours of Justice: Communities and Their Courts.* Boston: Little, Brown.

Emerson, R. (1983). "Holistic Effects in Social Control Decision Making." *Law and Society Review* 17:425–55.

Farrell, R., and M. Holmes (1993). "The Social and Cognitive Structure of Legal Decision Making." *Sociological Quarterly* 32:529–42.

Farrell, R., and V. Swigert (1978). "Prior Offense as a Self-Fulfilling Prophecy." *Law and Society Review* 12:437–53.

Flemming, R., Nardulli, P., and Eisenstein, J. (1993). *The Craft of Justice: Work and Politics in Criminal Court Communities.* Philadelphia: University of Pennsylvania Press.

Hawkins, D. (1981). "Trends in Black-White Imprisonment: Changing Conceptions of Race or Changing Patterns of Social Control." *Crime and Social Justice* 24:187–209.

Heumann, M. (1978). *Plea Bargaining: The Experiences of Prosecutors, Judges, and Defense Attorneys.* Chicago: University of Chicago Press.

Nardulli, P., Eisenstein, J., and Flemming, R. (1988). *Tenor of Justice: Criminal Courts and the Guilty Plea Process.* University of Illinois Press, Urbana.

Peterson, R., and J. Hagan (1984). "Changing Conceptions of Race: Towards an Account of Anomalous Findings of Sentencing Research." *American Sociological Review* 49:56-70.

Spohn, C., J. Gruhl, and S. Welch (1987). "The Impact of Ethnicity and Gender of Defendants on the Decision to Reject or Dismiss Felony Charges." *Criminology* 25:175–91.

Steffensmeier, D., J. Ulmer, and J. Kramer (1998). The Interaction of Race, Gender, and Age in Criminal Sentencing: The Punishment Cost of Being Young, Black, and Male. *Criminology* 36:763–97.

Sudnow, D. (1965). "Normal Crimes: Sociological Features of the Penal Code in a Public Defender Office." *Social Problems* 12:255–76.

Ulmer, J. (1997). *Social Worlds of Sentencing: Court Communities Under Sentencing Guidelines.* Albany: SUNY Press.

Weisburd, D., S. Wheeler, E. Waring, and N. Bale (1991). *Crimes of the Middle Class.* New Haven, CT:Yale UP.

Wheeler. S., D. Weisburd, and N. Bode (1982). "Sentencing the White-collar Offender: Rhetoric and Reality." *American Sociological Review* 47:541–659.

Zatz, M. (1985). "Pleas, Priors, and Prison: Racial/ethnic Differences in Sentencing." *Social Science Research* 14:169–93.

Further Reading

Blumberg, A. (1967). *Criminal Justice.* Chicago: Quadrangle.

Cressey, D. (1951). "Criminological Research and the Definition of Crimes." *American Journal of Sociology* 56:546–51.

Newman, D. (1956). "Pleading Guilty for Considerations." *Journal of Criminal Law, Criminology, and Police Science* 46:780–90.

THE DEFENSE ATTORNEY'S ROLE IN PLEA BARGAINING: ARE DEFENDANTS PRESSURED BY THEIR OWN ATTORNEYS TO PLEAD GUILTY?

Alschuler, A. (1975). "The Defense Attorney's Role in Plea Bargaining." *Yale Law Journal*84:1179–1314.

Background

As mentioned previously, guilty pleas are the dominant means to convict defendants and account for over 95 percent of all convictions. Although we take this for granted today, and consequently very little academic attention is currently paid to the issue, there was once much controversy over the ethics of attorneys encouraging their clients to forego their constitutional right to trial. This concern generated some of the most interesting *ethnographies* in court research to date. These studies were invaluable, not so much for the ethical discussions of plea bargaining per se, but for the more realistic descriptions of criminal courts, court politics, and court participants. These were the studies that changed our images of courts from being fair and impartial arbiters of justice to fallible organizations controlled by individuals who sometimes do not have the best interests of their clients in mind. The seemingly heavy focus of these works on plea bargaining, written primarily between the mid-1960s and late 1970s, reflected academics' questions regarding the wisdom of the American Bar Association and the President's Commission on Law Enforcement and Administration of Justice in their official approval of plea bargaining in 1967. (The Supreme Court also weighed in on the issue, declaring its constitutionality in 1971.) Scholars were critical of the fact that guilty pleas were the dominant mode of case disposition, which also contrasted with the public's conception of how business is conducted in our courts. Law schools do not even educate students about the underlying politics of the guilty plea process.

Plea bargaining occurs when a defendant submits a plea of "guilty" in exchange for reduced charges and/or a reduced sentence from the court. (Sentences are "reduced" relative to what the law recommends as well as what is likely to be handed out at trial.) The primary concerns of legal scholars with plea bargaining deal with the questionable ethnics surrounding how guilty pleas are solicited from defendants. After all, a defendant who pleads guilty implicitly agrees to forego their constitutional right to trial, and unlike a trial conviction s/he cannot appeal the verdict. There are other potential limitations as well, as articulated by Jonathan Casper (1972). First, plea bargaining contributes to different sentences for similarly situated offenders charged with the same crimes. Second, there is a risk under such a system that innocent persons will admit guilt out of fear of facing harsher sentences if convicted at trial. Third, sentences are not based on meaningful goals such as rehabilitation or even retribution. Fourth, the process might convey a sense of corruption to the defendant (an issue of key importance to Alschuler). Finally, there is very little formal control over the process.

On the other hand, several justifications for plea bargaining have been put forth as well (see also Casper 1972). First, there are not enough available resources to take all cases to trial without bottlenecking the system. Second, plea bargaining helps defendants to avoid mandatory sentences that may be overly severe in particular cases due to the circumstances of the case. Third, the process allows trial resources to be reserved for cases where the guilt of a suspect is truly in question. Fourth, defendants who acknowledge their guilt might be experiencing a first step toward their rehabilitation and therefore should be "rewarded" with a reduced sentence. Finally, the defendant actively participates in the plea bargaining process, thus providing input into his own punishment and (possibly) reducing his cynicism toward legal authority.

Albert Alschuler wrote a series of three articles focusing on the roles of prosecutors, defense attorneys, and judges in plea bargaining. The combination of these articles constitutes a scathing critique of the guilty plea process. The article described here has been cited in every subsequent (published) work on the topic, and it also offers some unique insights into defense attorneys that cannot be gleaned from the other studies discussed in this book. This is perhaps due to the scope of Alschuler's study, which included interviews with court participants across ten major cities in the United States. His observations now represent common knowledge among court scholars, and no other study has been applied so broadly to the topic.

The Study

Alschuler (1975) began his article with the acknowledgment that guilty pleas (more specifically plea bargains) were far and away the most common means to convictions in the criminal courts, accounting for roughly 90 percent of all *felony* convictions in the courts under study during the late 1960s. Although safeguards were in place to ensure that defendants who pled guilty understood the ramifications of their actions, Alschuler set out to interview court participants in ten major cities in order to explore the utility of defense attorneys for protecting the accused in the plea bargaining process. These interviews were unstructured and, therefore, did not constitute "scientific" data.

Interviews were conducted between 1967 and 1968 in Boston, Chicago, Cleveland, Houston, Los Angeles, Manhattan, Oakland, Philadelphia, Pittsburgh, and San Francisco.

Alschuler's companion piece, "The Prosecutor's Role in Plea Bargaining," was published in 1968 and was based on the same interviews.

Findings

Alschuler began his article with the cynical observation that the only way a defense attorney could be financially successful, aside from being an excellent trial attorney, was to handle large numbers of clients. This meant that trials could not be the norm for such attorneys since they required too much time, and so they spent the majority of their time pleading cases. Alschuler went on to describe examples of attorneys with very lucrative careers who had not tried a case in years (he referred to these attorneys as "pleaders," consistent with the jargon used by other attorneys). Only a vast minority of these attorneys were truly dishonest, however, even though a good portion never actually intended to go to trial (but would go if and when pressed to do so). The primary problem with "pleaders" was that, due to their impatience and desire to move cases, they often settled for less attractive plea agreements relative to those secured by other attorneys who more actively argued and negotiated with prosecutors (such as threatening to go to trial and thereby opening up the opportunity for an appeal).

If they performed so poorly, then, why did defendants choose them as their attorneys? First, the bail bondsman often recommended the names of attorneys who provided the bondsman with a cut of his/her legal fees (recall our earlier discussion of the bail system examined by Foote 1954). Second, some jail and police personnel also made recommendations in order to receive kickbacks from the attorneys. Finally, these attorneys occasionally hung out in the jails in order to drum up business. How did the attorneys induce their clients to plead guilty? If a client admitted guilt to his attorney, the attorney might later return and claim that the prosecutor had an unbeatable case against him, whether true or not. If the client claimed innocence, the lawyer might have gone to great lengths to get a confession. Another tactic involved attorneys approaching family members who, once convinced that pleading guilty was the "right" thing to do, would persuade the relative to plead guilty. Equally reprehensible, some attorneys would exaggerate to their clients the severity of the sentence if convicted at trial, or claim that the prosecutor's offer for a bargain was exceptionally lenient when in fact it was the going rate. Alschuler pointed out the absurdity of how, when convicted defendants tried to challenge their guilty pleas as a result of this corruption by defense attorneys, courts refused to treat those pleas as invalid. As a result of a system that permitted lawyers to perform their jobs informally and in private, there were "extraordinary opportunities for dishonest lawyers" (p. 1198) to take advantage of defendants. Alschuler talked at length, for example, of how some attorneys charged lower fees to clients who they felt were likely to plead guilty, thus contributing to a self-fulfilling prophecy where the attorney worked even harder to secure the plea. Unlike the situation where a defendant could challenge the quality of an attorney's defense in the courtroom, the absence of any oversight in the guilty plea process made it virtually impossible for defendants to challenge the circumstances under which pleas were negotiated.

Even the most honest attorneys often preferred plea bargaining over the prospect of going to trial, especially when an attorney questioned his or her own abilities. Also, going to trial meant taking a chance, no matter how good the defense, since jurors and some judges could be persuaded by factors aside from the evidence. Submitting a guilty plea also meant that the defendant would never know if s/he would have been acquitted at trial, so it could not be questioned later on. Another situation sometimes faced by private attorneys (not public defenders) involved the same attorney representing two defendants involved in the same case. In such cases, the attorney could not treat his clients equally because s/he must have perceived one as more culpable than the other. Under a guilty plea system, this might have resulted in defense attorneys bargaining with prosecutors to drop the charges against one defendant in exchange for a guilty plea from the other. This situation was unlikely with public defenders because most trial courts automatically assigned different defenders to different defendants involved in the same case in order to avoid the appearance of a conflict of interest. Private attorneys seemed less concerned about this phenomenon simply because these attorneys gained financially from defending more clients, regardless of the case.

The observations above were made in relation to private defense attorneys, and Alschuler recognized that the guilty plea process favored the economic interests of those attorneys more than public defenders who were salaried. Nonetheless, both groups used guilty pleas to the same degree, which implied (perhaps) a different set of motivations for public defenders. For example, PDs dealt with more socially and economically disadvantaged defendants who often had prior records, which might have provided attorneys with the incentive to pursue plea bargains in order to reduce the odds of more severe sentences at trial resulting from the defendant's criminal histories and/or from potential biases by some jurors toward poor, minority defendants. Another unique situation faced by PDs was their greater familiarity with prosecutors due to courtroom assignments and having to face the same attorney day after day. Friendships developed between these attorneys, and consequently they may not have vigorously debated the facts of a case when settling on a plea bargain.

The relatively heavy caseloads of PDs, especially in the cities examined by Alschuler, may have also affected attorneys' interests in bargaining. The variety of cases under a defense attorney's watch on any given day meant that for every defendant the attorney fought vigorously for, another client's case did not receive the same attention. On the other hand, even defendants who received less attention by their PD may have still fared better in plea bargains relative to the clients of private defense lawyers due to the prosecutor's greater "trust" of a public defender. This extended into the area of Discovery, where prosecutors generally were more willing to disclose evidence to PDs as opposed to private attorneys. Such unofficial access could work against a defendant, however, if the PD was looking for evidence that would convince a defendant to plead guilty, and Alschuler speculated that this was why prosecutors were more willing to disclose their evidence to PDs (especially in the strongest cases against defendants).

Eisenstein and Jacob (1977) once observed that, in Chicago, delaying case dispositions led to less appealing bargains offered to defendants. Alschuler observed the opposite, where defense attorneys received better offers with the passage of time. This trend occurred because witnesses became impatient with so many court appearances, their memories faded, and they sometimes backed out of the process altogether. As the odds of conviction declined, the prosecutor's plea bargains became more attractive. Private lawyers were better able than PDs to take advantage of this, however, because of the greater difficulty PDs had in requesting continuances. PDs assigned to one courtroom for weeks at a time would attract suspicion by the prosecutor and the judge if they developed a pattern of requesting continuances. It was also not in the best interest of many PDs' clients to delay trial since many did not obtain bond and were held in custody during the interim (see also Foote 1954).

Attorneys also anticipated how receptive particular judges would be to specific bargains, and so they sought out the more "lenient" judges. Due to a selection bias where "tougher" judges conducted more trials (because they were less likely to approve more lenient plea agreements), private attorneys could "shop around" for more lenient judges who were sympathetic to particular bargains. This was an advantage for private lawyers, however, since PDs in most of the cities examined were assigned to courtrooms and could not choose their judge. On the other hand, PDs who were more likely to push for trial faced a different problem involving more lenient judges who placed pressure on them to bargain. Alschuler related many examples of the insulting comments directed at defense attorneys by judges. Judges varied to the extent they favored the guilty plea process, and those who saw plea bargaining as effective case management were more apt to ridicule attorneys who were resistant to bargaining. Incurring the judge's wrath was not in the best interest of the defense lawyer who had to work with the same judge day after day.

Public defenders were also more likely to maintain antagonistic relationships with their clients relative to private attorneys and their clients, perhaps because indigent defendants did not choose their lawyers and may have been bitter due to their greater social and economic disadvantages. These types of relations between PDs and their clients may have contributed to higher odds of plea bargaining if the defenders were generally less interested in the welfare of their clients.

Although the greater caseload pressures on PDs would sometimes interfere with the best interests of his or her clients, PDs sometimes used their caseloads as leverage for more lenient plea agreements. PDs had the ability to slow down case processing by threatening trials for some (if not all) of their cases. Even when prosecutors were not amenable to such threats, judges sometimes placed pressure on prosecutors to "cooperate" with PDs.

Alschuler also made an important distinction between PDs and other "appointed" attorneys, including attorneys in the community who were ordered by judges to defend indigent defendants as well as those who volunteered to do so. These particular attorneys sometimes did not fit well in a system driven by guilty pleas. First, such attorneys were often paid hourly and so may have opted for trials in order to increase their earnings. Second, due to their (typical) lack of experience in the criminal courts, they were often not privy to courtroom cultures and the informal norms surrounding plea negotiations.

The article concludes with a discussion of ethical issues related to plea bargaining in practice, the most salient of which involves a system that places pressure on the truly innocent defendant to plead guilty. Most attorneys who believed their clients to be innocent did not claim to pressure them into pleading guilty, although some defense attorneys did so when prosecutors offered very large concessions relative to what the laws dictated in such cases. Alschuler also noted a hypocrisy in the observations of defense attorneys, namely that these attorneys did not apply the same rule (of not pressuring "innocent" clients into pleading guilty) when defendants claimed to have acted in self-defense, or when they argued entrapment or that there was an absence of intent. Of the "innocent" defendants who were not pressured to plead guilty, however, some public defenders may have acted out of self-interest in order to avoid client accusations of ineffective representation.

Limitations

Alschuler's work is a very interesting and informative piece on the abuses of plea bargaining, although he admitted that it was not a scientific study. As such, his observations were potentially tainted by *selection bias*. Alschuler was always one of the harshest and most outspoken critics of plea bargaining, and this was reflected in the interview excerpts he chose to include in the article. These passages focused overwhelmingly on court participants who were critical of plea bargaining. No direct quotes were offered from the "dishonest" attorneys who he claimed were the strongest advocates of the guilty plea system. The reader is not informed about how many attorneys and judges were interviewed and what proportions of these groups were advocates of the process. This method of argumentation is persuasive but does not meet the standard of scientific rigor. Alschuler might have focused only on instances where defendants received raw deals. For all we know, the vast majority of his subjects might have been advocates of the process and the vast majority of defendants might have benefited from not going to trial. His arguments were made based on selected "evidence," not unlike the arguments constructed by ex-cons regarding what bad places prisons are. The primary drawback to this strategy of argumentation is that it is flawed by nature of not offering a solution. Just as prisoners-turned-academics tend to criticize the use of prisons without offering a solution (short of decarceration), Alschuler's arguments are more difficult to defend without offering a viable alternative to the guilty plea system.

One of the criticisms of plea bargaining noted earlier is the possibility that sentencing disparities might emerge based on the extralegal characteristics of defendants. Speculations such as these can only be evaluated empirically with official data on the sentences of defendants who plead guilty versus those convicted at trial, and such evaluations are *quantitative* in nature. Eisenstein and Jacob (1977), described in the next section, conducted both qualitative *and* quantitative research on the guilty plea process in three urban trial courts. Alschuler, on the other hand, was limited to evaluating this criticism based only on the observations of somewhat critical attorneys. Despite his approach, however, Alschuler's assessment of possible biases in plea negotiations based on the economic status of defendants was surprisingly neutral. When alluding to this issue, he commented that while public defenders had proportionately more indigent clients than private attorneys, both types of attorneys seemed to engage in plea bargaining to the same extent.

Thirty years have passed since Alschuler's publications on plea bargaining, yet since that time it appears that most criminal defendants have found plea bargaining no less palatable than going to trial. There are several possible reasons for this, including a Supreme Court ruling *after* Alschuler's work that outlawed judicial participation in plea negotiations. Alschuler's description of how judges placed pressures on attorneys to settle their cases underscored the potential of judges to abuse their power by coercing subordinates into ignoring defendants' legal interests. Without these pressures, defense attorneys are better able to serve the interests of their clients. With the prosecution and the defense as sole arbiters in negotiations, it is more realistic to assume that one party or the other would insist on a trial if a plea agreement did not improve the positions of *both* the defendant and the state.

A second possible reason why the system of plea bargaining was not subsequently challenged is that, according to plea bargaining advocates, such negotiations permit compromises on both sides of the case. The defense is better able to avoid the maximum punishment, thus permitting sentences that are more apt to "fit" the circumstances of cases and defendants. Prosecutors, in turn, can secure convictions without having to spend the resources necessary to create stronger cases for the courtroom. This last observation reflects the economic advantage of guilty pleas, where failure to offer such "rewards" could lead a majority of defendants to opt for trial which, in turn, would slow case processing to a snail's pace. The prospect of such a scenario is unlikely, even with the abolition of plea bargaining, because the practice might simply be driven underground as it was in Alaska (where plea negotiations were displaced to bench trial proceedings, nicknamed "slow pleas of guilty" by Alschuler).

No less important is the potential benefit of plea bargaining to a defendant who wishes to avoid the stigmatization and degradation of a trial. Labeling theorists argue that the criminal trial is nothing more than a ritual for publicly redefining a defendant's life as deviant, thereby applying a negative stigma to the defendant's reputation. This process generates greater cynicism on the part of defendants toward legal authority because they are faced with constantly having to defend themselves while under attack, sometimes for months at a time. Plea bargaining, by contrast, allows the defendant to actively participate in this redefinition which is not under public view and (usually) results in a less negative stigma.

Significance and Subsequent Research

The literature on plea bargaining that took a decidedly negative view of the process, such as Alschuler's work which began several years before the study described here was published, ultimately had a significant impact on Alaska's ban on plea bargaining in 1975. The ban specifically prohibited negotiations regarding charge or sentence reductions for all offenses. Interestingly, this resulted in only a 30 percent increase in the number of trials (Rubinstein and White 1979), implying that most defendants continued to plead guilty. (A 30% increase in trial rates translated into a relatively small number of trials in Alaskan courts.) A few years later, however, Lynn Mather (1979) described how many of the bench trials in Alaska had become forums for plea bargaining, or "slow pleas of guilty," where judges basically encouraged defendants to plead out. Alaska's ban continued until 1993 even though the practice of charge bargaining eventually reemerged before then and became commonplace across the state. Regardless, the official ban did not slow down case processing to an appreciable degree, contrary to what critics expected. The Alaska Judicial Council conducted two evaluations of the reform. The first evaluation was conducted five years after implementation, and the second was conducted 15 years after. Together they revealed that the reform was fairly successful in preventing charge bargaining for about 10 years. Prosecutors also became more effective at screening cases and conducting more thorough investigations, ultimately leading to stronger cases, because they could no longer count on plea bargaining in order to secure convictions in cases with weaker evidence. Court delays were actually reduced rather than lengthened, perhaps because of the elimination of prosecutors' tactics to schedule cases for trial in order to persuade defense attorneys to accept their offers (as described by Alschuler). Finally, the ban did not lead to harsher sentences for most crimes although it did coincide with more severe sentences for a small minority of offenses. By the mid-1980s, prosecutors did not maintain the negative attitudes toward bargaining that characterized the 1970s. This change in court culture eventually led to the repeal of the ban in 1993.

The Alaska "experiment" served to vindicate critics of plea bargaining, including Alschuler, because the strongest argument favoring the preservation of plea bargaining was the speculation that courts would slow down and bottleneck if negotiations were abolished. Alaska courts do not deal with the caseload volume of the cities included in Alschuler's study, but the fact that trials increased by 30 percent instead of 100 percent was very revealing about the actual impact a ban on plea bargaining would have in other states. The return to bargaining in Alaska did not reflect a need to address any problems that emerged as a result of the ban, but instead reflected the interests of prosecutors to avert trials whenever possible in order to increase their chances of obtaining convictions.

Alschuler was also one of the first scholars to provide insight into the realities of Herbert Packer's (1967) theory on *assembly-line justice*. Packer observed that the criminal court system in the United States represents a compromise between due process and crime control. The due process model emphasizes the legal protections offered to criminal suspects so as not to wrongly convict individuals (e.g., right to counsel, right to trial, right to appeal, etc.). It is grounded in the presumption of innocence and in protecting the rights of the accused. Advocates of the crime control perspective, by contrast, emphasize the public's protection from crime rather than the protection of suspects. This emphasis has two implications for court proceedings. First, the demand of case processing must meet the supply of cases that flood the courts, so case processing must be swift. Second, the rights of the accused need not be emphasized at the expense of protecting the public since the vast majority of suspects are factually guilty, assuming that police officers perform their jobs adequately. Therefore, a preoccupation with trials and appeals is not necessary because most cases can be handled expediently with plea bargaining. The best way to handle cases is through an "assembly line" process whereby cases are handled efficiently and disposed of quickly. The focal point of the crime control model is therefore the guilty plea whereas the focal point of the due process model is the trial.

Alschuler's in-depth interviews with prosecutors, defense attorneys, and judges (reflecting all three of his publications from the same study) offered a very realistic assessment of Packer's framework. Not only did he capture attorneys' preoccupations with the assembly-line model, he also underscored the ideological conflict between due process and crime control. Regarding the latter, even most defense attorneys presumed their clients to be guilty. Alschuler also provided an important qualification to Packer's theory although he did not himself make the connection. That is, Packer theorized that prosecutors who followed a crime control strategy would pay more attention to their decisions at intake regarding whether to pursue formal charges against an arrested suspect, and that they would be careful to pursue prosecutions only in cases involving little doubt about the suspects' guilt. Alschuler countered this idea by describing interviews where attorneys either knew their clients were innocent or strongly suspected that they were innocent yet agreed to plea bargain, so as to avoid harsher sentences if the client was found guilty at trial. Along with scholars such as Jon Casper (1972), James Eisenstein and Herbert Jacob (1977), Milton Heumann (1978), and Lynn Mather (1979), Alschuler's research inspired a movement within political science and legal studies to more carefully assess how the conflict between due process and crime control impacts both criminal defendants and public perceptions of justice.

Alschuler's work also raised questions regarding the impact of plea bargaining on sentencing disparities, or differences in the sentences administered to similarly situated defendants (i.e., those charged with the same offenses under similar case circumstances and with similar criminal histories). Sentences derived through negotiations are necessarily void of considerations of punishment philosophies such as retribution, deterrence, or rehabilitation. The odds of disparate sentences across similar cases are greater without such guiding philosophies. The common observation in related studies that sentences are more severe when defendants are convicted by juries as opposed to guilty pleas is the most obvious evidence of sentencing disparity (Tiffany et al. 1975), but even among defendants who plead guilty there is reason to believe that disparities will exist based on Alschuler's observations regarding factors that influence the magnitude of a deal, such as stubbornness on the part of the defense attorney to engage in negotiations, the amount of time since formal charges were initially filed, and the amount of evidence against a defendant. None of these considerations have anything to do with sentences dictated by legal statutes, yet they are fundamental to determining the sentences of over 95 percent of all convicted felons in the United States. Alschuler provided a very cynical view of a process that has only become even more prevalent since he wrote. The various perversions of justice he described are important nonetheless and have contributed to a relatively broad literature on legal cynicism, even if policy makers have since ignored his original observations.

References

Alschuler, A. (1975). "The Defense Attorney's Role in Plea Bargaining." *Yale Law Journal* 84:1179–1314.

Casper, J. (1972). *Criminal Courts: The Defendant's Perspective.* Washington, DC: National Institute of Law Enforcement and Criminal Justice.

Eisenstein, J., and H. Jacob (1977). *Felony Justice: An Organizational Analysis of Criminal Courts.* Boston: Little, Brown.

Heumann, M. (1978). *Plea Bargaining: The Experiences of Prosecutors, Judges, and Defense Attorneys.* Chicago: University of Chicago Press.

Mather, L. (1979). *Plea Bargaining or Trial? The Process of Criminal Case Disposition.* Boston: Lexington Books.

Packer, H. (1967). *The Limits of the Criminal Sanction.* Palo Alto, CA: Stanford UP.

Rubinstein, M., and T. White (1979). "Alaska's Ban on Plea Bargaining." *Law and Society Review* 13:367–83.

Tiffany, L., Y. Avichai, and G. Peters (1975). "A Statistical Analysis of Sentencing in Federal Courts: Defendants Convicted After Trial, 1967-68." *Journal of Legal Studies* 4:397–417.

Further Reading

Alschuler, A. (1968). "The Prosecutor's Role in Plea Bargaining." *University of Chicago Law Review* 36:50–112.

Alschuler, A. (1976). "The Trial Judge's Role in Plea Bargaining." *Columbia Law Review* 76:1059–1154.

Alschuler, A. (1979). "Plea Bargaining and Its History." *Columbia Law Review* 79:1-43.

ORGANIZATIONAL DIFFERENCES IN CASE PROCESSING ACROSS COURTS: HOW DOES COURT "CULTURE" INFLUENCE CASE PROCESSING?

Eisenstein, J. and H. Jacob (1977). *Felony Justice: An Organizational Analysis of Criminal Courts.* Boston: Little, Brown.

Background

Sudnow examined the dynamics of case processing in one particular court whereas Alschuler's study of 10 courts was much broader in scope. James Eisenstein and Herbert Jacob (1977) conducted a study that fell between these other two in scope. Theirs was an in-depth *ethnographic* study that examined and compared case processing across three urban trial courts of general jurisdiction (Baltimore, Chicago, and Detroit). In contrast to Alschuler, Eisenstein and Jacob conducted a more scientific study by supplementing attorney interviews with observations of court proceedings as well as *quantitative* analyses of court data. Consequently, their work stands as one of the most cited pieces to date on court organization and provided important insights into the realities of case processing and how these processes vary based on the sociopolitical climate of the court under study. Aside from their subsequent related works with various colleagues, one might argue that no one else has carried out research on the topic that reached their level of depth.

This work is a good example of some of the differences in perspectives and methods between political scientists and sociologists. In the area of courts, sociologists more often focus on case outcomes and sentencing (Sudnow being an exception) with research grounded in conflict and/or labeling perspectives, the assumption being that due process rights are more often violated for more socially and economically disadvantaged defendants which, in turn, translate into harsher sentences for these defendants. Sociologists are also more willing to conduct statistical *multivariate* analyses of sentencing with data spanning several courts. Political scientists, on the other hand, focus more on case processing and less on outcome (since process shapes outcome), and they generally appear more neutral on the subject and act less as ideologues and more as objective observers. They also tend to stick with *ethnography* while emphasizing differences between courts as opposed to lumping different courts together under the assumption that there are no differences in case processing across courts. Some political scientists are quite vocal in their criticisms of *quantitative* analyses of multiple courts. After all, as described by Eisenstein and Jacob, differences in the social and political environments of courts have important consequences for differences in disposition rates and how the guilty plea process operates, and so analyses of cases from different courts may only mask important court differences that could very well contribute to differences in the sentences for those cases. Part of what feeds the belief that courts should be examined separately is a perspective that court actors' perceptions of "reality" can differ even within the same environment and differences in the environments themselves contribute further to different perceptions *across* courts. Interestingly, much of their work has been interpreted by sociologists as evidence of disparity in treatment even though political scientists themselves are less apt to offer such interpretations of their own findings.

The Study

Perhaps no other work has demonstrated the above differences more than *Felony Justice* where, on the first page of the preface, the authors referred to many common beliefs about courts and case processing as "myths," such as the idea that most guilty pleas resulted from actual "negotiations" between attorneys, sentences were harsher for African Americans relative to whites, pretrial detention led to harsher sanctions, and public defenders were inferior to privately retained counsel. Although these observations remain in question and continue to be examined, Eisenstein and Jacob offered one of the most scholarly treatments of these topics. Sudnow (1965) was one of the first scholars to focus on the ideas that most cases were disposed of with guilty pleas and that very little verbal negotiation actually took place, but Eisenstein and Jacob really drove these ideas home with their comparisons of guilty plea rates and levels of negotiations across urban courts, and with their explanations for these differences from an organizational perspective.

Eisenstein and Jacob conducted extensive observations of court participants (prosecutors, defense attorneys, and judges) involved in felony case processing both in and outside of the courtroom. They were permitted to observe plea negotiations behind closed doors, from which they gathered the majority of their most important observations regarding courtroom workgroups. They deliberately selected the cities of Baltimore, Chicago, and Detroit because their focus was on plea bargaining in urban courts and they knew that these procedures differed across the three cities. They also noted that these cities had crime rates comparable to the other 25 largest cities in the United States. The authors compiled data on samples of defendants charged with felony crimes in order to provide some simple descriptions of each city's felony caseloads, noting that the courts did not compile such aggregate statistics. This was an important observation by itself because of the implications for subsequent *quantitative* research on case processing.

The authors defined courts as "permanent organizations" (p. 20), treating the plea bargaining process (specifically) and case processing (more generally) as a series of exchange relationships between attorneys and judges within an organizational context. In order to understand these relationships, one had to understand the goals of the organization (both formal and informal), the unique goals of each actor, and how participants endeavored to balance these different goals. As Eisenstein and Jacob demonstrated, there were commonalities in these goals across courts but there were also important differences shaped by differences in political ideologies and resource constraints. All of these factors influenced the behaviors of court actors which, in turn, shaped case processing and the extent to which actors "relied" on plea bargaining and the guilty plea process to balance the goals of prosecutors (who sought convictions), defense attorneys (who sought reduced charges and no prison time), judges (who did not want their cases appealed), and the system overall (the expeditious movement of existing cases in order to keep pace with the influx of new cases).

At the center of Eisenstein and Jacob's focus was the "courtroom workgroup," consisting of the prosecutor, defense attorney, and the judge. These were the individuals responsible for plea bargaining and moving felony caseloads while operating within the organizational boundaries noted above. The authors drew parallels between the courtroom workgroup and other organizational workgroups by noting that both are characterized by (a) authoritative relationships, (b) "influence" relationships (i.e., each actor impacts the decisions of others which, in turn, influences the authoritative relationships), (c) cohesion among members based on common goals, (d) specialization of roles within the workgroup, (e) the use of a variety of work techniques, (f) a variety of tasks, and (g) different degrees of stability and familiarity (p. 20). From the authors' organizational perspective, understanding differences in plea bargaining practices across the three courts could be understood by focusing on differences in the dynamics of courtroom workgroups across these courts.

Findings

Eisenstein and Jacob's study revealed important differences in plea bargaining practices between the three courts which they ultimately attributed to differences in the ideologies of and interactions between members of the courtroom workgroup. Specifically, they found the lowest rate of plea bargaining (and, consequently, the highest rate of trials) in Baltimore due to (a) the higher turnover rate of attorneys relative to the other two cities, (b) the relatively weaker supervision over junior staff in the prosecutor's office, and (c) the pervasive ideology favoring severe sanctions for convicted defendants. Greater transiency among attorneys in the system interfered with the ability of prosecutors and defense attorneys to get to know each other's preferences and tolerances for particular plea agreements in specific types of cases. It also interfered with an attorney's ability to learn what judges were willing to accept or reject as legitimate charge and/or sentence reductions which accompanied guilty pleas. According to Eisenstein and Jacob, judges had little tolerance for defense attorneys who did not understand their ideologies and who continued to test their limits on leniency. On the other hand, knowing what judges were willing to accept helped to facilitate case processing because attorneys understood the parameters of charge/sentence reductions and did not waste the judges' time. Judges who were unpredictable in this regard tended to delay the process because attorneys could not make decisions in anticipation of how a judge would likely perceive a recommended package. This was also related to the second contributing factor to fewer guilty pleas, namely the inability of judges to keep attorneys in check through proper supervision and communication. The weak supervision over junior staff by senior staff in the prosecutor's office was a problem due to the transiency of personnel, and junior staff members were more likely to make mistakes because they had difficulty grasping the negotiation process.

In contrast to Baltimore, there was much more cohesion among members of the courtroom workgroups in Chicago where value was placed on "reducing uncertainty and maintaining cohesion" (p. 124). These priorities were so much a part of the court culture that negotiation and accommodation became important elements in the socialization of new attorneys. Negotiation was seen as acceptable even though there were no notable pressures to bargain in order to expedite case processing. Nonetheless, guilty plea rates were higher in Chicago relative to Baltimore because of the emphasis on accommodation coupled with the informal norms that encouraged "early" bargaining, such as less attractive offers as trial dates approached. Detroit, on the other hand, maintained the highest level of bargaining relative to the other two cities. There was pressure on attorneys to move their caseloads quickly, unlike in Chicago, and plea bargaining was expected and encouraged with very few incentives to go to trial, unlike in Baltimore. Eisenstein and Jacob referred to Detroit's system as "bureaucratic plea bargaining" in order to reflect the idea that both prosecutors *and* judges encouraged the process in cases where there was little ambiguity regarding guilt and/or defendants wanted to avoid trials. This allowed trials to be reserved for the relatively few remaining cases. The cost to defense attorneys, however, was that they were discouraged by judges to go to trial, and judges openly criticized and held grudges against attorneys who resisted the process. Court actors in Detroit also did not operate under "partisan politics," unlike attorneys and judges in the other cities, which allowed them more discretion when it came to plea negotiations.

Eisenstein and Jacob also conducted some rudimentary statistical analyses of the decision to go to trial and found that the best predictor was the court in which a defendant was processed (relative to both legal and extralegal characteristics of defendants such as seriousness of the offense, type of available evidence, a defendant's race, and his or her age). This finding was an early precursor to *multilevel* analyses of case outcomes which have appeared in academic journals recently and have focused on the relative importance of defendant characteristics versus court characteristics for influencing sentence severity (such as whether a convicted defendant was sent to prison and for how long). Other relevant findings included a high rate of dismissals in Chicago that reflected a fairly rigorous screening process and an ideology among prosecutors to only pursue cases that warranted prosecution based on the evidence and/or notoriety. Cases in Baltimore, on the other hand, were more likely to be fully prosecuted because the preliminary hearing workgroups had no vested interest in carefully screening cases based on evidence. This practice emerged due to the prevalence of inexperienced prosecutors combined with judicial apathy and the practice of private counsel to delay case processing in order to collect their fees. These different practices across courts, however, did not result in significant differences in the proportion of felony defendants who were convicted. Overall, Eisenstein and Jacob found that dismissals were far more common than convictions in these felony courts.

The authors also conducted a statistical analysis of the length of time to dispose cases and found that different factors influenced disposition times in each city. The "identity of the courtroom" (p. 237) was the best predictor in Baltimore, versus bail status in Chicago and strength of evidence in Detroit. Although downplayed in their text, Eisenstein and Jacob observed that many defendant characteristics that other scholars have speculated influence case outcomes (race, age, bail status, type of attorney, and criminal record) were irrelevant for predicting case outcomes across the three cities. Even more importantly, however, is that most of their statistical models did not account for more than 10–20 percent of the variation in case outcomes despite the inclusion of both legal and extralegal measures in those models. (Exceptions include the models predicting whether cases went to trial in Detroit and all of the models predicting length of prison sentences for convicted defendants.) This finding remains very common in related research today, including the observation that models predicting prison sentence length perform much better relative to models of any other case outcome.

An important link to Sudnow's work was made by the authors regarding the overall relevance of defendant characteristics based on the *ethnographic* and statistical findings: "Thus, a defendant's characteristics do not directly shape outcomes. Those characteristics are perceived by workgroup members; they shape outcomes only as they affect participants' behaviors" (p. 244). This observation was very important because it reflected an ideological difference between scholars who chose *qualitative* versus *quantitative* methods to study case processing. From Eisenstein and Jacob's perspective, defendant characteristics could *not* operate uniformly to affect case outcomes because the varying dynamics of workgroups and court cultures ultimately affected how defendant characteristics were perceived and considered in decision-making.

The organizational approach to understanding case processing adopted by Eisenstein and Jacob was grounded in a "cultural" perspective. Unlike the cultural perspective often adopted in sociological research, which focuses on the importance of "structural" features (or unalterable environmental characteristics) that might influence particular social processes and differences *across* organizations, their perspective focused on the form of decision-making *within* courts which might have ultimately shaped differences in case processing between them. Emphasis was placed on individual level considerations, which were believed to often be removed from the influence of external factors, and how these culminated to produce a specific product of decision-making (such as the degree of guilty pleas). The individual decision-maker or courtroom workgroup became the unit of analysis instead of the court itself. An understanding of guilty plea rates, for example, was sought by examining procedural norms within courts, the attitudes and perceptions of individual court participants, and the quantity and quality of social networks that developed between these participants. This method permitted a more intense examination of "process" by allowing for observations of the nuances between actors and groups within a system, thus offering a more profound discussion of underlying sources of more general relationships at the court level, such as those involving guilty plea rates.

Eisenstein and Jacob focused primarily on factors that influenced a defendant's submission of a guilty plea because most cases were disposed in this manner. While scholars such as Alschuler focused heavily on the ideological conflict between plea bargaining and due process, asking whether defendants were not "coerced" into foregoing their constitutional right to trial, Eisenstein and Jacob began their work under the assumption that guilty pleas were common place and did not necessarily result from the evil intentions of prosecutors to attain convictions on little evidence. On the contrary, they argued that the decision to submit a guilty plea could be understood by examining the personalities of *all* members of the courtroom workgroup in conjunction with the ideology toward the guilty plea process emphasized by prosecutors and judges in a particular jurisdiction. It was not simply a matter of whether a bargain was "attractive" or not to a defendant, but rather a matter of whether courtroom workgroup members were able to get along with each other while balancing the issues of crime control (the prosecutor's interest), fairness (the defense attorney's interest), and the judge's expectations and tolerance for particular agreements.

The "desirability" of plea bargaining must increase across courts in order for guilty plea submissions to increase. Public defenders, prosecutors, and judges also must share this desirability, since the occurrence of a plea agreement required the cooperation of all three court participants. Desirability was not enough by itself, however, in that levels of plea bargaining were also influenced by the quality of relations between workgroup participants, their degree of interaction, and the extent of involvement by each participant in decision-making. One of the central themes of Eisenstein and Jacob's work was that the plea bargaining rate increased as familiarity and rapport between court actors improved across the three courts because of a greater willingness by attorneys to communicate and to compromise.

Related to this last point, the degree to which judges involved themselves in plea negotiations also influenced guilty plea rates. It was legitimate for judges to actively engage in negotiations at the time of Eisenstein and Jacob's study. Eventually this practice was considered to conflict with the judge's role as an impassioned third party and arbiter, and so the judge's role in plea bargaining today is limited to reviewing the conditions under which the plea was submitted, and to approve or disapprove of the charge or sentence recommendation of the parties involved. Even today, however, judges indirectly convey their ideology regarding plea bargaining through their actions regarding the types of plea agreements they are willing to accept in particular cases, and attorneys are quick to learn what judges like and dislike about the process.

Limitations

The aforementioned criticism of *ethnographic* research regarding its limited *generalizability* also applied to Eisenstein and Jacob's work, although this criticism was offset somewhat by their supplemental *quantitative* analysis. Particular segments of their work did convey an overly confident tone regarding the generalizability of findings, such as the first sentence of their preface, which stated "Much of what the general and professional public believes to be true about criminal courts is not." Although they admitted that they were uncertain about whether their findings "apply fully in other cities . . .", they also add ". . . although we suspect that many of them do." This seems somewhat arrogant for a study of just three courts, and it was questionable that all courts across the United States could be divided into just three categories reflecting the sociopolitical processes operating in Baltimore, Chicago, and Detroit. This is the nature of ethnographic research on courts, however, in that the method provides valuable insights into details that cannot be quantified, yet the focus on a handful of systems, especially those purposefully selected based on size, necessarily prohibits generalizability. By its very nature, ethnography is more likely to generate conclusions of *dis*similarities rather than similarities based on the minutia of information involved, possibly contributing to the general criticism of quantitative research that such methods are void of detail and do not capture the "true" nature of the phenomenon under study. As a counterpoint, it should be noted that quantitative methods in the social sciences were originally applied to analyses of *parsimonious* models for the purpose of identifying the most important predictors of a particular phenomenon rather than the population of all possible predictors.

Also questionable was the authors' observation that sentencing disparities based on extralegal characteristics of defendants (such as race and sex) were not as prevalent as was once believed. Ironically, they came to this conclusion based on their statistical analysis rather than their *observational* research, yet statistical analyses are less able to identify such disparities due to the examination of pooled samples of cases. That is, the existence of bias in court proceedings is difficult to detect statistically unless it is very prevalent in the system because such analyses are designed to identify *general* relationships and trends that exist across an entire sample, producing "average" effects which can mask instances of bias in a subgroup of all cases. As several scholars have recently demonstrated, the general effect of a defendant's race on sentencing is more often *not* statistically significant although a defendant's race does appear to *condition* the effects of other extralegal as well as legal effects on case dispositions and outcomes. For example, there is evidence that minorities receive more severe sentences when they possess other attributes that reinforce court actors' stereotypes of more dangerous offenders, such as being male and/or unemployed (e.g., Daly 1989, 1994, Miethe and Moore 1985, Nobiling et al. 1998, Spohn and Holleran 2000, Steffensmeier et al. 1998).

Related to this theme, Steffensmeier et al.'s (1998) research on Pennsylvania's determinate sentencing scheme revealed that young African American men had the highest incarceration likelihood of any subgroup defined by age, race, and sex. In their analysis of three urban jurisdictions, Cassia Spohn and David Holleran (2000) also found higher likelihoods of imprisonment among young African American and Hispanic men compared to middle-aged white men, as well as higher likelihoods for unemployed African American and Hispanic men relative to employed white men. Tracy Nobiling, Cassia Spohn, and Miriam DeLone (1998) found that unemployment coincided with higher imprisonment likelihoods for African American men in Kansas City, Missouri. They also found that unemployment coincided with higher incarceration likelihoods for young Hispanic men in Chicago, and unemployment resulted in longer prison sentences for African American men in Chicago.

Also related to this theme, legal factors may be considered differently by court actors in order to justify harsher dispositions for groups of defendants they identify as "dangerous classes" (Black 1976, Quinney 2001, Sheldon 2001). Miethe and Moore (1985) argued that limiting an analysis of racial disparities in treatment to general race effects could mask potential differences in treatment if the effects of legal measures operated differently across race groups. They demonstrated the importance of examining legal effects on case outcomes broken down by a defendant's race in order to see if the structure of sentencing was different between race groups. Miethe and Moore's (1985) analysis of charge reductions and sentence negotiations in Minnesota revealed no significant general or *main effects* of race, but several significant *interaction effects* involving race and legal characteristics such as weapons use, number of counts charged, and severity of the initial charge. Scholars examining Pennsylvania's trial courts of general jurisdiction also offered additional evidence of interaction effects involving race and legal factors. Kramer and Steffensmeier (1993) originally found that the main effects of race and gender on sentencing were very weak, while subsequent analyses by Kramer and Ulmer (1996) and Ulmer and Kramer (1996) revealed that variables such as race and sex interacted with type of plea and jurisdiction in determining imprisonment and sentence length.

Also recall Albonetti's (1990) findings related to racial disparities in pre-trial dispositions which ultimately affect case outcomes. She observed that, relative to whites, African Americans were more likely to be detained prior to trial, were less likely to have private counsel, and were less likely to plead guilty in Norfolk, Virginia. Although she did not directly examine the ramifications of these differences for sentence severity, Albonetti discussed how such discrepancies might ultimately generate harsher outcomes for minorities. Subsequent research by Albonetti (1991, 1999) underscored her original argument. For example, she found that pretrial detention constituted a greater disadvantage at sentencing for African Americans relative to whites (Albonetti 1991). She subsequently argued that defendants of higher SES were better equipped to take advantage of particular options, which, in turn, increased their odds of obtaining more favorable dispositions (Albonetti 1999). Related to this line of research, Marjorie Zatz (1985) also found evidence of related disparities in the guilty plea process of California courts, where African Americans who plead guilty actually received shorter sentences compared to Hispanics who plead guilty. A separate analysis of California defendants revealed that race and ethnicity conditioned the effects of offense seriousness, guilty pleas, and prior record on sentence severity (Petersilia and Turner 1985). In short, Eisenstein and Jacob's observations regarding the absence of significant extralegal effects on case outcomes in Baltimore, Chicago, and Detroit did not imply the absence of *interaction* effects involving combinations of extralegal and legal characteristics.

Eisenstein and Jacob's work constituted an important description of case processing in large urban courts during the 1970s, but one might question the applicability of this understanding to case processing today. As we described earlier, both bench and jury trials are even less common in 2008 relative to 1978, and guilty plea rates do not appear to vary across courts nearly as much as they used to. It is quite common to see between 95 and 98 percent of all felony convictions resulting from guilty pleas across courts, and even higher rates for misdemeanor caseloads (e.g., Wooldredge et al. 2005). With guilty plea rates becoming more of a "constant," the types of nuances in case processing practices between courts described by Eisenstein and Jacob may have much less bearing on disposition rates today. The processes they described may still be relevant, however, in the context of understanding between-court differences in the magnitude of charge and sentence reductions as well as for understanding how particular courts may use plea bargaining in order to maneuver around restrictions placed on judicial discretion by the mandatory sentencing guideline schemes of the last 20 years.

Significance and Subsequent Research

The most immediate impact of Eisenstein and Jacob's study was on subsequent work with their students who continued their method of combining *qualitative* with *quantitative* methods (Eisenstein et al. 1988, Flemming et al. 1992, Nardulli et al. 1988). Ulmer (1997) followed this tradition more recently in his study of Pennsylvania courts. This combined body of research constitutes perhaps the richest body of *empirical* knowledge on case processing and has influenced the observations of some of the most notable legal scholars including Albert Alschuler (1983), James Jacobs (2001), Malcolm Feeley (1979), Milton Heumann (1979), and Michael Tonry (1996).

It was rare for court studies of this era to incorporate both qualitative and quantitative methods, and Eisenstein and Jacob's statistical analysis influenced a vast body of quantitative research on case dispositions and sentencing (described, in part, above). Some of the more prolific scholars of the topic can be grouped into separate "camps" based on differences in their frameworks and/or the outcomes examined. Individuals such as Albonetti, Hagan, Peterson, and Zatz fall into a group that have focused on decision points prior to sentencing, particularly guilty pleas and accompanying charge or sentence reductions, grounded in the idea (similar to Eisenstein and Jacob's) that this is the stage where sentencing "really" happens. The focus of much research on "judicial" decision-making conveys the impression that judges are primarily responsible for sentencing and, therefore, sentencing disparity. Eisenstein and Jacob underscored the idea that attorneys (particularly prosecutors) have *much* more of a role in the sentencing process than previously thought, due to the much higher rate at which defendants plead guilty rather than go to trial. Since then, Hagan and some of his students (such as Albonetti) have demonstrated the importance of focusing on decision points prior to sentencing in order to understand the magnitude of disparity in the treatment of criminal defendants throughout the system. As Feeley (1979) once argued, the process *is* the punishment in that the early decisions which a defendant must face in the system in and of themselves constitute punishment by nature of forcing defendants to do what they otherwise would not do. These decisions ultimately influence the odds of both conviction and imprisonment, and so prosecutors might be considered more powerful than judges in shaping case outcomes.

Another group of scholars who have focused on sentencing per se have also paid primary attention to the types of interaction effects between extralegal and legal factors described above. Brian Johnson, John Kramer, Daryl Steffensmeier, and Jeffery Ulmer have focused heavily on these types of issues in Pennsylvania, while David Holleran, Tracy Nobiling, and Cassia Spohn have focused on other states such as California, Nebraska, and Kansas (see also Rodney Engen, Randy Gainey, and Sara Steen for related studies of Washington, and Timothy Griffin and John Wooldredge for studies of Ohio) (Engen and Steen 2000, Engen et al. 1999, Gainey et al. 2005, Griffin and Wooldredge 2006, Holleran and Spohn 2004, Johnson 2003, 2005, 2006, Johnson et al. 2008, Kramer and Steffensmeier 1993, Nobiling et al. 1998, Spohn 1990, Spohn and Cederblom 1991, Spohn and Holleran 2000, Spohn et al. 1987, Steen et al. 1999, 2005, Steffensmeier et al. 1993, Steffensmeier et al. 1998, Ulmer and Johnson 2004, Wooldredge 2007, Wooldredge et al. 2005).

References

Albonetti, C. (1987). "Prosecutorial Discretion: The Effects of Uncertainty." *Law and Society Review* 21:291–313.

Albonetti, C. (1991). "An Integration of Theories to Explain Judicial Discretion." *Social Problems* 38:247–66.

Albonetti, C. (1999). "The Avoidance of Punishment: A Legal-Bureaucratic Model of Suspended Sentences in Federal White-Collar Cases Prior to the Federal Sentencing Guidelines." *Social Forces* 78:303–29.

Alschuler, A. (1983). "Implementing the Criminal Defendant's Right to Trial: Alternatives to the Plea Bargaining System." *University of Chicago Law Review* 50:931–1050.

Black, D. (1976). *The Behavior of Law.* San Diego: Academic Press.

Daly, K. (1989). "Neither Conflict nor Labeling nor Paternalism will Suffice: Intersections of Race, Ethnicity, Gender, and Family in Criminal Court Decisions." *Crime and Delinquency* 35:135–68.

Daly, K. (1994). *Gender, Crime, and Punishment.* New Haven, CT: Yale UP.

Eisenstein, J., and H. Jacob (1977). *Felony Justice: An Organizational Analysis of Criminal Courts.* Boston: Little, Brown.

Eisenstein, J., R. Flemming, and P. Nardulli (1988). *The Contours of Justice: Communities and Their Courts.* Boston: Little, Brown.

Engen, R., and S. Steen (2000). *The Implementation and Impact of Drug Sentencing Reform in Washington State.* Final Report to the Washington State Sentencing Guidelines Commission.

Engen, R., R. Gainey, and S. Steen (1999). *Racial and Ethnic Disparities in Sentencing Outcomes for Drug Offenders in Washington State: FY1996 to FY1999.* Final Report to the Washington State Minority and Justice Commission.

Feeley, M. (1979). *The Process is the Punishment.* Washington, DC: President's Commission on Law Enforcement and Administration of Justice.

Flemming, R., P. Nardulli, and J. Eisenstein (1992). *The Craft of Justice: Work and Politics in Criminal Court Communities.* Philadelphia: University of Pennsylvania Press.

Gainey, R., S. Steen, and R. Engen (2005). "Exercising Options: An Assessment of the Use of Alternative Sanctions for Drug Offenders." *Justice Quarterly* 22:488–520.

Griffin, T., and J. Wooldredge (2006). "Sex-based Disparities in Felony Dispositions Before versus

After Sentencing Reform in Ohio." *Criminology* 44:893–924.

Heumann, M. (1979). "Thinking About Plea bargaining." In *The Study of Criminal Courts*, edited by P. Nardulli. Cambridge, MA: Ballinger.

Holleran, D., and C. Spohn (2004). "On the Use of the Total Incarceration Variable in Sentencing Research." *Criminology* 42:211–40.

Johnson, B. (2003). "Racial and Ethnic Disparities in Sentencing Departures Across Modes of Conviction." *Criminology* 41:501-42.

Johnson, B. (2005). "Contextual Disparities in Guideline Departures: Courtroom Social Contexts, Guidelines Compliance, and Extralegal Disparities in Criminal Sentencing." *Criminology* 43:761–96.

Johnson, B. (2006). "The Multilevel Context of Criminal Sentencing: Integrating Judge and County Level Influences in the Study of Courtroom Decision Making." *Criminology* 44:259–98.

Johnson, B., J. Ulmer, and J. Kramer (2008). "The Social Context of Guidelines Circumvention: The Case of the U.S. District Courts." *Criminology* (forthcoming).

Jacobs, J. (2001). "The Evolution of U.S. Criminal Law." *Issues of Democracy* 6:6-15.

Kramer, J., and D. Steffensmeier (1993). "Race and Imprisonment Decisions." *Sociological Quarterly* 34:357–76.

Kramer, J., and J. Ulmer (1996). "Sentencing Disparity and Departure from Guidelines." *Justice Quarterly* 13:81–105.

Miethe, T., and C. Moore (1985). "Racial Differences in Criminal Processing: The Consequences of Model Selection on Conclusions About Differential Treatment." *Sociological Quarterly* 27:217–37.

Nardulli, P., J. Eisenstein, and R. Flemming (1988). *Tenor of Justice: Criminal Courts and the Guilty Plea Process.* Urbana, IL: University of Illinois Press.

Nobiling, T., C. Spohn, and M. DeLone (1998). "A Tale of Two Counties: Unemployment and Sentence Severity." *Justice Quarterly* 15:459–85.

Petersilia, J., and S. Turner (1985). *Guideline-Based Justice: The Implications for Racial Minorities.* Santa Monica, CA: RAND.

Quinney, R. (2001). *The Social Reality of Crime.* New Brunswick, NJ: Transaction.

Sheldon, R. (2001). *Controlling the Dangerous Classes: A Critical Introduction to the History of Criminal Justice.* Boston: Allyn and Bacon.

Spohn, C. (1990). "The Sentencing Decisions of Black and White Judges: Some Expected and Unexpected Similarities." *Law and Society Review* 24:1197–1216.

Spohn, C., and J. Cederblom (1991) "Race and Disparities in Sentencing: A Test of the Liberation Hypothesis." *Justice Quarterly* 8:305–27.

Spohn, C., and D. Holleran (2000). "The Imprisonment Penalty Paid By Young, Unemployed Black and Hispanic Male Offenders." *Criminology* 38:281–306.

Spohn, C., J. Gruhl, and S. Welch (1987). "The Impact of the Ethnicity and Gender of Defendants on the Decision to Reject or Dismiss Felony Charges." *Criminology* 25:175–91.

Steen, S., R. Engen, and R. Gainey (1999). *The Impact of Race and Ethnicity on Charging and Sentencing Processes for Drug Offenders in Three Counties of Washington State.* Final Report to the Washington State Minority and Justice Commission.

Steen, S., R. Engen, and R. Gainey (2005). "Images of Danger: Racial Stereotyping, Case Processing, and Criminal Sentencing." *Criminology* 43:435–68.

Steffensmeier, D., J. Kramer, and C. Streifel (1993). "Gender and Imprisonment Decisions." *Criminology* 31:411–46.

Steffensmeier, D., J. Ulmer, and J. Kramer (1998). "The Interaction of Race, Gender, and Age in Criminal Sentencing: The Punishment Cost of Being Young, Black, and Male." *Criminology* 36:763–97.

Sudnow, D. (1965). "Normal Crimes: Sociological Features of the Penal Code in a Public Defender Office." *Social Problems* 12:255–76.

Tonry, M. (1996). *Sentencing Matters.* New York: Oxford UP.

Ulmer, J. (1997). "Social Worlds of Sentencing: Court Communities under Sentencing Guidelines." Albany: SUNY Press.

Ulmer, J., and B. Johnson (2004). "Sentencing in Context: A Multilevel Analysis." *Criminology* 42:137–77.

Ulmer, J., and J. Kramer (1996). "Court Communities Under Sentencing Guidelines: Dilemmas of Formal Rationality and Sentencing Disparity." *Criminology* 34:383–407.

Wooldredge, J. (2007). "Neighborhood Effects on Felony Sentencing." *Journal of Research in Crime and Delinquency* 44:238–63.

Wooldredge, J., T. Griffin, and F. Rauschenberg (2005). "Sentencing Reform and Reductions in the Disparate Treatment of Felony Defendants." *Law and Society Review* 39:835–74.

Zatz, M. (1985). "Pleas, Priors, and Prison: Racial/Ethnic Differences in Sentencing." *Social Science Research* 14:169–93.

Further Reading

Hatch, M. (1997). *Organization Theory: Modern, Symbolic, and Postmodern Perspectives.* New York: Oxford UP.

Buchanan, D., and A. Huczynski (2006). *Organizational Behaviour: An Introductory Text.* Englewood Cliffs, NJ: Prentice-Hall.

PROCEDURAL INJUSTICES AND DUE PROCESS VIOLATIONS IN COURT: WHAT INFLUENCES DEFENDANTS' CYNICISM TOWARD THE LEGAL PROCESS?

Casper, J. (1972). *American Criminal Justice: The Defendant's Perspective.* Englewood Cliffs, NJ: Prentice-Hall.

Background

Ethnographic studies of court actors and the dynamics of case processing, such as those described previously, have focused heavily on interviews with attorneys and judges rather than defendants. When the authors of these studies provided commentaries on defendants and how they were treated, their observations were based only on what court actors had to say or were derived from observations of attorney/defendant interactions. This approach to understanding how defendants are treated, however, misses the emotional perspective of the person who stands to lose a great deal if found guilty. Recognizing this void in the literature, Jonathan Casper interviewed criminal defendants in order to capture this perspective. After the due process revolution of the 1950s and '60s, the ability to assess defendants' perceptions of their treatment by the criminal justice system was critical for evaluating the extent to which the system was following through on the protections of "life, liberty, and property" guaranteed by the Fifth Amendment to the US Constitution.

The origins of due process of law date back to England in the early 13th century when the previously unlimited power of King John over the citizenry was restricted under the Magna Carta (1215), most importantly regarding the unexplained seizures of persons or property by the government:

> "No free man shall be seized or imprisoned, or stripped of his rights or possessions, or outlawed or exiled, or deprived of his standing in any other way, nor will we proceed with force against him, or send others to do so, except by the lawful judgment of his equals or by the law of the land."

The last part of this passage referring to "law of the land" is synonymous with the contemporary phrase "due process of law." Both ideas concern the requirement that the state must follow particular procedures during their pursuit of apprehending and prosecuting any person accused of wrongdoing. These procedures exist to protect the truly innocent who, without these procedural safeguards, might otherwise be found guilty. Over time, "due process of law" came to be defined as procedural due process granted to anyone accused by the government of committing a crime.

The first procedural right of defendants is protection against being placed in the state's custody without notification of why they are being apprehended (or notification of criminal charges), which is granted by the Fifth Amendment: "No person shall be held to answer for a capital, or otherwise infamous crime, unless on a presentment or indictment of a Grand Jury," and by the Sixth Amendment: "In all criminal prosecutions, the accused shall . . . be informed of the nature and cause of the accusation." The second procedural safeguard involves a defendant's right to a hearing or a jury trial, also guaranteed by the Sixth Amendment, providing the opportunity to defend oneself against the state's accusations. At this point in the system defendants have the right to confront and cross-examine witnesses for the prosecution. Also relevant is that the state must prove their case against the defendant "beyond a reasonable doubt," or else the defendant must be declared innocent by the jury or the judge. Moreover, the defendant is not required to "prove" his or her innocence since s/he must only raise doubt about whether s/he committed the offense. No less important is the Sixth Amendment's provision of a defendant's right to legal assistance in order to prepare and execute his defense: "In all criminal prosecutions, the accused shall . . . have the Assistance of Counsel for his defense." Underlying these provisions, of course, is the presumption of the defendant's innocence until guilt has been proven by the state. To ensure this presumption, defendants also have the right to remain silent (i.e., the right against self-incrimination). All of these provisions reflect the great value placed on a person's life and freedom by the framers of the US Constitution, and they represent the means to ensure that truly innocent people do not lose their lives or liberty when faced with accusations by powerful government officials who otherwise might use coercion to exact confessions.

These aspects of procedural due process should be recalled when reading our summary of Casper's study. As Casper discovered throughout the course of his study, for many defendants these "rights" exist only in theory, particularly those pertinent to the presumption of innocence, representation by legal counsel, careful review of evidence, and trial by one's peers.

The Study

Casper (1972) conducted interviews with 71 criminal defendants charged with felonies in a Connecticut jurisdiction in order to observe and evaluate their attitudes toward police, attorneys, and judges, as well as their perceptions of case processing and how they were treated. All defendants were men and most were convicted. The pool included 49 men who were incarcerated in state correctional facilities, 16 probationers, and 6 defendants who were either acquitted at trial or had all charges dropped prior to trial. Casper's primary aim was to offer an important perspective that was missing from the *ethnographic* studies of court actors conducted up to that point in time. He believed that the defendant's perspective was vital for supplementing (and balancing) the views of police, attorneys, and judges on the realities of case processing and, perhaps more importantly, what is wrong with criminal justice in the United States. Since the defendant is the "'consumer' of criminal justice" (p. 3), his perspective should not be ignored when evaluating the process and developing strategies for improvement.

Findings

To demonstrate the disjuncture between the realities of case processing versus a defendant's preconceptions of what it was like (based on stereotypes derived from books and the media), Casper provided an excerpt from an interview with a convicted defendant whose first time through the system resulted in an 11–15 year prison term for manslaughter.

Although the man was atypical relative to other defendants (better educated with a better job and above average income), almost immediately he picked up on the motivations of both the pubic defender and the prosecutor to move their caseloads as quickly as possible, pushing for a plea bargain yet without any significant "bargain" except for the charge reduction from first-degree murder to manslaughter (which was irrelevant, since the original crime *was* manslaughter). The defendant also observed that the judge was not independent of the prosecutor's interests and acted only as a rubber stamp on the sentence recommended by the prosecutor. In other words, there was no effort to understand any unique circumstances surrounding the offense or the offender that might have been relevant for sentencing. This was important because Connecticut operated under *in*determinate sentencing during the 1970s. The defendant also spent over two months in jail waiting for the final disposition, and the conditions of confinement were deplorable even by the jail officers' standards. This was a perspective not entertained by Eisenstein and Jacob regarding a defendant's incentive to plea bargain, namely the motivation to get out of jail rather than wait for trial under poor living conditions. Such a scenario might have led a defendant to accept a plea agreement that was not in his or her best interest. Motivation to accept an agreement was also enhanced by pubic defenders who rarely communicated with their clients and, when they did, focused primarily on possible "deals" in plea negotiations (thereby assuming that the defendant was guilty). Other related observations made by this defendant as well as others that countered the notion of due process and the presumption of innocence included perceptions that:

> The prosecutor ran the show instead of the judge.
>
> The judge was not an objective mediator but instead acted primarily in the prosecutor's best interest.
>
> Sentences were based on "going rates" and/or whatever it took to convince a defendant to submit a guilty plea, rather than being based on specific case circumstances and the needs of the defendant.
>
> The assembly-line process could not educate the defendant about the morality of law and why he should not have engaged in the crime to begin with.
>
> Criminal charges actually changed throughout the process because they were dictated more by system needs rather than by careful consideration of the crime and the defendant.

Regarding police officers and their use of discretion, some of the defendants perceived officers as inefficient because so many criminals got away with so much crime before they were actually caught. This is due, they argued, to officers being "overworked and . . . lazy" (p. 21), leading them to violate rules in order to meet their job expectations and quotas (although officers were also viewed as basically honest). Police were not seen as negatively as Casper anticipated, but rather as performing an important job of maintaining order and protecting the public. Examples of rule violations, however, were offered by defendants in their descriptions of police arrest procedures. For example, defendants offered stories of illegal (warrantless) searches, failure to be Mirandized, their use of false witnesses, and entrapment. Unfortunately, unless challenged by the defendant, evidence collected illegally in this manner still helped to shape the odds of conviction and the severity of a sentence. Challenges were rare occurrences, although Casper's sample could not have been representative in that regard since he focused primarily on *convicted* defendants. Many defendants were repeat offenders who were very familiar with the court system and were so cynical that they considered their cases to be over at arrest. Any favorable outcomes were then seen as products of "luck" rather than justice since many of these individuals were unfamiliar with procedural safeguards and so did not try to take advantage of them. If they were familiar with such safeguards or when they talked about defendants who opted for trial, their perception was that persons who fought their charges faced even harsher sentences upon conviction. Of course, Casper tempered all of this with the realization that many defendants *were* in fact guilty as charged and simply resigned themselves to "fate." Nonetheless, this meant ". . . arrest rather than trial is the crucial step in the process from the defendant's perspective" (p. 37). He also inferred that some of the "less negative" views of defendants toward rule violations by police officers might have actually reflected the defendants' own predispositions toward deceit and deviance, and so they better understood those behaviors. On the other hand, the negative views of officers offered by a minority of the defendants might have been shaped much earlier in their lives when they encountered police as juveniles, whether as delinquents, as children of criminal parents or guardians, or as children in need of supervision. Even in the eyes of defendants with more favorable views of police officers, however, none of the defendants interviewed expressed *respect* for officers and their jobs.

Turning to defendants' experiences during arraignment when the conditions for pre-trial release were determined, except in capital cases, Casper observed a different type of "negotiation" that took place regarding bail amounts. In anticipation of a defendant exercising his right to a probable cause hearing, he was usually advised by counsel to waive that right in exchange for reduced bail and a better chance of obtaining pretrial release. This "deal" was in the best interest of the state because, even though sufficient evidence usually could be presented to justify prosecution in superior court, prosecutors did not want the defense to learn too much about the state's case too early in the process so they could see where the prosecutor's case was weak. Even before formal charges were filed, therefore, many defendants were essentially bribed into forgoing one of their due process rights. It is these initial encounters with public defenders that contributed to a defendant's level of distrust and disrespect for his attorney throughout the entire process.

For those who did not make bail, plea bargaining became an attractive alternative to enduring poor conditions of confinement in jail for an indefinite period of time. Moreover, pretrial detainees were less likely to fight very hard for a better bargain and were more likely to snitch on their accomplices in order to get out of jail. For defendants who even considered opting for trial, whether they made bail or not, there was a general fear about going to trial that was instilled in them by their own attorneys. Public defenders were quick to inform the defendant about the state's case against him, the odds of a conviction, and the fact that risking a trial could have easily increased the severity of the sentence if convicted. Defendants were also very suspicious that in the event of conflicting testimonies between the state and the defense, the state's witnesses would be perceived as more credible. All of this ultimately raised the possibility that even an innocent person might submit a guilty plea just to avoid inhumane conditions of confinement prior to trial and/or to reduce the risk of an even more severe sanction at trial.

Ironically, even though trials occurred for only a small portion of cases, most defense attorneys threatened prosecutors with the prospect of going to trial in order to negotiate a better plea agreement (since the prosecutor typically did not want to waste time and resources). Defense attorneys themselves were also reluctant to go to trial, but placing a case on the court docket did not mean that the trial would necessarily happen. Negotiations were possible up to the last minute and trials were often cancelled immediately before they were set to begin. One might perceive this process to have actually benefited (most) defendants in the long run, since they avoided both the economic and social costs of going to trial as well as harsher sentences, but the process reinforced an image of the court system as amoral and counterintuitive to due process. The plea bargaining experience appeared almost perverted to the defendant since outcomes were not based so much on the offense and case circumstances as much as they were based on the "game" of threatening to go to trial and being patient enough to wait for the prosecutor to come back with other offers rather than reacting too quickly and settling for the first or second offer. The process also exacted a toll on the defendant's self-image by essentially forcing him to negotiate the label that he had to live with for the rest of his life, referred to as a "successful degradation ceremony" by Abraham Blumberg (1967). Important to note, however, is that defendants could not offer an objective perspective of what a "fair" sentence would be in their own case. Casper observed that defendants generally perceived sentences as "fair" either when they received a much lighter sentence than expected, or when they did not get above the "going rate."

Although plea bargaining is counterintuitive to due process, there are many rationales for keeping it because the process (a) moves court caseloads more efficiently, (b) helps to avoid mandatory sentences, (c) saves trial resources for cases where guilt is really in question, (d) allows defendant's to acknowledge their culpability as a first step in their rehabilitation, and (e) provides defendants with a feeling that they have some control over the process. All of these rationales, however, are not actual *purposes* of bargaining and cannot be used to *justify* the process. The sentences derived through bargaining fail to reflect any guiding philosophy of justice such as retribution, deterrence, incapacitation, or rehabilitation. In the absence of a meaningful sentence (Enker 1967), the process lacks any moral element.

Casper described the origins of the public defender system in order to place some of the defendants' comments regarding public defenders in proper perspective. Generally speaking, the two methods of providing attorneys to indigent defendants included assigning private attorneys chosen from a state's bar association, who received small fees for their cases, versus assigning a public defender who was salaried and typically worked full time in a public defenders office. The public defender was considered preferable to assigned counsel because the latter took on a lot of cases due to their small fees and, consequently, spent very little time with any one defendant. Assigned counsel also was chosen from a wide range of attorneys, some of which did not have any experience in criminal law. Public defenders, on the other hand, focused full time on the criminal law. Regardless of the advantages of public defenders over assigned counsel, public defenders in the court under study had very heavy caseloads and were subjected to the first problem of not being able to spend much time with each of their clients. Casper examined each defendant's satisfaction with his or her attorney and then computed the percentage of satisfied defendants who had public defenders (49 defendants) versus privately retained counsel (12 defendants) versus legal assistants (10 defendants). Only 20 percent of the defendants with public defenders were satisfied with their attorneys, versus 100 percent of those with private counsel and 70 percent of those with legal assistants. One of the most common criticisms was that public defenders just did not fight very hard in their client's best interest, probably because there were no financial incentives to do so. Defendants also perceived public defenders as being more familiar with and politically tied to prosecutors as a consequence of working together in the same system. (This scenario, in turn, was perceived by defendants to increase the odds of public defenders pushing their clients to accept plea agreements.) Also, whereas private attorneys had to build reputations as good attorneys in order to attract clients, public defenders did not have to establish such reputations because they did not have to attract defendants (i.e., defendants were assigned to attorneys). With private attorneys, by contrast, defendants were in a position to buy a better defense. Defendants typically paid private attorneys a small fee up front and later paid another fee based on the severity of the outcome (i.e., more money for less severe sentences with the highest amount paid for an acquittal or dismissal). Of course, as Casper recognized, the nature of the relationship between a defendant and a private attorney was much different than with a public defender because paying for private counsel changed the tone of the relationship and placed the defendant in greater control of the situation. In short, money purchased satisfaction with one's defense, if only because it created the image that attorneys were more invested in their clients' interests.

Regarding defendant's perceptions of prosecutors, the general belief was that the prosecutor was the central figure in the court system rather than the judge. Although judges had the authority to dismiss formal charges brought by prosecutors as well as override their plea agreements, defendants observed that these were rare occurrences. Rather than placing power in the hands of the mediator, therefore, power instead fell with the prosecutor and the interests of the state to obtain convictions by any means possible. Consistent with their views of public defenders, defendants perceived prosecutors as deriving sentences based not so much on the offense and case circumstances but instead by chance and whatever would gain convictions. This reinforced defendants' beliefs that they were treated as objects rather than as human beings. As for judges, defendants saw them only as figureheads who relied on prosecutors to take care of business and who delegated power to them. This seemed logical to defendants, if only because prosecutors simply knew more about any one case compared to judges. Taking power away from the judge, however, was perceived by defendants as "the ultimate failure of American criminal justice" (p. 144).

Casper concluded his book with important linkages between defendants' accounts of their treatment during case processing and their attitudes toward the law. Adopting a social psychological perspective, Casper observed that criminal defendants typically viewed law-abiding behavior as a product of external controls placed on individuals' choices and behaviors rather than as a product of morality and proper socialization. In other words, they understood that what they did was "wrong" and agreed with the idea that their actions *should* be deemed illegal. However, they felt that all people were inherently immoral and in need of some form of external constraints. These observations were extremely important in that they reflected the idea that criminals may be more apt to perceive their criminal behavior as a failure of society to control them. As such, anything the justice system does to undermine an individual's allegiance to government authority will only push that person away from convention. In a nutshell, the disillusionment expressed by many of Casper's interviewees toward the justice system could ultimately impact their allegiance to legal authority and, in turn, to law-abiding behaviors.

Limitations

Casper's study filled an important void in the empirical literature on the dynamics of case processing and procedural (in)justices. The "truth" about due process in practice could only be determined with consideration of the perceptions of all actors involved, and the defendant's perspective was perhaps the most relevant given that s/he had the most to lose when the system failed to follow through on the guarantees promised in the Fifth and Sixth Amendments to the US Constitution. For example, any investigation into whether defendants are unduly pressured into pleading guilty must consider the defendant's viewpoint (Casale 1979) since only the defendant can perceive his or her own feelings of "pressure." As with any effort to scientifically assess a critical issue, however, there are criticisms of the methodological approach adopted by Casper. First, he interviewed defendants only and did not obtain counterpoints from attorneys and judges in order to provide a more "balanced" description of the process. Second, the sole focus on interview data as the basis for empirical assessments has come under attack more recently by sociologists.

Details on the sample of defendants described by Casper are a little fuzzy although he did infer that the sample should be treated more as a *convenience* sample rather than as a *probability* sample, and he stated that it was limited due to the small number of defendants interviewed. This description is offered in the preface to his book where he also stated that each interview lasted an average of 90 minutes. The 49 men interviewed in prison were selected *randomly* although the method of sampling was not described (*simple random, systematic random, stratified systematic random*, etc.). The other 22 men were "self-selected" in that a list was randomly generated from "various court records and newspaper reports" (p. vii), and these men were sent letters inviting them to participate in the study. Casper also did not reveal how many men were on the original list and received letters. This method might have generated a potentially biased sample of non-incarcerated defendants if those who participated differed from those who refused in terms of their perspectives of the justice system. For example, it is possible that only malcontented defendants agreed to participate so they could voice their dissatisfaction with the system. Those who refused might have offered more "balanced" views relative to those who participated, and the tone of some of Casper's themes might have changed (such as the defendants' general dissatisfaction with public defenders or the idea that most defendants felt pressured by their attorneys to quickly accept the plea bargains offered to them). Another possible contributing factor to the general disillusionment with plea bargaining was the over-representation of convicted defendants relative to those who were acquitted at trial or had their charges dropped (by a ratio of 10:1). Convicted defendants are more likely to be bitter about their case outcomes relative to non-convicted defendants, and *anyone* who ends up in prison might be the least likely to favor his or her attorney since s/he was convicted *and* incarcerated. Realistically, however, defense attorneys cannot always be blamed for cases ending in imprisonment. Perhaps a more rigorous design would have entailed interviewing each defendant as well as his attorney, the prosecutor involved in the specific case, and even the judge who ultimately approved the plea agreement or resided over the trial. Even without a more balanced pool of defendants, this approach could have provided different perspectives on the fairness of the outcome relative to other cases handled by the same court actors. Taking this criticism one step further, policy makers might be less inclined to consider defendants' observations as "proof" of procedural unfairness because they typically view defendants as unreliable sources of information on the subject of due process in practice (Casale 1977). The conundrum posed by this criticism is that the defendant's perspective is essential for an overall evaluation, so a difficult challenge lies in assessing just *how* biased these views might be.

Separate from the issue of focusing solely on defendants' interviews at the expense of interviews with attorneys and judges, the second criticism focuses on the use of interview data per se as a source of reliable information. Scholars have recently argued that social scientists who rely on interview data tend to treat the perspectives of interviewees as authentic truths. Jaber Gubrium and James Holstein (2002), however, argue that these "truths" are nothing more than reflections of the interview process itself, where researchers unconsciously feed the observations of their sample and thereby create "methodologically constructed social products" (p. 11). This criticism moves beyond an older criticism of interview data, similar to the first criticism above, regarding whether researchers can be sure that their subjects are not exaggerating or even lying (Dean and Whyte 1958). Other criticisms have included the incompleteness of interview data (Becker and Geer 1957), as well as inconsistencies between actions versus opinions (Deutscher 1973). The more recent criticism, however, actually brings into question the utility of *any* interview data. Taken literally, this also has implications for *quantitative* analyses of certain forms of *survey* data that capture the attitudes and opinions of individuals (i.e., data compiled from close-ended questions presented in a survey document or questionnaire). The argument is that the interview itself is a "social occasion" that is unique from a subject's everyday activities, and so anything said during the interview can only reflect a person's attitudes within that particular (and unusual) context and, therefore, is socially constructed by nature of the interview "event." For example, subjects are being asked questions that they otherwise would not necessarily even consider, let alone verbalize answers to, and so the interviewer acts as a "persuader" who necessarily influences a subject's response. Subjects are also thinking about how they are presenting themselves to these strangers. Both of these factors can interfere with accurate communication and responses. Interview data are used in various ways by social scientists, and Casper used his data "as a source of witness accounts of the social world" (Hammersley, 2003, p. 120). This use differs from other uses that focus more on how researchers *interpret* interview data as opposed to treating the data as accurate information. The focus of the above criticism is on the use of interview data as sources of accurate information. If taken as valid, this criticism brings into question the validity of observations from many studies included in this book.

Significance and Subsequent Research

The above criticisms must be given consideration although it is difficult to fathom how researchers can possibly gain insight into defendants' and court actors' attitudes without actually talking to them. Some might argue that participant observation might be less biased, but these methods can be criticized on similar grounds because the person(s) under observation may become self-conscious of their own behaviors and may react to that awareness. The context of being watched, therefore, also creates the possibility of a socially constructed reality fed by the researcher's presence. A second problem with participant observation in court research is that plea negotiations take place behind closed doors and outsiders are not allowed to witness them. Even as nonparticipant observers, plea bargaining is a process that often occurs spontaneously and in different contexts, and it often does not begin and conclude within a single context (i.e., the defense may be presented with several different offers before accepting the agreement). It would be highly unlikely that a researcher could even design a study that would provide reliable observations of such a process, unlike trials which are open to the public and the proceedings and transcripts of which are matters of public record. In short, interviews with defendants and court actors remain our richest source of information on the realities of due process in practice. Casper was at the forefront of this movement in criminal justice research.

Casper is credited as being one of the very first political science scholars to focus on "informal" justice and its impact on case outcomes. Driven by his passion for the due process rights of the accused, he appreciated how an understanding of case processing in practice might be facilitated by an interdisciplinary approach to studying the courts. His work was tempered by political science (through his understanding of political and organizational pressures that can ultimately lead well-intentioned attorneys and judges to divert their attention away from defendants' rights), by sociology (considering the environmental and cultural influences on defendants' preconceptions and stereotypes of attorneys and judges), and by psychology (with descriptions of how defendants' perceptions of the court system changed based on their unique experiences). This inter-disciplinary approach has broadened over time and is now often taken for granted, but Casper made conscious efforts to break down some of the barriers separating the social and behavioral sciences in order to get court researchers to think more comprehensively about their topics. Social psychologists will argue that they had already been doing this for decades within their realm of study, but Casper extended these ideas into research on legal issues while also adding the (necessary) political science perspective.

Court scholars including Albert Alschuler (1983), James Eisenstein (with Herbert Jacob, 1977), Malcolm Feeley (1979), Michael Finkelstein (1975), Milton Heumann (1978), Herbert Jacob (1973), Lynn Mather (1979), Peter Nardulli (1979), and Jeffrey Ulmer (1997) were all influenced by Casper's research to some degree, and his 1972 study of Connecticut defendants is one of his most cited works. Casper, in turn, was heavily influenced by the works of Albert Alschuler (1968), Abraham Blumberg (1967), Milton Heumann (1975), and Jerome Skolnick (1966). (Interestingly, there is no mention of Sudnow in Casper's work.) The work described here was actually a part of a larger study of defendants across three states, and Casper ultimately interviewed roughly 600 defendants on the subject of plea bargaining and trials. Simultaneous with this work he was also interviewing attorneys involved in civil rights litigation. Both of these projects contributed to his general theme that courts spend most of their time on the guilty plea process and informal justice, in contrast to media and textbook images of courts as being occupied solely with trials. Casper was one of the first scholars to study plea bargaining and the guilty plea process, following shortly after Sudnow and Blumberg. After considering all of his evidence compiled from defendants across three states, Casper subsequently concluded that defendants were more often satisfied with the guilty plea process compared to the trial process. He proceeded to examine why this might be the case. This interest ultimately led him to focus on the potential problems with jury trials and the applicability of psychological theories to an understanding of jury decision-making. From research on jury judgments regarding police searches and seizures he derived his famous theory of "hindsight bias" related to these judgments (Casper et al. 1989). He found that jurors were more likely to decide that a search was illegal when police did *not* confiscate any illegal contraband and less likely to decide a search was illegal when contraband was found. In other words, the outcome of the search dictated jury decisions even though officers in both types of cases were operating on the same assumptions and the same quality of information.

Casper's research expanded even further into the trial process, leading to several important observations regarding (a) the strong link between the quality of jury instructions and jury decisions, (b) how cross-examination of the state's witnesses could do very little to compensate for any unjustified claims made by those witnesses about a defendant's risk of future criminality, and (c) how attorneys' attitudes toward their clients were shaped by witness testimonies (Casper et al. 1988, 1989, Diamond and Casper 1992, Diamond et al. 1989). Underlying all of these themes, including "hindsight bias," were Casper's foci on procedural injustice, the cognitive (psychological) processes involved, and the sociopolitical barriers to due process. Casper eventually found that defendants were generally satisfied with the system, regardless of their case outcomes, as long as they perceived themselves as being treated "fairly" by legal authorities. His subsequent work throughout the '90s focused on the importance of citizens' favorable perspectives of government (and, more specifically, defendants' favorable perspectives of the justice system) for creating a stronger allegiance between citizens and government authorities. Again, the theme that "perceptions shape reality" reflected his social-psychological orientation to the topic. This is an important counterpoint to the criticism described earlier regarding the impact of the interview context on socially constructed realities. Casper understood the unique realities that defendants perceived during case processing and he did not claim to be examining an "objective" reality of procedural (in)justice. On the contrary, it was the variation in defendant characteristics and experiences that permitted variation in those realities, all of which could be linked to the legal cynicism of defendants and the strength of their allegiance to legal authority.

References

Alschuler, A. (1968). "The Prosecutor's Role in Plea Bargaining." *University of Chicago Law Review* 36:50–112.

Alschuler, A. (1983). "Implementing the Criminal Defendant's Right to Trial: Alternatives to the Plea Bargaining System." *University of Chicago Law Review* 50:931–1050.

Becker, H., and B. Geer (1957). "Participant Observation and Interviewing: A Comparison." *Human Organization* 16:28–32.

Blumberg, A. (1967). *Criminal Justice.* Chicago: Quadrangle.

Casale, S. (1977). "Review of 'Negotiated Justice: Pressures to Plead Guilty.'" *Law and Society Review* 13:655–60.

Casper, J. (1972). *American Criminal Justice: The Defendant's Perspective* Englewood Cliffs, NJ: Prentice-Hall.

Casper, J., K. Benedict, and J. Kelly (1988). "Cognitions, Attitudes, and Decision-making in Search and Seizure Cases." *Journal of Applied Social Psychology* 18:93-113.

Casper, J., K. Benedict, and J. Perry (1989). "Jury Decision Making, Attitudes, and the Hindsight Bias." *Law and Human Behavior* 13:291–310.

Dean, J., and W. Whyte (1958). "How Do You Know if the Informant is Telling the Truth?" *Human Organization* 17:34–38.

Deutscher, I. (1973). *What We Say/What We Do: Sentiments and Acts.* Glenview, IL: Scott, Foresman.

Diamond, S., and J. Casper (1992) "Blindfolding the Jury to Verdict Consequences: Damages, Experts, and the Civil Jury." *Law and Society Review* 26:513–63.

Diamond, S., J. Casper, and L. Ostergren (1989). "Blindfolding the Jury." *Law and Contemporary Problems* 52:247–67.

Eisenstein, J., and H. Jacob (1977). *Felony Justice: An Organizational Analysis of Criminal Courts.* Boston: Little, Brown.

Enker, A. (1967). *Perspectives on Plea Bargaining.* Washington, DC: President's Commission on Law Enforcement and Administration of Justice.

Feeley, M. (1979). *The Process is the Punishment.* Washington, DC: President's Commission on Law Enforcement and Administration of Justice.

Finkelstein, M. (1975). "A Statistical Analysis of Guilty Plea Practices in the Federal Courts." *Harvard Law Review* 89:292–315.

Gubrium, J., and J. Holstein (2002). *Handbook of Interview Research.* Thousand Oaks, CA: Sage.

Hammersley, M. (2003). "Recent Radical Criticism of Interview Studies: Any Implications for the Sociology of Education?" *British Journal of Sociology of Education* 24:119–26.

Heumann, M. (1975). "A Note on Plea Bargaining and Case Pressure." *Law and Society Review* 9:515–20.

Heumann, M. (1978). *Plea Bargaining: The Experiences of Prosecutors, Judges, and Defense Attorneys.* Chicago: University of Chicago Press.

Jacob, H. (1973). *Urban Justice.* Englewood Cliffs, NJ: Prentice-Hall.

Mather, L. (1979). *Plea Bargaining or Trial? The Process of Criminal Case Disposition.* Boston: Lexington Books.

Nardulli, P. (1979). "The Caseload Controversy and the Study of Criminal Courts." *Journal of Criminal Law and Criminology* 70:89–101.

Skolnick, J. (1966). *Justice without Trial: Law Enforcement in Democratic Society.* New York: Wiley.

Ulmer, J. (1997). *Social Worlds of Sentencing: Court Communities under Sentencing Guidelines.* Albany: SUNY Press.

Further Reading

Fisher, G. (2003). *Plea Bargaining's Triumph: A History of Plea Bargaining in America.* Stanford, CA: Stanford UP.

McDonald, W., and J. Cramer (1980). *Plea Bargaining.* Lexington, MA: D.C. Heath.

3

The Jury Trial

As conveyed in the last section, most criminal defendants who are convicted choose to submit guilty pleas instead of choosing to go to trial. Yet, the trial process itself remains the focal point in the criminal justice system. The criminal trial symbolizes the American system of jurisprudence where an accused person has the opportunity to defend him/herself against the government's charges. As opposed to a bench trial where the judge acts as both jury and referee, the jury trial is a trial by 12 of one's "peers." The jury trial is more symbolic of justice compared to the bench trial because it reflects a decision made by members of society who are separate from government officials. Underlying the process, however, is the assumption that 12 jurors can arrive at an intelligent and legally informed decision. Differences in education levels among jurors might interfere with this assumption. Rita Simon (1980) argued that because the education of many jurors is poor, personal characteristics such as a juror's sex, political party preference, income, and occupation might influence their verdicts. This is why prosecutors and defense attorneys prefer to select jurors with particular characteristics because these traits might make them more or less sympathetic toward a defendant. In short, jury verdicts might be influenced to some extent by the personal characteristics of jurors, also referred to as "lawyer's lore." If there is any truth to lawyer's lore, then there is a potential hypocrisy between the due process emphasis on equality under the law and the court system's reliance on citizens who might allow their subjective feelings, shaped by their personal characteristics, to interfere with an intelligent and carefully reasoned decision based only on the evidence presented at trial. Subjective decisions are discriminatory by their nature. Scholars have conducted research on the decision-making abilities of jurors, primarily through examination of *mock juries* where study volunteers are presented with simulated trials and then deliberate as a group to discuss the evidence and testimonies in order to determine whether the defendant in the hypothetical case should be found guilty. The two studies described in this section were among the first to examine jury decision-making and had an enormous impact on subsequent research (including studies of mock juries).

JURY DECISION-MAKING: WHY DO JURIES AND JUDGES SOMETIMES DISAGREE?

Kalven, H. Jr., and H. Zeisel (1966). *The American Jury.* Boston: Little, Brown (shortly thereafter published by University of Chicago Press).

Background

The jury trial has been criticized since its inception as an imperfect vehicle for arriving at an informed decision regarding a criminal defendant's guilt or innocence. The primary criticism of the jury trial is that jurors are not legal experts and are not trained in fact-finding, and so their abilities to carefully assess evidence and witness testimonies are questionable and may result in incorrect verdicts. The jury trial has survived in the United States primarily due to the symbolic nature of having citizens judge those accused of violating the laws created by the citizenry. In fact, it is the closest form of democratic justice short of vigilantism. Nonetheless, jury trial outcomes are often questioned, such as in cases resulting in jury pardons where the defendant is acquitted because the jurors felt that s/he should not be punished even though s/he is guilty of the crime(s) charged. Some jury deliberations also lead to actual bargaining between jurors voting to convict versus those voting to acquit, resulting in an agreement to find the defendant guilty of a lesser charge. Although these outcomes have been justified by some scholars as a way of keeping "the written rules of law from causing oppression by unfair or overzealous application" (Holten and Lamar 1991, p. 243), juries have also been accused of biasing against defendants based on their personal (extralegal) characteristics such as their sex, race, and age, and they have been criticized for not being sophisticated enough to appreciate complex evidence and expert testimonies. These and other criticisms mounted throughout the 20th century. The Chicago Jury Project emerged, in part, due to this negative focus on the utility of jury trials, although the Project would have never emerged without support the Ford Foundation provided to the University of Chicago's Law School in 1952. The grant from the Foundation was intended to fund and promote behavioral research on the law. The Chicago Jury Project, headed by Harry Kalven, Jr. (a legal scholar), Hans Zeisel (a methodologist), and Fred Strodbeck (a sociologist), was only one of a handful of related studies conducted at the University of Chicago during the 1950s, but it was also the most notable project and received the greatest attention from scholars, government officials, and the public. (Rita Simon also worked on the project and conducted her own jury simulation study on the insanity plea, also covered in this section.)

The Chicago Jury Project was not a single study but rather a series of studies that encompassed interviews with jurors, experimental jury simulations, analyses of trial statistics, observations of jury trials, and analyses of *survey* data compiled from judges. Kalven and Zeisel's *The American Jury* was the first study to emerge out of the Project and focused on analyses of the judges' survey data. The authors had originally intended to tape jury deliberations and to examine those recordings but there was an enormous backlash by government officials when they recorded and examined six jury deliberations in civil cases and presented some of those findings at a judicial conference. The recording of jury deliberations was subsequently outlawed and Kalven and Zeisel had to design another research strategy for studying juries. This compromise might have contributed to some of the disillusionment with their first study among scholars who were anticipating a psychology of jury decision-making but instead got *judicial interpretations* of the psychology of jury decision-making. Nonetheless, the authors received praise from many scholars for several of their insights on the topic, and it was ultimately hailed as a pioneering effort that generated a large volume of related research.

The Study

Kalven and Zeisel (1966) conducted a *quantitative* analysis of jury verdicts in criminal cases and judges' perceptions of those verdicts in order to measure the degree to which juries and judges disagreed. The authors examined verdicts and judges' opinions from 3,576 criminal trials, including 2,395 trials that occurred between 1954 and '55, and 1,191 trials from 1958. A different questionnaire was administered to a different set of judges during each time period. The total number of judges surveyed was 555 across the two time periods. The first questionnaire was less structured and included more *open-ended* survey questions (to which judges provided written responses) relative to the second questionnaire that included more *close-ended* survey questions (with judges selecting from a list of possible responses to each question, similar to multiple choice questions). The second questionnaire was developed from the researchers' evaluations of judges' responses to the first survey and was more detailed in terms of the topics covered. The authors wanted to obtain a *random* sample of judges from across the country, but the "sample" they ended up with was far from perfect. First, they obtained an incomplete list of all state judges of trial courts of general jurisdiction and all US District Court judges (N = 3,500). Second, rather than sample these judges, they solicited the cooperation of *all* judges on the list because they did not know which judges presided over *criminal* cases. Third, they received acknowledgements from roughly 40 percent of the judges (n = 1,646), but only 555 judges resided over criminal cases *and* provided completed surveys for the study. Moreover, roughly half of the trial verdicts examined by Kalven and Zeisel came from 15 percent of the responding judges, constituting only 2 percent of the judges on the original list. The authors admitted that their group of judges was more of a *convenience* sample because it consisted solely of volunteers. To their credit, however, they demonstrated that there was no regional bias in the responses of judges who participated, and they argued that there was no reason to suspect that the non-responding judges would have answered the questions any differently from those who participated.

The first survey covering cases processed between 1954 and 1955 compiled information on the details of criminal jury trials that each judge was presiding over at the time they received the survey, including the charges involved and other legal issues, whether the judge would have rendered a guilty verdict before hearing the jury's decision, the jury's verdict, what the sentence of a convicted defendant would have been if it had been a bench trial, reasons for the difference (if any) between the judge's and the jury's verdicts, prior record of the defendant, whether the defendant testified in court, trial length, juror's experiences with other jury trials, the actual sentence, and the prosecutor's and defense attorney's experiences with previous trials. The second survey covering 1958 was more detailed, with questions grouped into several categories including "Description of the Case," "The Verdict," "The Defendant," "The Victim," and "Court Procedure." Only one question was devoted to the quality of the prosecution and the defense, namely whether the judge thought that one side performed "better" than the other. For both surveys, judges were asked to comment on jury trials that they were *currently* presiding over. This was important so that each judge was able to record his decision of a defendant's guilt or innocence *before* the jury returned from deliberations with a verdict, and also because the observations would have been most accurate for their most recent trial experiences. Of course, the authors had to trust that the judges' decisions reflected their honest assessments before hearing each jury's decision as opposed to waiting to see what the jury decided (possibly inflating the correspondence between the judges' and juries' decisions). Also, it is never made clear why the authors generated a second survey with a second sample of judges, although it might have stemmed from weaknesses with the first survey and from lessons learned about how to improve the *response rates* and the quality of information provided to some of the original questions.

Results

With these important research limitations in mind, Kalven and Zeisel found that judges and juries agreed in roughly 78 percent of the 3,576 trials. In only 3 percent of the cases did the jury convict when the judge would have acquitted, and in 19 percent the juries acquitted the defendant when the judge would have convicted. In short, when judges and juries did not agree, juries tended toward acquittals whereas judges tended toward convictions. The remainder of the authors' work then turned to understanding *why* these differences occurred. The surveys included questions tapping why judges believed their opinions differed from those of the juries, and Kalven and Zeisel proceeded to analyze those reasons. They could not account for judge/jury discrepancies in ten percent of the cases but were able to categorize the sources of the remaining discrepancies into five groups: (1) evidence (in 54% of the disagreements), (2) facts unknown by jurors but known by judges (2%), (3) how unevenly the prosecution and defense were matched (4%), (4) jurors' attitudes toward the defendants (11%), and (5) jurors' attitudes toward the applicable laws (29%). Each of these categories were further divided into subcategories capturing more specific reasons for the disagreements. For example, category one was broken down into evidence for the prosecution versus the defense, and further into the specific types for each (police, eyewitness for prosecution, eyewitness for defense, expert for prosecution, expert for defense, etc.). Category two included 10 subcategories such as the judge knew the defendant personally, knew that other charges were pending, knew the defendant had a prior arrest for the same offense, etc. Category four was divided into jurors' perceptions based on the defendant's social status, family, physical appearance in court, occupation, etc. These categories, in turn, were broken down into specific demographics such as "young," "old age," "woman," "ill health," and so on. The subdivision of these groups into smaller and smaller categories was a mixed blessing. On the one hand, the authors had minimal numbers of cases in some of these groups, which did not bode well for the generalizability of their findings. On the other hand, this minutia provided insights that they otherwise would not have gained. Specifically, they found that jurors were often focused on the age of the victim (whether an adult or a minor), that jurors and judges were comparable in their assessments of a defendant's credibility, and that jurors were competent in their consideration and interpretation of evidence and testimonies. Other, less flattering findings included juries' tendencies to be more lenient in cases of voluntary intoxication, although not a legitimate defense, and the least tolerant of sex offenses involving sodomy (a reflection of a cultural bias toward homosexuals during this period).

The authors' analysis of disagreements in verdicts based on evidence also produced some interesting findings. In cases where the available evidence could have just as easily resulted in either a "guilty" or a "not guilty" verdict, juries were swayed more by extra-legal considerations such as their attitudes toward the defendant and toward the applicable laws. This led to the authors' formulation of the "liberation hypothesis," which stated that jurors were more likely to consider extralegal factors in their decisions when cases appeared more ambiguous, either because the evidence could be argued either way or because the cases were not particularly serious.

Regarding whether the prosecuting attorney was a better or worse attorney relative to the defense, Kalven and Zeisel concluded that this "disparity in counsel" did not account for many of the disagreements (only 4% of the total). Judges claimed that, for the most part, the two sides were evenly matched. The two questionnaires tapped this idea in different ways, however. The first questionnaire inferred the "superiority" of one attorney over the other by whether an attorney had more experience than another, yet the second questionnaire merely asked whether the judge perceived that the case was "tried equally well on both sides." One might argue that the second question was a better measure of one attorney's superiority over the other whereas the inference that differences in trial experience could be equated with differences in "superiority" was debatable.

Another aspect of the Jury Project that received much less attention in their book focused on jurors from two urban courts who provided their initial verdicts to the authors (i.e., the ballot votes cast at the beginning of jury deliberations). Kalven and Zeisel found that initial votes producing large majorities one way or the other most often led to final verdicts consistent with the initial majority. On the other hand, hung juries often began with relatively even splits in the initial votes. The authors interpreted this as evidence that it was the ambiguity of the case, not the stubbornness of particular jurors that contributed most to hung juries. Based on both of these findings, the authors inferred that the deliberation process had very little effect on the final verdict (i.e., initial votes were very similar to final votes). Overall, Kalven and Zeisel were favorably impressed by the performance of these juries. They argued that juries were generally competent (based on the compatibility of their verdicts with those of the judges') and that disagreements did not reflect any overarching ignorance or incompetence on the part of jurors. Rather, differences in verdicts occurred most often in "close" cases that were more ambiguous regarding the guilt of the defendant. These disagreements also were not more common in cases with more "difficult" evidence, suggesting that jurors were able to sort through the more complicated cases and still come to the same decisions as judges.

In their effort to understand the psychology of decision-making by jurors, Kalven and Zeisel concluded with a discussion of how "the mind of the jury . . . might . . . exhibit four dominant traits" (p. 493). The first trait involved "the niceness of its calculus of equities," where juries treated defendants with more or less leniency based on the role of the victim as well as what happened to the victim. For example, jurors considered a defendant's action against a victim to be justified when the victim provoked the defendant, but only if the reaction was equal to the provocation (e.g., a single punch). Also, juries sometimes viewed particular types of injuries to a defendant's partner, relative, or friend as punishment for the defendant when the injury was by accident (such as a father who accidentally runs over his child while backing down a driveway). The second trait was a jury's tendency to not perceive the state as the prosecution but instead to perceive the victim as the "other party . . . as though it were a private quarrel" (p. 493). Third, jurors tended to obscure distinctions between guilt and the actual punishment when considering the particulars of a case. The determination of guilt should be based solely on evidence whereas punishment (assuming guilt) can be influenced by such factors as victim impact statements or unique circumstances surrounding the events that might reflect an offender's level of culpability. Fourth, jurors sometimes made distinctions in the law that were not intended by the law itself, and so they might have been more or less lenient than the law dictated. For example, jurors (during the time at which the study occurred) were less inclined than the law to convict a defendant of rape, even though they recognized that the defendant was guilty of *some* crime. Similarly, some jurors were harsher than the law regarding adults accused of more minor sex offenses involving children, such as "sexual approach to children" (mentioned by the authors). Kalven and Zeisel observed that this last issue explained why some of the juries' decisions were harsher than the judges'.

Limitations

There were many critics of Kalven and Zeisel's study although much of the criticism might have been a product of the lackluster findings in light of the hype surrounding their much-anticipated book. Even so, a few of these criticisms were valid from an empirical standpoint. These included the administration and analysis of two different surveys from two different time periods, the types of questions that were ignored but would have been relevant to their inquiry, the ability of judges to offer reliable perceptions of attorneys' skills and experiences, not to mention of jurors' motivations to decide cases in particular ways that were inconsistent with judges' opinions, the honesty of the judges, and the lack of rigor in the statistical analysis of the *survey* data. The first criticism regarding two separate surveys is important because Kalven and Zeisel simply merged the two different samples of judges (and their trials) into one larger sample for their analysis. The use of different questions to measure the "same" phenomenon can be problematic if each set is interpreted differently by judges, such as measuring the skills of attorneys by years of experience during one period versus whether the judge perceived that one side performed better than the other during the second period (Waltz 1966). Also, based on the *non-probability* sampling methods employed, there was no way to be certain that the two groups of volunteers from the two time periods were similar enough to be pooled into the same sample. The assumption underlying such an approach is that the samples can be treated as if they were selected from the same population. It might seem logical that one set of judges can be pooled with another set of judges, but the difference in the time periods during which each group volunteered might have created differences between the two groups on unmeasured factors that were tied to the authors' variables. For example, improvements over time in jury selection techniques or procedures to educate jurors might have generated a tighter correspondence between judges' and juries' verdicts which, in turn, could have been correlated to differences over time in the quality of evidence (which also might have improved).

The second criticism related to the absence of important survey questions is also fair in light of Kalven and Zeisel's heavy focus on *why* jurors and judges disagreed in 23 percent of the verdicts. As discussed by Harris Steinberg (1966), there were no questions regarding differences between the personal characteristics of the defendant versus the jurors, the types of defense counsel involved (public defender, assigned counsel, private attorney), whether and how many challenges were made by each side, any publicity surrounding each case, and other extraneous factors that might have contributed to disagreements between judges and juries. This situation was potentially more problematic based on the all-volunteer sample because there was no way to determine whether some of the above confounding effects might have been more or less common in the cases heard by the particular judges examined. For example, given that 50 percent of the trial verdicts were provided by 15 percent of the responding judges, it is likely that those judges were from urban courts with heavy caseloads. Such courts were more apt to have public defenders and, based on Eisenstein and Jacob's (1977) work, judges might have been less inclined to rank those attorneys as superior to prosecutors. This raised the possibility that some of the disagreements attributed to "counsel disparities" by the authors actually resulted from political factors related to judicial biases toward PDs.

Also in question was how accurately judges were able to respond to questions regarding the experiences of attorneys as well as the possible motivations of jurors to vote in particular ways. Since the authors had no way of checking up on judges in order to *validate* the survey data, they also could not be sure that judges were commenting on trials currently underway at the time of the survey. Such a scenario opens up the possibility of *memory error* on the part of judges, and such errors might be compounded when judges are attempting to recall trials further in their past. Memory errors occur in survey research as a consequence of asking respondents specific questions about their past behaviors. A person's memory tends to fade as more time passes and respondents are more likely to recall events differently from what they actually experienced. These types of errors might be compounded with more detailed questions when efforts to provide more detail lead respondents to confuse different persons and/or events. In trying to retroactively interpret a jury's verdict, for example, a judge might not recall all of the jurors and/or all events that transpired during the course of the trial. Those he can remember then shape his definition of reality, thus leading to an interpretation of a decision that was not based on consideration of all relevant criteria.

Related to the fourth criticism regarding the authors' inability to be certain that judges were rendering their decisions *before* knowing the juries' decisions, the relatively high rate of correspondence in these decisions (78%) could have resulted from judges merely waiting until the jury's verdict was read before considering their own opinion. Somewhat related to this critique, there is also a question of whether a judge's perception of the "superiority" of the prosecution or the defense was based on the side that actually won the case. It would be logical for anyone to define a person's performance as "superior" to another's based on the outcome of that performance (a retrospective interpretation of past events).

The last criticism described here focused on the absence of any statistical *hypothesis* testing with the *survey* data (Hare 1967, Jacob 1967). Kalven and Zeisel displayed a variety of frequencies, percentages, and cross-tabulations, but they did not test whether juries' and judges' verdicts varied significantly by the five groups of information they identified (evidence, counsel disparity, knowledge of the defendant, etc.). Subjecting their data to some rudimentary *chi-square tests* (a test of *statistical significance*) might have narrowed down the list of contributing factors to the disagreements between juries and judges. Conversely, they might have found that many of these differences were attributable to mere chance, just as two judges might disagree on the same case once in a while.

Significance and Subsequent Research

Most of the above criticisms were either directly or indirectly expressed by Kalven and Zeisel themselves when they described the shortcomings of their data, and these self-criticisms might have actually generated the same criticisms made by others. Nonetheless, despite these criticisms, the book is now considered a classic of jury decision-making and is the most cited of any jury study to date (based on the Social Science Citation Index). More importantly, it contributed directly to growing interest in jury trials by academics and policy makers. Criticisms of jury trials in death penalty cases mounted during the 1970s and '80s when the death penalty was reinstated, and questions regarding jury biases in such cases led to research grounded in Kalven and Zeisel's discussion of the relevance of jurors' attitudes toward defendants. Related to this, jury selection procedures were being criticized for not providing an adequate representation of women and minorities. Issues of jury selection and size were dealt with by the US Supreme Court, which cited Kalven and Zeisel's work in related decisions.

In the area of academic research, the authors' work prompted many psychologists to study jurors' behaviors through jury simulation (mock jury) studies (e.g., Landy and Aronson 1969). It was this area of research that actually provided the majority of citations of Kalven and Zeisel's study. There were over 100 of such studies conducted within just 10 years after the authors' publication. Fred Strodtbeck and Rita Simon's work on the Project involved simulated trials with persons selected from actual jury rolls. The mock jurors listened to taped simulations of trials enacted by actual attorneys, complete with the presentation of evidence and witness testimonies. The jurors were then asked questions regarding their interpretations of the evidence and decisions on the legal debates. David Landy and Elliot Aronson (1969) modified their technique and studied college students in a similar context, asking about the sentences they would recommend in particular cases as opposed to the verdicts they would render. Their approach was then followed by many other academics, due to the ease with which such a project could be carried out on college campuses, until the method came under subsequent attack for the use of groups of college students rather than groups that were more similar to actual juries (Erlanger 1970, Vidmar 1979, Weiten and Diamond 1979). These critics observed that findings from many of the "college" jury studies often produced inconsistent results with those of Kalven and Zeisel even though the authors of those other studies tended to focus on the (fewer) similarities in findings across studies. Additional criticism subsequently led researchers during the 1980s and '90s *back* to the design originally employed by Strodtbeck and Simon (Diamond 1982, Hastie et al. 1983). The observations made by Kalven and Zeisel were eventually incorporated into studies of the cognitive abilities of jurors in the area of social psychology (Pennington and Hastie 1990).

Part of the larger plan of the Chicago Jury Project was to also focus on civil jury trials. There was equal (if not more) hype attached to that aspect of the Project, yet the authors failed to deliver any publication or report on the subject. This was somewhat disappointing since particular scholars were less critical of the criminal jury trial study only because it was seen as a predecessor to the more anticipated civil jury trial study. When referring to the relevance of Kalven and Zeisel's work, Jon Waltz (1966) stated "Perhaps its greatest importance resides in the circumstances that it may simply be a prelude to something much more important: the authors' forthcoming examination of the civil jury" (p. 385). Even so, their work drew more favorable attention over time and scholars arguing in favor of the use of juries in criminal litigation, based on Kalven and Zeisel's observations regarding jurors' competencies, have cited it often. Although Kalven and Zeisel stated that their work would offer evidence for *both* sides of that argument, most citations of this work have focused on findings that favored the use of jury trials (specifically, the general agreement between judges' and jurors' decisions, and the ability of jurors to sift through complicated evidence and testimonies and arrive at the same decisions as judges).

A separate but important area of research also emerged from the authors' study related to the "liberation hypothesis" derived from a segment of their analysis. According to their thesis, sentencing decisions may be less biased in the most heinous cases because offense seriousness is the *only* consideration of judges and juries in such cases. Sentencing may be *more* biased in *less* serious cases because those sentences are not clear-cut. Judges and juries might consider other factors reflecting their own prejudices that help them to rationalize their decisions. This thesis has been applied to studies of the death penalty, predicting that extralegal characteristics are *less* likely to matter in jury verdicts and sentences in homicide cases (Baldus et al. 1985, Barnett 1985, Keil and Vito 1989). It has also been applied in studies of racial and ethnic disparities in sentencing in the context of understanding why a defendant's race or ethnicity might matter more in some types of cases versus others. Based on the logic of the thesis, race and ethnicity should matter *less* in more serious cases. Cassia Spohn and Jerry Cederblom (1991) adopted this framework in their analysis of murder, robbery, rape, other sex offenses, and assault. They found that African Americans were more likely than whites to be incarcerated for assault but not for the other offenses. James Unnever and Larry Hembroff (1988) found support for the related idea that African American defendants were more likely than whites to be incarcerated when their cases did not fall into "an obvious dispositional category."

No less important were the impacts of the authors' work on the United States Supreme Court, federal appeals courts, and state appellate courts. The study was cited in 21 cases decided by the US Supreme Court (mostly death penalty cases), in 38 federal appellate court cases, and in 79 state appellate court decisions. Over 95 percent of the decisions cited Kalven and Zeisel in support of the majority opinions. Aside from the authors' discussion of death penalty cases, the most common cites involved their discussions of jury size, the decision rule, and jurors' perceptions of defendants. The context in which most of these cites were made involved arguments supporting the competence of juries. The authors were not pleased with all of the cites, however, such as when the Supreme Court ruled that Florida's use of six-member juries sufficed for an adequate determination of guilt. The Court drew from Kalven and Zeisel's finding that jurors with initial ballots reflecting a minority opinion (relative to the rest of the jury) often conceded to the majority in their final vote, suggesting that larger juries do not necessarily lead to dramatic changes in how the majority of jurors vote between the first and last ballots. Subsequent to that decision, Zeisel criticized the use of smaller juries because they tended to generate more variability in verdicts among jurors.

On the academic side, the vast majority of studies conducted since *The American Jury* have yielded similar conclusions regarding the ability of jurors to reach carefully reasoned decisions on the guilt or innocence of the accused. A relatively recent study involved a reanalysis of Kalven and Zeisel's data (Gastwirth and Sinclair 2004) and provided some new insights on the topic, suggesting that the original data remain of interest to scholars today. Two findings of particular interest emerged from the secondary analysis by Gastwirth and Sinclair. Elaborating on Kalven and Zeisel's original finding that the absence of a prior record had a significant impact on disagreements, the new analysis revealed that prior record had an important influence on whether jurors were sympathetic toward the defendant. Disagreements in serious crimes were also found to be influenced by superior defense attorneys and the apparent absence of prior records. By contrast, disagreements in lesser crimes were more often due to jurors' sympathy for a defendant. Related to the earlier criticism that Kalven and Zeisel failed to conduct statistical hypothesis tests with the survey data, Gastwirth and Sinclair presented results from hypothesis tests of some of the original data and found support for several of Kalven and Zeisel's observations.

References

Baldus, D., G. Woodworth, and C. Pulaski (1985). "Monitoring and Evaluating Contemporary Death Sentencing Systems: Lessons from Georgia." *University of California Davis Law Review* 18:1375–1407.

Barnett, A. (1985). "Some Distribution Patterns for the Georgia Death Sentence." *University of california Davis Law Review* 18:1327–74.

Diamond, S. (1982). "Growth and Maturation in Psychology and Law." *Law and Society Review* 17:1–10.

Erlanger, H. (1970). "Jury Research in America: Its Past and Future." *Law and Society Review* 4:345–70.

Gastwirth, J., and M. Sinclair (2004). "A Re-examination of the 1966 Kalven-Zeisel Study of Judge-Jury Agreements and Disagreements and their Causes." *Law, Probability, and Risk* 3:169–91.

Hare, A. (1967). "The American Jury (Book Review)." *American Sociological Review* 32:666–67.

Hastie, R., D. Penrod, and N. Pennington (1983). *Inside the Jury.* Cambridge, MA: Harvard UP.

Holten, G., and L. Lamar (1991). *The Criminal Courts: Structures, Personnel, and Processes.* New York: McGraw-Hill.

Jacob, H. (1967). "The American Jury (Book Review). *Midwest Journal of Political Science* 11:282–83.

Keil, T., and G. Vito (1989). "Race, Homicide Severity, and Application of the Death Penalty: A Consideration of the Barnett Scale." *Criminology* 27:511–35.

Kalven, H. Jr., and H. Zeisel (1966). *The American Jury.* Boston: Little, Brown (shortly thereafter published by University of Chicago Press).

Landy, D., and E. Aronson (1969). "The Influence of the Character of the Criminal and His Victim on the Decisions of Simulated Jurors." *Journal of Experimental Social Psychology* 5:141–52.

Pennington, N., and R. Hastie (1990). "Practical Implications of Psychological Research on Juror and Jury Decision Making." *Personality and Social Psychology Bulletin* 16: 90–105.

Simon, R. (1980). *The Jury.* Lanham, MD: Rowan and Littlefield.

Spohn, C., and J. Cederblom (1991). "Race and Disparities in Sentencing: A Test of the Liberation Hypothesis." *Justice Quarterly* 8:305–27.

Steinberg, H. (1966). "The American Jury (Book Review)." *Harvard Law Review* 80:477–84.

Unnever, J., and L. Hembroff (1988). "The Prediction of Racial/Ethnic Sentencing Disparities: An Expectation States Approach." *Journal of Research in Crime and Delinquency* 25:53–82.

Vidmar, N. (1979). "The Other Issues in Jury Simulation Research: A Commentary with Particular Reference to Defendant Character Studies." *Law and Human Behavior* 3:95–106.

Waltz, J. (1966). "The American Jury (Book Review)." *Journal of Criminal Law, Criminology, and Police Science.* 58:382–85.

Weiten, W., and S. Diamond (1979). "A Critical Review of the Jury Simulation Paradigm: The Case of Defendant Characteristics." *Law and Human Behavior* 3:71–93.

Further Reading

Levine, J. (1992). *Juries and Politics.* Pacific Groves, CA: Brooks/Cole.

Uviller, H. (1996). *Virtual Justice: The Flawed Prosecution of Crime in America.* New Haven, CT.: Yale UP.

Van Dyke, J. (1977). *Jury Selection Procedures: Our Uncertain Commitment to Representative Panels.* Cambridge, MA: Ballinger.

THE INSANITY DEFENSE: ARE JURORS ABLE TO UNDERSTAND DIFFERENT LEGAL RULES FOR ESTABLISHING A DEFENDANT'S CRIMINAL RESPONSIBILITY?

Simon, R. (1967). *The Jury and the Defense of Insanity.* Boston: Little, Brown.

Background

As part of the Chicago Jury Project, Rita Simon designed and conducted a study to assess the impact of "lawyer's lore" on jury deliberations and verdicts. If it were applicable, she argued, then different juror characteristics would coincide with differences in *how* they considered the facts presented at trial and with differences in their verdicts. Harry Kalven, Jr., and Hans Zeisel published *The American Jury* just one year before Simon published her study. Although Kalven and Zeisel's study received far more attention from both practitioners and academics, Simon's research had a larger impact on subsequent mock jury studies in the area of social psychology. Simon's study was also important due to her focus on the insanity defense and how well jurors understood related legal rules and instructions. How to process and sentence offenders who are mentally ill has been a preoccupation of legal scholars for over 150 years, and so her study captured two very important legal debates. Important to add is that Simon was also a statistical consultant solicited by Kalven and Zeisel to examine data from their 1966 publication.

Recall from our discussion of Kalven and Zeisel that their initial research efforts involving the observation and recording of actually jury deliberations ultimately led to legislation that prohibited researchers from engaging in those methods when studying jury decision-making. This posed a challenge to researchers because, without *observational* data on the process, related legal debates had to rely on mere speculations due to the secrecy of jury deliberations. Two approaches to the study of juries were subsequently developed. The first method involved analyses of actual jury verdicts sampled from court cases, or analyses of *archival* data. The primary foci of this type of research falls either on longitudinal trends in the verdicts delivered in specific types of cases (in order to evaluate changing public opinions of certain crimes), or on empirical relationships between these verdicts and case characteristics (to see if certain characteristics of defendants and cases increase the odds of acquittals versus convictions). The second approach involves the mock jury study, where research subjects listen to or watch a simulated trial and then engage in deliberations in order to derive a verdict. The analysis of archived data is limited because it provides little insight into how and why jurors reached their verdicts. Although relationships might be established between particular verdicts and case characteristics, a researcher cannot infer that the relationships are *causal* and must treat them instead as *correlations* (the distinction made in our previous discussion of Albonetti's study of prosecutorial discretion). The advantage of mock juries is the ability to conduct an *experiment* where the subjects are *randomly assigned* to different cases or the cases are randomly assigned to particular types of jurors. It is also easy to *replicate* (repeat) these types of studies for the purpose of *generalizablity*. Rita Simon adopted the mock jury approach but also incorporated elements of the first method (above) of studying jury decision-making by creating simulated trials from the official court transcripts of two actual trials involving the insanity defense. Merging the two methods in this way helped to reduce criticism that the mock trials did not deal with realistic subject matter.

Simon focused on cases involving the insanity defense for two reasons. First, as described below, there was a question about whether different legal rules on the insanity plea generated different decisions by jurors. Second, such cases provide an interesting context for examining whether and how jurors introduce their own biases into their evaluations of the evidence and instructions and, in turn, into their decisions. Beyond these factors, Simon's study of cases involving the insanity defense was important for assessing whether jurors can possess particular biases upon entering deliberations and yet still arrive at an intelligent decision *with* the group. In other words, did the jury process help to counter personal prejudices in order to generate more equitable decisions? If it did, then the existence of personal prejudices had no bearing on a court's ability to carry out due process. If the jury process did *not* counter personal prejudices, on the other hand, then there was hypocrisy between due process in theory versus in practice. Ironically, the court system holds "justice" as its primary goal while relying on persons to intelligently determine legal guilt even when they hold subjective values that interfere with the rational determination of a "just" decision.

Establishing the legal rule for criminal responsibility has preoccupied legal scholars for centuries. Prior to the 17th century, English courts followed "knowledge of good or evil" as the test for criminal responsibility. During the 17th century, it was held that only absolute madness was a defense for lack of criminal responsibility. It followed in the 18th century that the accused must lack any understanding and memory of his or her actions, similar to an infant, in order to be excused. English courts subsequently derived a legal rule under the case of Daniel M'Naghten whereby criminal responsibility was said to be absent when the offender did not understand the nature of his actions due to failure to distinguish "right" from "wrong." This was the legal rule applied in all courts of the United States until the mid-1990s when the case of *Durham v. United States* was tried in the US Court of Appeals for the District of Columbia. The legal rule emerging from *Durham* was that criminal responsibility was absent if the offense was a product of mental illness. This ruling provided psychiatrists with a more important role at trial and it seemed to be preferred by both defense attorneys and psychiatrists who, under *M'Naghten*, were limited in terms of the medical information they could introduce and describe at trial. At the time of Simon's 1967 study, most courts across the country still followed the *M'Naghten* rule. Questions arose, however, regarding whether juries differed in their understanding of *M'Naghten* versus *Durham* and, in turn, whether this resulted in differences in their ability to make informed decisions regarding criminal responsibility in cases involving the insanity defense.

The Experiment

Rita Simon, a sociologist, was solicited by Kalven and Zeisel to conduct an *experimental* study on jury deliberations in cases where the only defense is insanity. Simon's (1967) broader research question involved the decision making process of jurors and the extent to which their decisions were driven by rational thought, intelligence, and careful consideration of evidence versus by personal prejudices and accident. Simon's focus on cases involving the insanity defense allowed her to compare jury deliberations under two different types of related cases entailing different methods of consideration by jurors (i.e., *M'Naghten* versus *Durham*). If jurors came to similar decisions in each type of case, then perhaps they were not differentiating the facts and testimonies presented between the two types of cases, thus lending support to the idea that jurors do not carefully consider the details presented at trial.

The two types of cases focused on the *M'Naghten* rule versus the *Durham* rule, both of which guided the insanity defense throughout the history of the United States. Under *M'Naghten*, a defendant was determined to not be criminally responsible if s/he did not understand that the act was wrong (also known as the "right/wrong test"). The *Durham* rule, by contrast, stipulated that a defendant was not responsible if the act resulted from mental disease or mental defect. This rule generated a more important role for the psychiatrist at trial because of the requirement that the behavior be linked to a mental disorder which only a psychiatrist could officially determine. Simon took the transcripts of two actual trials that reflected each of these determinations: *Durham v. United States* (a case of breaking and entering into a private residence) and *United States v. King* (a case of incest). Both cases were renamed and the transcripts edited to constitute trials of 60–90 minutes in length. These edited transcripts were then recorded, with University of Chicago Law School faculty as the "players" (including the attorneys, witnesses, and judges involved in each case). There were 98 total trials held in Chicago, Minneapolis, and St. Louis with jurors selected from jury panels in each city. Each juror filled out a questionnaire on his or her personal demographic and socio-demographic information. Groups of 12 jurors listened to each trial with instructions provided at the end regarding the particular rule of law for determining criminal responsibility. Each juror submitted a written statement with his or her initial decision on the case *before* jury deliberations, and the jury's final decision (after deliberation) was reported to the bailiff. There were 30 trials conducted for the "breaking and entering" (*Durham*) trial, with half of those juries instructed that the defendant would be committed to a hospital if found not guilty by reason of insanity and would be hospitalized until determined to be of "sound mind" by authorities. The other half of the *Durham* juries was not given these instructions. The remaining 68 trials were devoted to the incest case. Of these trials, 20 juries were given instructions based on *M'Naghten*, 26 juries were given the *Durham* rule, and 22 juries were not instructed either way.

The study was designed to determine the effect of different legal rules on jurors' decision-making in cases where the defense was insanity. There was a question of whether there was a difference between the rules to the extent that jurors understood each rule and could apply it capably.

Results

Complications arose with the "breaking and entering" trials due to Simon's strict adherence to the original trial transcripts. In the original *Durham* case, the testifying psychiatrists were bound by the *M'Naghten* rule and so refused to express an opinion on the "right/wrong" question. The trial ended in a conviction that was subsequently overturned. The defendant was tried a second time under the *Durham* rule, at which time the psychiatrists provided obscure answers to the attorneys' questions. Simon concluded that, under these ambiguous conditions, neither the *M'Naghten* rule nor the *Durham* rule was reliably examined and so the "breaking and entering" trials were discontinued. Regardless, Simon found that the two sets of jurors who heard this case with two different rules of law generally came to the same decisions. That is, most jurors in each group believed that defendants found not guilty by reason of insanity would be hospitalized until "cured."

Turning to the "incest" trials, Simon found significant differences in the verdicts across the three groups (*M'Naghten* applied, *Durham* applied, no rule applied). For the *M'Naghten* cases, the psychiatrists stated that the defendant was mentally ill yet knew right from wrong during the crime. For the *Durham* cases, the psychiatrists stated that the crime (incest) resulted from the defendant's mental illness. For the cases with no instruction of a legal rule, the psychiatrists limited their statements to observations about the defendant's mental condition. The uninstructed juries produced similar findings to the juries instructed under *Durham*, contrary to Simon's prediction that the former would be more similar to the *M'Naghten* juries. The defendant was acquitted in 4 of the 22 uninstructed trials versus 5 of the 26 *Durham* trials, and hung juries occurred in 4 of the uninstructed trials versus 6 of the *Durham* trials. The M'Naghten juries delivered guilty verdicts in 19 of the 20 trials, with one hung jury. In short, jurors were much less likely to acquit under *M'Naghten* relative to *Durham*. She noted, " . . . the criterion for criminal responsibility as defined under *Durham* is closer to the jury's natural sense of equity than is the *M'Naghten* rule" (p. 216).

Simon interpreted these results as suggesting that jurors were unambiguous in their interpretations and applications of *M'Naghten* (due to the consistency in guilty verdicts), but they were less clear on the elements of *Durham* and how to apply it (reflected by the mix of guilty, not guilty, and hung verdicts). The similarity in findings between the Durham and no rule cases indicated that the *Durham* standard was no more effective than providing jurors with *no* legal standard.

Another empirical question examined by Simon was whether different verdicts would result from trials with "typical" expert testimony versus "model" expert testimony. The typical expert testimony involved what was offered in the original incest trial, whereas the model expert testimony offered a more comprehensive description of the defendant's psychiatric history. The model testimony was created in consultation with psychiatrists who perceived the need to enhance the role of expert testimonies in related cases. A comparison of findings for the two sets of juries revealed no significant differences in decisions based on the typical versus the model testimonies.

Simon also examined the validity of lawyers' claims that the personal attributes of jurors influenced their verdicts in ways that reflected their own personal attitudes and biases (i.e., "lawyer's lore"). For example, whether women tended to be more punitive than men, Englishmen more punitive than Irishmen, and less educated jurors more punitive than more educated jurors. Simon found evidence favoring the applicability of "lawyer's lore" to the *initial* votes of jurors. Her analysis of 1,176 jurors revealed that persons with less education were more likely to vote not guilty by reason of insanity, African Americans acquitted more often than all other race and ethnic groups, proprietors were more likely than laborers to vote guilty, and housewives were most likely to vote guilty.

Overall, Simon concluded that while jurors might have brought their personal prejudices into the jury room, which, in turn, affected their initial votes, the jury deliberations typically countered those initial reactions and helped to generate more reasonable decisions.

Simon also found that most of the juries spent several hours on deliberations, with many reflecting what would be expected from a trial lasting 2 or 3 days. The jurors in her study also did not reinforce the stereotype that typical jurors were punitive and wanted retribution. These findings generally supported the traditional jury system in the United States although they also suggested a need for greater reliance on expert testimony. Aside from the specific conclusions described here, Simon's study was pioneering in the application of an *experimental* design to a *quantitative* analysis of jury deliberations.

Limitations

One of the legal criticisms of *M'Naghten* was that the rule punished the sick because, relative to *Durham*, its application was more likely to result in a guilty verdict (i.e., mentally ill defendants were sometimes determined to have known right from wrong under *M'Naghten*). *Durham* was not as severe because the defendant was exonerated if a link was established between the mental illness and the crime. In other words, *M'Naghten* better protected society whereas *Durham* protected the offender. Whether society or the defendant should have been the focus was a policy debate that was brewing when Simon conducted her study although she never discussed the implications of her findings for this debate. The lack of any related discussion seemed odd given her ability to assess what jurors seemed to prioritize through their deliberations and verdicts.

Another criticism of the study came from Simon herself, who observed that the *M'Naghten* verdicts (19 guilty verdicts out of 20 trials) might have been influenced by how the trials were set up. All of the psychiatrists formally stated that the defendant understood right from wrong, and this clear absence of ambiguity might have led to the (basic) consensus across juries. She also recognized several other standard criticisms of research on mock juries. First, recorded trials were not as realistic as actual trials because the conditions under which jurors watched or listened to the proceedings were artificial. Second, the original trials lasted several days as opposed to 90 minutes. The additional details that would have emerged from longer trials could have also influenced the jurors' decisions. Third, jurors knew it was an *experiment* with no real consequences for either the defendant or the public. Under these circumstances, study participants might have been harsher than they otherwise would have been if the future of the defendant was really at stake. Conversely, they might have been more lenient in the experiment because their decision would have no real impact on the protection of society. Finally, the recording of the jury deliberations might have prevented some jurors from being honest in their opinions. There is always a risk that study participants will alter their behaviors when being observed by ethnographers, and some of the mock jurors might have altered their decisions based on what they believed the "appropriate" decisions should have been in such cases.

Some researchers have compared differences between jury decisions in simulated versus actual trials although their analyses produced mixed findings, including more lenient decisions by mock juries relative to actual juries, harsher decisions by mock juries, and no differences between the two groups (Kaplan and Krupa 1986, Kerr et al. 1979, Wilson and Donnerstein 1977, Zeisel and Diamond 1978). A couple of studies have also found that mock trials lead to findings of stronger effects of defendant characteristics on jury verdicts relative to actual trials (Kassin and Juhnke 1983, Tanford and Penrod 1984). Overall, however, it appears that the process whereby jurors reach their decisions does not differ between mock and actual trials (Hastie et al. 1983). Studies of differences between decisions made by college students versus adults have also been conducted because some researchers have used college students as mock jurors, as previously discussed. Findings from these studies have typically revealed no differences in verdicts between the two groups (Bray et al. 1978, MacCoun and Kerr 1988, Sue et al. 1974).

The "model" expert testimony examined by Simon was also criticized for its content. The model testimony offered in the simulated trials constituted a more objective review of medical facts as opposed to allowing the experts to place these facts in the context of the crime committed and the defendant's criminal history, yet jurors needed to hear the linkages between the defendant's history of mental illness and how that history might have influenced his criminal behavior since the jurors were not experts on those linkages (Diamond 1982). Simon observed that the lack of differences in verdicts between the "typical" and "model" expert testimonies suggested that the traditional expert testimony should suffice, but the absence of any differences could have also suggested the need to further improve expert testimony by allowing experts to tie a defendant's medical history to the facts of the case so that jurors (and even judges) could make better informed decisions. Given the case of incest, it also would have been helpful if the experts had commented and provided insights into the behaviors of the family members who, in the original case, knew of the sexual acts for several years before police became involved. It must be recognized that many judges prefer the more objective and dispassionate statements of psychiatrists in related cases. The criticism of dispassionate testimony, however, is that jurors were less likely to become interested in and concerned with the expert testimony.

Finally, Robert MacCoun (1989) argued that the two most policy-relevant questions in related research on jury deliberations were (a) under what conditions can jury performance be enhanced, and (b) how did the jury perform relative to other legal decision-makers? Simon's research could not really address either of these questions.

Significance and Subsequent Research

Most states came to reject the *Durham* test after Simon's study. Recall her finding that the *Durham* rule produced inconsistent verdicts that did not differ significantly from those obtained when jurors were not instructed on any applicable rule regarding the insanity defense. She interpreted this finding as *Durham* was no better than providing *no* guidance to jurors. This observation helped to fuel arguments against the use of *Durham*, which, in turn, contributed to its demise as a legal rule. Today, most states use one of three tests for insanity: *M'Naghten*, the "Irresistible Impulse Test," and the "A.L.I." (A few states do not apply these legal rules due to the existence of the "guilty but insane" verdict in these states.) The Irresistible Impulse Test involves determining whether a mental disorder led the defendant to be uncontrollably "drawn" to the criminal act even when s/he understood that the act was wrong. The A.L.I. focuses on the defendant's inability, or "lack of substantial capacity", to appreciate that the criminal behavior was wrong or that the defendant had a more general inability to conform to the law. Consistent with the continued use of *M'Naghten* was Simon's finding that 19 of the 20 juries instructed on *M'Naghten* delivered guilty verdicts, suggesting greater uniformity in jurors' understanding of this legal rule.

Simon's work also offered a methodological contribution to subsequent research on jurors' biases in decision-making. MacCoun (1989) underscored the importance of assessing juror's initial verdicts *before* deliberations took place due to findings such as Simon's regarding differences in jurors' verdicts before versus after their deliberations. This aspect of her study sets it apart from many other jury simulation studies and is the only reliable method of determining whether the deliberation process serves to offset the subjective views that individuals bring into the jury room.

Simon's work, in conjunction with Kalven and Zeisel's study, sparked an era of research on the American jury system beginning in the late 1960s. This era might have also been influenced by some of the sensational trials that received national attention during the 1960s and '70s, particularly those related to protests over the Vietnam War (e.g., the Chicago Seven), the assassinations of political figures (e.g., Martin Luther King, Jr., by James Earl Ray), and Watergate (e.g., John Ehrlichman). Nonetheless, Simon's work was an important contribution to this interest. Research on jury trials has taken several directions, all of which can be traced back to some aspect of Simon's study and findings. First, researchers continued to examine the ability of jurors to make rational and intelligent decisions as a group even though they each maintained particular biases (e.g., Diamond 1982, Erlanger 1970, Hastie et al. 1983, Landy and Aronson 1969, Pennington and Hastie 1990, Vidmar 1979, Weiten and Diamond 1979). Related to this topic was the social psychology of jury deliberations and whether decision-making was influenced by factors such as the number of jurors and the mandate to reach unanimous verdicts. Although Simon argued that her findings generally supported the idea that jury verdicts did reflect intelligent decision making, and that the whole was much more than the sum of its parts, the body of related empirical research produced mixed findings overall. Second, scholarly interest has grown regarding the influence of the media on jurors' decisions, specifically when the media "leaks" information on a defendant, and the importance of *voir dire* (jury instructions provided by the judge) to counter prejudices that may result from media bias (e.g., Friendly and Goldfarb 1968, Meyer 1969, Siebert 1970, Singer and Barton 1975). For the most part, related studies have suggested that voir dire can effectively counter such initial biases stemming from media coverage of the case and of the defendant. Related to this topic are discussions regarding the conflict between freedom of the press and granting defendants the right to a fair trial. Third, some scholars have explored the argument that the jury system no longer serves a useful function in modern society, and they have examined public support for either abandoning the system altogether or modifying the system (with the use of fewer jurors and majority verdicts instead of unanimous verdicts, for example). The literature on this issue generally supports maintaining the current system, consistent with Simon's observations.

A fourth area of research, also the most common, involved studies of juror characteristics and their links to both verdicts and how they were derived (how evidence was considered by jurors, what they generally paid attention to and why, if and how they considered the extralegal characteristics of defendants, etc.) (Adler 1975, Bing and Rosenfeld 1970, Boehm 1968, Crockett 1971, Gerard and Terry 1970, Griffitt and Jackson 1973, Hermann 1970, Kaplan and Simon 1972, Kuhn 1968, Landy and Aronson 1969, Mitchell and Byrne 1973, Sigall and Ostrove 1975, Snyder 1971, Stephan 1974, 1975). Simon examined some of these issues by having study participants fill out a survey at the beginning of the experiment that tapped information on their personal characteristics, and then asking the participants for their initial verdicts before jury deliberations began. This permitted her analysis of empirical relationships between juror characteristics and guilty verdicts both before *and* after deliberations (i.e., the examination of "lawyer's lore" described earlier). This area of research is tied to the first area mentioned above because of the theoretical argument that jurors' incompetence might be driven, in part, by their personal characteristics.

Yet another area of research focused more specifically on the voir dire procedure and its impact on jurors' decisions. All jury trials begin with the process of selecting jurors and informing them of their roles in the trial and what they can and cannot do. There are three primary functions of voir dire: to compile information on jurors in order to facilitate their selection by the prosecution and the defense, to allow the prosecutor and the defense attorneys to develop rapport with the jurors, and to allow the attorneys to influence jurors regarding how they should consider the evidence and arguments. Michael Fried, Kalman Kaplan, and Katherine Klein (1975) introduced a social psychological framework for understanding jury selection in this context, providing information on the motivations of prosecutors and defense attorneys to exclude or retain jurors with particular characteristics.

Other issues have also emerged in this literature although they have not been subjected to empirical research and were also not the focus of Simon's study. Specifically, a defendant's competency to stand trial has received a fair amount of debate but without direct examination. This topic might appear tied to Simon's focus on the insanity defense although "sanity" regarding a defendant's competency to stand trial is distinct from the insanity *defense*, the latter focusing on whether the defendant was sane *at the time the crime was committed*. Another subject of debate is the eligibility requirements for jurors. Most states maintain the same requirements but controversy stems from the issue that prospective jurors can be excused for particular "hardships." Different judges are more or less tolerant of excuses provided by solicited jurors, possibly generating inequities in jury pools across cases (such as when some judges are willing to exclude teachers but other judges are not). A final topic that has received much discussion but without much empirical attention is whether juries are in fact representative cross-sections of the populations from which they are drawn. Since voir dire allows attorneys to approve and excuse particular jurors, the question is whether this procedure is potentially discriminatory for a defendant. For example, prosecutors may attempt to remove minority jurors from the pool if the defendant is a minority. They can accomplish this through use of peremptory challenges, which allow prosecutors and defense attorneys to excuse a certain number of jurors without having to justify their decisions to the judge. These three topics pose particular challenges to either ethnographic or quantitative research designs because of the privacy of related proceedings. The fact that these are the only controversies excluded from study, however, bodes well for research on American juries.

References

Adler, F. (1975). "Socioeconomic Factors Influencing Jury Verdicts." *New York University Review of Law and Social Change* 3:1–10.

Bing, S., and S. Rosenfeld (1970). *A Report by the Lawyer's Committee for Civil Rights Under Law, to the Governor's Committee on Law Enforcement, and Administration of Justice and the Quality of Justice in the Lower Criminal Courts of Metropolitan Boston.* Unpublished manuscript.

Boehm, V. (1968). "Mr. Prejudice, Miss Sympathy, and the Authoritarian Personality: An Application of Psychological Measuring Techniques to the Problem of Jury Bias." *Wisconsin Law Review* 1968(3):734–47.

Bray, R., C. Struckman-Johnson, M. Osborne, J. McFarlane, and J. Scott (1978). "The Effects of Defendant Status on the Decisions of Student and Community Juries." *Social Psychology* 41:256–60.

Crockett, G. Jr., (1971). "Racism in the Courts." *Journal of Public Law* 20:384–89.

Diamond, S. (1982). "Growth and Maturation in Psychology and Law." *Law and Society Review* 17:1–10.

Erlanger, H. (1970). "Jury Research in America: Its Past and Future." *Law and Society Review* 4:345–70.

Fried, M., K. Kaplan, and K. Klein (1975). "Juror Selection: An Analysis of Voir Dire." In *The Jury System in America*, edited by R. Simon, 47–66. Beverly Hills: Sage.

Friendly, A., and R. Goldfarb (1968). *Crime and Publicity*. New York: Random House.

Gerard, J., and T. Terry (1970). "Discrimination Against Negroes in the Administration of Criminal Law in Missouri." *Washington State University Law Quarterly* 2:415–37.

Griffitt, W., and T. Jackson (1973). "Simulated Jury Decisions: The Influence of Jury-Defendant Attitude Similarity-Dissimilarity." *Social Behavior and Personality* 1:1–7.

Hastie, R., D. Penrod, and N. Pennington (1983). *Inside the Jury*. Cambridge, MA: Harvard UP.

Hermann, P. (1970). "Occupations of Jurors as an Influence on Their Verdict." *Forum* 5:150–55.

Kaplan, K., and S. Krupa (1986). "Severe Penalties Under the Control of Others Can Reduce Guilt Verdicts." *Law and Psychology Review* 10:1–18.

Kaplan, K., and R. Simon (1972). "Latitude and Severity of Sentencing Options, Race of the Victim, and Decisions of Simulated Jurors: Some Issues Arising From the 'Algiers Motel' Trial." *Law and Society Review* 7:87–98.

Kassin, S., and R. Juhnke (1983). "Juror Experience and Decision Making." *Journal of Personality and Social Psychology* 44:1182–91.

Kerr, N., D. Nerenz, and D. Herrick (1979). "Role Playing and the Study of Jury Behavior." *Sociological Methods and Research* 7:337–55.

Kuhn, R. (1968). "Jury Discrimination: The Next Phase." *Southern California Law Review* 41:235–328.

Landy, D., and E. Aronson (1969). "The Influence of the Character of the Criminal and His Victim on the Decisions of Simulated Jurors." *Journal of Experimental Social Psychology* 5:141–52.

MacCoun, R. (1989). "Experimental Research on Jury Decision-Making." *Science* 244:1046–50.

MacCoun, R., and N. Kerr (1988). "Asymmetric Influence in Mock Jury Deliberation." *Journal of Personality and Social Psychology* 54:21–33.

Meyer, B. (1969). "The Trial Judge's Guide to News Reporting and Fair Trial." *Journal of Criminal Law, Criminology, and Police Science* 60:287–98.

Mitchell, H. and D. Byrne (1973). "The Defendant's Dilemma: Effect of Jurors' Attitudes and Authoritarianism on Judicial Decisions." *Journal of Personality and Social Psychology* 25:123–29.

Pennington, N., and R. Hastie (1990). "Practical Implications of Psychological Research on Juror and Jury Decision Making." *Personality and Social Psychology Bulletin* 16:90–105.

Siebert, F. (1970). "Trial Judges' Opinions and Prejudicial Publicity." In C. Bush (ed.), *Free Press and Fair Trial*. Athens: University of Georgia Press.

Sigall, H., and N. Ostrove (1975). "Beautiful but Dangerous: Effect of Offender Attractiveness and Nature of the Crime on Juridical Judgment." *Journal of Personality and Social Psychology* 31:410–14.

Simon, R. (1967). *The Jury and the Defense of Insanity*. Boston: Little, Brown.

Singer, A., and A. Barton (1975). "The Impact of Pretrial Publicity on Jurors' Verdicts." In R. Simon (ed.), *The Jury System in America*. Beverly Hills: Sage.

Snyder, E. (1971). "Sex Role Differential and Juror Decisions." *Sociology and Social Research* 55:442–48.

Stephan, C. (1974). "Sex Prejudice in Jury Simulation." *Journal of Psychology* 88:305–12.

Stephan, C. (1975). "Selective Characteristics of Jurors and Litigants: Their Influences on Juries' Verdicts." In R. Simon (ed.), *The Jury System in America*. Beverly Hills: Sage.

Sue, S., R. Smith, and R. Gilbert (1974). "Biasing Effects of Pretrial Publicity on Judicial Decisions." *Journal of Criminal Justice* 2:163–71.

Tanford, S., and S. Penrod (1984). "Social Inference Processes in Juror Judgments of Multiple Offense Trials." *Journal of Personality and Social Psychology* 47: 749–65.

Vidmar, N. (1979). "The Other Issues in Jury Simulation Research: A Commentary with Particular Reference to Defendant Character Studies." *Law and Human Behavior* 3:95–106.

Weiten, W., and S. Diamond (1979). "A Critical Review of the Jury Simulation Paradigm: The Case of Defendant Characteristics." *Law and Human Behavior* 3:71–93.

Wilson, D., and E. Donnerstein (1977). "Guilty or Not Guilty? A Look at the "Simulated" Jury Paradigm." *Journal of Applied Social Psychology* 7:175–190.

Zeisel, H., and S. Diamond (1978). "Effect of Peremptory Challenges on Jury and Verdict: An Experiment in a Federal District Court." *Stanford Law Review* 30:491–532.

Further Reading

Simon, R., and D. Aaronson (1988). *The Insanity Defense: A Critical Assessment of Law and Policy in the Post-Hinckley Era.* New York: Praeger.

Goldstein, A. (1967). *The Insanity Defense.* New Haven, CT: Yale UP.

Kassin, S. (1988). *The American Jury On Trial: Psychological Perspectives.* Oxford, UK: Taylor & Francis.

Strier, F. (1996). *Reconstructing Justice: An Agenda for Trial Reform.* Chicago: University of Chicago Press.

4

Sentencing

Most of the attention paid to courts by academics as well as by the public and the media seems to focus on the sentences meted out to convicted criminals. Judges are often at the center of the media's or the public's focus, particularly when the sentences appear to be too lenient relative to the offenses involved. Academics' interests in sentencing, on the other hand, tend to focus on the issue of inequities (*disparities*) in sentencing across similarly situated offenders, or differences in the severity of sentences for persons convicted of the same offenses under similar circumstances. This last interest is somewhat related to the media's and the public's focus because a particularly lenient sentence is defined as "lenient" relative to what others have received in the past for the same offense, thereby reflecting a disparity in sentences between convicted criminals. Whereas the media and the public tend to focus on this issue with greater emotion due to their interest in just deserts, however, academics generally focus on this issue because of their interest in understanding *why* sentencing disparities occur. The reasons for sentencing inequities are important to understand from a due process perspective, not to mention that consistency and proportionality in punishment are necessary prerequisites for maintaining the credibility of the court system in the public's eyes. One of the problems with this much attention given to the sentencing process, however, is that judges often receive the most criticism for sentencing disparities. Based on our previous discussions of prosecutorial discretion and plea bargaining, judges do not have complete control over the determination of sentences except for a small minority of convicted defendants who go to trial. Even then, when defendants opt for jury trials in cases where the juries also make sentence recommendations, judges may not necessarily agree with those recommendations. Judges must approve all sentence recommendations nonetheless, thereby making them ultimately responsible for both public and academic dissatisfaction with the sentencing process.

JUDICIAL DISCRETION IN SENTENCING DECISIONS: DO JUDGES DISCRIMINATE AGAINST INDIVIDUALS OF LOWER SOCIOECONOMIC STATUS?

Hagan, J. (1974). "Extra-legal Attributes and Criminal Sentencing: An Assessment of a Sociological Viewpoint." *Law and Society Review* 8:357–83.

Background

The concept of "justice" is grounded in the idea of equal treatment under the law. Judges are granted a fair amount of discretion in their sentencing decisions, however, even in many states with mandatory sentencing guidelines (as described in the next section). Concerns regarding judges' abuse of their discretion stem from commonly observed differences in the sentences meted out to similarly situated offenders, or those who are convicted on the same charges and have similar prior records. The sources of these sentencing disparities have been popular topics of criminal justice research for decades, with much attention paid to whether sentences differ by the personal attributes of defendants such as their race or sex. It is difficult, however, to objectively gauge our current state of knowledge on the subject of whether judges actually discriminate against certain types of defendants based on their extralegal characteristics (or non-legally relevant factors). This is due, in part, to the proliferation of ideologues that firmly believe that judges are biased, and so they engage in questionable research tactics to provide "evidence" favoring their perspective. In short, methodologically rigorous studies with findings that are described objectively are less common.

Research on differences in the treatment of criminal defendants based on their personal (extralegal) characteristics became more popular in the United States throughout the 1960s and into the '70s due to the civil rights movement, the women's movement, the public's anti-government sentiment due to the Vietnam War and Watergate, and a liberal US Supreme Court. Not surprisingly, much of this research was grounded in the early conflict perspectives mentioned in the discussion of Albonetti. For research on inequities in the sentencing process, the conflict perspective offered by William Chambliss and Robert Seidman (1971), outlined in their book *Law, Order and Power*, was particularly popular. In their explanation of how decision-making processes throughout the criminal justice system are automatically geared toward biasing against suspects of lower socioeconomic status (SES), they argued that *any* decision-making body necessarily restricts the types of information that can be considered by decision-makers, such as the presentence investigation (PSI) reports considered by judges in their sentencing decisions. By placing limits on this information, decision-making bodies are automatically placing limits on their actual decisions. For example, judges are forced to make predictions about an offender's risk of future criminality based on limited information in PSI reports that define "higher risks" as persons with fewer community ties, such as those who are unemployed and have resided at their current address for short periods of time. This process might only reinforce stereotypes of "more dangerous offenders" as persons of lower SES, and it ignores other relevant information that is too costly or too time-consuming to compile. Therefore, based on the inherently limited and biased information considered in sentencing decisions, these "value loaded" decisions are likely to result in harsher sanctions for convicted defendants of lower SES.

As described previously, early conflict theories treated a person's race almost synonymously with his or her economic status due to segregation practices that forced-African Americans and other minorities into poverty and powerlessness. In conjunction with the gross over-representation of minorities in prison relative to their distributions in the general population, scholars were led to question whether the court system was biased towards minorities and the poor. Much of the early sentencing research focused heavily on disparities in treatment based on a defendant's race and economic status. Herbert Blumer's (1955) relatively early discussion of race relations in the United States focused on how the "myths" associated with particular race groups can promote fear among members of the more socially, politically, and economically powerful groups in society. Such fears can lead to "discrimination, segregation, and repression" (pp. 13–14) of the less powerful group in order to insulate the dominant group from any "threat" to their social and economic interests. These processes then perpetuate the original myths and stereotypes surrounding particular race groups. Blumer noted that the quality of race group relations varies across different contexts, implying that levels of perceived threat, fear, repression, etc. might be higher or lower depending on the social environment. These ideas set the stage for "racial threat" theories that were bi-products of the conflict perspective (e.g., Blalock 1967). (Technically speaking, a conflict perspective focuses only on differences in power based on economic inequalities.) Both conflict and racial threat theories constituted most of the frameworks in related research throughout the 1960s and '70s. This research continued to be fed by studies that produced findings of significant differences in the treatment of defendants based on their race and/or SES. Related studies of other extra-legal effects on sentencing were also conducted and included analyses of a defendant's age and sex, under the assumption that less powerful groups in a capitalist society also consist of females and younger individuals.

The Study

John Hagan's (1974) analysis of extralegal sentencing disparities was actually a review and re-analysis of findings produced from 20 *quantitative* studies that had been conducted on the subject prior to 1974 (spanning from 1931 to 1973, with half of the studies conducted in the 1960s). Hagan's synthesis was prompted by his concern for whether the authors of these studies were providing realistic assessments of the importance of extralegal factors in shaping case outcomes.

The "sociological viewpoint" Hagan referred to in his article dealt with a conflict perspective of crime and the treatment of criminal defendants by legal authorities. The conflict perspective is one of the three sociological *paradigms* or methods of viewing the world (which also include structural functionalism and symbolic interactionism). Throughout the 1960s and '70s, conflict theory was commonly applied to an understanding of inequities in the treatment of particular groups across the United States. The distribution of wealth and power is inherently uneven in a capitalist economy, and legal authority is concentrated in the hands of the wealthy. These individuals seek to protect their own interests (i.e., the preservation of their wealth, status, and power), and in doing so will make decisions that conflict with the interests of the economically disadvantaged. These decisions might lead to the segregation and oppression of particular groups in order to remove any "threat" to the social and economic interests of the more powerful group. Since the criminal justice system is controlled by the wealthy, the decisions of criminal justice officials (including police officers, prosecutors, and judges) might result in disproportionate overrepresentations of lower SES persons in the pools of arrested, convicted, and incarcerated offenders. Given the close link between a person's economic status and his or her race throughout the history of the United States, African Americans might also be disadvantaged relative to whites in the criminal justice system. Standing in contrast to the conflict perspective is the *legalistic perspective*, which states that legal factors such as the seriousness of the crime and the individual's prior record will determine how severely defendants are treated by the courts.

Hagan reviewed and re-analyzed data from 20 studies of differences in the sentences of convicted defendants based on their extralegal characteristics including race, sex, age, and SES. These studies varied in terms of their focus on non-capital and/or capital crimes (ten studies involved mostly capital crimes), and they were not all "equal" in methodological rigor in that some of the researchers controlled for legal factors while others did not. Hagan observed that these differences might have generated some differences in the findings for extralegal effects on sentencing across the 20 studies. Only 11 of the studies actually conducted *hypothesis tests* for these effects (see our discussion of Kalven and Zeisel). These tests involved empirical assessments of whether there were relationships between a defendant's extralegal characteristics and the severity of case outcomes (in order to determine whether particular race, sex, age, or SES groups tended to receive harsher sentences than other groups). Only four of the studies presented information on the strength of these relationships, or *measures of association*, which moves beyond a simple determination of whether relationships exist between a defendant's extralegal characteristics and the severity of case outcomes to how closely these factors correspond (i.e., the extent to which case outcomes can be determined simply by knowing the extralegal characteristics of defendants). The remaining eight studies did not offer these types of statistics. The *dependent* variables (case outcomes) also varied across studies and included whether prosecuted defendants were convicted, whether convicted defendants were incarcerated, whether they were sentenced to death (in capital cases), and whether their cases received appellate review.

Most of the researchers who conducted *hypothesis tests* found evidence of *statistically significant* relationships between a defendant's race and case outcome severity, and the researchers interpreted these findings as evidence of important extralegal effects. Hagan questioned this interpretation, however, due to the important distinction between *statistical significance* and *substantive significance*. The term "statistically significant" refers to a finding that favors the research hypothesis, such as evidence that African Americans are more likely than whites to be incarcerated. Such evidence does not reveal the degree of association between two variables, however, or how closely the two scales correspond with each other. For example, a hypothesis test might reveal that a defendant's race and sentence are related, so a researcher then proceeds to calculate a measure of association and finds that predicting whether convicted defendants were sent to prison was improved by 20 percent just by knowing a defendant's race (relative to making predictions based only on the proportion of the total sample sent to prison). This last observation constituted a finding that described the "degree of association" between two variables, or what Hagan implied by "substantive significance." Improving the accuracy of predictions by 20 percent would reflect a strong (substantively significant) relationship between race and sentencing. On the other hand, it is possible to find evidence of a relationship between two variables only to discover that the relationship is weak, such as improving prediction by only 1 percent. The relationship is *statistically significant* but not substantively significant. This is often a characteristic of relationships found to be statistically significant in large samples because hypothesis tests are designed to make it easier to establish significant relationships when more cases are included in the analysis (Blalock 1979).

Hagan also criticized how some of the authors interpreted their *statistically significant* findings as evidence of "discrimination" by the courts. As described previously in the discussion of Albonetti, failure to control for factors related to the variables of interest could lead a researcher to find a *spurious* relationship between the two variables. The relationship cannot be treated as a *causal* relationship if it becomes nonsignificant when controlling for these other factors. For example, a significant relationship between race and sentencing might exist when the severity of convicted charges is not controlled. However, if minorities were more likely to be convicted on more serious charges relative to whites, and more serious charges increased the odds of going to prison, then a spurious link between race and imprisonment would emerge when charge severity was ignored. Several of the studies reexamined by Hagan were methodologically weak in terms of not controlling for extraneous factors related to both defendants' extralegal characteristics and their case outcomes.

Findings

Results for each extralegal characteristic were described separately. Regarding a defendant's race, Hagan evaluated the results from 17 related studies. In some cases it was necessary to compute statistics that were not discussed or displayed in the original studies in order to conduct a more rigorous evaluation. (These statistics were computed from information displayed or described in the original studies.) Despite the fact that the vast majority of these studies uncovered *statistically significant* relationships between race and sentencing, Hagan found that most of these relationships were weak regardless of the focus on capital or non-capital cases. Judson et al.'s (1969) analysis of capital cases did not even produce a statistically significant finding for a defendant's race, however, and this was one of the more methodologically rigorous studies in the pool examined by Hagan. In several studies, prediction of sentences by knowing a defendant's race was improved by less than 1 percent. Edwin Lemert and Judy Rosberg (1948) provided the exception with their finding that prediction was improved by 8 percent. Interestingly, Hagan found that studies which controlled for offense seriousness actually produced stronger relationships between race and sentencing, although the median increase in strength was only 1.4 percent. He also noted that in one of the studies that controlled for offense seriousness, the author (Bullock 1961) displayed the results in such a way as to convey an artificially stronger race effect. Bullock examined whether incarcerated defendants received "short" versus "long" sentences and he broke these findings down by offense type and a defendant's race. He observed that in the pool of "short" sentences overall (regardless of offense type), African-Americans constituted only 45 percent whereas whites constituted 55 percent, thus suggesting a greater use of short sentences for whites. These differences were even more dramatic when broken down by particular offense groups including burglary, rape, and murder. These data were percentaged incorrectly, however, in that Bullock calculated the percentage of each sentence group ("short" versus "long") consisting of a particular race. Instead, he should have determined the percentage of each race group that received a particular sentence. When Hagan computed these new percentages he found a four percent difference between race groups overall in the use of short versus long sentences. That is, 56 percent of whites received short sentences versus only 52 percent of African Americans. When these figures were broken down by offense type, Hagan found that African Americans were more likely to receive *shorter* sentences relative to whites in rape and murder cases.

Hagan's reanalysis of the few studies that controlled for prior record revealed statistically nonsignificant race effects on sentencing for defendants with no prior convictions, yet significant race effects for defendants with one or more priors. The *statistically significant* effects were relatively weak, however, with only a 2.5 percent median improvement in the prediction of sentences by knowing a defendant's race (but ranging from 1.5 to 8 percent, depending on the study). This method of controlling for prior record is also a method for examining an *interaction effect* between variables, or whether a defendant's race *interacts* with his or her prior record to influence sentencing (covered in greater detail in our subsequent discussion of Steffensmeier, Ulmer, and Kramer, 1998). Although Stuart Nagel (1969) did not specifically examine this particular interaction effect, Hagan reanalyzed Nagel's data in order to do so. He found very similar results to those for the other studies.

Also relevant to the issue of race is whether interracial offenses involving African American offenders and white victims resulted in more severe outcomes relative to other racial dyads. The one related study of noncapital cases (Green 1964) did not produce any evidence of disparities based on racial dyads although most of the studies of capital cases revealed a *statistically significant* yet modest impact (with a median improvement in prediction of 2.5%). Marvin Wolfgang and Marc Reidel's (1973) study, however, found dramatic differences in outcome severity in rape cases across 11 southern states, with prediction of sentences improved by nearly 23 percent by knowing the race of both the offender and the victim.

Turning to a defendant's SES, all three of the studies that examined the role of a defendant's SES in non-capital cases revealed *statistically significant* relationships with sentencing, even when controlling for offense type. Nagel's (1969) study, however, produced a nonsignificant relationship once a defendant's prior record was controlled. The three related studies of capital cases produced mixed results, with two producing no significant SES effects versus a *statistically significant* and modest effect found by Charles Judson et al. (1969). They found that the prediction of case outcomes improved by 3.2 percent when a defendant's SES was known, even with controls for prior record and other legal factors.

Three of the four studies examining the effects of a defendant's age in noncapital cases uncovered *statistically significant* yet very weak relationships, even without controlling for legal factors. Only one of the five studies of capital cases produced a significant relationship that was also very weak. A similar theme of weak effects emerged for a defendant's sex, although in the two relevant studies of capital crimes these effects became weak only after controlling for type of offense and prior record.

Overall, the only substantively meaningful extralegal effects on case outcomes identified by Hagan included (1) the dramatic differences in sentencing based on racial dyads in capital crimes across the south, and (2) the modest effect of a defendant's SES on sentencing in capital cases. The absence of substantive findings in noncapital cases led Hagan to speculate that the disparities observed in capital cases might have been due to biases by jurors as opposed to judicial bias, given that jury trials were more common in capital versus noncapital cases (even more so back in the 1960s and '70s compared with today). Considered in conjunction with the pervasive weak effects found in noncapital cases, many of the original authors' accusations of "discrimination" by judges toward defendants were not firmly grounded in their data. Most of these authors focused only on statistical significance as opposed to the strength of these relationships, thereby ignoring the lack of substance to most of the extralegal effects examined.

Hagan concluded with recommendations for more rigorous research on the subject beyond the methods he adopted for his review. Perhaps the recommendation with the biggest impact on subsequent research involved a focus on *longitudinal* data capturing what happens to defendants throughout the court system (at the various stages of case processing). Since the dispositions at previous stages ultimately affect what happens at subsequent stages, Hagan underscored the need to examine arrest decisions, charging decisions, types of plea bargains, bail decisions, and the recommendations of probation officers in presentence investigation reports (some of which were examined in the studies described previously under Albonetti's study). Another important set of recommendations dealt with legal factors that might be important to consider as *control* variables in related research, such as court caseloads, community crime rates, media attention to particular types of crimes, and the characteristics of court actors and jurors. He added that researchers might also consider possible *interaction effects* involving a defendant's extralegal characteristics on the dispositions at these various stages, similar to his reanalysis of the race (x) prior record interaction effect on sentencing. This recommendation subsequently influenced a large body of research generated by Albonetti.

Limitations

Perhaps the most obvious drawback to Hagan's synthesis of research studies was the limited number of *quantitative* analyses that had been conducted up to that point in time, particularly those that he considered to be more methodologically rigorous. There have been well over 300 studies of racial and ethnic disparities in sentencing published in some form since 1974, in part a consequence of Hagan's research, and reviews of those studies paint a much more ambiguous picture of race effects on sentencing. Based on his analysis of only 20 studies, with even smaller numbers in the subgroup analyses, he found only a couple of exceptions to his more general conclusion regarding the relatively weak relationship between a convicted defendant's race and the sentence s/he received. Today, this conclusion has changed to reflect anomalous findings of null, weak, moderate, and strong race effects, with the added confusion that minority status coincides with harsher sentences relative to those for whites in some jurisdictions (e.g., Albonetti 1991, 1997, Holmes and Daudistel 1984, LaFree 1985, Kramer and Steffensmeier 1993, Myers and Talarico 1987, Nelson 1992, Spohn 1990, Steffensmeier and Demuth 2000, Steffensmeier et al. 1998, Zatz 1985), yet it corresponds with *less* severe sentences in other jurisdictions (e.g., Kleck 1985, Holmes et al. 1987, Peterson and Hagan 1984, Swigert and Farrell 1977, Thomson and Zingraff 1981, Unnever et al. 1980, Weisburd et al. 1991, Wheeler et al. 1982). These differences could merely reflect differences in the jurisdictions examined and/or differences in methodological rigor across studies. Hagan himself raised both of these possibilities several years after his article was published (Peterson and Hagan 1984).

It is also possible, however, that the much larger number of extant studies currently available for review reflects the same cross-section of studies examined by Hagan, and the sheer number of studies merely produced a larger number of "exceptional" findings. Recall that Hagan always found an exception to his general observation regarding each extralegal effect on sentencing, ranging from one to two studies per analysis, or from 10% to 33 percent of the pool of all relevant studies. Even if only 10 percent of the larger pool of currently available studies produced findings that countered the majority, this would still reflect over 30 studies of an even larger number of jurisdictions (since many of these studies included several courts). In short, Hagan's original conclusions regarding generally weak race effects on sentencing might have been unduly influenced by the limited number of studies, even if the findings from all of those studies were accurate.

A second potential limitation of Hagan's discussion involves his definition of a "weak" effect on sentencing. The weak effects he described ranged anywhere from a one to three percent reduction in error. Although we agree with Hagan that such effects are not substantively significant, some scholars might argue that the raw numbers of convicted minorities involved in these differences should not be ignored and are "substantively" important. Empirical studies of race differences always have the potential to spark debate no matter what the findings are, but applying definitions of "substantive significance" to evaluation studies of racial bias does seem rather cold and ignores the issue that *any* disparity in treatment based on an individual's race is immoral and needs to be addressed. In fairness to the original authors of the studies reexamined by Hagan, this might have been their perspective all along.

Also important to recognize is that earlier studies of racial disparities in sentencing often included crude measures of race consisting of "white" and "nonwhite" defendants. With only two categories, such a scale does not meet the standard that each category must be a "natural group" consisting of cases with identical characteristics. A category of "nonwhite" potentially includes a number of different race as well as ethnic groups such as Latinos, Asians, Native Americans, Indians, etc., depending on the jurisdictions examined. Yet, scholars have demonstrated significant differences in the treatment of African American and Latino defendants (e.g., Albonetti 1997, Nobiling et al. 1998, Spohn and Holleran 2000, Steffensmeier and Demuth 2000), and so these pooled categories could mask important differences in sentencing and contribute to the overall conclusion of a generally weak race effect on sentencing.

Significance and Subsequent Research

Hagan's study is currently his most cited publication to date and it is rare to find any other related publication that does not pay tribute to his study. *Quantitative* analyses of extra-legal effects on sentencing increased after the mid-1970s and really took off beginning in the early '80s. Part of this dramatic increase in related research is likely due to the greater availability of electronic data bases now compiled by many urban courts across the country and made available to interested academics. It is clear, however, that Hagan influenced much of the current interest in these data sets as well as how to examine them. In particular, his work can be interpreted as shaping analyses related to (a) the *interaction effects* of a defendant's race on sentencing, (b) the effects of racial dyads in cases involving violent crimes, and (c) meta-analyses of existing studies.

Some of the studies included in Hagan's project involved analyses of potential *interaction effects* on sentencing between a defendant's race and other legal characteristics, such as Bullock's (1961) analysis of race effects broken down by offense type. Hagan underscored the potentially greater relevance of these types of interactions relative to analyses of *general* race effects only. Focusing solely on the latter ignores how legal as well as other extralegal factors might influence sentences differently for minority defendants relative to white defendants. This observation sparked interest in examining race group differences in the effects of a defendant's sex, SES, prior record, and pretrial release status (in addition to many other factors) on whether a convicted defendant was sentenced to prison. For example, there is evidence that minorities receive more severe sentences when they possess other attributes that reinforce court actors' stereotypes of more dangerous offenders, such as being male and/or unemployed (e.g., Daly 1989, 1994, Miethe and Moore 1985, Nobiling et al. 1998, Spohn and Holleran 2000, Steffensmeier et al. 1998). Evidence has also been found indicating significant race and ethnic group differences in sentencing based on pretrial release status, offense seriousness, whether a defendant pled guilty, and prior record (e.g., Albonetti 1991, Petersilia and Turner 1985, Zatz 1985).

Hagan's reanalysis also generated more interest in the role of racial dyads in sentencing decisions, particularly in death penalty cases. Some studies conducted since Hagan's publication have indicated that African Americans and other minorities convicted of murdering whites were at especially high risk to receive the death penalty (Baldus et al. 1983, Gross and Mauro 1989, Keil and Vito 1990, Paternoster and Brame 2003). A possible explanation for racially disparate outcomes in capital cases is the inability of majority-white juries to empathize with African American victims (Gross and Mauro 1989). A different perspective was offered by Donald Black (1976), who suggested that minorities who victimized members of dominant groups would be regarded as especially repugnant by the functionaries of the law. In the case of the death penalty, white-dominated courts could view the murder of a white victim by a minority perpetrator as an especially shocking crime. Relatively sensational media coverage of interracial murders and the subsequent triggering of racial biases or stereotypes about minority offenders could result in the harshest outcomes in such cases (Bright 1995).

Hagan's synthesis of findings from different empirical studies also contributed to a more recent interest in *meta-analyses* of race effects on sentencing (e.g., Mitchell 2007, Pratt 1998). Meta-analysis is a *quantitative* method for synthesizing findings from multiple studies of the same (or similar) relationships. It is designed, in part, to estimate an average effect "size" for the empirical relationships of interest, such as the effect of a defendant's race on sentence severity. Meta-analysis can be a powerful technique in that the weighted effect produced from consideration of multiple studies should be more accurate than the effect produced from each study separately, under the assumption that analysis of a distribution of repeated studies should bring us closer to the "true" relationship in the population (analogous to the idea that an average of repeated sample means should be an unbiased estimate of the true population mean). Although desirable in theory, however, there are potential weaknesses of the technique when applied to *non-experimental* data of the sort reexamined by Hagan. If there are different research biases operating across the original studies included in the meta-analysis, then an "average" effect of already biased effects is also likely to be biased (Slavin 1984). Nonetheless, the pursuit of a more rigorous synthesis of findings related to extralegal effects on sentencing is clearly worthwhile given the sheer volume of research that has been influenced by Hagan's study.

References

Albonetti, C. (1991). "An Integration of Theories to Explain Judicial Discretion." *Social Problems* 38:247–66.

Albonetti, C. (1997). "Sentencing Under the Federal Sentencing Guidelines: Effects of Defendant Characteristics, Guilty Pleas, and Departures on Sentence Outcomes for Drug Offenses, 1991–1992." *Law and Society Review* 31:789–822.

Baldus, D., C. Pulaski, and G. Woodworth (1983). "Comparative Review of Death Sentences: An Empirical Study of the Georgia Experience." *Journal of Criminal Law and Criminology* 74:661–753.

Black, D. (1976). *The Behavior of Law.* San Diego: Academic Press.

Blalock, H. (1967). *Toward a Theory of Minority-Group Relations.* New York: Wiley.

Blalock, H. (1979). *Social Statistics.* New York: McGraw-Hill.

Blumer, H. (1955). "Reflections on Theory of Race Relations." In *Race Relations in World Perspective,* edited by A. Lind, 3–21. Honolulu: University of Hawaii Press.

Bright, S. (1995). "Discrimination, Death and Denial: The Tolerance of Racial Discrimination in the Infliction of the Death Penalty." *Santa Clara Law Review* 35:433–54.

Bullock, H. (1961). "Significance of the Racial Factor in the Length of Prison Sentences." *Journal of Criminal Law, Criminology, and Police Science* 52:411–17.

Chambliss, W., and R. Seidman (1971). *Law, Order, and Power.* Reading, MA: Addison-Wesley.

Daly, K. (1989). "Neither Conflict nor Labeling nor Paternalism will Suffice: Intersections of Race, Ethnicity, Gender, and Family in Criminal Court Decisions." *Crime and Delinquency* 35:135–68.

Daly, K. (1994). *Gender, Crime, and Punishment.* New Haven: Yale UP.

Green, E. (1964). "Inter- and Intra-racial Crime Relative to Sentencing." *Journal of Criminal Law, Criminology, and Police Science* 55:348–58.

Gross, S., and R. Mauro (1989). *Death and Discrimination: Racial Disparities in Capital Sentencing.* Boston: Northeastern UP.

Hagan, J. (1974). "Extra-legal Attributes and Criminal Sentencing: An Assessment of a Sociological Viewpoint." *Law and Society Review* 8:357–83.

Holmes, M., and H. Daudistel (1984). "Race and Justice in the Southwest: The Sentencing of Anglo, Black, and Hispanic Defendants." *Social Science Quarterly* 65:265–77.

Holmes, M., H. Daudistel, and R. Farrell (1987). "Determinants of Charge Reductions and Final Dispositions in Cases of Burglary and Robbery." *Journal of Research in Crime and Delinquency* 24:233–54.

Judson, C., J. Pandell, J. Owens, J. McIntosh, and D. Matschullat (1969) "A Study of the California Penalty Jury in First Degree Murder Cases." *Stanford Law Review* 21: 1306-1497.

Keil, T., and G. Vito (1990). "Race and the Death Penalty in Kentucky Murder Trials: An Analysis of Post-Gregg Outcomes." *Justice Quarterly* 7:189–207.

Kleck, G. (1985). "Life Support for Ailing Hypotheses: Modes of Summarizing the Evidence for Racial Discrimination in Sentencing." *Law and Human Behavior* 9:271–85.

Kramer, J., and D. Steffensmeier (1993). "Race and Imprisonment Decisions." *Sociological Quarterly* 34:357–76.

LaFree, G. (1985). "Adversarial and Non-Adversarial Justice: A Comparison of Guilty Pleas and Trials." *Criminology* 23:289–312.

Lemert, E., and J. Roseberg (1948). "The Administration of Justice to Minority Groups in Los Angeles County." *University of California Publications in Culture and Society* 11:1–10.

Miethe, T., and C. Moore (1985). "Racial Differences in Criminal Processing: The Consequences of Model Selection on Conclusions About Differential Treatment." *Sociological Quarterly* 27:217–37.

Mitchell, O. (2005). "A Meta-Analysis of Race and Sentencing Research: Explaining the Inconsistencies." *Journal of Quantitative Criminology* 21:439–66.

Myers, M., and S. Talarico (1987). *The Social Contexts of Criminal Sentencing.* New York: Springer-Verlag.

Nagel, S. (1969). *The Legal Process From a Behavioral Perspective.* Homewood, IL: Dorsey.

Nelson, J. (1992). "Hidden Disparities in Case Processing: New York State, 1985–1986." *Journal of Criminal Justice* 20:181–200.

Nobiling, T., C. Spohn, and M. DeLone (1998). "A Tale of Two Counties: Unemployment and Sentence Severity." *Justice Quarterly* 15: 459–85.

Paternoster, R., and R. Brame (2003). *An Empirical Analysis of Maryland's Death Sentencing System with Respect to the Influence of Race and Legal Jurisdiction: Final Report.* College Park: University of Maryland.

Petersilia, J., and S. Turner (1985). *Guideline-Based Justice: The Implications for Racial Minorities.* Santa Monica, CA: RAND.

Peterson, R., and J. Hagan (1984). Changing Conceptions of Race: Towards an Account of Anomalous Findings of Sentencing Research. *American Sociological Review* 49:56–70.

Pratt, T. (1998). "Race and Sentencing: A Meta-analysis of Conflicting Empirical Research Results." *Journal of Criminal Justice* 26:513–23.

Slavin, R. (1984). *Research Methods in Education: A Practical Guide.* Englewood Cliffs, NJ: Prentice-Hall.

Spohn, C. (1990). "The Sentencing Decisions of Black and White Judges: Some Expected and Unexpected Similarities." *Law and Society Review* 24:1197–1216.

Spohn, C., and D. Holleran (2000). "The Imprisonment Penalty Paid By Young, Unemployed Black and Hispanic Male Offenders." *Criminology* 38:281–306.

Steffensmeier, D., and S. Demuth (2000). "Ethnicity and Sentencing Outcomes in U.S. Federal Courts: Who Is Punished More Harshly?" *American Sociological Review* 65:705–29.

Steffensmeier, D., J. Ulmer, and J. Kramer (1998). "The Interaction of Race, Gender, and Age in Criminal Sentencing: The Punishment Cost of Being Young, Black, and Male." *Criminology* 36:763–97.

Swigert, V., and R. Farrell (1977). "Normal Homicides and the Law." *American Sociological Review* 42:16–32.

Thomson, R., and M. Zingraff (1981). "Detecting Sentencing Disparity: Some Problems and Evidence." *American Journal of Sociology* 86:869–80.

Unnever, J., C. Frazier, and J. Henretta (1980). "Race Differences in Criminal Sentencing." *Sociological Quarterly* 21:197–205.

Weisburd, D., S. Wheeler, E. Waring, and N. Bale (1991). *Crimes of the Middle Class.* New Haven: Yale UP.

Wheeler, S., D. Weisburd, and N. Bode (1982). "Sentencing the White-Collar Offender: Rhetoric and Reality." *American Sociological Review* 47:641–59.

Wolfgang, M., and M. Reidel (1973). "Race, Judicial Discretion, and the Death Penalty." *The Annals of the American Academy of Political and Social Science* 407:119–33.

Zatz, M. (1985). "Pleas, Priors, and Prison: Racial/Ethnic Differences in Sentencing." *Social Science Research* 14:169–93.

Further Reading

Edelman, B. (2006). *Racial Prejudice, Juror Empathy, and Sentencing in Death Penalty Cases.* El Paso, TX: LFB Scholarly Publishing LLC.

Rex, S., and M. Tonry (2002). *Reform and Punishment: The Future of Sentencing.* Uffculme, UK: Willan.

Tonry, M. (1998). *Sentencing Matters (Studies in Crime and Public Policy).* New York: Oxford UP.

JUDGES' ASSESSMENTS OF AN OFFENDER'S RISK FOR FUTURE CRIMINALITY: ARE SENTENCES AFFECTED BY STEREOTYPES OF "DANGEROUS OFFENDERS"?

Steffensmeier, D., J. Ulmer, and J. Kramer (1998). "The Interaction of Race, Gender, and Age in Criminal Sentencing: The Punishment Cost of Being Young, Black, and Male." *Criminology* 36:763–97.

Background

Between the time of Hagan's publication up to the late 1990s, considerable advancements were made in the methodological rigor of *quantitative* research on sentencing disparities. Specifically, methods were developed and applied to adjust for biases inherent in the types of samples examined (since defendants are never *randomly* assigned to groups of "convicted defendants") (e.g., Zatz and Hagan 1985), scholars began to examine other stages of case processing aside from sentencing (e.g., Albonetti 1987, Crutchfield et al. 1994, LaFree 1985, Petersilia 1983, Zatz 1985), different measures of prior record and offense seriousness were examined to better reduce the chance of finding spurious extra-legal effects (Welch et al. 1984), other *control* variables were explored for their relevance to sentencing models (e.g., Spohn and Cederblom 1991, Zatz 1987), and the types of interactions examined by Hagan (such as those involving a defendant's race and prior record) were more frequently examined (e.g., Wooldredge 1998). Still, aside from Albonetti's "uncertainty avoidance" perspective, most research was heavily tied to the more traditional conflict perspectives that treated race almost synonymously with social class. While these older perspectives might have been adequate for framing extra-legal effects on case outcomes, a broader perspective was needed in order to incorporate *both* extralegal and legal effects on sentencing under a unified framework. Moreover, very little research had been conducted up to that point on possible *interaction effects* involving extralegal characteristics only, such as a defendant's race *(x)* sex *(x)* age, and the limited work that had been done was fairly atheoretical in the sense that readers were not provided with logical explanations that might explain *why* these characteristics might interact to produce harsher sentences for defendants. Darrell Steffensmeier, Jeffery Ulmer, and John Kramer (1998) introduced a unified framework that would meet these requirements.

The Study

Steffensmeier, Ulmer, and Kramer (1998) began with the observation that previous research on extralegal disparities in sentencing had ignored the *interaction effects* of a defendant's race, gender, and age on sentence severity. This was an important lack, they argued, because the effect of a defendant's race might not be a general effect but instead might depend on a defendant's sex and age combined. Their prediction was consistent with Albonetti's argument (described previously) that African Americans *overall* were not likely to be treated more harshly than white defendants by the courts because it was only particular subgroups of minority defendants that fit with court actors' stereotypes of "more dangerous" offenders. In particular, younger African American males not only fulfilled this stereotype more than any other age *(x)* race *(x)* sex combination, they were also more likely to be perceived by judges as being able to "handle" incarceration better than other subgroups.

As described in our discussion of Hagan's study of extralegal effects on sentencing, empirical research on the general (main) effects of a defendant's race on sentencing had more recently produced mixed results, often leading to very different conclusions such as no race effects, weak effects, moderate to strong effects, and significant yet counterintuitive effects (where minority defendants were treated more *leniently* relative to white defendants). Research on the general effects of a defendant's sex have been much more consistent, however, with the common finding that males were sentenced more severely than females (Daly 1987, 1989, Griffin and Wooldredge 2006, Koons-Witt 2002, Kruttschnitt 1982, Kruttschnitt and McCarthy 1985, Steffensmeier et al. 1993). Related to a defendant's age, most researchers had found only moderate to weak effects on sentencing until Steffensmeier and his colleagues (1995) discovered that the relationship between age and sentence severity was U-shaped, meaning that the harshest sentences were administered to defendants in their 20s while defendants under 21 as well as those in their 30s received less severe sentences. They also found that defendants over 50 received the least severe sentences of all four age groups. The authors speculated that judges were reluctant to send very young defendants to prison because they were seen as more easily harmed by incarceration. Judges might have also viewed defendants over 50 as having lower odds for recidivism. All of these findings of *general* race, sex, and age effects might be misleading, however, if the "true" effects of these characteristics lie in how they interact with each other to shape judicial decisions.

Steffensmeier, Ulmer, and Kramer introduced a theory of "focal concerns" in order to frame their prediction of harsher sentences for young, black males. They argued that court actors' decisions were influenced by three focal concerns, namely "offender's blameworthiness, protection of the community, and practical implications of sentencing decisions" (p. 766). The first two concerns were related to the punishment philosophies of retribution and incapacitation, respectively. Regarding blameworthiness, they argued that judges sentenced offenders to more severe punishments as the harm inflicted by their behaviors increased, which was why offense severity was usually the strongest predictor of sentencing and was the primary consideration in sentencing guideline schemes. This also explained why a defendant's criminal history was considered in sentencing even though it was secondary in importance relative to offense severity. A history of criminal behavior suggested to judges that the defendant was more culpable for the current offense since they had already established their disrespect for the law.

The second focal concern of protecting the community was very similar to Albonetti's (1987) discussion of "bounded rationality" which, in turn, stemmed from the work of James March and Herbert Simon (1958). In order to reduce uncertainty in their prediction of an offender's future behavior, for the purpose of protecting the community, judges fall back on the limited information available to them which includes both case information *and* defendant characteristics. The latter might include extralegal factors such as history of drug abuse, marital status, number of children, job stability, and so on.

Finally, the third focal concern regarding implications of a judge's decision involved a judge's considerations of the consequences of a particular sentence for both the court system and for the defendant and his or her family. Organizational (court) concerns involved such things as making sure not to overextend existing jail and prison resources in order to reduce crowding, not disrupting case processing by avoiding sentences that were overly severe for the offenses committed (which increase the odds of appeals), and maintaining functional relationships with attorneys. Concerns regarding the defendant included, among other things, the implications of incarceration for his or her children, whether the defendant would have a more difficult time adapting to incarceration relative to other offenders, and any medical conditions that might also interfere with adaptation as well as increase the state's costs in caring for the individual.

The authors borrowed from Darnell Hawkins' (1981) discussion of "perceptual shorthand" in their speculations of whether judges derive "shorthand" methods to efficiently address the above focal concerns. That is, whether judges observed certain "cues" that suggested the defendant was a better or worse risk than others, and whether these cues included a defendant's race, sex, and age. Stereotypes are easily reinforced in someone's mind when the person sees an individual who "fits" the stereotype (Kluegel 1990), such as when a young, black male actually possesses a very serious criminal record. Based on this framework,

Steffensmeier and his colleagues predicted that a defendant's race, sex, and age would interact to provide a stronger effect on sentencing relative to each of these characteristics considered separately. The credibility of the authors' arguments were advanced by their discussion of Kathleen Daly's (1994) *qualitative* research on sentencing judges where her interviews revealed that some judges actually believed that young, black males were more crime-prone than other groups defined by age, race, and sex.

Steffensmeier, Ulmer, and Kramer examined sentencing data from Pennsylvania spanning 4 years (1989–1992). Pennsylvania developed presumptive sentencing guidelines in 1982 in order to reduce sentencing discretion, but the authors noted that the scheme was not as rigid as other guideline schemes and still permitted a fair amount of judicial discretion in sentencing decisions (a topic discussed in the next section). Almost 139,000 cases were examined. The sentences they examined included whether a convicted defendant was incarcerated in prison or jail, and the length of incarceration in prison or jail.

Results

The authors found that offense severity and prior record were the most important predictors of both outcome measures, consistent with their predictions based on the focal concern of *blameworthiness*. They also found that the variables race, sex, and age *each* maintained significant relationships with both outcome measures. Ten percent more African Americans were sentenced to incarceration relative to whites, nearly 15 percent more men than women were incarcerated, and defendants over the age of 50 were the least likely of any age group to be incarcerated (with 18% fewer incarcerated relative to defendants under 30). Regarding the latter finding and consistent with Steffensmeier et al.'s (1995) previous research, the relationship between age and sentence severity was U-shaped in that defendants under 21 and those over 50 were the least likely to be incarcerated, and defendants between 21 and 29 were the most likely to be incarcerated. This *curvilinear* relationship also held for each race (*x*) sex group separately although it was less pronounced (weaker) for women in general.

Turning to their findings for *interaction effects* involving a defendant's race, sex, and age, the authors found that the highest likelihoods of incarceration and the longest sentences for *males only* were distributed to African Americans aged 18–29. The odds of incarceration for white males 18–29 was 12 percent lower than for the first group. Differences in sentence length were not as dramatic although still significant, with white males 18-29 serving roughly three months less time than African American males 18–29. Race differences were reduced for older age groups, particularly for males over 50, although whites still fared (slightly) better than African Americans between the ages of 30 and 50. The odds of incarceration for *both* race groups over 50 was roughly 25 percent lower than for African American males 18–29. These dramatic differences in incarceration rates demonstrated that race differences in sentencing relied heavily on a defendant's age. The authors also examined whether these differences held up for different types of crimes (violent, property, and drug) and found very similar results for the odds of incarceration across all three offense groups. In their analysis of sentence length, however, age was more important for African Americans convicted of drug offenses.

Their analysis of females revealed that white females were much less likely than African-American females to be incarcerated, regardless of the age group examined. The smaller race differences found in the older age groups for males, therefore, did not hold for females. Similarly, for the length of incarceration, white females were sentenced to terms roughly 2 months shorter than African American females, regardless of the age group examined. The authors concluded that the race effect was much more consistent across age groups for women compared to men.

Taken altogether, the analysis revealed that African American males aged 18–29 maintained the highest odds of incarceration and the longest sentences relative to any other race *(x)* sex *(x)* age group. Also, there was a decrease in race group differences in the odds of incarceration as a male defendant's age increased (from 18–29 to 30–49 to 50–69), but this decline was not nearly as dramatic for women. Race group differences in the odds of incarceration for women declined only when moving from ages 30–49 to ages 50–69. Race group differences in sentence length also varied by a defendant's sex, with differences narrowing among older men yet becoming *broader* for older women. African American women aged 50–69 served an average of 6 months more than white women in the same age group.

The authors also described some of the observations of the judges they interviewed, arguing that many of the judges' observations favored a focal concerns perspective. Some of the themes they identified from these interviews included common observations by judges that:

1. The criminal records of young black males were more serious and, in turn, more reflective of higher risks for recidivism than those of other subgroups.
2. Some white offenders should not be sent to prison because black inmates may victimize them.
3. Decisions to incarcerate women and older offenders should include considerations of their higher odds of victimization during incarceration.
4. Women and older offenders were more costly to incarcerate.
5. Women and older offenders have more community ties and were, therefore, better risks for community sanctions.

These observations were consistent with the authors' empirical findings related to the more severe sentences for young, black males as well as the least severe sentences for both women and older offenders in general. In short, while judges focused primarily on legal factors when determining the sentences of convicted offenders, they also based their decisions in part on extra-legal factors, particularly the interaction of a defendant's age, race, and sex.

Limitations

Steffensmeier, Ulmer, and Kramer's study was subject to several common criticisms of research on sentencing disparities, such as failure to examine extralegal effects on earlier decision points in the process (from filing formal charges through conviction). This is an important criticism because such studies cannot determine the demographic composition of the arrested suspect pool, thus opening up the possibility that the pools of convicted African American and white defendants differed in some unknown ways that could have affected their sentences. For example, suppose that African American suspects were *less* likely than white suspects to be formally charged in Pennsylvania. The higher rate of dismissals for minority defendants could have generated a more serious pool of prosecuted African-Americans, assuming that prosecutors were less likely to pursue charges for less serious cases and for those with weaker evidence. This situation would have increased the odds of more serious sanctions for African Americans relative to whites based on differences in how prosecutors screened the cases of these two groups.

Also missing from the authors' analyses were legally relevant factors deemed to be important predictors of case outcomes in other court studies, including pretrial release status (Goldkamp 1979), type of counsel (Moore and Miethe 1986), and familiarity between the offender and the victim (Albonetti 1991). Failure to hold constant or control for the effect of pretrial release, for example, could have generated a spurious relationship between a defendant's race and incarceration if African Americans were less likely to make bail, and defendants who did not make bail were more likely to be convicted and incarcerated. In the context of Steffensmeier, Ulmer, and Kramer's study, young African American males might have been the subgroup *least* likely to make bail because of the overrepresentation of minorities in the poverty class, the generally lower socioeconomic status of younger (versus older) persons, and the generally more serious offenses committed by males (versus females) that lead to higher bond amounts. By holding constant the effect of pretrial release on sentencing, the differences in the odds of incarceration between the age *(x)* race *(x)* sex subgroups might have disappeared.

Another potential flaw with the authors' analysis involved some of their assessments of *interaction effects*, such as the statement, "The effect of race depends on gender and age, the effect of gender depends on race and age, and the effect of age depends on race and gender" (p. 783). The problem with this statement is that it was based on analyses of *non-experimental* data and so it is impossible to actually disentangle these "separate" effects. For example, to say that the effect of a defendant's sex on sentencing is different across race groups meant that the effect of a defendant's race would also vary by his or her sex, given that the same defendants were involved in each analysis. Assuming that (a) males *in general* were sentenced more severely than females regardless of race, (b) African American females were sentenced more severely than white females, and (c) males were sentenced even more severely than females in the pool of African American defendants relative to white defendants, then African Americans *must* have been sentenced more severely than whites in the pool of male defendants. In the pool of African Americans, males might be five times more likely than females to be incarcerated whereas males were only three times more likely in the pool of whites. This implied that judges were more severe with men relative to women when they were African American. Assuming that the odds of incarceration were also higher for African American females relative to white females, then, among men only, judges must also have been more severe with African Americans relative to whites. In short, one could not reliably determine the portion of the odds of incarceration that was due to a male defendant being African American versus an African American being a male.

Turning to the authors' outcome measures, it has recently been argued that combining jail and prison terms into one general category of "incarcerated" might mask important differences in sentencing convicted defendants to jail *or* prison (Holleran and Spohn 2004). On the one hand, it makes sense to combine jail and prison sentences because both outcomes entail removing an offender from the community and placing him or her in confinement. On the other hand, different types of offenders are sentenced to jail versus prison, and so combining the two might obscure results for both the legal and extralegal effects on sentencing. For example, both very serious and less serious offenders are likely to be confined even though very serious offenders go to prison whereas less serious offenders are more likely to go to jail. Also consider that jail sentences are much shorter in length than prison sentences and so any measure of sentence length that combines the two dispositions is somewhat misleading in terms of "severity." For example, jails are filled with offenders serving 6-month terms whereas prisons are filled with offenders serving at least 5-year terms.

David Holleran and Cassia Spohn (2004) examined differences in findings between the outcome examined by Steffensmeier and his colleagues versus outcomes that separated whether offenders went to jail or prison or were placed on probation. They also examined a jurisdiction within Pennsylvania (Philadelphia County), the same state examined by Steffensmeier (although Holleran and Spohn purposely did not examine the entire state, for reasons described below). Findings revealed substantial differences between the effects on jail versus prison sentences, with differences between whites and African Americans most pronounced in their models predicting prison sentences. Holleran and Spohn also found that offense severity maintained different effects on prison versus jail sentences depending on a defendant's race, where increasing severity coincided with consistently higher odds of jail sentences for whites but not for African Americans and Latinos. In short, the findings described by Steffensmeier and his colleagues might have been different if they had examined prison and jail sentences separately.

Also recall the authors' focus on all county courts in Pennsylvania. Related to Holleran and Spohn's (2004) decision to examine a single jurisdiction, a criticism of sentencing studies which have focused on statewide data is that combining cases from different jurisdictions could hide potential disparities that exist only in particular jurisdictions. This criticism follows logically from the observations of Sudnow (1965) and Eisenstein and Jacob (1977) related to differences in social and political climates between courts which, in turn, influence differences in plea bargaining and sentencing practices. Without conducting court-specific analyses, Steffensmeier, Ulmer, and Kramer's findings reflected statewide "averages" and did not convey the extent to which particular jurisdictions differed from these figures. Some jurisdictions might have exhibited no age *(x)* race *(x)* sex differences in sentence severity while others might have exceeded the differences described by the authors. At a minimum, simply testing for differences in the incarceration rates of young, African-American males across Pennsylvania courts might have placed their general findings in a more proper context.

Significance and Subsequent Research

Steffensmeier, Ulmer, and Kramer's study offered a fresh theoretical perspective for understanding extralegal disparities in sentencing and provided an important methodological contribution to *quantitative* studies of the topic. The authors' research also led others to recognize the relevance of *multi-level modeling* for related research. Regarding their theoretical contribution, one could argue that the "focal concerns" perspective in conjunction with Albonetti's "uncertainty avoidance" perspective contributed greatly to court scholars' abandonment of the older conflict perspective that dominated extant studies for decades. Relative to Albonetti's perspective, focal concerns theory offered a broader paradigm for understanding both prosecutorial and judicial decision-making via its incorporation of an offender's *blameworthiness* and related considerations of legal factors that were typically the strongest predictors of sentence severity.

Also in conjunction with Albonetti's contributions throughout the 1990s, Steffensmeier, Ulmer, and Kramer's study made it virtually impossible for any subsequent study to not recognize the possibility of interaction effects involving a defendant's race and sex on sentencing, and every published analysis of sentence severity since 2000 has at least included an acknowledgement of this possibility. We have also never seen a study published after 1998 that did not cite Steffensmeier et al.'s study. (Many more authors seem to miss Albonetti's equally important contributions.) Another important scholar in this regard is Cassia Spohn who, along with many of her colleagues, also examined interaction effects on sentencing throughout the late 1990s, though without a unique theoretical perspective. Spohn's contributions included analyses of (a) sentencing disparities based on a defendant's race *and* ethnicity (which revealed several differences in the treatment of Latino defendants relative to African American and white defendants in many United States jurisdictions from the southwest to the northeast), (b) interaction effects involving a defendant's race/ethnicity *(x)* sex *(x)* economic disadvantage (such as a defendant's unemployment status), and (c) interaction effects involving a defendant's race/ethnicity *(x)* offense type (particularly drug offenses, which were stereotypically associated with Latinos and African Americans) (e.g., Nobiling, Spohn, and DeLone 1998, Spohn 1990, Spohn and Cederblom 1991, Spohn and Holleran 2000, Spohn et al. 1987). Spohn's study with Holleran (described above) was a direct result of Steffensmeier et al.'s analysis, and her prolific works reflect the frameworks of both Albonetti and Steffensmeier.

A second methodological contribution of the authors' study was not intentional but had a major impact on subsequent research. Related to Holleran and Spohn's observation that statewide analyses might obscure jurisdiction differences in sentencing disparities, and in conjunction with the observations of political scientists such as Eisenstein, Jacobs, Flemming, and Nardulli, several researchers began to focus on sentencing disparities at *two* levels of analysis, the defendant and the jurisdiction, in order to examine jurisdiction differences in sentencing practices within states. As described previously in the discussion of Eisenstein and Jacob, ethnographic studies of court communities have uncovered important jurisdiction-level differences in court cultures and case processing practices (Eisenstein and Jacob 1977, Flemming et al. 1992, Nardulli et al. 1988, Ulmer 1997), and so it is important to recognize these differences in statewide analyses of sentencing. Chester Britt (2000), Paula Kautt (2002), and Jeffery Ulmer and Brian Johnson (2004) initially demonstrated the usefulness of analyses that "nest" defendants within jurisdictions in order to more reliably estimate the types of models examined by Steffensmeier and his colleagues. The procedure of *multilevel modeling* (the label reflecting recognition of more than one level of analysis, such as defendants and jurisdictions) essentially estimates separate *individual level* models within the *aggregate units*. In sentencing research, this involves estimating the types of models examined by Steffensmeier for each jurisdiction separately, and then testing whether these defendant (individual) level effects are different depending on the jurisdiction. This represents an application of *analysis of covariance*, or the examination of the relationship (covariance) between two individual level measures and how it becomes stronger or weaker across aggregates. With statewide sentencing data, for example, one can examine whether the effect of a defendant's race on the odds of incarceration is stronger in some jurisdictions relative to others. Researchers can take this one step further, if they find significant differences in the strength of this relationship, by examining whether jurisdiction differences in the race effect correspond with differences in particular jurisdiction characteristics (such as crime rates, court caseloads, dominant political party, etc). On the other hand, finding that a race effect does *not* differ in strength across courts is equally as important because it indicates that the level of racial disparities in sentencing is essentially the same across all courts in a state. This method also can be applied to legal effects on sentencing in order to see if the effects of offense severity on the odds of incarceration are the same across courts, which is particularly important for sentencing guideline states due to interest in making these effects more uniform across courts in the state.

Several of the more recent multilevel sentencing studies were conducted by Brian Johnson and Jeffrey Ulmer, both who have ties to Steffensmeier, Kramer, and the Pennsylvania sentencing data. Johnson has applied this method to an understanding of differences in sentencing practices across judges (with defendants and judges as the two levels of analysis), of differences in filing rates across prosecutors (cases and prosecutors), and of differences in rates of guideline departures across federal district courts (Johnson 2003, 2005, 2006, Johnson et al. 2008, Ulmer and Johnson 2004). The second author of this book also conducted a series of multilevel studies on sentencing practices in Ohio in order to see whether the effects of a defendant's race and sex on sentencing varied across courts as well as across neighborhoods, the latter focus which stemmed from a national concern over very high incarceration rates of African American men from poor neighborhoods (Wooldredge, Griffin, and Rauschenburg 2005, Griffin and Wooldredge 2006, Wooldredge 2007).

When examining multiple jurisdictions, there is always a possibility that jurisdiction differences in the types of defendants processed might be the reason for some of the differences in incarceration likelihoods and in the length of prison sentences across courts, even aside from the effects of court cultures. For example, larger portions of more serious cases might lead to a greater use of incarceration in some jurisdictions relative to others. Multilevel modeling is useful in controlling the effects of these types of *compositional differences* in individuals across jurisdictions, which may, in turn, affect differences in sentencing practices across courts.

References

Albonetti, C. (1987). "Prosecutorial Discretion: The Effects of Uncertainty." *Law and Society Review* 21:291–313.

Albonetti, C. (1991). "An Integration of Theories to Explain Judicial Discretion." *Social Problems* 38:247–66.

Britt, C. (2000). "Social Context and Racial Disparities in Punishment Decisions." *Justice Quarterly* 17:707–32.

Crutchfield, R., G. Bridges, and S. Pitchford (1994). "Analytical and Aggregation Biases in Analyses of Imprisonment: Reconciling Discrepancies in Studies of Racial Disparity." *Journal of Research in Crime and Delinquency* 31:166–82.

Daly, K. (1987). "Structure and Practice of Familial-based Justice in a Criminal Court." *Law and Society Review* 21:267–90.

Daly, K. (1989). "Neither Conflict nor Labeling nor Paternalism will Suffice: Intersections of Race, Ethnicity, Gender, and Family in Criminal Court Decisions." *Crime and Delinquency* 35: 135–68.

Daly, K. (1994). *Gender, Crime, and Punishment.* New Haven: Yale UP.

Eisenstein, J., and H. Jacob (1977). *Felony Justice: An Organizational Analysis of Criminal Courts.* Boston: Little, Brown.

Flemming, R., P. Nardulli, and J. Eisenstein (1992). *The Craft of Justice: Work and Politics in Criminal Court Communities.* Philadelphia: University of Pennsylvania Press.

Goldkamp, J. (1979). *Two Classes of Accused.* Cambridge, MA: Ballinger.

Griffin, T., and J. Wooldredge (2006). "Sex-based Disparities in Felony Dispositions Before versus After Sentencing Reform in Ohio." *Criminology* 44:893–924.

Hawkins, D. (1987). "Beyond Anomalies: Rethinking the Conflict Perspective on Race and Criminal Punishment." *Social Forces* 65:719–45.

Holleran, D., and C. Spohn (2004). "On the Use of the Total Incarceration Variable in Sentencing Research." *Criminology* 42:211–40.

Johnson, B. (2003). "Racial and Ethnic Disparities in Sentencing Departures Across Modes of conviction." *Criminology* 41:501–42.

Johnson, B. (2005). "Contextual Disparities in Guideline Departures: Courtroom Social Contexts, Guidelines Compliance, and Extralegal Disparities in Criminal Sentencing." *Criminology* 43:761–96.

Johnson, B. (2006). "The Multilevel Context of Criminal Sentencing: Integrating Judge and County Level Influences in the Study of Courtroom Decision Making." *Criminology* 44:259–98.

Johnson, B., J. Ulmer, and J. Kramer (2008). "The Social Context of Guidelines Circumvention: The Case of the U.S. District Courts." *Criminology* (forthcoming).

Kautt, P. (2002). "Location, Location, Location: Interdistrict and Intercircuit Variation in Sentencing Outcomes for Federal Drug-Trafficking Offenses." *Justice Quarterly* 19:633–71.

Kluegel, J. (1990). "Trends in Whites' Explanations of the Black White Gap in SES." *American Sociological Review* 55:512–25.

Koons-Witt, B. (2002). "The Effect of Gender on the Decision to Incarcerate Before and After the Introduction of Sentencing Guidelines." *Criminology* 40:297–328.

Kruttschnitt, C. (1982). "Women, Crime, and Dependency: An Application of the Theory of Law." *Criminology* 19:495-513.

Kruttschnitt, C., and D. McCarthy (1985). "Familial Social Control and Pretrial Sanctions: Does Sex Really Matter?" *Journal of Criminal Law and Criminology* 76:151–75.

LaFree, G. (1985). "Official Reactions to Hispanic Defendants in the Southwest." *Journal of Research in Crime and Delinquency* 22:213–37.

March, J., and H. Simon (1958). *Organizations.* New York: Wiley.

Moore, C., and T. Miethe (1986). "Regulated and Unregulated Sentencing Decisions: An Analysis of First-year Practices Under Minnesota's Felony Sentencing Guidelines." *Law and Society Review* 20:253–77.

Nardulli, P., J. Eisenstein, and R. Flemming (1988). *Tenor of Justice: Criminal Courts and the Guilty Plea Process.* Urbana: University of Illinois Press.

Nobiling, T., C. Spohn, and M. DeLone (1998). "A Tale of Two Counties: Unemployment and Sentence Severity." *Justice Quarterly* 15:459–85.

Petersilia, J. (1983). *Racial Disparities in the Criminal Justice System.* Santa Monica, CA: RAND.

Spohn, C. (1990). "The Sentencing Decisions of Black and White Judges: Some Expected and Unexpected Similarities." *Law and Society Review* 24:1197–1216.

Spohn, C., and J. Cederblom (1991). "Race and Disparities in Sentencing: A Test of the Liberation Hypothesis." *Justice Quarterly* 8:305–27.

Spohn, C., and D. Holleran (2000). "The Imprisonment Penalty Paid By Young, Unemployed Black and Hispanic Male Offenders." *Criminology* 38:281–306.

Spohn, C., J. Gruhl, and S. Welch (1987). "The Impact of the Ethnicity and Gender of Defendants on the Decision to Reject or Dismiss Felony Charges." *Criminology* 25:175-91.

Steffensmeier, D., J. Kramer, and C. Streifel (1993). "Gender and Imprisonment Decisions." *Criminology* 31:411–46.

Steffensmeier, D., J. Kramer, and J. Ulmer (1995). "Age Differences in Sentencing." *Justice Quarterly* 12:701–19.

Steffensmeier, D., J. Ulmer and J. Kramer (1998). "The Interaction of Race, Gender, and Age in Criminal Sentencing: The Punishment Cost of Being Young, Black, and Male." *Criminology* 36:763–97.

Sudnow, D. (1965). "Normal Crimes: Sociological Features of the Penal Code in a Public Defender Office." *Social Problems* 12:255–76.

Ulmer, J. (1997). *Social Worlds of Sentencing: Court Communities under Sentencing Guidelines.* Albany: SUNY Press.

Ulmer, J., and B. Johnson (2004). "Sentencing in Context: A Multilevel Analysis." *Criminology* 42:137–77.

Welch, S., J. Gruhl, and C. Spohn (1984). "Sentencing: The Influence of Alternative Measures of Prior Record." *Criminology* 22:215–27.

Wooldredge, J. (2007). Neighborhood Effects on Felony Sentencing. *Journal of Research in Crime and Delinquency* 44:238–63.

Wooldredge, J., T. Griffin, and F. Rauschenberg (2005). "Sentencing Reform and Reductions in the Disparate Treatment of Felony Defendants." *Law and Society Review* 39:835–74.

Zatz, M. (1985). "Pleas, Priors, and Prison: Racial/ Ethnic Differences in Sentencing." *Social Science Research* 14:169–93.

Zatz, M. (1987). "The Changing Forms of Racial/Ethnic Biases in Sentencing." *Journal of Research in Crime and Delinquency* 24:69–92.

Zatz, M., and J. Hagan (1985). "Crime, Time, and Punishment: An Exploration of Selection Bias in Sentencing Research." *Journal of Quantitative Criminology* 1:103–26.

Further Reading

Corley, C., and H. Hawkins (2006). "The Michigan Firearms Statute: Are There Racial/Ethnic Implications?" *Journal of Ethnicity in Criminal Justice* 4:67–79.

Sudbury, J. (2005). *Global Lockdown: Race, Gender and the Prison-Industrial Complex*. New York: Routledge.

5

Structuring Sentencing Decisions

O ver the past few decades there has been a political movement towards "getting tougher" with criminals, which has led many state court systems to place a higher priority on *retribution*, or punishing offenders in proportion to the harms they inflicted on others, as opposed to *rehabilitation*, or reforming the offender into more pro-social and law-abiding citizens. Prior to this movement, both state and federal governments followed indeterminate sentencing schemes in which convicted felons sent to prison received varying prison terms falling within broad ranges (e.g., 5–20 years) based on the court's assessment of each offender's amenability to rehabilitation. This practice was consistent with the philosophy of rehabilitation and the idea that sentences of indeterminate length were necessary to ensure that offenders were kept under supervision and treatment until successfully reformed. The onset of the "get tough" movement during the 1970s resulted in changes to state and federal schemes from indeterminate to more structured sentencing, often called "determinate" sentencing, where sentence ranges for particular crimes were much narrower relative to those under indeterminate schemes. The "get tough" movement, however, was not the sole impetus for more structured sentencing. Equally relevant was the criticism of indeterminate schemes as providing judges with unbridled discretion that often resulted in grossly disparate sentences across similarly situated offenders. For example, judges were permitted to consider many factors in their sentencing decisions that might have reflected an offender's amenability to treatment, such as family ties, work history, and residential stability. Given all of these possible considerations, different sentences could result for offenders who committed the same offenses simply because these other factors were considered or weighed differently in each case. Moreover, if these factors were also related to an offender's race or other extralegal characteristics, then judges could impose more severe sanctions on minority defendants while justifying their decisions under the guise of these other factors that are correlated to a defendant's race. Changes in sentencing policies from indeterminate to determinate/presumptive sentencing schemes over the last three decades have been driven, in part, by a belief that determinate sentencing can overcome the problem of unwarranted disparities in sentencing that often beset indeterminate models. Thus, the movement toward more structured sentencing schemes was seen by conservatives as a way to get tougher with criminals and was seen by liberals as a way to reduce the discretion of judges that might have been contributing to inequities in sentencing based on judicial biases toward defendants with particular extralegal characteristics, such as those examined by Hagan (1974).

SENTENCING GUIDELINES: CAN A SENTENCING SCHEME BE DEVELOPED TO REDUCE INEQUITIES IN PRISON SENTENCES?

Wilkins, L., J. Kress, D. Gottfredson, J. Calpin, and A. Gelman (1978). *Sentencing Guidelines: Structuring Judicial Discretion.* Washington, DC: National Institute of Law Enforcement and Criminal Justice, US Department of Justice.

Background

The two major criticisms of sentencing practices prior to the 1980s, primarily under indeterminate sentencing schemes, was that sentences were not equitable (similarly situated offenders often received different outcomes), and that sentences were unfair (too lenient or too harsh relative to the severity of the offenses convicted for). The second issue cannot be addressed in light of differences in public opinions regarding what constitutes "fair" outcomes, but the issue of equity can be addressed because everyone can agree on whether two sentences are the same or not (regardless of whether they meet some moral standard of "fairness"). Important to consider, however, is whether two different sentences are truly inequitable based on other information that judges have access to. Two offenders with the same prior record and who are convicted of the same offense might receive different sentences based on other information contained in a pre-sentence investigation report that reflects differences in, for example, their community ties (related to employment stability, residential stability, having dependent children, etc). In other words, the identification of *unwarranted* differences in sentences requires an understanding of *all* information judges have at their disposal when determining whether to send someone to prison and for how long.

Although judges have at their disposal a wide range of sentencing options (confinement in prison, confinement in jail, residential treatment programs, halfway houses, community treatment, community supervision, community service, fines, restitution, etc.), the greatest source of contention has emerged over apparent inequities in decisions of whether to send a convicted felon to prison (the "in/out" decision) and the length of confinement for those sent to prison. Several proposed sentencing reforms aimed at reducing discretion were seriously considered even before the study conducted by Wilkins and his colleagues described here. These tactics included the use of appellate review for addressing disparities across cases, sentencing councils or panels involving a group of three judges assigned to each case as a check on any one judge's decision, the use of flat-time sentences with a fixed number of years to be served in prison rather than a range of possible time served (such as a minimum of two years but no more than four years), mandatory prison terms for particular types of crimes, and presumptive sentences dictated by state legislatures that judges can depart from *only* with written justifications. Wilkins et al. argued that none of these tactics would be effective because they involve removing sentencing authority from the judges who continue to implement these sentences, and "attempts to impose solutions by fiat rarely work" (p. 4).

The Study

Leslie Wilkins and his colleagues conducted a study of whether disparities in the "in/out" decision and the length of imprisonment could be reduced by providing judges with *sentencing guidelines* that would indicate recommended sentences for offenders based on the characteristics of both the offenders and their crimes. Consistent with their criticisms of the alternate reform strategies mentioned above, their intent was not to derive a scheme that would eliminate judicial discretion but instead to help "guide and structure" this discretion. The findings from their study led to the creation and adoption of sentencing guideline schemes across the country. The fact that different states use somewhat different sets of guidelines is consistent with one of the authors' primary findings regarding differences across jurisdictions in the information considered by judges when they determine the "in/out" decision.

Wilkins et al. (1978) conducted a *quantitative* analysis of the feasibility of implementing sentencing guidelines for decisions regarding whether a convicted felon should be sent to prison and for how long. Their use of the term "guidelines" referred to "a system of data which functions as a tool in assisting decision-makers in arriving at individual and policy determinations" (p. 4). Their focus on developing guidelines originated from a previously successful feasibility study conducted by Don Gottfredson and Leslie Wilkins on federal parole guidelines. The parole study had a similar focus on reducing disparity in decision-making, specifically the decision to parole an incarcerated offender. Results of the study revealed that a vast majority of decisions by the Parole Commission could be predicted by knowing only a few pieces of information including (a) offense seriousness, (b) risk of recidivism, and (c) the conduct of the offender during incarceration (although this last piece of information was dropped from the scheme before it was ultimately implemented). In extending these ideas to judicial discretion, the authors examined whether most sentencing decisions could be predicted by knowing only a few items of information. However, Wilkins et al. stated at the outset that they were not interested in promoting legislatively mandated sentences since that would counter a philosophy of individualized justice, possibly generating an even greater problem with the second issue described earlier regarding "unfair" sentences.

The project ran from July 1974 through June 1976 and focused on several different possible instruments for judges. Wilkins et al. first had to assess all available information that judges might consider in their sentencing decisions. Items in this pool of information were determined by the empirical literature on sentencing as well as by judges who participated in the study as consultants. There were 205 items of information identified as being potentially relevant, and these items fell into three categories: offense seriousness, social stability, and prior record. Regarding "offense seriousness," debate ensued over whether it is the offense convicted on versus the actual behavior that is or should be considered in sentencing. Wilkins argued that consideration of the actual behavior would undermine plea bargaining since defendants engaged in bargaining in order to obtain a reduced sentence relative to the one corresponding with their "actual" crime. Consideration of "social stability" items was also problematic because they were often missing from court files and presentence investigation reports, meaning that judges often did not have this information at their disposal. Of all the social stability items, the authors determined that employment information was the most commonly available and should be relied on more heavily than other items such as marital status, school records, broken homes, etc. Finally, issues arose regarding relevant "prior record" items because of debate over whether only serious offenses should be considered, whether the number of offenses should be considered, whether only recent offenses should be considered, and whether priors should even be considered at all since offenders have already "paid" for those crimes.

The next step in the study involved compiling information on the 205 items from *random* samples of 400 sentenced cases in order to identify items that were the best predictors of sentencing in those cases. The sample was divided between the Denver District Court in Denver, Colorado (200 cases) versus all Vermont district courts (200 cases). These cases were drawn randomly from court dockets, and only one defendant was selected per case (since some cases involved multiple codefendants). Courts were selected deliberately based on the authors' interest in obtaining (1) a mix of urban and rural courts, (2) jurisdictions with moderate numbers of judges to facilitate communication with research staff, and (3) judges who determined sentences in plea bargained cases (as opposed to judges who allow prosecutors to do so during negotiations). These courts were referred to as "participant" courts whereas two other courts were treated as "observer" courts, including Essex County Court in Newark, New Jersey, and Polk County Court in Des Moines, Iowa. These observer courts provided judges who could more objectively assess the findings from these other courts since they were not involved in those sentencing decisions.

Results

The authors conducted a preliminary analysis of the quality and quantity of data available to judges in Colorado and Vermont for the 400 cases mentioned above. They found that many of the 205 potentially relevant items were not consistently found in the case files and pre-sentence investigation reports, and that this was more common for the social stability and personal history items (although missing data occurred randomly across the files and were not more common in particular types of cases). If some items were missing in large portions of cases, however, then those items could not be used to assemble a guideline system.

The authors' challenge was not only to identify information relevant to predicting sentencing decisions, but to also determine the relative importance of each item for prediction so that the information could be weighted differently in the guideline scheme (where stronger predictors receive more weight). The authors used *multivariate regression* analysis to determine the "best" predictors of prison sentences. Although not explicitly stated by the authors, it appears that they used a *step-wise regression* technique where variables were added to a model predicting type of sentence in the order of each variable's contribution to reducing error in prediction. That is, the best predictor was added first, followed by each subsequent variable until adding any of the remaining variables did not improve the prediction of sentence type. There were similarities and differences in the models derived from each court system. The analysis of cases from the Denver District Court revealed six significant predictors of sentencing that reduced error in prediction by 50 percent. These predictors included number of charges a defendant was convicted on, number of prior incarcerations (as a juvenile and as an adult), offense seriousness based on the maximum prison term possible, weapon use during the offense, whether the defendant was under court supervision at the time of the offense, and the defendant's length of employment before the arrest. Only four variables were significant predictors of sentences in Vermont, reducing error in prediction by 27 percent. These variables included number of prior incarcerations, weapon use, offense seriousness, and alcohol abuse. Note that the first three variables were important in both court systems.

The next step in the study was to develop several different matrix-style grids which all employed the information above but in different combinations across the instruments. The authors recognized that "decisions are not made about people, but about *information*" (p. 15), and this information is potentially infinite because "human beings are capable of a virtually infinite variety of behaviors." An effective guideline scheme, therefore, must contain ample information and offer a variety of options to adapt to the complexity of human behaviors. The challenge was how best to integrate this information in order to achieve this goal. They developed five sentencing models for comparison, three for Denver and two for Vermont (based on the differences in results from the authors' prediction models of sentencing in Denver versus Vermont).

The first three models were relevant to the Denver District Court. The first model (Model A) was the simplest model and involved a two-dimensional matrix with categories of offense seriousness placed along the vertical axis and categories of an "offender score" on the horizontal axis. Offense seriousness was a four-category scale developed by staff (judges') rankings of the conviction offenses, with seriousness increased if a dangerous weapon was used and/or the victim suffered physical harm. The Offender Score was an additive scale consisting of legal status at time of offense (whether the offender was already under court supervision at the time of arrest), prior conviction record, age at first conviction, prior incarceration record, probation/parole revocations, and employment (or school attendance) at sentencing. The second grid model (Model B) involved more dimensions than Model A. The primary difference was that a separate Offender Score index was developed for *each* statutory offense class (eight classes in Colorado), with 18 items used to determine a convicted defendant's score (15 items related to offense seriousness and prior record and 3 items related to social stability). Personal crimes and drug crimes were treated as more serious than other crimes in this model, with points added to an offender's score if they engaged in these offenses. Model B also focused on an offender's adult criminal history *only* rather than also considering juvenile records. The third model (Model C) was more similar to Model B than A, which also created a series of guidelines for each offense classification. Model C differed from B in that the Offender Score was based on both personal offender variables (age, alcohol abuse, narcotics abuse, employment status, legal status, residential stability, and community ties) in addition to the history of prior convictions as an adult. Model C also included a "harm/loss modifier" (p. 17), thereby ranking an offender by offense seriousness as well as the amount of harm in conjunction (interaction) with offense seriousness.

The next two models were developed for Vermont. The first (Model D) was similar to Model A for Denver, with a two-dimensional grid matrix of offense severity (x) Offender Score. The Offender Score was also computed similarly, which included legal status at arrest, prior adult and juvenile conviction records, age at first conviction, prior incarceration records as an adult and as a juvenile, probation/parole revocation, employment or school attendance at arrest, drug dependency, and alcohol dependency. The second model (Model E) was more similar to Model C above, with multiple dimensions of offender scores based on Vermont's eight offense categories, as well as consideration of the harm/loss modifier. Unlike Model C, however, the harm/loss modifier was considered separately as opposed to its interaction with offense seriousness.

The next stage of the project involved testing the five models by (1) applying each state's set of models to a *nonrandom* sample of cases selected from that state in order to determine what the sentence would have been under each set of guidelines, (2) comparing the predicted sentences to the actual sentences, and (3) having the judges responsible for the sampled cases indicate the most important pieces of information from the grid models that were used in their decisions. These judges also provided insights into any additional information they considered in the different cases. Regarding steps (1) and (2), each model was evaluated based on the number of cases that were not classified correctly as well as the reduction in prediction error when using the model as opposed to predicting a non-prison sentence for a convicted defendant (given that community sanctions were more common). A sample of 221 cases was examined in Denver, versus 113 cases in Vermont. In Denver, all three models predicted roughly 80 percent of the "in/out" decisions accurately. In Vermont, Model D accurately predicted 73 percent of these decisions, versus 83 percent accuracy from Model E. The authors concluded that all three of the Denver models were comparable in prediction.

Regarding step (3), the Denver judges considered the probability of an offender's recidivism as the most important consideration, followed by offense seriousness. The Vermont judges, on the other hand, identified the seriousness of an offender's prior record as the most important information, also followed by offense seriousness. The authors interpreted these differences as evidence that different jurisdictions might require different grid models to better reflect their unique social and political environments. Also interesting was the finding that offender variables (odds of recidivism and criminal history) were more relevant to sentencing than offense seriousness.

The final stage of the project focused on development of a single grid model that reflected a synthesis of the different sentencing models predicting the "in/out" decision. The synthesized model was then applied to roughly 400 additional sentencing decisions in Denver. When the model failed to predict accurately in particular cases, judges were asked to explain why they thought the predicted and actual sentences were different. The synthesized model included the determination of Offender Scores by prior incarcerations, probation/parole revocations, legal status at time of offense, prior convictions, and employment history. The harm/loss modifier was also included as an additive (not an interaction) effect. Histories of juvenile delinquencies and incarcerations were *not* incorporated into the scheme. The "Denver Demonstration Model" predicted 80 percent of the "in/out" decisions accurately, similar to the performance of each of the original three models (A, B, and C).

Although the models examined by Wilkins et al. ultimately included only a fraction of the original 205 items, they argued that "only a limited amount of information can be processed in making a decision" (p. 25). Also, even though additional accuracy (beyond the 80%) might have been obtained with additional items of information, the small gain in accuracy might not be worth the price of compiling and incorporating those items into the grid. As few as 6 to 12 items predicted 85 percent of what they called the "more usual" cases, and those items did not have to be weighted differently in order to improve prediction. On the other hand, there was a small minority of unusual cases for which the guidelines performed poorly, and for which other information might have significantly improved prediction. For this reason, Wilkins et al. recommended that judges be permitted to sentence outside the ranges set forth by the guidelines as long as they justify their decisions in writing. They were also quick to underscore the necessity of *not* abandoning judicial discretion in such cases, since the "guideline sentence is intended as a statistical aid and in no way provides a binding, prescriptive sentence to be automatically imposed in every case . . . the sentencing judge, as human decision-maker, still retains the discretion to override any suggested determination" (p. 28). Also, guidelines were intended to supplement rather than replace the presentence investigation report. When preparing these reports, probation officers could also compute the recommended sentence very quickly by referencing the guidelines. The authors also recommended that the guidelines be reviewed and revised as needed, with judges meeting bi-annually for this purpose. Therefore, by deriving a sentencing scheme based on past judicial behaviors while also placing control over its revisions in the hands of the judiciary, such a sentencing scheme was less likely to be subverted by judges as opposed to a scheme determined solely by the legislature.

Limitations

Wilkins et al. recognized the possible criticism that guidelines might only serve to "structure" unfair sentencing practices. Marc Mauer (1999) voiced this concern 20 years later, after the implementation of guideline schemes in 18 states and the District of Columbia, arguing that the development of guidelines based on past sentencing practices might only codify certain forms of discrimination into the formal sentencing process. Judges who would otherwise not discriminate in their decisions would necessarily do so simply by following the guideline recommendations. Yet, Wilkins et al.'s method of building a grid system should help to avoid this problem. The applicability of Mauer's criticism of guidelines developed using the authors' method depends on the assumption that the average behaviors of judges were discriminatory to begin with, yet "averages" should balance the extreme sentences that were more likely to coincide with conscious biases toward particular groups of defendants. In other words, following Wilkins et al.'s approach would render Mauer's criticism inapplicable. Several of the guideline systems currently in effect, however, were not developed based on average sentences distributed in the past, such as Oregon's scheme. Some states as well as the Federal Courts have relied on presumptions derived by state and federal legislatures and sentencing commissions. Both judges and academics have criticized these practices for the very reasons Wilkins and his colleagues presented in their report. Most importantly, legislatively derived guidelines developed without judicial input essentially reduces judges' authority and undermines their ability to apply their expertise.

The Federal Guidelines in particular have been heavily criticized since their implementation in 1987. Michael Tonry (1993) most effectively summarized the criticisms made by both academics and practitioners. He observed that the federal guidelines removed too much judicial discretion and might have led some prosecutors to use more of their discretion in order to cater sentences to defendants' unique case circumstances (through their discretion in the types of charges filed and in the plea bargaining process). Related to this criticism, Tonry also argued that court actors had incentives to try and maneuver around the recommended sentences that do not really "fit" the crimes. Important to underscore, however, is the emphasis Wilkins and his colleagues placed on the importance of developing a sentencing scheme that would help "guide and structure" judicial discretion as opposed to remove it altogether, which is yet another of the authors' recommendations that was not heeded in the early development of guideline schemes. We return to these particular criticisms in our subsequent review of Charles Moore and Terance Miethe's (1986) empirical evaluation of whether discretion was "displaced" from judges to prosecutors under Minnesota's sentencing guidelines.

A less common criticism noted by Tonry is that the federal guidelines were too complicated and were difficult to apply in practice. Although this might seem unwarranted in light of the simplicity of the schemes proposed by Wilkins et al. (with only eight offense classifications in their synthesized model), the federal guidelines included 48 offense classifications. Another criticism involved the "fairness" aspect that the authors stated outright was irrelevant to the development of a guideline scheme. Nonetheless, critics have argued that considerations of *only* offense seriousness and prior record tend to generate very similar sentences for very different individuals. The final criticism noted by Tonry dealt with the perception that the guidelines contributed to higher rates of incarceration in prison and that sentences overall had increased in severity. Altogether, both the federal guidelines as well as other "rigid" state guideline schemes (such as those operating in Minnesota, Florida, and Washington) have been widely criticized by judges and attorneys as being inflexible and unwieldy, often mandating outrageously severe sanctions that defy common sensibilities about fairness (Diroll 1989, National Council on Crime and Delinquency 1982). Erik Luna (2002) took one of these criticisms even further and argued that the rigidity of the federal guidelines actually led court actors to engage in dishonest and deceptive behaviors in order to avoid the prescribed outcomes. He also echoed the sentiments of Wilkins et al. that removing the determination of sentences from judges and placing it in the hands of the legislature would only create resentment and resistance by judges. According to Luna, "Justice in sentencing requires an individualized assessment of the offender and the offense, leading to a moral judgment imposed by judges with skill, experience, and wisdom" (2002, p. 1).

The criticisms described above are not really criticisms of Wilkins et al.'s study per se, but rather criticisms of how their ideas were ultimately implemented. It is clear that, in practice, most of what the authors warned about was ignored (such as basing sentences on past practices, using the scheme to "guide" rather than to dictate sentencing decisions, and revisiting the guidelines on a regular basis in order to revise as necessary). On the other hand, some criticisms have been aimed at the empirical method used by the authors to determine items for inclusion in guideline models as well as the method of validating different models. Wilkins et al.'s empirically based sentencing models were derived from the multivariate regression analyses described earlier. Using this method, they determined the final pool of 6 to 12 items (from the initial pool of 205 items), how they would be weighted, if at all, and how they would be combined for use as a predictive instrument. The technique was then used to determine the predictive power of each of their five models that were all roughly 80 percent "accurate" (except for one model). The primary criticism of this approach was that *multivariate regression* could not adequately model the complexities of judicial thought because judges do not necessarily consider items separately, nor do they necessarily weigh each item the same across cases. Minnesota's sentencing guidelines, for example, once consisted of a two-dimensional grid reflecting offense seriousness and the offender's criminal history. Such a scheme was an oversimplification of judicial decision-making even if these items predicted sentencing accurately in the majority of cases. While it is possible to evaluate the interactions of various items using multivariate regression, the technique is limited in terms of the types of interactions that can be assessed. As such, the instruments produced with this technique would not predict accurately in a certain portion of cases.

Even assuming perfect prediction, however, it is possible that judges came to many of the same decisions using different criteria than those included in the grid. Such a process could result from the consideration of information that is highly correlated to criteria structured into the guidelines. This issue is related to an argument raised by Richard Sparks (1983) regarding the atheoretical approach to prediction that has characterized the development of guideline schemes at the state and federal levels. He argued that the absence of any theory about judicial sentencing practices means that we lack an understanding and an appreciation of the complexity of these decisions. Without formulating a theory and allowing the model to be built with theoretically relevant predictors, items are explored that tend to maximize prediction whether they make sense or not. The inherent drawback to this approach is that guideline schemes may only include information that proxies the "real" information considered by judges, and so any changes in the relationships between those proxies and the more relevant criteria over time will weaken the reliability of the instrument. "Without some sort of theory, we can have no real idea what sort of information to collect in order to give a useful description of past sentencing practice" (Sparks 1983, p. 206).

Significance and Subsequent Research

Wilkins et al.'s study contributed directly to the implementation of sentencing guideline schemes in 23 states, in the District of Columbia, and in the federal courts. Gottfredson, Wilkins, and Hoffman (1978) were the first to examine empirically based decision-making guidelines in the context of parole decisions, and their success led to a similar application to sentencing decisions. Since the late 1970s and early 1980s, when Minnesota, Pennsylvania, and Washington established sentencing commissions and enacted new criminal sentencing guidelines, an increasing number of states along with the federal government have adopted similar reforms. Not all guideline schemes have been based on the synthesized model developed by Wilkins and his colleagues. At the federal level, for example, the US Sentencing Commission developed mandatory sentencing guidelines that were implemented in 1987 (although they became voluntary in 2005 after a Supreme Court ruling). The Federal Guidelines include 43 levels of offense seriousness and consider both the seriousness of the crime and the offender's criminal history. Wilkins et al. proposed only eight offense levels, by contrast, but also considered offense seriousness and prior record. Despite the widespread criticisms of the schemes currently in use, no one can debate the fact that Wilkins and Gottfredson played primary roles in the sentencing reform movement across the United States. (Determinate sentencing actually began prior to their work, in the early years of the "get tough" movement, and so many determinate sentencing states do not currently operate under "guidelines.")

The implementation of sentencing guidelines across the country generated two areas of research on the subject. Although both bodies of research are quite limited, the topic of sentencing guidelines remains very important from both academic and policy perspectives. The limited research only reflects difficulties in actually conducting empirical studies of the topic. The first area of research involved evaluations of whether sentencing guideline schemes were effective for reducing the unwarranted disparities in prison sentences that they were designed to address, or whether the discretion lost by judges was merely displaced to prosecutors. This topic is covered in our subsequent discussion of Moore and Miethe's (1986) study of the Minnesota Guidelines and so we do not spend any time on it here.

The second area of research focused on judicial attitudes toward guidelines, which was particularly important given that many of the schemes in place today were *not* shaped by judicial input and evaluation as Wilkins and his colleagues had recommended. As Wilkins et al. speculated, a sentencing scheme that was shaped by those who will use it was more likely to be supported by judges and less likely to be subverted as opposed to one that was derived strictly through the legislature (and more specifically through a sentencing commission). Indeed, anecdotal evidence from federal district courts and states implementing sentencing guidelines suggests there was a prevailing wisdom that judges generally disfavor restrictions on their sentencing practices (Knapp 1993, Tonry 1987). Furthermore, negative judicial reception of sentencing reforms has often been inferred from data revealing courtroom adaptation to them via charge reductions through plea bargaining, especially mandatory sentences (Loftin and Heumann 1979, Wicharaya 1995). Negative judicial reaction to the Federal Sentencing Reform Act of 1984 was implied by the complicity of many judges in prosecutors' subversion of the guidelines through plea bargaining (Nagel and Schulhofer 1992). A similar inference follows from the fact that more than 200 federal judges had ruled the federal sentencing guidelines to be unconstitutional during the months preceding the *Mistretta* decision in which the Supreme Court upheld the constitutionality of the Sentencing Reform Act (Knapp and Hauptley 1989, Stith and Cabranes 1998).

Although the best way to determine judicial reaction to sentencing reform is through direct *survey*s, these are quite rare. The few we could find were generally consistent with the anecdotal reports and inferences based on the noncompliance or subversion noted above. For example, a majority of federal judges attending a conference at the University of Chicago indicated in a small survey that they had frequently allowed plea agreements that were contrary to the federal sentencing guidelines (Alschuler and Schulhofer 1989). In a survey of federal district court judges, the Federal Courts Study Committee (1990) reported strong opposition to the rigidity of the federal guidelines, although a specific response percentage was not provided. Favoring greater judicial discretion, the committee recommended that the guidelines be nonbinding. The United States Sentencing Commission (1991) reported findings from face-to-face interviews with a select number of officials associated with the federal courts, including 45 judges. The commission found that a majority of the judges (65%) believed that sentences under the guidelines were "mostly appropriate" but that those who found the sentences "mostly inappropriate" were almost equally divided as to whether the guidelines were too harsh or too lenient. Half of the responding judges believed that disparity in sentencing had been reduced by the guidelines, and majorities did not believe that the guidelines reduced judicial discretion, were inflexible, or would overburden the prison system. The findings were mixed, however. For example, the commission found that the judges interviewed generally did not agree that the federal guidelines increased predictability, were well constructed, or made sentencing easier.

Two detailed surveys of federal judges come from the Federal Judicial Center. In the first, more than 80 percent of district court judges and 65 percent of circuit court judges supported a repeal of mandatory minimum penalties, whereas almost 50 percent and 40 percent, respectively, favored elimination of the federal guidelines (Jeter et al. 1994). A second survey from the center provided findings consistent with this although with some qualifications (Johnson and Gilbert 1997). Majorities of judges believed mandatory determinate sentencing guidelines were unnecessary and that plea bargaining had become an arena of hidden disparity. However, there were other important findings from this second survey that painted a more complex picture. Most judges surveyed (70%) did not favor a return to indeterminate sentencing. Furthermore, there was moderate support for the overall fairness and clarity of the guidelines.

We are aware of only one other direct examination of state judges' perspectives on state sentencing reforms. Miethe and Moore (1988) surveyed court actors in Minnesota six years after Minnesota's 1981 Sentencing Reform Act, which created presumptive dispositions for whether to incarcerate and for how long based on the intersection of an offender's criminal history and offense severity on a grid. Included in the sample were 66 of Minnesota's 125 felony court judges. Significant majorities of responding judges reported that the guidelines were an improvement over the previous system and had made sentencing in Minnesota more equitable. However, more than 80 percent of responding judges agreed that judicial discretion had been reduced by the guidelines, and roughly 55 percent recommended *either* complete abolition or major restructuring of the guidelines. Miethe and Moore concluded that given the long gap between implementation of the guidelines and the survey, there was still a remarkably high level of opposition to Minnesota's sentencing laws and that this sort of hostility might be inevitable if the presumptive guidelines are to be successful in achieving the goals of controlling prison populations and promoting more equitable sentences by restricting judicial discretion. Along with the recent surveys addressing the federal guidelines, these findings suggest that judicial reactions to sentencing reform are complex.

References

Alschuler, A., and S. Schulhofer (1989). "Judicial Impressions of the Sentencing Guidelines." *Federal Sentencing Reporter* 2:94–99.

Diroll, D. (1989). *Use of Community Corrections and the Impact of Prison and Jail Crowding on Sentencing.* Columbus, OH: Ohio Governor's Office of Justice Services.

Federal Courts Study Committee (1990), *Report of the Federal Courts Study Committee.* Washington, DC: Administrative Offices of the Federal Courts.

Gottfredson, D., L. Wilkins, and P. Hoffman (1978). *Guidelines for Parole and Sentencing.* Lexington, MA: D.C. Heath.

Jeter, Y., B, Kreiswirth, P. Lombard, M. Pecherski, C. Sutelan, C. Witcher, and M. Gottheiner (1994). *Planning for the Future: Results of a 1992 Federal Judicial Center Survey of United States Judges.* Washington, DC: Federal Judicial Center.

Johnson, M., and S. Gilbert (1997). *The U.S. Sentencing Guidelines: Results of the Federal Judicial Center's 1996 Survey.* Washington, DC: Federal Judicial Center.

Knapp, K. (1993). "Allocation of Discretion and Accountability within Sentencing Structures." *University of Colorado Law Review* 64:679–705.

Knapp, K., and D. Hauptley (1989). "U.S. Sentencing Guidelines in Perspective: A Theoretical Background and Overview." In *The U.S. Sentencing Guidelines: Implications for Criminal Justice,* edited by D. Champion, 3–17. New York: Praeger.

Loftin, C., and M. Heumann (1979). "Mandatory Sentencing and Abolition of Plea Bargaining: The Michigan Felony Firearms Statute." *Law and Society Review* 13:393–430.

Luna, E. (2002). "Misguided Guidelines: A Critique of Federal Sentencing." *Policy Analysis* 458:1–31.

Mauer, M. (1999). *Race to Incarcerate.* New York: New Press.

Miethe, T., and C. Moore (1988). "Officials' Reactions to Sentencing Guidelines." *Journal of Research in Crime and Delinquency* 25:170–87.

Moore, C., and T. Miethe (1986). "Regulated and Unregulated Sentencing Decisions: An Analysis of First-year Practices Under Minnesota's Felony Sentencing Guidelines." *Law and Society Review* 20:253–77.

Nagel, I., and S. Schulhofer (1992). "A Tale of Three Cities: An Empirical Study of Charging and Bargaining Under the Federal Sentencing Guidelines." *Southern California Law Review* 66:501–66.

National Council on Crime and Delinquency (1982). *California Summit Seminar on Prison Crowding–Final Report.* San Francisco: Crocker National Bank Foundation.

Sparks, R. (1983). "The Construction of Sentencing Guidelines: A Methodological Critique." In *Research on Sentencing: The Search for Reform,* vol. 2, edited by A. Blumstein, J. Cohen, S. Martin, and M. Tonry, 194–264. Washington, DC: National Academy Press.

Stith, K., and J. Cabranes (1998). *Fear of Judging: Sentencing Guidelines in the Federal Courts.* Chicago: University of Chicago Press.

Tonry, M. (1987). *Sentencing Reform Impacts.* Washington, DC: U.S. Department of Justice, National Institute of Justice.

Tonry, M. (1993). "The Failure of the U.S. Sentencing Commission's Guidelines." *Crime and Delinquency* 39:131–49.

Wicharaya, T. (1995). *Simple Theory, Hard Reality: The Impact of Sentencing Reforms on Courts, Prisons, and Crime.* Albany: State University of New York Press.

Wilkins, L., J. Kress, D. Gottfredson, J. Calpin, and A. Gelman (1978). *Sentencing Guidelines: Structuring Judicial Discretion.* Washington, DC: National Institute of Law Enforcement and Criminal Justice, U.S. Department of Justice.

Further Reading

Alschuler, A. (2005). "Disparity: The Normative and Empirical Failure of the Federal Guidelines." *Stanford Law Review* 58:85–117.

Cassell, P. (2004). "Too Severe? A Defense of the Federal Sentencing Guidelines." *Stanford Law Review* 56:1017–48.

Griffin, T., and J. Wooldredge (2001). "Judicial Reactions to Sentencing Reform in Ohio." *Crime and Delinquency* 47:491–512.

THE EFFECTIVENESS OF MANDATORY SENTENCING GUIDELINES FOR REDUCING JUDICIAL SENTENCING DISCRETION: WHAT IS THE EVIDENCE THAT GUIDELINES ACTUALLY "WORK" TO REDUCE SENTENCING DISPARITIES?

Moore, C., and T. Miethe (1986). "Regulated and Unregulated Sentencing Decisions: An Analysis of First-year Practices Under Minnesota's Felony Sentencing Guidelines." *Law and Society Review* 20:253–77.

Background

Sentencing disparities based on the extralegal characteristics of defendants (race, sex, income, etc.) pose significant barriers to the goals of due process and proportionality in punishment. Especially under indeterminate schemes, there is always the potential that judicial discretion may result in higher rates of imprisonment for defendants with particular extralegal characteristics (Zatz 1987). The sentencing reforms of recent years, such as the guideline schemes described previously, were designed to elevate the importance of legally relevant factors (severity of offense and criminal history) and reduce the influence of extra-legal factors on sentencing decisions. As described in our coverage of Wilkins et al. (1978), however, the mere existence of such reforms does not necessarily mean that judges will completely abide by the new policies and not attempt to maneuver around them in order to regain some of their discretion. Research on the effectiveness of sentencing guidelines for promoting more equitable sentences is therefore essential in order to assess the utility of such reforms. Charles Moore and Terance Miethe (1986) were the first to examine this issue for one of the first states to adopt sentencing guidelines (Minnesota).

Opinions vary on whether restructuring the sentencing process will reduce, have no effect on, or even exacerbate extralegal disparities in case outcomes. Proponents of sentencing reform have argued that racial and other extralegal disparities in sentencing should be less likely under schemes that reduce judicial discretion, especially determinate sentencing schemes with guidelines that specifically outline the weight of legal factors in decisions regarding imprisonment and the length of imprisonment (e.g., Davis 1971, Frankel 1972, compare Smith and Cabranes 1998). In conjunction with narrower sentence ranges relative to those under indeterminate sentencing, determinate schemes might be more effective for prohibiting general racial inequities that were once introduced by judges inclined toward sentencing minorities at the higher end of a range. The more specific guidelines for how legally relevant characteristics are to be considered should also reduce a judge's ability to focus more heavily on some of these characteristics versus others in order to distribute harsher sentences to defendants s/he perceives as more dangerous. In short, guideline proponents argue that legal effects on sentencing should become stronger while extralegal effects become weaker under more structured sentencing.

At the other extreme, Mauer (1999) contended that a move from indeterminate to determinate sentencing might only make matters worse for minorities:

> "In many jurisdictions around the country, minorities constitute two thirds or more of the defendants in many offense categories. To what extent are 'get tough' sentencing policies a reflection of the race and ethnicity of those likely to be affected by such policies? As the hue of the defendant population changes, do legislators and judges set different sentencing standards?" (p. 132)

For example, if a sentencing scheme dictated more severe sanctions for selling crack cocaine, then this might affect African Americans more than whites if the former were arrested more often for the offense. Between these opposite views is the argument that such reforms might coincide with little to no change overall. If legally relevant factors operate differently for African Americans and whites under indeterminate sentencing, then these differences might persist under determinate sentencing either because legal factors could still be weighed differently by prosecutors (in plea agreements) (Alschuler 1978, McCoy 1984, Savelsberg 1992, Tonry and Coffee 1987), or because judges still retain some discretion when considering these factors (in the form of sentence ranges and reasons for departures from sentence ranges) (Kramer and Ulmer 1996, Miethe 1987, Ulmer 1997). Regarding the idea of displacing discretion from judges to prosecutors, sentencing guidelines could lead prosecutors to use more discretion in order to maneuver around the restrictions placed on judicial discretion (Lagoy et al. 1979), and so disparities might persevere through the guilty plea process via charge reductions (Rathke 1982). Women could still face less severe sentences than men, for example, if prosecutors are more reluctant to expose women to mandatory prison terms.

The discussion of efforts by judges and prosecutors to circumvent sentencing guidelines was especially relevant to Minnesota, the focus of Moore and Miethe's study, because of the state's adoption of one of the most rigid determinate schemes. That is, efforts to maneuver around structured sentencing schemes might be more likely in states with the most rigid systems. Minnesota's scheme went into effect on May 1, 1980. As previously described, the term "guidelines" refers to the idea that prison sentences are presumed for specific types of crimes (e.g., first degree felonies) in conjunction with particular types of offenders (e.g., repeat or habitual offenders). There were also presumptions for probation, or "zero months imprisonment", for less serious offense groups. At the time of Moore and Miethe's study, the length of a prison sentence was mechanically derived from a two-dimensional grid based on the nature of the offense and prior criminal history, with strict limitations on departures. (The federal government followed suit and subsequently implemented this type of model in 1987, under the 1984 Sentence Reform Act.) Unlike other guideline states that followed Wilkins et al.'s suggestions, Minnesota's scheme was not derived from past sentencing practices. In some states, guidelines merely "structured" the average sentences distributed by judges in the past for particular types of cases. Minnesota, by contrast, implemented a scheme reflecting "modified just-deserts", whereby sentences were dictated primarily by the offense and secondarily by the offender's criminal history. Under other punishment philosophies, such as rehabilitation, offender characteristics were considered in the sentencing decision as they reflected the offender's amenability to treatment and helped to determine the need for specific types of treatment.

This was the norm prior to 1980, and so Minnesota's sentencing commission chose not to develop guidelines based on past sentencing patterns. For this reason, and consistent with Wilkins et al. (1978), Moore and Miethe speculated that Minnesota's scheme "would probably increase resistance to implementation" (p. 256).

Minnesota's scheme and others like it have been widely criticized by judges and attorneys as being overly rigid and excessive in the degree to which judicial discretion is reduced (Diroll 1989, National Council on Crime and Delinquency 1982, Tonry 1996). A drawback to more rigid schemes is the greater difficulty in crafting sentences to the unique circumstances of cases, leading to a perception that sanctions are overly severe for specific cases. This apparent shortcoming led some state sentencing commissions to reject such models in favor of more flexible presumptive guidelines, such as the sentencing guidelines implemented in Ohio in 1996 (Wooldredge et al., 2002). As a comparison of the difference between Minnesota's and Ohio's guidelines, consider a first offender that used a gun to commit robbery. Under the prototypical Minnesota Sentencing Guidelines Grid, such an offender had a presumed sentence of 48 months. The judge had discretion within a range of 44–52 months. In sentencing that same armed robber under Ohio's template, the judge had a range of 36 to 120 months. There were factors to guide the judge toward a stated prison term within the range but the judge still had broad discretion across the range. A Minnesota judge had a range of nine months; an Ohio judge had a range of 84 months.

The Study

Minnesota's Presumptive Sentencing Guidelines were evaluated by the Minnesota Sentencing Guidelines Commission (MSGC) immediately after their implementation in 1980, but Moore and Miethe criticized their methods of evaluation. The authors set out to reexamine whether the guidelines coincided with more uniform decisions regarding sentences that were regulated ("prescribed") by the guidelines relative to sentencing decisions that were not regulated by the guidelines during the first year of the reform. Minnesota was not the first state to implement a determinate sentencing reform although previous state reforms had "generally fallen short of expectations" (p. 254) while also contributing to harsher sentencing practices and larger prison populations. By contrast, the Minnesota guidelines were seen as more hopeful, and the MSGC's evaluation of first-year sentencing practices under the reform offered evidence that the guidelines helped to reduce sentencing disparities without generating harsher sanctions and larger prison populations. Another report issued by the MSGC three years later stated that this pattern had been maintained during the first 3 years under the guidelines.

The statistical analyses offered by the MSGC, however, were not particularly rigorous. Most of the presentation of findings involved simple descriptive statistics such as a breakdown of a defendant's race by type of sentence. Additional analyses controlled for possible confounding effects on the relationship between a defendant's race and sentence severity, but the controls were limited to "offense severity, prior convictions, and jurisdiction" (p. 255). In short, these more simple analyses were not rigorous enough to determine whether judges were less likely under the guidelines to consider a defendant's race and/or sex in sentencing decisions that fell under the guidelines. Moore and Miethe conducted more rigorous analyses of the same data, therefore, which consisted of a sample of 1,523 "useable" cases processed across the state during the first year under the guidelines. The *dependent* variables reflecting the types of sentences that guidelines were designed to control included whether a convicted felony defendant was sent to prison (an "executed" or non-suspended prison term), and the length of prison sentences for those sent to prison. Also examined were the types of sentences not falling under the constraints of the guidelines, including the types of sentences imposed when prison sentences were "stayed" (or suspended), the length of those sentences, and jail/workhouse sentences. The *independent* variables (predictors of sentences) examined by the authors included an array of measures tapping type and seriousness of the offense(s), weapon use, criminal history score, mitigating and/or aggravating circumstances, number of charges, plea bargain on charge or sentence, jurisdiction, whether the conviction was by trial, and various extralegal characteristics including race, sex, employment status, and job stability at sentencing, highest education level, and marital status. The logic of comparing the effects of these variables on both regulated and unregulated sentencing decisions is that legal factors should be more relevant for predicting the regulated decisions relative to the unregulated decisions while extra-legal factors should be *less* relevant for predicting the regulated decisions relative to the unregulated decisions. It should be emphasized that these models were far more rigorous than any other academic study of extralegal disparities in case processing that had been conducted up to that point in time.

Findings

Moore and Miethe's analysis revealed that prison sentences and the length of imprisonment were driven primarily by the presumptive sentence (i.e., the sentence prescribed by the guidelines), and by "allowable departures" (p. 266). Both the presumptive sentence and presumptive duration were also most affected, in turn, by offense severity and criminal history (as intended). Although these expected relationships were not as strong as they probably should have been, meaning that there was still a fair portion of variation in each outcome that could not be explained by *any* variables in the model (with the exception of non-suspended prison sentences), Moore and Miethe concluded that these findings offered substantial support for the idea of greater sentencing uniformity under the presumptive guidelines. Their analysis of departures from the prescribed sentences, however, produced very weak results for the predictors and led them to speculate that the use of departures might not be in line with the MSGC's policies. A defendant's extralegal characteristics mattered more in these decisions although the authors did raise the possibility that they might not have controlled for other relevant legal factors that were correlated with the extralegal characteristics examined.

In contrast to the models of regulated sentencing decisions, the models of unregulated sentencing decisions were much weaker for predicting those decisions. Whereas over 60 percent of the error in predicting regulated outcomes was reduced in those models, with a 98 percent reduction in the model of prison sentences, there was no more than a 30 percent reduction in error when predicting the unregulated outcomes. Moore and Miethe deduced that the regulated decisions were influenced more by offense factors whereas the unregulated decisions were driven more by judges' assessments of *both* the offenses and the offenders. Jail sentences were more common for defendants "who were single, male, unemployed, and poorly educated . . . (and) it would appear that unregulated sentencing decisions were more prone to direct and indirect socioeconomic biases than regulated decisions" (pp. 272–73).

These findings provided evidence favoring the effectiveness of the guidelines for promoting greater uniformity in prison sentences and the length of those sentences, but Moore and Miethe also concluded that their results were not as optimistic as those offered by the MSGC regarding sentencing decisions falling outside the scope of the guidelines. The latter were more heavily influenced by offender traits, suggesting that Minnesota judges remained somewhat committed to individualized justice and acted on that commitment when possible. The authors' comments implied that control over judicial discretion might have to be total in order to avoid disparities in case outcomes based on extralegal factors. When decisions were open to judicial interpretation, such as the departure decisions or the unregulated jail sentences, judges might have been influenced by other philosophies not encompassed by the guidelines (such as rehabilitation, deterrence, or incapacitation). The authors added the important caveat that any presumptive sentencing scheme must have provisions for allowing deviations from the prescribed sentences even though this opens the door to disparity in outcomes. As such, they recommended that departures be subject to greater monitoring and that the appellate review process be used more frequently.

Moore and Miethe's article concluded with the cautionary note that, while Minnesota's guidelines appeared to be effective, the state's rather unique population, culture, and historical use of imprisonment in moderation suggested that its rigid scheme might not work as well in other states. Ironically, the federal guidelines implemented in 1987 were very similar to Minnesota's grid system yet were criticized for being draconian and were subsequently replaced with a more discretionary scheme.

Limitations

Considering when their study was conducted, Moore and Miethe's *quantitative* analysis was one of the most rigorous studies of racial disparities in sentencing conducted up to that time. During this period, however, several issues emerged regarding the nature of research on sentencing disparities *in general* (not aimed specifically at Moore and Miethe). These issues involved the importance of possible sample biases in related studies, possible *interaction effects* of a defendant's extralegal characteristics, and the relevance of examining stages of case processing prior to sentencing (briefly mentioned in the discussion of Albonetti). Here we add a fourth (potential) limitation of sentencing evaluations per se, namely the importance of considering differences in sentencing patterns across courts *in the same state* and whether state level reforms can necessarily address such differences.

It is logical that samples of cases in related studies should have included convicted defendants. Convicted defendants are typically not *random* samples of all defendants, however, in that persons who are more likely to be convicted are also more likely to be sent to prison (such as murderers or habitual offenders). So, if a sample of convicted defendants differs from a random sample in particular ways that the researcher is unaware, this could bias the race effect on the odds of imprisonment if these other (unknown) differences are also tied to a defendant's race. For example, suppose there are higher proportions of convicted defendants who do not make bail relative to the proportion of *all* defendants who do not make bail (recall our discussion of Foote, 1954). As a consequence of its linkage to higher odds of conviction, this means that failure to make bail is also linked to higher odds of imprisonment because only convicted persons are eligible for prison sentences. Failure to make bail also might be linked to a defendant's race, however, as a consequence of the overrepresentation of minorities in the poverty class. Therefore, an inability to control for whether a defendant made bail could generate a spurious relationship between a defendant's race and the odds of imprisonment. The opposite scenario is also possible where a researcher finds *no* relationship between a defendant's race and the odds of imprisonment because s/he did not control for factors related to race but *un*related to conviction likelihoods (Berk et al. 2005). In short, the relationship between race and sentencing may be over- or underestimated depending on variables excluded from the model (Klepper et al. 1983, Myers and Talarico 1992, Zatz and Hagan 1985).

Another criticism of related studies is the failure of some researchers to examine *interaction effects* involving a defendant's race on sentencing (as described previously in the discussion of Hagan). In fairness to Moore and Miethe, they subsequently conducted a study of race-related interaction effects on sentencing with the same data (Miethe and Moore 1986). Until the 1980s, however, most researchers of the topic focused only on whether African American or Latino defendants *overall* received harsher sentences relative to similarly-situated white defendants. As we detailed previously, several scholars have recently demonstrated that the general effect of a defendant's race on sentencing is more often not statistically significant, but a defendant's race does appear to *condition* the effects of other extralegal as well as legal effects on case dispositions and outcomes. This issue is also salient to research on the effectiveness of sentencing guidelines for reducing extralegal disparities in sentencing. Sentencing policies aimed at reducing judicial discretion are not developed by policy makers who are cognizant of the underlying processes that more realistically contribute to race-related disparities (i.e., these processes do not involve *general* race effects).

The third limitation of Moore and Miethe's approach involved their focus on the sentencing stage only, thereby missing case dispositions prior to sentencing. This might be most relevant for studies of rigid guideline schemes such as Minnesota's because the resistance on the part of court participants toward rigid sentencing schemes has implications for other stages of case processing. Some researchers have suggested that judges are able to circumvent legal policies that constrain their exercise of discretion (Heumann and Loftin 1979). Specifically, they may attempt to maneuver around guidelines by being more tolerant of certain plea agreements (e.g., Albonetti 1990, 1997, Ulmer 1997). In this way, the discretion that sentencing guidelines were intended to curb might simply be "displaced" to prosecutors. This "hydraulic displacement" (McCoy 1984) might result in greater prosecutorial discretion in decisions related to the types of charges filed against a suspect, decisions to subsequently drop charges, and the types of charge and/or sentence reductions accompanying guilty plea agreements. In his discussion of the federal guidelines, Joachim Savelsberg (1992) argued that charge and sentence bargaining should be most affected because prosecutors could manipulate the charges/sentences accompanying plea agreements in order to ultimately avoid sentences dictated by the guidelines.

Miethe (1987) subsequently examined the issue of displaced discretion in Minnesota before versus after implementation of guidelines. He speculated that the displacement of discretion, if it occurred, should be most apparent in Minnesota because the state operated under the most rigid sentencing scheme. Interestingly, he found no supporting evidence for the thesis of displaced discretion. Miethe presented several logical observations regarding why significant changes in prosecutorial decision-making under determinate sentencing schemes *in general* might not occur. Specifically, both formal and informal limits exist over prosecutorial discretion based on rules of evidence (formal) and the prosecutor's role in courtroom workgroups that also include judges and public defenders (informal). As described in the discussion of Eisenstein and Jacob, members of the workgroup learn what to expect from each other in terms of the types of plea agreements that are more likely to be offered, accepted, and ultimately approved (Eisenstein and Jacob 1977, Flemming et al. 1992, Nardulli et al. 1988). Prosecutors who deviate from these expectations run the risk of interfering with the "flow" of case processing and being labeled as unpredictable. Prosecutors also might not attempt to maneuver around sentencing guidelines because they do not wish to advertise any attempts to individualize justice since political attention would eventually turn towards them in order to curb any abuse of their discretion. Another reason why prosecutors might not exercise more discretion under sentencing guidelines is that most determinate schemes retain some judicial sentencing discretion in the form of sentence ranges and reasons for departures. Many schemes are also derived based on the "average sentences" distributed in the past, as recommended by Wilkins et al. (1978), and there is no reason to think that judges would want to suddenly deviate from the sentences that they had approved/distributed in the past. These observations were completely logical, and so the popularity of "displaced discretion" might be misguided. There is no consensus on this issue, however, which might be due to the much more limited research on stages of case processing *prior* to sentencing.

The final limitation involves the state-level scope of related studies in which researchers have pooled together cases from multiple jurisdictions in a state. Some scholars argue that jurisdictions within states need to be examined separately because the "culture" of racial bias could vary considerably across jurisdictions within a state, such as between urban and rural areas (Mitchell 2005). Pooling cases across jurisdictions could potentially mask disparities that existed in some (but not all) of the courts. Also, when considering an approach such as jurisdiction-specific studies, this raises an even larger issue about the implications of jurisdiction differences existing within a particular state (e.g., Wooldredge et al. 2005). Efforts to generate greater equity in the treatment of women and men or African Americans and whites across an entire state might not be very successful when levels of discrimination vary by social context. In other words, an understanding of how to reduce sentencing disparities based on defendants' extralegal characteristics might require an understanding of *contextual* differences between the social climates in which defendants were processed. A state-level reform may be limited in its impact when it cannot address these types of environmental effects on case processing.

Significance and Subsequent Research

Moore and Miethe's study was an important prototype for future research. Their work also sparked interest in whether the short-term effects they found for reduced sentencing disparities under Minnesota's guidelines would necessarily prevail in the long run. Lisa Stolzenberg and Stewart D'Allessio (1994) addressed this issue with data spanning several years and found that extralegal variables were very weak predictors of sentences immediately after the implementation of Minnesota's guidelines, consistent with Moore and Miethe's findings, but became stronger predictors over time. In short, the guidelines had only a short-term impact on reducing extralegal disparities in sentencing. Barbara Koons-Witt (2002) found the same pattern when examining sex differences in prison sentences before the Minnesota guidelines are implemented, shortly afterward, and several years later. These types of findings are particularly salient for a broader issue regarding criminal justice policies and the general criticism that many crime control strategies have been effective immediately after their implementation, but few have had any enduring effects over time. More importantly, these subsequent findings reified Moore and Miethe's original speculations that any reductions in extralegal disparities under sentencing guidelines might have been short-lived as judges eventually learned to maneuver around the guidelines in order to retain their control over the sentencing process.

There were several state-level, internal evaluations of other state guideline schemes that followed Moore and Miethe's study of Minnesota. All of these studies rendered the general conclusion that guidelines successfully reduced disparities in Florida, Oregon, and

Washington (Bales 1997, Bureau of Justice Assistance 1996, National Institute of Justice 1996) although none of these examined long-term effects. An illustrative example of this research came from Florida, which enacted a scheme whereby sentences were guided by a point system that considered primary and secondary offenses, criminal history, and a host of "enhancements" based on other legally relevant variables. Uniformity and neutrality in sentencing were stated goals of these sentencing guidelines. One early study showed that *pre*-guideline, parole-based sentencing in Florida was racially biased, even after controlling for legally relevant variables (Sentencing Study Committee 1979). In contrast, research from the Florida Department of Corrections on *post*-guideline imprisonment rates found that higher imprisonment rates and sentence lengths for African Americans were a function of offense severity and prior record, not racial bias (Bales 1997). However, the findings from the Florida Department of Corrections were limited because some of the measures used to analyze post-guideline cases were not available for pre-guideline cases.

A potential problem with internal evaluations is that they are conducted by government personnel who may have a vested interest in finding results that favor the policies under examination. Nonetheless, other studies conducted by outside agencies and academics have reached similar conclusions regarding short-term effects of guidelines. Specifically, analysis of sentencing outcomes under determinate sentencing in California showed very weak race effects on sentencing (Petersilia and Turner 1985). Similarly, in their study of disparity and sentencing under the Pennsylvania Sentencing Guidelines, John Kramer and Darrell Steffensmeier (1993) found that race and gender were very weak predictors of case outcomes in statewide sentencing decisions while the most powerful factors included severity of offense and criminal history. An important limitation to both of these studies, however, is the absence of comparisons between pre-guideline and post-guideline sentencing data.

In contrast to the "favorable" results of these studies, recent before–after studies of the impact of Ohio's guidelines on sentencing disparities found little evidence that the guidelines significantly altered sentencing patterns across 24 trial courts of general jurisdiction, with the exception that the imprisonment rates of convicted defendants dropped by six percent after the guidelines were implemented (Griffin and Wooldredge 2006, Wooldredge et al. 2002, Wooldredge et al. 2005). For the two time periods examined (one year prior to and one year after the implementation of guidelines), the evidence indicated that legal factors were much more important for predicting the types and lengths of sentences when compared to extralegal factors. In contrast to Minnesota, Ohio implemented guidelines that permitted a fair amount of flexibility in prison sentence length as well as the in/out decision for particular offenses and types of offenders. Interestingly, Ohio's mandatory guidelines were declared unconstitutional by the Ohio Supreme Court in 2006 (*State v. Foster*), at which point the state shifted to voluntary guidelines that judges were not required to follow (which also meant they no longer had to provide written justifications for guideline departures). Some state officials fear that the reintroduction of broad judicial discretion will lead to greater disparities in prison sentences as well as more crowded prisons (Worner 2006). Yet, despite a widely held belief that presumptive guidelines effectively reduce judicial discretion (as described by Bushway and Piehl 2007), the Ohio studies offered very little empirical evidence to this effect.

In light of their findings of reduced disparities under Minnesota's guidelines, Moore and Miethe made the very pertinent qualification that *departures* from presumptive sentences were apparently biased in favor of whites and females. This observation has been followed by a recent surge in research on possible causes of guideline departures, particularly in the states of Pennsylvania (Britt 2000, Johnson 2003, 2005, 2006, Kramer and Steffensmeier 1993, Kramer and Ulmer 1996, Steffensmeier et al. 1993, 1995, 1998, Ulmer and Johnson 2004) and Washington (Engen et al. 1999, Engen and Steen 2000, Gainey et al. 2005, Steen et al. 1999, 2005). For example, Kramer and Ulmer (1996) found that the use of guideline departures in Pennsylvania seemed to favor whites and females, consistent with Moore and Miethe's observation regarding Minnesota. Provisions for guideline departures are necessary to ensure proportionality in presumptive sentencing schemes but also carry the potential to foil the purpose of increased uniformity in sentencing because they introduce greater discretion in the sentencing process (Tonry 1996).

References

Albonetti, C. (1990). "Race and the Probability of Pleading Guilty." *Journal of Quantitative Criminology* 6:315–34.

Albonetti, C. (1997). "Sentencing Under the Federal Sentencing Guidelines: Effects of Defendant Characteristics, Guilty Pleas, and Departures on Sentence Outcomes for Drug Offenses, 1991–1992." *Law and Society Review* 31:789–822.

Alschuler, A. (1978). "Sentencing Reform and Prosecutorial Power: A Critique of Recent Proposals for 'Fixed' and 'Presumptive' Sentencing." *Univ. of Pennsylvania Law Review* 126:550–77.

Bales, W. (1997). *The Impact of the 1994 and 1995 Structured Sentencing Policies in Florida.* Tallahassee, FL: Bureau of Research and Data Analysis.

Berk, R., A. Li, and L. Hickman (2005). "Statistical Difficulties in Determining the Role of Race in Capital Cases: A Re-analysis of Data from the State of Maryland." *Journal of Quantitative Criminology* 21:365–90.

Britt, C. (2000). "Social Context and Racial Disparities in Punishment Decisions." *Justice Quarterly* 17:707–32.

Bureau of Justice Assistance (1996). *National Assessment of Structured Sentencing.* Washington, DC: Government Printing Office.

Bushway, S., and A. Piehl (2007). "Social Science Research and the Legal Threat to Presumptive Sentencing Guidelines." *Criminology and Public Policy* 6:461-82.

Davis, K. (1971). *Discretionary Justice: A Preliminary Inquiry.* Urbana: University of Illinois Press.

Diroll, D. (1989). *Use of Community Corrections and the Impact of Prison and Jail Crowding on Sentencing.* Columbus, OH: Ohio Governor's Office of Justice Services.

Eisenstein, J., and H. Jacob (1977). *Felony Justice: An Organizational Analysis of Criminal Courts.* Boston: Little, Brown.

Engen, R., and R. Gainey (2000). "Modeling the Effects of Legally Relevant and Extralegal Factors under Sentencing Guidelines: The Rules Have Changed." *Criminology* 38:1207–29.

Engen, R., and S. Steen (2000). *The Implementation and Impact of Drug Sentencing Reform in Washington State.* Final Report to the Washington State Sentencing Guidelines Commission.

Engen, R., R. Gainey, and S. Steen (1999). *Racial and Ethnic Disparities in Sentencing Outcomes for Drug Offenders in Washington State: FY1996 to FY1999.* Final Report to the Washington State Minority and Justice Commission.

Flemming, R., P. Nardulli, and J. Eisenstein (1992). *The Craft of Justice: Work and Politics in Criminal Court Communities.* Philadelphia: University of Pennsylvania Press.

Frankel, M. (1972). *Criminal Sentences: Law without Order.* New York: Hill and Way.

Gainey, R., S. Steen, and R. Engen (2005). "Exercising Options: An Assessment of the Use of Alternative Sanctions for Drug Offenders." *Justice Quarterly* 22:488–520.

Heumann, M., and C. Loftin (1979). "Mandatory Sentencing and the Abolition of Plea Bargaining: The Michigan Felony Firearm Statute." *Law and Society Review* 13:393-430.

Johnson, B. (2003). "Racial and Ethnic Disparities in Sentencing Departures Across Modes of Conviction." *Criminology* 41:501–42.

Johnson, B. (2005). "Contextual Disparities in Guideline Departures: Courtroom Social Contexts, Guidelines Compliance, and Extralegal Disparities in Criminal Sentencing." *Criminology* 43:761–96.

Johnson, B. (2006). "The Multilevel Context of Criminal Sentencing: Integrating Judge and County Level Influences in the Study of Courtroom Decision Making." *Criminology* 44:259–98.

Klepper, S., D. Nagin, and L. Tierney (1983). "Discrimination in the Criminal Justice System: A Critical Appraisal of the Literature." In *Research in Sentencing: The Search for Reform*, vol. 2, edited by A. Blumstein, J. Cohen, S. Martin, and M. Tonry. Washington, DC: National Academy Press.

Koons-Witt, B. (2002). "The Effect of Gender on the Decision to Incarcerate Before and After the Introduction of Sentencing Guidelines." *Criminology* 40:297–328.

Kramer, J., and D. Steffensmeier (1993). "Race and Imprisonment Decisions." *Sociological Quarterly* 34:357–76.

Kramer, J., and J. Ulmer (1996). "Sentencing Disparity and Departure from Guidelines." *Justice Quarterly* 13:81-105.

Lagoy, S., F. Hussey, and J. Kramer (1979). "The Prosecutorial Function and its Relation to Determinate Sentencing Structures." In *The Prosecutor*, edited by W. McDonald, 209–38. Beverly Hills, CA: Sage.

Mauer, M. (1999). *Race to Incarcerate*. New York: New Press.

McCoy, C. (1984). "Determinate Sentencing, Plea Bargaining Bans, and Hydraulic Discretion in California." *Justice System Journal* 9:256–75.

Miethe, T. (1987). "Charging and Plea Bargaining Practices under Determinate Sentencing: An Investigation of the Hydraulic Displacement of Discretion." *Journal of Criminal Law and Criminology* 78:155–76.

Mitchell, O. (2005). "A Meta-Analysis of Race and Sentencing Research: Explaining the Inconsistencies." *Journal of Quantitative Criminology* 21:439-66.

Moore, C., and T. Miethe (1986). "Regulated and Unregulated Sentencing Decisions: An Analysis of First-year Practices Under Minnesota's Felony Sentencing Guidelines." *Law and Society Review* 20:253–77.

Myers, M., and S. Talarico (1987). *The Social Contexts of Criminal Sentencing*. New York: Springer-Verlag.

Nardulli, P., J. Eisenstein, and R. Flemming (1988). *Tenor of Justice: Criminal Courts and the Guilty Plea Process*. Urbana: University of Illinois Press.

National Council on Crime and Delinquency (1982). *California Summit Seminar on Prison Crowding–Final Report*. San Francisco: Crocker National Bank Foundation.

National Institute of Justice (1996). *Key Legislative Issues: The Impact of Sentencing Guidelines*. Washington, DC: Government Printing Office.

Petersilia, J., and S. Turner (1985). *Guideline-Based Justice: The Implications for Racial Minorities*. Santa Monica: RAND.

Rathke, S. (1982). "Plea Negotiating Under the Sentencing Guidelines." *Hamline Law Review* 5:271–91.

Savelsberg, J. (1992). "Law That Does Not Fit Society: Sentencing Guidelines as a Neoclassical Reaction to the Dilemmas of Substantivized Law." *American Journal of Sociology* 97:1346–81.

Sentencing Study Committee (1979). *A Report on the Analysis of Sentencing Procedures in Florida's Circuit Courts*. Tallahassee, FL: Bureau of Research and Data Analysis.

Smith, K., and J. Cabranes (1998). *A Fear of Judging: Sentencing Guidelines in the Federal Courts*. Chicago: University of Chicago Press.

Steen, S., R. Engen, and R. Gainey (1999). *The Impact of Race and Ethnicity on Charging and Sentencing Processes for Drug Offenders in Three Counties of Washington State*. Final Report to the Washington State Minority and Justice Commission.

Steen, S., R. Engen, and R. Gainey (2005). "Images of Danger: Racial Stereotyping, Case Processing, and Criminal Sentencing." *Criminology* 43:435–68.

Steffensmeier, D., J. Kramer, and C. Streifel (1993). "Gender and Imprisonment Decisions." *Criminology* 31:411–46.

Steffensmeier, D., J. Kramer, and J. Ulmer (1995). "Age Differences in Sentencing." *Justice Quarterly* 12:701–19.

Steffensmeier, D., J. Ulmer, and J. Kramer (1998). "The Interaction of Race, Gender, and Age in Criminal Sentencing: The Punishment Cost of Being Young, Black, and Male." *Criminology* 36:763–97.

Stolzenberg, L., and S. D'Allessio (1994). *Sentencing and Unwarranted Disparity: An Assessment of the Long-Term Impact of Sentencing Guidelines in Minnesota*. Santa Monica, CA: Rand.

Tonry, M. (1996). *Sentencing Matters*. New York: Oxford.

Tonry, M., and J. Coffee (1987). "Enforcing Sentencing Guidelines: Plea Bargaining and Review Mechanisms." In *The Sentencing Commission and its Guideli*, edited by A. Von Hirsch, K. Knapp, and M. Tonry, 152–63. Boston: Northeastern UP.

Ulmer, J. (1997). *Social Worlds of Sentencing: Court Communities under Sentencing Guidelines*. Albany: SUNY Press.

Ulmer, J., and B. Johnson (2004). "Sentencing in context: A Multilevel Analysis." *Criminology* 42:137–77.

Wooldredge, J., F. Rauschenberg, T. Griffin, and T. Pratt (2002). *Final Report: The Impact of Ohio's Senate*

Bill 2 on Sentencing Disparities. Washington, D.C.: National Institute of Justice.

Worner, N. (2006). *Ohio Supreme Court Decision Eliminates Sentencing Guidelines.* Mount Vernon, OH: Mount Vernon News.

Zatz, M., and J. Hagan (1985). "Crime, Time, and Punishment: An Exploration of Selection Bias in Sentencing Research." *Journal of Quantitative Criminology* 1:103–26.

Further Reading

Hofer, P., K. Blackwell, and R. Ruback (1999). "The Effect of the Federal Sentencing Guidelines on Inter-Judge Sentencing Disparity." *Journal of Criminal Law and Criminology* 90:239–306.

Nagel, I., and B. Johnson (1994). "The Role of Gender in a Structured Sentencing System: Equal Treatment, Policy Choices, and the Sentencing of Female Offenders under the United States Sentencing Guidelines." *Journal of Criminal Law and Criminology* 85:181-221.

Reitz, K. (2005). "The Enforceability of Sentencing Guidelines." *Stanford Law Review* 58:155–73.

Corrections

The correctional system in the United States was created to administer punishment and oversee the care and treatment of criminal offenders. Today, corrections refer to the broad range of community and institutional sanctions and programs used to supervise and manage our offender population. Early American colonists relied primarily upon physical punishments. Criminals were subjected to various forms of corporal punishment such as whipping, flogging, branding, or mutilation. The colonists also had an extensive list of capital offenses. Offenders could be put to death for murder, treason, stealing horses, and adultery. Punishments were intended to be painful to achieve retribution and punishment was administered in public to shame an offender and to set an example for the community. Banishment and fines were also used as punishment in colonial America. The only correctional institutions were *gaols*, or short term holding facilities for offenders awaiting trial or for their corporal or capital punishment to take place (Johnson and Wolf 2003). Offenders were housed in dirty, unsanitary cells with little food or provisions. By the late 1700s, a need for change was recognized. Critics of the physical forms of punishment pushed for a reform of the correctional system that would include more humane forms of punishment. At the center of this reform was an idea that involved removing offenders from society and isolating them in facilities where they could be reformed.

In 1790, a Pennsylvania Quaker by the name of Benjamin Rush converted a section of the Walnut Street Jail to house offenders. For the first time in America, incarceration was used as punishment. The concept was borrowed from John Howard, an English prison reformer who had developed the *penitentiary* in England 20 years earlier. Penitentiaries were places where offenders could repent for their crimes and emerge as law-abiding citizens of the community. The Pennsylvania system of confinement consisted of a rigid structure of hard work and penance in an isolated, silent environment. Two prisons were opened in the early 1800s. Western Penitentiary outside of Pittsburgh opened in 1826, and three years later Eastern Penitentiary opened near Philadelphia. Both of these penitentiaries operated under the silent, solitary confinement system started at the Walnut Street Jail.

About the same time, the Quakers were implementing their system of confinement; New York opened a facility in Auburn. The original plan was to operate the institution according to the same philosophy as the Pennsylvania model; however, in 1823 the facility was modified to allow the inmates to congregate in work groups during the day. The Auburn model of confinement became the preferred system across the United States because it was less costly to build and maintain inasmuch as the inmates could work to defray the cost of confinement.

Over the next several decades, several large penitentiaries were constructed. Despite the construction boom, early facilities very quickly became crowded prompting another reform. This time the push for change was widespread. In 1870, a congregation of prison administrators, concerned citizens, and political leaders met in Cincinnati and established the National Prison Association (known today as the American Correctional Association). The group met to discuss the current state of American prisons and ideas for future developments (Allen et al. 2006). The general consensus among members was that the penitentiary had become a revolving door. Released offenders returned to a life of crime only to return to prison. One of the most popular topics for discussion was the Irish prison system operated under Sir Walter Crofton. Crofton had implemented a system of graduated release, a practice he duplicated from another prison administrator, Captain Alexander Maconochie, who was in charge of the British penal colony on Norfolk Island, Australia. The Irish system involved preparing the inmates for release into society by gradually allowing them to earn more freedoms in exchange for their good behavior. Offenders were sentenced under an *indeterminate* sentence where their release date was based on how they performed in prison. Delegates at the Cincinnati conference adopted the Irish system with the use of the indeterminate sentence and agreed that programs to help the offenders once they were released back into society should be added to the penitentiary regimen. The name of our prison facilities changed as well. They became known as *reformatories* because of the expanded educational and vocational programs to help the offenders upon release.

An alternative form of punishment was being used in Massachusetts. In 1878, Massachusetts passed a statute that allowed judges to place juvenile offenders on probation. Offenders on probation remained in the community under court-imposed conditions designed to limit opportunities for crime. The concept dated back to 1841 when a Boston judge turned over custody of an offender to a shoemaker named John Augustus. Augustus took care of the offender and kept the court informed of this progress. By 1938, 37 states and the federal government had statutes in place recognizing probation as a correctional sanction. In the 1960s, other alternatives to incarceration were developed (i.e., community service and intermediate sanctions) and the United States experienced a tremendous growth in its community correctional population. Two-thirds of all offenders today receive some type of community sentence.

In the first three decades of the 20th century, the United States experienced massive growth in its prison population as well. New prisons were constructed and the focus changed from trying to reform the inmates to using inmate labor to support the increasing costs of prison. By 1929, many prisons had become self sufficient by selling goods and services on the open market. In response to criticisms by organized labor groups, Congress passed legislation in 1929 and again in 1935 that restricted the sale of prison made goods. Prisons had to find other ways to not only generate revenue but also occupy the inmates' time. The next several decades were difficult for prisons. Without resources to expand programs for the increasing prison population, many inmates acted out with violence. Several riots and major disturbances took place. Inmates were dissatisfied with the quality of their living conditions and had no recourse to complain. The courts had decided a long time ago that they would not interfere in the management of prisons. This sentiment changed in the landmark case of *Cooper v. Pate* (1964) when the US Supreme Court began accepting cases filed by inmates. From 1964 to the mid-1980s, the federal courts maintained an active agenda addressing the grievances of inmates and the result was significant improvements in the conditions of confinement.

Correctional Research

The riots of the 1960s and 1970s focused national attention on prisons in the United States. To address the problems and concerns, in December 1971, Attorney General John Mitchell organized a corrections conference in Williamsburg, Virginia. Participants discussed the need for professionalism in the correctional field. This would be achieved by improving the training for correctional officers and administrators *and* by encouraging research and providing forums for the dissemination of research and ideas (American Correctional Association 1983). Three years later, the National Institute of Corrections was established to help coordinate these efforts. Correctional research has flourished over the past 35 years. Administrators and policy makers have access to an enormous amount of information to help govern prisons and manage inmates. The research included in this section was derived from various social science disciplines such as sociology, psychology, political science, and economics. The studies became the foundation of an impressive body of knowledge that continues to influence the correctional field today. Included in this section are studies examining the effectiveness of correctional strategies designed to rehabilitate, deter, and incapacitate offenders, as well as research on inmate social systems, prison conditions, and correctional officers. Studies of both institutional and community corrections are included.

References

Allen, H., E. Latessa, B. Ponder, and C. Simonsen (2006). *Corrections in America* 11th ed. Upper Saddle Ridge: Prentice Hall.

American Correctional Association (1983). *The American Prison: From the Beginning.*

Johnson, H., and N. Wolfe (2003). *History of Criminal Justice.* Cincinnati: Anderson.

Further Reading

Blumstein, A., and A. Beck (1999). "Population Growth in U.S. Prisons, 1980–1996." In *Crime and Justice: A Review of Research*, vol. 26, edited by Michael Tonry and Joan Petersilia, 17–61.

Jacobs, J. (1980). "The Prisoners' Rights Movement and Its Impact, 1960–1980." In *Crime and Justice: A Review of Research*, vol. 2, edited by Norval Morris and Michael Tonry, 429–70.

Morris, N., and D. Rothman (eds.) (1997). *The Oxford History of the Prison: The Practice of Punishment in Western Society.* New York: Oxford UP.

Rothman, D. (1980). *Conscience and Convenience: The Asylum and Its Alternatives in Progressive America.* Boston: Addison-Wesley.

Tonry, M., and J. Petersilia (eds.) (2000). "Prisons: Crime and Justice." Special Issue, *Crime and Justice: A Review of Research*, vol. 26.

1

Correctional Goals

The correctional system in the United States attempts to accomplish several different (and sometimes competing) goals. Underlying all of our efforts to punish criminals is the goal of *retribution*. Retribution or *just desserts* is the oldest and most enduring goal. We punish offenders because they deserve it. Society has an obligation to inflict harm upon those who harm others. As a correctional goal, retribution is non-utilitarian. There is no interest on the part of the state in the actual or predicted consequences of the punishment. Retribution focuses solely on *past* behavior. Nothing is achieved in terms of preventing *future* criminal behavior. Goals that attempt to prevent crime include rehabilitation, deterrence, and incapacitation. These goals are considered to be utilitarian since each involves the purpose of reducing crime. *Rehabilitation* is based upon the assumption that individuals commit crime because of some underlying psychological, biological, or environmental problem. The correctional system attempts a diagnosis and offers treatment. Addressing the causes of crime reduces recidivism by turning criminals into law-abiding members of society. Rehabilitation (originally called reformation) was the goal of our correctional system for most of the 20th century. *Deterrence* attempts reduce crime by making an example out of the offender. Punishment helps to prevent an offender from committing any more crimes and can also prevent others who may be contemplating crime from doing so. Isolating criminals from society to keep them from breaking the law is the premise of *incapacitation*. Society is protected from recidivists by reducing the opportunity for offenders to continue breaking the law. Each utilitarian goal involves predictions made by the state regarding the potential *future* benefits of punishing offenders. Inherent in any of these predictions is the possibility of error because of imprecise information used for evaluation. Beginning in the late 1960s, America launched a "get tough" strategy to combat increasing crime rates with policies designed to achieve both the goals of deterrence and incapacitation. These two correctional goals continue to dominate current correctional policies. Included in this next section are four empirical studies of the three utilitarian goals: rehabilitation, deterrence, and incapacitation. This research not only provided a better understanding of the goals' underlying assumptions, it also contributed to several policy debates about the underlying purpose(s) of our correctional system.

REHABILITATION

Efforts to change offenders into law-abiding members of society can be traced back to the development of the first penitentiaries of the 18th century. Penitentiaries were designed to reform criminals through isolation, deprivation, and religion. Inmates were housed in institutions located in remote areas away from the corruption of society and were expected to read the bible and repent for their crimes. These efforts were largely unsuccessful as evidenced by high recidivism rates. The concept of reformation was expanded as part of the New Penology to include educational and vocational training. Teaching inmates to read and write as well as employment skills that could be used upon their release would reduce their likelihood of returning to crime. Rehabilitation became the stated goal of our correctional system at this time. In the early 1900s, the Progressives introduced a Positivist School approach to rehabilitation. Social scientists were busy developing theories to explain criminal behavior and the Progressives believed this knowledge could be used to help offenders. Rehabilitation centered on a medical model. Each inmate brought into the correctional system was evaluated, diagnosed, and prescribed some type of treatment (i.e., medical, psychological, educational, vocational). By the early 1960s, the emphasis turned to attempts to help inmates reintegrate back into society *after* they had been rehabilitated in prison.

THE EFFECTIVENESS OF CORRECTIONAL TREATMENT: CAN CRIMINALS BE REHABILITATED?

Martinson, R. (1974). "What Works? Questions and Answers About Prison Reform." *The Public Interest* 35:22–54.

Background

Rehabilitation remained the goal of our correctional system until the early 1970s, when the efficacy of rehabilitation was questioned. Violent crime was on the rise and many politicians placed the blame on the criminal justice system. Some believed the system was too lax on offenders (Cullen and Gilbert 1982). The due process revolution resulted in criminals being set free because of "loopholes" and "technicalities." Prisoners were equally successful in the courts securing their constitutional protections. The perception of prison as a place of punishment was diminished because inmates were perceived as too comfortable and well cared for. Other critics took issue with the individualized treatment model put forth by the Progressives. Treating offenders differently based on their unique needs was viewed as contradictory to the Equal Protection Clause of the 14th Amendment. Aside from the philosophical debates, questions were also raised about whether or not correctional treatment programs reduced recidivism. Research examining the effectiveness of correctional treatment began to surface in the 1950s, and the results showed little evidence to support existing rehabilitative efforts. Interest in the effectiveness of correctional treatment remained low, however, until 1974 when an article published in *Public Interest* titled "What Works? Questions and Answers About Prison Reform" generated enormous political and public attention to the effectiveness of correctional treatment (Cullen and Gilbert 1982).

The Research

In the mid-1960s, the governor of New York appointed a special committee to address the problem of high recidivism rates within the state. The committee began its work operating under the assumption that prisons were capable of rehabilitating offenders; therefore they attributed the high recidivism rates to a problem with the structure and administration of the current prison system. David Rothman (1980) observed that rehabilitation was never completely implemented into our correctional system. Treatment always took a back seat to security and many correctional programs lacked the necessary funding and staff to provide adequate treatment. In order to successfully rehabilitate criminals, prisons would have had to change from a custodial model (with a primary emphasis on security) to a true rehabilitative model. The problem faced by the committee was that there was no comprehensive research demonstrating which treatment programs were the most effective in reducing recidivism. Criminologist Robert Martinson and his colleagues Douglas Lipton and Judith Wilks were commissioned by the state of New York to address this void. Over a six-month period, the researchers reviewed all of the existing literature on correctional treatment published in English from 1945 to 1967. Each of the articles was evaluated according to traditional standards of social science research. Only studies that utilized an *experimental design*, included a *sufficient sample size*, and could be *replicated* were selected. One of the most important tasks involved in research using *available data* is assessing the quality of the data. Martinson and his colleagues were relying on the *validity* of research conducted by other social scientists. Many studies were excluded simply because the researchers did not provide enough information to determine the accuracy of the findings. Two hundred and thirty-one studies examining a variety of different types of treatment were chosen. All of the treatment studies included at least one measure of offender recidivism, such as whether or not offenders were rearrested or violated their parole. The recidivism measures were used to examine the "success" or "failure" of a program in terms of reducing crime.

Martinson and his colleagues reviewed published research on the following types of correctional treatment:

Educational and vocational training. Efforts to teach prisoners how to read and write and skills to help secure employment upon release were part of the reform movement during the 1870s. Programs were based on the assumption that criminals typically had poor work histories and turned to crime as an alternative means of support. Typical prison programs included literacy and high school equivalency courses and vocational programs such as auto mechanics and carpentry.

Individual and group counseling. Counseling programs in prison developed in the early 1900s as part of the medical model approach to corrections. Criminal behavior was believed to result from an underlying psychological problem. Under the guidance of a trained therapist, offenders learned to recognize their problems and were taught better ways to cope with everyday life stresses.

Therapeutic milieus. Correctional treatment has always taken a backseat to security. While rehabilitation may have been the predominate goal of our correctional system for most of our history, prisons were always designed and administered to protect the public from criminals. Beginning in the 1960s, prisons began experimenting with therapeutic communities as part of efforts to assist inmates with their reintegration back into the community. The prison environment was transformed into a complete treatment atmosphere. The staff was supportive and non-threatening. All of the interactions between inmates presented an opportunity for self-discovery and healing.

Medical treatment. Efforts to change behavior through drugs or surgery were also part of the medical model of the early 1900s. Correctional treatment took advantage of medical advances to treat biological problems with hormone therapy, psychotropic medications, and brain surgery.

Differences in length and type of incarceration. The development of prisons during the early 1800s provided reformers a method of punishment that could be varied according to the severity of the crime. Serious offenders received longer sentences than offenders who committed less serious crimes. Beginning in the 1970s, the Federal Bureau of Prisons began classifying inmates on the basis of security, and prisons were structured accordingly. States adopted this practice of placing inmates in minimum, medium, or maximum-security prisons based upon an assessment of risk.

Community corrections. Most of our correctional clients are currently housed within the community either on probation, parole, or other community treatment program. In response to rising crime rates and prison crowding, the number of offenders receiving some type of community sanction increased significantly in the 1970s. The growth of community corrections was also based on an assumption that rehabilitation was more effective if administered within a non-institutional setting.

Conclusions

After reviewing all 231 studies, Martinson reported that there was no consistent evidence that correctional treatment reduced recidivism. Specifically, he wrote: ". . . with few and isolated exceptions, the rehabilitative efforts that have been reported so far have had no appreciable effect on recidivism" (p. 25). Martinson further indicated that the lack of empirical support for correctional treatment could be a consequence of poorly implemented programs. If the quality of the programs were improved, the results may have proved more favorable. This conclusion was for the most part ignored by the media and policy makers as was the more thorough report coauthored with Lipton and Wilks published one year later.[1] Martinson's article became referred to as "nothing works" and was subsequently used as the definitive study detailing the failures of rehabilitation. The article had implications that went beyond questioning whether or not specific types of correctional treatment reduced recidivism. The entire philosophy of rehabilitation was now in doubt because of Martinson's conclusion: ". . . our present strategies . . . cannot overcome, or even appreciably reduce, the powerful tendencies of offenders to continue in criminal behavior" (p. 49). Not only had our treatment programs not "worked," it appeared as if no treatment *could* work. Our efforts to help criminals were being wasted on a population incapable of change.

Martinson turned his report over to the state of New York, but officials decided not to publish it. The governor's committee had already agreed to continue funding programs aimed at rehabilitating offenders. The state also forbid Martinson from publishing the findings on his own,

---

[1] Lipton, D., R. Martinson, and J. Wilks (1975). *The Effectiveness of Correctional Treatment: A Survey of Treatment Evaluation Studies.* New York: Praeger.

but copies began circulating until Martinson wrote the article for *Public Interest*. The article received considerable media attention. Martinson appeared on the popular news magazine series *60 Minutes* three months after his report was published touting his "nothing works" findings.

Criticisms

Despite the widespread appeal of Martinson's study, many proponents of rehabilitation took issue with the report and condemned his pessimistic conclusions. Much of the criticisms centered on the approach Martinson and his colleagues used in determining the effectiveness of treatment. Distinguishing between programs that "failed" or "succeeded" was a subjective process. Martinson himself pointed out several instances where particular types or specific programs showed enough promise of success to warrant additional consideration. One year after the report was published, Ted Palmer (1975) a psychologist and principal investigator with the Community Treatment Project, wrote an article for the *Journal of Research in Crime and Delinquency*, outlining all of the positive results and partial successes cited by Martinson. Forty-eight percent of the studies actually revealed a reduction in recidivism. For example, male offenders who successfully completed vocational training on the use of IBM equipment had lower rates (48%) of recidivism compared to the control group of non-participants (66%). Studies of individual counseling showed that participants deemed amenable to treatment had lower rates of recidivism. The same finding was consistent for group counseling where success was achieved with programs whose therapists demonstrated empathy for the participants. Palmer also noted that the research on sentence length revealed different effects for different types of offenders. Shorter sentences reduced recidivism for "anti-social" inmates while longer sentences worked better for "manipulative" inmates. Successes were also achieved for various types of community programs. Community treatment programs that targeted an offender's antisocial attitudes and included motivated therapists were shown to reduce recidivism. Martinson's conclusion that "nothing works" was unsubstantiated by his own research. There was evidence that *some* programs did reduce recidivism for *some* offenders. Many of the programs labeled as ineffective were never properly funded or implemented nor were the programs based on a sound theoretical explanation of criminal behavior (Gendreau and Ross 1979).

Critics also took issue with Martinson's decision to only examine recidivism rates as measures of success. Whether or not an offender was rearrested for violating parole is not always the best indicator of an effective treatment program. The research on therapeutic communities showed that while overall participants had comparable rates of recidivism to offenders housed in traditional prisons, therapeutic communities cost less to administer. The same was true for programs administered within the community. These programs offered the same level of community protection, but at a savings. Martinson also failed to consider *time to recidivism*. For example, the research on therapeutic communities found that participants spent longer periods in the community before re-arrest and were arrested for less serious crimes compared to the control group. A delay in time to recidivism could be an important factor in assessing the effectiveness of a program. Palmer further argued that research evaluating the effectiveness of intensive supervision probation (ISP) should not include technical violations (i.e., failing to make curfew) as indicators of failure. Offenders placed on were monitored more closely because they were high risk. A high number of technical violations would be an indicator of success because it demonstrated community protection.

The same year Palmer published his article debating the merits of Martinson's conclusions, the National Academy of Sciences convened a panel to assess the *validity* (accuracy) of Martinson's findings. The panel reviewed the same studies cited by Martinson and found no fault with the overall conclusions. However, the panel also reported that based on the empirical evidence presented in the report, no recommendations regarding the future of rehabilitation could be made (Secrest, White, and Brown 1979). Martinson himself recanted his original statements in 1979 in an article published in the *Hofstra Law Review* when he wrote, ". . . contrary to my previous position, some treatment programs do have an appreciable effect on recidivism." (p. 244). His attempt to set to the record straight was for the most part ignored by the press and policy makers. One year later, Martinson committed suicide. According to an article written by Jerome Miller for the *Washington Post*, Martinson's ". . . melancholy suicide was to be a metaphor for what would follow in American corrections" (Miller 1989). The controversy surrounding his findings was a valuable lesson for social scientists. Research findings are subject to interpretation and while scientists have little control over how their conclusions will be construed, results should be reported in such a way as to minimize the likelihood that readers will misinterpret or read too much into them.

Significance and Subsequent Research

Martinson's article provided policy makers the evidence to justify spending cuts on rehabilitative programs. Furthermore, it allowed politicians to respond to growing concerns about crime with punitive get-tough strategies. States began implementing strict mandatory sentences that resulted in more criminals being sent to prison and for longer periods of time. Over the next 15 years, Martinson's article was used over and over to support abandoning efforts to treat offenders until rehabilitation became virtually nonexistent in our correctional system. The US Supreme Court supported the transition in the 1989 case of *Mistretta v. United States* by upholding the constitutionality of federal sentencing guidelines that removed the consideration of rehabilitation as a sentencing factor. In spite of these changes, the debate over the effectiveness of correctional treatment continued. Other scholars confirmed Martinson's findings. Lee Sechrest, Susan White, and Elizabeth Brown (1979) analyzed the same 231 studies examined by Martinson as well as other evaluation studies of correctional treatment programs from 1968 to 1977 and concluded that there was no treatment program ". . . guaranteed to reduce the criminal activity of released offenders." (p. 3). David Greenberg (1977) reviewed 115 published studies from 1967 to 1975 and reported that while Martinson's claim that "nothing works" was exaggerated, his basic conclusion was justified. Greenberg uncovered only a small number of studies that showed a "modest" success in reducing recidivism.

Beginning in the early 1980s researchers began to use *meta-analysis* as a statistical technique to evaluate the effectiveness of correctional treatment. Meta analysis was believed to be a better way to examine prior studies of correctional treatment. The technique involves collecting previously published studies of a particular type of correctional treatment. Next, the researcher computes the effect size (the difference in recidivism between the treatment and control groups) for each of the studies and then calculates a summary statistic for the entire group of studies. The advantage of the meta-analysis over a simple review of study findings is that it allows the researcher to evaluate studies with different sample sizes. John Whitehead and Steven Lab (1989) utilized the meta-analysis technique in their study of correctional treatment programs for juvenile offenders. They examined 50 prior studies published from 1975 to 1984 and also found that very few programs had any appreciable effect on recidivism.

Other academics and professionals working in the correctional field utilized the meta-analysis to launch a campaign to demonstrate the effectiveness of correctional treatment with the goal of convincing policy makers not to abandon rehabilitation as the goal of our correctional system. In 1985, Carol Garrett (1985) published a meta-analysis of 111 studies of correctional treatment for juveniles between 1960 and 1983 and found that rehabilitation did "work." Participants in the treatment group performed .37 standard deviations above the control group. Garrett also showed that certain programs had better success rates compared to others. Mark Lipsey (1992) also set out to prove the "nothing works" doctrine wrong. He performed a meta-analysis on 443 treatment programs for delinquents and found that 64 percent of the programs demonstrated positive outcomes. Furthermore, consistent with Garrett's research, he established that there were observable differences between the programs that worked versus those deemed ineffective. Support for correctional treatment was also offered by two studies conducted by Paul Gendreau and Robert Ross (1979, 1987). Both studies involved extensive literature reviews of published research on correctional treatment after Martinson published his article, and both reviews found clear evidence that rehabilitation did work. In fact, some studies revealed reductions in recidivism by as much as 80 percent.

It soon became apparent that there was evidence of the effectiveness of correctional treatment. While some programs failed to reduce recidivism, other programs were deemed successful. The next task for researchers was to identify the successful components of the programs that worked. Two Canadian psychologists undertook this challenge by developing a theory of correctional treatment known as the *principles of effective intervention.* Don Andrews and James Bonta (1998) created the principles after reviewing prior studies documenting the success of correctional treatment, particularly the work of Gendreau and Ross. Successful treatment programs adhered to the principles of *risk, need,* and *responsivity.* Offenders varied in their levels of risks and treatment intensity should be administered accordingly. Programs should also target "criminogenic needs" correlated with offending. Criminogenic needs were offender characteristics that could be changed and include such things as antisocial attitudes and associates as well as insufficient problem solving skills. The responsivity principle involved matching offenders based on their learning or personality styles to particular types of programs. Overall, social learning and cognitive-behavioral approaches had been shown to be the most effective (consistent with Gendreau and Ross's findings). Andrews et al. (1990) conducted a meta-analysis of 45 treatment programs for delinquents. Their analysis revealed that programs operating under the principles of risk, needs, and responsivity were effective in reducing recidivism. On average, these programs reduced recidivism by 50 percent. It should be noted that most of the programs reviewed by Andrews were the same programs examined by Whitehead and Lab one year earlier, only Whitehead and Lab concluded that *overall* the programs had no appreciable impact on recidivism.

Researchers have not only been able to identify which correctional treatment programs work, they have also discovered what does not. The *principles of ineffective treatment* include (Gendreau 1989):

traditional psychodynamic therapies

non-directive relationship oriented therapies

radical nonintervention

traditional medical model approaches (i.e., changes in diet) intensive treatment administered to low-risk clients

    treatment that encourage clients to displace anger or externalize blame

    punishing smarter strategies (i.e., bootcamps, shock probation)

Martinson's conclusion that rehabilitation was a waste of effort had a profound impact on our correctional system. The impact had more to do with timing than the strength of the evidence he presented. The intent behind Martinson's quest to demonstrate the ineffectiveness of rehabilitation was to convince policy makers that incarceration was a poor policy choice because offenders were not being reformed. Instead, policy makers eager to respond to escalating crime rates and heightened public fear of crime embraced the goals of deterrence and incapacitation. If offenders were incapable of change, then the solution was to implement harsher sentences resulting in more offenders being sent to prison and for longer periods of time.

Just as police practices have become more "evidence-based," according to Don Andrews and Robert Hoge (1995) corrections would benefit from the same approach. Martinson himself argued that correctional policy making should be based on empirical evidence of what works to reduce recidivism. The rehabilitation debate resulted in an extensive body of research that suggests the right types of correctional treatment do work to reduce recidivism for some offenders.

References

Andrews, D., and R. Hoge (1995). "The Psychology of Criminal Conduct and Principles of Effective Prevention and Rehabilitation." *Forum on Corrections Research* 7:34–36.

Andrews, D., and J. Bonta (1998). *The Psychology of Criminal Conduct*, 2nd ed.) Cincinnati: Anderson.

Andrews, D., I. Zinger, R. Hoge, J. Bonta, P. Gendreau, and F. Cullen (1990). "Does Correctional Treatment Work? A Clinically Relevant and Psychologically Informed Meta-Analysis." *Criminology* 28:369–404.

Cullen, F., and K. Gilbert (1982). *Reaffirming Rehabilitation*. Cincinnati: Anderson.

Garrett, C. (1985). "Effects of Residential Treatment on Adjudicated Delinquents: A Meta-Analysis." *Journal of Research in Crime and Delinquency* 22:287–308.

Gendreau, P., and R. Ross (1979). "Effective Correctional Treatment: Bibliotherapy for Cynics." *Crime and Delinquency* 25:463–89.

Gendreau, P., and R. Ross (1987). "Revivification of Rehabilitation: Evidence from the 1980s." *Justice Quarterly* 3:349–407.

Gendreau, P. (1989). "Programs That Do Not Work: A Brief Commend on Brodeu and Doob." *Canadian Journal of Criminology* 3:133–35.

Greenberg, D. (1977). "The Correctional Effects of Corrections: A Survey of Evaluations." In *Corrections and Punishment*, edited by D. F. Greenberg, 111–48. Beverly Hills, CA: Sage.

Lipsey, M. (1992). "Juvenile Delinquency Treatment: A Meta-Analytic Inquiry into the Variability of Effects." In *Meta-Analysis for Explanation: A Casebook*, edited by T. Cook, H. Cooper, D. Cordray, H. Hartmenn, L. Hedges, R. Light, A. Louis, and F. Mosteller, 83–127. New York: Russell Sage Foundation.

Martinson, R. (1974). "What Works? Questions and Answers About Prison Reform." *The Public Interest* 35:22–54.

Martinson, R. (1979). "New Findngs, New Views: A Note of Caution Regarding Sentencing Reform." *Hofstra Law Review* 7:243–58.

Miller, J. (March 1989). "The Debate on Rehabilitating Offenders: Is It True That Nothing Works?" *Washington Post*. Available at: http://www.prisonpolicy.org/scans/rehab.html.

Palmer, T. (1975). "Martinson Revisited." *Journal of Research in Crime and Delinquency* 12:133–152.

Rothman, D. (1980). *Conscience and Convenience: The Asylum and Its Alternatives in Progressive America*. Boston: Addison-Wesley.

Sechrest, L., S. White, and E. Brown (1979). *The Rehabilitation of Criminal Offenders: Problems and Prospects.* Washington, DC: National Academy of Sciences.

Whitehead, J., and S. Lab (1989). "A Meta-Analysis of Juvenile Correctional Treatment." *Journal of Research in Crime and Delinquency* 26:276–95.

Further Reading

Antonowicz, D., and R. Ross (1994). "Essential Components of Successful Rehabilitation Programs for Offenders." *International Journal of Offender and Comparative Criminology* 38:97–104.

Cullen, F. (2005). "The Twelve People Who Saved Rehabilitation: How the Science of Criminology Made a Difference." *Criminology* 43:1–42.

Cullen, F., and P. Gendreau (2000). *Criminal Justice 2000.* Vol. 3, *Policies, Processes and Decisions of Criminal Justice System.* Washington, DC: Office of Justice Programs, US Department of Justice.

Gibbons, D. (1999). "Changing Lawbreakers—What Have We Learned Since the 1950s?" *Crime and Delinquency* 45:272–93.

Lipsey, M., and D. Wilson (1999). "Effective Intervention for Serious Juvenile Offenders." In *Serious Juvenile Offenders: Risk Factors and Serious Interventions,* edited by R. Loeber and D. Farrington, 313–45. Thousand Oaks, CA: Sage.

Lipton, D., R. Martinson, and J. Wilks (1975). *The Effectiveness of Correctional Treatment: A Survey of Treatment Evaluation Studies.* New York: Praeger.

Palmer, T. (1992). *The Re-Emergence of Correctional Intervention.* Newbury Park, CA: Sage.

DETERRENCE

Deterrence involves punishment for the purpose of teaching a lesson. There are two types of deterrence: specific and general. Specific deterrence seeks to prevent recidivism. An offender is punished so that he/she learns not to do it again. General deterrence is about punishing an individual to set an example for the rest of society. In order for punishment to deter behavior, punishment must be certain, severe, and swift. Individuals need to be confident that if they break the law they will be punished for doing so. Offenders and the general public must perceive punishment as harsh. Finally, punishment must be administered within a reasonable time period after the crime was committed (so that offenders and society can associate the punishment with the crime). Deterrence rests on the assumptions that individuals are rational in their decisions to engage in crime and make choices that serve to maximize pleasure and minimize pain. According to Jeremy Bentham (1748–1832), if the "pains" of engaging in crime (i.e., the punishment) outweigh the benefits for an individual, that person will alter their behavior in the future to avoid similar pains. The colonists relied on physical forms of punishment that consisted of corporal punishment, banishment, and the death penalty. Punishment was for the goal of retribution and deterrence (primarily general deterrence). Persons who had not yet engaged in crime may refrain from doing so because they do not wish to endure the same punishment as the "example" offender. Therefore, making the public aware of an offender's sanction was a key element of general deterrence. In his *Essay on Crimes and Their Punishment,* Cesare Beccaria (1738–1794) argued that public awareness of society's laws and the sanctions for violating those laws should be enough to achieve general deterrence. This logic of course rests on the additional assumption that all offenders convicted of a particular crime necessarily face the same sanction.

CAPITAL PUNISHMENT: DOES THE DEATH PENALTY DETER MURDER?

Ehrlich, I. (1975). "The Deterrent Effect of Capital Punishment: A Question of Life and Death." *American Economic Review* 65:397–417.

Background

During the colonial period, there were over 50 different crimes that carried a possible death sentence. Hanging was the preferred method of execution, which was always public to achieve the goal of general deterrence. Despite the fact that executions are no longer public, capital punishment is frequently supported on the grounds that its use deters crime. There are only two crimes that carry a possible death sentence: murder and treason (a handful of states have enacted statutes authorizing capital punishment for rape of child, however, the US Supreme Court recently declared Louisiana's law unconstitutional). Because of its rare occurrence in our country, very few people are executed for treason. Any deterrent value really only applies to the crime of murder, and only certain types of murder qualify for the death penalty. Thirty-seven states and the federal government currently recognize the death penalty as a sanction for murder but its use varies tremendously between these states. Over half of the 42 executions that took place in 2007 occurred in a single state (Texas) with the remaining taking place in only nine other states.

Capital punishment has always been recognized as a legitimate form of punishment in the United States, but its use remains controversial. Capital punishment is the most expensive sanction, costing two to three times more than a life sentence for an incarcerated offender. There are also concerns over the application of the death penalty. Claims of racial disparity led the US Supreme Court to declare capital punishment unconstitutional in 1972. The Court reinstated its use four years later, but minorities continue to be an over represented group among death row populations. Given the finality of capital punishment, concerns have also been raised over whether the procedural safeguards in place are sufficient to ensure that the innocent do not end up on death row. Any deterrent value of capital punishment should not occur at the expense of discriminating against minorities or at the risk of executing an innocent person. For most of our history, the belief that capital punishment served as a deterrent for the crime of murder went unquestioned. Public support for the death penalty has always been high, and most supporters include the deterrent value in their arguments. The logic is quite simple if you subscribe to the notions that people exercise free will and that crime is a product of rational choice. Criminals weigh the benefits of a particular crime against the possible consequences, and as long as the former outweighs the later, the probability for crime is increased. If someone is contemplating killing another human being and they do not think they will get caught, or if they are caught the punishment is not severe, they are likely to follow through with the crime. If, however, someone contemplating murder knows that if they are caught they could get the death penalty, they might think twice before committing the crime and choose an alternative (non criminal) course of action.

One the earliest empirical studies to test the deterrent effect of capital punishment was conducted by Thorsten Sellin in 1959. Sellin examined homicide rates between states that had capital punishment statutes and states that had abolished its use. He examined these rates for the years 1920–1955 and 1920–1965. Sellin grouped states according to size, social, and economic characteristics and then compared homicide rates for states with and without capital punishment statutes. His data showed no significant difference in homicide rates between the two groups of states. He concluded that capital punishment provided no deterrent value beyond that of a life sentence. Other comparative studies of capital punishment confirmed Sellin's findings, but an economist by the name of Isaac Ehrlich set out to prove these findings invalid. Ehrlich (1975) believed that Sellin's conclusions were based on a flawed analysis. Sellin's research only took into account whether or not a state *permitted* the use of capital punishment. Ehrlich believed that an economic model would provide a better test of the deterrent value of capital punishment by taking into account the *certainty* or actual risk of being executed. Ehrlich had previously developed an economic theory of crime, and he wanted to apply this theory to murder in an effort to test the deterrent value of capital punishment.

An Economic Model of Murder

Isaac Ehrlich, an economist at the University of Chicago and the National Bureau of Economic Research, conducted an empirical test to determine if capital punishment deterred murder. According to Ehrlich (1975), murder was a deliberate act committed with the intent of causing harm. Most murders in the United States occurred between people who knew one another: family and acquaintances. Most murders were considered "crimes of passion" and either resulted from some type of interpersonal conflict or was a consequence of property or drug crime. Assuming we are all rational in our decision-making, the choice to commit murder would be dependent upon the benefits resulting from such a crime (i.e., getting rid of someone who is causing problems in your life) being greater than the consequences (getting caught and going to prison or being executed by the state). The benefits of committing murder must also outweigh the benefits derived from another course of action. Ehrlich also believed that a certain amount of planning was involved in all crime. Some plans were highly sophisticated and required a lot of time and forethought while others were more spontaneous. Even spontaneous murders involved some forethought (however brief it may be). If murder could be explained as a function of choice wherein the offender weighed the benefits and consequences of their crime, the probability of being executed *should* enter into a criminal's deliberations.

Ehrlich set out to test whether or not capital punishment deterred murder *beyond* that of a life sentence. Both forms of punishment incapacitated the offender, but Ehrlich was interested in whether or not capital punishment could actually *prevent* murder. He relied on *existing data* gathered from official measures of crime, census data, and published government expenditure reports. He derived the capital murder rate from the FBI's Uniform Crime Report (UCR). While data from the UCR are subject to error because they do not include crimes that go unreported to the police, this is typically not a problem for murder. In 1975, capital punishment was authorized for crimes other than murder including rape, kidnapping, and armed robbery, however, its use for these other crimes was limited. Prior research had focused primarily on murder as well.

According to deterrence theory, punishment must be perceived as *severe* to influence behavior. While some may have questioned whether or not capital punishment constituted a *more* severe form of punishment compared to a life sentence, there was evidence to suggest the contrary. Most offenders on death row appealed their sentence to seek commutation, and capital punishment was reserved for only the most serious crimes. Punishment must also be perceived as *certain* to deter. The likelihood of receiving a death sentence must be high enough to influence perceptions of certainty. Ehrlich examined the certainty of capital punishment by including the probabilities of apprehension, conviction, and execution. Execution risk was measured by the ratio of executions to convictions. In addition, Ehrlich's model took into account trends in the use of capital punishment during the study period.

In order to establish a deterrent effect for capital punishment, Ehrlich had to examine a variety of other aggregate level factors that had been shown to influence murder rates. He included several economic and demographic measures obtained from the US Census Bureau in his model in order to *statistically control* for these influences. *Experiments* are considered to be the most ideal way for researchers to control for outside influences, but experiments are not always an option. Researchers still have the ability to control for outside influences with the statistics used to analyze their data. Controlling for *extraneous* influences allows a researcher to eliminate possible sources of bias that can produce inaccurate findings. Economic influences were measured by labor force participation, unemployment, and per capita income. Ehrlich also included population size, portion of the population age, 14–24, and the portion of nonwhites in the population. Data on government expenditures were acquired from the Survey of Current Business. Two measures of expenditures were included: per capita expenditures by all governments and per capital expenditures on police.

Results

Ehrlich conducted a *time series analysis* to examine the relationship between capital punishment and murder. This type of analysis is appropriate for establishing *correlations* between trends. In his analysis, Ehrlich compared the capital murder rate and the probability of being executed and discovered that the two were related. Specifically, he found that an increased probability of execution corresponded to an increase in murder. This finding was the opposite of what was expected, but once he included the additional *control* variables in his analysis, Ehrlich found that an increased probability of execution produced a *decrease* in murder. He concluded that increasing the probability of being executed by as little as 1 percent would yield a .06 decrease in murder. This finding offered support for the argument that capital punishment deterred crime. In fact, it was Ehrlich's contention that every execution carried out between 1933 and 1967 actually prevented (deterred) 7–8 murders. His analysis further showed a deterrent effect beyond that of a life sentence in prison. He also believed that the 25 percent increase in murder that occurred between 1960 and 1967 might have been due to the decline in executions during that same time period. According to Ehrlich, his analysis provided empirical support for the deterrent effect of capital punishment. In his conclusions, he pointed out that his findings were not offered as justification for the continued use of the death penalty. He argued that other forms of punishment might be equally effective in preventing murder. His model also showed unemployment and crime to be related to homicide rates. Economic policies geared toward reducing unemployment and increasing earning potentials might also prevent murder.

Criticisms

It came as no surprise that Ehrlich's study generated criticism from death penalty opponents. Numerous criticisms from the academic community also surfaced almost immediately after the study was published. David Baldus and James Cole (1975) published an article in the *Yale Law Journal* the same year Ehrlich's study was released. In their article, they discussed the methodological flaws of Ehrlich's research and defended Sellin's approach. Remember, Sellin compared murder rates between death penalty states and abolitionist states and found no appreciable difference between the two (an approach that Ehrlich disapproved of). According to Baldus and Cole, the *probability* of being executed only existed in states that had death penalty statutes. Sellin's comparisons were appropriate given the debate over whether states should retain or get rid of capital punishment. Baldus and Cole acknowledged the sophistication of Ehrlich's analysis, however, argued that his research only dealt with execution trends in states with capital punishment statutes. In his model, Ehrlich predicted what would happen if a state abolished capital punishment by looking at a zero probability of execution. This measure failed to take into account the difference in states that have capital punishment statutes but do not use them, and abolitionist states. The existence of a statute alone could have also exerted a deterrent effect because of the mere possibility of its use.

Baldus and Cole also criticized Ehrlich's use of aggregate data to examine relationships across individual states. Ehrlich's findings may have been influenced by *aggregation bias*. Ehrlich's conclusions were based on inferences he made regarding individual states and national crime and execution data. These inferences are suspect because they are not derived from data collected at the state level. Ehrlich's approach also failed to consider regional differences in murder rates across the United States. Ehrlich contended that his study offered a better test of the deterrent effect of capital punishment because he included in his analysis other factors that have been shown to influence murder rates (i.e., economic and demographic factors). Sellin also took these factors into account with his study; only he used a "matching" technique to control for these influences (states were grouped according to size, economic characteristics, and social characteristics). The extent to which Ehrlich's approach yielded more valid results depended on whether he included *all* of the important influences in his model. There were numerous factors that influenced murder rates during the time periods examined by Ehrlich that were not included in his model, such as rates of gun ownership, migration patterns, and rates of violence in general. William Bowers and Glenn Pierce also published a critique of Ehrlich's study in 1975. They questioned Ehrlich's use of UCR data to obtain murder rates. UCR data published before 1958 (and particularly in the 1930s) underestimated the official count of crime. Numerous police agencies did not participate in the reporting program. Even fewer agencies provided information on clearance and conviction rates.

In 1978, the National Academy of Sciences appointed a panel of experts to review Ehrlich's study. The panel issued strong criticisms of Ehrlich's work and reported his findings to be misleading because of several methodological flaws. For example, Ehrlich analyzed data from 1933 to 1969; however, his finding that as the risk of execution dropped, murder increased, was only true for the years 1962–1969 (Panel on Research on Deterrent and Incapacitative Effects 1978). The United States witnessed an increase in all types of crime during a period when there were fewer executions. According to the panel's report, Ehrlich's failure to account for variations in murder rates between 1933 and 1962 demonstrated a lack of evidence supporting a deterrent effect for capital punishment. The panel not only concluded that there was no credible evidence that capital punishment worked as deterrent, it also suggested that additional research was not likely to provide any new insight on the issue and should not be used by policy makers (Panel on Research on Deterrent and Incapacitative Effects 1978). Ehrlich published a defense to the panel's criticisms. He pointed out that a major focus of the panel's attack on deterrence was against research conducted by economists yet there were no economists on the panel (Ehrlich and Randall 1977). He further criticized the panel for failing to offer "constructive" suggestions for improving his statistical techniques or demonstrating that including more influences would have improved his model (Ehrlich and Randall 1977).

Significance and Subsequent Research

Ehrlich's research not only contributed to the continuing debate over the use of capital punishment in the United States, it also had an influence on criminal justice policy. In 1976, the US Supreme Court reinstated the use of capital punishment in the case of *Gregg v. Georgia*. The Court cited Ehrlich's findings as evidence of the deterrent value of capital punishment.

Efforts to replicate Ehrlich's findings have produced mixed results. Bowers and Pierce (1975) analyzed Ehrlich's data using the same statistical technique but found that the deterrent value inferred by Ehrlich vanished when they excluded the last five years that were included in Ehrlich's analysis. Bowers and Pierce found Ehrlich's results to be a "statistical artifact," not evidence of a deterrent effect for capital punishment. Murder rates increased significantly between 1962 and 1969 during a time period when very few executions took place. A *statistical artifact* is a spurious (nonexistent) relationship between two variables. Ehrlich erroneously concluded that low execution risk was related to the increase in murder.

In 1977, Ehrlich published findings from another study of capital punishment that addressed some of the criticisms of his earlier study. He utilized a *cross sectional* research design as opposed to the time series analysis used in his prior study. Cross sectional research involves data collected at one point in time. Ehrlich analyzed murder and execution data from 1940 and 1950 and examined data from both "executing and nonexecuting states." He chose these two particular years because the number of executions was sufficient to permit the analysis and because of the consistency in crime reporting for these years. Ehrlich once again reported support for a deterrent effect of capital punishment. Data showed not only an effect for murder but also other violent crimes. Ehrlich was not the only economist that found capital punishment deterred crime. Stephen Layson (1985) conducted a time series analysis that involved several improvements over Ehrlich's original study. He included data on the additional years of 1968–1977, and he used murder rates from Vital Statistics records instead of the UCR estimates. He also used a different statistical technique and included a better measure of the probability of punishment. His findings confirmed Ehrlich's contention that capital punishment deterred murder. In fact, his deterrent effect was much larger. He found that every execution deterred on average 18 murders. Layson also reported that a 1 percent improvement in the clearance rate for murder would result in 250 fewer murders.

Despite repeated criticisms of the econometric approach, economists have continued to find support for a deterrent effect of capital punishment. Recently, Zhiqiang Liu (2004) conducted a study utilizing data from both capital punishment and abolitionist states. Between 1940 and 1950, five states with capital punishment statutes abolished it while four states instated the death penalty. This permitted an analysis of how *changes* in capital punishment statutes influenced crime. The reinstatement of capital punishment appeared to have been preceded by an increase in murder. Liu not only found that capital punishment deterred murder, but the existence of a death penalty statute corresponded with an increase in the probability of conviction for murder. He concluded that abolishing capital punishment would weaken other legal deterrents for murder.

Other studies of capital punishment produced results that suggested that the death penalty actually *increased* crime. According to the *brutalization theory*, the murder rate goes up in the months following an execution. Bowers and Pierce (1984) analyzed execution and homicide data in the State of New York for the years 1906–1963. New York had executed a total of 695 offenders since 1890 (more than any other state). They found that each execution resulted in 2–3 homicides in the month following the execution. Bowers and Pierce believed that when the state took the life of a convicted criminal, it communicated a message to those contemplating murder that vengeance was acceptable. Research conducted in Arizona, Georgia, and Illinois produced findings consistent with the brutalization theory (Bailey 1983, Stack 1993, and Thompson 1997) and Brian Forst (1983) found support for a brutalization effect when he examined capital punishment data for all states between 1960 and 1970.

The reinstatement of capital punishment in 1976 generated additional research on the deterrent and brutalization effect of capital punishment. A study by Ruth Peterson and William Bailey published in 1991 examined the use of capital punishment between 1976 and 1987. Their study explored the influence of capital punishment on felony murder. Most of the 93 executions that took place between 1976 and 1987 were for felony murder. Like Ehrlich, Peterson and Bailey utilized time series analyses of monthly felony murder rates and the incidence of executions. They also examined the amount and type of television exposure related to each execution. Media coverage is an important consideration in arguments that capital punishment deters crime. Their study found no support for capital punishment as an overall deterrent for felony murder. Further, they also failed to find support for the brutalization argument.

In 1990, Charles Troy Coleman became the first murderer executed by the State of Oklahoma in 25 years. This presented a unique opportunity to assess the impact of capital punishment in a single state. John Cochran, Mitchell Chamlin, and Mark Seth (1994) analyzed weekly time-series data on homicides in Oklahoma for the years 1989–1991. They examined several different types of murder in their study including felony, stranger, and total homicides. Researchers found no support for a deterrent effect on homicide, but they did find evidence to support brutalization theory. Homicides involving an offender and victim who did not know one another increased in the months following the execution of Coleman. According to researchers, "Coleman's execution led to an increase of approximately one additional stranger-related homicide incident per month" (p. 129). A subsequent analysis of Oklahoma's return to capital punishment produced consistent findings (Bailey 1998). Evidence of brutalization added to the continued debate over the impact of capital punishment. While most criminologists believe that capital punishment has no effect on homicides one way or the other (Radelet and Akers 1996), Cochran and Chamlin (2000) argued that the death penalty could have both deterrent and brutalization effects. In an analysis of California's return to capital punishment, Cochran and Chamlin found that after the execution of Robert Alton Harris, there was a decrease in "non-stranger felony murders", but an increase in "stranger-argument homicides".

The large number of offenders executed in Texas (compared to the rest of the United States) presented another unique opportunity for testing the deterrent and/or brutalization effect of capital punishment. Texas accounts for nearly one-third of the total executions since 1976. Jon Sorensen, Robert Wrinkle, Victoria Brewer, and James Marquart (1999) examined executions and homicide rates for the years 1984 and 1997. The number of executions increased dramatically in the 1990s at a time when homicide rates in Texas dropped significantly. While this appeared to offer support for a deterrent effect, the decrease in homicide continued even after legal challenges led to a temporary stop to executions in the State. Furthermore, the decrease in homicide corresponded with decreases across the rest of the United States. This suggests that something other than capital punishment was responsible for the decline.

Death penalty research continues to fuel the debate between those who advocate abolition and those who argue that capital punishment provides a needed deterrent. A majority of Americans support the use of capital punishment; therefore many lawmakers are quick to defend its value. Ehrlich's study continues to be used as evidence that capital punishment deters despite a general consensus among "expert" criminologists that there is no discernable relationship between the use of the death penalty and murder (Radelet and Akers 1996).

References

Bailey, W. (1983). "Disaggregation in Deterrence and Death Penalty Research: The Case of Murder in Chicago." *Journal of Criminal Law and Criminology* 74:827–59.

Bailey, W. (1998). "Deterrence, Brutalization, and the Death Penalty: Another Examination of Oklahoma's Return to Capital Punishment." *Criminology* 36:711–34.

Bailey, W., and R. Peterson (1991). "Felony Murder and Capital Punishment: An Examination of the Deterrence Question." *Criminology* 29:367–95.

Baldus, D., and J. Cole (1975). "A Comparison of the Work of Thorstein Sellin and Isaac Ehrlich on the Deterrent Effect of Capital Punishment." *Yale Law Journal* 85:170–86.

Bowers, W., and G. Pierce (1975). "The Illusion of Deterrence in Isaac Ehrlich's Research on Capital Punishment." *Yale Law Journal* 85:187–208.

Bowers, W., and G. Pierce (1980). "Deterrence or Brutalization: What Is the Effect of Executions." *Crime and Delinquency* 26:453–84.

Cochran, J., M. Chamlin, and M. Seth (1994). "Deterrence or Brutalization? An Impact Assessment of Oklahoma's Return to Capital Punishment." *Criminology* 32:107–34.

Cochran, J., and M. Chamlin (2000). "Deterrence and Brutalization: The Dual Effects of Executions." *Justice Quarterly* 17:685–706.

Ehrlich, I. (1975). "The Deterrent Effect of Capital Punishment: A Question of Life and Death." *American Economic Review* 65:397–417.

Ehrlich, I. (1977). "Capital Punishment and Deterrence: Some Further Thoughts and Additional Evidence." *Journal of Political Economy* 85:741–88.

Ehrlich, I., and M. Randall (1977). "Fear of Deterrence: A Critical Evaluation of the 'Report of the Panel on Research on Deterrent and Incapacitative Effects." *Journal of Legal Studies* 6:293–316.

Forst, B. (1983). "Capital Punishment and Deterrence: Conflicting Evidence?" *Journal of Criminal Law and Criminology* 74:927–42.

Layson, S. (1985). "Homicide and Deterrence: A Reexamination of the United States Time-Series Evidence." *Southern Economic Journal* 52:68–89.

Lu, Z. (2004). "Capital Punishment and the Deterrence Hypothesis: Some New Insights and Empirical Evidence." *Eastern Economic Journal* 30:237–58.

Panel on Research on Deterrent and Incapacitative Effects (1978). *Deterrence and Incapacitation: Estimating the Effects of Criminal Sanctions on Crime Rates.* edited by A. Blumstein, J. Cohen, and D. Nagin. Washington, DC: National Academy of Sciences.

Passell, P., and J. Taylor (1977). "The Deterrent Effect of Capital Punishment: Another View." *American Economic Review* 67:445–51.

Radelet, J., and R. Akers (1996). "Deterrence and the Death Penalty: The Views of the Experts." *Journal of Criminal Law and Criminology* 87:1–16.

Sorensen, J., R. Wrinkle, V. Brewer, J. Marquart (1999). "Capital Punishment and Deterrence: Examining the Effect of Executions on Murder in Texas." *Crime and Delinquency* 45:481–93.

Stack, S. (1993). "Execution Publicity and Homicide in Georgia." *American Journal of Criminal Justice* 18:25–39.

Thomson, E. (1997). "Deterrence vs. Brutalization: The Case of Arizona." *Homicide Studies* 1:110–28.

Further Reading

Archer, D., and R. Gartner (1983). "Homicide and the Death Penalty: A Cross-National Test of a Deterrence Hypothesis." *Journal of Criminal Law and Criminology* 74:991–1013.

Bailey, W., and R. Peterson (1989). "Murder and Capital Punishment: A Monthly Time Series Analysis of Execution Publicity." *American Sociological Review* 54:722–43.

Bailey, W., and R. Peterson (1999). "Capital Punishment, Homicide, and Deterrence: An Assessment of the Evidence." In *Studying and Preventing Homicide,*

edited by M. Smith and M. Zahn. Thousand Oaks, CA: Sage.

Bedau, H., and P. Cassell (2005). *Debating the Death Penalty: Should American Have Capital Punishment? The Experts on Both Sides Make Their Case.* New York: Oxford UP.

Ehrlich, I. (1975). "Rejoinder." *Yale Law Journal* 85:368–69.

McGahey, R. (1980). "Dr. Ehrlich's Magic Bullet: Economic Theory, Econometrics, and the Death Penalty." *Crime and Delinquency* 26:485–502.

Paternoster, R. (1991). *Capital Punishment in America*. New York: Lexington Books.

Peck, J. (1975). "The Deterrent Effect of Capital Punishment: Ehrlich and His Critics." *Yale Law Journal* 85:359–67.

Zimring, F., and G. Hawkins (1973). *Deterrence: The Legal Threat in Crime Control*. Chicago: University of Chicago Press.

INCAPACITATION

Protecting society from individuals who refuse to abide by the laws underlies the correctional philosophy of incapacitation. Incapacitation is a crime control strategy that involves isolating an offender from the community to reduce the opportunity for crime. Incapacitation is typically accomplished with incarceration (community sanctions like probation can achieve only a limited incapacitation effect). The use of incarceration can be used to achieve two types of incapacitation effects: selective or collective. Estimates of the amount of crime reduced as a result of efforts to incarcerate offenders rest on three assumptions (Cohen 1983). First, offenders share the same risk of being apprehended, convicted, and incarcerated. Second, other offenders will not replace the criminal activities of those sent to prison. Third, the experience of being in prison has no effect on an offenders' behavior (i.e., the offender was not rehabilitated) once released (see Cohen 1983 for a more thorough discussion of these assumptions).

SELECTIVE INCAPACITATION: CAN CRIME BE REDUCED WITHOUT INCREASING PRISON POPULATIONS?

Greenwood, P., and A. Abrahamse (1982). *Selective Incapacitation*. Santa Monica: Rand.

Background

The impact that locking up offenders has on crime rates depends upon the number of offenses each criminal commits. If each of the offenders currently incarcerated committed only the crime for which they were incarcerated for, then a large number of criminals would need to be incarcerated to reduce crime. Researchers, however, have found this not to be the case. In 1972, criminologists at the University of Pennsylvania published findings from a *cohort* study that involved all males born in the city of Philadelphia in 1945 (Wolfgang et al. 1972). Cohorts are persons who share the same life event (i.e., birth or marriage). Cohort studies are a type of *longitudinal* research that attempts to measure the effects of age, history, or generational influences on attitudes and behavior. The Philadelphia birth cohort study examined the delinquent histories of juveniles to determine age of onset and the progression or termination of delinquency. The sample consisted of 9,900 males who lived in the city that were between the ages of 10 and 18. Thirty-five percent of the sample was involved in at least one delinquent act, but the most interesting finding was that less than 6 percent of the delinquents were responsible for over half of all delinquency (Wolfgang et al. 1972). Five years later, researchers began administering self-report surveys to adult prison inmates in an effort to uncover how many crimes went undetected by authorities. Asking the criminals to report on their own offending provided a more accurate measure of the extent of crime in society. A similar finding to the Philadelphia study emerged. A small percentage of inmates reported committing a significant number of crimes. These high-rate offenders became known as "career criminals," and a new field of study was born. Theories of crime were developed to explain the offending patterns of the career criminal, and policy makers began exploring ways to use this information in their strategies to reduce crime.

The crime rate began to climb upward beginning in the early 1960s exerting pressure on an already overburdened criminal justice system. From 1960 to 1970 the index crime rate increased 111 percent, and by 1980 another 49 percent (Bureau of Justice Statistics 1981). By the late 1970s, there were over 300,000 adults incarcerated in state or federal prisons throughout the United States—more than what the institutions were constructed to house. The correctional system appeared to be in the midst of a crisis if the growth continued. To address this issue, Rand researcher Peter Greenwood (1982) began working on a sentencing model based upon a philosophy of selective incapacitation. Selective incapacitation is a crime control strategy that targets the career criminals and sentences them to a lengthy period of incarceration. The advantage of selective incapacitation over collective (incarcerating large numbers of offenders) is that crime can be reduced without having to increase prison populations. If a small number of career criminals are responsible for a significant amount of crime, then by locking up these offenders, crime control can be achieved with less cost.

The Proposal

Greenwood's proposal was based upon estimates derived from a large-scale inmate survey conducted previously by the Rand Corporation. The purpose of the inmate study was to determine the extent that imprisoned offenders were involved in crime *before* their incarceration. Inmates from three states (California, Michigan, and Texas) participated in the study. Researchers selected three states located in different geographical regions of the country and then chose a combination of medium and large size counties within each state. This would help reinforce the *generalizability* of the findings to a diverse group of inmates across the United States. The sample consisted of 2,190 prison and jail inmates. Jail inmates were included to gather information on less serious offenders (only misdemeanors are sentenced to jail) (Chaiken and Chaiken 1982). To make sure the sample was representative of the inmate population, a *cohort* of incoming inmates was sampled. By restricting the sample to incoming inmates, researchers were able to include a wide variety of offenses and sentence lengths. Participation in the study was voluntary and each participant received five dollars for completing the survey (Chaiken and Chaiken 1982). Researchers frequently offer some type of incentive to help increase *response rates*. Surveys were administered in a controlled setting with trained survey administrators. Prison authorities assigned the inmates to sessions consisting of 20–30 inmates per session. The inmates were given instructions on how to complete the survey and each had to sign a form agreeing to participate. Inmates were informed that their responses would be *confidential* but not *anonymous*. Protecting the confidentiality of research subjects is one of the *ethical standards* of research where the researcher promises not to release the subjects' responses without first obtaining the subjects' permission. When a researcher guarantees anonymity, it means that even the researcher will not be able to identify the subjects based on their responses. The survey administrators remained in the room while the inmates completed the survey and provided assistance to the inmates who requested help (Chaiken and Chaiken 1982).

The questionnaire asked inmates to report on their own involvement in crime. Self-report studies are useful in measuring the extent of crimes that go undetected by authorities. Inmates were asked questions about their prior involvement in crime, including the age of first arrest, prior convictions, and prior incarcerations. In addition, questions were asked to measure the inmates' attitudes about crime and the criminal justice system, motives for committing crimes, alcohol and drug use, and participation in treatment programs while incarcerated. Inmates were also asked to indicate basic demographic information such as race/ethnicity, age, prior employment and residential status (Chaiken and Chaiken 1982).

The results of the inmate surveys revealed some noteworthy findings regarding the offending patterns of those offenders who eventually ended up in jail or prison. First, offenders typically did not specialize in their crimes (Chaiken and Chaiken 1982). Most offenders engaged in a variety of crimes throughout their criminal careers. This became an important consideration when measuring incapacitation effects because any estimated crime reduction must take into account other types of crimes and not just the incarcerated offense. Second, individual crime rates were not evenly distributed for all offenders. Most offenders reported limited involvement in crime, but a small number were high rate offenders in that they committed numerous crimes (Chaiken and Chaiken 1982). These findings were consistent with prior inmate self report studies. The survey results also showed some patterns across offense type. For example, convicted robbery offenders, were more likely to commit other types of crimes compared to drug or assault offenders. In California, convicted robbers reported committing an average of 53 robberies per year, but this group also reported an average of 4 assaults, 90 burglaries, 163 thefts or fraud, and 646 drug offenses. The results were similar for Michigan and Texas (Chaiken and Chaiken 1982). Locking up a robbery offender not only reduced robbery but other crimes as well. Not all of the surveyed inmates reported a high number of crimes. This was important to recognize because when researchers speak in terms of the mean or average number of offenses for a sample of inmates, the averages can be misleading. If the reported offenses are not evenly distributed across all inmates, the average is not a good indicator of what is typical for the sample. For example, convicted robbery offenders in California reported an average of 90 burglaries per year. In Michigan the average number was 50 and in Texas 24. These averages suggested that robbery offenders *in general* committed a significant number of burglaries, however, the median number of burglaries for this group was only 5.5 (Chaiken and Chaiken 1982). The median offered a better estimate of the typical number of burglaries each robbery offender committed each year. The averages were high because of the small number of offenders who committed a lot of burglaries. In fact, 10 percent of the robbery offenders reported at least 232 burglaries in a single year!

The key factor in Greenwood's selective incapacitation strategy was the ability to identify the high-rate offenders. This was an easy task with those already incarcerated—the inmates told the researchers how many crimes they committed. Selective incapacitation involves making predictions about which offenders are *likely* to commit a lot of crimes if permitted to stay in the community. Two types of prediction could be utilized to identify who the high rate offenders were. The first was *clinical* or subjective. Trained psychiatrists or psychologists would conduct interviews and examinations with offenders and then offer their best guess as to whether or not the offenders were a threat to the community. The second type of prediction was *actuarial* or objective prediction. This type relied on offender and/or offense characteristics that were correlated with future risk of offending. Greenwood chose the actuarial method because it was believed to be more accurate than subjective prediction. He utilized the inmate survey data to create a scale consisting of factors related to high rate offending. Thirteen items emerged as strong correlates of inmate criminal activity, but six were excluded because they were not legally relevant factors (i.e., race). The scale consisted of the following seven items:

prior conviction for the currently incarcerated offense

incarcerated for more than half of the preceding two years

conviction prior to age 16

prior juvenile incarceration

drug use in the past two years

prior drug use as a juvenile

employed less than 50 percent of the time during the past two years.

These seven items were strongly correlated with the inmates' reported involvement in crime and were all factors that could guide sentencing decisions. The scale was designed to be simple to use with offenders receiving either a 1 or 0 for each item. The items were then added together and the higher the offenders' score, the higher their predicted risk of future offending.

Once the risk scale was constructed, Greenwood proposed six different hypothetical incapacitation strategies. The first one involved a collective incapacitation approach to sentencing, and the remaining five proposed a change in the way offenders could be sentenced to prison or jail. Each strategy predicted a reduction in crime and estimated the change in prison populations. The six strategies are presented below:

Strategy one: Sentence a larger number of low, medium, and high-risk offenders to prison.

Strategy two: Sentence the same number of offenders to prison but increase the length of incarceration for low, medium, and high-risk offenders.

Strategy three: Sentence high-risk offenders to a longer period of incarceration. Sentences for low and medium risk would remain unchanged.

Strategy four: Sentence high-risk offenders to a longer period of incarceration and sentence all low-risk offenders to one year in jail. Sentences for medium-risk offenders would remain unchanged.

Strategy five: Sentence high-risk offenders to a longer period of incarceration; sentence all low-risk offenders to one year in jail while reducing the sentence lengths of medium-risk offenders by half.

Strategy six: Sentence high-risk offenders to a longer period of incarceration, while sentencing *both* low and medium-risk offenders to one year in jail.

Each of the strategies predicted an overall reduction in crime, but they differed with respect to predicted increases/decreases in incarceration rates. Greenwood predicted that in California, strategies three and five would result in a 20 percent reduction in crime, but with a 10 percent *increase* in prison populations. Strategy six would achieve the same reduction *without* any increase in prison populations. Selective and collective incapacitation both offers the potential to reduce crime. The advantage of selective incapacitation over collective is that crime can be reduced without overburdening prisons. Locking up the

FIGURE 3.1 Selective Incapacitation Prediction Table

Offender Score	Predicted Risk of Re-offending
0–1	Low
2–3	Medium
4–7	High

high rate offenders for long periods of time would achieve the same, if not greater, reduction in crime as locking up all offenders. The strategies were flexible in the sense that minimum periods of incarceration could be altered depending on a jurisdiction's specific crime and incarceration rates. The logic underlying selective incapacitation did rest on the critical assumption that the high rate offenders could be identified. The implementation of selective incapacitation as a sentencing policy required a determination of individual offense rates and factors related to high rate offending for each jurisdiction. Jurisdictions would also need to examine their current sentencing trends as a basis of comparison with any alternative selective policies.

Ethical considerations were raised with the Rand sentencing model. Our criminal justice system was founded on a philosophy of equal treatment under the law. Two offenders who commit similar crimes should receive similar punishments. Under a selective incapacitation model, offender characteristics such as prior record and history of drug use were used to either increase or decrease an offender's sentence. Offenders who scored high on the prediction scale received a much longer sentence than a low-risk offender even though their current conviction was for the same crime. In a sense, some offenders would be punished for crimes they had not yet committed but was predicted to commit in the future. There could also be a potential negative consequence of selective incapacitation. Ernest van den Haag (1983) argued that reducing the sentences for low-risk offenders might actually *increase* their future involvement in crime. They may perceive the benefits of crime to be greater than the punishment. Additionally, concerns were raised over items included in the risk predictor scale. Two of the seven indicators were factors related to an offender's juvenile record. Our juvenile justice system was established to help protect adolescents from negative labels into adulthood. Using an offender's juvenile record as a sentencing factor contradicted that philosophy.

Criticisms

Greenwood's selective incapacitation sentencing model was based upon the Rand inmate study. Samples of prison and jail inmates in three states were asked to report on their involvement in crime prior to being incarcerated. The inmate responses became the estimates used to predict how much crime locking up the career criminals could reduce. The Rand study of inmates has been subject to much criticism. Self-report studies do help researchers tap into crimes that go unreported to the police. They are an important part of measuring how much crime takes place in our society, but their accuracy depends upon the honesty of the subjects being questioned. Allen Lynch (1994) questioned the *reliability* of inmate responses arguing that some inmates were reluctant to report their involvement in crime while others likely overestimated involvement to boost their status. Rand defended the study based on *reliability checks* that showed inmates were truthful when reporting their convictions and arrest (remember, the study was not anonymous, so researchers could compare responses to official records). The *survey* design also included reliability checks by asking redundant questions throughout the survey. This is a common technique to improve reliability in survey research. The response rates for the institutions selected for the study varied between 40 and 90 percent, despite the fact that a $5 fee was paid for participation (Greenwood 1982). The potential for *response bias* existed if the inmates who chose not to participate differed on important characteristics related to offending compared to the sample of participants. This was shown not to be a problem when Greenwood analyzed response rate patterns. There was no significant difference in terms of age, prior record, race, or custody level between the participants and non-participants. Hispanic inmates were underrepresented in California so the *generalizability* of the sample to this particular group remained questionable.

Validity is also a concern with survey research. It is important to make sure that the survey questions and responses precisely measure what they allege to (in this study the inmates actual involvement in crime). Jan and Marcia Chaiken (1982) constructed a *validity scale* that was used to eliminate any problematic responses in the Rand inmate survey. Next they compared the eliminated responses to the rest of the sample and found no significant difference between the two. An additional problem had to do with estimates derived from samples of *incarcerated* offenders. These samples may not have reflected the characteristics of criminals who were never caught or received some type of community sanction. Selective incapacitation, however, targeted incarcerated offenders and not those who remained in the community.

Greenwood's model was also criticized because it failed to take into account the age at which involvement in crime began to diminish. Prior criminal career research had shown careers to be finite lasting from five to fifteen years (Blumstein and Cohen 1982). Incarcerating an offender *beyond* the age they would be committing crimes would not yield any decrease in crime. Greenwood's crime reduction estimates assumed that the high-risk offenders targeted for longer prison sentences would continue their crimes if allowed to remain in the community. An estimated 35 percent of the high-risk offenders would be kept in prison longer than their actual criminal careers (Blumstein et al. 1986).

Critics also took issue with the prediction scale developed to identify the high-risk career criminals. The scale was created with offender characteristics that maintained a strong *correlation* with criminal activity. The utility of the scale depended upon its *predictive validity*. Did the seven items accurately predict the high, medium, and low-risk offenders? The scale was applied to the Rand study of inmates. The scale accurately categorized the sample 51 percent of the time (Greenwood 1982). Efforts to predict future criminal behavior are subject to two types of mistakes or errors. Predicting a low-risk offender to be high risk is an example of a false positive. The Rand predictive scale had a false positive rate of 4 percent. The second type of error is a false negative: predicting a high-risk offender to be low risk. False negatives occurred with 3 percent of the inmate sample (Greenwood 1982). The capability to accurately predict only half of the time implied that the same results could have been achieved by simply flipping a coin. A comparison between the Rand scale and the criteria that judges were already using to sentence offenders revealed that the Rand scale was a better instrument. Based on the sentences already imposed for the sample of inmates, judges accurately categorized offenders according to risk only 42 percent of the time (with a 7% false positive and a 5% false negative rate) (Greenwood 1982).

Significance and Subsequent Research

The Rand study of selective incapacitation sparked an interest among policy makers concerned with reducing crime and prison populations as well as with researchers trying to estimate the effects of incapacitation. The study was based on prior research indicating that small numbers of "career criminals" were responsible for a significant amount of crime. After the study was published, career criminal research became a top priority. Greenwood estimated that sentencing all high-risk robbery offenders to a minimum eight years in prison would result in a 15–20 percent reduction in robbery, all without any increase in prison populations. Jacqueline Cohen (1983) and Christy Visher (1986) reanalyzed data from the same sample of inmates and found at most a 14 percent reduction. William Spelman (1986) also analyzed the same Rand inmate data and was only able to predict an 8 percent reduction. In 1985, Michael Janus conducted a similar study of selective incapacitation with federal prison inmates.

The federal prison system was already using a risk scale to predict recidivism among parolees. He estimated a 7 percent reduction in serious crime with no change in prison populations. All of these studies utilized risk prediction as the basis for the estimates of crime reduction. Cohen used a different approach. She developed a sentencing model that targeted *all* robbery and burglary offenders, not just those identified as high risk. This strategy avoided the risk of error in predicting the high-risk offenders. Her sample included arrestees in Washington, DC. Adding two additional years to their sentences would yield an 8 percent reduction in robbery and burglary. The reduction would occur at a price. The extra two years would result in an *increase* in prison populations by as much as 25 percent (Visher 1987).

Subsequent research has also focused on efforts to improve the accuracy at which the high-risk offenders are identified. The Salient Factor Score, Wisconsin Risk Assessment, and the Level of Service Inventory-Revised are examples of other instruments that are used in the criminal justice system to predict risk. Improvements in the *validity* and *reliability* of risk prediction have occurred in the past two decades and there is currently a considerable body of literature on the validation of risk assessments to special population offenders.

Selective incapacitation is a very appealing strategy. Reduce crime and prison populations by incarcerating the offenders who pose the biggest threat to society. Greenwood's sentencing model offered policy makers an alternative to collective incapacitation (incarcerating large numbers of inmates), which is expensive and requires building more prisons. The concept of targeting career criminals was not a new idea when Greenwood put forth his proposal. Many states already had laws in place to target career criminals. Recidivist statutes and habitual offender laws imposed lengthy periods of incarceration for offenders with extensive prior records. Greenwood's strategy was introduced at a time when prison expenditures were out of control and prison populations kept increasing. The public supported increasing sentence lengths but for all offenders, not just the career criminals. Selective incapacitation came to the forefront of criminal justice policy making in 1993 when the state of Washington passed a "three strikes law." Offenders convicted of their third qualifying felony offense would receive a mandatory life in prison sentence without the possibility of parole. One year later, California passed their version of three strikes and the trend quickly took off. By 2004, 26 states and the federal government enacted similar legislation. Three strikes became the new fad among lawmakers who used the initiative to respond to public concerns that our criminal justice system was soft on crime. Research does not support the contention that three strikes laws reduce crime (Zimring, Kamin, and Hawkins 1999). Policy makers in California tried to attribute the decline in violent crime that occurred in 1995 to its three strikes law, but crime rates dropped even lower in states without the laws. Three strikes laws face the same criticisms and problems discussed above with selective incapacitation. Until we can predict with greater precision which offenders are likely to commit crimes in the future, efforts to selectively incapacitate our career criminals becomes more about retribution for past offenses than a plan to reduce crime.

References

Blumstein, A., and J. Cohen (1982). *The Duration of Adult Criminal Careers.* Final Report to the National Institute of Justice. School of Urban and Public Affairs, Carnegie-Mellon University, Pittsburgh.

Blumstein, A., J. Cohen, J. Roth, and C. Visher, eds. (1986). *Criminal Careers and "Career Criminals."* Panel on Research on Criminal Careers. National Research Council. Washington, DC: National Academy Press.

Bureau of Justice Statistics (1981). *Sourcebook of Criminal Justice Statistics.* Washington, DC: U.S. Department of Justice.

Chaiken, J., and M. Chaiken (1982). *Varieties of Criminal Behavior.* Santa Monica, CA: Rand.

Cohen, J. (1983). "Incapacitation as a Strategy for Crime Control: Possibilities and Pitfalls." In *Crime and Justice: An Annual Review of Research,* vol. 5, edited by M. Tonry and N. Morris. Chicago: University of Chicago Press.

Greenwood, P., and A. Abrahamse (1982). *Selective Incapacitation.* Santa Monica: Rand.

Janus, M. (1985). "Selective Incapacitation: Have We Tried It? Does It Work?" *Journal of Criminal Justice* 1:539–47.

Lynch, A. (1994). *The Cost Effectiveness of Incarceration: A Critical Review of the Literature.* Tallahassee: Florida Corrections Commission.

Spelman, W. (1986). *The Depth of a Dangerous Temptation: Another Look at Selective Incapacitation.*

Final Report to the National Institute of Justice. Washington, DC: Police Executive Research Forum,

Wolfgang, M., R. Figlio, and T. Sellin (1972). *Delinquency in a Birth Cohort.* Chicago: University of Chicago Press.

Van den Haag, E. (1983). "Thinking About Crime Again." *Commentary* December:73–77.

Visher, C. (1986). "The Rand Inmate Survey: A Reanalysis." In *Criminal Careers and "Career Criminals,"* edited by A. Blumstein, J. Cohen, J. Roth, and C. Visher, 161–211. Panel on Research on Criminal Careers. National Research Council. Washington, DC: National Academy Press.

Visher, C. (1987), "Incapacitation and Crime Control: Does a 'Lock' Em Up' Strategy Reduce Crime?" *Justice Quarterly* 4:513–43.

Zimring, F., S. Kamin, and G. Hawkins (1999). *Crime and Punishment in California.* Berkeley, CA: Institute of Government Studies Press.

Further Reading

Blumstein, A., and S. Moitra (1980). "The Identification of 'Career Criminals' from 'Chronic Offenders' in a Cohort." *Law and Policy Quarterly* 2:321–34.

Chaiken, M., and J. Chaiken (1984). "Offender Types and Public Policy." *Crime and Delinquency* 30:195–226.

Forst, B. (1983). "Selective Incapacitation: An Idea Whose Time Has Come?" *Federal Probation* 46:19–23.

Gottfredson, S., and D. Gottfredson (1985). "Selective Incapacitation?" *Annals of the American Academy of Political and Social Sciences* 478:135–49.

Klein, S., and M. Caggiano (1986). *The Prevalence, Predictability, and Policy Implication of Recidivism.* Santa Monica, CA: Rand.

Shinnar, R., and S. Shinnar (1975). "The Effect of the Criminal Justice System on Crime Control: A Quantitative Approach." *Law and Society Review* 9:581–612.

Tonry, M. (1987). "Prediction and Classification: Legal and Ethical Issues." In *Prediction and Classification: Criminal Justice Decision Making,* edited by D. Gottfredson and M. Tonry, 367–413. Chicago: University of Chicago Press.

Von Hirsch, A. (1984). "The Ethics of Selective Incapacitation: Observations on the Contemporary Debate." *Crime and Delinquency* 30:175–94.

COLLECTIVE INCAPACITATION: DOES INCARCERATION REDUCE THE COSTS OF CRIME?

Zedlewski, E. (1987). *Making Confinement Decisions.* Washington, DC: National Institute of Justice.

Background

Collective incapacitation attempts to reduce crime through the imprisonment of large numbers of criminals. The more criminals behind bars, the safer society will be. Locking up large numbers of criminals would appear to be an effective way to reduce crime, but an important question to consider is how many offenders we have to put behind bars before we can achieve a reduction in crime. Cost is also a consideration. Incarceration is expensive, but the cost is justified if in the long run reducing crime saves money.

The United States leads the world in its use of incarceration. With over two million people currently behind bars, there are more offenders locked up (per 100,000 people) than any other country across the globe. Our commitment to the use of incarceration dates back to 1790 when the Quakers converted a section of the Walnut Street Jail to be used as a place for housing convicted offenders. Incarceration was viewed as more humane than the physical punishments that dominated the colonial era. In addition, incarceration allowed lawmakers the opportunity to create punishment that would be proportionate to the offense. The length of incarceration could be altered to reflect the seriousness of the crime.

One problem that has always existed in our correctional system is overcrowded prisons. The United States has a history of exceeding the constructed capacity of a facility by sentencing more offenders to prison than the prison was designed to hold. The belief that there is always room for more has led to many prisons being placed under court orders for conditions that stem from overcrowding. Proponents of incarceration argue that it achieves the correctional goal of incapacitation. By restricting an offender's opportunity to engage in criminal behavior, society is protected. As long as an offender is behind bars the public is safe (this philosophy completely ignores the crime that takes place in our prisons and jails). With the exception of the death penalty, incarceration is the most expensive sanction utilized in the United States. State and federal spending on corrections now exceeds 36 billion dollars, with the average cost of incarcerating a single inmate per day of $62.22 (Camp and Camp 2002). Proponents of incarceration argue that the expense is necessary to protect the public from dangerous criminals. Policy makers continue to respond to public concern over crime by creating laws that increase the number of offenders sent to prison and the length of time they are incarcerated.

The Analysis

In the late 1980s the prison population had reached half a million—an increase of almost 150 percent in a 15-year period and was growing at a rate of 1000 inmates per week. Policy makers became interested in determining whether or not the money spent on incarceration was money well spent. Edwin Zedlewski, a staff economist with the National Institute of Justice, was the first to attempt a systematic approach to try and answer this question. Zedlewski (1987) carried out a *cost-benefit analysis* to assess whether or not an investment in the use of incarceration paid off in terms of money saved compared to *not* putting offenders behind bars. A popular technique in the field of economics, the cost-benefit analysis is used to make decisions on the overall value of social policies. Mathematical techniques are used to determine whether policies and programs should continue or be terminated. Relevant criteria are expressed in monetary terms wherein a researcher estimates the amount of money spent to develop and implement a policy and compares these costs to the benefits derived from the policy. A policy is deemed "cost-effective" if the net benefits are greater than the net costs.

Estimating the cost of incarceration seemed like an easy task. In the 1980s the average cost of incarcerating a single felony offender in a state prison was $25,000.00 per year (the net cost of incarceration). To determine the benefits, Zedlewski considered a recently published study by the Rand Corporation that surveyed prison inmates in three states (Michigan, Texas, and California) asking them to estimate the number of crimes they committed in the year prior to being incarcerated (this is the same Rand inmate study used by Greenwood for his selective incapacitation proposal). The survey revealed that inmates were responsible for anywhere from 187 to 287 property crimes per year (Chaiken and Chaiken 1982). Zedlewski used the more conservative estimate of 187 in his analysis. The average cost per crime was determined to be $2,300.00. This amount was calculated by dividing the total annual expenditures on crime by the total number of crimes. In 1983, expenditures on crime was $99.8 billion, which included money spent to operate the criminal justice system, private security, property loss, and personal injury. According to the National Crime Survey, there were 42.5 million crimes reported that same year (*$99.8 billion/42.5 million = $2,300.00*). The National Crime Survey measures individual and household victimization and is published annually by the Bureau of Justice Statistics.

If each offender committed an average of 187 crimes per year, then a single offender would be responsible for $430,100 in crime costs each year (*187 × $2,300.00*). Compare this figure to the $25,000 spent to incarcerate a single offender, and it was easy to understand Zedlewski's conclusion that for every felony criminal sent to prison, money was saved. Put in simplified terms, for every dollar spent on incarceration, states saved $17.00 in reduced crime. His findings offered clear support for an increased use of incarceration. According to Zedlewski's report ". . . the results overwhelmingly support the case for more prison capacity." The study presented policy makers the evidence they needed to defend their "get tough" crime control strategies and helped justify the continued growth in prison populations.

FIGURE 3.2 Zedlewski's Cost-Benefit Analysis

Cost of Incarceration		Cost of Crime	
Average Annual Cost of Incarceration Per Offender	$25,000	Average Number of Crimes Committed Per Offender Annually	187
Cost of Incarcerating 1,000 Felony Offenders Per Year (1,000 x 25,000)	$25,000,000	Average Cost Per Crime	$2,300
		Cost of Crime for Each Felony Offender Per Year ($2,300 x 187)	$430,100
		Cost of Crime for 1,000 Felony Offenders Annually (1,000 x 430,100)	$430,000,000

The annual cost of incarceration for 1,000 felony offenders is $25,000,000; however **not** locking up these offenders would cost $430,000,000—a savings of $405,000.000. In other words for every dollar spent on incarceration, $17 is saved.

Criticisms

Despite the apparent straightforwardness of Zedlewski's conclusions, there were many criticisms that surfaced almost immediately after the report was published. Prior to publication, scholars had not reviewed the study and yet it was widely disseminated to lawmakers all around the country (Clear 1994). Many of the criticisms had to do with the Rand survey data used by Zedlewski to estimate the number of crimes committed each year by an average offender. The *reliability* of the inmate responses was questionable. Inmate surveys can be biased if inmates are either reluctant to report their involvement in crime or overestimate their involvement (Lynch 1994). In response to Zedlewski's report, Franklin Zimring and Gordon Hawkins (1988) published an article in *Crime and Delinquency* detailing the problems with his findings. They concluded that if Zedlewski's numbers were accurate, crime rates would have already diminished to zero in the year before his analysis was even conducted. The Rand study (also sponsored by the National Institute of Justice) revealed the highest rate of individual offending published at that time. No other study produced numbers close to 187.

There were also problems with the sample of inmates. Over half of the inmates who answered the survey did not report any involvement in any of the property crimes included in the survey. In addition, half of the inmates reported less than 15 crimes per year (Greenberg 1991). Criticism of Zedlewski's benefit estimate was also derived from the fact that his study did not take into account the number of drug offenders behind bars. Twenty percent of the prison population consisted of offenders who were incarcerated for drug crimes and whose involvement in property crime was minimal (Feldman 1993). If Zedlewski's estimates were based on an erroneous assumption that the mean property rate for prison inmates was 187, then he overestimated the money saved through incarceration.

Regardless of the estimates, the issue of *generalizability* was raised. Zedlewski sampled inmates from three prisons located in different geographical areas to make sure his results would generalize to other states. The three states (Michigan, Texas, and California), however, had crime rates higher than the national average. It is doubtful that Zedlewski's findings would have been replicated in jurisdictions with more typical amounts of crime (Piehl et al. 1999). Zedlewski also failed to consider crimes committed by offenders who were not incarcerated (Greenberg 1991). Offenders who received some type of sentence in the community (i.e., probation) were typically different from those who were incarcerated, yet Zedlewski was generalizing from his sample to an entire criminal population. Research suggested that factors including prior record, offense seriousness, and socioeconomic status were relevant in understanding which criminals went to prison and which did not (Lynch 1994).

Critics also took issue with Zedlewski's cost estimate. While a measure of the cost of incarceration should include money spent on the housing of an inmate, additional expenditures should have also been considered such as construction costs. Funds used to construct prisons were (and continue to be) often diverted from educational and other social welfare programs (Lynch 1994). Spending money on prisons instead of on programs that may have helped to prevent crime in the first place become important (although more difficult to estimate) secondary costs. The use of the cost-benefit analysis to evaluate social policies has also been subject to criticism. Applying monetary considerations when making decisions about continuing and/or expanding various social policies can be problematic. If a policy (such as the use of incarceration) is shown to be cost effective does this mean it should automatically be expanded? Following the presumption that policies should only be continued if the benefits outweigh costs ignores important ethical and moral considerations that can be just as important in our decision-making about crime.

Significance and Subsequent Research

Zedlewski's study generated interest among other researchers and policy makers looking for a way to empirically determine the true benefits of incarceration and whether the benefits outnumbered the costs. Several other cost-benefit analyses were conducted in different states with different estimates. Some of the studies revealed an overall cost benefit, although no study produced a benefit ratio anywhere close to Zedlewski's 17:1. A reanalysis of Zedlewski's data utilized the median number of crimes per year instead of the mean (remember means can be misleading when data are not evenly distributed). Half of the inmates who participated in the Rand survey had committed less than 15 crimes per year. Using the median number of 15 instead of the average 187 offenses still produced a positive ratio of 1.38 (Logan and DiIulio 1992). John DiIulio (1990) conducted his own cost-benefit analysis for the Wisconsin Policy Research Institute. He also used the median number of crimes committed by a typical offender (his data produced a median of 12 offenses per year). In Wisconsin, the cost of incarceration outweighed the benefits by as much as 4:1. Other studies estimated the crime reduction anywhere from 1 (Clarke 1974) to 53 percent (Shinnar and Shinnar 1975). Regardless of the findings, these studies were subject to the same criticisms discussed above.

Zedlewski responded to the criticisms and defended his findings. The estimated 187 crimes per offender per year he argued was based on inmate self-reported data, and while inmates may not have been completely truthful; the self-reported data addressed many of the limitations of relying on official counts of crime. Crimes that frequently go unreported to the police tend to show up in self-reported studies. He contended that his calculations were based on estimates, and even if the estimates were not be completely accurate, the overall finding that the cost of incarceration was less that the cost of crime still held true. A *natural experiment* involving collective incapacitation was taking place during this debate. The United States doubled its prison population between 1970 and the early 1980s. According to Visher (1987) the impact of such an increase in incarceration was an estimated crime reduction of 10–30 percent. Her findings offered support for Zedlewski's contention that collective incapacitation reduced crime.

Zedlewski's analysis raised other questions as well. Would his calculations hold true with an even larger prison population? Or would the benefits of incarceration start to diminish once the costs reached a particular level? Zimring and Hawkins (1988) argued that increasing the number of offenders in prison could lead to an increase in court costs. Offenders facing lengthy prison sentences are more likely to take their case to trial and to appeal their convictions thereby creating additional costs for the criminal justice system. It was an erroneous assumption to think that because crime rates decreased, expenditures also decreased.

For most of our correctional history, we have operated under an assumption that crime control is primarily achieved through incarceration. Incapacitating offenders who would otherwise be free to continue their crimes is how we reduce crime. This strategy is based upon the logic that there is a strong negative relationship between incarceration and crime rates. If incarceration rates go up and crime goes down, this justifies our incapacitation efforts. Over the past 30 years, crime was at its highest when imprisonment rates were at their lowest. Zedlewski's analysis rendered support for the contention that sometimes you have to spend money to save money. The assumption underlying incapacitation is that if all of the criminals were locked up there would be no crime. This assumption fails to consider an important issue associated with certain interventions that may appear to be effective in reducing crime: crime displacement. Removing an offender from the streets today opens up opportunities for other offenders to come along and take their place. Crime remains a constant; only the particular offenders change. Finally, it is important to consider that while crime rates influence the use of incarceration, there are many other factors such as economic conditions, policy change, and prison construction that impact these rates as well.

Applying the cost-benefit technique to an understanding of prison expenditures can help determine if the enormous expense underlying our collective incapacitation policies offers a return on the investment. Incarceration is an expensive way to control crime in our society, but if the savings achieved once an offender is incarcerated offsets the cost, then this would be money well spent. The underlying premise of weighing the costs and benefits of incarceration is easier to accomplish in theory than in practice. Estimating both the costs and benefits of incarceration becomes difficult without a clear consensus on how each of these is calculated. Despite the limitations of Zedlewski's analysis, he provided valuable insight into our ability to use prison as a mechanism of social control. Instead of forging forward in our quest to lock up as many criminals as possible, policy makers began to evaluate the utility of these endeavors and question many traditionally held beliefs about incapacitation and crime.

References

Camp, C., and G. Camp (2003). *The Corrections Year-book, Adult Corrections 2002.* Middletown, CT: Criminal Justice Institute.

Chaiken, J., and M. Chaiken (1982). *Varieties of Criminal Behavior.* Santa Monica, CA: Rand.

Clark, S. (1974). "Getting' Em Out of Circulation: Does Incarceration of Juvenile Offenders Reduce Crime?" *Journal of Criminal Law and Enforcement* 4:528–35.

Clear, T. (1994). *Harm in American Penology: Offenders, Victims, and Their Communities.* Albany: State University of New York Press.

DiIulio, J. (1990). *Crime and Punishment in Wisconsin: A Survey of Prisoners.* Milwaukee: Wisconsin Policy Research Institute.

Feldman, D. (1993). "Imprisoner's Dilemma: Why More Jails Aren't the Answer." *The American Prospect.* Summer.

Greenberg, D. (1991). "The Cost-Benefit Analysis of Imprisonment." *Social Justice* 17:49–73.

Logan, C., and J. DiIulio (1992). "Ten Deadly Myths About Crime and Punishment in the U.S." *Wisconsin Interest* 1:21–34.

Lynch, A. (1994). *The Cost Effectiveness of Incarceration: A Critical Review of the Literature.* Tallahassee: Florida Corrections Commission.

Piehl, A., B. Useem, and J. DiIulio (1999). *Right-Sizing Justice: A Cost-Benefit Analysis of Imprisonment in Three States.* Civic Report for the Manhattan Institute for Policy Research.

Shinnar, R., and S. Shinnar (1975). "The Effect of the Criminal Justice System on the Control of Crime: A Quantitative Approach." *Law and Society Review* 9:581–612.

Visher, C. (1987). "Incapacitation and Crime Control: Does a 'Lock' Em Up' Strategy Reduce Crime?" *Justice Quarterly* 4:513–43.

Zimring, F., and G. Hawkins (1988). "The New Mathematics of Imprisonment." *Crime and Delinquency* 34:425–36.

Zedlewski, E. (1987). *Making Confinement Decisions.* Washington, DC: National Institute of Justice.

Zedlewski, E. (1989). "New Mathematics of Imprisonment: A Reply to Zimring and Hawkins." *Crime and Delinquency* 35:169–73.

Further Reading

Austin, J., and B. Krisberg (1985). "Incarceration in the United States: The Extent and Future of the Problem." *Annals of the American Academy of Political and Social Science* 48:15–30.

Baird, C. (1993). *The "Prison's Pay" Study: Research or Ideology.* Washington, DC: NCCD Focus.

Cohen, J. (1983). "Incapacitation as a Strategy for Crime Control: Possibilities and Pitfalls." In *Crime and Justice: An Annual Review of the Research,* vol. 5, edited by M. Tonry and N. Morris, 1–84. Chicago: University of Chicago Press.

Petersilia, J., P. Greenwood, and M. Lavin (1977). *Criminal Careers of Habitual Felons.* Santa Monica, CA: Rand.

Van Dine, S., S. Dinitz, and J. Conrad (1979). *Restraining the Wicked: The Dangerous Offender Project.* Lexington, MA: Lexington Books.

Zimring, F., and G. Hawkins (1991). *Scale of Imprisonment.* Chicago: University of Chicago Press.

2

Community Corrections

PROBATION

Most convicted offenders receive a sentence of probation. Offenders who are on probation are permitted to remain in the community under court-imposed conditions. Judges are afforded wide discretion over the specific conditions imposed, but typical conditions include refraining from criminal activity, reporting requirements, and curfews. Judges may also order offenders to participate in treatment or educational programs. In theory, if an offender fails to abide by their conditions, probation is revoked and the offender is sent to jail or prison. The practice dates back to 1841 when a Boston shoemaker by the name of John Augustus posted bail for a defendant charged with public drunkenness. Augustus convinced the judge to defer sentence and release the defendant to his custody and care. Augustus is considered to be the nation's first "unofficial" probation officer. It is estimated that he bailed out more than 1,800 offenders. The practice was not officially recognized until Massachusetts passed their first probation statute for juveniles in 1878. New York was the first state to officially authorize probation for adults in 1901. By 1938, 37 states, the District of Columbia, and the federal government all had probation statutes. Today there are over four million people on probation in the United States (Glaze and Bonczar 2006). Supporters of probation argue that probation is beneficial to the offender. Offenders can maintain their family, social, and employment ties and earn money to pay their fines or restitution orders (Petersilia 1985). In addition, it costs less to supervise an offender on probation compared to putting them in jail or prison.

FELONY PROBATION: IS IT SAFE TO PUT FELONS ON PROBATION?

Petersilia, J., S. Turner, J. Kahan, and J. Peterson (1985). *Granting Felons Probation: Public Risks and Alternatives.* Santa Monica, CA: Rand.

Background

The number of offenders on probation began to significantly increase beginning in the mid-1970s. In 1983, probation was the most frequently used sentence in the state of California and its use was not limited to misdemeanor crimes and juveniles. Prisons were already operating above capacity due to rising crime rates and a lack of construction to keep pace with increasing incarceration rates. Many states were under federal court orders for prison conditions associated with crowding. Increasing numbers of felony offenders were being placed on probation because judges had no other alternative forms of punishment. From 1975 to 1983, the number of adult felony offenders sentenced to probation increased almost 13 percent (Petersilia 1985). Many of the offenders sentenced to probation were convicted of serious crimes. For example, 17 percent of convicted rapists, 30 percent of offenders convicted of robbery, and 80 percent of offenders convicted of assault in California received a sentence of probation (Petersilia 1985). At the same time judges were sentencing more offenders to probation, the state was allocating *less* money to cover the cost of supervision. From 1975 to 1983, the state was spending almost 25 percent less per offender and the average caseload for probation officers had increased (Petersilia 1985). These trends were not unique to California. It had become apparent by the early 1980s that the criminal justice system was becoming more reliant on the use of probation as a means of punishment. The increased use of probation for serious offenders coupled with less supervision raised important questions about the effectiveness of probation. Did probation offer the same level of public protection as incarceration? Despite the increase in the use of probation in the 1980s, few empirical studies of probation (particularly its use with felony offenders) had been published. In his report on the effectiveness of correctional intervention, Robert Martinson (whose study was discussed previously) deemed probation to be a failure. Early research included inconsistent measures of recidivism with various follow-up periods making it difficult to determine the effectiveness of probation (Vito 1986). In the early 1980s, the Rand Corporation (at the request of the National Institute of Justice) conducted an extensive study of probation to learn more about the offenders sentenced to probation and the effectiveness of probation as a criminal sanction. At the time the study began, over one-third of California's probation population were convicted felons (Petersilia et al. 1985).

The Study

In 1985, Joan Petersilia, Susan Turner, James Kahan, and Joyce Peterson published findings from a large-scale study of felony probation in California. They examined data on a large number of probationers to address the following research questions:

1. What were the recidivism rates for offenders who received probation?
2. What were the characteristics of the probationers who recidivated?
3. What criteria did the Courts use in deciding which offenders received probation versus who went to prison?
4. Was it possible to accurately predict which probationers would recidivate?

Data for the study was obtained from the California Board of Prison Terms (CBPT). The Board had been collecting comprehensive data for all offenders sentenced to prison since 1978 and on a sample of adult males from 17 counties who received probation. From these two data sources, researchers selected a sample of male offenders who had been convicted of the following crimes: robbery, assault, burglary, theft, forgery, and drug offenses. These crimes were selected because an offender could receive *either* prison or probation if convicted. Approximately 16,500 felony male offenders were included in the study. For each offender, researchers had access to their personal characteristics, information on their crimes, court proceedings, and disposition.

Analyzing *existing data* is both convenient and cost effective. Researchers sometimes run into problems, however, if the data do not provide the exact information needed. The CBPT database included information on all offenders sent to prison, but information for only a sample of probationers and the sample was not *random*. This was problematic because the likelihood of an offender being sent to prison differed across the counties studied. Researchers were able to access additional data from the California Bureau of Criminal Statistics. This information was used to estimate the likelihood of receiving a prison sentence in each county. Recidivism data had to be collected separately from offender rap sheets. Researchers chose two counties (Los Angeles and Alameda) because they had a large number of probationers and officials were willing to provide adequate information on the recidivists. Two hundred and six probationers were selected from Alameda. These were all probationers for which information was available. The number of probationers in Los Angeles was too large to include all offenders, so researchers selected all drug offenders and a *randomly* selected sample of violent and property offenders. The total number of offenders from Los Angeles was 1,466 (for a combined total of 1,672). The offenses for which probationers had been convicted were representative of the offenses in the data derived from CBPT. Researchers recorded arrest and conviction data for each probationer from the time he was granted probation in 1980 to May 1, 1983. Most of the probationers had also received a jail sentence in conjunction with probation so researchers had to subtract any time served from their follow-up period. Follow-up periods varied for the sample. The maximum follow-up was 40 months and the average follow-up period was 31 months.

Findings

The Rand study of felony probation in California included a substantial amount of data and involved numerous analyses. Researchers used this data to address several important research questions about the use and effectiveness of probation. The findings from this endeavor are summarized below.

Recidivism rates. The majority of offenders sentenced to probation recidivated during the follow-up period. Over all, 65 percent of the sample was re-arrested and 51 percent were charged and convicted. A total of 18 percent were convicted of a violent crime.

Property offenders were more likely to recidivate compared to violent or drug offenders. Researchers also discovered that probationers tended to recidivate by committing the same crime they were originally convicted of and sentenced to probation for. Recidivism is often measured by whether or not an offender is arrested, charged, and/or convicted of a new offense. Another informative way to measure recidivism is to examine the time it takes for an offender to recidivate. Rand researchers included time to recidivism in their analysis and found that property and violent offenders recidivated sooner than drug offenders. The

Felony Probationers: Percent Recidivating

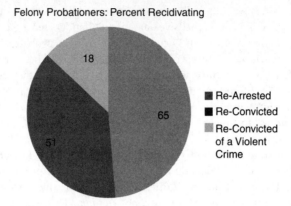

FIGURE 3.3 Results of the Rand Study of Felony Probation

median time to the first filed charge was 5 months for property offenders and 8 months for violent offenders. In addition, very few property or violent offenders recidivated after 27 months. The median time for drug offenders was 5 months. Researchers also looked at whether or not the factors used in the pre-sentence investigation (PSI) report were correlated with probationer recidivism. Probation departments prepared the PSI for offenders who were eligible for probation. The report consisted of background information on the offender and any other information relevant to the sentencing decision. The reports were designed to assist judges in their decisions. In their study, researchers did find that when the PSI recommended probation based on a favorable family situation, consistent employment, and lack of prior record that the probationer actually did have lower reconviction rates. Some of the factors included in the report, however, were not related to recidivism as expected. For example, if the PSI recommended prison for the offender because he had used a weapon or did not provide information on any accomplices, reconviction rates were lower.

Prison/probation decision. Researchers examined several legal and extralegal factors to determine which offenders were most likely to receive probation compared to prison. The offenders who received prison had typically been convicted of two or more charges or had been on probation or parole when arrested. Prior record also influenced the prison/probation decision, but the number of priors was different across crime type. For example, burglars only needed one prior conviction but drug offenders needed five or more to be sent to prison. These findings were consistent with California statutes regarding the use of probation. Age and education did not influence the decision, but race did. Blacks and Hispanics were more likely to be sentenced to prison compared to whites even after controlling for offense characteristics. Robbery, theft, and drug offenders with drug addiction were more likely to go to prison as well as offenders who used a weapon or seriously injured their victim. Researchers also explored relationships between several "process variables" such as the type of legal representation, use of pretrial detention, and method of conviction. Offenders who had been released prior to their trial, were represented by a private attorney or were willing to agree to drug treatment were less likely to be sentenced to prison. This finding was true for offenders across all crime types. For all crimes except forgery, offenders who were convicted at trial (no plea bargaining) were more likely to go to prison. Contrary to prior research on the influence of the PSI, judges in Alameda and Los Angeles counties frequently ignored the recommendation made by the probation department in their PSI report.

One of the objectives of the Rand study of felony probation was to determine the extent to which the above factors could be used to *predict* who receives probation versus prison. The predicted sentences failed to correspond with the actual sentences for 20–25 percent of the cases. Many of the offenders who received probation shared the same characteristics of those who were imprisoned. This could have been a consequence of not examining other factors that were relevant to the prison/probation decision. Researchers then wanted to find out if serious felons *as a matter of routine* were sentenced to prison and less serious felons to probation. Offenders were assigned one point for each of the following risk factors:

two more convictions

two or more prior adult convictions

currently on parole

possessed a gun

used a weapon

seriously injured the victim

addicted to drugs or under the influence at the time the crime was committed

Each offender received a score ranging from *zero* (no risk factors) to *seven* (all of the risk factors). Those with a score of three or higher had an 80 percent chance of being incarcerated and those with scores of five or higher had a 100 percent chance of incarceration. This finding applied to all crimes except assault.

Predicting recidivism. Researchers *hypothesized* that the factors found to influence the prison/probation decision would also predict recidivism for those on probation. They tested this hypothesis by exploring the recidivism rates for probationers with low, moderate, and high-risk scores. Fifty-five percent of the low-risk probationers were rearrested while on probation compared to 78 percent of the high-risk probationers. An interesting finding emerged for the moderate risk group. Seventy-one percent were rearrested while on probation. This finding questioned the ability of the courts to accurately identify offenders likely to succeed on probation.

Based on their findings, Rand researchers attempted to develop a recidivism prediction model to improve the courts' decision-making capabilities. They first identified all of the factors that were correlated with recidivism (rearrest, reconviction, and reconviction for a violent crime). Next, researchers categorized these factors into four levels based on their importance in making the prison/probation decision. Level one consisted of the type of crime committed (personal or property). Level two included several "culpability" factors such as prior record, probation or parole revocations, and history of drug/alcohol abuse). Level three included the PSI recommendation and level four contained the offenders' demographic information. An analysis revealed that offenders convicted of a property crime with more prior convictions (adult or juvenile) were more likely to recidivate. On the other hand, offenders with an income at the time of their arrest who were living with their spouse and/or children were less likely to recidivate. Researchers then examined whether or not these factors could predict recidivism. Level one information (type of crime) predicted rearrest accurately for 56 percent of the sample. Adding prior record and history of drug/alcohol abuse (level two information) improved the accuracy by 11 percent. Level three information (derived from the PSI) added very little predictive power. Demographic information (level four information) improved the accuracy of prediction by 2 percent (the complete model was therefore able to predict rearrest with 69% accuracy). By chance alone, researchers could have predicted with 54 percent accuracy. These same factors predicted reconvictions with 64 percent accuracy and reconvictions for violent crimes with 71 percent accuracy. Mistakes are an inevitable part of prediction. The mistakes that are made when predicting behavior are referred to as false positives and false negatives. A false positive occurs when an offender is predicted to recidivate but does not. False negatives occur when a good risk offender recidivates. Researchers were also unsuccessful in their efforts to predict offenders likely to do well on probation. Less than 3 percent of offenders coming into the criminal justice were recognized as good risks for probation (meaning they had at least a 75% chance of not recidivating).

Recommendations

According to Rand researchers, these findings raised serious doubts about the effectiveness of probation for felony offenders. Most of the felons sentenced to probation recidivated and researchers were unable to develop an accurate prediction model to improve the courts' decision-making. Continuing to use probation as a sanction for felony offenders appeared to be putting the public at risk. Without adequate prison space, the courts had no other alternatives besides probation to use as punishment. In their report, researchers made several recommendations to address the limitations of using probation for felony offenders. First, states needed to formally acknowledge that the purpose of probation had changed. Probation was originally used as a means of furthering the goal of rehabilitation in the correctional system. As the United States moved away from that goal in the late 1960s, the expectations of probation changed. Probation was now used as a way to exercise "restrictive supervision" over more serious offenders. Second, probation departments needed to redefine the responsibilities of their probation officers. Probation officers were expected to be surveillance officers, which may have required special training. In addition, states needed to explore the possibility of broadening the legal authority of its probation officers by allowing them to act as law enforcement officers if necessary. Third, states should adopt a formal client management system that included risk/need assessments of every client. Such a system would help establish uniform, consistent treatment of those on probation and would also help departments allocate their resources efficiently and effectively. Finally, researchers encouraged states to develop alternative forms of community punishment that offered more public protection than regular probation.

Criticisms

Rand researchers provided the first large scale study of felony probation by examining the effectiveness of probation as a criminal sanction and the criteria used by the courts in deciding which offenders should be placed on probation. Researchers articulated a concern for public safety based on the large number of probationers who recidivated, but they cautioned against using their findings as the definitive evaluation of probation. The Rand study focused exclusively on felony offenders, and the results should not be applied to other probation populations. The issue of whether or not the findings would *generalize* to other counties in California and to other states was raised. Data for the study came from probation and prison records from two counties in California. These two counties were not *randomly* selected, but were chosen because of their large probation populations and the willingness of departments to provide information (*purposive sampling*). Further, the probation departments in these counties had experienced significant budget cuts. Supervision may have become compromised as a result and this could have explained why these counties had high rates of recidivism. Researchers did articulate that their findings ". . . have significance for other states . . ." (p. vi). Studies of probation recidivism in other states, however, had found recidivism rates to be much lower suggesting that the Rand results may not have applied elsewhere (Vito 1986, McGaha et al. 1987).

One of the limitations of previous evaluations of probation was the inconsistent measures of recidivism. Recidivism can be measured using arrest, prosecution, or conviction statistics. In addition, researchers can examine whether or not an offender recidivates, how many times they recidivate, and time to recidivism. While each measure provides valuable insight into offender recidivism, each measure is subject to bias. For example, arrest statistics may have overestimated recidivism if a significant number of those arrested were never charged (Morgan 1994). Convictions may have underestimated the amount of recidivism if charges were dismissed for reasons other than insufficient evidence. The measurement of recidivism had implications for failure rates. Rearrest measures produced higher failure rates compared to reconviction (Geerken and Hayes 1993). The number of offenders who were reincarcerated could have also been misleading. Incarcerations could occur as a result of technical violations. Probationers committed technical violations when they failed to abide by their probation conditions (i.e., failure to report). Some believed that technical violations were an important consideration in determining the effectiveness of probation (Vito 1986, Morgan 1994). A recent study of felony probation in Michigan found that most probation violations were related to the conditions of probation not new criminal offenses (Gray et al. 2001). Rand researchers examined multiple measures of recidivism including rearrests, filed charges, convictions, and incarcerations, but each of the measures were for new criminal offenses. Researchers did not include technical violations as an indicator of failure.

Rand researchers maintained that the large number of probation failures in California posed a significant risk to public safety. One of the questions raised after the report was made public was whether or not the Rand findings provided support for increasing the use of incarceration. If those on probation were sentenced to prison they could not commit any crimes against the public. In an effort to answer that question, Michael Geerken and Hennessey Hayes (1993) analyzed burglary and robbery arrests for probationers in New Orleans, Louisiana, between 1974 and 1986. They wanted to determine whether or not incarceration would have resulted in a significant decrease in crime due to its incapacitation effect. According to their data, 8 percent of the total arrests for burglary and 8 percent of the total arrests for robbery involved offenders on probation. Replacing probation with incarceration would yield only a small reduction in crime. What remained unknown, however, was the likelihood of recidivating once inmates were released from prison back into the community. To address this question, Rand published a study titled *Prison versus Probation in California: Implications for Crime and Offender Recidivism* one year after their original report. Researchers compared recidivism measures for a sample of probationers from their original 1985 study with a "matched" sample of prison inmates. Both groups performed poorly, but the prisoners had higher rates of recidivism compared to probationers (72% compared to 53%) (Petersilia et al. 1986). While prison may have incapacitated offenders, it did not appear to be deterring them from future crime. Putting more offenders in prison may have reduced crime in the short term but had no lasting impact. The second Rand study received very little attention. In fact, the

National Institute of Justice (which funded the study) criticized the findings and tried to keep Rand from disseminating the report (Clear 1994).

Significance and Subsequent Research

The Rand study of felony probation received a considerable amount of attention within the field of corrections. According to one scholar, the study was acclaimed as ". . . the most important criminological research to be reported since World War II" (Conrad 1985, p. 71). Summaries of the report were reprinted in other forums (*Federal Probation* and *Crime and Delinquency*) and the National Institute of Justice disseminated the report to criminal justice agencies across the country and even "highlighted" the study in their monthly newsletter (Clear 1994). Today, the study remains one of the most highly cited piece of corrections research (Wright and Miller 1999). The report generated interest in the use of probation as a sanction for felony offenders. Several studies examining the effectiveness of probation and the factors correlated with probation outcomes were published after 1985. Much of this research failed to produce results consistent with the Rand study.

One year after the Rand study was published; Gennaro Vito (1986) reported findings from a study of felony probation in Kentucky. A sample of 317 felony probationers from five counties was followed for 36 months. Like California, Kentucky had also experienced an increase in its probation population. Vito examined several standard indicators of recidivism including rearrest, conviction, and incarceration for a new offense. In addition, he included technical violations (failure to complete the conditions of probation) and incarceration for a probation violation. Vito's study produced rates much lower than the Rand study. Only 22 percent of the probationers were rearrested and 18 percent reconvicted. Incarceration rates were similar to those found by Rand. Twelve percent were incarcerated for a new crime and another 7 percent were incarcerated for violating probation conditions. The Rand study, however, only included incarcerations for a new offense. If researchers had included the number of technical violations, this rate probably would have been much higher. Probationers in California were rearrested for more serious offenses than in Kentucky where most of the rearrests were for minor crimes and technical violations. A study of felony probation conducted in Missouri produced results consistent with Vito. Twenty-two percent of the sample was rearrested and 12 percent reconvicted during a 40-month follow-up period (McGaha et al. 1987).

John Whitehead (1991) conducted a study of felony probation in New Jersey. He examined a group of offenders sentenced to probation in 1976 and 1977. Probationers had been convicted of robbery, assault with intent to rob, burglary, or drug crimes. Whitehead found recidivism rates in between those reported by Vito and Rand. Forty percent of probationers in New Jersey were rearrested and 35 percent reconvicted (within a 48 month follow-up period). The number of probationers incarcerated (16%) was found to be consistent with Vito. Robbers and Burglars had higher rates of recidivism compared to drug offenders. Whitehead also examined several legal and extralegal factors to determine their relationship with recidivism. Consistent with the Rand study, prior convictions, offense type, and income at the time of arrest were correlated with recidivism. However, living arrangements had no relationship as it did in California. Whitehead also found employment to be related to recidivism. Based on his findings and those of Vito and McGaha, Whitehead cautioned against using the Rand study as an affirmation of the failure of probation.

Attempts to replicate the Rand study in other jurisdictions failed to produce the high recidivism rates found in California. Most of the studies were limited to data collected from a single state. In 1992, results were published from a study of probation across 17 states. Patrick Langan and Mark Cunniff (1986) examined recidivism rates for 79,000 felony probationers. Within three years of being sentenced to probation, 62 percent of the sample had either been rearrested for another felony or appeared at a disciplinary hearing for violating probation conditions. Forty-six percent had been reincarcerated or failed to appear in court. Langan and Cunniff also found that 21 percent of those sentenced to probation had not been recommended by the probation department as suitable candidates and were more likely to fail compared to those who had been recommended. In another multi-state study of felony probation, W. Reed Benedict and Lin Huff-Corzine (1997) examined recidivism rates for a sample of male offenders sentenced to probation for property crimes. Sixty-seven percent of the offenders successfully completed their probationary terms (compared to the 65% that failed in California). Recidivism measures were examined separately for whites, blacks, and Hispanics. Whites had the lowest rate of recidivism (25%), followed by blacks (35.8%) and Hispanics (39.8%). Prior drug use was related to rates for whites and Hispanics, but not blacks.

In their study, Rand researchers explored the relationship between several legal and extralegal factors to determine which were related to probationer recidivism. Subsequent research has identified additional offense and offender characteristics that are associated with the likelihood of success or failure for probationers. Kathryn Morgan (1994) examined probation outcomes for 266 male and female felons in Tennessee. She found gender, marital status, education, employment, income, and prior record were all related to probation outcome. Females were more likely to succeed than males. In addition, offenders who were married, employed making at least minimum wage, had fewer prior convictions and institutional commitments were more likely to succeed. She also found that the amount of time on probation influenced the likelihood of success. Felons with longer sentences (more than five years) were less likely to succeed. Morgan included all of the significant relationships in a *multivariate analysis* to determine the "best predictors of probation outcome." Multivariate analysis is a statistical technique used to examine the simultaneous influence of several factors (variables) on a *dependent* variable. Gender, martial status, employment, prior record, and conviction offense were the strongest predictors of recidivism. Probationers who were female, married, employed, had fewer prior felony commitments, and were convicted of either a violent or public disorder crime were more likely to succeed. Barbara Sims and Mark Jones (1997) studied probation outcomes for 2,850 offenders in North Carolina and found relationships consistent with Morgan.

Important changes occurred after the Rand study was published. California and other states began increasing the use of probation for felony offenders in response to rising crime rates and overcrowded prisons. The courts lacked alternative forms of community sanctions that would provide greater public protection. One of the recommendations made in the Rand report was for states to develop alternatives that would allow offenders to remain in the community but under closer court supervision. At the time the report was published, a handful of states had already implemented ISP programs. ISP offered a means of protecting the community by increasing the level of supervision over an offender. There is wide variation in how these programs are administered across the country, but the typical program includes more frequent reporting requirements and more restrictive curfews compared to regular probation. Greater surveillance is achieved from reduced caseloads of probation officers. These programs became so popular that by 1990, ISPs were "hailed by many as the 'new wave' in corrections" (Petersilia and Turner 1990). Early evaluations of ISP showed great promise with recidivism rates less than 10 percent (Petersilia and Turner 1990). Probationers on ISP were reported to have more technical violations but this could have been a consequence of the increased monitoring (they were just more likely to get caught). Other evaluations of ISP have found recidivism rates to be comparable between ISP and regular probation (Petersilia and Turner 1993). Despite the mixed findings on the effectiveness of ISP, it remains a viable sentencing option for the courts. Furthermore, courts are no longer restricted in their sentencing decisions either. Other options include house arrest, electronic monitoring, and day reporting centers. These alternatives offer more protection and control compared to regular probation but with the benefits of allowing offenders to remain in the community. Probation departments today also utilize Community Classification Systems to more accurately determine the appropriate level of supervision for their clients. These systems provide an assessment of probationers' risks and needs.

References

Benedict, W., and L. Huff-Corzine (1997). "Return to the Scene of the Punishment: Recidivism of Adult Male Property Offenders on Felony Probation, 1986–1989." *Journal of Research in Crime and Delinquency* 34:237–52.

Clear, T. (1994). *Harm in American Penology: Offenders, Victims, and Their Communities.* Albany: SUNY Press.

Conrad, J. (1985). "Research and Development in Corrections." *Federal Probation* 49:69–71.

Geerken, M., and H. Hayes (1993). "Probation and Parole: Public Risk and the Future of Incarceration Alternatives." *Criminology* 31:549–64.

Glaze, L., and T. Bonczar (2006). *Probation and Parole in the United States, 2005.* Washington, DC: Bureau of Justice Statistics.

Gray, M., M. Fields, and S. Maxell (2001). "Examining Probation Violations: Who, What, and When." *Crime and Delinquency* 47:537–57.

Langan, P., and M. Cunniff (1992). *Recidivism of Felons on Probation 1986–1989.* Washington, DC: Bureau of Justice Statistics.

McGaha, J., M. Fichter, and P. Hirschburg (1987). "Felony Probation: A Re-Examination of Public Risk." *American Journal of Criminal Justice* 1:1–9.

Morgan, K. (1994). "Factors Associated with Probation Outcome." *Journal of Criminal Justice* 22:341–53.

Petersilia, J. (1985). "Probation and Felony Offenders." *Federal Probation* 49:4–9.

Petersilia, J., and S. Turner (1993). *Evaluating Intensive Supervision Probation/Parole: Results of a Nationwide Experiment.* Washington, DC: National Institute of Justice.

Petersilia, J., S. Turner, J. Kahan, and J. Peterson (1985). *Granting Felons Probation: Public Risks and Alternatives.* Santa Monica, CA: Rand.

Petersilia, J., S. Turner, J. Kahan, and J. Peterson (1985). "Granting Felons Probation: Public Risks and Alternatives." *Crime and Delinquency* 31:379–92.

Petersilia, J., S. Turner, and J. Peterson (1986). *Prison versus Probation in California: Implications for Crime and Offender Recidivism.* Santa Monica, CA: Rand.

Sims, B., and M. Jones (1997). "Predicting Success or Failure on Probation: Factors Associated with Felony Probation Outcomes." *Crime and Delinquency* 43:214–327.

Vito, G. (1986). "Felony Probation and Recidivism: Replication and Response." *Federal Probation* 50:17–25.

Whitehead, J. (1991). "The Effectiveness of Felony Probation: Results from an Eastern State." *Justice Quarterly* 8:525–43.

Further Reading

Clear, T., and A. Braga (1995). "Community Corrections." In *Crime: Twenty-Eight Leading Experts Look at the Most Pressing Problem of our Time,* edited by J. Wilson and J. Petersilia, 421–44. San Francisco: Institute for Contemporary Studies.

Clear, T., P. Harris, and S. Baird (1992). "Probationer Violations and Officer Response." *Journal of Criminal Justice* 20:1–12.

Crouch, B. (1993). "Is Incarceration Really Worse? Analysis of Offenders' Preferences for Prisons over Probation." *Justice Quarterly* 10:67–88.

Dressler, D. (1962). *Practice and Theory of Probation and Parole.* New York: Columbia UP.

Harris, P. (1994). "Client Management Classification and Prediction of Probation Outcome." *Crime and Delinquency* 40:154–74.

Klein, A. (1997). *Alternative Sentencing, Intermediate Sanctions, and Probation.* Cincinnati: Anderson.

Langan, P. (1994). "Between Prison and Probation: Intermediate Sanctions." *Science* 264:791–93.

Maltz, M. (1984). *Recidivism.* Orlando, FL: Academic Press.

Petersilia, J. (1997). "Probation in the United States." In *Crime and Justice: A Review of Research*, vol. 22, edited by Michael Tonry. Chicago: University of Chicago Press.

Taxman, F., and R. Cherkos (1995). "Intermediate Sanctions: Dealing with Technical Violators." *Corrections Today* 57:46–57.

Tonry, M., and M. Lynch (1996). "Intermediate Sanctions." In *Crime and Justice: A Review of Research*, vol. 20, edited by Michael Tonry. Chicago: University of Chicago Press.

PAROLE

Parole is the conditional release of inmates from prison prior to the expiration of their term of imprisonment. The practice of allowing inmates to be released early from prison can be traced back to 1840, when Alexander Maconochie developed a "mark system" while he was superintendent of a British penal colony on Norfolk Island. Under the mark system, offenders received an indeterminate, or open-ended, prison sentence. Inmates earned marks, or credits, for demonstrating self-discipline and hard work. The marks allowed inmates to progress through four progressive stages of imprisonment, with inmates enjoying greater freedom in each successive stage. Inmates who reached the last stage were issued "tickets of leave" wherein they were released into the community. The concept gained the attention of Sir Walter Crofton, who became the director of the Irish prison system in 1854. Crofton implemented a similar system of graduated release. Under Crofton's system, however, offenders continued to be supervised in the community. Offenders were required to regularly report to an employee of the prison system who also visited their homes and helped offenders find employment. Offenders who failed to abide by the conditions of their release had their ticket of leave revoked and returned to prison. In 1870, Zebulon Brockway introduced all of these practices (the indeterminate sentence, mark system, and supervised release) at the American Prison Association's first meeting in Cincinnati, Ohio. Prison administrators from all over the United States embraced the ideas, and by 1900 several states had implemented the indeterminate sentence and supervised early release. Indeterminate sentencing was consistent with the correctional goal of reformation because offenders had different needs. The decision of when an offender was "reformed" was left up to prison officials who were in a position to witness a change in attitudes and behaviors. The ability of an inmate to earn early release provided the motivation for change. Supervised release allowed the prison to continue its control over the offenders, while the threat of having to return to prison offered incentive to stay out of trouble. New York was the first state in 1930 to establish a parole board. The parole board was a separate entity responsible for deciding if and when inmates should be released early. All states had implemented indeterminate sentencing and parole by 1944.

PAROLE PREDICTION: IS IT POSSIBLE TO PREDICT WHO WILL SUCCEED OR FAIL ON PAROLE?

Burgess, E. (1928). "Factors Determining Success or Failure on Parole." In *The Workings of the Indeterminate-Sentence Law and the Parole System in Illinois*, edited by A. Bruce, E. Burgess, and A. Harno, 205–49. Springfield: Illinois Board of Parole.

Background

The state of Illinois was among the first to pass legislation authorizing the use of parole in the late 1800s. The intent of the law was: ". . . to make good citizens out of felons . . ." (Bruce et al. 1928). The state also incorporated indeterminate sentencing into its penal code for all crimes except treason, murder, manslaughter, and rape (Bruce 1928). Originally, the Board of Prison Management was responsible for all parole decisions. In 1917, a new board called the Board of Pardons and Paroles was created under the Department of Public Welfare and then in 1927, a separate parole board was established. This board consisted of a supervisor of parolees and nine members. The governor appointed members to the board. Parole decisions were to be made by the newly established parole board, while responsibility for supervision remained with the Department of Public Welfare. The state was experiencing increases in its prison population and faced with the choice of funding the operation of parole or constructing new prison facilities, the legislature allocated close to one and half million dollars in 1927 for parole (Bruce 1928). Parole was not only considered to be beneficial to the offenders, it also seen as a cost effective way to supervise them.

The Illinois Parole Board was given authority over inmate release decisions. Members were divided into three subcommittees that rotated between three state prison facilities: Joliet, Menard, and Pontiac. Inmates became eligible for parole after serving their minimum sentence. The subcommittees reported to the general board once a month with recommendations for release. The board was afforded a tremendous amount of discretion over release decisions. The criteria used by the board in their decision-making included the severity of the crime the inmate was incarcerated for, prior record, behavior while in prison, whether or not the inmate had been sufficiently punished, the likelihood of the inmate committing any more crimes upon release, and any other relevant information (including information provided by the public, the inmate's family, etc.). According to the board's procedures,

> Before a prisoner will be paroled, his mental condition and institutional record
> must be satisfactory and the Board must be satisfied that he is desirous of leading
> a better life, and that society will not be injured by his release. (Harno 1927)

Six of the ten members had to approve the release before such could be granted. All decisions by the board were final (Harno 1927).

In 1926, the chairman of the Illinois Parole Board, Hinton Clabaugh, commissioned a study of the state's indeterminate sentence law and parole system. To avoid any appearance of conflict of interest, outside researchers from three Illinois Universities were solicited to conduct the study that took two years to complete. The objective of the study was to determine whether or not indeterminate sentencing and parole should be retained or abolished within the State. The final research report known as *The Workings of the Indeterminate-Sentence Law and the Parole System in Illinois* was submitted to Chairman Clabaugh on August 16, 1928. As part of the comprehensive study, Ernest Burgess, a sociology professor from the University of Chicago, was charged with the task of examining the institutional and criminal records of a sample of males recently paroled from prison in order to determine the factors that influenced parole success or failure. The extent to which parole was deemed a "success" or "failure" depended upon the recidivism rates of offenders released on parole. Members of the Illinois Parole Board (as well as parole boards around the country) had been using their professional judgment in deciding who were good risks for parole release. The accuracy of their subjective decisions was not known. Burgess wanted to create an objective prediction scale that would provide a more efficient and precise assessment of an offender's risk to the community.

Burgess was not the first to attempt this type of research on parole outcomes. In 1923 Sam Warner published findings from his study of parole in Massachusetts. He analyzed data on 600 offenders released on parole and another 80 offenders who were released after serving their entire sentences. Warner gathered 64 pieces of information about each offender from their parole records and correlated each with parole success or failure. Based on his assessment of the 64 items, he concluded that the only real difference between the parole violators and non-violators was the subjective assessment of the offenders by the board's physician. According to Hornell Hart (1923), Warner's conclusion was in error. Hart applied a statistical method that had not previously been used in social science research. Based on his analysis, 35 of the items examined by Warner maintained *statistically significant* (meaning the differences were not likely due to chance) relationships with parole outcome. While Burgess was not the first to look for relationships between offender characteristics and parole outcomes, he was the first to propose a prediction table to be used by parole boards to improve their decision-making.

The Study

Data for the study came from the Illinois Parole Board who granted full access to their files. Burgess examined the parole records of 3,000 male inmates paroled from three prisons in Illinois: the Illinois State Penitentiary at Joliet, the Southern Illinois Penitentiary at Menard, and the Illinois State Reformatory at Pontiac. The sample consisted of 1,000 male inmates from each prison. Burgess selected the sample by choosing inmates that had been paroled prior to January 1, 1925. All of the inmates had been released from their institution a minimum of two-and-a-half and a maximum of five years prior to the start of the study. Most of the offenders remained on parole for one year after their release so the majority of the offenders in sample had expired parole terms.

Findings

One objective of the study was to determine how many offenders succeeded and failed on parole. If an offender became a law-abiding citizen (evidenced by no new criminal offenses or parole violations) and a productive member of society (evidenced by his gainful employment), he was labeled a "success." All others were considered parole failures. There was little variation across the three prisons in the percentages of successes and failures. Nearly three-fourths (74.3%) succeeded and 25.7 violated their parole. It was estimated that an additional 10 percent of the non-violators actually committed a new criminal offense *after* their parole had expired. At the time of the report, Illinois had increased the length of parole supervision to five years. Such an increase appeared to be warranted based on the additional 10 percent failures. According to Burgess, the more accurate percentage of failure was 35 percent. Almost 11 percent of the parole violators were returned to prison for violating a condition of parole. A slightly higher percentage (14.7%) returned for committing a new criminal offense. The largest proportion of offenders who violated their parole did so within the first month of release.

The second objective was to find out what factors influenced the likelihood of parole success or failure. It was the opinion of members of the parole board that there were individual characteristics associated with parole outcomes but there was no empirical research verifying such. To help address the research void, Burgess compiled a list of 22 factors found in the offenders' parole records. The 22 factors and their relationship with parole outcomes are presented below.

1. *Current offense.* Offenders who were convicted of personal crimes generally had a lower percentage of violations compared to property offenders. Murderers and sex offenders had the lowest percentage, while offenders convicted of fraud, forgery, or burglary had the highest. Burgess attributed this finding to the possibility that offenders who committed violent crimes may have been more amenable to rehabilitation or may have been supervised more closely in the community.

2. *Number of associates involved in the crime.* A large number of offenders were convicted along with another offender(s). Offenders with three or more associates in crime had lower percentages of failure compared to offenders without associates.

3. *Race/ethnicity.* The race or ethnicity of an offender was ascertained by looking at the listed race or nationality of their father. Over half of the offenders were born to native white fathers. Nearly 20 percent were black and the rest were divided among other ethnic groups. Irish, British, and German natives had the highest rate of violations.

4. *Parental status.* Only a small percentage of offenders came from two parent households and these offenders had lower than average parole violations.

5. *Marital status.* Nearly 60 percent of the offenders were single at the time of the conviction. Single offenders from Menard and Joliet had above average parole violations. At Pontiac this group had lower percentages than the married offenders.

6. *Offender type.* Burgess used the information contained in each of the offenders' records and parole reports and created a typology of the paroled men that consisted of four categories. *First offenders* had no prior criminal record (although a few of the inmates put into this category had committed one or two minor offenses). Most of the offenders paroled from the three institutions were first offenders (55.8%). This group had the lowest percentages of parole violations. *Occasional offenders* were those who had committed several crimes in a short period of time. These offenders did not appear to be dedicated to a life of crime. Approximately one-third of the paroled offenders fit into this category (31.3%). This group also had low percentages of violations. First and occasional offenders were also more likely to commit technical violations as opposed to new criminal offenses. Eleven percent were *habitual offenders.* This group had a more continuous involvement in crime. Crime was a way of life for the *professional offenders.* These offenders supported themselves primarily through illegal activity and tended to specialize in their offending. Only a small percentage of those paroled were considered to be professional offenders (1.5%). Both the habitual and professional offenders had higher than average parole violations (five times higher than the first and occasional offenders) and were more likely to commit a new criminal offense.

7. *Social type.* Burgess tried to establish a social type for offenders based on the information contained in their parole records. Seven types emerged: the "hobo," the "ne'er-do-well," the "mean citizen," the "drunkard," the "gangster," "recent immigrant," "farm boy," and "drug addict." Farm boys and recent immigrants had the lowest percentages of violations while drug addicts, hobos, and ne'er-do-wells had higher than average percentages of violations.

8. *County of residence.* Burgess found no relationship between the offenders' county of residence and their parole outcome.

9. *Place of residence.* Burgess examined parole violations for offenders who had resided in stable residential communities or in neighborhoods with high crime rates and transient populations. Parole violators were more likely to come from crime ridden areas with transient populations.

10. *Community size.* Burgess did not uncover any significant differences in violations based on the size of an offender's community except that offenders residing on farms had the lowest percentages of violations.

11. *Residential status.* Approximately one-fourth of the offenders lacked a permanent residence at the time of their crime. This group was more likely to fail compared to offenders with stable residents.

12. *Recommendations by trial judge or prosecutor.* In most cases the judge or prosecutor presented information to the parole board with no recommendation as to whether the offender should be released. Offenders who had been released despite a negative recommendation had higher percentages of violations compared to those with recommendations of leniency.

13. *Whether or not sentence was the result of a negotiated plea.* Offenders sentenced as part of a negotiated plea had similar percentages of violations as those convicted of the original offense.

14. *Type and length of sentence.* Offenders convicted of treason, murder, rape, and kidnapping received a flat or fixed sentence under the law. All other offenders were sentenced to an indeterminate period of incarceration. Offenders sentenced to a flat period along with those who received a long indeterminate sentence (i.e., 3–20 years and one year to life) had lower percentages of violations.

15. *Amount of time served prior to being released on parole.* Offenders who were incarcerated for longer sentences were more likely to violate their parole. This finding was consistent with the high number of habitual and professional criminals who spent more time in prison compared to the first and occasional offenders.

16. *Prior record.* Offenders with no prior criminal record had the lowest percentages of parole violations compared to offenders with prior convictions and institutional commitments.

17. *Prior work history.* Offenders who were regularly employed at the time of their arrest had the lowest rates of violations, whereas offenders with no work history or even sporadic histories had rates much higher.

18. *Institutional conduct.* Offenders with a record of institutional misconduct had an above-average rate of parole violations compared to those with no record. It appeared as if the offenders most likely to violate their parole were the same as those who refused to follow the rules in prison.

19. *Age upon release.* The average age of inmates released from Joliet was 34.7 years, 33.9 years from Menard, and 21.6 years from Pontiac, however, across the entire sample the age range was 17–86 years. Burgess divided the offenders into age groups and found that the youngest and the oldest inmates had the lowest percentages of violations. Inmates between the ages of 25 and 29 had the highest percentages of violations.

20. *Intelligence.* Offenders were administered an intelligence test by Illinois State Criminologist, Herman Adler. This information was included in the offenders' parole reports. Adler had previously shown that low intelligence was *not* a major cause of crime. Offenders with low intelligence were more likely to succeed on parole compared to those with average or superior intelligence.

21. *Personality type.* Also included in the offenders' parole reports were results from a personality assessment that diagnosed certain offenders as "egocentric," "socially inadequate," or "emotionally unstable." Burgess found that the egocentric offenders had higher percentages of violations compared to the other diagnoses.

22. *Psychiatric prognosis.* Based on results from an offenders' personality assessment, the psychiatrist made a prognosis that was either "favorable," "doubtful," or "unfavorable" as to the offenders' likelihood of success or failure on parole. The prognosis found in the offenders' parole records from Pontiac and Joliet proved to be reliable indicators. The same was not true for offenders from Menard. Menard employed the services of a part-time psychiatrist and Burgess speculated that he might not have been able to conduct a thorough evaluation of each offender.

Recommendations

Based on his analysis of the 22 factors pulled from an offenders' parole report, Burgess proposed an assessment instrument that would include the 21 factors (all but county of residence) found to be related to parole violations. Members of the parole board could complete the instrument for each offender who became eligible for parole to determine their likelihood of success or failure. Offenders received one point for every favorable item (i.e., if an offender was employed at the time of their arrest they received one point). Burgess then created a prediction table where he calculated expectancy rates of parole violation for the sample of offenders from Joliet. Offenders that received more favorable items were predicted to succeed on parole. For example, 98.5 percent of the offenders with at least 16 favorable items or points had no parole violations. Parole boards could "expect" an offender with a minimum score of 16 to succeed. Seventy-six percent of offenders with four or less favorable items were parole violators. Parole boards could "expect" an offender with a score less than five to fail.

FIGURE 3.4 Expectancy Rates of Parole Violation and Non-Violation[*]

Points for Number of Factors Above the Average	Number of Men in Each Group	Expectancy Rate for Success or Failure			Percent Non-Violators of Parole
		Percent Violators of Parole			
		Minor	Major	Total	
16–21	68	1.5	—	1.5	98.5
14–15	140	.7	1.5	2.2	97.8
13	91	5.5	3.3	8.8	91.2
12	106	7.0	8.1	15.1	84.9
11	110	13.6	9.1	22.7	77.3
10	88	19.3	14.8	34.1	65.9
7–9	287	15.0	28.9	43.9	56.1
5–6	85	23.4	43.7	67.1	32.9
2–4	25	12.0	64.0	76.0	24.0

[*]E. W. Burgess, *Factors Determining Success or Failure on Parole*, in A. A. Bruce, A. J. Harno, E. W. Burgess, and John Landesco, The Workings of the Indeterminate-Sentence-Law and the Parole System in Illinois. Springfield (1928), p. 248.

Burgess also suggested his parole prediction table be used in determining appropriate supervision levels for offenders on parole. Offenders with fewer points should be monitored more closely than those with more points.

Criticisms

Burgess created an objective risk assessment instrument that offered the Illinois Parole Board a more efficient way of making release decisions. Few could disagree with the simplicity of such a system over the traditional subjective method of prediction. Points were assigned to offenders meeting certain criteria, and the points were then totaled into a score that indicated whether or not the offender should be released. One important question remained. Would Burgess' system offer an accurate assessment of risk? The ability to accurately predict which offenders would succeed or fail on parole depended on the *reliability* of the prediction instrument. A reliable instrument will yield the same predictions in repeated applications. Burgess performed no reliability checks on his prediction table. Clark Tibbitts (1931a) tested the reliability of the factors used in Burgess's prediction tables. He applied his outcome criteria to a group of 907 youths released on parole in the summer of 1927 and then again in 1928 to determine if their predicted likelihood of success or failure would be the same. This reliability assessment technique is known as the *test-retest* procedure. Several factors proved highly reliable: type of sentence, type of offense, age at time of parole, race/ethnicity, acceptance of a lesser plea, and length of time served. This was not surprising because these items were primarily objective with little or no room for interpretation. Seven items, however, were found to be unreliable: statement by the prosecuting attorney, personality type, offender type, size of residential area, residential mobility, associates in crime, and mental assessment. These items were more subjective in that they required a certain amount of interpretation on the part of the person completing the form. In addition, Burgess created his prediction table using factors that were related to parole outcome for a particular population of offenders. Burgess made no effort to test his instrument on offenders in different parts of the country.

Burgess' was also criticized for relying on official data obtained from the offenders' parole records (Vold 1931). Some of the information may have been inaccurate. For example, institutional conduct was based on the offenders' punishment records while incarcerated. Guards may have biased against particular inmates and overestimated the number of times they had been in trouble. As is often the case when researchers examine *existing data*, Burgess encountered missing information. For example, information on parental status was missing from a large number of cases. The data on offender residence did not permit Burgess to determine the type of neighborhood that an offender lived in prior to his arrest. He appropriately acknowledged when this occurred but it remained unclear whether the missing data influenced his results.

Burgess used an extensive list of factors in creating his prediction tables. In his scoring, each item was treated equally. In other words, the *strength* of the relationship for each factor was assumed to be same. This method could have been problematic in that it failed to take into account the likelihood that not all of the factors maintained *strong relationships* with parole outcome (Glueck and Glueck 1930, Kirby 1954). Under Burgess' system, an offender could be predicted a bad risk for not having enough total points. The offender may do well on parole if the points he received were derived from factors that had strong relationships with parole outcome. Some psychologists criticized Burgess' parole prediction instrument for relying primarily on objective criteria. Burgess had included a psychological assessment of the offenders' personality type, but the measure was somewhat limited in that it only differentiated between three personality types. In a study of 221 delinquents paroled from the New York State Training School for boys, researchers created a prediction scale that included 28 psychological traits such as apathy, defiance to authority, aggressive tendencies, and lack of remorse (Jenkins et al. 1942). There were observed differences between the youth who succeeded and failed on parole, but researchers failed to demonstrate that the inclusion of psychological criteria improved parole decision-making.

Significance and Subsequent Research

Burgess' efforts to develop a prediction table to improve parole decision-making made him a pioneer in the field of risk assessment. Over the next several decades, researchers worked on refining the system proposed by Burgess. Attempts were made to create instruments that were more efficient, reliable, and accurate. Around the same time Burgess was conducting his study, Sheldon and Eleanor Glueck (1930) began examining parole outcomes for a group of 510 offenders released from the Massachusetts Reformatory in 1921 and 1922. Data came from the offenders' parole records, as well as from interviews with their parole officers, and interviews with the parolees (to address the problems associated with official reports). Forty-three percent of the offenders had their parole revoked for either a technical violation or new criminal offense. Consistent with Burgess, they found that most violations occurred within the first few months of release. The Gluecks analyzed over 50 pieces of information on each offender to determine which factors were related to parole success or failure and identified 13 factors to be related to parole outcome. The factors were categorized as "pre-reformatory" (factors included type of crime, prior arrests, prior incarceration, work habits, economic responsibility and mental condition), "reformatory" (conduct while incarcerated), "parole" (conduct on parole) and "post-parole" (factors included work habits, family relationship, economic responsibility, type of home, and use of leisure time). In creating their prediction tables, the Gluecks "weighted" their factors according to how well each was able to distinguish between violators and non-violators. Their system included factors that were either "favorable" or "unfavorable" indicators of parole outcome. Offenders received one point for each favorable item but points were deducted for unfavorable items. Whether or not their method was superior to that used by Burgess was questionable. George Vold (1931) analyzed parole outcomes for offenders from two Minnesota prisons and compared the weighting procedure used by the Gluecks with Burgess' method and found little difference in results. Over the next 20 years, parole prediction benefited from advances in statistical techniques that allowed researchers to develop more efficient and accurate instruments. Bernard Kirby (1954) found a 10 percent improvement in accuracy when he applied a more sophisticated weighting procedure (compared to that used by Vold) to his prediction table.

Three years after Burgess put forth his parole prediction scale; Clark Tibbits (1931b) published findings from a similar study of parole in Illinois. Tibbitts examined parole records of 3,000 youths released from the Illinois State Reformatory at Pontiac on or before July 1, 1925. Consistent with Burgess, 24.7 percent of the offenders failed to successfully complete their parole due to a technical violation or a new criminal offense. In addition to the factors examined by Burgess, Tibbitts included the following four items: alcohol use, type of community the offender returned upon release, last work assignment while incarcerated, and first job obtained on parole. Information on alcohol use was found to be unreliable so it was dropped from the analysis. Offender marital status (one of Burgess' original factors) was also dropped because there were no observed differences between violators and non-violators. Tibbitts also classified the factors as either "favorable" or "unfavorable" to parole outcome. He then applied a statistical technique to determine if the differences between parole violators and non-violators were significant. Tibbitts eliminated items that were not *statistically significant* (meaning the relationships were due to chance). He did so by examining the offender violation rates for each factor and removing those factors that did not differ by more than five percentage points from the group violation rate. Twenty-two factors remained significant. The only factor eliminated was whether the offender was working at the time of their arrest. Tibbitts also calculated expectancy rates and found that offenders with 12 or more favorable items and no unfavorable items were expected to succeed 100 percent of time. Offenders with no favorable items and nine unfavorable items were the least likely to succeed (only 45% were expected to succeed).

The Illinois Parole Board began using parole prediction in 1933. Research on parole prediction continued after its implementation. Lloyd Ohlin, a research sociologist with the Illinois Division of Correction, conducted a large-scale study of parole outcomes. Ohlin (1951) collected information on several thousand offenders paroled from Joliet-Stateville and Menard prisons from 1925 to 1945. Ohlin examined 27 factors that were being used to predict parole outcomes. He then performed statistical tests of each factor and found only 12 were significant and reliable predictors.[1] Among those factors excluded were age, prior record, amount of time served, punishment record in prison and alcohol use. Ohlin created a new "experience table" that consisted of the predicted likelihood of an offender violating their parole. Like Tibbitts, Ohin included factors that were "favorable" or "unfavorable" to parole outcomes. Three percent of the offenders with five to ten favorable points had violated their parole while 75 percent of those with five or six unfavorable points were violators. Ohlin's research showed that more is not always better in terms of prediction. His 12 factors were just as accurate as the 21 factors used by Burgess. Ohlin further demonstrated the need to revise the experience tables on an annual basis. As institutions changed their parole preparation procedures for inmates and parole agencies altered their policies, the expected rates of violation changed as well.

Parole prediction instruments are valid only to the extent that the factors included are strong predictors of parole outcome. Other researchers have attempted to establish the *validity* of Burgess' prediction table. Burgess himself compared the expected violation rates to the actual rates for 2,701 offenders. The actual violation rates were significantly

---

[1] The twelve predictors were: type of offense, type of sentence, type of offender, home status, family interest, social type, work record, community, parole job, number of associates, personality rating, and psychiatric prognosis.

lower than what was predicted. He attributed this finding to a high proportion of "better risks" offenders released on parole. Michael Hakeem (1948) applied Burgess' prediction table to a sample of 1,108 male offenders released on parole. He found less than a 5 percent difference between the expected rates of violations to the offenders' actual rate of violations.

Efforts to improve parole prediction continued into the 1950s. Research up to this point focused on refining the procedures used to create prediction tables. Other scholars became interested in identifying additional factors to predict parole outcome. Daniel Glaser (1954) wanted to create a list of factors that would remain stable predictors from one time period to the next. Unlike his predecessors who relied on information that was readily available, Glaser allowed a theory of crime causation to guide his selection of factors. Offenders were scored on seven items derived from "differential identification" theory. Glaser's instrument proved more accurate than Ohlin's 12-item scale.

Despite numerous attempts to improve the efficiency and accuracy of parole prediction, its use did not become widespread until the 1970s. A significant advancement in this area occurred in 1966 when the National Council on Crime and Delinquency implemented the Uniform Parole Reports Program. The parole boards in several states worked together to develop common procedures for collecting parole data (Glaser 1987). The program was expanded to include data from all 50 states and the federal parole system. A second major advancement took place in the early 1970s when Don Gottfredson and Leslie Wilkens developed a new predictive device for the US Parole Commission. The objective risk assessment instrument was called the "salient factor score." Offenders were scored on seven items where a higher score predicted a favorable parole outcome. The items included number of prior convictions, number of prior institutional commitments, age of first institutional commitment, commitment offense, prior parole revocations, history of drug dependency, and employment stability. These items were consistent with a change in correctional philosophy away from rehabilitation to a "just desserts" model (Hoffman 1983). In 1981 the instrument was revised and employment stability was dropped. Peter Hoffman and James Beck (1985) demonstrated the accuracy of the revised SFS using a sample of over 1,800 offenders released from federal prison. Only 9 percent of the sample that scored eight to ten points committed a serious crime compared to 40 percent of those with scores of 0–3. Other risk assessment instruments emerged in the 1980s and their use was expanded beyond parole prediction. The Wisconsin Risk Assessment System and the Level of Supervision Inventory-Revised are examples of two instruments that are still used today in the criminal justice system. Risk assessment is used to make bail decisions, to determine appropriate levels of supervision for probationers, and in making housing assignments within correctional institutions. Despite the advances made in our ability to predict risk, there is still debate over whether or not objective instruments outperform the subjective determinations made by trained clinicians. A recent meta-analysis[2] performed on over 100 studies comparing accuracy rates of objective and subjective assessment methods addressed this issue. Researchers found that objective methods were, on average, 10 percent more accurate than subjective predictions (Grove et al. 2000).

---

[2] For a description of this statistical technique refer to Martinson's study presented earlier in this section.

References

Bruce, A., E. Burgess, and A. Harno (1928). *The Workings of the Indeterminate-Sentence Law and the Parole System in Illinois.* Springfield: Illinois Board of Parole.

Bruce, A. (1928). "The History and Development of the Parole System in Illinois." In *The Workings of the Indeterminate-Sentence Law and the Parole System in Illinois,* edited by A. Bruce, E. Burgess, and A. Harno, 3–63. Springfield: Illinois Board of Parole.

Burgess, E. (1928). "Factors Determining Success or Failure on Parole." In *The Workings of the Indeterminate-Sentence Law and the Parole System in Illinois,* edited by A. Bruce, E. Burgess, and A. Harno, 205–49. Springfield: Illinois Board of Parole.

Glaser, D. (1954). "A Reconsideration of Some Parole Prediction Factors." *American Sociological Review* 19:335–41.

Glaser, D. (1987). "Classification for Risk." In *Prediction and Classification: Criminal Justice Decision Making Crime and Justice a Review of the Research,* vol. 9, edited by D. Gottfredson and M. Tonry, 249–91.

Glueck, S., and E. Glueck (1930). *500 Criminal Careers.* New York: Knopf.

Grove, W., D. Zald, B. Lebow, B. Snitz, and C. Nelson (2000). "Clinical Versus Mechanical Prediction: A Meta-Analysis." *Psychological Assessment* 12:19–30.

Hakeem, M. (1948). "The Validity of the Burgess Method of Parole Prediction." *The American Journal of Sociology* 53:376–86.

Harno, A. (1928). "The Workings of the Parole Board and Its Relation to the Court." In *The Workings of the Indeterminate-Sentence Law and the Parole System in*

Illinois, edited by A. Bruce, E. Burgess, and A. Harno, 67–120. Springfield: Illinois Board of Parole.

Hart, H. (1923). "Predicting Parole Success." *Journal of Criminal Law and Criminology* 14:405–14.

Hoffman, P. (1983). "Screening for Risk: A Revised Salient Factor Score (SFS 81)." *Journal of Criminal Justice* 11: 539–47.

Hoffman, P., and J. Beck (1985). "Recidivism Among Released Federal Prisoners: Salient Factor Score and Five-Year Follow-Up." *Criminal Justice and Behavior* 12:501–07.

Jenkins, R., H. Hart, P. Sperling, and S. Axelrad (1942). "Prediction of Parole Success: Inclusion of Psychiatric Criteria." *Journal of Criminal Law and Criminology* 33:38–46.

Kirby, B. (1954). "Parole Prediction Using Multiple Correlation." *The American Journal of Sociology* 59:539–50.

Ohlin, L. (1951). *Selection for Parole: A Manual for Parole Prediction.* New York: Russell Sage.

Tibbits, C. (1931a). "Reliability of Factors Used in Predicting Success or Failure in Parole." *Journal of Criminal Law and Criminology* 22:844–53.

Tibbits, C. (1931b). "Success or Failure on Parole Can Be Predicted." *Journal of Criminal Law and Criminology* 22:11–50.

Vold, G. (1931). *Prediction Methods and Parole.* Hanover, New Hampshire: Sociological Press.

Warner, S. (1923). "Factors Determining Parole From the Massachusetts Reformatory." *Journal of Criminal Law and Criminology* 14:172–207.

Further Reading

Allen, R. (1942). "A Review of Parole Prediction Literature." *Journal of Criminal Law and Criminology* 32:548–54.

Andrews, D. (1982). *The Level of Supervision Inventory (LSI): The First Follow-Up.* Toronto: Ontario Ministry of Correctional Services.

Baird, C., R. Heinz, and B. Bemus (1979). *The Wisconsin Case Classification/Staff Deployment Project.* Project Report No. 14. Madison, WI: Department of Health and Social Services, Division of Corrections.

Berecochea, J., A. Himelson, and D. Miller (1972). "The Risk of Failure During the Early Parole Period: A Methodological Note." *Journal of Criminal Law, Criminology, and Police Science* 63:93–96.

Heilbrun, A., I. Knopf, and P. Bruner (1976). "Criminal Impulsivity and Violence and Subsequent Parole Outcome." *British Journal of Criminology* 16:367–77.

Hoffman, P., and J. Beck (1985). "Recidivism Among Released Federal Prisoners: Salient Factor Score and Five-Year Follow-Up." *Criminal Justice and Behavior* 12:501–07.

Lanne, W. (1935). "Parole Prediction as Science." *Journal of Criminal Law and Criminology* 26:377–400.

Meehl, P. (1954). *Clinical vs. Statistical Prediction: A Theoretical Analysis and a Review of the Evidence.* Minneapolis: University of Minnesota Press.

Monachesi, E. (1941). "An Evaluation of Recent Major Efforts at Prediction." *American Sociological Review* 6:478–86.

Schuessler, K. (1954). "Parole Prediction: Its History and Status." *Journal of Criminal Law, Criminology and Police Science* 45:425–31.

van Alstyne, D. (1978). "A Multidimensional Contingency Table Analysis of Parole Outcome: New Methods and Old Problems in Criminological Prediction." *Journal of Research in Crime and Delinquency* 15:172–93.

3

Inmate Subcultures

Prisons were originally established in this country as a means of providing criminals the opportunity to repent and become law-abiding members of society. Prison administrators and reformers focused their attention on the institution itself as a means of reforming criminals, rather than on the inmate social networks that might influence efforts to change inmate behaviors and attitudes. Criminals are isolated from free society upon their incarceration, but become integrated into an inmate social system commonly referred to as an *inmate subculture*. Two competing perspectives have been put forth to explain the existence of inmate subcultures. The first is known as the *deprivation* model. Inmates become part of a subculture as a means of adapting to the deprivations of prison. The second perspective is called the *importation* model. Inmate subcultures are not viewed as unique to the prison environment, but rather as a reflection of the criminal subcultures found on the outside. Elements of the inmate subculture are "imported" by criminals upon their incarceration. The research discussed in this next section pertains to inmate subcultures. Donald Clemmer (1940) was among the first to document the existence of inmate subcultures. Gresham Sykes (1958) followed with his description of the deprivations experienced by inmates as they assimilated into the prison environment. Rose Giallombardo (1966) provided an account of the differences between male and female inmate social networks. Finally, Leo Carroll (1974) explored the differences between black and white inmate subcultures and offered insight into how social and cultural processes at work in free society influenced the nature of these subcultures in prison.

INMATE SOCIAL NETWORKS: HOW DO INMATES BECOME SOCIALIZED INTO A PRISON CULTURE?

Clemmer, D. (1940). *The Prison Community.* Boston: Christopher.

Background

Prisons were for the most part ignored by researchers until the 1920s. Early studies document-ing the prison experience were written by inmates, prison administrators or those whose knowledge was derived from brief visits to a prison facility (Mannheim 1971). One exception was a published account by prison life by Hans Reimer in 1937. Reimer spent three months in prison as a *participant-observer*. In his report to the American Prison Association, Reimer described how the prison environment was shaped by a group of inmate leaders. The first systematic examination of the prison environment and the inmate social groups found inside is credited to Donald Clemmer. Clemmer was a sociologist working in the mental health unit at the Illinois State Prison at Menard.

The Study

Clemmer's (1940) objective was to provide a detailed, objective description of the formal and informal organization of a typical American penitentiary. The data for his *ethnographic* study of prison came from a variety of sources. Clemmer already had access to a prison through his employment as a sociologist at the Illinois State Prison for men located in Menard. He also drew upon his prior experience working in two other state prison facilities. Between 1931 and 1934, he interviewed over 2,500 male inmates, conducted over 1,000 intelligence and psycho-logical assessments of inmates, observed correctional administrators and staff, and conducted interviews with inmates after their release from prison. Clemmer also obtained information on the inmates from their prison records and he read over 50 inmate autobiographies describ-ing the prison experience.

Findings

Based on data collected through his observations, interviews, and review of inmate records, Clemmer gave a thorough account of the inmate population and described both the formal and informal prison organization.

The Inmates

Clemmer's first task was to collect data on the inmates incarcerated at the penitentiary. The state prison facility housed 2,300 male inmates. Over half of the inmates had resided in Illinois prior to their incarceration. Inmates came from both rural and urban areas within the state. Forty percent came from broken homes. Inmates ranged in age from 17 to 90 and the average age of the inmate population was 34 years. Twenty-two percent of the inmates were black. An assessment of the inmates' intellectual capacity revealed that most inmates were of average or borderline intelligence. Nearly one-fourth of the inmates were mentally deficient. Furthermore, less than 30 percent of the inmates had an eighth grade education. Over half of the population had worked as common or semi-skilled laborers prior to their incarceration, but many from this group had no stable work histories. Nearly 60 percent of the inmates had been married. The largest percentage of inmates had been convicted of property crimes, followed by robbery and murder. A review of the inmates' prior records showed that 42 percent had a previous history of incarceration.

The Formal Prison Organization

In addition to providing a description of the inmate population, Clemmer offered a detailed narrative of the institutional environment where the offenders were housed. Inmates resided in either one of three cell houses or in the single dormitory facility. Inmate facilities were situated on 13 acres of land surrounded by a 30-foot wall. In 1931, the state was spending approximately 278 dollars per inmate each year. By 1934, that amount had been reduced to 156 dollars. The penitentiary was administered under the control of a warden, two assistant wardens, 202 guards, and a variety of other treatment and clerical staff. Upon entering the prison, inmates were subject to a routine processing system. Inmates were stripped of their civilian clothes and issued a set of standard inmate garments (one pair of jeans, two shirts, one pair of socks and shoes, a hat, a towel, and a handkerchief). Every inmate received a shower, was sprayed for lice, and was given a haircut (inmates all had to shave their heads). Each inmate was then interviewed by prison staff and given a medical physical.

Inmate behavior was controlled with the use of rewards and punishments. Punishments consisted of solitary confinement, loss of privileges and good time (time off a sentence for good behavior). The prison had in place a "progressive merit system" where inmates progressed through a serious of five "grades" based on good behavior. During the initial months of incarceration, inmates earned no good time credit. Provided the inmates followed the rules and stayed out of trouble, they could start earning credit on their sentence after the first three months. Inmates adhered to a daily routine that began at 5:30 A.M. and ended with lights out at 9:00 P.M. Inmates received three scheduled meals per day, were required to work, and were given a specified time to bath and dress. Time was also set aside for educational, recreational, and religious activities. The most important part of the inmates' daily routine was the inmate "counts." At least twice a day the inmates were lined up and each inmate had to be officially accounted for. The rigid routine and the requirement that inmates strictly adhere to all prison rules and regulations was a dominant feature of the prison environment. Every aspect of the prison environment was geared towards the institutional goal of maintaining order, discipline, and security.

The Informal Prison Organization (The Prison Community)

Clemmer referred to his prison as a "community" because it was a self contained social system with its own social relations, rules, values, and behavioral patterns. Inmates were separated from the outside world and the culture of mainstream society, but once inside, the inmates became assimilated into a prison subculture. According to Clemmer, the same cultural elements and social processes found in free society could be observed inside of the prison. Inmates had their own means of communication, group affiliations, mechanisms of social control, divisions of labor, and leisure activities. Clemmer called the assimilation of inmates into this subculture "prisonization" where inmates take on ". . . in greater or less degree of the folkways, mores, customs, and general culture of the penitentiary" (p. 299). The prisonization experience began the same for all inmates. Inmates were stripped of their status as free men as soon as they entered the facility. Inmates were no longer referred to by name, but by a number. The state-issued clothing was the same for all inmates. Personal identities were no longer acknowledged on the inside. Inmates immediately became part of a nameless group of inferiors.

The prisonization continued as inmates adjusted to their new routine. All aspects of an inmate's life were controlled by the rules and regulations of the prison. Inmates were told when to get up, eat, work, and sleep. Because the prison relied upon the inmates to perform many of the day-to-day tasks essential to its operation (i.e., cleaning and general maintenance), inmates became aware that the needs of the institution were put ahead of their own. It was through their associations with other prisoners that inmates became integrated into the prison community. Clemmer acknowledged that there were differences in the degree to which inmates become assimilated into the prison subculture, but he believed that all inmates were affected by the subculture. All inmates were exposed to the language, social groups, norms and values that permeated the prison environment. Clemmer examined several cultural processes within the prison and described how each influenced inmate behavior.

Communication. Communication plays an important role in a community and this was particularly true in prison. According to Clemmer, inmates became acclimated to the unique aspects of the prison subculture through their communication with other inmates. Clemmer observed the significance of prison "argot" or slang words used by inmates in their verbal and written communications with one another. He developed an argot "dictionary" that consisted of 1,200 words or phrases along with their meanings. A knife was referred to as a "shiv," guards were called "screws," and narcotics were "packages" or "junk." Most of the terms (66%) referred to aspects of the prison or the crimes in which these men were incarcerated for. Nicknames were also common and tended to reflect the physical features of the inmates (i.e., a short inmate might be called "shorty"). Clemmer found that inmates used prison jargon as a means of excluding others from their group or to show status and identity. Not all inmates regularly used the slang terms, but all inmates were familiar with the words and their meanings. Communication was also an important part of the social relationships between inmates. Inmates were typically housed two to a cell providing ample opportunities for relationships to develop. Topics of conversation tended to center on the inmates' crimes and court experiences, discussions of prison officials, and other aspects of prison life.

The inmate social system. Clemmer observed that there existed in prison a type of class structure among inmates. Classes were not rigidly defined. Membership in a particular class tended to be based on the inmates' reputation prior to incarceration, their behavior in prison, as well as other personality traits. The "elites" had above average intelligence, were perceived as "urbanized" and "sophisticated" inmates. They tended to keep to themselves and usually only associated with others in this group. They were considered "anti-administration" and never tried to win favor amongst the guards. Most inmates fell into the "middle class." These inmates shared few distinguishing characteristics except for their disapproval of the inmates who belonged to the "hoosier" class. Members of the hoosier class were not even aware of their status. This particular inmate class was designated by members of the other two classes and consisted primarily of sex offenders, the less intelligent, and the physically weak.

Group affiliations. Interviews with a sample of the inmates revealed that 32 percent considered themselves to be part of a social group of inmates. Inmates organized themselves into groups according to certain shared characteristics such as backgrounds, associations in crime, or sexual attractions. Based on the inmates' responses, Clemmer created a typology of inmate affiliation. The "complete, clique man" was part of a stable, cohesive group of three or more inmates. These inmates spent a great deal of time engaged in activities as a group. Nearly 18 percent of the inmates fell into this category. They looked out for each other, protected one another, and shared a true group identity. The "group man" on the other hand was less affiliated with one particular group of inmates. These inmates (who comprised 35% of the inmate population) may have belonged to a primary group, but they were less integrated and also associated with inmates outside of their group. The "semi-solitary man" was not part of any inmate group. These inmates were cordial with other inmates and they would sometimes casually associate with them. Thirty-four percent of the inmates fell into this category. Finally, the "complete-solitary man" was a true loner. These inmates kept to themselves and associated with no one. Less than 4 percent of the inmates were considered this type. In addition, Clemmer determined that each inmate group had a leader, or one particular inmate who dominated and influenced the other members. Once identified, Clemmer examined the characteristics of inmate leaders. He found their average age to be 32, which was slightly younger than the average age of the total inmate population. Most leaders displayed higher intelligence, came from urban areas, were convicted of a violent crime, and had previously been incarcerated.

Social controls. There exists in every prison a system of formal social control. The inmates are governed by rules and procedures designed to maintain order and security. Preventing riots and escapes are the primary concerns of prison administrators. According to Clemmer, the institution relied on an unyielding system of prison discipline to make certain inmates complied. In addition, the prison used rewards (good time or privileges) and punishment (solitary confinement, loss of privileges) to maintain control. Clemmer reviewed disciplinary reports for a six-month period and found that for a sample of 200 inmates, there were only eight offenses.

Clemmer also observed within his prison a system of *informal* social control. In addition to the rules and procedures, inmates were governed by certain mores, folkways, customs, and dogma. The mores consisted of an "inmate code," a set of unwritten rules developed by the inmates themselves. Inmates were expected to remain loyal to their fellow inmates at all times. Cooperating with the prison staff, speaking to the guards, and ratting out fellow inmates were strictly prohibited. Inmates who violated these rules faced disciplinary action at the hands of the other inmates. Folkways and customs were reflected in the interactions and mannerisms of the inmates. For example, inmates were not permitted to speak in the dining hall so they used hand gestures to communicate. Inmates wore their caps tilted at an angle. Newcomers quickly adopted these behaviors. Inmates also shared similar beliefs and attitudes that were transmitted through rumors and stories. Parole boards and prison staff were perceived as corrupt, and it did not matter who occupied these positions. Aspects of the prison culture were also found in the inmates' songs and poems.

Work and leisure time. Every inmate that entered into the facility was given a work assignment. Inmates were not only responsible for the daily care and maintenance of the prison; they also tended to the fields or worked in one of the prison industries. Clemmer observed a hierarchy of work assignments (similar to that found in free society) that consisted of three groups of workers. The "convict workers" (the largest group) were assigned to one of the various prison "shops." These workers had no status. In the middle were the semi-trusties or "politicians." Politicians held jobs that required a certain amount of skill such as preparing meals, clerical tasks, or working in the prison barbershop or hospital. The inmates who held these positions were afforded special privileges like eating in the officers' kitchen or spending more time outdoors. Their status was further signified by their dress: politicians wore white shirts. At the top of the hierarchy were the inmate trusties. These inmates were permitted to work outside of the facility with little or no supervision. Inmates close to the end of their sentence with ties to the community were usually assigned to these positions. Trusties enjoyed better living arrangements and food.

Despite the strict routine and the fact that all inmates were required to work while incarcerated, there were opportunities for leisure activities. Clemmer estimated that an inmate spent about 44 percent of their "awake" time involved in either regulated or non-regulated free time. Regulated leisure activities consisted of sports (baseball, football, boxing, etc.). Inmates participated either as players or spectators. Clemmer himself coached the inmate football team while he was working at the prison. Inmates watched movies, listened to the radio, and read newspapers and books. Many inmates participated in religious services (if they chose to do so). Inmates were also afforded the opportunity to write letters and receive visits from family members. In addition to the regulated leisure time activities, inmates occupied their free time with activities that were against prison rules. They gambled and consumed alcohol (that was either made by the inmates or smuggled in from the outside). Homosexuality was also a common element of prison life.

Prisonization

Clemmer argued that the amount of time it would take, and the extent to which an inmate assimilated into the prison community, depended on several factors including both inmate and institutional characteristics. The most prisonized group included inmates with:

> long sentences
>
> unstable personalities
>
> few social ties to the outside
>
> an eagerness to belong to a prison primary group
>
> a willingness to accept subcultural values and attitudes without question
>
> a willingness to engage in deviant inmate behavior
>
> ample opportunities to interact with other inmates sharing these characteristics.

Clemmer believed that it was possible for researchers to determine the extent to which an inmate was assimilated into the prison community, but this could only be done through *qualitative* means. Researchers would have to conduct thorough *case studies* of individual inmates to make such a determination. This information he argued would be useful for parole boards in making release decisions. Clemmer believed that the more prisonized inmates would have a greater likelihood of violating their parole.

Limitations

Clemmer's portrayal of the prison community and inmate social networks was based on *qualitative* data that he gathered while working in an Illinois state prison. He acknowledged that his research was offered as a *descriptive* study of prison subcultures and he encouraged others to conduct research using more "refined" statistical measures. Several researchers were interested in determining whether or not Clemmer's findings would *generalize* to inmates and prisons located in other geographical areas. Researchers also tried to *quantify* Clemmer's findings to examine and test *hypotheses* that could *explain* rather than simply *describe* the prisonization experience. Stanton Wheeler (1961) developed a *survey* questionnaire that he administered to a *randomly* selected sample of 237 inmates from a state reformatory. Inmates were presented a series of "hypothetical conflict situations" designed to measure their conformity to the expectations held by staff members. According to Wheeler, inmates that conformed to staff role expectations were less influenced by the inmate subculture. Wheeler found only partial support for Clemmer's argument that inmates gradually progressed through several stages of prisonization. The extent to which an inmate assimilated into the prison community depended on several factors, the most important of which was the amount of time spent in prison. Longer periods of incarceration increased the degree of prisonization. Wheeler found that length of time in prison was correlated with prisonization measures; however, towards the end of their sentence, inmates became "deprisonized." Prior to their release from prison, inmates displayed fewer subcultural characteristics. This "u-shaped" relationship suggested that inmates became part of a subculture only as a means of adaptation. The subultural influences were short-lived. Research by Peter garabedian (1963) confirmed Wheeler's findings. Others however, have not produced results consistent with Wheeler. Robert Atchley and M. Patrick McCabe (1968) surveyed 856 inmates from a maximum-security federal prison located in the Southwest. The inmates were on average younger than the inmates studied by Clemmer and were serving shorter sentences. Atchley and McCabe found no relationship between length of time in prison and the degree of inmate prisonization. Studies of inmates in minimum security and boot camp prisons also raised doubts as to whether Clemmer's observations would apply to other types of prisons. Oscar Grusky (1959) and Bernard Berk (1966) found that inmates displayed favorable attitudes and less antagonistic behaviors towards staff in treatment oriented prisons.

Clemmer argued that the extent to which inmates became assimilated into the prison subculture had obvious implications for parole release decisions since many of the values held by subculture members countered the prison's efforts to rehabilitate offenders. Prisons in a sense had a criminogenic influence on the inmates. Again, this finding was based on Clemmer's observations and personal experiences derived primarily from a single prison environment. *Quantitative* research examining recidivism rates for released inmates refuted Clemmer's premise. A study by Donald Garrity (1961) failed to find support that extended contact with an inmate subculture influenced parole outcomes.

In his book *Governing Prisons*, John DiIulio (1987) criticized Clemmer and other sociologists for their failure to give adequate attention to the administrations that were an integral part of the prison community. Further, the "sociological view of prisons" offered few suggestions for making prisons better. DiIulio presented an *exploratory* analysis of three prison systems: California, Michigan, and Texas (the same states where Rand had completed their inmate survey discussed previously). He argued that prison management was the most important influence on the prison environment. Quality of life for inmates depended upon a prison providing inmates a safe environment where their basic needs were met and where there were programs to help inmates improve their chances of success after leaving the facility.

Significance and Subsequent Research

Clemmer's position as a sociologist with an Illinois state prison afforded him the necessary access to be able to observe and interact with the inmates in their natural environment. Clemmer offered the first systematic study of inmate social relationships. His study generated interest among other sociologists that resulted in several empirical studies of inmate social systems over the next two decades. About the same time Clemmer was conducting his study, Norman Hayner and Ellis Ash (1939), two sociologists at the University of Washington, were studying inmates at the Washington State Reformatory at Monroe. Ash spent four months as a participant-observer at the prison and then made several visits to the facility over a subsequent 12-month period. Like

Clemmer, Hayner and Ash documented the existence of an inmate subculture and they observed many of the same elements identified by Clemmer. Inmates communicated using slang vocabulary, adhered to an inmate code of behavior, and spent much of their leisure time gambling. There existed a division of labor and a hierarchy of inmate classes. According to Hayner and Ash, inmates relied upon the inmate social network to provide access to goods and services that were otherwise prohibited. Inmates spent a considerable amount of time "conniving" with one another to obtain these prohibited items. The prison community was counterproductive to the institution's goal of rehabilitation because participation in the inmate social network also allowed prisoners to acquire additional crime skills.

In 1941, the Washington State Legislature formed the Committee on Penal and Charitable Institutions. The Committee asked Hayner to conduct a study of inmate social networks across four state prison facilities, including the School for Girls and the Training School for Boys. Hayner (1943) assigned one of his students to each institution to collect data as participant-observers. He published segments of their findings in an article titled "Washington State Correctional Institutions as Communities." Hayner reported on several differences in the inmate social systems within each facility. Unlike at the adult male prisons, the delinquent girls were not organized into stable groups according to their institutional roles or backgrounds. Social networks constantly changed as the girls switched friends and group affiliations fairly regularly. The girls did, however, share some of the same values. "Snitching" was not tolerated. The social structure at the training facility for delinquent boys was more clearly defined compared to that found at the girls' facility, but not to the same extent as in the adult male prisons. Newcomers had to prove themselves before gaining acceptance into a social group. An inmate might be challenged to a fight and would also have to demonstrate that he could be trusted. Like the adult male inmates, the boys had a well-developed vocabulary of slang terms. In addition to the observed differences between adult and juvenile and male and female institutions, Hayner discovered that inmate social networks also changed over time.

One of the participant-observers was assigned to the same adult male prison Hayner had studied five years before (the State Reformatory at Monroe). Administrators at the State Reformatory at Monroe increased their enforcement of the prison's rule against alcohol that appeared to have decreased the inmates' consumption. As a result, there was less "conniving" among inmates. The final facility studied was the Penitentiary at Walla Walla. This facility housed over 1,600 inmates. In addition to being considerably larger than the other prisons, the inmates were older and had more extensive criminal histories. Clarence Schrag was the student assigned to collect data from this facility. According to Schrag, the inmate social system consisted of very distinct and stable groups. An inmate's status was determined by their membership with a particular group. In addition, he found that inmates could be categorized according to five social types. The "outlaws" held no allegiance to a particular group and were therefore not vulnerable to social pressures to conform. They were described as callous and heavily engaged in illegal activities within the prison. The "right guys" subscribed to the inmate code and demonstrated considerable loyalty to their inmate group. "Politicians" took advantage of the illegal activities of outlaws as a way to gain favor among the guards. They were willing to "snitch" on other inmates in exchange for some privilege or reward. The "square john" was not committed to a life of crime prior to their incarceration. They tended to follow the formal rules and regulations of the prison. "Dings" consisted of those inmates classified by erratic and impulsive behavior. These inmates were outcasts with no real group affiliation (Hayner 1943).

Research by Peter Garabedian (1963), another student from Washington University, found differences in prisonization according to the social types described by Schrag (reported in Hayner 1943). Garabedian studied 380 inmates from a maximum-security prison located in the western United States. Only the "outlaws" became prisonized in the progressive manner described by Clemmer. The "johns" and "right guys" followed the u-shaped prisonization pattern described by Wheeler. Both groups appeared less prisonized prior to their release from prison. Evidence of a progressive pattern of prisonization was least apparent for the "politicians" and "dings." These relationships presumed accurate measures of inmate social type. Garabedian differentiated inmates according to their level of agreement or disagreement with such items, as "Inmates can trust me to be honest and loyal in my dealings with them" (right guy) and "I worry a lot about little things" (ding). Subsequent research was unable to demonstrate that these measures were *reliable* or *valid* indicators of social type (Poole et al. 1980).

A second study of inmates housed at the Menard Penitentiary in southern Illinois was published in 1942. S. Kirson Weinberg argued that the inmate social structure developed in response to the conflict between guards and inmates. Upon incarceration, offenders were forced into a subordinate inmate position under the control of the guards. Inmates had little recourse except to complain and express their contempt for the guards. The guards countered these opinions by displaying their own negative attitudes towards the inmates. Inmates and guards formed stereotypes of one another and these attitudes and perceptions were communicated to new officers and inmates as part of the socialization process. As the tensions between inmates and guards escalated, their social distance only became more pronounced.

According to Clemmer, inmates affiliated into groups based on shared characteristics such as similar backgrounds. Morris Caldwell (1956) examined inmate social structures within prisons across five mid-western and southern states and found that group affiliations were also based on "the pursuit of common interests" while incarcerated. He created a typology consisting of 11 types of inmate social groups. The "politicians" or "big shots" were typically well known offenders with an interest in gaining control of the prison through riots, strikes, or escapes. "Right guys" maintained a strict adherence to the inmate code that they used to influence the other inmates. They had a reputation for taking advantage of all possible opportunities to improve their living conditions or prospects for early release. The "moonshiners" were responsible for the production and sale of alcohol within the prison. Inmates made their "moonshine" from virtually anything they could get their hands on, such as shoe polish, antiseptic, and sugar. In addition to the demand of alcohol, inmates sought illegal drugs. Guards and visitors smuggled the drugs into the prison and a small number of inmates took over their distribution and sale. The "larceny boys" supplied inmates with other material goods. These inmates stole items from the more vulnerable inmates and then sold them. Other inmates belonged to a "gambling syndicate." Inmates were organized into small gambling groups, each under the control of a "kingpin" who controlled their activities. The homosexuals or "wolves" engaged in both consensual and nonconsensual sexual activities. There were prostitutes who had sex for money or other favors. Other inmates were more predatory and used threats or force. Protection was another commodity for sale in prison. There was also an inmate group responsible for manufacturing and supplying weapons. Not all of the groups were organized in pursuit of disruptive or illegal activities. The "leather workers" spent their free time crafting leather goods such as purses and wallets that were sold to the general public. Prisons were also home to several groups of "religionists" who were zealous in their praying and reading of the scriptures. Finally, the "Spartans" were inmates who took great pride in their physical masculinity. They routinely paraded around the locker rooms nude. Caldwell further observed the same hierarchy of inmate groups as Clemmer. Class status was either "assigned" or "achieved" by inmates.

Caldwell believed that the existence of an inmate social system had implications for the management of inmates. The interactions and conflicts between the informal inmate social groups and the formal groups of prison guards and administrators shaped the entire prison environment. An understanding of how these groups operated within a prison was essential to explaining prison riots and disturbances as well as efforts to rehabilitate prisoners. Research by Matthew Zingraff (1975) offered support for Caldwell's argument that inmate social networks might undermine efforts to rehabilitate offenders. Zingraff surveyed 267 male delinquents incarcerated in a state juvenile correctional facility. He found that inmates who had become assimilated into an "inmate normative system" displayed attitudes that were opposed to the institution and to the law, which could hinder their effective resocialization.

Erving Goffman put forth additional support for the existence of an inmate subculture in 1957. Goffman described prisons as "total institutions" because the formal organizational structure dictated almost every aspect of the inmates' life. Inmates' activities took place under the control of a single authority, the daily routine of inmates occurred primarily in groups, and inmates were required to follow a strict schedule. The prison environment consisted of rules, regulations, and activities designed to fulfill a single purpose: to control the behaviors of the inmates. Goffman's account of how inmates became assimilated into the prison environment was consistent with Clemmer. Inmates were "stripped" of their personal identities upon entering the prison. Inmates adapted to the prison environment in different ways. Some inmates went through "situational withdrawal" where they isolated themselves from others. Others adapted through a "rebellious line" by refusing to submit to the authority of prison staff. Some inmates became "colonized" into the prison environment. These inmates appeared comfortable and at home in prison. Finally, some inmates adapted through "conversion" where they became well behaved model inmates.

As part of a larger study of prison and parole, Daniel Glaser (1964) interviewed inmates from five different federal prisons. The inmates were selected into three panels representing different phases of incarceration: entrance, mid-term, and near-release. *Panel* studies allow researchers to examine how individuals change over time. Glaser used this design to help determine if the prisonization process was *linear* (as suggested by Clemmer, where inmates become gradually more prisonized the longer they spend in prison) or followed a u-shape pattern (consistent with Wheeler, where prisonization becomes less towards the end of inmate's sentence). Glaser found that the younger inmates were more likely to conform to the prison subculture compared to older inmates. Consistent with Wheeler, inmates affiliated more with inmate groups towards the middle of their incarceration, but then displayed less affiliation near the end.

Gaining access to a prison in order to collect data on inmate subcultures was not an easy task for sociologists (Schmid and Jones 1993). Clemmer's position afforded him the necessary unlimited access to observe and interview inmates and staff. Inmates themselves have also provided several studies of the prison environment. In 1993, Thomas Schmid and Richard Jones published their study of inmate adaptation that was based upon data collected by Jones while he served a sentence in a maximum-security prison. Jones was enrolled in a graduate level sociology course during his incarceration. He teamed up with sociologist Schmid to conduct an empirical study of inmate adaptation. As an inmate, Jones was in a unique position to observe his fellow inmates. They accepted him because he was one of them. Schmid and Jones were interested in exploring the prisonization of "first-time, short-term" inmates. Jones himself was only serving a sentence of one year and one day.

They found that first-time; short-term inmates initially defined their status according to society's portrayal of the prison environment. Towards the middle of their sentences, the inmates' "outsider's perspective" was still apparent, but the inmates also began to define their experiences in terms of subcultural elements acquired from their fellow inmates. First-time, short-term inmates never became completely assimilated into an inmate subculture, but they still took part in certain subculture activities to ease their adjustment to prison life. Near the end of their sentences, first-time, short-term inmates displayed aspects of both their "outsider" and "insider" perspectives. Throughout their entire period incarceration, first-time, short-term inmates appeared unsure of their transitional status. Their "ambivalence" explained why total prisonization did not take place.

Clemmer pioneered the study of inmate social networks with his published work *The Prison Community*. Lee Bowker (1977) referred to Clemmer as the "father of the sociology of the prison." *The Prison Community* remains one of the most widely cited works in the field of corrections (Wright and Miller 1999). Clemmer not only documented the existence of inmate subcultures, he provided a detailed description of the content of these subcultures and process by which inmates became assimilated into the subculture. Numerous studies of inmate subcultures have been published in the past 69 years since Clemmer's book first appeared. Clemmer went on to become the director of the Department of Corrections in Washington, DC, where he continued to publish research on inmate social networks.

References

Atchley, R., and M. McCabe (1968). "Socialization in Correctional Communities: A Replication." *American Sociological Review* 33:774–85.

Berk, B. (1966). "Organizational Goals and Inmate Organization." *American Journal of Sociology* 71:522–34.

Bowker, L. (1977). *Prisoner Subcultures*. Lexington, MA: Lexington Books.

Caldwell, M. (1956). "Group Dynamics in the Prison Community." *Journal of Criminal Law, Criminology and Police Science* 46:648–57.

DiIulio, J. (1987). *Governing Prisons: A Comparative Study of Correctional Management*. New York: Free Press.

Garrity, D. (1961). "The Prison as a Rehabilitation Agency." In *The Prison: Studies in Institutional Organization and Change*, edited by D. Cressey, 358–80. New York: Holt, Rinehart, and Winston.

Glaser, D. (1964). *The Effectiveness of a Prison and Parole System*. Indianapolis: Bobbs-Merrill.

Goffman, E. (1957). *Characteristics of Total Institutions*. Symposium on Preventive and Social Psychiatry: Walter Reed Army Institute of Research.

Grabedian, P. (1963). "Social Roles and Processes of Socialization in the Prison Community." *Social Problems* 11:139–52.

Grusky, O. (1959). "Organizational Goals and the Behavior of Informal Leaders." *American Journal of Sociology* 65:59–67.

Hayner, N., and E. Ash (1939). "The Prisoner Community as a Social Group." *American Sociological Review* 4:362–69.

Hayner, N. (1943). "Washington State Correctional Institutions as Communities." *Social Forces* 21:316–22.

Mannheim, H. (1971). *Group Problems in Crime and Punishment and Other Studies in Criminology and Criminal Law*. Montclair, NJ: Patterson Smith.

Poole, E., R. Regoli, and C. Thomas (1980). "The Measurement of Inmate Social Role Types: An Assessment." *Journal of Criminal Law and Criminology* 71:317–24.

Reimer, H. (1937). "Socialization in the Prison Community." *Proceedings of the American Prison Association*. New York: American Prison Association.

Schmid, T., and R. Jones (1993). "Ambivalent Actions: Prison Adaptation Strategies of First-Time, Short-Term Inmates." *Journal of Contemporary Ethnography* 21:439–63.

Weinberg, S. (1942). "Aspects of the Prison's Social Structure." *American Journal of Sociology* 47:717–26.

Wheeler, S. (1961). "Socialization in Correctional Communities." *American Sociological Review* 26:697–712.

Wright, R., and J. Miller (1999). "The Most-Cited Scholars and Works in Corrections." *Prison Journal* 79:5–22.

Zingraff, M. (1975). "Prisonization as an Inhibitor of Effective Resocialization." *Criminology* 13:366–88.

Further Reading

Clemmer, D. (1938). "Leadership Phenomena in a Prison Community." *Journal of Criminal Law and Criminology* 28:861–72.

Clemmer, D. (1950). "Observations on Imprisonment as a Source of Criminality." *Journal of Criminal Law, Criminology and Police Science* 41:311–19.

Hawkins, G. (1976). *The Prison: Policy and Practice.* Chicago: University of Chicago Press.

Hayner, N., and E. Ash (1940). "The Prison as a Community." *American Sociological Review* 5:577–83.

Leger, R. (1978). "Socialization Patterns and Social Roles: A Replication." *Journal of Criminal Law and Criminology* 69:627–34.

McCorkle, L., and R. Korn (1954). "Resocialization Within Walls." *Annals of the American Academy of Political and Social Science* 293:88–98.

Schrag, C. (1954). "Leadership Among Prison Inmates." *American Sociological Review* 19:37–42.

Wilson, T. (1968). "Patterns of Management and Adaptations to Organizational Roles: A Study of Prison Inmates." *American Journal of Sociology* 74:146–57.

THE "PAINS OF IMPRISONMENT:" HOW DO INMATES ADAPT TO IMPRISONMENT?

Sykes, G. (1958). *The Society of Captives: A Study of a Maximum Security Prison.* Princeton, NJ: Princeton UP.

Background

In addition to the research discussed above, Clemmer's study also caught the attention of sociologist, Gresham Sykes. Upon earning his Ph.D. from Northwestern University, Sykes was assigned to teach criminology at Princeton University. As part of the course, Sykes facilitated small discussion groups to supplement his lecture materials. The warden of the New Jersey State Penitentiary located near the University led one such group and he encouraged Sykes to build a research agenda focusing on prisons. The warden offered his assistance by granting Sykes full access to his prison (Reisig 2001). Sykes extended Clemmer's work by providing an explanation for *why* inmate social groups develop in prison. Sykes examined the social psychological aspects of prison life and described the inherent frustrations faced by prison inmates. He argued that the prison subculture was a reflection of these "pains of imprisonment." With Sykes' classic work, *The Society of Captives*, the deprivation model emerged.

The Study

Sykes (1958) collected data from the New Jersey State Prison located in Trenton, New Jersey. The maximum-security prison, built in the late 18th century, held 1,200 inmates and employed approximately 300 guards, clerks, and other professionals. The prison was described as a typical maximum-security facility surrounded by a 20-foot wall. Several data sources were used for the study, including official prison records, prison policies and regulations, inmate files, inmate interviews, staff interviews, and personal observations. Sykes also administered a survey to a *random* sample of 200 inmates.

The Inmate Population

An analysis of the inmate population in October 1954 showed that 24 percent were serving time for homicide. Another 24 percent were incarcerated for burglary, 20 percent for robbery and 12 percent for some type of larceny offense. The median age for the inmates was 35 years old. Over half of the inmates had less than an eighth grade education, while less than half were considered mentally deficient. Roughly one-third of the inmates were classified as "psychopathic personalities." Sixty-five percent had prior institutional commitments and 84 percent had a prior record. This particular prison contained a significant number of black inmates (38%).

Sykes was interested in examining differences in how inmates adjusted to the prison environment. His intent was to formulate specific *hypotheses* related to inmate adjustment, collect data to test the hypotheses, and use the findings to *explain* differences in inmate adjustment. Sykes changed his objective upon realizing that the current knowledge base on inmate roles was insufficient. He opted instead for an *exploratory* study of the prison social system that he believed would be more meaningful.

The Defects of Total Power

Like Clemmer, Sykes wanted to study prison from a sociological perspective. A prison was best understood as a social system that centered on efforts to establish and maintain absolute authority over the inmates. This perspective was particularly applicable to maximum-security prisons where every aspect of the prison environment was geared towards security and control. Security was the responsibility of the guards who exercised authority over the inmates. Control was exerted through the use of rewards and punishment. According to Sykes, the ability of the institution to maintain complete control over the inmates, however, was more of an illusion than reality. This was apparent in the numerous crimes, and rule violations committed by inmates while incarcerated. Sykes derived this information from prison disciplinary records, but both inmates and guards were in agreement that authorities only discovered a fraction of the actual number of violations. Sykes believed that the custodial staff was ". . . engaged in a continuous struggle to maintain order . . ." (p. 42) but were largely unsuccessful in their efforts. The guards' insecurities became evident when asked to provide input on possible topics for training. Nearly every one of them responded with, "what to do in event of trouble." (p. 45). In a maximum-security prison, conflict permeated the relationships between guards and inmates. Guards were in a position to exercise power over the inmates, but inmates did not recognize their authority to do so. Inmates did not comply with prison rules and regulations out of a sense of obligation or duty. In other words, while the guards may have been granted legitimate control over the inmates by virtue of their position, the inmates did not acknowledge their authority. Guards had to rely on persuasion and bribery to make sure inmates complied with their orders. The use of physical force was viewed as "inefficient" given that the inmates outnumbered the guards by a ratio of nearly ten to one.

Sykes found the prison's use of rewards and punishment to be an ineffective way to control inmates. The formal means of punishment—solitary confinement, loss of privileges, and altered work assignments—were typically not viewed as punitive by the inmates. Inmates were already confined, with few privileges and little say over their work assignments. Even the use of such rewards as mail, visitation, and "good time" were flawed because they were things given to all inmates upon their incarceration. Inmates viewed these rewards as "rights," not privileges to be earned for their good behavior. The inmates instead determined their own rewards, which were acknowledged by the guards. In exchange for compliance, a guard might "look the other way" for rule violations or warn inmates of an impending cell search.

The Pains of Imprisonment

Incarceration replaced the more inhumane forms of physical punishments that were used prior to the 19th century. According to Sykes, incarceration inflicted a different type of suffering upon an inmate. Inmates were placed in a deprived environment where the living conditions differed significantly from those on the outside. He recognized that, while the incarceration experience might differ for inmates, most of the inmates in his study perceived the prison environment as ". . . depriving or frustrating in the extreme." Sykes called these deprivations "pains of imprisonment." Sykes described five commonly experienced pains: deprivation of liberty, deprivation of goods and services, deprivation of heterosexual relationships, deprivation of autonomy, and deprivation of security.

Deprivation of liberty. The most apparent deprivation was that of an inmate's liberty. Inmates were not only confined to an institution, their movements were restricted within the institution. Many inmates perceived incarceration as a form of social death. Incarceration removed inmates from their social network of family and friends. Inmates were permitted to communicate with those on the outside through correspondence and visits, but most inmates found their social ties diminished while incarcerated. Sykes reviewed the visiting records for a sample of the inmates and discovered that 41 percent had received no visits within the past year.

Deprivation of goods and services. Prison officials provided inmates only the absolute basic necessities. Inmates were clothed, fed, given a place to sleep, and provided with medical care. While many inmates may not have had all of these things in free society, one could not compare the quality of life inside of prison to life outside. An inmate's clothing consisted of a uniform with their number stenciled on it. There was little variety in the food and medical care only had to be "adequate." Inmates sought special amenities. Cigarettes, alcohol, more food (or at least a greater variety of food), and extra furnishings for their cells were the things highly desired by inmates. The fact that inmates were taken out of a society that emphasized material wealth further contributed to this deprivation in prison.

Deprivation of heterosexual relationships. Sykes observed the sexual frustration experienced by inmates to be significant. Inmates were not allowed conjugal visitation. Many inmates engaged in homosexual behavior as a means of alleviating that frustration, but a lack of heterosexual relationships also diminished the inmates' masculinity. In free society, a male's self identity was shaped by their interactions with members of the opposite sex. Inmates no longer had those interactions to make them feel like men.

Deprivation of autonomy. Inmates lost the ability to make their own decisions. Prison rules and regulations controlled virtually every aspect of an inmate's life. Inmates were told when to get up, eat, sleep, shower, and work. Even their free time was scheduled and regulated. Inmates perceived many of the prison rules to be unnecessary and used by the guards as an attempt to display authority over them.

Deprivation of security. Prisons were intended to protect society from criminals, but prisons did little to protect the inmates from each other. Prisons were full of inmates with extensive histories of aggression and violence. Inmates not only worried about physical and sexual attacks, they also worried about their reputations. Inmates wanted to appear tough so they often became aggressors simply to avoid being victimized themselves.

Inmate Adaptations

Sykes argued that incarceration was a form of punishment in which inmates experienced the deprivations or pains of imprisonment. The pains were not just felt by the inmates, they threatened the inmates' self-identity and worth. While the pains were an unavoidable part of being sent to prison, the inmate social networks found in prison could lessen their effect. Inmates who became part of an inmate social group (inmate subculture) took on a new collective identity. Inmates found their adaptation to the prison environment easier when they were part of a group of inmates who were all experiencing the same pains. In addition, belonging to an inmate subculture provided opportunities for inmates to acquire goods and services beyond those supplied by the prison.

In his study of inmate social networks, Sykes identified several "argot roles" occupied by the inmates. Inmates displayed certain characteristic behaviors that were acknowledged by other inmates as well as the prison staff. The inmates themselves defined the roles. Prison "rats" or "squealers" were inmates who reported illegal or prohibited activities to prison officials. Inmates either snitched on other inmates as a way to win favor amongst the guards, to eliminate competition in an illegal enterprise, or in retaliation. Regardless of the motive, ratting out fellow inmates was perceived to be the absolute worst thing a prisoner could do because it was an offense against all inmates. Most inmates also disliked the "center men." Center men identified more with the guards than the other inmates. They were not only cooperative with guards, but also went out of their way to be accommodating. Inmates acquired goods and services beyond those provided by the prison either legitimately by shopping at the prison store or through illegitimate inmate "channels." Inmates participated in a "barter system" where they traded items amongst themselves. Not all inmates were willing to participate. Those who used force to take things from others were called "gorillas." "Merchants," on the other hand, sold items for profit. Inmates disliked both the gorillas and merchants because their activities disrupted the traditional barter system.

Despite the fact that the prison prohibited homosexual activities, and the vast majority of inmates who engaged in these activities were not considered homosexual, inmates categorized the homosexuals into three groups. "Wolves" were aggressors who forced themselves upon other inmates as a way to confirm their masculinity. These inmates resorted to homosexual sex as a means of adaptation. Upon their release, they would resume heterosexual relationships. "Punks" and "fags" were passive participants. Punks were forced into having sex with another inmate, while fags enjoyed having sex with other men (those who were homosexual before coming to prison). Because of their passive participation in homosexual sex, other inmates perceived them as feminine. Some of the roles were shaped by the inmates' interactions with guards. Inmates who were openly defiant and antagonistic towards the guards were called "ball busters." Inmates were never expected to cooperate with the guards, but the ball busters were viewed as troublemakers. Their behavior often had negative consequences for all inmates. "Real men" displayed self-respect by appearing neither compliant nor hostile towards the guards. Other inmates admired them for their independence and self-restraint. Inmates also used violence as a means of displaying their masculinity. The "toughs" were quick tempered and always willing to fight. Inmates admired them, but were also afraid of them. The "hipsters" were inmates who pretended to be tough but were perceived as cowards because they selectively picked fights with weaker inmates. These inmates spent their time trying to gain acceptance into any social group that would have them.

Criticisms

Society of Captives generated few criticisms upon his publication. Sykes provided a thorough *ethnographic* study of the prison environment, which he supplemented with *surveys* and *existing data*, but like Clemmer based his observations on a single prison. Whether or not his findings would *generalize* to other prisons was an issue. Sykes described the deprivations of a maximum-security prison. It was doubtful that inmates in less secure facilities would experience the same pains (or at least not to the same extent).

The major criticism of Sykes' research came from researchers purposing an alternative perspective to his deprivation model. The deprivation model assumed prisons to be closed societies isolated from all outside influences. Others contended that the prison environment was shaped by the pre-institutional experiences of offenders sent to prison. According to John Irwin and Donald Cressey (1962), Sykes (as well as Clemmer) applied a "structural-functionalist" approach in their study of prison. As such, they concluded that it was the unique prison environment that shaped the behavior of the inmates. Irwin and Cressey offered a competing perspective with their importation model. The distinct prison environment observed by Clemmer and Sykes was actually the product of a *criminal* subculture. Offenders carried with them into prison certain cultural aspects (i.e., language, behaviors, norms, and values) from the criminal subcultures they belonged to in free society. The criminal subcultures were simply *imported* into the prison environment. Irwin and Cressey identified three types of subcultures found in prison. The "thief" subculture consisted of inmates who had been part of a criminal subculture prior to incarceration. This group of "professional thieves" adhered to a set of values that closely resembled those described by Clemmer and Sykes. Thieves did not cooperate with police, they did not provide information on their associates, and were even-tempered and trustworthy. Upon their incarceration, they affiliated with other thieves who shared their criminal values. These inmates perceived the prison experience as a temporary interruption from their criminal careers. The "convict" subculture included those inmates who had spent most of their lives behind bars. These inmates spent their time trying to improve their prison experience by taking advantage of the system and exerting influence over the other inmates. Their "utilitarian and manipulative behavior" was a product of the lower class lifestyle that dominated their existence on the outside. The "legitimate" subculture consisted of inmates not affiliated with either the thief or convict networks. In fact, these inmates shared no affiliation with any prison group. They kept to themselves, shared values similar to the staff, caused little problems, and participated in rehabilitative programs. Julian Roebuck (1963) called Irwin and Cressey's prison subculture typology "artificial and non-discriminating," but the idea that the prison environment could be influenced by preinstitutional characteristics generated considerable interest and empirical support among prison researchers.

Significance and Subsequent Research

Sykes built upon the work of Clemmer and offered not only a description of inmate social networks, but also an explanation for why they developed. He acknowledged his study of inmate social systems as *exploratory* in that he did not formulate or test any specific *hypotheses*. Subsequent researchers set out to do what Sykes did not: establish relationships between prison deprivations and inmate attitudes and behaviors. Charles and Drollene Tittle (1964) interviewed a *stratified random* sample of imprisoned narcotic addicts. Stratified random samples are a type of probability sample where the researcher divides a population into groups and then randomly selects cases from each group. This is done to make certain that relevant factors are sufficiently represented in the sample. The Tittles measured the addicts' adherence to the prison code, the amount of time spent in the facility, the addicts' perception of difficulty adjusting to the environment, levels of alienation, participation in therapy, and the difference between the addicts' aspirations and expectations for success outside of the institution. Their findings offered support for several of the ideas put forth by Sykes. Time spent in the institution was associated with the addicts' adherence to the prison code. The pains of imprisonment were also decreased for addicts with a strong observance of the inmate code.

Numerous studies have tested the deprivation model put forth by Sykes against Irwin and Cressey's importation model. Charles Wellford (1967) surveyed a random sample of 120 inmates incarcerated in a Washington, DC, prison. His survey consisted of questions designed to measure prisonization, including the amount of time spent in the prison, whether or not an inmate was at the beginning, middle, or end of their sentence, and criminal social type. For his *dependent* variable, Wellford examined the extent to which inmates adopted the inmate code. Inmates were presented with a series of "hypothetical" scenarios and asked to indicate their level of "approval" or "disapproval" with the behavior of the inmate presented in each scenario. Wellford found no significant relationship between the length of time in prison and adoption of the inmate code. Phase of incarceration and criminal social type were both significantly related to adoption of the code, however, independent of each other. He concluded that prisonization depended more on the characteristics of the inmates *prior to* their incarceration as opposed to the prison environment. Adoption of the inmate code was stronger for inmates who belonged to a criminal subculture on the outside. Barry Schwartz (1971) conducted a test of the deprivation and importation models using a sample of delinquents from the Glen Mills School for boys. His research also showed that several factors derived from an inmate's environment were significant predictors of their prison attitudes and behaviors, but pre-institutional characteristics were also found to be significant. "Those characteristics of the inmate which are influenced by his prison surroundings are also affected by what he brings into them" (Schwartz 1971, p. 542).

Wellford and Schwartz collected data from inmates in a single prison. In 1974, Ronald Akers, Norman Hayner, and Werner Gruninger published their study of inmate behavior using data collected from seven prisons located across the United States. They wanted to determine if the *type* of prison was important for understanding the influences of deprivation and importation. Prisons were classified along a treatment-custody continuum. Three prisons were classified as "treatment," three as "custodial," and one prison as "intermediate." A sample of inmates from each facility was administered a questionnaire to assess their affiliation with a inmate social system, their personal and criminal characteristics, participation in prison programs, as well as their drug use and homosexual activities while incarcerated. They found that institutions with considerable amounts of drug use also had high amounts of homosexual activity, both of which were more frequent in custody oriented prisons. This finding offered support for the deprivation model. The deprivations were greater in custody oriented prisons as reflected by the large number of inmates engaged in these activities. Researchers acknowledged, however, that their finding might have been due to the pre-prison drug use and homosexual behavior of the inmates prior to their incarceration. To explore this possibility, they examined several inmate characteristics, including whether or not the inmate was incarcerated for a drug or sex offense. None of the pre-institutional factors were related to drug use and only age was related to homosexuality in prison. Their findings provided greater support for the deprivation model. These same researchers conducted a study of prisonization with inmates from five different countries (including the United States) and also found that measures of deprivation were better predictors of inmate attitudes (Akers et al. 1977). More recently, Michael Reisig and Yoon Ho Lee (2002) verified the applicability of Sykes' deprivation model to prisons in other countries with their study of Korean prisons.

Aspects of both the deprivation and importation models have been empirically verified with research. This suggests that an integrated model might be more appropriate for a complete understanding of why these subcultures develop. Beginning in the mid-1970s, researchers became more interested in determining how elements from *both* perspectives influenced specific aspects of inmate adaptation. Charles Thomas took this approach in his 1977 study of prisonization. Thomas (1977) administered an anonymous questionnaire to 273 inmates confined in a medium security prison. The questionnaire included items designed to assess the inmates' degree of alienation and their length of confinement (deprivation variables) as well as the inmates' pre-prison characteristics and their post-prison expectations for success (importation variables). Three outcome measures were examined: the degree to which inmates subscribed to subculture values, the inmates' level of opposition to the prison organization and the degree to which inmates perceived themselves to be criminal. Thomas found that measures of deprivation maintained a stronger relationship with the first two outcome measures (subculture values and opposition), however, one aspect of importation (an inmate's post-prison expectations) was important for understanding the inmates' perceptions of themselves as criminal.

In his prison study, Sykes observed that guards relied upon bribery and persuasion to get the inmates to comply with prison rules because the inmates did not acknowledge the guards' authority. One year later, Richard Cloward made similar observations while he was collecting data for his dissertation. As part of his study, Cloward (1960) interviewed 90 prisoners in a northeast Army prison and found that there were some inmates who refused to accept their subordinate status and comply with prison rules and regulations. By adopting one of the argot roles described by Sykes, inmates secured positions within the prison's "illegitimate opportunity structure" that afforded them status. For example, the "merchant" gained status by controlling access to goods and services. The guards decided how much illicit activity would be tolerated through their control over the accessibility of these desirable positions.

Sykes provided a thorough description of the deprivations related to the prison experience. Schwartz identified one additional "pain" after reviewing several inmate autobiographical accounts of prison life. Schwartz (1972) argued that inmates also had to adapt to the *loss of privacy*. Virtually all of an inmates' time was spent in the presence of others. Activities that were once done in private, such as dressing or showering, took place under the watchful eyes of other inmates and guards. Visits with family members were supervised and personal letters opened and read by officials. Inmates were subjected to routine strip searches and searches of their cells. Assimilation into an inmate subculture appeared to be a contradictory way of adapting to the loss privacy; however, Schwartz believed that this particular deprivation helped explain two conflicting tenets of the inmate code. Inmates were expected to remain loyal to their group but at the same time to "do their own time."

In 1977 Hans Toch published *Living in Prison* in which he identified several needs of inmates that were consistent with the deprivations described by Sykes. Toch interviewed a random sample of 900 male inmates in five New York maximum-security prisons. He found that inmates consistently expressed concerns over their *privacy, safety, structure, support, emotional feedback, social stimulation, activity,* and *freedom*. Based on his findings, he developed the *Prison Preference Inventory,* an assessment tool used to measure the extent to which inmates expressed these needs. In 1985, Kevin Wright took this research one step further when he created the *Prison Environmental Inventory.* The Prison Environmental Inventory measured inmate perceptions of how well their needs were being met by prison officials. Researchers today frequently employ these instruments in their assessments of inmate adjustment.

In addition to providing a comprehensive description of the prison environment for those who have never been incarcerated, *Society of Captives* continues to have a major influence on prison research. Forty-three years after its publication, the work was judged to be the most influential book ever written on prison (Reisig 2001). Sykes' analysis of the prison environment and inmate social system generated a considerable amount of research in the decades that followed.

References

Akers, R., N. Hayner, and W. Gruninger (1974). "Homosexual and Drug Behavior in Prison: A Test of the Functional and Importation Models of the Inmate System." *Social Problems* 21:410–22.

Akers, R., N. Hayner, and W. Gruninger (1977). "Prisonization in Five Countries: Type of Prison and Inmate Characteristics." *Criminology* 14:527–54.

Cloward, R. (ed.) (1960). *Theoretical Studies in Social Organization of the Prison.* New York: Social Science Research Council.

Irwin, J., and D. Cressey (1962). "Thieves, Convicts, and the Inmate Culture." *Social Problems* 10:142–55.

Reisig, M. (2001). "The Champion, Contender, and Challenger: Top-Ranked Books in Prison Studies." *Prison Journal* 81:389–407.

Reisig, M. and Y. Lee (2000). "Prisonization in the Republic of Korea." *Journal of Criminal Justice* 28:23–31.

Roebuck, J. (1963). "A Critique of Thieves, Convicts and the Inmate Culture." *Social Problems* 11:193–200.

Schwartz, B. (1971). "Pre-Institutional vs. Situational Influence in a Correctional Community." *Journal of Criminal Law, Criminology and Police Science* 62:532–42.

Schwartz, B. (1972). "Deprivation of Privacy as a 'Functional Prerequisite': The Case of the Prison." *Journal of Criminal Law, Criminology and Police Science* 63:229–39.

Thomas, C. (1977). "Theoretical Perspectives on Prisonization: A Comparison of the Importation and Deprivation Models." *Journal of Criminal Law and Criminology* 68:135–45.

Tittle, C., and D. Tittle (1964). "Social Organization of Prisoners: An Empirical Test." *Social Forces* 43:216–21.

Toch, H. (1977). *Living in Prison.* New York: Free Press.

Wellford, C. (1967). "Factors Associated with Adoption of the Inmate Code: A Study of Normative Socialization." *Journal of Criminal Law, Criminology, and Police Science* 58:197–203.

Wright, K. (1985). "Developing the Prison Environment Inventory." *Journal of Research in Crime and Delinquency* 22:257–77.

Further Reading

Adams, K. (1992). "Adjusting to Prison Life." *Crime and Justice* 16:275–359.

Bowker, L. (1977). *Prisoner Subcultures.* Lexington, MA: Lexington Books.

Hagan, J. (1995). "The Imprisoned Society: Time Turns a Classic on its Head." *Sociological Forum* 10:519–25.

Johnson, R., and Toch, H. (1982). *The Pains of Imprisonment.* Beverly Hills: Sage.

Marquart, J., and B. Crouch (1984). "Coopting the Kept: Using Inmates for Social Control in a Southern Prison." *Justice Quarterly* 4:291–509.

Riley, J. (2002). "The Pains of Imprisonment: Exploring a Classic Text with Contemporary Authors." *Journal of Criminal Justice Education* 13:443–61.

Simon, J. (2000). "The 'Society of Captives' in the Era of Hyper-Incarceration." *Theoretical Criminology* 4:285–308.

Stojkovic, S. (1984). "Social Bases of Power and Control Mechanisms Among Prisoners in a Prison Organization." *Justice Quarterly* 1:511–28.

Sykes, G. (1957). "Men, Merchants, and Toughs: A Study of Reactions to Imprisonment." *Social Problems* 4:130–38.

Thomas, C., and S. Foster (1973). "The Importation Model Perspective On Inmate Social Roles: An Empirical Test." *Sociological Quarterly* 14:226–34.

FEMALE INMATE SUBCULTURES: ARE FEMALE INMATE EXPERIENCES DIFFERENT FROM THE EXPERIENCES OF MALE INMATES?

Giallombardo, R. (1966). *Society of Women: A Study of a Women's Prison.* New York: Wiley.

Background

The first studies of inmate social systems described how male inmates assimilated into the environments of male prisons. By the 1940s, female offenders were already being housed in separate prison facilities. The separation of female inmates has been credited to the efforts of Elizabeth Fry, an English Quaker who established the *Ladies' Society for Promoting the Reformation of Female Prisoners* in 1816 (Dobash et al. 1986). Her efforts to reform prisons for women led to the opening of the first separate building for female offenders in the United States. The New York House of Refuge opened in 1825 for female juvenile offenders. Almost 50 years later, Indiana opened the first separate state prison for women in 1873. Female prison facilities were constructed differently from the prisons built for men. Female prisons consisted of small housing units with kitchens, living rooms, and bedrooms designed to hold around 30 inmates each. This cottage-style design was used to create a domestic environment where women could learn or improve their homemaking skills.

The difference in environments between male and female prisons led sociologists to question whether or not female inmates adapted by assimilating into the same types of subcultures found in male prisons. One such sociologist was Rose Giallombardo from Northwestern University. Giallombardo spent a year inside of an all-female prison to examine the nature of female inmate social networks. She compared the pains of imprisonment identified by Sykes eight years earlier to the deprivations experienced by women in prison. Prior research on this topic consisted primarily of historical or autobiographical accounts of female prisons (Giallombardo 1966). One exception worth noting was an empirical study of female inmates published in 1964 by David Ward and Gene Kassebaum. Ward and Kassebaum examined prison records, conducted interviews, and administered a survey to female prison inmates in California. They found that at least 50 percent of the females engaged in homosexual behaviors while incarcerated as a means of adapting to the loss of heterosexual relationships. They further identified several different homosexual roles assumed by women. Giallombardo's goal was to provide an empirical study of the entire female prison environment and all of the deprivations experienced by female inmates.

The Study

Giallombardo's objective was to conduct a sociological study of a female prison environment to determine the similarities and differences between male and female inmate social systems (subcultures). Giallombardo collected data as a *participant-observer* at the Federal Reformatory for Women in Alderson, West Virginia. She referred to her study as *exploratory* because so few empirical studies had been published on the topic. Giallombardo did not formulate any specific *hypotheses* for her study, but her inquiry was based on the following assumptions:

1. Prisons were an ideal setting to examine interactions between individuals and groups within a small social community.
2. In order to collect *valid* and *reliable* data, a researcher had to make sure that their presence and participation did not influence the interactions being studied.
3. A complete understanding of how prisons influenced the behavior of inmates and correctional officers could not be derived from studying only the formal prison structure.
4. Female prisons also contained informal inmate social networks.
5. A comparison between male and female inmate social networks would provide a better understanding of inmate attitudes and behaviors.

Giallombardo spent one year (July 1962 to July 1963) as a *participant-observer* in a female prison. As with all *field* research, some important decisions had to be made regarding her role as a researcher. Once she obtained permission for her study, Giallombardo had to present herself to her study participants and decide what her membership role would be. How a researcher is presented to their subjects and the role played by a researcher can influence the type and quality of the data that is collected. For her study, Giallombardo became a *peripheral member* of the prison. She interacted with and observed inmate and staff activities without actually participating in them. The warden of the facility presented Giallombardo to her subjects when he issued a memorandum to the staff and inmates informing them that a sociologist would be arriving to conduct a study of "institutional living." The memo encouraged the full cooperation of inmates and staff and also issued a guarantee that any interviews would be kept *confidential*. The warden's memo to the inmates was posted on a bulletin board used for general announcements in each of the living cottages. Upon her arrival, Giallombardo realized that the inmates seldom read the information on the bulletin boards because correctional officers always announced the important information. She spent the first two weeks walking around and introducing herself to the inmates who appeared curious about who she was, her living arrangements, and the purpose of her research. Many of the inmates seemed doubtful of her identity until she showed them a Northwestern University bulletin that listed her as a lecturer for the sociology department. This apparently satisfied the inmates because in the entire year spent at the prison Giallombardo only had one inmate who refused to speak with her.

Giallombardo's peripheral membership role was tested a few times by the inmates in the early weeks of her study. She was asked to do small favors for the inmates like mailing a letter or bringing in a magazine. While this may have helped her gain favor among the inmates, it was against prison rules to grant these favors. Giallombardo told the inmates that she would not grant their favors, and the requests soon stopped. Giallombardo kept all conversations and interviews *confidential*, but some of the inmates tested her assurances of confidentiality. Within a few months, however, the inmates had accepted Giallombardo. When she would introduce herself to a new inmate, an inmate that she had already interviewed would frequently vouch for her.

Giallombardo observed all aspects of the inmates' formal and informal prison environment and experiences, including their orientation sessions, work assignments, vocational, educational, and treatment sessions, recreational and religious activities, as well as their unstructured leisure time. Giallombardo did not live at the prison because this would have required special sleeping accommodations separate from the inmates. She was concerned that the inmates would have perceived her to be aligned with the staff. Instead she would arrive around 8:00 A.M. and stay until approximately 10:00 P.M. She deliberately did not keep a fixed schedule out of concern that her daily routine might influence the interactions of inmates and staff. In addition, Giallombardo had access to the prison records for all 653 female inmates who were incarcerated during the study period. Her final source of data came from interviews with correctional officers, administrators and other staff members.

Findings

Giallombardo spent an entire year collecting data on the female inmates housed at the Federal Reformatory for Women. She provided a detailed description of the prison's physical structure, gave a thorough account of both staff and inmate characteristics, and offered an analysis of the prison environment and the adaptations of female inmates.

The Prison Facility

Built in 1927, the Federal Reformatory for Women housed 653 inmates convicted of federal crimes. The facility did not resemble the maximum-security male prisons described by Clemmer and Sykes. There was no conspicuous massive wall surrounding the facility. The prison was situated on 50 acres surrounded by wire fences. Most of the inmates were housed in one of 16 "cottages" that were self-contained living units. The cottages consisted of a kitchen, living room, library, and separate bedrooms for the inmates. Each cottage also had space set aside for the prison staff. The cottage style environment was consistent with other prison facilities for women and girls throughout the United States. The female inmate population was divided into "small housekeeping units" to facilitate the development of domestic skills and to create a home like environment that would be "less painful for women." The cottages were constructed to house 30 inmates, however, at the time of the study were holding between 45 and 55 inmates. To further accommodate recent increases in the inmate population, several buildings were converted into dormitories. Despite the homelike design of the cottages, they were furnished with only the basics: a bed, locker, rocker, dresser, and dressing table. Compared to the living conditions for men, Giallombardo described the facilities to be clean and generally pleasant.

The Prison Staff

The majority of correctional officers were women. The prison only employed ten male correctional officers compared to the 92 female officers. Giallombardo limited her discussions to only the female officers, but she did point out that the female inmates associated the male officers' presence with the use of force because the males were the ones called upon to use physical force on noncompliant inmates. Recruitment for the Federal Reformatory was a problem. The facility was located in a remote area with limited housing. Most of the officers were drawn from the community where the prison was located, whereas the inmates were predominately from urban areas all across the United States. Most officers were married with a high school education, had previously been employed outside of the home, and their primary motivation for working at the prison was to supplement their household income. Giallombardo found that the characteristics of the female correctional officers influenced how the inmates perceived them—primarily as "West Virginia hillbillies" who "know nothing of life." The role of the correctional officers was the same as that in a male prison. Officers were responsible for the security of the institution. Custody and control of the inmates consumed most of the officers' time.

Inmate Classification and Characteristics

Male inmates were housed in minimum, medium, or maximum-security prisons at the state and federal level based on their propensity for violence or escape risk. The small number of female inmates did not permit separate facilities. Females of all security levels were housed in the same facility. The few inmates deemed maximum security were usually kept in a separate wing of the facility. Their classification had more to do with problem behavior while incarcerated as opposed to a history of violent crimes. Rehabilitation was the stated goal of the prison (just as in most male facilities), but security always took precedence over treatment. Vocational training consisted primarily of work assignments that facilitated the maintenance needs of the prison even though the majority of these women would require full time employment upon release. Female inmates worked in the kitchen and laundry. They learned how to cook, set tables, clean, sew, and do needlepoint. The females were being trained to be housewives (even though less than 32% were actually married), waitresses, or to perform other domestic work.

The inmate population was varied in terms of their backgrounds and needs. Nearly half of the inmates were serving relatively short sentences (three years or less), which made it difficult for the institution to meet their needs prior to their release. About half of the inmate population had less than an eighth grade education, but only 13 percent were considered mentally defective. The inmates were confined for a wide range of offenses, including drug and property crimes. Very few of the females were incarcerated for violent crimes. The age of the inmates ranged from 15 to 67. The median age of the inmates was 30.5. A little over half had prior institutional commitments.

Pains of Imprisonment for Female Prisoners

One of Giallombardo's objectives was to determine if female inmates experienced the same deprivations described by Sykes. Based on her observations and interviews, it was her conclusion that ". . . prison life *is* depriving and frustrating for the Alderson inmates" (p. 93). Females experienced the same losses of liberty, autonomy, material goods and services, heterosexual relationships, and security, however, Giallombardo found differences in the *degree* to which the female inmates felt these pains and the *nature* of the experience. The prison environment was less severe for women, but the deprivations were still present.

Loss of liberty. Despite the fact that the prison facility was located in the countryside of rural West Virginia and was surrounded only by a fence, the inmates were acutely aware that they had lost their liberty. The female inmates were subjected to the same structure and routine found in male facilities. Being isolated from family and friends was particularly difficult for these inmates. Giallombardo noted that one of the problems with the limited number of female facilities was that many females were sentenced to prisons located far away from family members. This made it more difficult for female inmates to receive visitors. An examination of visitation records revealed that only 12 percent of the females had contact with at least one outside visitor during the past year (compared to the 59% noted by Sykes).

Loss of autonomy. The female inmates also had difficulty adjusting to the loss of autonomy. The fact that these women were unable to make decisions for themselves made them feel like dependent children. Upon entering the prison, the female inmates went through an initiation similar to their male counterparts. Their personal belongings, including most of their clothes, were taken away. Females were not required to undergo the degrading hair cut, but the loss of their personal possessions made their isolation from society apparent. Inmates were issued a dress (that was worn, faded and usually the wrong size), a petticoat, and underwear that looked a lot like men's boxers. Giallombardo believed that the standard prison uniform was particularly threatening to the female inmates' self-image because of the importance society placed on women's fashion.

Loss of goods and services. Even though female inmates were housed in facilities that were generally nicer than their male counterparts, female inmates were still only provided the basics (food, clothing, and housing) in terms of their possessions. Females relied on the same legitimate and illegitimate channels to acquire items not provided by the institution.

Loss of heterosexual relationships. Perhaps the most significant difference found between male and female inmates centered on the deprivation of heterosexual relationships. Female inmates expressed the same difficulty adjusting to the loss of heterosexual relationships as male inmates. These women took pleasure from relationships with men prior to their incarceration (except for the 5% who claimed to be practicing homosexuals). Just as the deprivation had a negative impact on the male's masculine identity, the females' self-concept also became threatened. Like their male counterparts, female inmates turned to heterosexual activities as a way to adjust to this deprivation, but there were differences in the *nature* of these relationships. Females engaged in homosexual behavior as a part of a meaningful, "marital" relationship. She derived pleasure not only from the sex, but also from the intimate, emotional connection made with another female. Another observed difference was the lack of coerced sex in the female prison.

Loss of security. The female inmates did not experience the loss of security the same way as male inmates. In a male prison, the inmates lived in almost constant fear of being assaulted and they were always preoccupied with maintaining a "tough" image. The female inmates expressed no anxiety over their physical safety. Instead, their insecurity stemmed from having to "live with other women." Inmates described each other as untrustworthy, devious, and cruel. The females worried about being taken advantage of by the other inmates.

Female Inmate Social Roles

According to Sykes, inmates adapted to the pains of imprisonment by taking on an "argot" role that collectively became the inmate social networks or inmate subcultures. Giallombardo also identified social roles within the Alderson female prison. Female inmates adhered to a code, where like their male counterparts, "snitching" was the worst thing an inmate could do. The "snitcher" was the female equivalent of Sykes' "rat." Giallombardo found that there were different degrees of snitching. The infrequent snitcher was usually motivated by jealously and snitched on a fellow inmate to achieve some specific purpose (i.e., to cause relationship problems). The "good girls" regularly snitched to correctional officers in an attempt to improve their situation (i.e., better work assignment). Good girls were not only looked down upon by other inmates, but by the officers as well. An officer might be forced to react to information received about another inmate even though they might have preferred to leave matters alone. Female inmates rarely snitched anonymously. Giallombardo attributed this to the fact that snitchers were almost never met with violence. Instead, the females displayed their disapproval by "panning" (talking bad about an inmate behind their back) or "signifying" (talking bad about an inmate in their presence). Giallombardo found panning and signifying to be effective control mechanisms. Being socially ostracized in prison made the physical isolation from society more difficult to tolerate.

Sykes described the "center man" as an inmate who identified more with the guards than other inmates. The "inmate cop" or "lieutenant" occupied this role in the female prison. These were inmates whose work assignments gave them authority over other inmates. Their positions of authority generated tremendous resentment from the other inmates. "Squares" and "jive bitches" were also despised. Squares also identified more with prison staff, not to improve their situation, but because they were considered "accidental criminals." "Cube squares" displayed no sense of loyalty to the other inmates, while "hip squares" showed the inmates some compassion but never engaged in any homosexual activities. Troublemakers were known as "jive bitches." These inmates did not cause the same types of trouble as Sykes' "ball busters" who were always antagonizing the guards. Jive bitches stirred up trouble amongst the inmates.

Giallombardo identified two inmate roles unique to the female prison. When two inmates developed a special friendship they became known as "rap buddies." The friendship usually grew out of a common interest, but the friendship was conditional on both parties meeting certain expectations. Friendships between "homeys" were permanent. Homeys were inmates from the same or nearby hometowns. Homeys never engaged in homosexual activities with one another.

Like their male counterparts, female inmates turned to illegitimate channels to obtain goods and services not provided by the institution. Some of the female inmates held positions that afforded them access to desired goods or information. Inmates that took advantage of their position to help out other inmates became known as "connects." Connects occupied a dual role by not only providing inmates with things they needed or wanted, they also used their positions to bargain with other inmates who could provide goods or services. "Boosters" on the other hand used their positions to acquire goods and then sold them to other inmates. Their activities made them unpopular with the other inmates. Sykes described a similar role with his "merchant." Giallombardo did not observe the female inmates using force to take things from each other. Female inmates also shared items, but this was usually only done between inmates engaged in a homosexual or family relationship. In order for the illegitimate economy to run smoothly, some inmates took on the important role of "pinner." Pinners served as lookouts to alert inmates of approaching staff. Inmates who could be trusted and knew the routines of the prison occupied this important role.

The significance of the loss of heterosexual relationships and its effect on inmates was apparent by the number of inmate roles associated with the inmates' homosexual behaviors. In the male prison studied by Sykes, there were only three homosexual roles: fags, punks, and wolves. Giallombardo identified several homosexual roles occupied by women. Ward and Kassebaum had previously documented many of these social roles in their study of female homosexuality in a California prison published two years earlier. Giallombardo identified the "penitentiary turnout" who engaged in homosexual activities as a means of adapting to life without men. "Lesbians" were homosexuals prior to incarceration. Like their male counterparts, female inmates expressed very different attitudes about the two roles. Lesbians were perceived as deviants, but there was nothing abnormal about being a penitentiary turnout. Females also occupied different roles within their homosexual relationships. Most women preferred the role of "femme" or "mommy" because it allowed them to play a part they were already comfortable with. The femme's masculine counterpart was a "stud broad" or "daddy." The inmates that occupied this role were referred to as "he" or "him" and gained the respect of other inmates because it was a more difficult role to play. Studs dressed the part, changed their names, and displayed male mannerisms and behaviors. Stable relationships between studs and femmes were perceived as marriages in prison. These marriages tended to be long-term alliances, but like in free society, these marriages could be threatened when one partner became attracted to someone else. When a stud became interested in another stud, this was called "dropping the belt."

Not all of the relationships between female inmates were sincere. Some inmates became involved in a homosexual relationship for self-serving reasons. For example, a "commissary hustler" had sex with several different inmates, known as "tricks" for economic gain. "Chippies" were promiscuous inmates who engaged in several short-term relationships with different inmates. "Kick partners" also engaged in sex with several different inmates, but these inmates were not perceived as promiscuous because their motives were clear. "Kick partners" were only looking for sexual fulfillment with no assurances of a relationship. Within the prison, there were a group of inmates who had not yet been "turned out." "Cherries" were typically younger inmates who had not participated in any homosexual activities. The "punk" role in a female prison was different from the punk role found in a male facility. Male punks were inmates forced into homosexual activities. Female punks were inmates who displayed feminine characteristics when they were supposed to assume a masculine role. "Turnabouts" were inmates who bragged about their ability to play *either* the feminine or masculine role.

An inmate subculture offered both male and female inmates a way to lessen the pains of imprisonment and adapt to the prison environment. But the nature of the social relationships between female inmates distinguished them from their male counterparts. Females engaged in homosexual activities to cope with the loss of heterosexual activities, but this was primarily done in the context of a meaningful relationship. Many of the relationships were stable, long-term arrangements where two inmates considered themselves to be married. For those inmates choosing not to participate in such a marital unit, many established "kinship links" or close knit family units. Inmates took on the roles of brother, sister, son, or daughter. Giallombardo believed that these family units helped the women adapt to an environment that deprived them of their female identities. Women were traditionally socialized to be caregivers and as such their status was determined by how well they played the role of wife and mother. Both male and female subcultures emerged in response to the deprivations associated with the prison environment, but the differences between male and female subcultures reflected the cultures from which males and females were apart of prior to their incarceration.

Limitations

Observational research is ideal for studying dynamic environments like that found inside of a prison, but the extent to which findings can be *generalized* beyond the scope of the study always becomes an issue. Giallombardo's findings were based upon observations of inmates confined in a single prison during a one-year period. At the time of her study there were fewer than 5,500 female inmates incarcerated in prison. Today there are nearly 112,500 incarcerated females (Sabol et al. 2007). The number of incarcerated women has been increasing at double the rates as men and is largely a consequence of our nation's drug control policies. A recent study published by Kimberly Greer explored the applicability of Giallombardo's findings to an understanding of current female institutions. Greer (2000) interviewed 35 female inmates about their relationships with other inmates. Most of the females considered themselves to be "loners" in the sense that they did not form close, personal friendships with other inmates. In fact, females expressed a reluctance to form close relationships. Only 10 inmates reported having homosexual relationships with other females. This number was considerably lower than that found by Giallombardo and other studies published around the same time period. The inmates in Greer's study also did not conform to the "femme" or "stud broad" roles to the extent observed by Giallombardo.

Furthermore, Greer did not observe the same clearly defined kinship networks described by Giallombardo. Greer attributed the apparent change in female inmate social networks to differences in living accommodations, length of incarceration, changes in the social roles occupied by women in free society today, and to changes in the prison environment. The females studied by Greer were housed in dormitories and had only served on average seven months of their current sentence. The female inmates also did not appear to conform to traditional gender stereotypes. Greer's observations could have also stemmed from the transformation of prisons away from being closed institutions cut off from society.

Giallombardo's findings offered additional support that inmate subcultures develop in response to the deprivations of the prison environment. She also recognized the importance of the importation perspective when she wrote, ". . . the content of male and female roles are brought into the prison setting and function to determine the direction and focus of the inmate cultural systems" (p. 187). According to Barbara Bradshaw (1967), Giallombardo's study was incomplete because she offered no explanation as to *why* female inmates occupied different social roles in prison. It would have been more insightful to learn how the individual characteristics of the women studied influenced the specific roles displayed by the inmates. Several studies published after 1966 addressed this criticism by including measures of both deprivation and importation in the analyses.

Significance and Subsequent Research

Giallombardo published the first comprehensive empirical study of the female inmate environment and the female social networks found in prison. Giallombardo found that both the deprivation and importation perspectives explained the inmate social systems found in a female prison. Like Sykes, she argued that the inmate subculture within a female prison emerged in response to the deprivations of the prison environment. However, it was also her contention that the nature of that subculture reflected the social roles occupied by women in free society. Females brought into prison with them traditional female characteristics that influenced their social networks. In an effort to test which perspective—deprivation or importation—provided a better explanation for the development of *female* inmate subcultures, Charles Tittle conducted a study of confined narcotics addicts in which he interviewed both male and female inmates. Tittle (1969) first set out to determine if in fact female inmate subcultures were different from male inmate subcultures. He found that females were more likely to affiliate with small, cohesive groups compared to their male counterparts. Tittle also interviewed inmates who were at different phases of their institutional experience: early, middle, and late. He found that while the percentage of males who affiliated with an inmate group remained fairly continuous throughout their incarceration, the percentage of female affiliations increased at a steady pace. Females and males were almost equal in their participation in homosexual activities, but Tittle observed, however, a difference in the *nature* of the homosexual activities. Consistent with Giallombardo, females formed longstanding homosexual relationships, while male inmates engaged in more casual homosexual activities for immediate gratification or economic gain. Female inmates were less committed to the inmate code and indicated fewer behaviors that reflected a "symbiotic inmate structure" compared to their male counterparts. Tittle concluded that there were apparent differences between female and male inmate social systems. The female and male inmates who participated in Tittle's study were confined within the same institution, which presented a rather unique opportunity to examine the influences of deprivation and importation because females and males were incarcerated within the same environment. He included in his analysis several criminal subculture measures, as well as preinstitutional inmate characteristics. Tittle found greater support for the deprivation perspective to explain the development of both female and male inmate subcultures.

Six years after Giallombardo published her study, Esther Heffernan published *Making it in Prison: The Square, the Cool, and the Life.* Heffernan (1972) conducted an extensive study of female inmates at the Virginia Women's Reformatory at Occoquan. Consistent with Irwin and Cressey (1962), Heffernan found no evidence of a single, identifiable female inmate subculture. Instead, she observed several criminal subcultures brought into the prison environment by female offenders. Differences in the criminal backgrounds of these women explained the type of subculture they belonged to prison. The "square" subculture was made up of women with little experience in crime. These women displayed a commitment to conventional social norms as evidenced by their unwillingness to participate in homosexual activities. Other females belonged to the "cool" subculture that was comprised primarily of professional property criminals. Crime was a way of life for these inmates and their goal in prison was to serve their sentence as fast and painless as possible. Finally, inmates in the "life" had spent a significant portion of their lives behind bars. Prison had become a way of life for these inmates who relied upon their subculture to meet virtually of their needs.

Subsequent research has also examined the assimilation of female inmates into their social networks to determine if females become prisonized the same way as their male counterparts. Gary Jensen and Dorothy Jones' (1976) examined a random sample of female inmates confined in the North Carolina Correctional Center for Women to determine whether or not the amount of time spent in prison was related to the female inmates' degree of prisonization. They found support for Wheeler's u-shaped perspective. Commitment to an inmate code was strongest for female inmates in the middle of their incarceration.

At the time of her study, Giallombardo found no evidence to indicate that the prison environment was any less depriving for women. Females experienced the same pains of imprisonment as their male counterparts, but the nature of some of the pains were experienced differently. In order to determine if there were *quantitative* differences in how females and males experienced the prison environment, Jean Wahl Harris (1993) administered Toch's Prison Preference Inventory (PPI) and Kevin Wright's Prison Environmental Inventory (PEI) (discussed previously in the discussion of Sykes) to a random sample of female inmates from both a minimum and medium security prison in New York State. For comparison, both instruments were also administered to random samples of male inmates from five medium and five maximum-security prisons within the same state. Harris discovered differences in the needs identified by both genders as important. Female inmates indicated that their need for freedom, social stimulation, and support was less important compared to male inmates. Females and males also differed in their perceptions of prison resources allocated to meet their needs. Females were more likely to perceive prison resources to be adequate in meeting their needs. Harris pointed out, however that neither the PPI nor PEI included items to measure one of the most important sources of stress for females: the loss of their children.

Because Giallombardo's study was carried out at a single female prison, she was unable to explore whether or not different prison environments resulted in observed differences for how female inmates adapt to prison. Several subsequent studies have examined female subcultures within two or more prisons. Candace Kruttschnitt, Rosemary, Gartner, and Amy Miller (2000) interviewed 70 inmates from two different female prisons in California. The first prison was the California Institution for Women built in 1952. The prison held 600 inmates and was originally designed according to the cottage architectural style. While several structural and environmental changes had occurred beginning in the 1970s, the facility still had a campus like atmosphere. The second prison was Valley State Prison, a newer facility that held 3,600 female inmates. Valley State resembled a maximum-security male prison with its layers of fencing and other security features. Researchers tested the applicability of the importation and deprivation perspectives to explain differences in how females adapted to their prison environments. The two prisons confined inmates that were similar in terms of age, race, and commitment offense, but the California Institution for Women housed more parole violators and females serving life sentences. Researchers found partial support for the importation perspective. Inmates' preinstitutional social class and age was related to their adjustment. Inmates from lower class backgrounds appeared to have an easier time adjusting to the deprivations of imprisonment compared to inmates removed from middle class backgrounds. Inmates in their 30s (the median age for the prisons) appeared more at ease with their environments compared to younger and older inmates. A third preinstitutional factor that was related to adjustment was whether or not the inmates had experienced any physical abuse. Many of the inmates drew parallels between being abused prior to incarceration and their incarceration experience. A comparison of the inmate interviews between the two facilities revealed several differences that offered support for the deprivation perspective as well. While inmates from both institutions expressed concerns over the trustworthiness of their fellow inmates, inmates from Valley State indicated a greater reluctance to form personal relationships with other inmates. Consistent with this finding, fewer Valley State inmates reported sharing their material possessions with other inmates, received less help from their fellow inmates, and revealed less interest in maintaining inmate contacts upon their release. Inmates from the California Institute for Women displayed more favorable attitudes towards their prison staff and institution. In fact, when asked where the inmates would prefer to do their time, most females from both institutions expressed a preference for the California Institute for Women.

Shanhe Jiang and Thomas Winfree (2006) published another recent study of female inmate adjustment that used samples of inmates from multiple prisons. Jiang and Winfree examined differences in social support and adjustment for male and female inmates from 275 state prisons across the United States. Female inmates had more social support from their children as evidenced by the frequency of communication and contacts (mail, telephone and visitation). Male inmates, however, had greater social support from their spouses. The number of rule violations in a 30-day period was used to measure the inmates' adjustment to prison. Married, male inmates had lower rates of rule violations compared to single, male inmates. Female inmates who maintained telephone communication with their children had fewer violations.

In her study Giallombardo found that only 12 percent of the inmates received a visitor during the past year of incarceration. Several other studies have documented the limited number of visits received by female inmates (Bloom and Steinhart 1993, Fuller 1993). More recently, Karen Casey-Acevedo and Tim Bakken (2002) published a study of female visitation at a maximum-security prison in the Northeast. They examined the visitation records of 180 women released from prison and they also observed the visitations that took place over a one-month period and conducted interviews with inmates and staff. The prison provided ample opportunities for visitation by allowing inmates to receive visitors every day from 8:30 A.M. to 3:00 P.M. In addition, the prison offered programs designed to help strengthen bonds between mothers and children and provided financial assistance to help pay for transportation costs. Seventy-nine percent of the women had received visits from family or friends. Researchers also explored the extent to which mothers received visits from their children. In their study, 158 inmates had children under the age of 18. Almost 20 percent of these inmates had children in foster care. Only 39 percent of the mothers received any visits from their children. The younger mothers received more visits compared to older mothers. The staff speculated that this was probably due to the age of the children. Older children may have been more reluctant to visit. Consistent with Giallombardo, researchers found that prison location explained why many inmates received no visits from their children.

Giallombardo made a valuable contribution to the literature on inmate subcultures with her detailed analysis of female inmate social networks. She compared the pains of imprisonment experienced by females to those described years earlier by Sykes and found that the same deprivations held true for females. Giallombardo discovered, however, important differences in the nature and extent of the pains felt by female inmates that she attributed to the different cultural experiences of women in free society. Her study offered further support for an integrated explanation of inmate subcultures that included elements of the deprivation and importation perspectives.

References

Bloom, B., and D. Steinhart (1993). *Why Punish the Children: A Reappraisal of Incarcerated Mothers in America.* San Francisco: National Council on Crime and Delinquency.

Bradshaw, B. (1967). "Society of Women: A Study of a Women's Prison." (Book Review) *Social Forces* 45:461–62.

Casey-Acevedo, K., and T. Bakken (2002). "Visiting Women in Prison: Who Visits and Who Cares?" *Journal of Offender Rehabilitation* 34:67–83.

Dobash, R., R. Dobash, and S. Gutteridge (1986). *The Imprisonment of Women.* Oxford: Basil Blackwell.

Fuller, L. (1993). "Visitors to Women's Prisons in California: An Exploratory Study." *Federal Probation* 57:41–47.

Giallombardo, R. (1966). "Interviewing in the Prison Community." *Journal of Criminal Law, Criminology and Police Science* 57:318–24.

Greer, K. (2000). "The Changing Nature of Interpersonal Relationships in a Women's Prison." *Prison Journal* 80:442–68.

Harris, J. (1993). "Comparison of Stressors Among Female and Male Inmates." *Journal of Offender Rehabilitation* 19:43–56.

Heffernan, E. (1972). *Making it in Prison: The Square, the Cool, and the Life.* New York: Wiley-Interscience.

Jensen, G., and D. Jones (1976). "Perspectives on Inmate Culture: A Study of Women in Prison." *Social Forces* 54:590–603.

Jiang, S., and T. Winfree, Jr. (2006). "Social Support, Gender, and Inmate Adjustment to Prison Life: Insights from a National Sample." *Prison Journal* 86:32–55.

Kruttschnitt, C., R. Gartner, and A. Miller (2000). "Doing Her Own Time? Women's Responses to Prison in the Context of the Old and the New Penology." *Criminology* 38:681–717.

Sabol, W., H. Couture, and P. Harrison (2007). *Prisoners in 2006.* Washington, DC: US Department of Justice.

Tittle, C. (1969). "Inmate Organization: Sex Differentiation and the Influence of Criminal Subcultures." *American Sociological Review* 34:492–505.

Ward, D., and G. Kassebaum (1964). "Homosexuality: A Mode of Adaptation in a Prison for Women." *Social Problems* 12:159–77.

Further Reading

Casey-Acevedo, K., and T. Bakken (2003). "Women Adjusting to Prison: Disciplinary Behavior and the Characteristics of Adjustment." *Journal of Health and Social Policy* 17:37–60.

Fox, J. (1982). "Women in Prison: A Study in the Social Reality of Stress." In R. Johnson and H. Toch (eds.), *The Pains of Imprisonment.* Beverly Hills: Sage.

Hannah-Moffat, K. (1991). "Feminine Fortresses: Women-Centered Prisons?" *Prison Journal* 75:135–64.

Johnson, P. (2003). *Inner Lives: Voices of African American Women in Prison.* New York: New York UP.

Leger, R. (1987). "Lesbianism Among Women Prisoners: Participants and Nonparticipants." *Criminal Justice and Behavior* 14:448–67.

Negy, C., D. Woods, and R. Carlson (1997). "The Relationship Between Female Inmates' Coping and Adjustment in a Minimum-Security Prison." *Criminal Justice and Behavior* 24:224–33.

Severance, T. (2005). "You Know Who Can Go To: Cooperation and Exchange Between Incarcerated Women." *Prison Journal* 85:343–67.

Sharp, S., and S. Marcus-Mendoza (2001). "It's a Family Affair: Incarcerated Women and Their Families." *Women and Criminal Justice* 12:21–49.

Ward, D., and G. Kassebaum (1965). *Women's Prison: Sex and Social Structure.* Chicago: Aldine.

INMATE RACE RELATIONS: DO PRISON SUBCULTURES DIFFER BY AN INMATE'S RACE?

Carroll, L. (1974). *Hacks, Blacks, and Cons.* Lexington, MA: Lexington Books.

Background

Early studies of inmate subcultures also paid little attention to the issue of race. In *The Prison Community*, Clemmer noted that some of the black inmates segregated themselves from the white inmates, however, found no wide spread racial prejudice among the inmate population. Sykes made a similar observation in his study. Inmates, both black and white, were housed within the same prison environment so it was believed that both groups adapted to their environment by becoming part of the same inmate subcultures. In some states, correctional administrators kept black inmates separated from white inmates by housing them in separate institutions or by work and housing assignments (Jacobs 1979). Prisons underwent many significant changes beginning in the late 1950s that transformed the prison environment. Various "humanitarian reforms" resulted in a lessening of the deprivations or pains of imprisonment originally experienced by inmates. Inmates benefited from greater access to counseling and educational programs and more opportunities for visitation, work release, and parole (Carroll 1974). The increased contact inmates enjoyed with the outside meant that prisons could no longer be considered closed institutions where the lives of inmates remained untouched by events taking place in free society.

The civil rights movement was one such event that would have a major influence on the prison environment. Racial tensions in society escalated as black Americans pushed for equality and an end to racial discrimination. In prison, black inmates were also no longer willing to accept their subordinate status. The Black Power movement became a catalyst for black inmates to unite themselves against white inmates and the predominately white correctional staff. As a result, race became increasingly relevant to our understanding of the inmate society.

The Study

Leo Carroll (1974) provided the first in-depth sociological examination of the racial conflict that characterized many prisons in the 1970s. He further documented important differences between black and white inmate subcultures that reflected changes in the prison environment. The data for Carroll's study came from a variety of sources including observations, interviews, prison records, staff reports, and inmate essays. Carroll spent 15 months (October 1970 to December 1971) as a *participant-observer* in a small state prison located in Rhode Island. He called the prison Eastern Correctional Institution, a fictitious name, to protect the *confidentiality* of the inmates and staff. Carroll assumed the role of an "interested observer" who was gathering data for a book about prison. He did not want to be perceived as associated with either the staff or inmates. His initial time was spent in the public parts of the prison (i.e., the yard) that afforded him access to a lot of inmates. He initiated contact with the inmates and then waited for them to reciprocate. Carroll found the inmates to be suspicious, but most of the inmates were curious enough about what he was doing in prison to strike up conversations with him, and some inmates even introduced him to their friends. In order to appear completely impartial, Carroll established different types of relationships with the various groups of inmates by aligning himself with one particular group at a time. He found this necessary because his personal characteristics influenced how the inmates perceived him. Carroll was a white, college-educated outsider who could come and go from the prison. The inmates were both white and black, had little education, and were not free to leave. Carroll's integration into the white and black inmate groups differed significantly. Carroll's preliminary contacts with the white inmates consisted of inmates on the periphery of an inmate social system. Once he was introduced to the leaders of several inmate organizations, he was able to gain access to the rest of the white inmate population. Carroll's integration into the black inmate society proved more difficult. His initial presentation was with the black inmate leaders to whom he was introduced by the white leaders. It took considerably longer for Carroll to develop relationships with the black inmates. It was not until he segregated himself completely from the white inmates that the black inmates became responsive. Carroll was able to further gain their cooperation by showing an interest in their politics and racial causes. Carroll knew that if the inmates perceived him to be aligned with the staff it would compromise his position with the inmates. He limited his contact with staff to areas of the prison that were off limits to the inmates, such as the officers' dining hall.

Carroll described his role as both "active" and "passive" participant. As an *active participant*, he wore clothing that resembled the inmates, spoke using the inmates' slang vocabulary, and took part in the inmates' daily activities. He played the role so well that sometimes inmates and staff mistook him for a fellow prisoner. At other times, Carroll would step back and observe the inmates as a non-participant. Carroll also conducted interviews with inmates and staff. Most of his interviews were "conversational interviews" in which he would informally ask inmates questions when the opportunity arose. These took place while inmates were engaged in their regular prison activities. Prior to the start of his study, Carroll read reports on the prison written by various investigatory commissions. He also completed his own "census" of the inmate population by recording their numbers and demographic profiles. In addition, Carroll was permitted to review the inmate disciplinary reports submitted each week as well as staff reports and court transcripts. Finally, some of the inmates that Carroll developed a close connection with provided him with essays and narratives of events he was unable to personally witness.

Findings

Carroll spent several months as an observer in a maximum-security prison. He gathered data on the prison environment, the staff, and the inmates. Carroll acknowledged his study to be *exploratory*, but throughout the course of his study he formulated and tested the following *hypotheses*:

1. The humanitarian reforms introduced in the mid-1950s decreased solidarity among white inmates, but increased solidarity among black inmates.
2. Black inmates were penalized more severely than white inmates by the prison disciplinary board.
3. Most of the sexual assaults involved black perpetrators against white victims.

In addition to testing these hypotheses, Carroll provided a thorough description of the prison environment and the differences between white and black inmate groups. He further offered a detailed account of the working environment for correctional officers.

The Prison Environment

Eastern Correctional Institution housed inmates of all security levels: minimum, medium; and maximum. Carroll chose to limit his study to the maximum-security facility because it contained the most inmates and was completely separate from the other facilities. The maximum-security building was constructed in 1878 and was surrounded by a huge wall with guard towers. Inmates were confined separately in their cells, yet spent most of their daytime hours at work or involved in recreational activities. Up until 1956, prison operations followed the same custodial model as the prisons described by Clemmer and Sykes. Inmates adhered to a strict regime of rules and procedures all designed to maintain discipline and security. The formal operations of the prison changed dramatically in 1956 when a new warden was appointed: Alfred King. King relaxed many of the institutional rules, did away with procedures designed to humiliate the inmates, and implemented changes that improved the overall quality of life for inmates. Inmates were permitted to wear their own clothes and were given more freedom to move about the facility, and visitation privileges were increased. Inmates accused of violating prison rules were afforded basic due process rights prior to being punished. In addition, King encouraged the development of several inmate organizations, including a prison newspaper, an art club, a chapter of Alcoholics Anonymous, and an organization for inmates serving life terms. These programs and improvements were considered to be rehabilitative in the sense that they could help promote positive inmate behavior. Carroll called these changes "humanitarian reforms." While they lessened the pains of imprisonment, they could not be considered treatment.

The "Hacks"

As part of his study, Carroll examined the work environment of the prison's custodial staff referred to by the inmates as "hacks." He found that officers were frustrated and experienced role conflict that stemmed from multiple sources. First, a new warden was appointed in 1969. Charles Knott replaced King who had occupied the position since 1956. Knott was charged with the task of continuing the institution's transition to a "correctional facility" geared towards treatment but was unable to secure the necessary financial resources to adequately fulfill his mission. In addition, the other members of his administrative staff displayed resistance to his treatment philosophy. Second, as part of the changes implemented under Warden King's administration, the role of the prison "guard" became less clear. Guards were responsible for enforcing prison rules and regulations in an effort to maintain order and security. Consistent with the goal of rehabilitation, the term "guard" was replaced with "correctional officer" in the mid 1950s. Correctional officers assumed the responsibility of aiding the rehabilitation of inmates. This added role was less clearly defined. Officers had not been trained as counselors, nor were they given any formal instructions for how to carry out this directive. The administration had relaxed many of the rules giving inmates more freedom and officers were instructed to use good judgment in enforcing the remaining rules left in place. Third, by the early 1970s the courts were longer maintaining their "hands off" policy with regards to inmate rights. Correctional officers believed that recent court rulings had diminished their authority making it more difficult to control the inmates.

The organizational conflict, uncertainty over job expectations, and court decisions affording inmates certain constitutional rights created a frustrating and stressful work environment for the correctional officers employed at Eastern Correctional Institute. Carroll found that some officers entered into exchange relationships with inmates as a means of gaining their compliance. Consistent with Sykes' observation, Carroll found that officers relied on persuasion and bribery to make sure inmates complied with their orders. Other correctional officers pushed for change by organizing work stoppages, which were largely unsuccessful. Officers were unable to secure the support of their state employee's union so they set up their own union: the Fraternal Order of Correctional Officers. The new union was successful in its efforts to secure better pay and benefits, but officers wanted more. Officers pressed the administration for formal rules and regulations to govern their interactions with inmates. Reluctantly, Warden Knott established a five-member panel to work on the rules. At the time of Carroll's study, the panel had just begun its work.

The "Cons"

When Carroll began his study, there were 186 inmates housed in the maximum-security facility. Inmates were convicted of a wide range of personal and property crimes, but over half were for breaking and entering, robbery, or homicide. Inmates were young with a mean age of 29.3 years and over half had completed some high school. The median sentence length for the inmates was 7.3 years, and most of them had prior institutional commitments. One hundred and forty-five of the inmates were white (referred to as "cons"). Consistent with Clemmer, Sykes, and Giallombardo, Carroll identified several inmate roles adopted by the white inmates. While many of the roles adopted were in response to the deprivations of prison, Carroll did not observe these roles to be a sign of an inmate code. Inmates did not adhere to a set of shared values. White inmates affiliated into various fragmented groups with no apparent inmate solidarity. Inmate roles reflected the diverse interests of the inmates who adopted them. There were the "stand-up guys" who displayed physical and mental strength. Stand-up guys (analogous to Sykes' real men) were loyal to the other inmates, but remained detached and did not consider them to be true friends. They never cooperated with staff and never complained. The "mafia" consisted of a tight knit group of inmates whose reputation for violence invoked fear from other inmates. Two other groups of inmates took on roles that allowed them to control certain aspects of the prison environment. The "wise guys" consisted of a group of 12 to 15 inmates who controlled many of the illegal activities in prison (i.e., gambling and drugs). The mafia and wise guys both exerted a considerable amount of power over other inmates, but it was the "politicians" who held elected positions with the prison "Jay Cees" and worked on the prison newspaper who were perceived by staff and outsiders to be the leaders of the white inmate groups. There were inmate groups observed by Carroll who maintained their conventional identities while in prison. "Administration men" not only deliberately separated themselves from other inmates they also did not associate much with each other. The "hippies" on the other hand, belonged to a tight knit group that remained detached from other inmate groups. Hippies did not consider themselves to be criminals but political prisoners.

Carroll observed the same homosexual roles described by Sykes. The "fags" were self-proclaimed homosexuals while other inmates ("punks") were forced into homosexual activities. When a punk became a regular sex partner for an inmate or a small group of inmates they were known as "kids." Homosexual activities were not the only illegal behaviors observed by Carroll. Drug use had also become prevalent and was reflected in the social roles adopted by inmates. Many inmates used drugs as a means of temporary escape from the everyday realities of prison, but the "dope fiends" were drug addicts who used drugs prior to their incarceration and spent most of their time on the inside obtaining drugs and getting high.

Carroll also observed a group of inmates he termed "others." Because of their short sentences, the others were a transient group of inmates who preyed upon the other inmates. They stole things from inmates' cells and charged items to other inmates' accounts. Their deceitfulness only fueled the inmates' suspicions of one another, which helped to explain the lack of inmate solidarity among white inmates. The inmates' response to snitches provided further evidence of the lack of inmate solidarity among whites. Despite the lack of adherence to an inmate code, inmates at Eastern Correctional Institute maintained a prohibition against snitching. Snitches were labeled as "rats" but inmates also used the term for inmates outside of their social group. Carroll also found that certain types of ratting were acceptable. For example, one inmate could rat on another who had previously snitched on him. Inmates perceived ratting to be an issue best settled between individual inmates as opposed to behavior that warranted a group response. In his book, Carroll offered a diagram to illustrate the interactions between white inmates:

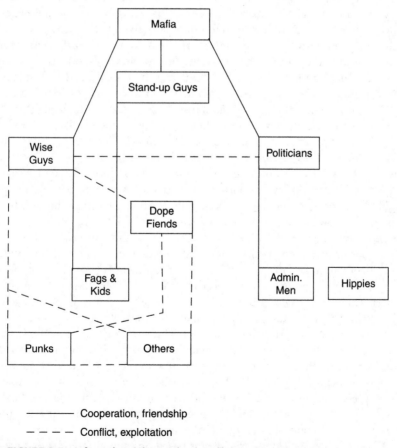

———— Cooperation, friendship

– – – – Conflict, exploitation

FIGURE 3.5 Informal social organization of the white prisoners

Source: Carroll, L. (1974). *Hacks, Blacks, and Cons.* Lexington, MA: Lexington Books

The quality of life for inmates confined at the Eastern Correctional Institute was significantly better than it had been for the inmates studied by Sykes. The pains of imprisonment had been lessened as a result of the "humanitarian reforms" introduced in the 1950s. Carroll *hypothesized* that the inmate solidarity among whites decreased as a consequence of the reforms. Inmates enjoyed greater access to the outside world and increased freedom on the inside. While Carroll was not able to test this hypothesis directly, interviews with the long-term white inmates supported his hypothesis.

The Blacks

At the time of Carroll's study, there were 41 black inmates in the maximum-security facility at Eastern. Blacks constituted only 22 percent of the total population but their numbers had grown significantly in the preceding years (an 8% increase in only four years). Unlike their white counterparts, black inmates maintained a high degree of inmate solidarity. Carroll *hypothesized* that the same humanitarian reforms that had weakened cohesion among white inmates actually increased unity among black inmates (which he again supported with interview data). Black inmates belonged to a single organization, the Afro-American Society. The primary purpose of this group was not to help alleviate the deprivations of prison, but rather to maintain a cohesive racial identity. Black inmates brought into prison with them the content of the Afro-American Society. During the 1960s, black culture experienced two important, but conflicting, social changes referred to by Carroll as "soul" and "nationalism." Soul signified a ". . . celebration of a black American culture that has developed as an adaptation to conditions imposed by racism" (p. 91). As a consequence of slavery, blacks lost their African cultural identity. The soul perspective afforded blacks a new identity that was uniquely theirs. Blacks shared a history marked by exploitation and discrimination. Soul acknowledged the struggles blacks have endured and their ability to survive continuing hardships. The perspective that black culture was rooted in African, not American, traditions and that blacks should have control of their own society was known as nationalism. African-American became the preferred term for blacks. African-American's embraced their African heritage through their dress, hairstyles, art, and language. Black nationalism also referred to revolutionary efforts by blacks to gain control over political, economic, and social institutions.

The perspectives of soul (a celebration of the unique American history experienced by blacks) and nationalism (efforts to establish an African identify) were not compatible. The conflict and tension between the two perspectives in free society influenced the adaptive roles of black inmates in prison. Black inmates acknowledged the same argot roles adopted by whites (i.e., the fags, punks, kids), but the primary roles adopted by black inmates centered on a need to assert their racial identity. Inmates affiliated with the Afro-American Society were known as "brothers." For some, an inmate had to be black to be called a brother, but others considered any minority group member to be a brother. Brothers were not necessary a close-knit group. Membership into the "brotherhood" was based on a collective understanding of the oppressed status occupied by minorities in free society. Brothers willingly shared their possessions with one another and stood as a unified group against the administration and the rest of the inmate population. The relationship between "partners" was more personal. These inmates developed friendships based on mutual interests or backgrounds.

Partners remained loyal and protected one another. Inmates who knew each other on the outside might become "street partners" on the inside, while "jail house partners" became friends after their incarceration. The only black inmates kept out of the brotherhood were "toms." Toms were black inmates who identified with the white inmate groups or were accommodating to staff members.

Carroll identified a group of six or seven inmates to be "revolutionaries." These inmates had adopted the perspective of Black Nationalism and considered themselves to be political prisoners. Revolutionaries kept to themselves in prison and as a group spent their time ". . . in preparation for the eventual revolution" (p. 103). Revolutionaries maintained a bare existence while incarcerated. Their cells contained minimal furnishings and they chose not to participate in the inmate barter system. Revolutionaries perceived inmates who spent their time trying to alleviate the pains of imprisonment with drug use and homosexual activities to be "weak." Instead, revolutionaries took advantage of programs offered by the Afro-American Society and various self improvement designed to heighten their awareness of black oppression. Other inmates, referred to as "half-steppers" professed to be revolutionaries, however, their behavior ran contrary to their beliefs. Whereas revolutionaries spent their time in pursuit of future endeavors, half-steppers were more concerned with creating an environment in prison reflective of their soul perspective. The soul perspective was reflected in the nicknames these inmates called each other, their dress, and their mannerisms. The incompatible perspectives of nationalism and soul became a source of conflict between the revolutionaries and half-steppers. The revolutionaries established the Afro-American Society with the intent of persuading the half-steppers to join their cause. Instead, the half-steppers used the organization as a means of alleviating some of the deprivations of prison. Half-steppers participated in the leisure activities sponsored by the organization, but displayed no real interest in the cultural awareness programs. In spite of this conflict, the organization remained stable. According to Carroll, the organization was able to carry on because the revolutionaries (although fewer in number) continued their mission to convert half-steppers to their way of thinking. In addition, all meetings of the Afro-American Society were "open" where members could voice their issues.

Race Relations

There was an overwhelming consensus among black inmates that they were discriminated against by prison administrators and staff. It was their perception that white inmates were provided better housing and work assignments. Black inmates also believed that they were victims of unfair disciplinary practices. Carroll tested this *hypothesis* by reviewing disciplinary reports for a four-month period. He found an overrepresentation of black inmates in these reports. In a four-month period, officers filed 210 reports. Sixty-nine, or 32.9, percent involved black inmates, yet blacks were only 22 percent of the inmate population. Another interesting finding emerged. Black inmates were more likely to be reported for major rule violations such as failure to comply with orders and threatening the officers. Despite the overrepresentation of black inmates found in the prison disciplinary reports, black inmates were not treated more severely by the Disciplinary Board.

Carroll observed what appeared to be racial bias on the part of the correctional staff. On one occasion an officer abruptly ended a black inmate's visit because he was displaying

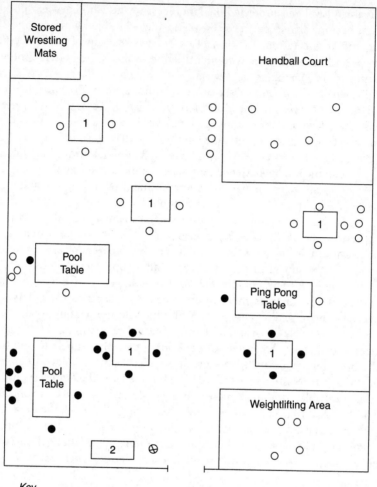

Key

○ White Prisoners
● Black Prisoners
⊕ Guards
1 Card Tables
2 Card Desk

FIGURE 3.6 Racial Segregation of Prisoners in the Gym

Source: Carroll, L. (1974). *Hacks, Blacks, and Cons.* Lexington, MA: Lexington Books

intimate behavior with a white female visitor. Although the contact between the inmate and visitor was a violation of the rules, inmates displaying the same behavior with visitors of the same race were left alone. Interviews with white correctional officers revealed that none of them disclosed having any black social contacts beyond the black officers they worked with. White correctional officers also verbalized various stereotypes of blacks as lazy and of low intelligence. At the same time, white officers perceived the black inmates as militants (a stereotype fed by the revolutionary inmates) interested in taking control over the prison through violent revolution. Because of these stereotypes, black inmates were watched more closely than white inmates (Carroll believed this could have explained why blacks were over represented in the prison disciplinary reports).

The racial biases of correctional officers coupled with the inmates' revolutionary status meant that black inmates were not in a position to enter into exchange relationships with the guards the same way as their white counterparts. White inmates manipulated the officers' authority by diffusing dangerous altercations before they got out of hand. Guards would return the favor by ignoring rule violations. Black inmates, on the other hand, challenged the authority of officers through various confrontational tactics. Officers were intimated by the solidarity among black inmates. Carroll believed that this also helped explain why black inmates received more disciplinary reports, but at the same time were not sanctioned more severely than whites.

Carroll tested his fourth *hypothesis* with data obtained from inmate interviews. He found that a majority of the sexual assaults (both reported and unreported) were interracial. The aggressor was usually black and the victim white. Black aggressors justified their attacks on the grounds that their white victims were ". . . primarily responsible for the psychological emasculation of the black male" (p. 187).

The black and white inmates at Eastern clearly preferred to remain segregated from one another as evidenced by their participation in inmate organizations, recreational and other activities. Despite the limited space and situations where inmates were forced to have contacts with members of the opposite race (i.e., work assignments), inmates still managed segregate themselves. Carroll provided the following diagram to show the segregation of inmates in the prison gym (a common area for all inmates).

Limitations

Carroll was among the first to document differences between blacks and whites in their experiences of the prison environment. Like his predecessors, his conclusions were derived from a single prison located in the eastern part of the United States. Blacks comprised only 22 percent of the inmate population in his prison, yet in many other prisons throughout the United States, blacks made up a significantly higher proportion of the inmate population. In 1974 blacks made up 47 percent of all inmates nationwide and had become the majority in many prisons (Gottfredson, Hindelang, and Parisi 1978). Whether or not Carroll's findings related to race relations would *generalize* to other prisons with different racial compositions became an issue. In addition, Carroll supplemented his observations with data obtained from prison disciplinary reports that could have been biased. Carroll found that black inmates had lower rates of minor rule violations but higher rates of major violations compared to white inmates. Inmate disciplinary records are potentially problematic for the same reasons as other official measures of crime. Not all inmate rule violations are detected, and even if detected, may not be reported. Researchers have uncovered racial bias on the part of correctional officers in that black inmates were more likely to be written up for rule violations even though self-report studies indicated similar rates of rule violations for white inmates (Poole and Regoli 1980).

Carroll included in his study a discussion of the correctional officers employed at Eastern Correctional Institution, but according to Eric Colvin (1976), he failed to examine how the daily responsibilities of correctional officers contributed to the prison organization. Instead, Carroll only wrote about the anxiety and role conflicts faced by officers.

Juliette Martin (1976) also believed that Carroll should have explored staff and inmate attitudes towards hiring black correctional officers as a possible means of reducing racial conflict within the prison.

Significance and Subsequent Research

Hacks, Blacks, and Cons was the first major sociological study to explore the influence of race on the prison environment. Carroll provided a systematic look at the racial segregation among inmates and the differences in adaptation between black and white inmates. In 1977, James Jacobs published his work *Stateville: The Penitentiary in Mass Society.* Jacobs spent three years gathering data from Stateville Penitentiary in Illinois. Consistent with Carroll, Jacobs observed the impact of nationalism on black inmate behaviors and attitudes. Black inmates used the ideology of the Black Muslim movement as justification for confronting the white correctional officers. Jacobs also found black inmates to be part of a highly cohesive group. The prison environment was further transformed by the infiltration of gangs. The city of Chicago increased its enforcement of gang related crime in the 1960s, and as a consequence, more and more gang members were incarcerated. Gang leaders perceived the increased enforcement to be racially motivated which only fueled their antagonism towards the correctional system. In prison, gang members sought to establish and maintain their status and power. Conflicts between rival gangs became a major source of prison violence and unrest. In an earlier study, Jacobs (1974) identified three major black prison gangs within Stateville Penitentiary: the *Black P. Stone Nation*, the *Disciplines*, and the *Vicelords*. These gangs were part of the largest street gangs in Chicago. Membership in a prison gang afforded inmates protection, access to goods and services, and psychological support.

A few years after *Stateville*, John Irwin published his *Prisons in Turmoil*. Irwin (1980) also described how the prison environment had undergone dramatic changes as a result of broad social movements and changes in the inmate population. The Black Muslim movement with its separatist ideology started having a major influence on black inmates at Soledad Prison in California (where Irwin himself had previously been incarcerated). Irwin observed an environment characterized by racial segregation, gang affiliations, drugs, and violence. Inmates organized themselves into informal social groups according to their race or ethnicity. According to Irwin, "the hate and distrust between white and black prisoners constitute the most power source of divisions" (p. 183). As the number of black inmates increased, their presence and radical separatist ideas were perceived as threatening to the white inmates. Racial tensions and conflict between black and white inmates frequently escalated into violence. The penetration of violent "cliques" and gangs also contributed to the increasingly violent prison environment.

Carroll documented several important differences between black and white inmates. Research by Ann Goetting and Roy Howsen (1983) examined data from a national sample of state prison inmates and identified other differences between black and white inmates. In 1981, blacks made up 45.6 percent of the nation's total prison population. Black inmates were younger, less likely to ever have been married, had more children and more siblings, and were less likely to have had steady employment prior to their incarceration compared to their white counterparts. There were more black inmates serving time for violent crimes compared to white inmates and blacks were serving longer prison sentences. While in prison, blacks had more disciplinary reports, but for less serious rule violations (a finding that contradicted Carroll). Goetting and Howsen also identified racial disparities in work assignments that could have reflected discriminatory prison procedures. Black inmates generally occupied low status positions such as food service and janitorial work.

Carroll, Jacobs, and Irwin based their findings primarily upon their *qualitative* observations of inmate interactions in a single prison. Subsequent research has attempted to examine inmate behavior and attitudes using large samples of inmates from multiple prisons and *quantitative* measures of inmate adjustment. In 1984, Lynn Goodstein and Doris MacKenzie published results from their study of inmates confined in five prisons located in four states. A random sample of 1,618 inmates completed a survey that included questions to assess their level of prison adjustment and prior institutional characteristics. Goodstein and MacKenzie found that black and white inmates differed in their prisonization experiences. Black inmates were more likely to come into prison with negative attitudes towards prison staff compared to white inmates. This difference, however, was the result of where the inmates lived prior to their incarceration. Urban blacks as well as urban whites possessed negative attitudes more so than rural blacks and whites. Prior involvement in the criminal justice system influenced the attitudes of white inmates but not black inmates. Negative attitudes towards staff appeared to be influenced more by the prison environment for white inmates compared to black inmates. The degree of radicalism among white inmates also increased with more criminal justice system contacts, but whites were still less radical than blacks. Contrary to what they expected, Goodstein and MacKenzie found that black inmates reported less prisoner-to-prisoner conflict compared to white inmates. This finding was attributed to higher degree of solidarity among black inmates. Blacks did, however, maintain higher levels of conflict with the staff compared to whites, which could have reflected discriminatory treatment by correctional officers. Research by Craig Hemmens and James Marquart (2000) also found that black inmates had lower opinions of correctional officers compared to white inmates. Hemmens and Marquart surveyed 775 inmates who had been recently released from the Texas Department of Corrections (TDC). Inmates were asked to indicate the extent to which they agreed with statements designed to measure their opinions about the correctional staff. Black inmates were less likely to agree with the item, "Overall they treated me pretty good in the TDC." White inmates were more likely to disagree with the statement, "Most guards in the TDC treat inmates like they are less than human." Hemmens and Marquart (1999) also found that white and Hispanic inmates were more likely than black inmates to perceive race relations to be a problem in prison. Finally, Goodstein and MacKenzie (1984) found no differences in levels of anxiety between black and white inmates, but black inmates did score higher on their measures of depression. These findings were contrary to previous research that found that black inmates experienced less stress and depression than whites while incarcerated (Johnson 1976, Fagan and Lira 1978). Research by Kevin Wright (1989) also found that black and white inmates experienced similar levels of stress and anxiety.

Robert Leger and Harvey Barnes (1986) conducted a study of black inmates from two maximum prisons in different parts of the United States. Potomac Correctional Facility was located on the East Coast and Piedmont in the South. Inmates completed a questionnaire that contained items designed to measure the perspectives identified by Carroll to have a major influence on the attitudes and behaviors of black inmates: degree of *black radicalism, class-consciousness,* and *soul orientation.* In addition, inmates were assessed according to the extent to which they adhered to the inmate code, their orientation towards violence, and conflicts with authority. Leger and Barnes found that increased contact with the criminal justice system influenced black inmates' perceptions of discrimination and their reported conflicts with staff. These results did not support those of Goodstein and MacKenzie. In their examination of inmate violence and aggression, Leger and Barnes found that inmates who scored high on the black radicalism and soul measures reported more fights with other inmates. Further, they found that longer periods of incarceration corresponded with the inmates' adherence to the inmate code, greater levels of class-consciousness and black radicalism. This finding, which supported Clemmer's (1958) prisonization theory, only applied for inmates from Potomac. Results from Piedmont offered support for Wheeler's (1961) u-shaped relationship. The difference was attributed to the political environments of each institution. Potomac was described as more "politicized" than Piedmont.

Carroll extended the research on inmate subcultures by examining the influence of race on inmate experiences of the prison environment. Prisoners could no longer be viewed as isolated societies of inmates far removed from events and changes taking place on the outside. The social and cultural movements that drew attention to racial inequality and injustice in free society penetrated the prison walls and had a profound impact on black inmates and transformed the once stable and relatively peaceful prison environment. Today, prisons are no longer allowed to segregate inmates based solely on race. In the 2005 case of *Johnson v. California*, the US Supreme Court ruled that prisons were not exempted from the laws prohibiting segregation in free society. Prisons are only allowed to segregate according to race in situations where it is necessary to protect the safety of inmates and staff. Clemmer, Sykes, Giallombardo, and Carroll all contributed to an expansive body of literature on inmate subcultures that is important to our understanding of how prisons function as a mechanism of social control.

References

Clemmer, D. (1940). *The Prison Community*. Boston: Christopher.

Colvin, E. (1976) Hacks, Blacks, and Cons: Race Relations in a Maximum Security Prison. Book Review. *British Journal of Criminology* 16: 201–202

Fagan, T., and F. Lira (1978). "Profile of Mood States: Racial Differences in a Delinquent Population." *Psychological Reports* 43:348–50.

Goetting, A., and R. Howsen (1983). "Blacks in Prison: A Profile." *Criminal Justice Review* 8:21–31.

Goodstein, L., and D. MacKenzie (1984). "Racial Differences in Adjustment Patterns of Prison Inmates—Prisonization, Conflict, Stress, and Control." In *The Criminal Justice System and Blacks*, edited by D. Georges-Abeyie, 271–306. New York: Clark Boardman.

Gottfredson, M., M. Hindelang, and N. Parisi (1978). *Sourcebook of Criminal Justice Statistics—1977*. Washington, DC: U.S. Government Printing Office.

Hemmens, C., and J. Marquart (1999). "The Impact of Inmate Characteristics on Perceptions of Race Relations in Prison." *International Journal of Offender Therapy and Comparative Criminology* 43:230–47.

Hemmens, C. and J. Marquart (2000). "Friend or Foe? Race, Age, and Inmate Perceptions of Inmate-Staff Relations." *Journal of Criminal Justice* 28:297–312.

Irwin, J. (1980). *Prisons in Turmoil*. Boston, MA: Little, Brown.

Jacobs, J. (1974). "Street Gangs Behind Bars." *Social Problems* 21:395–409.

Jacobs, J. (1977). *Stateville: The Penitentiary in Mass Society*. Chicago: University of Chicago Press.

Jacobs, J. (1979). "Race Relations and the Prisoner Subculture." *Crime and Justice* 1:1–27.

Johnson, R. (1976). *Culture and Crises in Confinement*. Lexington, MA: DC Health.

Leger, R., and H. Barnes (1986). "Black Attitudes in Prison: A Sociological Analysis." *Journal of Criminal Justice* 14:105–22.

Martin, J. (1976). "Hacks, Blacks, and Cons" (Book Review). *Criminal Justice and Behavior* 3:101–02.

Poole, E., and R. Regoli (1980). "Race, Institutional Rule-Breaking, and Institutional Response: A Study of Discretionary Decisionmaking in Prison." *Law and Society Review* 14:931–46.

Wheeler, S. (1961). "Socialization in Correctional Communities." *American Sociological Review* 26:697–712.

Wright, K. (1989). "Race and Economic Marginality in Explaining Prison Adjustment." *Journal of Research in Crime and Delinquency* 26:67–89.

Further Reading

Carroll, L. (1998). *Lawful Order: A Case Study of Correctional Crises and Reform.* New York: Garland.

Cole, D. (1999). *No Equal Justice: Race and Class in the American Criminal Justice System.* New York: Holt, Rinehart, and Winston.

Jacobs, J. (1975). "Stratification and Conflict Among Prison Inmates." *Journal of Criminal Law and Criminology* 66:476–82.

Johnson, R. (1976). *Culture and Crises in Confinement.* Lexington, MA: DC Health.

Johnson, R. (2001). *Hard Time: Understanding and Reforming the Prison.* Belmont, CA: Wadsworth.

Johnson, R., and H. Toch (1982). *The Pains of Imprisonment.* Beverly Hills, CA: Sage.

Petersilia, J. (1983). *Racial Disparities in the Criminal Justice System.* Santa Monica, CA: Rand.

Trulson, C., J. Marquart, C. Hemmens, and L. Carroll (2008). "Racial Desegregation in Prisons." *Prison Journal* 88:270–99.

4

Inmate Violence

Correctional facilities are full of people who have histories of violent behavior so it should come as no surprise that our prisons and jails are full of violent activity. It is estimated that one-half of the prison population consists of inmates convicted of a violent offense (Harrison and Beck 2005). For many offenders, the tables are turned once incarcerated when they find themselves victimized by other inmates. Correctional administrators assume responsibility for the care and safety of their inmate populations, but violence in correctional facilities is considered to be a regular occurrence and a normal part of the incarceration experience (Johnson 1987). Violence became more prevalent in correctional facilities beginning in the 1960s as a consequence of crowding and the emergence of prison gangs. In addition, inmates were granted several constitutional protections that made it more difficult to discipline them (McCorkle 1992). There are two types of inmate violence. *Interpersonal* violence takes place between two or more inmates as a result of some interpersonal conflict while *collective* violence is usually against the prison administration and includes prison disturbances, riots, and gang conflicts (Braswell et al. 1994). Research on both types of violence is explored in the following section.

INTERPERSONAL VIOLENCE

Violence between inmates can take several forms. Inmates commit physical assault (with or without a weapon), sexual assault, and even murder while incarcerated. Violence is a resource used by inmates to accomplish some goal. *Instrumental* violence is used to assert authority, achieve status, or exert power. Violence can be a means of lessening the deprivations of imprisonment. Violence can help an inmate establish their dominance, which can result in better living conditions and greater access to goods and services (Bowker 1985). Other acts of violence are considered to be *expressive*. Expressive violence is not linked to any tangible goal, but rather is used as a means of reducing tension (Bowker 1985). Both types of violence are problematic for prison administrators. Violence among inmates is one of the most serious problems facing correctional administrators today.

INMATE VICTIMIZATION: ARE PRISONS SAFE FOR INMATES?

Fuller, D., and T. Orsagh (1977). "Violence and Victimization within a State Prison System." *Criminal Justice Review* 2:35–55.

Background

While prisons have long been recognized as violent institutions, *quantitative* research into the extent and causes of inmate violence did not surface until the 1960s. Early research focused on the inmates who engaged in violent behaviors while incarcerated and relied on either inmate self report data or on official inmate disciplinary records which tended to underestimate the extent of violence (Wooldredge 1994). Initial efforts to explain inmate violence focused on the individual characteristics of the inmates (i.e., age, race, and prior history of violence) and the characteristics of the institutions (i.e., security level, crowding) in which inmates were confined. Beginning in the early 1970s, researchers began using victimization surveys as a way of obtaining more accurate measures of crime. Victimization surveys are valuable for uncovering offenses that make up the *dark figure of crime*. Two economists published the first *quantitative* analysis of inmate victimization in 1977. Dan Fuller and Thomas Orsagh conducted a large-scale study of victimization across ten prison institutions (housing 4,495 inmates) in North Carolina.

The Study

Fuller and Orsagh (1977) wanted to obtain an accurate estimate of the most common type of inmate violence (assault) in order to explore its *correlates* and *causes*. Their study on inmate victimization was designed to answer the following four research questions:

1. How much assault occurred within the prison system?
2. What were the characteristics of assault victims?
3. What were the causes of assault?
4. What could be done within the prison system to reduce assault?

Fuller and Orsagh utilized three separate databases for their study. This was done to address the potential bias associated with one particular source. Prison officials may have underestimated the extent of violence within their facilities while the inmates may have exaggerated its occurrence. The first data set was the *Offense Report Data Base* that included all official reports of assault during a three-month period in 1975. The second source of data came from the *Superintendent Data Base*. This consisted of data collected from interviews with superintendents from each of the ten correctional facilities. The third source was the *Inmate Data Base*. Approximately 400 inmates (representing a *stratified random* sample) from six prisons were interviewed over a two-month period in 1971. Stratified random samples involve a researcher first dividing up a population into two or more groups (strata) and then selecting a random sample from each group. Inmates were asked if someone had hit them, whether or not their assailant used a weapon, and if they had assaulted someone during the specified time frame.

Results

Fuller and Orsagh had access to an impressive amount of data from a variety of sources that they used to answer several research questions about the extent and nature of inmate victimization. Their results are summarized below.

Victimization rates. According to the official reports, there were 126 reported assaults during the study period. This translated into a quarterly victimization rate of 1.7 percent. After reviewing the superintendent data, Fuller and Orsagh deduced that 29 percent of all assault went unreported to officials. They adjusted for this and came up with a corrected assault rate of 2.4 percent. Aside from the underreporting issue, the superintendents were asked to provide an estimate of the total number of assaults that took place during the same three-month period used in the official reports. Based on their estimates, researchers calculated a victimization rate ranging from a low of 3.4 percent to a high of 10.6 percent. The 3.4 percent was still higher than the adjusted official rate of 2.4 percent. Fuller and Orsagh provided three possible explanations for the discrepancy. First, offense reports provided a specific definition of assault while the superintendents may have used a more inclusive definition. Second, superintendents were asked to provide two estimates: the actual amount of assaults and the amount that went unreported. Both of these estimates may have been inaccurate.

Two victimization rates were calculated from the inmate data. The "net victimization rate" was 5.8 percent. This rate was based on the number of inmates who had reported being the victim of an assault (with or without a weapon) and had not been involved as an assailant during the same time period. The "gross victimization rate" was 19.4 percent. This rate included the inmates who reported being victimized and also reported involvement as an assailant. According to Fuller and Orsagh, the difference between net and gross victimization rates illustrated one of the limitations of most victimization data—the victims' involvement in their own victimization. To address this issue, researchers went back into the offense reports to determine whether or not the victim played a role in their own victimization. This was possible because the offense reports included statements provided by witnesses. Taking this information and the sources of bias mentioned above into account, Fuller and Orsagh came up with a "pure victimization rate" of 2.4 percent *per year*. To give this rate more meaning, Fuller and Orsagh also calculated a victimization rate for males of the same age range in the general population and found that an inmate serving time in a North Carolina prison was 50 percent *more* likely to be assaulted than a male citizen on the street. Nonetheless, a rate of 2.4 percent was lower than what was assumed by the general public.

The rate of sexual victimization was also low. Only one report of sexual assault was found in the Offense Report Data Base. The superintendents estimated that nine took place during the three-month period. Inmates were no more likely to be the victim of sexual assault than a female from the same age group in free society. Fuller and Orsagh also calculated an assault rate for the custodial staff (1,543 staff members working in the ten institutions). Twelve staff members reported being the victim of an assault. Taking into account the number of hours worked in a week and the amount of contact with inmates, researchers determined that the quarterly assault rate for staff was 1.1 percent (put another way, one out of every ten assaults involved a staff member).

Victim characteristics. In addition to the finding that many assault victims had at one time committed an assault, researchers also uncovered two other correlates of victimization: age and race. As anticipated, the probability of victimization declined with age. Sixty-eight percent of victimizations involved an inmate between the ages of 18 and 25. The relationship between age and victimization was attributed to the fact that younger inmates also committed more assaults in prison. Whites had higher rates compared to black inmates. A few interesting findings pertaining to race were noted. In 61 percent of the reported assaults, the victim and assailant were of the same race. Of those occurrences where the victim and assailant were of different races, whites were more likely assaulted by a black assailant compared to blacks assaulted by whites. This helped explain why whites had higher victimization rates.

Precipitating causes. Fuller and Orsagh wanted to advance their study of victimization by exploring the underlying causes of assault in prison. They examined all 126 reported assaults and were able to determine the precipitating cause for 96 of them. The causes were categorized into two categories of variables: inmate interaction and economic factors. The inmate interaction variable included such items as verbal abuse, revenge or horseplay. This variable explained 62 percent of the total assaults. The economic variable consisted of gambling, some type of debt, or property, and explained 31 percent of the total assaults. A third cause, mental illness, was also explored, and this variable accounted for six percent of all assaults. Researchers further examined variables derived from the inmate data designed to measure an inmate's attitudes towards violence. Inmates were presented with a serious of scenarios involving an inmate assault and were then asked if the assault was justified. Inmates were also asked if it was appropriate to use force to obtain something and whether or not the inmate had any weapons. These factors were not significant predicators of victimization. Researchers further examined data from offense reports and found that 43 percent of all incidents involving a victim actually started while a correctional officer was present. This percentage was lower than the percentage of incidents without a victim. According to Fuller and Orsagh, this suggested that inmates were aware of their risk of getting caught and took steps to avoid detection. By far the most significant predictor of assault victimization in prison was whether the victim had also been an assailant.

Policy recommendations. Based on the findings presented above, Fuller and Orsagh made several suggestions for protecting inmates from assault. The finding that fewer inmates were victimized in the presence of a correctional officer, compared to incidents with no victim, suggested greater supervision would reduce assault victimization. This, however, would require an increase in custodial staff. Fuller and Orsagh explored ways of increasing supervision by reallocating some of the non-supervisory duties of the custodial staff. They discovered that only 2.5 percent of the staffs' hours were spent on such activities. Any reallocation would produce only a modest increase in supervision. The most feasible and inexpensive approach would be to reorganize the prison population. Inmates should be classified according to their predicted likelihood of violence. A classification system based on age alone would be beneficial. Younger inmates were already segregated from those inmates over the age of 21, and further segregation for those inmates 21 to 25 would offer greater protection.

Criticisms

Fuller and Orsagh's study was offered as the first "comprehensive quantitative profile of in-prison victimization" (Fuller and Orsagh 1977, p. 36).[1] Using three different data sources, researchers attempted to estimate the extent to which inmates became victims of assault. In spite of their efforts, their incidence rates have been criticized. Subsequent research has found victimization rates to be much higher. Official records of inmate assault are subject to the same criticisms as the official reports of crime in free society. Many offenses are never reported to authorities. The inmate code (discussed in the previous section on inmate subcultures) discouraged snitching on fellow inmates. Inmates tended to be reluctant to report out of fear of retaliation (by other inmates or even the guards) (Wolff et al. 2007). Comparisons of official assault rates across jurisdictions can also be problematic because of differences in definitions of assault. Further, Fuller and Orsagh calculated their official assault rate based on the number of disciplinary reports that involved an assault. This calculation was misleading because it did not consider the size of the total inmate population (O'Mahoney 1994).

Fuller and Orsagh recognized the limitations of official measures of inmate assault so they also surveyed inmates and asked them to report on their own victimization experiences. While victimization surveys can help uncover those offenses not reported to authorities, they have their own potential drawbacks. Memories fade and inmates may not be truthful in their reporting (Bowker 1980, Cooley 1993). Reporting a sexual assault even on a *confidential* survey questionnaire can be stigmatizing for inmates as well. Fuller and Orsagh discovered more inmates reporting an assault compared to official prison records, but even their victimization rates derived from inmates were significantly lower than most research has found (Bowker 1980, Wooldredge 1994, 1998, Wolff et al. 2007).

Fuller and Orsagh's incident rate for sexual assault has also been criticized. They calculated an incident rate based on the 31 incidents reported by the superintendents during a one-year period. Their calculation was inaccurate because they divided 31 by the total number of inmates (4,495). Incident rates should only be computed using only those inmates at risk for sexual assault because it was common practice for prisons to transfer at risk populations out of the general population for safety reasons (Gaes and Goldberg 2004). Fuller and Orsagh reported that the official records only indicated one incident of sexual assault, but they did not report how sexual assault was defined. According to Gaes and Goldberg (2004), the official reports probably only included completed rapes. Fuller and Orsagh also failed to include sexual victimization in their inmate survey. If this had been included, they probably would have discovered more sexual victimization.

In their analysis, Fuller and Orsagh explored the relationship between race and victimization and found that blacks were more likely to be an assailant compared to whites.

---

[1] Fuller and Orsagh were the first to publish a quantitative study of victimization; however, the first published quantitative study of prison violence was Ellis, D., H. Grasmick, and B. Gilman (1974) "Violence in Prison: A Sociological Analysis." *American Journal of Sociology* 80(1):16–43.

This finding was based on the data contained in the offense reports. Other research has found this relationship to be spurious. Factors such as age and prior record explained why blacks appeared to be more aggressive when examining official sources (Goodstein and MacKenzie 1984, Wright 1989). Furthermore, racial discrimination on the part of prison administrators could have also accounted for the disparity. Research by John Ramirez (1983) found that black inmates were more likely to be charged with misconduct compared to their white counterparts.

Significance and Subsequent Research

Numerous studies of prison violence have been published. Most of this research has focused on the behavior of inmates as offenders primarily because of a lack of concern with inmates as victims. The pervasive sentiment toward inmates is one of indifference. Research on inmate offending frequently utilize official measures of misconduct that have been shown to underestimate the extent of violence within our penal institutions. Several informative studies of inmate victimization have been published since 1977. Researchers have uncovered additional factors that are either related to or help explain inmate victimization. These studies have explored both inmate and institutional characteristics. In addition, different types of victimization including personal, property, and sexual have been examined.

Fuller and Orsagh observed that younger inmates were more likely to be victims of assault compared to older inmates. Robert Mutchnick and Margaret Fawcett (1991) offered a further test of this finding by exploring the incidence of victimization within juvenile correctional facilities. Juveniles sentenced to one of Pennsylvania's nine juvenile group homes were asked to report on their victimization experiences. Seventeen percent of the juveniles reported being a victim of minor assault (being pushed or shoved by another juvenile). Percentages were also low for major assault (9.5 %), assault with a weapon (7.1%), and sexual assault (3.6%). The juveniles ranged in age from 13 to 17 years old. Age, however, was not related to any of the different types of assault. The relatively low rate of assault victimization and the lack of a relationship between age and assault were inconsistent with Fuller and Orsagh's (1977) findings. Mutchnick and Fawcett speculated that this might have been because the juveniles in their sample had relatively short periods of incarceration and were adequately supervised. In another test of the age–victimization relationship, Angela Maitland and Richard Sluder (1998) found personal victimization rates that were consistent with Fuller and Orsagh. They sampled inmates incarcerated in a medium security prison for youthful offenders. The inmates were between the ages of 17 and 25. A small percentage reported personal victimization involving a weapon (5.5%) or being bitten by another inmate (7.3%). Only one inmate reported sexual assault. Over half of the inmates, however, reported verbal harassment (58.6%) and almost half (48.6%) reported having their property stolen. Inmates with reported victimization also reported higher levels of fear and measured lower on several prison adjustment indicators. Maitland and Sluder also identified racial differences in victimization experiences. Whites were more likely to have been victims of mind games and property extortion and were more likely to have had a weapon used against them and suffered physical injury compared to nonwhites. In a study comparing victimization rates for inmates incarcerated in adult facilities and inmates housed in young offender institutions researchers found rates to be significantly higher for youthful inmates (O'Donnell and Edgar 1998).

Recently, Jon Kerbs and Jennifer Jolly (2007) examined victimization rates among a group of older male inmates. Past research had shown older inmates to be among the least victimized, yet one of the critical issues facing correctional administrators today is protecting the safety of a rapidly growing older inmate population. The number of inmates aged 50 and older doubled between 1994 and 2001, and as of 2006 there were an estimated 160,000 inmates in this age group. Kerbs and Jolly surveyed and interviewed a sample of inmates aged 50 and older who were all incarcerated in a single prison. Inmates reported on various types of psychological, property, physical and sexual victimization. Psychological and property victimization occurred most often. The most frequently reported types of psychological victimization were having other inmates cut in line (85%), being insulted (40%) and being threatened with fake punches (25%). The threatening behaviors were primarily by younger inmates trying to exert control over public spaces. Almost 30 percent of the inmates reported being cheated out of money, while 28 percent reported having items stolen from their cells. Not only were the older inmates vulnerable to "con games," they were also frequently taken advantage of. For example, an inmate might "borrow" something from an older inmate with no intent of returning it. Most of the physical victimization was in the form of being pushed, hit or kicked (10.8% reported this type of assault). Eleven percent of the inmates reported some type of sexual harassment, but only one inmate reported being raped.

Fuller and Orsagh distinguished between "pure victims" and victims who also participated in an assault and found that the most significant predictor of assault victimization in prison was whether the victim had also been an assailant. Kevin Wright (1991) examined the characteristics of inmates who had committed an act of violence and inmates who were the victims of a violent act to determine if these groups were truly distinct from one another. A random sample of 942 inmates from five medium and five maximum security New York State prisons were administered questionnaires. Significant differences between the offenders and victims were revealed. Violent inmates tended to be younger, were brought into the criminal justice system at a young age, and had been incarcerated before. Involvement in the criminal justice system and prior institutional experience was less for victimized inmates. Victimized inmates were rarely charged with assault, yet they considered themselves to be aggressive (i.e., they argued with staff and other inmates). According to Wright, the aggressive nature of victimized inmates may be a precipitating cause of their victimization. Wright also identified personality differences between the two groups of inmates and recommended that prisons use a personality inventory in their internal classification decisions (i.e., housing assignments).

In 1993, Dennis Cooley published findings from a study of inmate victimization within the Canadian Prison System.[2] The study was known as the Prison Victimization Project. A randomly selected sample of 117 male inmates across five Canadian prison were administered a victimization survey. The survey asked participants if they had been victims of robbery, sexual assault, assault, theft, vandalism, and/or extortion. A total of 55 (47%) of the sampled inmates reported being victimized during a 12-month period. Twenty-three of these inmates (42%) reported multiple victimizations.

---

[2] In a previous study, Cooley found the rates of victimization to be higher compared to US prisons. See Cooley, D., (1990). *Prison Violence in the Correctional Service of Canada: An Analysis of Security Incidents and Cross-Jurisdictional Data*. Ottawa: Research and Statistics Branch. Correctional Service of Canada.

Theft was the most commonly reported victimization; however, the total number of personal victimizations (robbery, sexual assault, assault, extortion) was more frequent than property victimizations (theft and vandalism). Assault was the most frequently reported personal victimization. In a comparison between the victimizations reported by inmates and the official prison statistics, Cooley found the victimization rate for assault to be three times *higher* than what the official records revealed. Cooley further compared the number of personal victimizations reported by inmates to members of the general public. The victimization rate for male prison inmates was 538.46 per 1,000 inmates. For males in the general population, the rate was only 214 per 1,000. In an effort to better understand the causes of inmate victimization, Cooley examined several aspects of inmate life. He found that inmates adhered to a set of informal rules that were somewhat consistent with the inmate code previously identified by Sykes (1958). The rules included "do your own time," "avoid the prison economy," "don't trust anyone," and "show respect." These rules created a sense of cohesion among inmates that was beneficial to the overall management of a prison; however, violation of the rules explained inmate victimization. A significant amount of personal victimization resulted from inmates not "showing respect" for their fellow inmates.

Research on inmate victimization within a correctional facility located in the southwest revealed that Mexican Americans were more likely than whites to be the victims of personal crime. In addition, younger inmates and inmates with a prior history of violent behavior were more likely to be victimized by personal crime (Wooldredge 1994). Several factors related to an inmate's likelihood of victimization were identified. Inmates who regularly participated in recreational programs, spent little time watching television, had close friends inside the facility, received monthly visits from friends or family, and had positive attitudes toward the facility were significantly less likely to be victimized. In fact, the predicted likelihood of personal victimization for these inmates was only .0007. Inmates with no regular participation, who spent several hours per week watching television, received no monthly visitors, had few close friends, and expressed negative attitudes toward the facility, had a predicted victimization likelihood of .95 (Wooldredge 1994). In a later study of inmate victimization across three prisons in Ohio, it was revealed that one out of every two inmates reported some type of victimization within a six-month period (Wooldredge 1998).

In 2007, a group of researchers published a large-scale study of inmate victimization across 14 prisons located in a mid-Atlantic State. Using a random sample of 7,221 male inmates and 564 female inmates, researchers administered a questionnaire asking respondents to report if they had been the victim of physical assault by another inmate or staff member within the past six months or at any time while incarcerated for their current offense (Wolff et al. 2007). Researchers utilized *computer-assisted* survey equipment to administer the survey. This technology is considered ideal for asking sensitive questions. Twenty-five percent of the male inmates reported being assaulted by another inmate while incarcerated, compared to 20 percent of the females. Males were significantly more likely than females to have reported an assault by a staff member. Consistent with prior research, younger inmates were significantly more likely to report being assaulted by either an inmate or staff member. Prevalence rates for males and females were similar for assaults by an inmate during the past six months, but males were more likely to report an assault involving a weapon and were three times more likely to report an assault by a staff member. Researchers also discovered variation in assault rates across institutions. Inmate-on-inmate assault was more common in small facilities, but staff-on-inmate assault was lower. The opposite was true for large facilities, which had fewer inmate-on-inmate assaults but more staff-on-inmate assaults (Wolff et al. 2007).

In addition to efforts to determine the extent of inmate victimization and the causes, researchers have also examined how victimization impacts an inmate's behavior. Using data from a sample of male inmates within the Tennessee State Prison, Richard McCorkle (1992) identified eight types of "precautionary behaviors" inmates engaged in to try and avoid violent victimization. The most common reported behaviors were keeping to oneself, avoiding certain areas, spending more time in ones' cell, and acting tough and lifting weights. One fourth of the sample reported keeping a weapon nearby. A few inmates reported limiting their participation in activities or requesting protective custody. Inmates took these precautionary steps out of fear. Older inmates used more "passive, avoidance techniques" while younger inmates used "aggressive, proactive" behaviors.

While Fuller and Orsagh (1977) uncovered only one incident of sexual assault, subsequent research has shown this type of victimization to be much more common. Research by Cindy Struckman-Johnson and her colleagues found that 22 to 25 percent of inmates reported being the victims of sexual pressuring, attempted sexual assault or rape. One out of every ten inmates had been raped in prison and two-thirds of inmates were sexually victimized on repeated occasions (Struckman et al. 1996). Despite these figures, in a national survey of prisoner sexual assault carried out in 2001, very few correctional administrators confirmed the wide spread occurrence of sexual assault (Mariner 2001). The effects of sexual abuse can be devastating for the victims and most prisons are not equipped to help victims cope with their suffering. Victims frequently exhibit symptoms of post-traumatic stress disorder, depression, and anxiety (Cotton and Groth 1982). In response to concerns of inmate sexual assault, in 2003 Congress passed the Prison Rape Elimination Act. This piece of legislation was designed to facilitate research and policy changes to protect the adults and juveniles incarcerated in our prisons and jails. The Act established the National Prison Rape Elimination Commission that was charged with overseeing correctional policies related to the detection, prevention, and punishment of sexual assault in correctional facilities across the United States. The Act further called upon the Bureau of Justice Statistics to develop a research plan to determine the extent of sexual victimization. In a report issued by the Bureau in December of 2007, 4.5 percent of the inmates surveyed from 146 state and federal prisons reported at least one incident of sexual victimization within the past year (Bureau of Justice Statistics 2007). Despite efforts to accurately determine the extent of inmate sexual abuse, the Bureau acknowledged that their estimates were probably less than the actual occurrence due to the reluctance of some victims to report their experiences.

Correctional facilities are designed to protect society from those who break the law but they offer little protection for the inmates inside. Fuller and Orsagh provided the first *quantitative* study of inmate victimization by examining the extent, correlates and causes of violent victimization in prison. In addition, they offered suggestions for how prisons could use their findings to reduce the incidence of assault. Specifically, they advocated segregating younger adult inmates from older inmates. The relationship between age and victimization has been well documented in subsequent research and additional risk factors for victimization have been identified. Correctional facilities today utilize these risk factors as part of their internal inmate classification systems. Administrators attempt to protect vulnerable inmates by making housing, work, and program assignments with risk assessment instruments that predict an inmate's likelihood of misconduct.

References

Bowker, L. (1980). *Prison Victimization*. New York: Elsevier: North Holland.

Bowker, L. (1985) An Essay on Prison Violence. In *Prison Violence in America*, edited by M. Braswell, S. Dillingham, and R. Montgomery (pp. 7–17). Cincinnati: Anderson

Braswell, M., R. Montgomery, and L. Lombardo (1994). *Prison Violence in America*, 2nd Edition. Cincinnati: Anderson.

Cooley, D. (1993). "Criminal Victimization in Male Federal Prisons." *Canadian Journal of Criminology* 35:479–95.

Cotton, D., and A. Groth (1982). "Inmate Rape: Prevention and Intervention." *Journal of Prison and Jail Health* 2:47–57.

Fuller, D., and T. Orsagh (1977). "Violence and Victimization within a State Prison System." *Criminal Justice Review* 2:35–55.

Gaes, G., and A. Goldberg (2004). *Prison Rape: A Critical Review of the Literature, Working Paper*. Washington, DC: National Institute of Justice.

Goodstein, L., and D. MacKenzie (1984). "Racial Differences in Adjustment Patterns of Prison Inmates: Prisonization, Conflict, Stress, and Control." In *The Criminal Justice System and Blacks*, ed. D. Georges-Abeyie, 271–306. New York: Clark Boardman.

Harrison, P., and A. Beck (2005). *Prisoners in 2005, Bureau of Justice Statistics Bulletin*. Washington, DC: US Department of Justice.

Johnson, R. (1987). *Understanding and Reforming the Prison, 2nd Edition*, Boston: Wadsworth

Kerbs, J., and J. Jolley (2007). "Inmate-on-Inmate Victimization among Older Male Prisoners." *Crime and Delinquency* 53:187–218.

McCorkle, R. (1992). "Personal Precautions to Violence in Prison." *Criminal Justice and Behavior* 19:160–73.

Maitland, A., and R. Sluder (1998). "Victimization and Youthful Prison Inmates: An Empirical Analysis." *Prison Journal* 78:55–73.

Mariner, J. (2001). *No Escape: Male Rape in US Prisons*. New York: Human Rights Watch.

Mutchnick, R., and M. Fawcett (1990). "Violence in Juvenile Corrections: Correlates of Victimization in Group Homes." *International Journal of Offender Therapy and Comparative Criminology* 34:43–56.

O'Donnell, I., and K. Edgar (1998). "Routine victimization in Prisons." *Howard Journal of Criminal Justice* 37:266–79.

O'Mahoney, P. (1994). "Prison Suicide Rates: What Do They Mean?" In *Deaths in Custody: International Perspectives*, edited by A. Liebling and T. Ward, 45–57. London: Whiting and Birch.

Ramirez, J. (1983). "Race and the Apprehension of Inmate Misconduct." *Journal of Criminal Justice* 11:413–27.

Struckman-Johnson, C., D. Struckman-Johnson, L. Rucker, K. Bumby, and S. Donaldson (1996) "Sexual Coercion Reported by Men and Women in Prison." *Journal of Sex Research* 33:67–76.

Wolff, N., C. Blitz, J. Shi, J. Siegel and R. Bachman (2007). "Physical Violence Inside Prisons: Rates of Victimization." *Criminal Justice and Behavior* 34:588–99.

Wooldredge, J. (1994). "Inmate Crime and Victimization in a Southwestern Correctional Facility." *Journal of Criminal Justice* 22:367–81.

Wooldredge, J. (1998). "Inmate Lifestyles and Opportunities for Victimization." *Journal of Research in Crime and Delinquency* 35:480–502.

Wright, K. (1989). "Race and Economic Marginality in Explaining Prison Adjustment." *Journal of Research in Crime and Delinquency* 26:67–89.

Wright, K. (1991). "The Violent and the Victimized in the Male Prison." *Journal of Offender Rehabilitation* 16:1–25.

Further Reading

Dumond, R. (2000). "Inmate Sexual Assault: The Plague Which Persists." *Prison Journal* 80:407–14.

Ekland-Olson, S., D. Barrick and L. Cohen (1983). "Prison Overcrowding and Disciplinary Problems: An Analysis of the Texas Prison System." *Journal of Applied Behavior Science* 19:163–76.

Ellis, D., H. Grasmick, and B. Gilman (1974). "Violence in Prisons: A Sociological Analysis." *American Journal of Sociology* 80:16–43.

Farrington, D., and C. Nutall (1980). "Prison Size, Overcrowding, Prison Violence, and Recidivism." *Journal of Criminal Justice* 8:221–31.

Flanagan, T. (1980). "Correlates of Institutional Misconduct among State Prisoners." *Criminology* 21:29–39.

Huebner, B. (2003). "Administrative Determinants of Inmate Violence: A Multilevel Analysis." *Journal of Criminal Justice* 31:107–17.

Lockwood, D. (1980). *Prison Sexual Violence.* New York: Elsevia/Thomond.

MacKenzie, D. (1987). "Age and Adjustment to Prison." *Criminal Justice and Behavior* 14:427–47.

COLLECTIVE VIOLENCE

Collective forms of inmate violence do not occur as frequently as interpersonal violence among inmates, but the impacts can be more devastating for a correctional facility. Collective violence includes a wide range of activities from minor inmate disturbances, protests, and work stoppages to prison riots. A riot is the most severe form of inmate collective violence; however, researchers have defined riots differently. According to Bert Useem and Peter Kimball (1991), ". . . a prison riot occurs when the authorities lose control of a significant number of prisoners, in a significant area of the prison, for a significant amount of time" (p. 4). This definition helps to distinguish riots from other forms of inmate protests and disturbances. Vernon Fox (1971) described riots in terms of five progressive stages. In the first stage, some event ignites the inmates into violence. Inmate leaders emerge in the second stage and assume control over the course of the riot while administers become organized. During the third stage, communication between inmates and administrators begins (usually in the form of negotiations). Custodial control is reestablished in the fourth stage. The final stage takes place after the riot. This is when investigators attempt to determine the cause of the riot and establish blame. The first reported prison riot took place in 1774 at Newgate prison in Simsbury, Connecticut. There have been over 300 prison riots since that time, but most of them have occurred since 1952 (Martin and Zimmerman 1990).

PRISON RIOTS: WHAT CAUSES INMATES TO RIOT?

Wilsnack, R. (1976). "Explaining Collective Violence in Prisons: Problems and Possibilities." In A. Cohen, G. Cole, and R. Bailey (eds.), *Prison Violence*. Lexington, MA: Lexington Books.

Background

Early research into the causes of prison riots focused primarily upon the deprivations that are part of the prison environment. Gresham Sykes (1958) provided one of the first analyses of prison riots when he explored the causes of two riots that took place at the New Jersey State Prison in the spring of 1952. Sykes attributed the riots to changes in the inmate social system that had stripped the inmates of their control. From the late 1930s up until the mid-1940s, inmates exercised a considerable amount of power and influence within the institution. The inmates controlled housing and job assignments, recreational activities and privileges. The institution benefited from a relatively calm and stable environment. This all changed beginning in the mid-1940s when administrators started to assert their authority and tightened their control over the inmates. Inmates lost their influence while the "pains of imprisonment" were intensified. Over the next several years, the tension between inmates and administration continued to increase until the inmates revolted in early 1952. Based on his observations, Sykes believed that the transfer of power from the inmate social system to prison staff exaggerated the deprivations experienced by inmates and contributed to the riots. His insights, however, failed to provide a complete understanding of why inmates rioted. Overcrowding, poor living conditions, lack of programming, guard brutality, poor administration, and a concentration of violence-prone inmates have all been cited as contributing factors despite the fact that these conditions also exist in prisons where no riots have ever taken place. Further, Sykes' explanations of prison riots were based on data collected from a single prison facility where a riot had occurred. In an effort to formulate a more comprehensive explanation for why inmates riot, Richard Wilsnack (1976) examined data from 48 state prisons. Included in his sample were prisons that had experienced a riot, some other type of collective inmate violence, as well as prisons with no reported collective violence.

The Study

Wilsnack was the first to conduct a large-scale *quantitative* study of collective inmate violence. In order to develop an explanation for why inmates riot, Wilsnack's first task was to identify a list of prison conditions associated with previous riots. He wanted to gather as much information as possible from a large number of prisons so he constructed a survey that asked prison officials to indicate whether or not their facility had experienced any type of collective violence during an 18 month period between January 1971 and June 1972. *Survey* research is ideal for collecting large quantities of information from multiple sources. Respondents were asked to distinguish between riots and other types of collective disturbances such as work stoppages and hunger strikes. Wilsnack defined a riot ". . . as a seizure by inmates of prison territory where they can move freely but staff cannot, plus a presentation of demands that affect more inmates than those actively participating in the disturbance" (p. 67). Wilsnack wanted to determine if both riots and other forms of collective violence could be explained by the same factors. The survey also asked respondents to indicate whether or not certain prison conditions existed or had changed within the facility before, during and/or after each type of violence. The list of conditions was derived from previously published *case studies* of various prison riots. In addition, Wilsnack included factors drawn from prior research on collective violence in other settings such as mental hospitals and universities.

The 160-question survey was mailed to a sample of 51 correctional institutions. The sample consisted of the largest state prison institutions for each state and the District of Columbia. All of the prisons housed adult males convicted of felony crimes and were medium-or maximum-security facilities. Institutions were selected to be representative of the types of prisons where riots were most likely to occur. Only three states—Alabama, Kansas, and Mississippi failed to provide adequate information. To improve the *reliability* of responses, questions were constructed in such a way that respondents had to only provide simple replies. Wilsnack believed that this would reduce the likelihood of bias on the part of the individuals completing the survey. Some of the questionnaires had incomplete responses to the survey questions. Missing data is a common problem in survey research. Reliability becomes an issue if, for example; officials in prisons that had experienced a disturbance were more willing to report certain conditions compared to institutions with no disturbances. Researchers should always be forthright in explaining any occurrences of missing data and what was done to address the problem. Wilsnack checked for reliability by comparing the incomplete responses between prisons reporting riots, other forms of disturbances, and those with neither and found no significant differences in responses. He also made sure to collect information that could be verified through official reports and media accounts.

Findings

Wilsnack examined data from institutions that had experienced a prison riot, institutions with other forms of collective violence, and institutions with no reported collective violence. This allowed him to determine if the same conditions found in rioting institutions were also present in facilities where no riots had occurred. Further, he could find out if the same conditions could explain both riots and other forms of collective violence. Based on the results of his survey, Wilsnack identified several conditions that were present in prisons that had experienced a riot, some other type of inmate collective violence, or both. There was, however, no single precondition present in every case where such a disturbance occurred. In other words, the existence of these conditions was not a guarantee that the institution would experience collective forms of violence. Results of the survey also revealed that riots and other forms of collective violence were unique in that the same conditions were not related to both types.

Conditions associated with prison riots. Twelve of the prisons surveyed reported a riot during the study period. An analysis of prison conditions revealed that inmate deprivation and disorganization, administrative instability and conflict as well as external pressures existed in prisons where riots had taken place. Riots were more likely to occur in maximum-security prisons with overcrowding and unoccupied inmates. In addition, riots were more likely to occur in facilities where inmates of different ages, convictions, and prior records were all housed together. Two-thirds of the prisons that reported a riot had experienced these conditions. Inmate disorganization and conflict were also related to rioting. Three-fourths of the prisons reporting a riot had experienced an increase in inmate assault and/or had at least one occurrence of an inmate assault on a guard. The same number of facilities had experienced major administrative changes (i.e., turnover or extended absences) and conflict among staff members. While a shortage of correctional staff was not related to the occurrence of a riot, low salaries and high staff turnover were found to be associated. Finally, Wilsnack found that pressure and publicity from outside of the prison was also related to the occurrence of a riot. All of the riots had taken place in institutions where legislators and concerned citizens had tried to influence prison operations. Further, 80 percent of these institutions had received some type of media coverage prior to the riot. Wilsnack's findings did not support Sykes' contention that riots occurred as a result of a disruption to the inmate social structure.

Conditions associated with non-riot forms of collective violence. Eighteen prisons experienced other forms of inmate disturbances. Wilsnack discovered that the same conditions associated with a riot were not all related to other forms of collective inmate violence. Inmate deprivation was the only condition related to both forms of violence, while non-rioting behaviors were more likely to occur in prisons that had experienced a change in its inmate population (i.e., changes in offenses or ethnicity), had inmate populations over 1,000, and had segments of politically motivated inmates. Several indicators of staff deficiencies were also related to non-riot forms of violence. Disturbances were found in institutions with lax hiring requirements, inadequate training for guards, and a security staff less than one-fourth the size of the inmate population.

Toward a theoretical explanation. After Wilsnack determined which factors were associated with prison riots and other forms of collective inmate violence, he then used these factors to formulate a theory to explain why the disturbances occur. Inmate collective violence was most likely to occur in prisons where the deprivations were greatest. In overcrowded maximum-security prisons, inmates were forced to adapt using only their own resources. To distinguish between riots and other forms of collective violence, Wilsnack borrowed two concepts used by political scientists to describe collective action in free society. If a group of frustrated citizens had the resources to bargain with an opposing group they tended to rely on *direct confrontation* (Lipsky 1968). This practice was analogous to inmates who engaged in non-riot forms of inmate collective violence to persuade administrators to take action. The inmates were in a position to negotiate because they were well organized and had resources (i.e., manpower and cooperation) that the administration relied upon. On the other hand, if a group was powerless to negotiate with an adversary and lacked the resources needed for a direct confrontation they were more likely to *protest* and involve an influential outsider to negotiate for them (Lipsky 1968). Inmate riots shared many of the same features of a protest. The inmates were disorganized and left with no option but to riot in order to gain attention from the outside (i.e., the media). Security became threatened in institutions with unstable administrations and staff conflicts. This provided inmates the opportunity to take control and riot.

All of the institutions that had reported a riot had also indicated some other from of collective inmate behavior either before or after the riot. Wilsnack offered two possible reasons for this finding. First, if the riot preceded other forms of violence it may have been because the riot was successful in terms of improving conditions for inmates so the inmates relied on non-rioting behavior in their future negotiations with administrators. Second, in those institutions where the riot occurred *after* the inmates had participated in non-rioting violence, the riot may have been in response to the perceived failure of non-rioting behavior.

Limitations

Wilsnack was the first to examine the causes of prison riots using data collected from a large number of prison facilities in the United States. While he was successful in obtaining information from 48 state prisons (including the District of Columbia), the prisons were not *randomly* selected. He deliberately chose the largest medium or maximum-security prison facility in each state to increase the likelihood of selecting prisons that had experienced a riot. This type of sampling (known as *purposive sampling*) was appropriate given Wilsnack's objective of including prisons where riots had taken place; however, his findings may not have *generalized* to other institutions. In addition, responses to his questionnaire came from individuals that occupied different administrative positions within the prisons (Wilsnack 1976). If position influenced the responses, the *reliability* his findings can be questioned.

Wilsnack identified several conditions that maintained significant relationships with both riots and other forms of collective violence. He derived his list of conditions from prior studies of inmate violence as well as collective violence in other institutional settings. His objective was to formulate a theory based upon his findings that would explain inmate collective violence. In his analysis, Wilsnack examined only *bivariate* relationships with no *control* variables. Bivariate analysis measures the likelihood of a relationship between two variables and the strength of the relationship. This technique is insufficient for establishing *causation* because it does not allow the researcher to statistically control for possible *extraneous* influences. According to Useem and Reisig (1999), Wilsnack may have obtained different results if he had used a *multivariate* analysis. In a multivariate analysis, the researcher can determine the influence of several *independent* variables on one *dependent* variable while simultaneously controlling for the separate effects of each variable. Multivariate studies of inmate riots are more challenging for researchers because of their infrequent occurrence. There are usually more factors needed to explain riots compared to the number of riots that have taken place.

Significance and Subsequent Research

Wilsnack's *quantitative* study of inmate collective violence enhanced our understanding of prison riots and other forms of collective prison disturbances. He was among the first to offer a general explanation for why riots occur. His explanation was derived from a comprehensive study of prison conditions related to previous prison riots. By expanding the focus of his research to include prisons without a reported riot, Wilsnack was also able to identify conditions related to other forms of collective violence. Prison riots are a rare occurrence in the United States making it a difficult phenomenon to study. There have been, however, several studies conducted in the last 30 years on this topic. Much of the research has been *qualitative*. Several in depth *case studies* have been published on major prison riots (i.e., Colvin 1982, Useem 1985, Mahan 1994, Martin and Zimmerman 1990). These case studies have provided detailed descriptions of the events leading up to the riots, inmate and administrative actions during the riots, as well as the aftermaths. Although less numerous, there have also been other *quantitative* studies of riots similar to the study published by Wilsnack.

The New Mexico prison riot is considered to be the most brutal and costly US prison riot (Colvin 1982, Useem 1985). On February 2, 1980, at approximately 1:40 A.M., several inmates at the New Mexico Penitentiary in Santa Fe took control of the institution. The riot lasted 36 hours during which 33 inmates were killed, 400 were injured, and property damage was estimated at 100 million dollars (Colvin 1982, Useem 1985). Inmates gained access to prisoner records and obtained the names of several prison informants who had provided information to prison staff. The informants were viciously tortured and killed. Other inmates as well as seven[3] correctional officers were beaten, stabbed or raped. The New Mexico State Legislature ordered an official investigation of the riot events. Mark Colvin was the principle researcher and he wrote the final report (*The Report of the Attorney General on the February 2 and 3, 1980 Riot at the Penitentiary of New Mexico*, Office of the Attorney General 1980). Over an eight-month period he analyzed information from 299 interviews with former and current inmates, guards, and prison officials. Colvin provided a detailed analysis of the changes in the inmate social structure that occurred in the decade prior to the riot. His findings were consistent with sykes' observations of the inmate social system at the New Jersey State Prison several years prior. Between 1970 and 1975, the prison environment was relatively calm as evidenced by the low level of escapes and inmate violence. The number of inmates held in disciplinary segregation during this time was less than 5 percent of the inmate population and the

---

[3]A total of twelve correctional officers were taken hostage.

administration relied primarily upon "voluntary" informants. The high level of order and stability was attributed to the informal system of inmate control found within the institution. Control was maintained by two groups of inmates. The first were a group of "inmate administrators." The inmate administrators were associated with several prison programs that were started at the prison in 1968 (i.e., educational and vocational programs). Inmate administrators exercised a considerable amount of power by controlling access to these programs (inmate administrators recommended particular inmates for participation). Inmates sought out these programs because participation was used as a consideration in parole decisions. To maintain their power, inmate administrators had to ensure the continuation of the programs so they used their power to keep the other inmates in line. Despite the fact that many of the inmate administrators were in prison for violent crimes, they exercised their power using non-violent means. Another group of inmates controlled the drug trade in prison. In order to protect their trafficking activities, these inmates maintained control over other inmates. Prison staff tolerated their activities because the prison benefited from the control exercised by both groups of inmates over the rest of the inmate population.

The prison environment started to become less stable and more violent beginning in 1975 (five years before the riot) as a result of changes in the inmate control structure. Consistent with Wilsnack, Colvin found that the prison administration had also become increasingly fragmented. A turnover in prison administration occurred when the warden and his top officials were transferred. Allegations of corruption and inefficiency prompted the state Attorney General and Governor to take action. A new warden was hired and the Governor brought in officials from out of state to run the facility. During the next five years, the institution was under the control of four different wardens. Each new administrative team maintained tighter control over the inmates. The informal use of "incentives" to control the inmates (i.e., rewards, transfers) was replaced with formal control mechanisms. Administrators took control away from the inmates by removing the inmate administrators from their positions, restricting inmate movement within the prison, increasing the use of disciplinary segregation, and cracking down on the drug trafficking. In June 1976, the inmates arranged a work strike to protest the new policies. The administration responded with force and the instigators were placed in disciplinary segregation or transferred to another prison facility. Inmates attempted one last unified campaign against the administration in 1977 when two of the inmates responsible for organizing the work strike filed a class action suit against the prison.

The informal social control structure was undermined as inmates lost their authority and influence. The administrator could no longer rely on "voluntary informants" and instead began coercing inmates to "snitch" on one another. Inmate solidarity was decreased as inmates became increasingly suspicious and distrustful of one another. When the administration took away the inmates' ability to exert power through non-violent means, inmates became fragmented and many turned to violence as a way to assert control. The violence only escalated as other inmates resorted to violence as a means of protection.

Three years after Colvin published his case study of the New Mexico prison riot, Bert Useem (1985) analyzed data from a random sample of guards and inmates who were interviewed by the State Attorney General's Office after the riot. Useem also interviewed inmates himself. Consistent with Colvin, he found that the riot resulted from a breakdown in the control mechanisms within the prison. This explained not only why the riot occurred, but also the disorganized nature of the riot itself. Contrary to Colvin, however, he believed that the breakdown was a consequence of worsening prison conditions and not changes in the inmate social control structure. He found no evidence of a unified inmate social system prior to 1975. According to the inmates, the deprivations of imprisonment had become noticeably worse beginning in 1975 (when a new administration assumed control). Many prison programs were reduced or eliminated leaving inmates with little to occupy their time. As a result, inmates had no incentive to comply with prison rules. Useem also documented an increase in inmate violence beginning in the mid-1970s. Guards had become increasingly hostile toward the inmates and complaints of staff brutality were common. The guards also reported that prison conditions had worsened, but they also indicated that the changes implemented by the new administration were necessary to regain control of the prison back from the inmates. Despite the lack of organization displayed by inmates during the riot, Useem concluded that the riot resulted in significant improvements for the inmates. In the years following the riot, there was less crowding, better treatment by the guards, fewer restrictions, and more programs.

Bert Useem and Peter Kimball (1991) examined several major prison riots that occurred between 1971 and 1986 and found evidence of a "breakdown in administrative control" prior to each of the riots. The deprivations became more apparent to inmates housed in prisons with less stable administrations. Inmates perceived guards and supervisors as useless and lacking legitimate authority. Security was weakened in institutions lacking administrative control, which provided inmates the opportunity to riot. Useem and Kimball (1991) also provided an explanation for why many prisons experienced such a breakdown. Several prisons were under court order to improve inmate living conditions but were not provided the resources to implement such changes. Building upon this perspective, Arjen Boin and Willian Rattray (2004) argued that administrative breakdown over a long period of time could lead to institutional breakdown. Institutional breakdown took place when a prison implemented changes (regardless of how minor) to the inmates' routine or activities. Changes to the structure of prison life were often put into action without administrative concerns over how rules and regulations were applied under a new system. Inconsistent procedures created confusion for the inmates and lost their legitimacy. When the staff attempted to reestablish order, the inmates challenged their authority. This set off a cycle of conflict and tension between the staff and the inmates. In addition, staff morale declined. Under these conditions, the probability of a riot increased. Riots were most likely to erupt in facilities with no effective system of crises management.

Richard McCorkle, Terance Miethe, and Kriss Dass published another large-scale study of collective inmate violence in 1995. They examined data from 371 state prisons. Information from minimum, medium, and maximum facilities were included in the study. Consistent with Wilsnack, researchers found that riots were more likely to occur in higher security facilities. Measures of deprivation were not related to prison riots. In 1999, Bert Useem and Michael Reisig conducted a study of inmate collective action. They analyzed data from a sample of 317 state prisons across the United States. Three types of collective action were examined: riots, inmate disturbances, and non-violent protests. Useem and Reisig also examined a fourth outcome measure—increased severity of an unlawful protest. Results from their multivariate analysis revealed a significant relationship between their measure of administrative control and the occurrence of a riot. Riots were more likely to occur in prisons where moral was low among correctional officers and tensions were high between officers and the administration. Additionally, they found that two measures of administrative control were significant predictors of an increase in the severity of violence.

Collective violence escalated in prisons where the use of administrative sanctions was perceived as "ineffective" and the prison contained a large number of inmates that belonged to a prohibited organization (i.e., prison gang). Useem and Reisig found greater support overall for the "administrative control" perspective compared to the "inmate balance" theory (the perspective put forth by Sykes and Colvin). Administrative control not only explained inmate riots, but other inmate disturbances and non-violence protests.

Despite the difficulties in researching prison riots, our understanding of the causes has grown significantly over the past three decades. Researchers have uncovered many of the conditions associated with prison riots and several theories have been developed to explain their occurrence. Theories have focused on the informal social networks among inmates, environmental conditions, and administrative breakdowns. Prison administrators today are better equipped to respond to prison riots with emergency response teams. These teams consist of officers trained in hostage negotiation and disturbance control. This body of research has also helped prison administrators develop preventative measures to reduce the likelihood of riots. Regular security audits, consistent enforcement of rules and procedures, maintaining effective communication between inmates, staff, and administrators, providing inmates with structured activities and appropriate programs, and using inmate classification systems are all important strategies for preventing the occurrence of riots (Henderson et al. 1987). The number of prison riots has significantly declined since the 1970s, despite the large increases in the number of inmates. According to Useem and Piehl (2006), this trend can be attributed to more effective prison management.

References

Boin, A., and W. Rattray (2004). "Understanding Prison Riots: Towards a Threshold Theory." *Punishment and Society* 6:47–65.

Colvin, M. (1982). "The 1980 New Mexico Prison Riot." *Social Problems* 29:449–63.

Fox, V. (1971). "Why Prisoners Riot." *Federal Probation* 35:9–14.

Henderson, J., W. Rauch, and R. Phillips (1987). *Guidelines for Developing a Security Program* (2nd ed.). Washington, DC: U.S. Department of Justice, National Institute of Corrections, NIC Accession Number 006045.

Lipsky, M. (1968). "Protest as a Political Resource." *American Political Science Review* 62:1144–58.

Martin, R., and S. Zimmerman (1990). "A Typology of the Causes of Prison Riots and an Analytical Extension to the 1986 West Virginia Riot." *Justice Quarterly* 7:711–37.

McCorkle, R., T. Miethe, and K. Drass (1995). "The Roots of Prison Violence: A Test of the Deprivation, Management, and 'No-So-Total' Institution Models." *Crime and Delinquency* 41:317–31.

Mahan, S. (1994). "An 'Orgy of Brutality' at Attica and the 'Killing Ground' at Santa Fe: A Comparison of Prison Riots." In *Prison Violence in America, 2nd Edition,* edited by M. Braswell, S. Dillingham, and R. Montgomery, Jr., 253–64. Cincinnati: Anderson.

Office of the Attorney General (1980). *Report of the Attorney General on the February 2 and 3, 1980 Riot at the Penitentiary of New Mexico, Part One.* State of New Mexico.

Sykes, G. (1958). *The Society of Captives: A Study of a Maximum Security Prison.* Princeton, New Jersey: Princeton UP.

Useem, B., and A. Piehl (2006). "Prison Buildup and Disorder." *Punishment and Society* 8:81–115.

Useem, B., and M. Reisig (1999). "Collective Action in Prisons: Protests, Disturbances, and Riots." *Criminology* 37:735–59.

Useem, B., and P. Kimball (1991). *States of Siege: U.S. Prison Riots 1971–1986.* New York: Oxford UP.

Useem, B. (1985). "Disorganization and the New Mexico Prison Riot of 1980." *American Sociological Review* 50:677–88.

Wilsnack, R. (1976). "Explaining Collective Violence in Prisons: Problems and Possibilities." In *Prison Violence,* edited by A. Cohen, G. Cole, and R. Bailey, pp. 61–78. Lexington, MA: Lexington Books.

Further Reading

Braswell, M., S. Dillingham, and R. Montgomery, Jr., eds. (1985). *Prison Violence in America*. Cincinnati: Anderson.

Cohen, A., G. Cole, and R. Bailey, eds. (1976). *Prison Violence*. Lexington, MA: Lexington Books.

Colvin, M. (2007). "Applying Differential Coercion and Social Support Theory to Prison Organizations: The Case of the Penitentiary of New Mexico." *Prison Journal* 87:367–87.

Flynn, E. (1980). "From Conflict Theory to Conflict Resolution: Controlling Collective Violence in Prison." *American Behavioral Scientist* 23: 745–76.

Hartung, F., and M. Floch (1956). "A Social-Psychological Analysis of Prison Riots: A Hypothesis." *Journal of Criminal Law, Criminology and Police Science* 47:51–57.

Useem, B., and P. Kimball (1987). "A Theory of Prison Riots." *Theory and Society* 16:87–122.

Useem, B., C. Camp, and G. Camp (1996). *Resolution of Prison Riots: Strategies and Policies*. New York: Oxford UP.

5

Correctional Officers

The responsibility for maintaining security and order lies with the correctional officers (formally called guards) employed in our prisons and jails. Correctional officers are separated from the inmates by the authority they have over them. Their function is unique in that they exercise control over a group of individuals (the inmates) who do not acknowledge their authority and are held against their will (Jacobs and Retsky 1975). Researchers interested in exploring the nature of the prison environment and its influence on the attitudes and behaviors of inmates also focused on correctional officers. In their *ethnographic* studies of prison, Clemmer, Sykes, Giallombardo, and Carroll described the correctional officers' influence on the prison environment. The attitudes of prison guards toward inmates were considered relevant to a complete understanding of the prison environment. According to Boaz Shamir and Amos Drory (1981), ". . . due to the number of contacts between guards and inmates, the guard becomes a very salient feature of the prison experience of inmates . . ." (p. 233). Prisons were originally established in the United States to be institutions in which convicted criminals could be reformed into law-abiding members of society. Prison advocates put their faith in the institution itself believing that a "proper" environment would have a positive influence on behavior. Despite these good intentions, the deplorable conditions and abusive treatment of inmates by guards in our early prisons rendered them ineffective in terms of reducing recidivism. Early efforts to bring about reforms resulting in more humane treatment were largely unsuccessful. A lack of government oversight, along with the courts' unwillingness to intervene, left inmates without recourse to complain. Instead of being reformed, inmates usually developed strong negative attitudes about prison and the authority figures that held them captive. The prison riots that took place in the 1960s brought many of these abuses out in the open and administrators became concerned with the quality of their custodial staff as part of efforts to improve prison conditions. The field of corrections witnessed an increase in the number of empirical studies on correctional officers in the 1970s as researchers became interested in explaining the attitudes and behaviors of those who exercised control over the inmates. It was even suggested that prison guards (like inmates and police officers) were socialized into a guard subculture consisting of shared values, attitudes, and behaviors (Duffee 1974, Jacobs and Retsky 1975, Kaufman 1981). As an occupational group, guards were perceived as being "anti-inmate" and "procustodial" (Klofas 1984). Two competing perspectives for explaining the content of the guard subculture emerged out of this research (just as there were two perspectives to explain police officer and inmate subcultures). One theory was that the subculture emerged in response to the unique occupational environment in which guards worked. Others believed the shared values; attitudes and behaviors reflected characteristics held by guards long before they entered into their profession. The studies presented in this next section explored these perspectives and offered valuable insight into our understanding of the intrinsic structural conflict between the guards and inmates confined in our correctional facilities.

THE STANFORD PRISON EXPERIMENT: WHAT EXPLAINS THE COERCIVE BEHAVIOR OF PRISON GUARDS?

Haney, C., C. Banks, and P. Zimbardo (1973). "Interpersonal Dynamics in a Simulated Prison." *International Journal of Criminology and Penology* 1:69–97.

Background

According to the "dispositional hypothesis", the prison environment reflected the characteristics, behaviors, and attitudes of both the inmates and the guards (Haney et al. 1973). Guards lacked empathy and were cruel toward inmates because of their aggressive nature. Inmates, by virtue of their confinement, were criminals incapable of conforming to the rules and laws of society. Their destructive and reckless tendencies could only be controlled through physical and/or psychological coercion. This perspective is analogous to the importation theory used to explain inmate attitudes and behaviors and the idea that police work attracts certain types of individuals prone to abuse. A team of psychologists from Stanford University led by Philip Zimbardo devised a research study to test the dispositional hypothesis as an explanation of both guard and inmate behavior. The US Navy and Marine Corps funded the study because they were interested in explaining the conflict between guards and prisoners in their own facilities. The obvious approach would have been to gain access to a prison and observe the interactions and behaviors of guards and inmates. The problem with this approach was that the inmates and guards were already part of the prison environment (Haney et al. 1973). It would have been difficult to separate out the individual characteristics of the two groups from the environment itself so the researchers came up with a clever alternative—construct a "mock" prison whose inhabitants would be selected from the general population. Researchers would *randomly* assign normal functioning adults to play the roles of "prisoners" and "guards" and observe the interactions between the two groups. The "prison experiment" became one of the most controversial and criticized studies in criminal justice.

The Experiment

In the summer of 1971, Stanford University researchers, Craig Haney, Curtis Banks, and Philip Zimbardo (1973)[1] conducted an *experiment* to better understand the conflict between guards and inmates. A simulated prison was assembled in a 35-foot section of the basement of the psychology building at Stanford University. The goal was to create a "functional representation" of a prison environment so that researchers could observe the influence of this environment on behavior. Ex-prisoners were consulted on the design. Laboratory rooms were turned into six-by-nine foot cells with black steel bars as doors. Each cell contained a cot, mattress, sheet, and pillow. A small room was set aside as the prison yard, and a tiny closet was designated to be the solitary confinement cell (this cell measured two-by-two-by-seven feet and had no lighting). In another section of the basement, guard quarters were constructed that consisted of a break room, a room for the prison warden and superin-tendent, and an interviewing area.

The research subjects were recruited from a newspaper advertisement requesting male volunteers for a psychological study of prison life. Seventy-five college students responded. The selection process consisted of questionnaires to assess family upbringing, physical and mental health, and prior involvement in crime. The researchers also interviewed each of the respondents. The 24 subjects selected were deemed to be mature, well-adjusted college students. Subjects were predominately white middle-class students, with the exception of one Asian student. Subjects were *randomly* assigned to play either the role of "prisoner" or "guard" (this was literally done by flipping a coin). *Random assignment* would allow researchers to determine the influence of the prison environment separate from the characteristics of the individuals playing the roles. Efforts were made to ensure that the participants did not know one another and each subject underwent a series of psychological tests prior to the start of the experiment. Four subjects were assigned as alternates leaving nine guards and nine inmates. Zimbardo himself assumed the role of superintendent and one of his research assistants played the part of prison warden.

All of the details of the experiment were not disclosed to the subjects. Participants were informed that they would be assigned to either the role of guard or prisoner for two weeks in exchange for monetary compensation. Each subject signed a contract giving their consent to participate and agreeing to certain conditions of the experiment. Inmates were told that they would be provided minimal food, clothing, housing, and privacy. They were also informed that they might be subjected to verbal abuse. No other information was provided. Researchers wanted the subjects to enter into the experiment with only their own preconceived ideas about how inmates behaved in prison.

Researchers went so far as to create a realistic prison induction experience for the inmates. With assistance from the Palo Alto City Police Department, participants assigned to the prisoner group were all arrested without warning at their place of residence. The public nature of the arrest was meant to humiliate them. Suspects were arrested for either burglary or armed robbery, they were read their Miranda rights, searched, handcuffed, and taken to the police station for booking. At the police station, subjects were photographed, fingerprinted, and placed in a detention cell. Next, they were blindfolded and driven to the simulated prison.

---

[1]Additional information on the Stanford Prison Experiment was obtained from Phillip Zimbardo's website: http://www.prisonexp.org/.

The prisoners were unaware of the location of the prison so they would think they were being taken to a "real" prison institution. After the inmates arrived, they were stripped of their clothing and sprayed for lice. Each prisoner was issued a uniform that consisted of a simple "smock" with an inmate number on the front. Inmates were not permitted to wear anything under the smock and had to wear a stocking cap on their head (to symbolize having their head shaved as real inmates did). The issued shoes were rubber sandals. Each inmate had to wear a small lock and chain around one ankle. The uniforms were not typical of what a real inmate would wear, but the purpose of the uniform was the same: to strip the prisoners of their old identities and remind them of their confined status. All the inmates dressed the same to solidify their status as inmates. The entire induction process was designed to degrade and demoralize the inmates. Inmates were not referred to by name, but by their inmate number. The prisoners were to remain in their cells 24 hours a day for a two-week period.

Subjects playing the role of guard were also issued a standard uniform to help create a common identity among them and to further remind the prisoners of their subordinate status. The guards' uniforms were very similar to what a real prison guard might wear. Guards wore khaki shirts, pants and mirrored sunglasses so the inmates could not make eye contact with them. They were given a whistle and a police nightstick as symbols of authority. The guards were assigned to eight-hour shifts with three guards working per shift. While "off duty," the guards were told to resume all normal activities. Guards attended an orientation meeting prior to the start of the experiment. They were provided with work assignments, prisoner schedules, and procedures for completing reports. Researchers explained that the purpose of the experiment was to create a realistic prison environment. Their job was to "maintain the reasonable degree of order within the prison necessary for its effective functioning" (p. 7). No other instructions were provided. Researchers were purposely vague to make sure the guards also brought with them only their own ideas about how to maintain control over a group of subordinates.

After the subjects were placed in their "cells" the warden (one of the researchers) welcomed the inmates and read them the institutional rules that were written by the warden with the help of the guards. Inmates had to memorize the rules and recite them back to the guards during the scheduled inmate counts. The daily routine of the inmates consisted of the following:

> three meals (that consisted of a bland diet)
>
> three toilet visits (all supervised)
>
> two hours of free time (to read or write letters)
>
> work assignments
>
> daily exercise
>
> two visiting periods per week

The routine became the inmate's only indication of time, as there were no clocks or windows in the prison.

Observations

All of the interactions between guards and inmates were continuously observed. Both the warden and superintendent (also played by a researcher) were present at various times to document what took place and all of the events were recorded. Intercoms secretly recorded conversations between the inmates as well as the guards. During the first day of the experiment, both groups appeared to have had some difficulty with their prospective roles. The scheduled counts created an opportunity for the guards to assert their authority, and the inmates complied. When the inmates did not follow the rules, the guards required them to do "pushups" as punishment. Remember, the guards were not given any instructions on *how* to punish. The pushups were their own idea. Punishments were also administered for disrespecting the guards (something the guards felt they were entitled to by nature of their position). What happened on the second day completely surprised researchers. The day began with a revolt from the inmates. They removed their caps and inmate numbers and refused to leave their cells. Next, they barricaded their cells with their cots and verbally abused the guards. When the day shift arrived, they became angry at the nightshift and blamed them for the rebellion. The guards immediately attributed the inmates' behavior to lenient treatment by the guards the night before. Reinforcements were called in (the alternate guards) and the night shift guards stayed on duty to help quieten the disturbance. To gain access to the cells, the guards sprayed inmates with a fire extinguisher. Next, they proceeded to strip the inmates of their smocks and removed their cots. The alleged "leaders" of the revolt were taken to solitary confinement while the other inmates were subjected to verbal abuse and physical intimidation by the guards. The guards successfully ended the disturbance.

Realizing that all nine guards could not remain on duty, one of the guards came up with a plan to use "psychological tactics" to keep the inmates in line. A "privilege" cell was set up for the three inmates believed to be the least responsible for the disturbance. These inmates were given back their clothes and beds, were allowed to wash and brush their teeth, and were given a special meal that was eaten in the presence of the other inmates. The guards were deliberately trying to break the inmates' solidarity. The next day, the "good" inmates were taken back to the "bad" inmate cell and the "bad" inmates taken to the privilege cell. This was all done to confuse the inmates and to trick the alleged leaders into thinking that their fellow inmates had turned on them and were now cooperating with the guards. Guards wanted to turn the inmates against each other to divert their aggression away from them (it was interesting that the guards came up with this plan on their own). These actions also appeared to be increasing the cohesiveness of the subjects playing guards. Their roles became more defined. The guards started to perceive the inmates as a threat and in response began to intensify their efforts to control them. Guards no longer followed the daily routine. Bathroom visits became privileges dispensed at the whim of the guards. The guards went so far as to place buckets in the inmates' cells to use as toilets and then refused to empty them. One inmate had his smoking privileges taken away and others were denied access to their mail.

Thirty-six hours into the experiment one inmate (#8612) started to exhibit intense emotional symptoms such as uncontrollable crying and bouts of aggression. The researchers believed he was faking so he could be released early. Even the researchers had assumed the role of prison administrators by treating the inmate as a "con." The prison consultant was brought in to interview the inmate. He called the inmate "weak" and explained that his treatment was mild compared to what real inmates received. The consultant then bargained with the inmate by telling him that if he continued with the experiment and served as an informant, the guards would leave him alone. He was sent back to his cell and told to think it over. At the next count, the inmate started screaming to the other inmates that they could not leave or quit the experiment. His erratic behavior intensified, and the guards were unable to bring him under control. The prison administrators finally realized his symptoms were real and released him.

Day four was visiting day. The researchers were concerned that family members might find the prison environment alarming and would be shocked at the appearance of the inmates, so they decided to manipulate the situation. The inmates were washed, allowed to shave, and fed a large meal. A nice-looking former Stanford cheerleader was brought in to play the role of greeter, and music was pumped in over the intercom during the visits. Despite the fact that the visitors were made to wait an hour to spend ten supervised minutes with their family members, most cooperated. Some of the parents expressed concern over the physical appearance of their sons, but the warden and superintendent alleviated their worries. One father was asked if he felt his son could handle the experiment, and he indicated that he could. Most of the parents left with the impression that the experiment was all in fun and that their loved ones were well taken care of.

After visiting hours were over, the guards picked up on a rumor that the released inmate (#8612) was planning on returning to the prison with friends to help the other inmates escape. The guards called a meeting with the warden and superintendent to discuss strategies for preventing the escape. One idea was to bring in an informant to pose as an inmate to try and get information on the plan. The researchers also went so far as to try and have the inmates moved back to the Palo Alto jail, but the sheriff refused because of liability concerns. What the researchers did instead was to dismantle the jail and move the inmates to another floor of the building. If anyone from the outside showed up they would be told the experiment ended and everyone had gone home. The only person who showed up was a colleague of one of the researchers who was curious about the experiment. The escape rumor turned out to be false. The jail was reconstructed, and the inmates returned to their cells. The guards became furious after spending all that time taking apart and putting back together the mock prison. They took out their frustration on the inmates who had made them look foolish. The guards punished the inmates by having them do strenuous exercises and more chores. Each count lasted over an hour and the inmates were subjected to continuous verbal abuse.

Researchers decided to bring in a Catholic priest who had served as a prison chaplain to provide feedback on the reality of the prison environment. The inmates were allowed to speak with the priest individually. The priest was quite surprised when the inmates introduced themselves by their number and not their actual name. He then proceeded to ask the inmates what they were doing to try and get out of prison. The inmates appeared confused by the question so the priest told them they needed a lawyer. He even offered to call their parents to tell them to get legal assistance. Some of inmates consented. One particular inmate (#819) had refused to see the priest. He complained of feeling sick and requested to see a doctor. When he came out of his cell, he started crying uncontrollably. He was taken to a room to rest and was given some food. The guards became angry with this and made the other inmates start chanting that inmate #819 was a "bad inmate" (knowing that inmate #819 could hear this). The inmate became more upset and was asked if he wanted to go home. He responded that he couldn't because the other inmates would think he was bad. He asked to go back to his cell. Zimbardo told the inmate that he was not bad, that this was just an experiment, not a real prison, and the inmate agreed to leave.

The next day researchers decided to schedule a parolee hearing. Some of the inmates were brought before a parole board that consisted of college staff and graduate students. The prison consultant was also present. The inmates were asked if they would forfeit their pay in exchange for parole, and most said yes. However, when they were told to go back to their cells they all complied. The last rebellious act on the part of the inmates occurred right before the experiment ended. The new inmate, brought in as an alternate, went on a hunger strike. The prison experience was different for this inmate. He came in and immediately immersed into the hostile environment created by the guards. The other inmates experienced a more gradual introduction to the environment. The others also told the inmate that the prison was real because they were not free to leave. When he refused to eat, the guards placed him in solitary confinement and held him three times longer than the rules allowed. Instead of sympathizing with the inmate, the others labeled him a troublemaker. The guards took advantage of this and gave the inmates a choice: give up their blankets and the inmate would be released from solitary. The inmates chose to keep their blankets.

On the fifth night, some visiting parents asked Zimbardo to contact a lawyer (just as the priest had suggested) to help get their sons out of prison. An attorney showed up the next day and met with each of the prisoners. It was at this point that Zimbardo and the other researchers decided to end the experiment—less than one week after it began. The researchers felt that the simulated prison environment had become too real for both the guards and the prisoners. The inmates continued to become passive and withdrawn and showed signs of depression. Some of the guards became overzealous in their actions to control the inmates, while the other more humane guards felt helpless to intervene. One of the interviewers brought in to question the guards and inmates expressed strong objections to how the inmates were being treated and was shocked that the experiment had been allowed to continue as long as it did. The prisoners were elated to be released early, but the guards expressed discontentment that the study was over. During the entire experiment, no guard ever showed up late for work, called in sick, or requested overtime pay for the extra time on duty. The guards genuinely appeared to like their position of authority over the inmates.

Conclusions

Based on their observations, Zimbardo and his research team contended that they had refuted the *dispositional hypothesis*. The subjects recruited to play the roles of guards and prisoners were normal, middle-class adults put into an environment where the guards were given almost total authority over the prisoners. With little direction on how to exert and maintain that authority, the guards increasingly demonstrated negative and hostile behaviors. They quickly immersed themselves into their positions relying on both physical and psychological techniques to control the inmates. Three types of guards were observed. The "tough but fair" guard adhered to the prison rules consistently for all inmates. The "good guys" gave the inmates special privileges and never punished them. A third of the guards were antagonistic and harsh toward the inmates. Rules were enforced arbitrarily, and they seemed to enjoy coming up with new ways to exert power over the inmates. None of the psychological testing or personal interviews provided any insight into why the guards behaved differently.

There were also observed differences in the coping styles of the prisoners. Initially, the inmates all complied with the orders and followed the rules. This quickly changed, when several inmates became rebellious and antagonistic toward the guards. Eventually, they became more passive as the experiment continued. Four prisoners experienced severe emotional distress, and one even developed a psychosomatic rash. A few inmates actually tried to endure the conditions as best they could by cooperating at all times with the guards. The solidarity between inmates that existed at the beginning of the study very quickly diminished as evidenced by their loss of personal identities (remember how each of them introduced themselves by their inmate number). All of the inmates expressed relief when the experiment was terminated early. The only personality trait uncovered in the psychological testing that appeared to be linked to differences in coping styles was that prisoners who tested high on a measure of authoritarianism seemed to adapt better to the environment.

Researchers believed their observations of the simulated prison environment offered support for the contention that the prison environment, not the individuals who inhabited it, influenced the behavior of real inmates and guards. Prisons were designed to be dehumanizing, degrading, and instill a sense of despair among the people who were being held against their will. Guards were put in a position of having to exercise control and maintain authority over the prisoners under circumstances in which they were outnumbered and disrespected by the prisoners. Inmates and guards became immersed into roles that were shaped by their environment. Some inmates adapted by lashing out against the guards through violence or verbal insults, while others shut down emotionally and became depressed and submissive. Knowing that it was the responsibility of the guards to maintain control over the inmates, some guards exerted their authority in an aggressive and hostile manner. According to the researchers, this explained the volatile interactions that frequently occurred between guards and inmates in real prisons.

Criticisms

Researchers put forth great effort in creating their simulated prison, but an obvious question raised after the study was published was whether or not the environment was authentic enough for the subjects. The *ecological validity* of Zimbardo's study depended upon the extent to which his participants perceived the prison environment to be real. No matter how much Zimbardo and his team tried to simulate a real prison environment, the fact remained that the prison was not real. Certain conditions of prison could not be imitated. At no time were the inmates or guards in any physical danger, and the experiment was to last only two weeks. It was possible that the prisoners and guards had just put on a good show for the researchers by behaving in stereotypical ways because this was what was expected of them. Both groups knew their behaviors were being recorded. In response to the issue of ecological validity, researchers pointed out that the guards believed the experiment focused solely on the inmates. When the guards were in the break room, they did not know their conversations were recorded. Instead of using this time to get to know their fellow employees, most of their conversations focused on work. They spoke about the inmates and discussed prison related details. It was also discovered from interviews conducted after the experiment ended that there were interactions between the guards and prisoners that were not observed, such as trips to the bathroom. These interactions were reportedly more negative than those observed. The harassment continued and was often more intense. Also, the hostility of the guards intensified as the experiment went on suggesting the guards might have become consumed in their roles. According to Zimbardo, the guards were not given any specific instructions on how to exert control, yet they relied on physical and psychological coercion. Certain aspects of the prisoners' daily routine such as watching television, reading, and even going to the bathroom became privileges that were granted or denied at the whim of the guards. The guards knew they had power over the lives of the prisoners, and they had no difficulty exhibiting that power. Several guards even reported in their interviews they found the control "exhilarating." According to Erich Fromm (1973), however, Zimbardo's experiment failed to adequately distinguish between "behavior" and "character." The guards were assigned a role, and some behaved negatively toward the prisoners according to their perceptions about how guards should act, but it was misleading to suggest that the guards *enjoyed* treating the prisoners poorly.

Conversations between prisoners were also recorded without their knowledge. The prisoners spent most of their time talking about their prison experience. They complained to each other about the food, guards, and punishments. This was a group of students who did not know one another outside of the experiment and yet they had very little interest in each other. When interviewed by the priest, the inmates introduced themselves by their number, and at the parole hearing; three inmates were willing to forfeit their pay to go home. The prisoners became passive and emotionally distraught as the experiment progressed. Despite the fact that the prisoners knew their incarceration was not real, researchers believed that the experience influenced them. The loss of personal identity, arbitrary control, dependency, and emasculation appeared to have had an impact on their behavior. The helpless behaviors observed from the prisoners may have been a manifestation of the initiation technique used in the study. Subjects were unknowingly arrested by real police officers and taken to a police station for booking. It would have been natural for them to be confused as to whether or not they were free to end the experiment at any time (Fromm 1973). There continues to be doubts as to whether or not the inmates and guards acted on their own accord. Carlo Prescott, the ex-inmate who served as a consultant for the experiment, wrote an article for the *Stanford Daily* in 2005 in which he reported that researchers had prompted some of the participants' actions (http://daily. stanford.edu/article/2005/4/28/the Lie Of The Stanford Prison Experiment).

Zimbardo's sample of research subjects could also be criticized. His subjects were selected from of group of volunteers who had answered an ad in the newspaper. Each underwent psychological testing and interviews so that 24 "normal" white male college students could be selected to participate in the experiment. Study participants shared very few characteristics with real prison guards and inmates. It is questionable whether the results would have *generalized* to a larger more diverse population.

Most of the criticisms focused on alleged *ethical violations* of Zimbardo's research. All of the details of the experiment were not disclosed to the participants. The fake arrests that took place at the beginning of the study were a complete surprise. This was intentional because the researchers wanted the prisoners to go through the same type of induction as real criminals. The vagueness of the instructions left the guards under the impression the researchers were only interested in studying the behaviors of the prisoners. Researchers made no attempt to correct this because they wanted the guards to feel comfortable playing their roles. *Full disclosure* is not always possible when conducting research, but it becomes an important consideration when making sure that subjects give their *informed consent* to participate. Zimbardo himself admitted he became so caught up in his role of prison superintendent that his objectivity may have been compromised. When confronted with the rumor of the impending prison break, he helped devise a strategy to stop it. Despite the fact that Zimbardo was assigned a role to play in the experiment, as a researcher he should have allowed the guards to come up with their own plan.

The most significant ethical issue surrounding the Stanford Prison experiment was the *harm* inflicted upon the subjects. Researchers wanted to explore the influence of a prison environment on the behaviors of individuals assigned to play the roles of prisoners and guards. Researchers never anticipated the extent both groups would become absorbed into those roles. The prisoners suffered harm and became so emotionally distraught that the experiment had to be terminated after only six days. The guards became immersed into their roles as well by demonstrating a willingness to use physical and psychological methods of control. Their position of authority carried with it a sense of power that the guards freely exercised. No one questioned their tactics or intervened to stop the abuse. While the experiment was taking place, over fifty curious individuals visited the prison and observed what was going on. No one voiced any concerns or disapproval until the sixth day when a colleague of Zimbardo showed up and expressed shock and condemnation at what was taking place. Before the subjects left the prison, everyone participated in discussion sessions to allow the guards and prisoners to openly express their thoughts and feelings. The researchers also participated by questioning the moral and ethical concerns of some of their actions. It is important to point out that the researchers followed all guidelines specified by the Stanford human ethics committee who granted approval for the study. Predicting harm can be difficult, but the experiment should have been terminated once the researchers started to observe the prisoners' distress and the guards' willingness to inflict suffering.

Significance and Subsequent Research

The Stanford Prison experiment became one of the most widely cited pieces of social science research primarily because of the alleged ethical violations. Numerous social science research texts cite the study as an example of *unethical* research. The experiment has never been replicated in the United States for this very reason. In 2002, the British Broadcasting Corporation produced a reality television show based on the original prison experiment. Fifteen participants were assigned to play the roles of prisoners and guards in a simulated prison constructed in a television studio. Two psychologists, Alex Haslam and Stephen Reicher, watched over the project, and an independent ethics committee was on hand to supervise as well. In this experiment, the prisoners formed a unified front against the guards. Prisoners mocked and ridiculed the guards and refused to comply with their orders (Reicher and Haslam 2006). This study met a similar fate as the original in that it was terminated early after participants started to exhibit severe emotional symptoms (namely the guards).

The Stanford Prison experiment gained further notriety in 2004 when the news media reported on the torture of Iraqi inmates held by US soldiers at Baghdad's Abu Ghraib prison. Images of inmates being abused and humiliated left many wondering how American soldiers could be responsible for such behavior. The military placed the blame on a few dishonorable guards, but Zimbardo provided another explanation. In fact, he testfied as an expert witness for one of the soldiers who was court-martialed. Zimbardo believed the abuse stemmed from some of the same "situational forces" that existed in his simulated prison (Zimbardo 2004). The total power exercised by guards over the inmates, a lack of oversight and accountability, and an environment where inmates were viewed as less than human helped explained the guards' actions.

The Stanford Prison experiment provided valuable insight into the dynamic roles of inmates and guards and how the prison environment can shape these roles. During the experiment, the guards relied primarily upon coercive tactics to force inmates to comply with their orders even though they had not been instructed to do so. Research that followed explored differences in how correctional officers controlled inmates. John Hepburn (1985) conducted a study of correctional officers to determine the extent to which officers relied upon particular "bases of power" in their control over inmates. Three hundred and sixty correctional officers completed surveys designed to measure five different power bases: legitimate, coercive, reward, expert, and referent. *Legitimate* power was derived from the correctional officers' position. Officers were placed in a rightful position to control the inmates. Officers were also in a position to exercise *coercive* power because they could punish inmates who refused to comply with their orders. Officers further had the ability to *reward* inmates for their obedience either with recommendations for housing and work assignments or by ignoring minor rule violations. *Expert* power was based on the inmates' perception that officers possessed some special knowledge that made them experts in their field. Finally, inmates who complied with officers because they liked and respected them recognized the officers' *referent* power. Hepburn found that most officers believed inmates complied primarily because of legitimate and expert power, despite the fact that inmates typically did not acknowledge the officers' rightful authority over them and usually did not perceive officers' as skilled professionals. Coercive and reward power were ranked last among officers as reasons for inmate compliance. According to Hepburn, this finding was not surprising because inmates usually did not perceive the punishments handed out by guards separate from their general incarceration experience, and the availability of rewards issued by officers was limited.

When the first prisons were constructed back in the late 1700s, incarceration was intended to replace physical forms of punishment, such as corporal punishment. Corporal punishment continued to be used, however, as a means of enforcing inmate discipline within prison. It was not until 1963 that the Eighth Circuit Court of Appeals ruled in *Jackson v. Bishop* that corporal punishment violated inmates' protection against cruel and unusual punishment. Despite the court's ruling, research demonstrated that correctional officers continued to use physical coercion against inmates. James Marquart (1986) conducted an *ethnographic* study of correctional officers by becoming a prison guard in a Texas state prison. He spent 19 months observing correctional officers' interactions with inmates and he also developed relationships with several other guards who became his informants. The institution had in place a formal disciplinary system for inmates who refused to follow the rules; however, Marquart found that officers also utilized their own unofficial system of punishment. Over a two-month period, there were 30 episodes that were witnessed by Marquart or reported by one of his informants in which officers used unofficial physical coercion over inmates. Marquart found that officers relied upon three types of unofficial physical coercion: "tune-ups," "ass whippings," and "severe beatings." Tune-ups included verbal insults, pushing, slapping, or kicking inmates who engaged in minor rule violations (i.e., failure to comply with an order or cursing at an officer). Officers used the tune-up as an "attention getter" for inmates. Inmates who committed more serious rule infractions (challenging an officer's authority or threatening an officer) were likely to receive an ass whipping. Officers used some type of weapon (i.e., flashlight or riot baton) to injure the inmate, but not to the point of requiring major medical care. Severe beatings were the least common type of physical coercion. Severe beatings were only used for inmates who had assaulted a correctional officer, instigated some type of inmate rebellion, or escaped. Inmates who received a severe beating suffered serious physical injuries (some requiring hospitalization). In each of the observed situations, officers used force that violated prison policy and was against the law. According to Marquart, the unofficial use of force was so common and routine for the officers it became "legitimized." The tune-ups, ass whippings, and severe beatings were all considered by the officers to be necessary means to achieve control over the inmates. Officers also relied upon these coercive tactics to demonstrate their superiority over inmates. The unofficial use of force was well established in the guard subculture. New officers were socialized into the guard subculture and part of their socialization involved instructions on the "appropriate" use of force to control inmates. Officers that adhered to subcultural norms were rewarded with promotions and desirable work assignments. Finally, the use of unofficial force increased the group cohesion among subculture members.

Zimbardo and his research team identified three types of guards through their observations of the guards' interactions with inmates. Other researchers have created additional typologies. Kelsey Kauffman (1988) identified five types of correctional officers based upon his interviews with 60 correctional officers from different prisons. The typology reflected the officers' attitudes toward each other and the inmates. The "pollyanna" officers displayed positive attitudes toward the other officers and to the inmates. The "white hats" held favorable attitudes toward inmates, but not for their fellow officers. "Hard asses" on the other hand were unsympathetic toward inmates, but held other officers in high regard. "Burnouts" displayed negative attitudes toward both inmates and other officers. The last type included the "functionaries," who were described as "indifferent" toward the inmates and officers. According to Kauffman, officers entered their careers as either pollyannas, white hats, or hard asses, and then some of these officers became burnouts or functionaries later in their career. This suggested that the occupational experiences of the officers shaped their attitudes.

The Stanford Prison experiment remains one of the most controversial studies ever conducted by social scientists. The study even attracted the attention of film makers. A German film titled *Das Experiment* (released in 2001), was based on Zimbardo's experiment, and an American version is currently in production. The notoriety stems primarily from the ethical violations of the researchers, but findings from the experiment did contribute to our understanding of the conflict between correctional officers and inmates.

References

Fromm, E. (1973). *The Anatomy of Human Destructiveness*. New York: Holt, Rinehart, and Winston.

Duffee, D. (1974). "The Correction Officer Subculture and Organizational Change." *Journal of Research in Crime and Delinquency* 11:155–72.

Haney, C., C. Banks, and P. Zimbardo (1973). "Interpersonal Dynamics in a Simulated Prison." *International Journal of Criminology and Penology* 1:69–97.

Hepburn, J. (1985). "The Exercise of Power in Coercive Organizations: A Study of Prison Guards." *Criminology* 23:145–64.

Jacobs, J., and H. Retsky (1975). "Prison Guard." *Urban Life* 4:5–29.

Kauffman, K. (1988). *Prison Officers and Their World*. Cambridge, MA: Harvard UP.

Klofas, J. (1984). "Reconsidering Prison Personnel: New Views of the Correctional Officer Subculture."

International Journal of Offender Therapy and Comparative Criminology 28:169–75.

Marquart, J. (1986). "Prison Guards and the Use of Physical Coercion as a Mechanism of Prisoner Control." *Criminology* 24:347–63.

Prescott, C. (April 28, 2005) "The Lie of the Stanford Prison Experiment." *Stanford Daily*. Available at: http://www.daily.stanford.edu/article/2005/4/28/ the Lie Of The Stanford Prison Experiment.

Reicher, S., and S. Haslam (2006). "Rethinking the Psychology of Tyranny: The BBC Prison Study." *British Journal of Social Psychology* 45:1–40.

Zimbardo, P. (May 2004) "Power Turns Good Soldiers Into 'Bad Apples'" *Boston Globe* Available at: http://www.prisonexp.org/.

Further Reading

Crouch, B. (1982). *The Keepers*. Springfield, IL: Thomas.

Emerson, R. (1962). "Power-Dependence Relations." *American Sociological Review* 27:31–41.

Israel, M., and I. Hay (2006). *Research Ethics for Social Scientists*. Thousand Oaks, CA: Sage.

Farkas, M. (2000). "A Typology of Correctional Officers." *International Journal of Offender Therapy and Comparative Criminology* 44:431–49.

Lombardo, L. (1989). *Guards Imprisoned*. Cincinnati: Anderson.

Martin, S. (2006). "Staff Use of Force in U.S. Confinement Settings: Lawful Tactics Versus Corporal Punishment." *Social Justice* 33:182–90.

Sales, B., and S. Folkman (2000). *Ethics in Research with Human Participants*. Washington, DC: American Psychological Association.

Zimbardo, P., C. Haney, W. Banks, and D. Jaffe (1974). "The Psychology of Imprisonment: Privation, Power and Pathology." In *Doing Unto Others: Explorations in Social Behavior*, edited by Z. Rubin, pp. 61–74. Englewood Cliffs, NJ: Prentice Hall.

Zimbardo, P. (2006). *The Lucifer Effect: Why Good People Turn Evil*. London: Random House/Ebury.

CORRECTIONAL OFFICERS' ATTITUDES: DO CORRECTIONAL OFFICERS' ATTITUDES DIFFER BY RACE?

Jacobs, J., and L. Kraft (1978). "Integrating the Keepers: A Comparison of Black and White Prison Guards in Illinois." *Social Problems* 25:304–18.

Background

Correctional officers were traditionally white, uneducated, conservative males who lived in the rural areas were most prisons were located (Philliber 1987). The correctional officer's essential role in protecting the public by maintaining control over incarcerated criminals was historically not reflected in the hiring requirements, training, or pay scales of most prisons where even a high school education was not mandatory. Beginning in the 1950s prison populations started to change as more urban blacks were sent to prison. Racial tensions between inmates and guards escalated. Black inmates had not only become more prevalent in number, they stood as a unified group against the guards who perceived them as a greater threat compared to the white inmates. Many reformers advocated increasing the number of black prison guards as a way to reduce conflict and antagonism between guards and inmates. The assumption was that black guards would be able to relate better to the black inmates because they shared similar backgrounds (Jacobs and Kraft 1978). Whether or not the attitudes held by black prison guards toward inmates were any different from those held by white guards remained an untested assumption until the late 1970s when James Jacobs and Lawrence Kraft conducted an empirical test of correctional officers' attitudes.

The Study

Jacobs and Kraft (1978) conducted a study to determine if there was a relationship between correctional officers' race and their attitudes toward inmates, correctional goals, administrators, and correctional officer roles. They administered a *survey* to a sample of 252 in-service guards from two prisons in Illinois: Stateville and Joliet. Both prisons were maximum-security facilities, located within seven miles of each other. Three-fourths of the inmate populations in both prisons were black, and most of the prisoners came from the Chicago area (the prisons were 35 miles southwest of the city). At the time the survey was administered, 12 percent of the correctional officers employed by the Illinois Department of Corrections were black and most of them were working at Stateville and Joliet. The survey was administered to guards while they attended the Correctional Academy between the summer of 1974 and fall of 1975. One hundred and sixty-five white guards and sixty-six black guards completed the survey. Twenty-one guards were excluded from the sample because they either did not indicate their race and/or rank on the questionnaire.

There were several differences between the white and black prison guards that completed the surveys. Most of the black guards were hired in the 1970s and as a result were younger and had less seniority than the white guards. Black guards were also better educated. More black guards had graduated high school and had completed some college compared to white guards. Finally, more black guards had grown up in urban metropolitan areas and considered themselves to be politically liberal and working class compared to their white counterparts.

Jacobs and Kraft's objective was to determine whether or not black prison guards expressed different attitudes than white guards, and if so whether or not the differences could be attributed to the individual characteristics of the guards or to their occupational roles. They formulated four *hypotheses*:

1. Black guards had more sympathetic attitudes toward inmates compared to white guards.
2. Black guards were more supportive of rehabilitation compared to white guards.
3. Black guards conveyed less support for their superiors compared to white guards.
4. Black guards were less committed to institutional goals and to their occupations compared to white guards.

To test for these differences, black and white prison guards were administered an *anonymous* survey and asked to respond to a series of questions that consisted of both *closed-ended* (respondents had to choose a response from those provided) and *open-ended* (free response) questions. Closed-ended questions are typically used when researchers are interested in creating a common frame of reference for respondents. This was important because researchers were looking for differences in the responses between black and white guards. On the other hand, open-ended questions can be a source of new information not considered by the researchers. Questions were designed to assess the guards' attitudes toward inmates, their occupation, superiors, and the correctional system in general. Researchers were also interested in whether or not there were any racial differences in attitudes based on age and years of experience. They created two subgroups: guards under the age of 40 (which was younger than the mean age of all guards in the sample) and guards with less than four years experience.

Findings

Jacobs and Kraft analyzed survey responses from a sample of 231 prison guards working for two Illinois state prisons. They compared responses between black and white guards to determine any significant differences. In addition, researchers examined the responses for younger guards and those with less experience. A summary of their findings is presented below.

Attitudes toward inmates. Based on their responses, black prison guards did not express attitudes that were more sympathetic toward inmates compared to white guards. The responses of black guards to several questions actually revealed *less* sympathy. No racial differences were found in response to a question designed to measure social distance that asked, "How similar are correctional officers and inmates?" Most of the guards, including the younger black guards, indicated that inmates "try to take advantage of officers whenever they can." Black guards were less likely to agree that most inmates were "decent people," however, black guards indicated that a smaller number of inmates actually "belong in prison" compared to responses by white guards. There was no difference in responses to the item "most inmates lack morals." Researchers expected the black guards with less experience to display the most empathic attitudes toward inmates, but this was not revealed in their responses. Many of them indicated, "inmates take advantage of officers whenever they can," although less experienced black guards also felt that fewer inmates should be in prison and inmates had not been given too many constitutional rights. Less experienced white guards displayed the most negative attitudes toward inmates. Black guards (and particularly less experienced black guards) were more likely than white guards to agree with the statement, "Black guards get along better with inmates than whites do." Most of the black and white officers disagreed with the statement, "Correctional officers should be rough with inmates occasionally to let them know who is boss," but more of the less experienced blacks agreed with the statement. Guards were also asked about the number of disciplinary reports they issued each week. Black guards indicated they issued more reports compared to white guards. While the responses to most questions indicated that black guards did not have more favorable attitudes toward inmates, blacks expressed a preference for job assignments that involved greater contact with the inmates. White guards on the other hand indicated they preferred assignments with less contact with inmates. Jacobs and Kraft speculated that black guards might be more comfortable interacting with inmates compared to their white counterparts.

Attitudes toward rehabilitation. Black and white prison guards both indicated that rehabilitation was the primary purpose of prison, but fewer black guards agreed with the statement, "Rehabilitation programs are a waste of time and money." Younger, white guards were more likely to indicate the primary reason was to protect society. When asked what the "primary purpose of prison should be," more black guards than white chose punishment. Guards were also asked to indicate the reason why minorities were over represented in the prison system. Blacks were more likely than whites to believe the reason was due to "lack of opportunity."

Support for superiors. Most of the prison administrators and supervisors at the two prisons were white. In a previous study, researchers discovered that nearly three-fourths of the nonwhite guards who resigned or were terminated expressed difficulties with superior officers (Jacobs and Greer 1977). In this study, however, black prison guards responded more favorably to their superiors than the white guards. Jacobs and Kraft attributed the inconsistent findings to a "highly effective process of (de)selection operating with the guard force" (p. 314). Black guards who identified with the inmates over the administration either left their positions or were fired. According to Jacobs and Kraft, the guards that continued in their positions may have experienced changed attitudes as they started to acknowledge the administration's authority.

Occupational commitment. The responses of both black and white guards indicated a strong sense of institutional commitment. Two-thirds of the guards sampled responded that they planned to be working at the prison for at least the next five years. Many of the guards expressed a preference for their current occupation over other alternative options (such as private security and police work). Among those guards that desired another occupation, private security followed by police work was chosen most frequently. A majority of both white and black guards indicated that they did not want their sons to become prison guards. Young black guards were twice as likely to admit they were embarrassed to tell others they were prison guards.

Researchers uncovered only a few significant differences between black and white prison guards. For the most part, both groups displayed similar attitudes toward the inmates, rehabilitation, their superiors, and jobs. Jacobs and Kraft speculated that their inability to find any consistent differences might have been attributed to the screening process. Black guards who displayed greater empathy for inmates either left or were terminated early in their careers. It was also possible that guards became socialized into a guard subculture (whose content was anti-inmate) almost immediately upon entering their occupation. There were no significant differences in responses between guards with more or less seniority.

Limitations

Jacobs and Kraft failed to support their *hypothesis* that black prison guards were more inmate oriented compared to white guards based on the guards' responses to their survey questions. Surveys are considered to be ideal for measuring attitudes, but one of the inherent difficulties of using survey questions to measure attitudes is constructing questions that accurately capture an individual's way of thinking. Jacobs and Kraft acknowledged that some of their questions designed to measure such differences might have been worded improperly. For example, social distance between guards and inmates was measured with the question, "In your opinion, when just considered as people, how similar are guards and prisoners?" Guards may have interpreted the question as "most guards" as opposed to answering from their own perspective. The guards' responses to this question, however, were consistent with their responses to other questions. Jacobs and Kraft recognized one of the potential sources of bias with their questions known as *social desirability effect*. The guards may have responded to their questions in terms of how they felt they should respond not based on their own personal feelings. The extent that social desirability influenced the guards' responses was not known. Social desirability effect is a source of measurement error that threatens the *validity* of a researcher's measures. Survey questions are valid only if they correctly assess the phenomenon under study.

When constructing survey questions, researchers must also be concerned with the *reliability* of their measures. Whereas validity refers to the extent a researchers' questions accurately measure a particular concept, reliability is concerned with consistency. Jacobs and Kraft created an inmate orientation scale from ten survey questions; however, they presented no reliability data with their analysis. Furthermore, Jacobs and Kraft administered their survey to a sample of guards from two prisons, but they failed to mention whether or not the sample was randomly selected. The results of their study may not have applied to the other guards working at the two study prisons or to guards across the United States. In addition, both prisons were maximum-security facilities. Security level has been found to influence guard attitudes. Correctional officers working in minimum-security prisons displayed more punitive attitudes toward inmates compared to officers from medium- or maximum-security prisons (Smith and Hepburn 1979).

Significance and Subsequent Research

Jacobs and Kraft found that black and white prison guards were very similar in their attitudes toward inmates despite differences in background characteristics (more black guards came from urban areas and were more educated). Neither group displayed attitudes that indicated they were "inmate oriented." The similarities suggested that the attitudes might have been formed as a result of their socialization into the prison environment. Just as police officers developed "working personalities" that influenced their interactions with the public, guards displayed particular attitudes and behaviors toward inmates (Jacobs and Kraft 1978). Numerous studies published after Jacobs and Kraft have identified various organizational influences on guards' attitudes. In addition, researchers have also found evidence to suggest that certain individual characteristics (including race) are also important predictors.

Early studies of prison guards discovered that many guards perceived a conflict between their primary function of maintaining security and the institutional goal of rehabilitation (Cressey 1960, Jacobs and Retsky 1975, Jacobs and Grear 1977, Farmer 1977, Poole and Regoli 1980). The term "guard" was even changed to "correctional officer" in the 1960s to better reflect officers' changing role. Correctional officers were still responsible for preventing inmate disturbances and escapes, but were also told to minimize their use of formal disciplinary procedures (Cressey 1960). These contradictory directives became a source of stress and frustration for officers. In response, officers either quit or continued to emphasize their custodial function because this was the role they were most comfortable with (Jacobs and Retsky 1975). Research by Eric Poole and Robert Regoli (1980) found that correctional officers adapted to role stress by displaying punitive attitudes toward the inmates. Officers not only emphasized their custodial functions in response to stress, they also issued more disciplinary reports against inmates. Conflict between the custodial and treatment staff was also a source of stress for officers. There existed in prison a division of labor between the "non-professional" custodial staff and the "professional" treatment staff. According to James Jacobs and Harold Retsky (1977), the social distance between custodial and treatment staff was equally apparent as the distance between officers and inmates. Conflict between staff was an added source of role stress and contributed to feelings of alienation and cynicism among correctional officers (Farmer 1977, Jacobs and Grear 1977). John Hepburn and Celesta Albonetti (1980) found that treatment staff experienced more role conflict than custodial staff and role conflict was also more pronounced in minimum-security prisons. Role conflict was responsible for job dissatisfaction and the punitive attitudes held by prison staff.

Other studies failed to offer evidence that correctional officers experienced role conflict. Hans Toch and John Klofas (1982) assessed levels of alienation among 832 New York prison correctional officers. Officers from urban areas (which tended to be nonwhite) and those in the middle of their careers (those with five to nineteen years of experience) reported higher levels of discontentment with their work but held similar attitudes toward rehabilitation as other officers. Unlike Jacobs and Kraft, Toch and Klofas uncovered racial differences in correctional officers' attitudes toward inmates. They found that black officers expressed a preference for greater social distance compared to white officers. This finding was further confirmed in a study by John Whitehead and Charles Lindquist (1989) who additionally found that black offers displayed less punitive attitudes compared to white officers.

Ben Crouch and Geoffrey Alpert (1982) conducted a longitudinal study to determine if punitive and aggressive attitudes toward inmates changed during the guards' first months on the job. They also examined the influence of guard background characteristics such as age, sex, race, and education. Three consecutive classes of recruits from the Texas Department of Corrections were surveyed and interviewed during their orientation at the training academy and again six months later. Sixty-eight males and 16 females participated in both stages of data collection. Consistent with Jacobs and Kraft, researchers found no significant differences in attitudes based on the race of the guards. Education also failed to maintain a relationship with punitive and aggressive attitudes. Males and females displayed similar punitive and aggressive attitudes toward inmates when they first became guards. Males, however, became more punitive and aggressive while females reported less punitive and aggressive attitudes. Crouch and Alpert attributed the difference in attitudes to differences in the environments and cultures of male and female institutions. The female prisons were smaller and had a more relaxed atmosphere compared to the male facilities.

Nancy Jurik published a comprehensive study of correctional officers' attitudes in 1985. Jurik surveyed 179 correctional officers from a prison institution located in the western United States. The prison housed both male and female inmates in medium- and minimum-security units. Jurik examined both organizational and individual officer characteristics to determine the influence of each on correctional officers' attitudes toward inmates. Contrary to Jacobs and Kraft, she found minority correctional officers displayed more positive attitudes toward inmates compared to white officers. The difference in findings could have been explained by regional differences between the samples of guards (Jacobs and Kraft surveyed guards in the Midwest), differences in security level (Jacobs and Kraft surveyed guards from maximum-security prisons), or the inclusion of other minority groups (Jacobs and Kraft only examined black guards). Jurik also uncovered differences in attitudes based on age, but opposite to what was expected. Older guards responded with more positive attitudes. Male and female guards displayed similar attitudes, and there were no significant differences in attitudes based on level of education. Two organizational measures were found to maintain significant relationships with correctional officers' attitudes. More years of experience corresponded to more negative attitudes toward inmates. Officers working in minimum-security prisons held more favorable attitudes. This finding was inconsistent with research by Carol Smith and John Hepburn (1979) who found the opposite relationship between security level and attitudes.

Almost of the half of the officers surveyed by Jacobs and Kraft indicated that rehabilitation was "the main reason for putting an offender in prison." Ten years later, the sentiment appeared to have changed. A study of 155 correctional officers from a southern prison facility found that only 10.3 percent of the officers agreed that rehabilitation was the primary goal of prison (Cullen et al. 1989). A majority of the officers, however, also disagreed that rehabilitation programs "allow criminals who deserve to be punished to get off easily" and agreed that rehabilitation was equally important as punishment. The study also discovered differences in attitudes toward rehabilitation according to shift assignment. Officers working the night shift held less favorable attitudes toward rehabilitation. This could have been explained by the lack of contact these officers had with the inmates. Black officers were also found to be more supportive of rehabilitation compared to white officers. Jerome Jackson and Sue Ammen (1997) reached the same conclusion in their study of Texas correctional officers.

The number of black correctional officers employed in prisons across the United States has increased in the 30 years since Jacobs and Kraft published their study, but the percentage of black correctional officers remains low at 21 percent (Camp and Camp 2003). Jacobs and Kraft were the first to explore the influence of race on correctional officer attitudes. Numerous studies of correctional officers' attitudes have been published since 1978. Correctional officers are no longer the ignored figures in corrections research. The debate over whether or not hiring more black correctional officers will ease racial tensions between officers and inmates continue because of contradictory research findings, but according to Jurik (1985), it would be unrealistic to expect significant improvements to the prison environment by simply hiring officers with particular demographic characteristics.

References

Camp, C., and G. Camp (2003). *The 2002 Corrections Yearbook.* Middletown, CT: Criminal Justice Institute.

Cullen, F., F. Lutze, B. Link, and N. Wolfe (1989). "The Correctional Orientation of Prison Guards: Do Officers Support Rehabilitation?" *Federal Probation* 53:33–42.

Crouch, B., and G. Alpert (1982) "Sex and Occupational Socialization Among Prison Guards: A Longitudinal Study." *Criminal Justice and Behavior* 9:159–76.

Cressey, D. (1960). "Limitations on Organization of Treatment in the Modern Prison." In R. Cloward, *Theoretical Studies in Social Organization of the Prison.* New York: Social Science Research Council.

Farmer, R. (1977). "Cynicism: A Factor in Corrections Work." *Journal of Criminal Justice* 5:237–46.

Hepburn, J., and C. Albonetti (1980). "Role Conflict in Correctional Institutions." *Criminology* 17:445–59.

Jacobs, J., and H. Retsky (1975). "Prison Guard." *Urban Life* 4:5–29.

Jacobs, J., and M. Grear (1977). "Drop-outs and Rejects: An Analysis of the Prison Guard's Revolving Door." *Criminal Justice Review* 2:57–70.

Jacobs, J., and L. Kraft (1978). "Integrating the Keepers: A Comparison of Black and White Prison Guards in Illinois." *Social Problems* 25:304–18.

Jackson, J., and S. Ammen (1996). "Race and Correctional Officers' Punitive Attitudes Toward Treatment Programs or Inmates." *Journal of Criminal Justice* 24:153–66.

Jurik, N. (1985). "Individual and Organizational Determinants of Correctional Officer Attitudes Toward Inmates." *Criminology* 23:523–39.

Philliber, S. (1987). "Thy Brother's Keeper: A Review of the Literature on Correctional Officers." *Justice Quarterly* 4:9–37.

Poole, E., and R. Regoli (1980). "Role, Stress, Custody Orientation, and Disciplinary Actions: A Study of Prison Guards." *Criminology* 18:215–26.

Shamir, B., and A. Drory (1981). "Some Correlates of Prison Guards' Beliefs." *Criminal Justice and Behavior* 8:233–49.

Smith, C., and J. Hepburn (1979). "Alienation in Prison Organizations: A Comparative Analysis." *Criminology* 17:251–62.

Toch, H., and J. Klofas (1982). "Alienation and Desire for Job Enrichment Among Correction Officers." *Federal Probation* 46:35–44.

Whitehead, J., and C. Lindquist (1989). "Determinants of Correctional Officers' Professional Orientation." *Justice Quarterly* 6:69–88.

Further Reading

Cullen, F., B. Link, N. Wolfe, and J. Frank (1985). "The Social Dimensions of Correctional Officer Stress." *Justice Quarterly* 2:505–33.

Jurik, N., and G. Halemba (2008). "Gender, Working Conditions and the Job Satisfaction of Women in a Non-Traditional Occupation: Female Correctional Officers in Men's Prisons." *Sociological Quarterly* 25: 551–66.

Jurik, N. (1985). "An Officer and a Lady: Organizational Barriers to Women Working as Correctional Officers in Men's Prisons." *Social Problems* 32:375–88.

Johnson, R., and S. Price (1981). "The Complete Correctional Office: Human Service and the Human Environment of Prison." *Criminal Justice and Behavior* 8:343–73.

Klofas, J., and H. Toch (1982). "The Guard Subculture Myth." *Journal of Research in Crime and Delinquency* 19:238–54.

Lombardo, L. (1989). *Guards Imprisoned*. Cincinnati: Anderson.

O'Toole, S. (2000). "Prison Officer Training—The Link with Prison Reform." *Journal of Correctional Education* 51:282–84.

Poole, E., and R. Regoli (1980). "Examining the Impact of Professionalism on Cynicism, Role Conflict, and Work Alienation Among Prison Guards." *Criminal Justice Review* 5:57–65.

Robinson, D., F. Porporino, and L. Simourd (1997). "The Influence of Educational Attainment on the Attitudes and Job Performance of Correctional Officers." *Crime and Delinquency* 43:60–77.

Roucek, J. (1935). "Sociology of the Prison Guard." *Sociology and Social Research* 20:145–51.

Tewksbury, R., and E. Mustaine (2008). "Correctional Orientations of Prison Staff." *Prison Journal* 88:207–33.